Yearbook on

International

Communist Affairs

1979

Yearbook on International Communist Affairs 1979

EDITOR: Richard F. Staar

Associate Area Editors:

Eastern Europe and the Soviet Union	Milorad M. Drachkovitch
Western Europe	Dennis L. Bark
Asia and the Pacific	Ramon H. Myers
The Americas	William E. Ratliff
Africa and the Middle East	Lewis H. Gann
International Communist Front Organizations	Alex N. Dragnich

HOOVER INSTITUTION PRESS
STANFORD UNIVERSITY, STANFORD, CALIFORNIA

Hoover Institution Publication 215

© 1979 by the Board of Trustees of the
    Leland Stanford Junior University
All rights reserved
International Standard Book Number 0-8179-7151-3
Library of Congress Catalog Card Number 76-51879
Printed in the United States of America

CONTENTS

Asia and the Pacific

The Americas

Africa and the Middle East

International Communist Front Organizations (Alex N. Dragnich)

Biographies (Richard F. Staar)

INTRODUCTION

The purpose of the 1979 *Yearbook on International Communist Affairs*, the thirteenth consecutive volume in this series, is to provide basic data concerning organizational and personnel changes, attitudes toward domestic and foreign policies, and activities of communist parties and international front organizations throughout the world. Much of the information comes from primary source materials in the native languages. Profiles on each party include founding date, legal or proscribed status, membership, electoral and parliamentary (if any) strength, leadership, auxiliary organizations, domestic activities, ideological orientation, views on international issues, attitude toward the Sino-Soviet dispute, and principal news media. Identity as a Marxist-Leninist party remains the criterion for inclusion and hence pro-Soviet, pro-Chinese, Castroite, Trotskyist, as well as other rival communist movements, are treated whenever applicable.

Excluded from the *Yearbook* are Marxist liberation movements and Marxist ruling parties that specifically disclaim being communist. The Frente de Libertação de Moçambique (FRELIMO), for example, transformed itself into a political party and governs the People's Republic of Mozambique. It has announced a Marxist program and is organized on the basis of "democratic centralism," but is not, properly speaking, a communist party. The Movimento Popular de Libertação de Angola (MPLA) reorganized itself into the Popular Movement Workers' Party and rules most of the People's Republic of Angola; it derives support from Soviet advisers and Cuban armed forces in a continuing struggle against opposition. The Partido Africano de Indépendence de Guiné e Cabo Verde (PAIGC) is the ruling party of Guinea-Bissau. MPLA and PAIGC both share FRELIMO's general orientation; they also have been excluded.

The ruling movement in the Congo People's Republic, the Parti Congolaise du Travail, claims to be Marxist-Leninist; its leaders state that they are communists committed to "scientific socialism." But the party is not regarded as an orthodox Marxist-Leninist movement by its peers. The president of the Congo People's Republic has stated that, while Marx's writings remain valid, they must be adapted to local conditions. The same applies to the National Front in the People's Democratic Republic of Yemen and the Party of the People's Revolution in the People's Republic of Benin (previously knows as Dahomey).

Leftist organizations of an oppositional type, such as the Mouvement National pour l'Independence de Malagasy (Monima), the Eritrean Liberation Front, as well as the so-called national liberation movements in Bahrain, former Spanish Sahara (Polisario), Rhodesia (ZANU and ZAPU), and South-West Africa (SWAPO) are not discussed. Omitted also because of insufficient data are groups such as the communist parties of the Faroe Islands, Hong Kong, Jamaica,[1] Malta, Nigeria (the Socialist Workers' and Farmers' Party), and Saudi Arabia, even though their Marxist-Leninist orthodoxy may not be in dispute. The following is a brief summary of *Yearbook* highlights for calendar year 1978.

---

[1]The Jamaican Workers' Party held a founding congress at Kingston in December, and a brief profile is included in this *YICA*.

Membership. The number of communist parties recognized as orthodox by their peers reached 99 with the addition of the one in Afghanistan. The latter is among the 17 currently in power. Only 29 operate clandestinely, having been proscribed by the authorities. Ten of these are in Africa or in the Middle East.

Membership world-wide is estimated to be approximately 71 million, which represents a 1.4 percent annual growth rate over the previous year. The Soviet and East European ruling movements claim to have registered a gain in excess of one-half million members. Those in Western Europe remained at about the same levels, although French and Spanish communists reported increases of almost 10 and 35 percent respectively. The latter may be exaggerated.[2]

Almost no change was registered throughout Asia and the Pacific, except for the possibly inflated figure in Afghanistan. The same applies in general to the Americas, with a noteworthy exception in Mexico where the discrepancy between claim and estimate is four to one. The 25 percent increase throughout Africa and the Middle East can be explained by the new estimates which had not been made a year ago.

No new figures have been published on the strength of the international communist front organizations, and only one change has been entered. The CGIL in Italy withdrew from the World Federation of Trade Unions and hence four million members have been subtracted from the latter. The eleven fronts claim over one half billion supporters or more than seven times the total number of card-carrying communist party members throughout the world. They comprise a powerful instrument of Soviet foreign policy that can be relied upon to disseminate the Moscow line whenever and wherever necessary.

The table that follows provides a convenient checklist on the status of 99 communist movements and the 11 most important front organizations. The last column gives the attitude of each party toward the Sino-Soviet dispute. In this connection, 51 of the political entities designated with an asterisk reportedly have pro-Chinese splinter groups which sent greetings to the recent eleventh CCP congress.

USSR and Eastern Europe. The dominance which Leonid Brezhnev had attained at the recently held twenty-fifth CPSU congress appeared to lessen during much of 1978 but became stronger by the end of the year. The death on 17 July of Fedor D. Kulakov (60), politburo member and secretary for agriculture, eliminated one of Brezhnev's protegés who also had been considered a potential successor. Next came the unexpected retirement of Kyril T. Mazurov (64), politburo member as well as a first deputy premier, on 27 November, and promotion of another Brezhnev protegé, Konstantin U. Chernenko (67), to full membership in the politburo.[3] However, the concept of "collective leadership" continued to be extolled by prominent CPSU leaders more frequently than in the past.

Efforts to upgrade party propaganda work were very much in evidence. One significant aspect involved the attempts at homogenization of Soviet society in terms of class and structure. These efforts went hand in hand with the amalgamation (*sliianie*) approach to the nationalities question. The latter increasingly has become one of the more delicate and potentially most disruptive issues in the Soviet Union. An unusual spontaneous demonstration held at Tbilisi on 14 April to protest deletion from the draft republic constitution of a reference to Georgian as the official language was followed three days later by its restoration.[4] The same developments, without reported demonstrations, occurred in Armenia and Azerbaidzhan.

---

[2] See *YICA, 1978*, p. xii, for evidence of falsification.

[3] *Pravda*, 28 November 1978.

[4] *New York Times*, 18 April 1978.

CHECKLIST OF COMMUNIST PARTIES AND FRONTS

Eastern Europe and the Soviet Union (9)

Area	Population (est)	Communist party membership	Percent of vote; seats in legislature	Status	Sino-Soviet dispute
Albania	2,569,000	101,500 claim	99.9 (1978); all 250 Democratic Front	in power	independent
Bulgaria	8,864,000	812,000 claim	99.9 (1976); 272 of 400 Fatherland Front	in power	pro-Moscow
Czechoslovakia	15,136,000	1,473,000 claim	99.9 (1976); all of 200 National Front	in power	pro-Moscow
East Germany (GDR)	16,757,000	2,077,262 claim	99.9 (1976); 127 of 500 National Front	in power	pro-Moscow
Hungary	10,693,000	770,000 claim	99.6 (1975), all 352 Patriotic People's Front	in power	pro-Moscow
Poland	35,000,000	2,758,000 claim	99.4 (1976); 262 of 460 Front of National Unity	in power	pro-Moscow
*Romania	21,868,000	2,747,000 claim	99.9 (1975); all 349 Front of Socialist Unity	in power	neutral
USSR	261,200,000	16,300,000 claim	99.9 (1974); all 1,517 CPSU-approved	in power	– –
Yugoslavia	21,968,000	1,629,082 claim	– – (1978); all 380 Socialist Alliance	in power	independent
Total	394,055,000	28,667,844			

Western Europe (24)

Area	Population (est)	Communist party membership	Percent of vote; seats in legislature	Status	Sino-Soviet dispute
*Austria	7,517,000	22,500 est.	1.2 (1975); none	legal	pro-Moscow
*Belgium	9,840,000	10,000	2 to 3 (1978); 4 of 212	legal	pro-Moscow
Cyprus	641,000	11,500 est.	30.0 (1976); 9 of 35 Greek Cypriot seats	legal	pro-Moscow
*Denmark	5,106,000	8,000 est.	3.7 (1977); 7 of 179	legal	pro-Moscow
*Faroe Islands	42,000	insignificant	– – (1977); none	allowed	split
*Finland	4,770,000	48,000 est.	19.0 (1975); 40 of 200	legal	pro-Moscow
*France	53,446,000	650,000 claim	20.6 (1978); 86 of 491	legal	pro-Moscow
*Germany (FRG)	61,520,000	46,380 claim	0.3 (1976); none	legal	pro-Moscow
West Berlin	2,100,000	7,500 est.	1.9 (1975); none	legal	pro-Moscow
*Great Britain	55,894,000	25,938 claim	0.5 (1974); none	legal	pro-Moscow
*Greece	9,309,000	27,500 est.	9.3 (1977); 11 of 300	legal	split (3)
*Iceland	224,000	3,000 est.	22.9 (1978); 14 of 60	legal	independent
Ireland	3,288,000	600 est.	– – (1977); none	legal	pro-Moscow
*Italy	56,711,000	1,800,000 claim	34.4 (1976); 228 of 630	legal	pro-Moscow
*Luxembourg	358,000	600 est.	9.0 (1974); 5 of 59	legal	pro-Moscow
*Malta	334,000	100 est.	– – (1976); none	legal	pro-Moscow
*Netherlands	14,000,000	14,500	1.7 (1977); 2 of 150	legal	pro-Moscow
*Norway	4,061,000	2,250 est.	5.2 (1977); 2 of 155	legal	independent
*Portugal	9,786,000	142,000 claim	14.6 (1976); 40 of 263	legal	pro-Moscow
*San Marino	20,000	300 est.	21.1 (1978); 16 of 60	legal	pro-Moscow
*Spain	36,734,000	270,000 claim (200,000 est.)	9.2 (1977); 20 of 350	legal	independent
*Sweden	8,273,000	17,000 est.	2.5 (1976); 17 of 349	legal	split
*Switzerland	6,293,000	5,000 est.	2.5 (1975); 6 of 200	legal	pro-Moscow
Turkey	43,059,000	2,000 est.	– – (1977)	proscribed	pro-Moscow
Total	393,326,000	2,986,868			

Asia and the Pacific (22)

Area	Population (est.)	Communist party membership	Percent of vote; seats in legislature	Status	Sino-Soviet dispute
Afghanistan	14,381,000	50,000 claim	no elections scheduled	in power	pro-Moscow
*Australia	14,227,000	3,900 est.	-- (1977); none	legal	split (3)
*Bangladesh	85,771,000	2,500 est.	-- (1973)	proscribed	split
*Burma	32,205,000	7,000 est.	-- (1974)	proscribed	pro-Peking
*Cambodia	8,148,000	10,000 est.	100.0(1976); all 250	in power	pro-Peking
China	1,003,835,000	35,000,000 claim	no elections scheduled	in power	--
*Hong Kong	4,584,000	2,000 est.	city council @ 2 years	legal	pro-Peking
*India	660,722,000	100,000 CPM est. 85,000 CPI est.	4.3 (1977); 22 of 244	legal	neutral pro-Moscow
*Indonesia	140,680,000	1,000 est.	-- (1977)	proscribed	split
*Japan	114,983,000	350,000 est.	10.4 (1976); 17 of 511	legal	independent
*Korea (DPRK)	18,000,000	1,800,000 est.	100.0(1977); all 579	in power	neutral
*Laos	3,500,000	15,000 est.	no elections scheduled	in power	neutral
*Malaysia	12,860,000	3,150 est.	-- (1978)	proscribed	pro-Peking
Mongolia	1,587,000	67,000 claim	99.9(1973); all 336	in power	pro-Moscow
Nepal	13,680,000	6,500 est.	-- (1959)	proscribed	split
*New Zealand	3,116,000	500 est.	0.2 (1978); none	legal	split
Pakistan	77,786,000	1,500 est.	-- (1977)	proscribed	pro-Moscow
*Philippines	45,880,000	2,250 est.	-- (1978)	proscribed	split
Singapore	2,400,000	500 est.	-- (1976)	proscribed	pro-Peking
*Sri Lanka	14,283,000	6,000 est.	1.9 (1977); none	legal	split
*Thailand	45,850,000	1,200 est. (plus 10,500 guerrillas)	-- (1976)	proscribed	pro-Peking
*Vietnam	51,226,000	1,533,000 claim	99.0(1976); all 492	in power	pro-Moscow
Total	2,369,705,000	39,048,500			

The Americas (27)

Area	Population (est.)	Communist party membership	Percent of vote; seats in legislature	Status	Sino-Soviet dispute
*Argentina	26,487,000	70,000 est.	no elections scheduled	legal	pro-Moscow
*Bolivia	5,081,000	500 est.	-- (1978)	proscribed	split
Brazil	115,415,000	6,000 est.	-- (1974)	proscribed	split
*Canada	23,632,000	2,000 est.	-- (1974); none	legal	split
*Chile	10,770,000	unknown	elections promised	proscribed	pro-Moscow
*Colombia	25,559,000	12,000 est.	1.9 (1978); 3 of 311	legal	pro-Moscow
Costa Rica	2,119,000	3,200 est.	2.7 (1978); 2 of 57	legal	pro-Moscow
Cuba	9,797,000	200,000 est.	91.7(1976); 441 of 481	in power	pro-Moscow
*Dominican Republic	5,393,000	5,000 est.	-- (1978); none	legal	factions
Ecuador	7,550,000	1,000 est.	5.1 (1978); none	legal	split
El Salvador	4,515,000	225 est.	-- (1976)	proscribed	pro-Moscow
*Guadeloupe	331,000	3,000 est.	-- (1976); 7 of 36	legal	pro-Moscow
Guatemala	6,621,000	740 est.	-- (1974);	proscribed	pro-Moscow
Guyana	813,000	250 est.	26.0(1973) 14 of 53	legal	pro-Moscow
*Haiti	5,534,000	unknown	-- (1973)	proscribed	pro-Moscow
*Honduras	3,517,000	650 est.	promised 1979/80	proscribed	split
Jamaica	2,201,000	200 est.	-- (1976); none	allowed	pro-Moscow
Martinique	327,000	1,000 est.	-- (1976); 3 of 36	legal	pro-Moscow
Mexico	65,833,000	25,000 est. (100,000,000 claim)	-- (1976); none	legal	pro-Moscow
Nicaragua	2,409,000	160 est. (1,200 claim)	-- (1974)	proscribed	split
Panama	1,812,000	500 est.	-- (1972); none	allowed	pro-Moscow
Paraguay	3,095,000	3,500 est.	-- (1973)	proscribed	split
*Peru	16,818,000	3,200 est.	5.9 (1978); 6 of 100	legal	split
Puerto Rico	3,200,000	125 est.	-- (1976); none	legal	pro-Moscow
*United States	220,000,000	18,000 claim	0.2 (1976); none	legal	pro-Moscow
*Uruguay	2,893,000	10,000 est.	elections scheduled 1980	proscribed	pro-Moscow
*Venezuela	14,058,000	6,000 est.	9.0 (1978); 22 of 195	legal	factions
Total	585,780,000	372,260			

Africa and the Middle East (17)

Area	Population (est.)	Communist party membership	Percent of vote; seats in legislature	Status	Sino-Soviet dispute
Egypt	39,890,000	500 est.	-- (1976); 3 of 360	proscribed	pro-Moscow
Iran	35,286,000	1,500 est.	-- (1975)	proscribed	pro-Peking
Iraq	12,000,000	2,000 est.	no elections since 1958	allowed	pro-Moscow
Israel	3,654,000	1,500 est.	4.6 (1977); 5 of 120	legal	pro-Moscow
Jordan	2,990,000	500 est.	no elections since 1967	proscribed	pro-Moscow
Lebanon	2,500,000	2,500 est.	-- (1972); none	legal	pro-Moscow
Lesotho	1,277,000	negligible	unsuccessfully called for elections since 1970	proscribed	pro-Moscow
The Maghreb					
Algeria	17,639,000	500 est.	-- (1976)	proscribed	pro-Moscow
Morocco	18,915,000	700 est.	-- (1977); none	allowed	pro-Moscow
Tunisia	6,242,000	100 est.	-- (1974)	proscribed	pro-Moscow
Nigeria	68,486,000	unknown	-- (1976)	proscribed	pro-Moscow
*Reunion	500,000	2,000 est.	32.8 (1978); none in Paris	legal	independent
Saudi Arabia	7,862,000	negligible	no elections scheduled	proscribed	pro-Moscow
Senegal	5,380,000	2,000 est.	0.32 (1978); none	legal	pro-Moscow
South Africa	27,432,000	unknown	-- (1977)	proscribed	pro-Moscow
Sudan	17,624,000	3,500 est.	-- (1978); no parties	proscribed	pro-Moscow
Syria	8,700,000	4,000 est.	-- (1977); 6 of 195	allowed	pro-Moscow
Total	276,359,000	21,300			
Grand Total:	4,019,225,000	71,096,772			

Note: *Based on fraternal greetings sent to the most recent communist party congress in Peking, these 51 countries either have pro-Chinese splinter groups or ruling movements that are at least neutral in the Sino-Soviet dispute. Many of them have more than one organization, e.g., Indonesia, North Kalimantan, and Surinam. Not listed above are CP (M/L) organizations in the Faroe Islands, Macao, and South Korea.

International Communist Front Organizations (11)

	Claimed Membership	Headquarters
Afro-Asian People's Solidarity Organization	no data[a]	Cairo
Christian Peace Conference	no data	Prague
International Association of Democratic Lawyers	25,000	Brussels
International Federation of Resistance Fighters	3,000,000[b]	Vienna
International Organization of Journalists	150,000	Prague
International Union of Students	ca. 10,000,000[c]	Prague
Women's International Democratic Federation	over 200,000,000[d]	East Berlin
World Federation of Democratic Youth	ca. 150,000,000[e]	Budapest
World Federation of Scientific Workers	300,000[f]	London
World Federation of Trade Unions	ca. 146,000,000[g]	Prague
World Peace Council	(affiliates in 120 countries)	Helsinki

Sources: Official figures on CP membership claimed during 1978 by party newspapers or journals; estimates are from Central Intelligence Agency, *National Basic Intelligence Factbook* (Washington, D.C., January 1979), passim; and *International Front Organisations* (London, April 1977), passim.

Notes: [a] AAPSO-affiliated committees exist in most countries of Asia and Africa.
[b] Forty "national" organizations exist in 20 countries of Europe plus Israel.
[c] The bulk of membership comes from communist-ruled states.
[d] Figures for 1966; none issued since then. Affiliates in over 100 countries, but most of membership is in Soviet Bloc.
[e] Most members live in CP-ruled countries; others generally represent small groups attached to local communist parties.
[f] Bulk of membership is from communist-ruled states.
[g] Some 90 percent live in CP-ruled states, including 107 million from the USSR. Communist China is not a member. The Italian CGIL, with over four million members, withdrew in 1978 from WFTU.

Fear by the regime of a linkage between this nationalistic ferment and the general dissident movement led to harsh treatment of nonconformists, especially during the spring and summer. Yuri F. Orlov, organizer of a group to monitor implementation of the Helsinki agreements, and Aleksandr Ginzburg, administrator of a fund established by Solzhenitsyn to aid families of political prisoners, were given heavy jail and labor camp terms in May and July respectively. Likewise the sentencing to thirteen years in prison of Anatoly B. Shcharansky, a leader of the Jewish emigration movement, precipitated severe criticism throughout the noncommunist world. It also led to tension in Soviet-American relations. Apart from groups and individuals struggling for political, artistic, religious and nationality rights, there emerged for the first time, in January, an attempt to establish an unofficial labor union. Its organizers were arrested and disappeared.

Overall functioning of the Soviet economy remained uneven. The Central Committee plenum at mid-year largely concentrated on agriculture. Brezhnev sharply criticized its performance and demanded that increased production efficiency be given top priority. During the November plenum he made the toughest, harshest domestic speech in years, lashing out at basic flaws in the economy: poor management, waste, and low productivity. A record 235 million ton grain harvest could not compensate for shortages of meat, milk and metals. This criticism led to announcement[5] of increased targets for consumers' goods and food supplies in 1979. Economic decentralization is not being considered. Instead, more centralized control will be the planned remedy.

USSR diplomacy, buttressed by military power and propaganda, had to cope with several challenges: new U.S. weapons systems, efforts at revitalization of NATO, and increased anti-Soviet activism by China in the international arena. Vis-à-vis the United States, USSR leaders aimed at two objectives: convince American public opinion of their peaceful intentions and prevent deployment of new American systems, particularly the neutron weapon. Addressing U.S. congressmen on 23 January, CPSU secretary Boris N. Ponomarev insisted on peaceful Soviet aims but also warned that deployment of the neutron weapon would force the USSR to follow suit. President Carter's decision in early April to postpone production was considered unsatisfactory.[6]

American protests over the trial of dissidents in the Soviet Union, as well as Carter's denunciation of USSR and Cuban activities in the Horn of Africa, brought forth strong reactions from Moscow. Georgi A. Arbatov, director of the influential USA Institute, placed full blame on Washington for deterioration in relations.[7] At the end of June, in a speech televised at Minsk, Brezhnev charged Carter with pursuing a short-sighted policy of trying to play the China card against the USSR. Arrest for espionage of two Soviet diplomats in May and the subsequent retaliatory arrest of an American businessman in Moscow had contributed to more tension. Yet officials in both countries stated that disagreements in other fields did not inhibit a favorable outcome of strategic arms limitation talks. Secretary of State Cyrus R. Vance and foreign minister Andrei Gromyko met at Geneva for a "final" round of negotiations which did not result in agreement.[8]

Highlights of Soviet relations with Western Europe included visits by Brezhnev to the Federal Republic of Germany (FRG) in May and by Gromyko to France during October. The Bonn trip was interpreted in many circles as a move designed to weaken West German commitment to NATO, if not to

---

[5]However, plans for 1979 heavy industry expansion (5.8 percent versus 4.7 percent in 1978) surpass those for light industry (4.6 versus 3.7). *Washington Post*, 10 December 1978.

[6]Moscow radio, 8 April 1978.

[7]*Pravda*, 28 March 1978.

[8]*New York Times*, 24 December 1978.

establish a special relationship with the FRG at a time when Moscow was critical of French intervention in Zaire. After his talks in Paris, however, Gromyko emphasized the "privileged relations" between France and the Soviet Union.

Through the so-called Third World, the USSR stepped up its support for Arab "rejectionist" forces. It also became the first to recognize the new regime in Afghanistan after the communist-led coup in late April. Ties between the two countries soon intensified, with economic agreements reached, Soviet advisers arriving at Kabul, and a twenty-year treaty signed in early December. Brezhnev had warned during the previous month that any military interference in the affairs of Iran would be regarded by the USSR as affecting its security interests. One day later, a Soviet-Ethiopian treaty of friendship and cooperation was signed,[9] consolidating the USSR position in the Horn of Africa.

Sino-Soviet relations fluctuated early in the year but deteriorated progressively during the second half of 1978. Two border incidents during February were followed by conciliatory diplomatic gestures from Moscow. Peking's unresponsiveness led to pressure of a different kind. Brezhnev and defense minister D. F. Ustinov visited the Far East and conspicuously observed Soviet maneuvers being held in early April. After a strong protest against organized "military provocation" on 9 May, the USSR formally apologized for "inadvertent" penetration of Chinese territory by Soviet troops. A series of international issues further complicated Sino-Soviet relations. In the bitter military and political conflict between Vietnam and Cambodia, Peking not only supported Phnom Penh but engaged in a violent war of words with Hanoi. Moscow supported the latter, and on 13 December the two concluded a treaty of friendship and cooperation. Chairman Hua Kuo-feng's visit to Romania and Yugoslavia during August had been considered by the USSR as anti-Soviet provocation. During the same month, its press and radio mounted a barrage of attacks against "Great Han chauvinism," accusing China of "joining up with the most aggressive forces of imperialism and reaction."[10] Soviet diplomatic pressure to prevent ratification of a treaty between Peking and Tokyo failed, and the document was signed in October.

In the international communist movement, the CPSU increased its efforts to maintain or reassert a semblance of global leadership. "Eurocommunism" remains an unacceptable ideological concept,[11] although Moscow supports domestic tactics of the Italian communists. Relations with the party in France further soured, and Soviet commentators strongly attacked the "revisionism" of noted communist intellectuals. Closer to home, tighter control was extended over all East European ruling movements except for those in Albania, Romania, and Yugoslavia. Five multilateral meetings of party secretaries convened at Budapest (February), Warsaw (September and mid-October), Prague (24–26 October), and Budapest (same time). Subjects discussed included ideology and international relations, human rights under a "socialist" system, mass media and their role in education and propaganda as well as organizational affairs.

While the objectives at all meetings had been to enhance bloc-wide "homogenization," and while Soviet control remained uncontested, each client state in Eastern Europe had its own significant peculiarities. East Germany maintains (together with Bulgaria, Czechoslovakia, and Romania) the most severely repressive domestic system but has been singled out to play an important role through military advisors and other personnel in support of the pro-Moscow regimes of Ethiopia, Angola, and Mozambique.

The situation in Poland, despite the unswervingly orthodox policies of its communist leaders, is markedly different. Early in the year there appeared signs of factional ferment within the ruling party. The ailing leader, Edward Gierek, faces mounting economic difficulties. Moreover, active opposition against his domestic policies has expanded, with social dissent now a permanent feature of political life.

---

[9] Moscow radio, 20 November 1978.

[10] *Pravda*, 4 August 1978.

[11] See the article by Vadim Zagladin, first deputy director of the CPSU Central Committee's international department, in *Pravda*, 6 November 1978.

Specific illustrations of dissident activities, reluctantly tolerated by the regime, include "flying universities" which offer academic courses at private homes in cities, and self-defense committees protesting official agricultural policies in villages. Attempts to organize a free trade union among miners in Silesia resulted in prompt arrests. Another "first" was a border meeting between Polish and Czechoslovak human rights activists.[12] The most important event, however, took place in church affairs, with the election on 16 October of Karol Cardinal Wojtyla as pope. General expectations are that the Roman Catholic church in Poland will be strengthened in its long struggle to achieve fair treatment by the state.

Czechoslovakia celebrated three momentous anniversaries: sixty years since the establishment of the republic, three decades since the communist seizure of power, and ten years of occupation by Soviet troops. They were celebrated as follows: the national "bourgeois" holiday, with official restraint; the second, with government pomp; and the third, by speeches justifying foreign intervention which had "saved" socialism. Despite steady police harassment, the Charter 77 movement continued to maintain its vitality.[13]

Hungary remains the quietest communist-ruled state in Eastern Europe. The tenth anniversary of its New Economic Mechanism elicited numerous analyses of achievements and shortcomings. Without any sign of disloyalty toward the Soviet Union, the Kadar regime substantially improved its relations with the United States: at the beginning of the year, the crown of St. Stephen was returned to Budapest, and in July that country received most-favored-nation trading status from the U.S. Congress. After 1 January 1979 Hungarian exiles will be issued passports for regular visits. The only sign of open bloc discord remains the dispute with Romania over treatment of the Szekely minority in Transylvania.

Romania's domestic affairs in 1978 included continuation of internal repression, a sweeping shake-up of the party and state leadership, intensification of economic problems, lingering worker unrest, and the growth of leader Nicolae Ceauşescu's "cult of personality." At the same time, Bucharest accentuated its insistence on national independence. Hua Kuo-feng was warmly greeted in August. At the political consultative committee meeting of the Warsaw Pact, held in Moscow during 22-23 November, the Romanian delegation opposed Soviet demands for increased military spending and closer integration of member states' armed forces. Justifying this stand, Ceauşescu subsequently declared at a public meeting in Bucharest that "it is the sacred right of each nation to decide its own destiny without interference from the outside." At the same time, he stressed that Romanian armed forces would seek to cooperate with other Pact armies and pledged to work for "collaboration, friendship and solidarity" among communist-ruled states.[14]

Little of major political importance happened in Bulgaria. Noteworthy, however, was the clandestinely published "Declaration 78" as a first sign of human rights ferment. Relations with Yugoslavia remained tense throughout the year, despite exchanges of high level party and state delegations. The essential reason involves the Sofia claim that there are no Macedonians living in Bulgaria and Belgrade assertions to the contrary. In an extremely blunt interview, Milovan Djilas stated that "behind the [Macedonian] issue stands most certainly the Soviet Union," with its hidden objective "to work through Bulgaria toward shattering Yugoslavia."[15]

An international theoretical conference on the "Construction of Socialism and Communism and World Progress" opened in Sofia. Sponsored by the Central Committee of the Bulgarian Communist Party, in cooperation with the *World Marxist Review* monthly, the conference was attended by repre-

---

[12]*The Times* (London), 18 August 1978.

[13]*La Stampa* (Turin), 9 March 1978; *Frankfurter Allgemeine Zeitung*, 11 April, 1978.

[14]*New York Times*, 2 December 1978. Ceauşescu also had refused to sign a Warsaw Pact statement attacking China and another one criticizing the Camp David talks on the Middle East.

[15]*Die Welt* (Hamburg), 22-23 July, 1978.

sentatives of 73 communist and workers' parties. The Soviet delegation was headed by Boris Ponomarev, candidate politburo member and secretary, according to Sofia radio for 12 December 1978.

The League of Communists (LCY) held its eleventh national congress during 20–23 June. The most important decision involved reducing the decisionmaking body or presidium from 48 to 24 members. As explicitly stated by Tito, the parallel existence of a collective state presidency (all 9 members belong to the LCY presidium) and of the new party presidium composed of his trusted supporters, guarantees a smooth transition after he leaves the political scene. However, writings and speeches of the most prominent theoretician, Edward Kardelj, suggest how difficult the task will be to reconcile exclusive political rule with the main Titoist concepts of sociopolitical decentralization and worker self-management. Kardelj likewise asserted that "Eurocommunism" is not applicable to countries already ruled by communist parties, even though LCY maintains close relations with corresponding Italian, Spanish, and French movements. Yugoslav-American relations continued to improve. On the occasion of Tito's stay in Washington, D.C. the official communiqué announced "continued support of the United States for the independence, territorial integrity and unity of Yugoslavia." Addition of the word *unity* carried this beyond previous U.S. policy statements.[16] Chairman Hua received an enthusiastic greeting when he came to Belgrade in August, although Tito emphasized that the visit was not directed against the Soviet Union.

In neighboring Albania, however, the journal *Rruga e partisë* for February republished an article from the "Maoist" Brazilian communist party's monthly which attacked Peking for attempts to split the Marxist-Leninist movement throughout the world. Direct criticism by a politburo member four months later described the Chinese theory of the three worlds as an attempt to replace orthodoxy with opportunism.[17] The following month China stopped all economic and technical assistance, which reportedly had totaled almost five billion dollars over the preceding quarter century. Tirana sent a 56-page letter to Peking, harshly reviewing relations between the two countries.[18] Enver Hoxha revealed in a speech that he would seek friends selectively in the "bourgeois" world and approached India for help. Foreign trade delegations subsequently visited Sweden and Finland, offering agricultural products in return for assistance in developing unexplored mineral wealth.[19]

Western Europe. The same two principal themes continued to dominate policy positions of the area's 24 communist movements: unity of the Left and détente between communist-ruled and democratic states. They represent subjects which these parties can address in the alleged interest of stable government and peaceful relations between East and West. At the same time, their spokesmen freely criticize capitalism and oppose the neutron weapon as well as the development of nuclear power plants in Western Europe but not in the Soviet bloc. The subject of "Eurocommunism" continued to receive attention, especially because of the emphasis placed upon it by communists in France, Italy, and Spain.

During 1978, however, it became clear that Eurocommunism does little for unity even among those parties which espouse the concept. Many of them not only proclaim independence from Moscow, but also independence from one another. At the beginning of the year this trend was described by a political observer as representing[20]

> largely, though perhaps not entirely, a manifestation of the postwar nationalist revival in Europe. It is Gaullism of the left. . . . If aggressive nationalism is now the fashion among Communists and the extreme left, there is no cause for jubilation. It means that the follies of nationalism are being superimposed on parties whose attachment to dictatorships hasn't changed. This bodes ill for the future of freedom and democratic rule.

[16]*New York Times*, 10 March 1978.
[17]Tirana radio, 10 June 1978.
[18]Ibid., 30 July 1978.
[19]*Christian Science Monitor*, 14 December 1978.
[20]Walter Laqueur, *Wall Street Journal*, 5 January 1978.

Although "unity of the Left" continued to be endorsed as a desirable and effective means to gain power through the establishment of credible reputation as legitimate participants in the democratic electoral process, almost all of the West European communist movements emphasized the necessity of pursuing their own independent paths toward eventual replacement of capitalism with "socialism." Sixteen of the twenty-four parties held representation in parliaments during 1978, the same as last year. They include Belgium, Cyprus, Denmark, Finland, France, Greece, Iceland, Italy, Luxembourg, Netherlands, Norway, Portugal, San Marino, Spain, Sweden and Switzerland. By contrast, Austria, Faroe Islands, Federal Republic of Germany, West Berlin, Great Britain, Ireland, Malta, and Turkey have no communists in their legislatures. Three party members hold ministerial positions in Iceland, the same number in Finland, with tiny San Marino having four at cabinet or sub-cabinet levels.

National elections took place in four countries. The party vote declined in France, but increased slightly in Belgium, Iceland, and San Marino. Representation continues to be largest in Italy, where it comprises just over one-third of the seats in parliament (228 out of 630). Among the remaining parties, San Marino communists had the next highest percentage (26.67), followed by those in Cyprus (25.71), Iceland (23.33), Finland (20.0), France (17.52), Portugal (15.21), and Luxembourg (8.47). None of the other eight parties held more than 6 percent.

Italian, French, and Spanish movements all have endorsed Eurocommunism as a vehicle for achieving power. During 1978 close attention was given to efforts by the Communist Party of France (PCF) to win a major victory in national elections.

Extraordinary success at municipal levels during March 1977 had suggested that electoral alliance with the socialists (PS) would result in the attainment of a majority the following year. Public opinion polls supported this, despite unsuccessful efforts to renegotiate the "common program" in September. Most forecasts predicted that the PCF—PS coalition would win in March 1978 and promptly nationalize all large companies and the banks. Thus, the prospect of "socialism with a French hue"[21] occupied the attention of most observers. Electoral success in France, together with the growing strength of the party in Italy, would have made it considerably easier for other Western European movements to endorse Eurocommunism.

The outcome of the French elections came as a surprise and may have helped bring about the relative quiescence among other West European communist parties for the remainder of the year. PCF received 20.55 percent, almost one point less than in 1973 and the lowest vote since 1945 (with the exception of 1958). More important, the party failed to obtain the one-fourth that PCF leader George Marchais had declared would be necessary to form a coalition government with the socialists. PS captured 22.58 percent, laying claim to the title of "first party in France."

The long-term effect on PCF, as well as on the electoral future of PS, is not at all clear. Prominent communists, like Jean Elleinstein, severely criticized the PFC leadership and stressed that it should accelerate the growing independence from Moscow. At the same time, others condemned the PS for its "slide to the Right." In the fall, Marchais described participation by socialists in the governments of all countries where they hold power as a "recourse of the grand bourgeoisie, permitting it to preserve its policies and its domination."[22]

Toward the end of the year it became known that the PCF political bureau remained divided concerning a strategy to follow vis-à-vis the socialists. One group advocated restoring "unity of the Left." Another concluded that PS had compromised with the bourgeoisie and that PCF must rely on itself, even if this meant a new period of isolation.[23] The party's twenty-third congress, to be held in May 1979, assumes additional significance with regard to these policies.

---

[21]Klaus-Peter Schmidt, *Die Zeit*, 27 January 1978.

[22]Quoted in *Le Monde* (Paris), 30 September 1978.

[23]T. Pfister in ibid., 19 and 23 October 1978.

While the most significant event unquestionably involved the French election, activities of the Communist Party of Italy (PCI) also warranted special attention. The Italian movement exercises a more powerful role in government at municipal, province and national levels than is the case in any other European country. PCI clearly stood to gain in stature had a French cabinet included PCF members. While PCI is not in the Italian cabinet, without its support no government could survive.[24] During the year, however, politics continued as usual. Hence, PCI devoted primary attention to emphasizing its commitment to achieve a "revolution" through observance of democratic rules. Consistent with this position, it condemned the murder of Aldo Moro and maintained that the decision against negotiating with the kidnappers had been correct.

Support for the government coalition also reflected an increasing emphasis on independence from Moscow. This point was highlighted during PCI leader Enrico Berlinguer's visit to Paris, Moscow and Belgrade. He claimed that Eurocommunism had become stronger as a result of the trip to France. The communiqué[25] released by the two parties also stressed "full independence in the activities of both parties," and recognized the "diversity of conditions under which the parties pursue their policies and differences existing with respect to certain aspects of the European Economic Community."

After the visit to Belgrade, some observers thought PCI might advocate restoration of relations with the Communist Party of China while seeking CPSU approval for its continued advocacy of independence. The communiqué[26] following Berlinguer's visit to Moscow could have been interpreted as Soviet endorsement for PCI domestic strategy, i.e., "cooperation between communists, socialists, social democrats and other democratic forces—including Christian ones—can make its own contribution to strengthening the process of détente and cooperation between states with different social systems." The fifteenth PCI congress has been scheduled for 20—25 March 1979.

Eurocommunism's foremost champion emerged in Spain after publication in 1977 of *Eurocommunism and the State* by Santiago Carrillo, chairman of that country's communist party (PCE). During 1978 he continued his movement's avowed commitment to the democratic process. This was stressed at the party's ninth congress held in April—the first legal one in almost half a century. PCE had described itself previously as a "thorough-going Eurocomunist" party, no longer intent on armed insurrection or the dictatorship of the proletariat.[27] Most controversial at the national congress was the decision to change the PCE designation from "Marxist-Leninist" to "Marxist, revolutionary and democratic." This, Carrillo had contended, would mean eliminating capitalism within the framework of parliamentary democracy. By the end of the year indications suggested that public support for the PCE had increased. With parliamentary elections scheduled for 1 March 1979, it could be expected that the party would continue to strengthen its image as a legitimate participant in political life.

Activities of the smaller communist movements in Western Europe were not without significance and might have increased substantially had PCF entered the new French cabinet. In Portugal, where the party had played a major role in the 1974 revolution and held a portfolio in every government for almost two years thereafter, it had no cabinet posts. Strongly pro-Soviet, it frequently criticized Eurocommunism and particularly its Spanish counterpart. While the influence of the movement on Portugal's government continued to pose a security problem for other NATO states, party activity did not exert any decisive effect on the country itself.

---

[24]At a press conference toward the end of the year, Berlinguer called for a "government of national unity" that would include PCI members. *New York Times*, 21 December 1978.

[25]*L'Unità* (Rome), 6 October 1978. These differences, apart from EEC, also include PCI support for supranational and legislative powers in the European parliament to be elected during June 1979. Ibid., 9 November 1978.

[26]Moscow radio, 9 October 1978.

[27]*Mundo Obrero* (Madrid), 26 January 1978.

Cypriot, Greek and Turkish communists played a minimal role in political life. The movement is proscribed in Turkey, and in Greece it remains split. The communist party on Cyprus (AKEL) is the best organized in these three countries, although its support comes primarily from the Greek majority on the island. While the proportion of party members to national adult population probably ranks AKEL second only to its Italian counterpart, it has never been represented in any cabinet even though it holds one-fourth of all Greek seats in the legislature.

Neither British nor Irish communists have attracted much attention since the 1977 split among the former, resulting in a Eurocommunist majority, even though they have at least one party member on almost every trade union executive board. This penetration is of considerable significance for Britain's political life because about 80 percent of Labour Party funds comes from trade union contributions. In addition, almost 88 percent of the votes at the annual Labour Party conference is controlled by trade unions.

In Denmark, the Netherlands, and Belgium, communist activities did not include major developments. To some extent this was also the case in the Nordic countries of Finland, Iceland, Norway and Sweden. The Marxist Left in Norway is divided into three competing factions and remains electorally weak. In Sweden the party is split, with Eurocommunists in the majority. Parliamentary elections are scheduled for September 1979. If these should result in a return of social democrats to power the Swedish communist party may assume a more important role than heretofore. In Iceland communists polled 22.9 percent of the vote (up 4.6 points) and won 14 out of 60 seats in parliament, for a gain of three. The coalition government, with progressives and social democrats, includes three communists in cabinet posts: education and communications, industry, and commerce. In Finland the communist party holds one-fifth of all parliamentary seats and participates in the coalition government, holding posts of deputy education minister as well as labor and traffic ministers. It is also split, but the factions remain within a single movement.

No developments of major significance were reflected in the activities of the Austrian, Luxembourg or Swiss movement, although the last party elected Armand Magnin (58) to replace long-time party chairman Jean Vincent (72). The only other change in leadership occurred in the SEW or Socialist Unity Party of West Berlin. The sudden death of chairman Gerhard Danelius required an extraordinary congress which elected former deputy chairman Horst Schmitt to succeed Danelius in July.

Throughout the Federal Republic of Germany traditional pro-Soviet positions were maintained by DKP. Its fifth national congress met during October and confirmed the leadership of Herbert Mies. DKP reiterated the aim of establishing "real socialism," as practiced in the German Democratic Republic, and endorsed "unity of the Left." The latter represents the first phase in a three-part strategy which later foresees a "united front," finally leading to a "popular front." DKP does not support the Eurocommunism in France, Italy, and Spain.

One of the smallest movements of Western Europe is located in San Marino, yet in national elections held during May it received one-fourth of the vote and now holds 16 of 60 parliamentary seats. Formation of a leftist cabinet during the summer gave communists the departments of internal affairs, industry and crafts, health, and education. In September party chairman Ermenegildo Gasperoni was elected to a six-month term as one of the captain-regents who are heads of state.

Asia and the Pacific. Three new developments during 1978 may have far reaching significance for peace and economic prosperity throughout the region. First, the People's Republic of China (PRC) reversed certain Maoist policies of the past and initiated a number of new activities to speed up modernization. Second, the Socialist Republic of Vietnam became embroiled in a small war with the communist regime in Cambodia, and that conflict threatened to involve the PRC and even the USSR. Finally, a new revolutionary Marxist regime seized power in Afghanistan.

In the PRC deputy premier Teng Hsiao-ping continued to consolidate power. His policy of the four modernizations (industry, agriculture, science, and defense) gained momentum. The party convened a number of high-level conferences that discussed how to revive the educational system, promote a lagging industry and agriculture, and consider the means to obtain advanced technology and capital.[28] During the fall China and the United States agreed to exchange students and scholars. Top PRC leaders traveled abroad to convey their government's intention to expand trade and purchase foreign technology. Even former chairman Mao came under criticism for serious mistakes during the Great Cultural Revolution and for nearly restoring a fascist leadership under the "gang of four," now under house arrest.

The PRC is bent on obtaining credits from the capitalist West and initiating domestic organizational exchanges[29] to create a more beneficial environment for economic development. Peking's new outward reach probably achieved its greatest success when on 15 December the United States agreed to long-standing PRC prerequisites for normalization: break the 1953 treaty with the Republic of China; cut diplomatic ties; remove all American troops from Taiwan. It was announced that Teng would arrive in Washington, D.C. on 29 January 1979.

In former Indo-China the Socialist Republic of Vietnam (SRV) moved rapidly to eliminate the middle class throughout the south. During the month of March urban businessmen of all types were forced to cease activities and their assets nationalized. Meanwhile, the communist leadership pressed for more collectivization of agriculture. A poor rice harvest, however, caused extreme hardship. As the economy became affected by adverse developments, SRV angered its former ally China by stepping up military operations against Cambodia. The Vietnamese have established a rival Cambodian communist party and a provisional government[30] which they hope will replace the Pol Pot regime either through a coup in Phnom Penh or by defeating the Cambodian military on the battlefield.

The SRV Government signed a new treaty[31] with the USSR, and the Soviets are supplying much needed food grains and military equipment by airlift or sea. Hanoi has moved closer to Moscow and its relations with Peking have worsened. One-half million refugees have fled the south of Vietnam, attesting the economic crisis and repressive measures against the middle class.

In Afghanistan a military coup created a Marxist state, the first of its kind in this part of Asia. The new leader, Nur Mohammed Taraki, has denied that his People's Democratic Party is communist[32] or even Marxist. But to carry out regime goals of expanding state ownership, control over the economy, and agrarian reform, he signed 29 trade and aid agreements with the USSR which have brought in 5,000 Soviet military and civilian advisers.[33] Taraki's movement is establishing youth organizations on the Pioneer and Komsomol model, co-opting the trade unions, and setting up party committees and their organs throughout the country. These tactics can only mean consolidating the power of the People's Democratic Party supported by the twenty-year treaty signed in Moscow.[34] This unprecedented event has given the Soviet Union a new sphere of influence in this strategically important part of the world.

---

[28]China has signed during 1978 over $60 billion in import contracts compared with an export total of only $9 billion. *San Francisco Examiner & Chronicle*, 24 December 1978.

[29]A five-day Central Committee plenum rehabilitated several persons who had been purged by Mao and added three new members to the politburo, including the widow of Chou-En-lai. *New York Times*, 24 December 1978.

[30]This so-called National United Front of Kampuchea has adopted an action program, a summary of which was broadcast by Moscow radio on 5 December 1978. Insurgents, supported by Vietnamese regulars, had occupied three province capitals and about one-fourth of Cambodia by the end of the year.

[31]*Washington Post*, 13 December 1978.

[32]Identified as such by the *Socialist* (Sydney), 24 November 1976.

[33]*U.S. News & World Report*, 11 December 1978, pp. 55-56.

[34]Moscow radio, 5 December 1978.

Such developments suggest two new trends. First, the USSR will increase its role throughout Asia, particularly in the western and southeastern parts of that continent. Second, China's new pragmatic leadership is committed to building the PRC into an economic and military superpower by the end of the century as well as reversing many policies of Mao Tse-tung. Peking still remains hostile toward Moscow and has publicly declared that it will not renew the 30-year friendship treaty which expires on 13 February 1979. President Carter's announcement of U.S. normalization with the PRC takes effect two weeks later and will produce new and unpredictable international developments.

The communist parties and other left-wing movements in Asia and the Pacific made little or no advances in increasing their membership or expanding their political or ideological influence. The Japanese Communist Party (JCP) was confronted by a major crisis when politburo member Satomi Hakamada exposed inner party secrets through several articles published by a popular weekly.[35] These revelations concerning the top JCP echelon are bound to tarnish its image but probably will not create any major setback which cannot be overcome with time.

Meanwhile, the North Korean communist regime has tried to cure an ailing economy and bolster its military forces. Pyongyang now definitely manipulates both allies, USSR and PRC, yet does not seem to have obtained much from either one recently. The question remains how much , if any, leverage either of these states can exert. As economic growth in the south continues to outstrip that of the north, the Korean peninsula remains an area of great potential conflict that could envelop neighboring countries in war.

The Americas. Communists and their supporters throughout Latin America flocked to the polls in unprecedented numbers during 1978, as some of the military governments instituted reforms and democratic governments also held scheduled elections for congressional or presidential offices. The most successful of these parties was the Movement Towards Socialism (MAS) in Venezuela—a break-away from the pro-CPSU Communist Party of Venezuela (PCV)—whose presidential candidate drew a mere 6 percent of the vote in the December balloting. MAS elected eleven deputies and two senators and firmly established itself as the third most important party in the country, far ahead of PCV.

Communist movements also won congressional seats in most of the region's other democratic countries—Colombia, Costa Rica, Martinique, Guadeloupe—as well as contesting elections in alliance with leftist movements in a number of other countries, including Bolivia, Peru, and Ecuador, where military governments loosened the reins slightly during the year.

The People's Progressive Party under Cheddi Jagan continued to participate in Guyana's legislature, while protesting prime minister Forbes Burnham's alleged manipulation of votes in an important constitutional referendum.[36] Another pro-Soviet movement boycotted the election in Guatemala. On the other hand, pro-Chinese communists who had wanted to participate in the election held by Ecuador were not permitted to do so. Maoists took part in electoral fronts of Bolivia and Peru with little success.

Meanwhile, governments which formerly had been the most democratic on the continent—Chile and Uruguay—continued to suppress communist activities. The parties in those countries operated underground at home but openly and often rather actively abroad from the major capitals of Eastern and Western Europe, Cuba and Mexico. Repression of all communist activities continued in Paraguay, Haiti, and most of the states throughout Central America.

Pro-Soviet movements influenced labor affairs in several countries, particularly Guyana, Colombia, and Peru, while pro-Chinese groups continued to attract support from workers in Colombia and students

---

[35] *Shukan Shincho* (Tokyo), 12 January 1978, p. 105.

[36] Leader of the People's Temple, Jim Jones, who ordered the mass suicide or execution of 913 followers, reportedly had been an American communist since the 1950s according to the *Chronicle* of Guyana. He also bequeathed $7 million, never transmitted, to the CPSU. *New York Times*, 18 and 20 December 1978.

in several of the Andean countries. The pro-Soviet communist party in Peru evidently suffered from serious internal dissensions, due to its relatively moderate line in domestic affairs. The (formerly pro-Chinese) Communist Party of Brazil broke with the Peking government over recent shifts in policies pursued by the People's Republic of China.

Guerrilla and terrorist activities erupted into virtual civil war throughout Nicaragua, as Sandinist Liberation Front (FSLN) forces challenged Anastasio Somoza Debayle's government. A similar situation seemed to be brewing in El Salvador.[37] Pro-Soviet and other guerrillas remained active from time to time in certain areas of Colombia, Mexico, and several other countries. Argentine guerrillas—particularly the Marxist-Peronist Montoneros—attracted attention through their international terrorist activities rather than in opposition to the Videla government at home.

Cuban troops and other personnel increased to almost 50,000 in fifteen African countries, particularly in Angola and Ethiopia. They played a decisive role, with heavy Soviet support, in the Ethiopian counteroffensive against Somali guerrillas and troops in the Ogaden desert. Toward the end of the year there were also indications that Cubans might be used to eliminate the secessionist movement from Eritrea. In domestic affairs Fidel Castro agreed to release 3,200 political prisoners if they would be received by the United States. Officials in Washington indicated the government would accept 400 per month.[38]

The Communist Party of the United States (CPUSA) attempted to project greater independence in political campaigns, its candidate winning only 11,279 votes in the November 1978 election for governor of New York State. It also increased efforts to establish center-Left labor cooperation. CPUSA called for nationalization of the energy industry and, in the most important shift of the year, supported the Equal Rights Amendment. The movement to the north defended a united Canada but at the same time paid lip service to self-determination for nationals of French extraction, while the Maoists came out unequivocally in support of an independent Quebec.

Africa and the Middle East. Moscow's strategy in sub-Saharan Africa envisages a series of so-called national democratic revolutions as stepping stones on the road to power. Tactics to assure this objective vary widely. They entail cooperation with incumbent governments, not necessarily "pro-socialist"; support for pro-Soviet communist parties; and participation by the latter in self-styled liberation movements or in fronts designed to develop Marxist-Leninist parties of an orthodox type. Communist movements remain of negligible importance at present. The once-powerful party in the Sudan has not recovered since 1971, when it was smashed. The Parti Africain de l'Indépendence of Senegal[39] is small; the Communist Party of Lesotho and the Socialist Workers' and Farmers' Party in Nigeria have remained insignificant since their inception. The South African Communist Party (SACP) wields some influence through intimate links with the also banned African National Congress. Nevertheless, SACP essentially is a party in exile and influential mainly among a small group of intellectuals.

On the face of it, communism has made enormous gains through the emergence of regimes in countries as different as Angola, Mozambique, Ethiopia, the People's Republic of the Congo, and Benin, all of which claim to be operating on Marxist-Leninist principles. In practice, they vary widely. However, none of their ruling movements can be described as orthodox communist. Instead, they might be called "Afro-Marxist," rather than using the Soviet designation of "revolutionary democratic." Despite the great differences that divide them, they usually share certain common features.

---

[37]The three guerrilla groups in El Salvador are called Armed Forces of National Resistance, Popular Revolutionary Bloc, and Popular Forces of Liberation. *New York Times*, 21 December 1978.

[38]*San Francisco Examiner & Chronicle*, 10 December 1978.

[39]Senegal has two communist parties, one actually legal but controlled by the government; the other clandestine group is supported by Moscow and bears the same PAI designation.

These characteristics comprise the following: (1) the formal structure of a Marxist-Leninist party, ostensibly based on "democratic centralism"; (2) a privileged position for the new salaried class of party functionaries and politicized soldiers; (3) widespread lack of discipline and poor organization, especially at the village level; (4) the eclectic nature of the ruling movement's Marxist-Leninist ideology, developed in countries where the urban proletariat is small and where most of the population makes a living from agriculture; (5) the prominence given to the armed forces within both government and ruling party; (6) widespread willingness to collaborate for limited objectives with Western and, in the case of Mozambique, even with South African, business interests; (7) heavy reliance on military support from the Soviet bloc and, less so, from China; (8) a striking contrast between the ruling party's claimed economic achievements and actual performance, with widespread economic dislocation; (9) dependence, despite a formal non-racist ideology, on particular ethnic groups; (10) strong commitment to guerrilla warfare to attain revolutionary objectives, especially for the purpose of "liberating" all of southern Africa; (11) extensive collaboration with "progressive bourgeois" groups in Western countries which have developed an extensive propaganda network. Many of these characteristics are shared by African nationalist movements of a non-Marxist variety, so that a distinction between them often remains blurred.

Soviet-bloc military intervention in Africa has come to be regarded as a potent form of international solidarity among progressive forces in the Third World. Cuba has sent ground troops and instructors to countries like Angola,[40] Ethiopia, and the People's Republic of the Congo. East Germany provides specialists and instructors, especially for uniformed and secret police units. The Soviet Union, in addition to making available weapons and training facilities, also assigns its own senior staff officers for military planning.

In the political arena there has developed a tendency for popular fronts to expand into parties, complete with secretariats and political bureaus, functioning on the Marxist-Leninist principle of democratic centralism. For example, the Popular Movement for the Liberation of Angola transformed itself at the end of 1977 from a "movement" into a Marxist-Leninist party called MPLA-PT or MPLA Party of Labor. MPLA-PT operates as a self-styled "vanguard of the proletariat," uniting workers, peasants and intellectuals in a country overwhelmingly dependent on backward farmers. The new party depends to a considerable extent on support from mestizos who are of mixed Afro-European ancestry and among the best-educated in the country. Its influence is weak, on the other hand, among dissident ethnic groups such as Bakongo in the north and Ovimbundu in the south. About half of the central committee membership comes from military professionals.

Stressing the virtues of "scientific socialism," MPLA-PT considers religion as no more than "a distorted reflection . . . of reality that is basically determined by the living conditions of men."[41] Angola supports USSR foreign policy, while it relies for much of its hard currency on the Gulf Oil Corporation. At present the regime depends heavily on Cuban, and to a lesser extent Soviet, military assistance against guerrilla movements. MPLA-PT also must cope with dissension within its own ranks concerning personalities,[42] the reportedly privileged position of mestizos, economic problems, and ethnic issues. It attempts to deal with the chaotic economic situation by regime control over foreign trade, organizing villagers into cooperatives, and nationalization of processing industries. None of these measures appear to have improved the situation.

Mozambique has managed to steer a somewhat more independent course. FRELIMO, the Marxist-Leninist ruling party, looks to the Chinese as well as the Soviet model, having placed special emphasis on

---

[40]By the end of January 1979 there were expected to be about 30,000 Cubans in Angola, including 5,000 civilian technicians. *Washington Post*, 10 December 1978.

[41]Central Committee report to the MPLA congress. *Granma* (Havana), 14-15 December 1977.

[42]President Agostinho Neto apparently strengthened his position when two members of the eleven-man politburo were dismissed. *Pravda*, 10 December 1978.

development of communal villages. At the same time, the country depends on South African assistance in operating its railways, the main port of Maputo, and the Cabora Bassa hydro-electric project.

The People's Republic of the Congo is controlled by the Parti Congolais du Travail (PCT) which describes itself as a Marxist-Leninist movement. It claims to operate along principles of "scientific socialism" and relies heavily on Cuban advisers. With its heavily ethnic overtones, PCT can in no way be regarded as an orthodox communist party.

Ethiopia is controlled by the armed forces high command. This ruling group has destroyed the traditional power positions of monarchy, church, and landed gentry. The new rulers depend to a considerable degree on Cuban and Soviet military assistance[43] against Eritrean and other rebels. They use Marxism as an ideological tool with which to rebuild an Ethiopian empire and, for all practical purposes, maintain Amhara ethnic predominance. The military junta places special emphasis on the value of the USSR connection. According to Mengistu Haile Miriam,[44] chairman of the provisional military administrative council, "the international assistance given to Ethiopia by the Soviet people, party and government during the hard period of radical social reform holds a special place in the history of the Ethiopian revolution." Thanks to this help, "the national democratic revolution has now reached a point of no return." From the Moscow point of view, this is a "progressive" policy[45] but remains far from entitling the Ethiopian ruling group to a place among the ruling communist parties.

The USSR would support an alliance among FRELIMO, MPLA-PT, SWAPO (South-West Africa/Namibia), ANC, and ZAPU (Rhodesia/Zimbabwe), the last as part of the so-called Patriotic Front. SWAPO, ZAPU and ANC all benefit from Soviet weapons and training facilities. ANC attempts to infiltrate guerrillas into South Africa through Botswana. ZAPU is engaged in building up something like a regular armed force in Zambia, while leaving the bulk of the fighting to ZANU, which is a ZAPU partner in the Patriotic Front. There exists bitter political dissension between ZAPU and ZANU, the latter looking to North Korea and China as well as to the Soviet Union. There are also disputes between MPLA-PT and SWAPO, as the former, along with the Cubans in Angola, has carried out a savage counter-insurgency campaign against ethnic groups that support SWAPO.[46] Formally, these movements are all committed to the struggle for national liberation, "socialism," and (except for ZANU), to a pro-Soviet foreign policy. However, their ideological, political, and military discipline still leaves much to be desired.

Orthodox communist parties have made even less of an impact throughout the Moslem world, including Syria and Iraq where they command a certain degree of support and nominally participate in their respective governments. Soviet influence has diminished in the latter country,[47] but this loss has been more than balanced by USSR successes in the People's Democratic Republic of [South] Yemen. Here, the government was overthrown by a rival faction within the ruling National Front. The army as well as the Front's political bureau underwent a purge. Groups remaining in the National Front agreed to

---

[43]USSR aid has surpassed $1 billion. *New York Times*, 21 November 1978.

[44]Addis Ababa radio, 10 March 1978.

[45]The USSR has signed a twenty-year treaty of friendship and cooperation with Ethiopia. *Washington Post*, 22 November 1978.

[46]L. H. Gann and Peter Duignan, *South Africa: War, Revolution or Peace?* (Stanford, CA.: Hoover Institution Press, 1978), pp. 50-52.

[47]Note however that Iraqi vice-president Saddam Hussein traveled to Moscow, the first high level visit since the Baghdad regime executed several communists early in the year. Communiqué broadcast over Moscow radio, 13 December 1978.

establish a single "vanguard party," based on Marxist-Leninist principles, known as the Yemen Socialist Party. The new organization held its constituent congress in October 1978 at Aden. The movement considers its goal to be "scientific socialism." It wishes to avoid the "mistakes" made by Arab leaders, like former Egyptian president Gamal Abdul Nasser, who failed to go beyond the national democratic phase of the "bourgeois revolution" with its loose alliance of class interests.[48] South Yemen's ruling faction, headed by Abdul Fatah Ismail, supports the USSR and in turn derives assistance from Cuban troops as well as East German instructors and specialists. The Yemen Socialist Party as yet has not been recognized as communist by Moscow.

Farther to the east, the widespread unrest in Iran owes little to activities of the Tudeh [communist] Party. Opposition is derived from many different groups: conservative shopkeepers, traditionally minded mullahs, discontented workmen and state employees, left-wing intellectuals, and others. The shah's problems have been aggravated by covert warfare ably waged against him by the USSR, which maintains an extensive network of intelligence agents throughout the country[49] and also makes use of front organizations like the Iran-Soviet Cultural Society. Pro-communist underground publications in Farsi support the new regimes of Afghanistan and South Yemen, criticize the Iraqi government (previously pro-Soviet in its outlook), and call for a united front between Moslems and Marxists. Iranian terrorists reportedly receive arms, funds, and training facilities from countries as varied as Algeria, Cuba, Lebanon, South Yemen, and above all, Afghanistan, which reportedly has become the main center for anti-shah activities.[50]

The Soviet-Afghan treaty of 5 December 1978, mentioned above, now brings to seven the number of such agreements in force between the USSR and countries of Africa, the Middle East, and South Asia. These included India (9 August 1971), Iraq (8 April 1972), Angola (8 October 1976), Mozambique (31 March 1977), Vietnam (3 November 1978),[51] and Ethiopia (20 November 1978). Two other similar treaties had been abrogated unilaterally by Egypt on 14 March 1976 and Somalia on 13 November 1977, respectively. Soviet strategic objectives with regard to control over maritime choke-points, like approaches to the Persian Gulf or the Red Sea and ultimately the Cape of Good Hope, are worthy of consideration.

International communist front organizations continued, for the most part, to support the foreign interests and policies of the Soviet Union. Indeed, on no issue did they openly criticize the USSR. There were heard, however, a number of dissenting voices within certain of these organizations. Internal differences could be noted especially in the World Federation of Trade Unions, where the Italian delegation on several occasions spoke up in opposition to what it called inadequate attention paid to the problems of the socialist states, i.e., the communist-ruled countries of Eastern Europe. It also described the WFTU as "an outdated and useless instrument."[52]

Interwoven with their basic effort to expand membership and influence by attracting the collaboration of nonpolitical organizations through the use of such slogans as "defend détente, disarmament, and peace," were general denunciations by the fronts of the governments in Chile, South Africa, Israel, Nicaragua, and the United States, the last specifically for its efforts to promote peace in the Middle East as well as for its development of the neutron weapon. The Palestine Liberation Organization and other

---

[48] *Washington Post*, 23 November 1978.

[49] A former Iranian general officer and three Russians were arrested in Teheran on espionage/subversion charges. *Siam Roth* (Bangkok), 29 May 1978.

[50] Robert Moss, *New Republic*, 2 December 1978.

[51] Vietnam and Afghanistan, of course, are communist-ruled states.

[52] *L'Unità*, 15 March 1978.

such movements received nothing but praise. Consistent adherence to Soviet propaganda lines were the hallmark of all fronts.

In a review of the year's activities, three tend to stand out. Most important was the eleventh youth festival held at Havana in July, and sponsored by the World Federation of Democratic Youth and the International Union of Students. Two features tended to overshadow everything else: a carnival atmosphere, prepared and staged by the Cubans, and the discordant note struck mainly by Western delegates who wanted to condemn violations of human rights in communist-ruled as well as other countries. The delegation from Yugoslavia refused to sign the final document.

The second notable activity involves the ninth congress held by the World Federation of Trade Unions. It also witnessed disunity, brought on by actions of the two strongest West European labor organizations, those in Italy and France, both dominated by communists. The Italians withdrew from WFTU. The French demonstrated their displeasure by not permitting a colleague to be nominated for secretary general, a post held by a citizen of France ever since the WFTU had been founded.

Third, but perhaps of lesser importance, were the border clashes and pitched battles between Vietnam and Cambodia. Although fronts followed the Soviet lead in backing Vietnam, also in criticizing China for supporting Cambodia, it clearly bothered the leaders that two communist-ruled states were fighting each other. They could only urge a settlement on the "reasonable terms" suggested by Vietnam.

*   *   *

Staff members and several of the associate editors were responsible for some of the writing, research, and most of the data-collecting effort that produced this *Yearbook*. Profiles were contributed by a total of 65 outside scholars, many of whom prepared more than one. Names and affiliations appear at the end of individual essays. Mrs. Ica Juilland and Mrs. Lynn Ratliff assisted in the processing and filing of research materials as well as assembling some of the data. Much of the final typing was done by Mrs. Margit Grigory, who also handled most of the correspondence with contributors. Special appreciation is due to the curators and their staff as well as members of the readers' services department at the Hoover Institution for their response to emergency requests and for the bibliography.

Sources are cited throughout the text, with news agencies normally identified by generally accepted initials. Abbreviations are also used for the following widely quoted publications:

FBIS   *Foreign Broadcast Information Service*

NYT   *New York Times*

WMR   *World Marxist Review*

IB   *Information Bulletin* (of the *WMR*)

YICA   *Yearbook on International Communist Affairs*

January 1979   Richard F. Staar

EASTERN EUROPE AND THE SOVIET UNION

Albania

The Albanian Communist Party was established on 8 November 1941. At its First Congress, November 1948, the name was changed to the Albanian Party of Labor (Partia e Punës e Shqipërisë; APL). As the only legal political party in Albania, the APL exercises a monopoly of power. Party members hold all key posts in the government and the mass organizations. All 250 seats in the People's Assembly, the national legislature, are held by members of the Democratic Front (DF), the party-controlled mass organization to which all Albanian voters belong.

At the Seventh APL Congress (1−7 November 1976), it was announced that there were 101,500 party members. Of these, 88,000 were full members and 13,500 candidate members. In 1976, 37.5 percent of APL members were reportedly laborers, 29.0 percent peasants, and 33.5 percent white-collar workers (*Zëri i popullit*, 2 November 1976). Women in 1978 comprised about 27 percent of the party's membership (ibid., 2 June). Approximately 4 percent of the Albanian people are party members, the lowest ratio of party members to the general population among the communist-ruled states of Eastern Europe.

The population of Albania in mid-1978 was approximately 2,597,600. According to 1975 census data, peasants comprise 49.4 percent of the population, laborers 36.2 percent, and white-collar workers 14.4 percent. In 1975, about 42 percent of the population was under the age of fifteen (ibid., 28 May, 8 June 1975).

Leadership and Organization. There were no significant leadership changes in the top echelons of the APL during 1978.

Politburo member and Minister of Finance Haki Toska, who had not been mentioned in the Albanian communications media since November 1977, did make a public appearance with his polit-buro colleagues in October (ibid., 3 October). Toska, a long-time associate of APL First Secretary Enver Hoxha, was also re-elected to the People's Assembly in November (ibid., 14 November). Both these developments suggest that, if Toska had in fact run afoul of the APL leadership, he had managed to regain their confidence by the end of 1978.

APL First Secretary Enver Hoxha, the party leader since 1941 and the dominant personality in the ruling elite, observed his 70th birthday in October (ibid., 17 October). Although there have been persistent rumors that Hoxha has been plagued by serious health problems (see *YICA, 1977*, p. 1), he nevertheless continued to maintain an active schedule. In keeping with his practice of recent years, Hoxha attended numerous functions in Tirana and made several trips outside the Albanian capital.

Between 15—28 March the Albanian party leader toured his home district of Gjirokaster as well as the Sarandë district. This trip was unusual with respect to both the length of time Hoxha spent away from Tirana and the detail in which it was covered by the Albanian press, radio, and television (see e.g., *Zëri i popullit*, 16-31 March; *Yllia* [Tirana], April). It appears that Hoxha's lengthy sojourn in southwestern Albania was intended to rally support for his policies and, perhaps, to recapture some of the popularity he seems to have lost as a consequence of his extensive purges of the party leadership and government bureaucracy during the mid-1970s. The APL first secretary's endorsement of the regime's efforts to raise the nation's standard of living, his acknowledgment that the goals of the Ideological and Cultural Revolution would have to be implemented over a long period of time, and his strong appeals to patriotism further suggest that he was interested in fostering greater national unity—especially as Tirana's relations with Peking continued to deteriorate (*Zëri i popullit*, 28 March; *Rruga e partisë*, March). In August Hoxha also briefly visited the Pogradec district in east central Albania (*Zëri i popullit*, 15 August).

Auxiliary and Mass Organizations. The Eighth Congress of the Union of Albanian Women (UAW) met in Durrës on 1—4 June. APL Central Committee member Vito Kapo was re-elected UAW president, a post she has held since 1955 (ibid., 6 June). In her report to the congress Kapo asserted that it was the "correct Marxist-Leninist policy" of the APL which had made possible the emancipation of Albanian women. As a result of the "cooperative efforts" of the party and UAW to bring women into the mainstream of Albanian life, females in 1978 comprised 46 percent of the country's labor force, 47 percent of the students enrolled in the nation's school system, 33 percent of the deputies to the People's Assembly, and 44 percent of the members of district and local legislative bodies. In addition, 29 percent of all elected offices in APL organizations were held by women (ibid., 2 June). Kapo denounced the women's liberation movement in "bourgeois and revisionist countries" for having abandoned the "correct road" to female emancipation by turning "the struggle of women for equal rights with men into a battle of the sexes [and] a conflict within the bosom of the family." Specifically, Kapo condemned those "foreign advocates of women's liberation" who called for the "destruction of the family, abandonment of children, and total disregard of every moral standard." Finally, the UAW president admonished her colleagues never to lose sight of the fact that the ultimate goal of the campaign for female equality was the overthrow of the capitalist system (ibid.).

The Central Committee of the Union of Albanian Labor Youth (UALY) met twice during 1978. Both the April and October UALY Central Committee meetings were devoted to the development of programs of patriotic as well as physical and military education to ensure that the nation's youth would be equal to the task of defending their homeland should the need arise (*Zëri i rinisë* [Tirana], 19 April, 21 October). In his address to the October session, Prime Minister and Defense Minister Mehmet Shehu suggested that the present generation of Albanian youth may be required to play the decisive role in preserving the communist system that their World War II counterparts had brought to power "by defeating the party's internal and external enemies" (Tirana radio, 21 October).

The plenum of the Albanian League of Writers and Artists (ALWA), which met in Tirana on 28—29 June, was devoted to an evelution of developments in the field of drama since the 1973 party cultural crackdown (see *YICA, 1974*, pp. 3-5). Although there was a consensus among the discussants at this meeting that most of the "alien manifestations" and "ideological shortcomings" in Albanian drama, which had resulted from the "pernicious influence" of the former secretary of the Tirana district party organization, Fadil Pacrami, had now been eliminated, they also agreed that the quality of Albanian drama had declined in the past five years. The problems which have arisen in drama are mainly attributable to the silencing of a number of the country's more promising dramatists and the understandable reluctance of those still permitted to write to be innovative in their work. To surmount the difficulties in this sector, Albania's successful, ideologically-reliable writers were urged to help upgrade the work of their younger colleagues. The plenum also suggested that fledgling drama-tists be encouraged to study the works of such "masters" as Sophocles, Euripides, Shakespeare, and Schiller, among others, in order to improve their own skills (*Nentori* [Tirana], August).

Enver Hoxha, in his capacity as chairman of the Democratic Front, presided over the 20 Sep-tember meeting of the organization's general council (*Zëri i popullit*, 21 September). This one-day session was devoted to planning for the 12 November People's Assembly election (see below). Hoxha delivered a major address titled "Proletarian Democracy Is True Democracy," which established the regime's theme for the election campaign. In summary, Hoxha sought to refute the negative image which Albania's Stalinist political system has for many foreigners, and apparently some Albanians, by claiming that the People's Socialist Republic of Albania (PSRA) is the "most truly democratic and socialist country in the world." According to the Albanian party leader, "there is no other state in the world where citizens are as equal before the law or where wage differences between laborers and administrators are as small." He further declared that "only in Albania is the government the instru-ment of the people and not of special interests." For these reasons, Hoxha concluded, "only in Socialist Albania can one speak of democracy in the fullest sense of that term" (ibid.).

Party Internal Affairs. There were two APL Central Committee plenums in 1978. The issues considered at these meetings reflected the major concerns of the party leadership during the year.

The Fourth Central Comittee Plenum (30−31 January) was devoted to a discussion of the per-formance of the economy during 1977 and a consideration of the proposed economic goals for 1978 (ibid., 1 February). An editorial on this meeting in the party daily left no doubt that Albania's rulers were distressed that several key economic goals had not been realized during the first two years of the current (1976-80) five year plan (see below). The Central Committee apparently expects that the accumulated deficits will be made up during 1978, and that greater efforts will be made to improve the quantity, quality, and distribution of consumer goods. In addition, the January plenum, perhaps anticipating an economic break with China, emphasized that the Albanian people must learn to rely more heavily than ever before on their own economic resources (ibid., 4 February).

At its Fifth Plenum, 26−27 June, the Central Committee focused on the situation in the armed forces (ibid., 28 June). Specifically, the Central Committee evaluated the extent to which the "harm-ful influences" of ousted Defense Minister Balluku and his associates (see *YICA, 1975*, pp. 3-4) had been eliminated from the military establishment. The plenum considered reports on the restructur-ing of the organizational aspects of the armed forces, the "ideopolitical education" programs for military personnel, and the revamped military training programs. Apparently the Central Committee concluded that satisfactory progress is being made in implementing its program for the armed forces. At the same time, however, Hoxha seems determined to take whatever steps may be required to ensure that the military establishment remains subordinate to the party (*Rruga e partisë*, August). Although the Albanian press did not report or comment on Hoxha's remarks to the Central Com-mittee Plenum, his address, less than two weeks later, commemorating the thirty-fifth anniversary of the establishment of the Albanian army did receive wide publicity (e.g., *Zëri i popullit*, 11 July; *Zëri i rinisë*, 12 July; *Shqipëria e re* [Tirana], July). On this occasion, the APL first secretary accused Balluku and his followers of advocating a "capitulationist policy" in the event Albania was invaded by a major power. Hoxha indicated that in order to defend Albania against any type of external ag-gression, the armed forces would have to be well schooled in modern military strategy and weaponry. He also stated that in the event of a foreign invasion all of Albania would be transformed into a battlefield and that the Albanian army and people would be expected to fight to the end. Hoxha's position on this issue apparently represents a reversal of the Balluku line, which held that Albania was incapable of resisting an invasion without external aid and that the country's armed forces should engage an invader in guerrilla-type operations rather than by means of direct confrontation (*Zëri i popullit*, 9 November).

Domestic Attitudes and Activities. *Political Developments.* The quadrennial election campaign for the People's Assembly began on 22 September and the nomination process was completed a month later (ibid., 22 September, 24 October). As usual, there was only one nominee for each seat in the Assembly. Throughout the campaign period, however, the Albanian press bitterly and repeatedly attacked the "so-called" democratic-style elections in the United States and Western Europe, which were allegedly controlled by wealthy individuals and corporations and subject to "manipulation" by the CIA, and contrasted this situation with the "freedom," "openness," "honesty," and "lack of coercion" which supposedly characterized Albanian elections (ibid., 8, 21, 29 October; 2, 4, 5 November). The national elections were held on 12 November. According to the official returns, only 4 of the nation's 1,436,289 voters failed to cast their ballots for the DF candidates (ibid., 14 November). The APL daily hailed the election results as "another expression of the fervent approval of the general party line by the working masses and the magnitude of the unity of the people around the Party and its Central Committee headed by Comrade Enver Hoxha" (ibid., 15 November).

On the occasion of its thirty-fifth anniversary, the Albanian state security organization (Arma e Sigurimit të Shtetit) was commended for having successfully thwarted all efforts to overthrow the regime. It was emphasized that the organization will continue to play an important role in the country's life so long as Albania's "foreign and domestic enemies, the imperialists and revisionists of every variety, harbor designs to topple the regime [and] divert Albania from its true Marxist-Leninist course" (*Zëri i popullit*, 21 March).

During 1978 Albania celebrated the hundredth anniversary of the formation of the League of Prizren, a major turning point in the nineteenth century Albanian National Renaissance. In their commentaries on this significant event, both party and government spokesmen maintained that the country's rulers have remained true to the ideals of pioneers of the Albanian renaissance by defending Albania's independence and territorial integrity and by encouraging the preservation and appreciation of the nation's cultural heritage (ibid., 5 March, 8–12 June; *Nentori*, June). The Albanian leaders also sought to use this occasion to raise the morale of the masses by reminding them that throughout their long history the Albanian people had successfully fought to preserve their national identity and freedom against what often seemed to be impossible odds (e.g., ibid., 11, 12 June).

The Economy. The unsatisfactory performance of the economy was obviously a major concern of Hoxha and his associates even before the Chinese halted their economic and military aid programs in July (see below). The planned goals in such key sectors as industry, agriculture, and construction have not been realized during the first two years (1976, 1977) of the current five year plan, and it seemed unlikely that the 1978 targets would be attained. Albania's present economic difficulties stem mainly from China's inability or unwillingness to furnish capital imports on schedule, unfavorable weather conditions, worker apathy and reluctance to adopt new technology and techniques, and administrative shortcomings (*Probleme ekonomike* [Tirana], January-March; *Zëri i popullit*, 16 November, 2 December). Most likely the cessation of Chinese aid will temporarily aggravate the country's economic problems.

Albania's leaders have been especially distressed by the poor performance of the agricultural sector. For the second consecutive year heavy rains during the spring planting season coupled with extended late summer-fall droughts have made it impossible to achieve planned increases in farm productivity (e.g., *Zëri i popullit*, 21 April, 13 May, 23 November, 10 December). The serious shortfalls in cotton and sugar beet production during 1976 and 1977 prompted the APL Central Committee to issue special decrees mandating that the cumulative deficits in both these crops be made up in

1978. Since virtually every hectare of potentially arable land in the country is now under cultivation, the People's Assembly in February approved a new "law on the protection of the land." This legislation establishes regulations governing the use of farm and grazing land and establishes penalties for individuals who and enterprises which "abuse" the land (ibid., 22 February). In the hope of spurring peasant productivity, Hoxha has emphasized that the regime has no immediate plans to reduce further the size of private plots and individually owned livestock holdings on the collective farms (ibid., 28 March, 9 November).

The prolonged drought which Albania experienced again this year has apparently significantly reduced the amount of electricity generated by the nation's hydropower stations. This situation has in turn put a heavy strain on the country's thermal power stations, which have been operating at peak capacity since late summer. The consequent drop in the quantity of electricity available has resulted in the rationing of electrical power both for industrial and for domestic consumers. Despite this measure, some factories have apparently been required to curtail their operations. In addition, the regime has expressed dismay at the heavy use of oil by the thermal power stations and has stepped up its efforts to convert these plants to the use of coal (ibid., 7 May, 23 November, 10 December).

It was evident that the Albanian leadership is exceedingly sensitive to the concerns of the masses regarding the state of the economy. In numerous statements and press articles regime spokesmen have attempted to convince their compatriots that they are better off than the inhabitants of "capitalist and revisionist" countries whose standards of living and purchasing power are being eroded by inflation. In Albania, on the other hand, prices have remained steady or declined as more consumer goods have become available (ibid., 28 March, 27 May, 9 November). The Albanian people, however, have continued to complain about the inadequate supplies, poor quality, and inefficient distribution of consumer goods (ibid., 18 April, 21 June, 13 December).

In the aftermath of the discontinuance of China's aid programs in Albania, the leadership sought to minimize the significance of this action for the Albanian economy by announcing with much fanfare the installation of the first two turbines of the Fierza hydropower station, the inauguration of several new departments in the Elbasan Metallurgical Complex, the production of the first Albanian-made tractor, and the completion of the Ballsh oil refinery (ibid., 13, 14, 15 October; 28 November). All these projects had been undertaken with Chinese material and technical assistance and they were near completion when China ended its aid programs.

International Views and Policies. The People's Socialist Republic of Albania (PSRA) during 1978 established diplomatic relations with Panama (*Shqipëria e re*, August), and at the year's end had diplomatic relations with 82 countries.

The most important development in Albanian international relations in 1978 was the termination of the economic relationship between Tirana and Peking. Additionally, there was a further escalation, on Tirana's part, of the ideological polemics between these former allies.

Following the Sino-Albanian economic rupture, Hoxha, in two major addresses (*Zëri i popullit*, 21 September, 9 November) declared that this incident would not result in any changes in Albania's foreign policy. He sought to end the speculation in the Western press (*NYT*, 30 July; *Chicago Sun-Times*, 17 August) concerning the possibilities of an Albanian-Soviet or Albanian-American rapprochement by announcing that the PSRA had no intention of establishing diplomatic relations or any other ties with either the United States or the Soviet Union. The APL first secretary left no doubt that he continued to regard "U.S. imperialism" and "Soviet social-imperialism" as the two most serious threats to world peace and obstacles to the world revolutionary movement. Furthermore, Hoxha ruled out any ties between Albania and Israel or with "fascist states." Aside from these nations, the PSRA is apparently willing to maintain diplomatic, economic, and cultural relations with "capitalist" and "revisionist" states according to the principles of "equality, respect for sovereignty, noninterference in internal affairs, and mutual benefit." Hoxha expressed an especially strong desire to maintain good relations with Albania's Balkan neighbors, Greece and Yugoslavia, as well as Turkey. He also emphasized that the PSRA regarded itself as a member of the international community and that it was not interested in pursuing a policy of isolation. In this connection, he noted that while Albania was interested in cultural contacts with foreign countries, it did not wish to make its culture a carbon copy of those of the Western European countries. Rather, the PSRA would be open to "progressive influences" from abroad and would adapt these to meet its own needs.

The Albanian leader, however, also made it clear his regime would continue to support "legitimate" national-liberation and revolutionary movements throughout the world. Thus, Albania during 1978 endorsed the anti-Shah movement in Iran and asserted that the "Shah's terrorism and murder would not deter the Iranian people in their struggle against his rule" (*Zëri i popullit*, 17 May). Tirana also expressed sympathy for the anti-Somoza Nicaraguan movement (ibid., 20 September), and reaffirmed its backing for the Palestinian "liberation movement" (ibid., 9 November). So far as the Albanians are concerned, the world is on the brink of a revolt against the "oppression" of the superpowers, and thus it is the duty of all "genuine" Marxist-Leninists to do everything possible to promote this revolutionary upheaval (ibid., 27 October). According to Tirana, China and other "former socialist states," by refusing to recognize this situation and by placing their respective national interests above those of the world revolutionary movement, are guilty of having betrayed the teachings of Marx and Lenin (ibid., 3 October).

Albanian-Chinese Relations. On 7 July the Chinese Foreign Ministry informed the Albanian Embassy in Peking of China's decision to halt its economic and military aid programs in Albania. The Chinese action came exactly one year after Albania had escalated its polemics with Peking by publishing a bitter condemnation of Mao Tse-tung's "three worlds theory" in *Zëri i popullit* (see *YICA, 1978*, p. 6). In their note to the Albanians (see *Peking Review*, 21 July), the Chinese indicated they had decided to take this drastic step only after their specialists in Albania had been subjected to continued harassment and Tirana had failed to respond to Peking's proposal of 7 June calling for bilateral negotiations to resolve the problems that had arisen regarding the implementation of the Chinese aid program in Albania.

In their lengthy response to the Chinese note (*Zëri i popullit*, 30 July), the Albanians acknowledged that differences over economic issues had developed between Tirana and Peking. The PSRA, however, maintained that the Chinese were solely to blame for these difficulties. Specifically, the Albanians accused China of having hampered their country's economic development by delays of one to six years in shipping equipment and materials, in violation of the provisions of various Sino-Albanian economic agreements. In addition, the Chinese were taken to task for attempting to dictate the priorities for Albania's economic development, overestimating the value of their aid, betraying Albanian military secrets, and removing or destroying the blueprints for all projects being built with their aid when they withdrew their specialists from Albania.

The Albanian note also outlined the factors that had, from Tirana's standpoint, contributed to the Sino-Albanian estrangement during the late 1960s and 1970s. This account confirms the existence of Sino-Albanian differences over domestic and foreign issues from the inception of their special relationship in the 1960s. The Albanians were unhappy with both the slowness with which China moved towards its ideological break with the USSR and the excesses of the Chinese Cultural Revolution. But the major strains in the Peking-Tirana axis did not emerge until the late 1960s and 1970s when China abandoned its cultural revolution and moved toward rapprochement with the West. Hoxha and his associates resented the fact that the Chinese were unwilling even to discuss these and other matters of concern to the Albanians. Hua Kuo-feng's alignment with the Chinese "pragmatists" following the death of Mao Tse-tung inspired the first round of Albanian polemics with the Chinese. In this stage the Albanians, for the most part, used their supporters in the Marxist-Leninist movement as proxies in their war of words with Peking. Even with the escalation of the Sino-Albanian dispute following the publication of the 7 July 1977 *Zëri i popullit* editorial, neither side seemed anxious to expand the scope of their ideological quarrel (*Frankfurter Allgemeine Zeitung*, 1 November 1977; Tirana radio, 30 December 1977; *NYT*, 30 July). It appears the Albanians expected that their new relationship with China would be similar to their relationship with Yugoslavia, i.e., they would be able to engage in ideological polemics without fear of jeopardizing their economic and diplomatic ties.

By early 1978, however, China and Albania had become embroiled in a series of disputes regarding the implementation of various aspects of Peking's aid program. These conflicts had taken on serious overtones by late March and reached crisis stage in May when the Albanian government refused to accept Chinese invoices for the equipment and materials delivered to the PSRA between December 1977–April 1978. China's patience seems to have been worn thin by early June when Tirana refused to negotiate over this and related issues. Subsequently, the Albanians inaugurated a new round of polemics against Peking (e.g., *Zëri i popullit*, 11, 12 June). The Chinese appear to have been especially irked by the allegation that they had resorted to "imperialist tactics" in their conflict with Vietnam (ibid., 24 June). At this point Peking's leadership seems to have concluded that all Chinese aid programs in Albania should be terminated, since they no longer served a useful purpose.

It does not appear that the Chinese move caught the Albanians by surprise. Prime Minister Shehu in mid-June had reminded Peking that when Yugoslavia and the Soviet Union had moved to extend their ideological disagreements with Albania into the sphere of state relations, both had "met with failure" and so presumably would the Chinese effort (ibid., 12 June). The most important consequences for Tirana of the Sino-Albanian economic break were the loss of the unexpended balance of the $250 million Chinese credit for the 1976-80 plan period, the services of 513 technicians and specialists, and the unspecified military aid Peking had been furnishing. As a result of the dramatic dropoff in Chinese-Albanian trade, the Albanians renounced the 1961 agreement establishing the Chinese-Albanian Joint Stock Company (ibid., 28 September).

Since the end of the Chinese-Albanian economic relationship, Tirana has again escalated its polemics with Peking. Hua Kuo-feng's tour of Yugoslavia, Romania, and Iran during August evoked extremely negative reactions from the Albanians, who for the first time publicly and directly criticized the Chinese leader. Hua was accused of seeking to transform the Balkans into a base from which to launch a new war designed to promote Chinese world dominance (ibid., 3 September). The APL's two leading theoreticians, Enver Hoxha and Ramiz Alia, both publicly attacked Mao Tse-tung (ibid., 9 November, 3 October). Tirana further charged that Peking's efforts to improve relations with Japan and the United States provided additional evidence of the extent to which Peking was willing to go to advance its "hegemonistic aims" (*Zëri i popullit*, 11 November; Tirana radio, 19, 20 December).

Although the Albanians are obviously displeased with both Peking's domestic and foreign policies, Tirana has, for the moment, no intention of breaking diplomatic relations with China. On this point, Prime Minister Shehu has declared that "despite the repeated treachery of the Chinese leaders, we are for the continuation of state relationships with the People's Republic of China on the basis of peaceful coexistence" (*Zëri i popullit*, 7 November).

Albanian-Soviet Relations. The Soviet Union persisted in its efforts to lure Albania back into its fold. In anticipation of a possible Sino-Albanian break, Moscow revived the Soviet-Albanian Friendship Society (Moscow radio, 11 January). It was also clear that the USSR was carefully monitoring the course of Chinese-Albanian relations during the first half of 1978 (ibid., 3 July). Following the announcement of the Peking-Tirana economic rupture, Moscow did indicate it was prepared to replace the assistance programs the Chinese had withdrawn (ibid., 11, 12 July). Albanian spokesmen, however, left no doubt that Tirana had no intention of turning to the USSR (*Zëri i popullit*, 3 September, 9 November).

Relations with Eastern Europe. Although a majority of the East European communist party states have expressed a willingness to normalize relations with the PSRA (*NYT*, 30 July), Tirana does not appear to have responded to their overtures. In fact, Albania's relations with several of the CMEA-member states seem to have cooled somewhat. Romania's decision to receive Hua Kuo-feng did not meet with Tirana's approval (ibid., 24 August). The Albanians were also harshly critical of Hungary for seeking credits from capitalist countries (ibid., 25 May) and of Bulgaria and Czechoslovakia for "submitting" to Soviet economic exploitation (ibid., 14 May, 17 September).

Albanian-Yugoslav economic and cultural relations continued to flourish during the year. At the same time, however, the APL persisted in its ideological polemics with its Yugoslav counterpart. Hoxha, for example, charged that Tito had liquidated "the former Yugoslav Communist Party" and "transformed Yugoslavia into a capitalist country" (*Rruga e partisë*, March).

Greek-Albanian economic and cultural relations continued to expand in 1978. It is estimated that the 1978 Greek-Albanian trade agreement provides for a total trade volume of $20 million, an increase over the previous year (Tanjug, 30 March). The Greek press commented favorably on Hoxha's call for a "good neighbor" relationship between the two countries (*Zëri i popullit*, 2 April). On 28 March, Greece's Olympic Airways inaugurated weekly flight service between Athens and Tirana (ibid., 29 March).

Turkish-Albanian relations, which had deteriorated somewhat following Tirana's rapprochement with Athens, were more cordial in 1978. The DF daily, *Bashkimi* (April), hailed the signing of a two-year cultural exchange pact as a positive step in strengthening relations between the two countries. Tirana also regarded Turkey's decision to permit the return to Albania of the remains of Abdyl Frashëri, one of the leaders of the League of Prizren, as a friendly gesture (*Zëri i popullit*, 21 March).

Relations with Western Europe and the United States. Although Enver Hoxha again emphasized Albania's desire to improve its economic and cultural ties with Western Europe, Tirana's contacts with these countries are still limited. In part this situation results from the PSRA's desire to cultivate those individuals or groups who are sympathetic to the Albanian regime. Since the Albanian constitution prohibits the government from obtaining credits from "bourgeois or revisionist countries," the prospects for a significant rise in Albania's trade with the countries of the region are minimal. The Albanian party leader believes the prospects for expanding trade and cultural contacts are most promising in the Scandinavian countries, Holland, Belgium, France, Austria, and Switzerland (ibid., 9 November).

The U.S. decision to recognize the People's Republic of China coupled with Hoxha's rejection of a rapprochement with Washington (ibid.) ensure there will be no change in U.S.-Albanian relations in the near future.

International Activities and Contacts. The APL organized a conference on "Problems of Contemporary World Development" which met in Tirana on 2–4 October. This meeting was apparently designed to coordinate the activities of the pro-Albanian faction of the Marxist-Leninist movement and to demonstrate to the Chinese that Tirana intended to press its quarrel with them. Twelve Marxist-Leninist parties—those of Brazil, Ecuador, West Germany, Iran, Italy, Japan, Canada, Chile, Mexico, Spain, Portugal, and Venezuela—sent delegations to the conference. Not surprisingly, the speakers who addressed the meeting condemned the "three worlds theory" and other "anti-Leninist" Chinese positions (ibid., 3—5 October).

Albania's relative isolation in the world communist movement was reflected in the fact that only twenty foreign delegations, five fewer than in 1973, and fourteen fewer than in 1967, attended the UAW Congress. Vietnam was the only ruling party represented at this gathering (ibid., 2 June). Le Duan of Vietnam and Kim Il-song of North Korea were the only ruling communist party leaders to send Hoxha greetings on his 70th birthday (ibid., 17 October).

December 1977 marked the thirtieth anniversary of the appearance of *New Albania* magazine. This illustrated monthly is currently published in eight languages: Albanian, French, English, Spanish, German, Russian, Italian, and Arabic. It has an estimated circulation of 70,000 and is distributed in about 60 countries (*New Albania*, January-February).

Publications. The APL daily newspaper (with a claimed circulation of 108,000) is *Zëri i popullit*. The party's monthly theoretical journal is *Rruga e partisë*. Another major publication is *Bashkimi*, the daily organ of the DF (claimed average circulation of 45,000). The newspapers of the Union of Albanian Labor Youth, *Zëri i rinisë*, and the Albanian Trade Unions, *Puna*, are published twice weekly. The official news agency is the Albanian Telegraphic Agency (ATA).

Western Illinois University   Nicholas C. Pano

Bulgaria

The Bulgarian Communist Party (Bulgarska komunisticheska partiya; BCP) originated from the Bulgarian Socialist Democratic Party of 1891. However, its separate existence resulted from the split of the mother party in 1903 into "broad" and "narrow" socialists, the latter officially becoming the Bulgarian Communist Party in 1919 and joining other parties as a charter member of the Communist International, under Soviet guidance. Tactical considerations counseled a change in name to "Workers' Party" in 1927 and to "Bulgarian Workers' Party (Communist)" in 1934. The BCP designation was restored in 1948 after the consolidation of power. Its best-known leader was Georgi Dimitrov, a secretary general of the Comintern, 1935—43, and the Bulgarian premier between 1946 and his death in 1949.

The BCP, which had a small membership during World War II (about 15,000), came to power quite unexpectedly when between 5 and 9 September 1944 the USSR declared war on the pro-Western Bulgarian Government of Muraviev, the Red Army moved unopposed into the country, and the Communist-inspired "Fatherland Front" (FF) coalition carried out a coup d'etat with the connivance of Muraviev's minister of war. The consolidation of power took several years and included the destruction of the "United Opposition" by force and violence, culminating in the hanging of opposition leader Nikola Petkov in 1948. A purge within the BCP's own ranks, including the hanging of Traycho Kostov as a Titoist in 1949, turned the party into the obedient Soviet tool which it has remained ever since. Domestically, the BCP has installed one of the most oppressive communist regimes. Although a second political party, a purged remnant of the once important Bulgarian Agrarian People's Union, is permitted to coexist, it subscribes officially and in fact to the monopoly of the BCP. The current leader of the BCP, Todor Zhivkov, has been its first secretary since 1954 and is now also head of state, maintaining a firm hold on the levers of power with obvious Soviet backing.

Party membership as of 1 January 1978 was given as 812,000 (an increase of about 22,000 since the Eleventh Congress of 1976). The population of Bulgaria is about 8,864,000.

The social composition of the membership was reported as including 41.8 percent blue-collar workers (41.1 in 1975), 30.3 white-collar workers (30.2 in 1975), and 22.4 percent peasants (23.1 percent in 1975), the rest being students, retired people, etc. The share of women members was given as 28.2 percent, a meager increase over the 1975 figure of 27.5. The share of members under 40 years of age was listed as 40 percent. In sum, the avowed goal of the party to increase the shares of workers, women, and youth have been only marginally achieved.

Leadership and Organization. The party structure follows the familiar Soviet pattern, with "democratic centralism" the basic principle; also a form of "personality cult" *à la* Brezhnev has become increasingly evident with regard to Zhivkov, who has successfully elminated any potential rival, most recently (in 1977) his second-in-command, Boris Velchev. This purge was followed by significant changes in the Politburo and Secretariat; thus, at a Central Committee plenum on 19 December 1977, the Politburo size—temporarily reduced to eight—was restored to eleven persons by the inclusion of Defense Minister Dobri Dzhurov, Foreign Minister Petur Mladenov, and Party Secretary Ognyan Doynov—all three, loyal Zhivkov supporters. (The other eight members are Zhivkov, Tsola Dragoycheva, Grisha Filipov, Pencho Kubadinski, Aleksandur Lilov, Ivan Mikhaylov, Stanko Todorov, and Tano Tsolov.) The number of candidate members was reduced from six to four. The number of Central Committee secretaries (to be distinguished from the party secretaries) also changed. At first, the December 1977 plenum added Dimitur Stanishev, Petur Dyulgerov (both members of the Secretariat), and Georgi Atanasov to the previously four-person body, but—later on—a July 1978 plenum dropped Ivan Prumov while adding two new secretaries, Todor Bozhinov and Stoyan Mikhaylov, steadying the number of secretaries at eight. The promotion of Stanishev and Dyulgerov and the addition of Nacho Papazov to the party Secretariat left the latter body with four members.

The new secretaries became heads of departments of the Central Committee (Stanishev, international relations; Dyulgerov, organization; Atanasov, personnel records; and Mikhaylov, propaganda), except for Bozhinov, who was a first deputy chairman of the State Planning Committee.

The average age of the current Politburo is 59 (Zhivkov himself is 67) as against the previous average of 63; some rejuvenation is noticeable in the Secretariat as well. The most influential members after First Secretary Zhivkov seem to be Filipov and Lilov, as well as the young though colorless Doynov, all of whom combine Politburo membership with a secretary's position. Prime Minister Todorov's role has diminished.

The two plenums mentioned above expanded in uncustomary fashion the Central Committee by 21 new members to its present size of 173. There are also 106 candidate members. Among the new full members are Finance Minister Belchev, Foreign Trade Minister Christov, Deputy Prime Minister Lukanov, and Zhivkov's brother-in-law Atanas Maleev, president of the Medical Academy.

Auxiliary and Mass Organizations. The Fatherland Front, the largest mass organization, has over four million members and includes as its collective members the Agrarian Union (120,000), the trade unions (2.5 million), and the Communist Youth (1.4 million). No secret is made of the undisputed party leadership and control of the Fatherland Front.

Party Internal Affairs. Paralleling the many changes in the highest party organs, there were also replacements in provincial leaderships and within the central government. Thus, Plovdiv—the second largest district city—as well as Ruse, changed party secretaries. At the governmental level Zhivkov's rumored girl friend and Politburo candidate member, Drazha Vulcheva, assumed the post of minister of education, a field in which reforms and indoctrination-tightening were announced as party priorities. Although the real reasons behind the purge of Velchev remained nebulous, speculations that he had become more tolerant of domestic relaxation (his son Iliya had been one of the leaders of the artistic vanguard) and supported some modicum of independence from the Soviet line, under the influence of Eurocommunism, gained greater credence in knowledgeable circles.

Another consequence of Zhivkov's seeming obsession with total loyalty was the drive to exchange party membership cards. This move, announced by the first secretary himself at the 1976 party congress, was confirmed at the December 1977 plenum and began in September 1978, to last until 1980 (*Rabotnichesko delo,* 20 December 1977, and 11 September 1978; hereafter cited as *RD*). Although the professed intent is to check cadres' commitment to party goals, it seems that this potential purge is more of a threat and a call to rally around Zhivkov's policies than an actual program to reduce the party rank and file drastically, which would in fact prove embarrassing. The two previous card replacements took place in 1953−5, after Stalin's death, and in 1967−68, during the Czechoslovak Spring.

A major event of the year was the National Party Conference (20−21 April), which meets every four years, between party congresses. The main thrust of the conference was on economic matters (see below). Other topics discussed at the conference included the party's role in international relations; the struggle for greater effectiveness, quality, and further construction of a developed socialist society; and the complex improvement of the socialist organization of labor. References to party life in particular claimed that the party was gradually becoming a mass party of the entire people and that the 29,000 primary party organizations bore prime responsibility for the building of an advanced socialist society. Zhivkov, in his report, complained, however, that these primary organizations were not taken seriously because they were run formalistically from above. He pleaded for more individual initiative despite the risks involved. (Ibid., 7 April.)

Domestic Affairs. As in the past, "proper communist attitudes" and creative activities in all aspects were extolled and familiar shortcomings denounced. In more specific terms, the year saw a renewed attention to youth, to the press, and to younger writers, as well as the first official mention of "dissenters" in Bulgaria.

Youth. At the turn of the year, Zhivkov spoke before the first meeting of professional schoolmasters (*nastavnitsi*) about their responsibility to train youth in professional skills as well as ideological-political values. He complained that neither secondary nor higher education had done enough to prepare young people for real life and for productive work. (Ibid., 28 December 1977.) Similarly, Zhivkov's letter, read at the Fourth Plenum of the Communist Youth Central Committee in July, mixed some praise with criticism. He stressed weaknesses in ideological and vocational training, alarming divorce rates, interest in Western music, and apathy. Zhivkov tried to explain these shortcomings by blaming the cultural heritage and character of the Bulgarians in general as averse to working habits. Moreover, he criticized the educational system and suggested that it should be thoroughly revised. The youth leadership was singled out for failing in its main responsibilities. (Radio Sofia, 19 July.) All this tends to prove that the goals set in Zhivkov's "Theses on Youth" of 1967 have not had much success in the past decade. (Cf. Radio Free Europe Research, *Bulgaria: Situation Report,* 27 July, item 2.)

Press. Other controversies affected the press. Professor Dimitur Georgiev, deputy editor-in-chief of the party daily *Rabotnichesko delo,* engaged in self-criticism in the columns of the organ of the Journalists' Union, citing a score of shortcomings in his paper's editorial policy (*Bulgarski zhurnalist,* no. 6). For its part, *Rabotnichesko delo* (6 March) chose to attack *Anteni,* the weekly journal for politics and culture sponsored by the Ministry of the Interior, for having allowed the publication of two articles indirectly criticizing certain government decisions related to agriculture. *Anteni* (15 March) admitted its errors but also argued that the views of the authors of these articles had been supported widely and thus were not atypical. Similarly, a critical article by maverick Professor Krustyu Goranov deplored excessive centralization and bureaucratization in the cultural field, possibly having in mind Zhivkov's daughter Lyudmila, head of the Committee on Culture (*Narodna kultura,* no. 16, 28 April). These and other seemingly minor disputes indicate some movement in this otherwise uniform and dull area.

Dissidence and Defection. The Third National Conference of Young Writers (a section of the Writers' Union), held in December 1977, heard Zhivkov vent familiar concerns, while other speakers called for "curbing" the younger poets, complained about following foreign styles, and appealed for "politically committed" art. However, Zhivkov's long speech, published belatedly (*RD,* 3 February), was less significant because of his defense of the "only valid model of the Great October Socialist Revolution" as the "prototype of the new society," than because of the first known official reference to dissidence in Bulgaria. Zhivkov seemed obviously uncomfortable asserting that dissidence was a political phenomenon and as such did not exist in Bulgaria, while at the same time admitting that there were "a few people who think differently." He ascribed their behavior to misguidance, confusion, and also to "purposeful siding with our enemies." He also castigated "several potential dissidents," stating that "dissidence in Bulgaria is condemned to inevitable failure in advance, to a disgraceful and ignominious end."

While Zhivkov treated the phenomenon of dissidence in general terms, the West European press some time later reported the clandestine publication of "Declaration 78," dated 2 March. It contained a six-point list of demands, including observance of human and civil rights, respect for constitutionally guaranteed freedoms, freedom of information and emigration, and a variety of legal guarantees and requests for improvements in living standards (see *Die Presse,* Vienna, 3 April). Another Western source (*L'Aurore,* Paris, 24 May) reported an anticommunist demonstration. Although the regime denied these reports, the speech by Zhivkov seemed to corroborate earlier speculations about the reasons surrounding Velchev's dismissal and other critical references made by the respected poetess Blaga Dimitrova in an interview in *Nouvelles littéraires* in 1977. (See also L. L. Kerr, Radio Free Europe Research, *Dissidence in Bulgaria,* 10 July.)

Denunciations of dissenters at home seemed to have echoes abroad. Thus, the mysterious deaths of two well-known Bulgarian defectors in London who worked for the BBC, Zhivkov's former confidant Georgi Markov and his friend Vladimir Simeonov, raised serious suspicions about assassination by communist agents. The British press reported widespread indignation, and voices in Parliament called for expulsion of the Bulgarian ambassador (*Observer,* 17 September; *London Times,* 30 September, 4 October). Scotland Yard ordered an around-the-clock guard of other Bulgarian defectors broadcasting for the BBC (*Boston Herald American,* 6 October). Markov's exposures of intraparty and family feuds among the regime's leaders, especially Zhivkov, were cited as one possible reason for the alleged assassinations.

The Economy. The slowdown in economic growth continued, with official reports for 1977, corroborated also by Premier Todorov in his report to the National Assembly in March, indicating widespread underfulfillments of even scaled-down targets. The goals of the 1978 plan, revealed as usual during the December session of the National Assembly (*RD,* 21−23 December 1977), showed a further scaling down of 1977 targets, although not of the actual 1977 performance, as follows: national income, 6.8 percent; industrial production, 7.7 percent; agriculture, 5.0 percent; labor productivity, 6.7 percent; retail trade, 4.4 percent; services, 9.2 percent; and real per capita income, 3.6 percent. Foreign trade was to increase 11.5 percent. Given performances over the past two years of the Seventh Five-Year Plan and the 1978 goals, the fulfillment of the five-year targets is highly doubtful, especially in view of already reported shortfalls in agriculture.

The critical agricultural situation, evidenced also with unusual frankness in Zhivkov's speech to the leadership of the satellite Agrarian Union (*RD,* 13 March), brought its usual scapegoats: the former chief planner and current Deputy Premier Sava Dulbokov, together with Deputy Premier Mako Dakov, Minister of Agriculture and Food Supply Gancho Krustev, as well as the Central Committee's head of the agricultural department Vulkan Shopov, were dismissed.

In view of the many economic problems, the leadership devoted much time and effort to improving overall efficiency. In fact, the emphasis of the National Party Conference, held in April, was put on "Improving the Socialist Organization of Labor and the Planned Management of the Economy"—the titles of Zhivkov's report and of the conference theses. Since much of Zhivkov's report was devoted to foreign policy, the economic portion revealed little that was new. Instead it belabored familiar shortcomings, such as the underutilization of the country's human and material resources, the slowness of modernization, and the impelling need for economies. The remedies were also of a familiar nature: expansion to a two and three-shift workday and introduction of a six-to seven-day workweek equivalent, avoidance of rejects and of squandering scarce resources, and greater reliance on labor brigades based on self-support and self-control. Zhivkov complained about outdated labor norms which penalize or reward workers unfairly but did not suggest any specific remedies. It should be mentioned in this connection that the new wage system, outlined in 1977, makes a worker's pay dependent on complicated criteria, eliminates bonuses and replaces them with wage flexibility. Due to its inherent complications and the criticism it evoked, this system began to be applied in November on a selective basis, as its intended incentive-promoting goals seem to allow also for considerable arbitrariness by supervisors and to require sufficient funds should pay increases be warranted. The extreme labor shortage in agriculture led to a Politburo decision to reduce the further outflow by promising better working conditions and greater social benefits (*RD,* 30 August).

As to the improvement of planned management, Zhivkov also exhumed old slogans, such as more "planning from below." However, this time he cited it as proof of "democratic centralism," though in fact it was an exhortation to step up "socialist competition" and labor discipline. Zhivkov also singled out planning bottlenecks resulting from failure of supply enterprises to comply with their contractual obligations as a major problem and called for strict penalties. He also asked for longer term plans, complaining that in reality the economy is geared to short-term tasks. The lack of competitiveness of Bulgarian products on the world market was openly admitted. Zhivkov called for enterprises to finance imports with exports; otherwise, they would be refused extremely scarce foreign exchange.

Last but not least, Zhivkov reemphasized the crucial role of concentration, terming the large combines, based on the horizontal-integration principle, the most important organizational form and calling for their greater independence. (*RD,* 26 April, 29 April. See also R.N., "The BCP's National Party Conference on Organization of Labor and Planning," *RFE Research,* 1 June.) In fact, a subsequent decree (*Durzhaven vestnik,* no. 51, 30 June) reduced the number of compulsory indicators, enlarged the funds at the disposàl of the economic units, and gave greater leeway to directors in decision making. At the same time, however, controls were to be increased by banks, party groups, and other superior bodies.

A similar zigzagging was noticeable in the lagging agricultural sector, where the 170 huge agro-industrial complexes, instead of the promised greater autonomy of their components, have become increasingly centralized and bureaucratized (see *RD*, 27 February, 14 April, and 5 May). Not much different was the attitude toward "private plots," which were to be supported on a par with the public sector; yet at the same time they are not provided with needed breeding stock and fodder and are strictly supervised (*Zemedelsko zname*, 7 June).

In sum, it seems clear that the conflict between the pressing economic need for greater flexibility and decentralization and the political imperatives of rigid party controls persists and even intensifies. Consequently, the economy does not respond favorably either to half-measures and mutually exclusive priorities or to administrative rearrangements, such as the new territorial division of the country into 252 "settlements" based on vague criteria of mutuality of daily needs and the site of major production units (see the decree in *Durzhaven vestnik*, no. 10, 3 February) or Zhivkov's idea of dividing the country into six large regions based on the specialized economic activities (report to the April National Conference).

The domestic difficulties called for increased help from the Soviet Union and other bloc nations and for drastic curtailment of imports from the industrial West due to the accumulated large deficits. Foreign trade volume was reported to have increased by 13 percent (larger than in 1976), and total trade turnover of about 12 billion leva accounted for nearly 74 percent of national income, thus dramatizing the great dependence on trade, which is conducted overwhelmingly with socialist countries and especially with the Soviet Union (*RD*, 3 and 9 February, 22 March).

Foreign Affairs. *The Soviet Union.* The strict attachment of the Zhivkov leadership to the Soviet line has continued unabated. At the April Party Conference Zhivkov supported the whole gamut of Soviet positions—from deploring "the U.S. weakening of détente" through supporting the Palestinians and calling for a Geneva conference to extolling "proletarian internationalism" and unity under Moscow's aegis and lashing out at Chinese leadership.

The regime's attitude toward the Soviet Union was summarized as follows by Zhivkov on the same occasion: "The Bulgarian Communist Party will continue to place in the center of its party-political, ideological, economic, cultural, and defense activities the . . . consolidation and deepening of fraternal Bulgaro-Soviet friendship and will work tirelessly for an ever fuller, organic rapprochement between Bulgaria and the great Soviet Union." He personalized these relations by referring to the "historic contribution" of Leonid Brezhnev. In June the Dimitrov Prize was bestowed on Brezhnev as "the worthy heir to and continuer of the great Lenin . . . a synonym and symbol of true love of peace and consistent internationalism" (*Radio Sofia*, 17 June).

Economic ties to the Soviet Union have also been intensified. Total trade with the USSR for 1978 is planned to exceed 5.6 billion rubles, placing Bulgaria in third place among all Soviet trading partners. This intensification is due to a variety of factors but—most recently—to the gradually increased prices of Soviet oil and other materials and to increased Bulgarian investments in Soviet resource developments, which necessitates greater Bulgarian exports. Bulgaria received most of its machinery and equipment as well as its petroleum, natural gas, cooking coal, cotton, and cellulose from the Soviet Union, exporting in return calcined soda, knitwears and garments, tobacco and cigarettes, and other traditional agricultural products.

As has been the case in the past, Zhivkov paid his annual visit to the Crimea in August, this time as the last East European communist leader to do so. While no specifics were given in the official announcements, mention was made of the deepening of cooperation and rapprochement and the unanimity of views on international issues.

The BCP sponsored jointly with the *World Marxist Review* an international theoretical conference on the theme "Construction of Socialism and Communism and World Progress." it opened on 12 December in Sofia in the presence of representatives of 73 communist and workers parties. Boris Ponomarev, candidate-member of the Politburo and secretary of the CC of the CPSU headed the Soviet delegation. Todor Zhivkov made a lengthy and rousing opening speech (Radio Sofia, 12 December).

Other East European and Balkan countries. Relations with the other CMEA partners showed no noticeable changes, and no head-of-state visits took place in 1978. Prime Minister Todorov visited Warsaw in September and then received his East German counterpart, Stoph, in Sofia in October; the Cuban foreign minister had visited Sofia in August.

Relations with Balkan neighbors remained stable, except for Yugoslavia (see below). Bulgaria stuck to its preference for bilaterial over multilateral dealings (as suggested on occasions by its neighbors) for fear of remaining isolated or in a minority position. It remains paradoxical that the country now has more stable relations with its noncommunist than with its communist neighbors. Thus, relations with Turkey remained quite active as evidenced by the visit of Prime Minister Ecevit to Bulgaria (3—5 May)—the fifth high-level visit in the last three years—and visits by Bulgarian dignitaries to Turkey. New elements included discussions about Bulgarian credits for the construction of industrial plants in Turkey, exports of their products to Bulgaria, a joint port on the Sea of Marmara to benefit Bulgaria, and arrangements for further emigration of Turks from Bulgaria (the current agreement is about to expire). Relations with Greece were even more friendly. Prime Minister Caramanlis visited Bulgaria on 6—7 July and was cordially greeted. Many aspects of economic cooperation were stressed, such as joint ventures for marketing Oriental tobacco abroad, to which Turkey might also be a party. The Greco-Turkish conflict over Cyprus, in which Bulgaria, like the Soviet Union, leans toward Greece, had permitted Bulgarian inroads in both countries' Balkan policies. Relations with Romania remained correct, but the latter's maverick position in the Soviet bloc keeps Bulgaria at a certain distance. Prime Minister Todorov visited Bucharest in October, with discussions centering on economic cooperation. Careful openings for reestablishing normal relations with Albania were made as a result of the Albanian disenchantment with China. A veiled warning was made to Balkan countries not to let themselves become "objects of intrigues by hostile forces," with an open mention of China's hostile course (Radio Sofia, 14 August).

Bulgaro-Yugoslav Controversies. Relations with Tito's Yugoslavia did, on the other hand, deteriorate because of the heating-up of the Macedonian issue. "Opportunities" for this multiplied in 1978 as Bulgaria celebrated the centenary of its liberation from Turkey when Bulgaria's "San Stefano" frontiers included almost all of Macedonia. The Yugoslavs, long on the offensive in their insistence that a "Macedonian minority in Bulgaria" be assured its rights as part of the "Macedonian nation" (a position supported in Sofia between the end of World War II and the mid-fifties), remained particularly sensitive about any mention of Macedonia, not only in contemporary but also in historic terms. The Bulgarian regime, for its part, refrained for a while from engaging in polemics, following its denial some time ago of the existence of any Macedonians in Bulgaria by calling the listing in the 1956 census of about 180,000 Macedonians in the Pirin area of Bulgaria (revised to 1,500 by the 1965 census), an error made under pressure of events. From the Bulgarian point of view, there is no Macedonian minority in Bulgaria, implying the artificiality of the concept of a Macedonian nationality but not questioning the right of the inhabitants of the Yugoslav Macedonian Republic to consider themselves as they choose as long as their present feelings are not projected back into history. Therefore, for the Bulgarians there is and should be no Macedonian problem outstanding.

This dispute reached inflammable proportions when the continued Yugoslav attacks included accusations of the existence of forced labor camps in present-day Bulgaria (*Večernje novosti,*

Belgrade, 4–24 November 1977) and claimed that "Bulgarian historians and politicians made territorial demands against Yugoslavia" (*Nin*, Belgrade, 29 January). The Bulgarian regime then decided to abandon its rather passive and defensive attitudes. First, the 3 March celebrations gave occasion for the historians to stress the ethnic basis of the Treaty of San Stefano, which included Macedonia among Bulgarian lands (*RD*, 16 February), and the role of the Macedonian Bulgarians in the years-long struggle for liberation (*Trud*, 11 March). Then came statements about Pirin Macedonia as an integral part of the Bulgarian nation by politicians such as Politburo member and Secretary Lilov (*Pirinsko delo*, 22 March), and the major speech by Zhivkov himself, given in the largest city of Bulgarian Macedonia, Blagoevgrad, on 15 June. After describing the current state of relations with the other Balkan nations, he zeroed in on relations with Yugoslavia and mixed conciliation with firmness. While acknowledging "complex problems inherited from history," he was confident of their solution in the name of the "common socialist cause." Bulgaria had no territorial claims and was ready to sign a declaration about the inviolability of common borders, "even tomorrow morning." But the attempts by the Yugoslavs to put preconditions or impose one country's view on the other was "a false, fruitless, and nearsighted approach." (*RD*, 16 June.)

Zhivkov's statement, obviously timed to influence the impending congress of the League of Yugoslav Communists, did not generate the expected positive reaction in Belgrade. Instead, the congress included in its resolution on 23 June a stern reference: by denying the Macedonian minority in Bulgaria its legitimate rights, Sofia was violating the U.N. Charter and the Helsinki agreements (Tanjug, 23 June). The Bulgarian delegate to the Yugoslav party congress on his return expressed his disappointment and regrets and stated emphatically that the population of Bulgarian Macedonia had always been "an inseparable part of the Bulgarian people." The official Bulgarian press agency also drew the conclusion from the failure of the Yugoslavs even to acquaint the Yugoslav public with the Zhivkov offer that it was Yugoslavia which had territorial claims on Bulgaria. (BTA, 24 June.)

The Bulgarian position was spelled out by the Ministry of Foreign Affairs in a fifteen-page brochure dated 24 July (reprinted in *RD*, 25 July) and entitled "For All-Round Development of Bulgaro-Yugoslav Relations." This declaration found the major obstacle to normal relations in the Yugoslav claim to "the so-called Macedonian national minority in Bulgaria" and asserted that it was up to the citizens of each country to determine their own national awareness. It maintained that the population of Bulgarian Macedonia considered itself Bulgarian historically and presently, but the censuses of 1946 and 1956 were the result of prolonged pressure to forcefully inculcate a different national consciousness in that population. The declaration categorically rejected any validity in the Yugoslav position linking the inviolability of frontiers and Bulgarian recognition of a Macedonian minority and termed such linkage "concealed territorial aspirations."

This open accusation aimed at the Yugoslavs introduced a new element in the dispute and raised questions about the reasons for its escalation. Some speculations have it that this was in answer to Yugoslavia's constant pressure and increasingly aggressive stance, which are ascribed to Tito's attempt to divert attention from growing domestic nationality problems. In view of the previously passive Bulgarian attitude to similar Yugoslav claims, however, this sudden outburst may indicate Soviet backing if not instigation. The possible Soviet role may be found in the unsettled state of Soviet-Yugoslav relations and they may be using the all too willing Bulgarian regime as a threat of intervention after Tito's death. In fact, Tanjug, the Yugoslav news agency, accused a Soviet writer in the Moscow *Novoe vremya*, 14 July, of having endorsed the Bulgarian position, thus implicating the Soviet leadership indirectly.

Asia, Africa, and the Middle East. The Bulgarian leadership, following the Soviet line, continued its attacks on China's new leadership but maintained diplomatic and trade relations. As if to underscore its anti-Chinese attitudes, Bulgarian Foreign Affairs Minister Mladenov visited Hanoi in the spring, expressed support for Vietnam in its conflict with Cambodia, and signed further long-term agreements for scientific and cultural cooperation in addition to existing trade agreements.

Zhivkov's state visit to Japan in March, during which he was also received by the emperor, confirmed his continued search for recognition. During the visit, an Intergovernmental Commission for Trade Cooperation was formed, and stress was laid on scientific and technical cooperation, especially in the field of agriculture and fishing (*RD*, 18 March).

Between 16 and 29 October Zhivkov visited four African countries (Nigeria, Angola, Mozambique, and Ethiopia) as well as South Yemen. He signed treaties of friendship and cooperation with Angola and Mozambique, and declarations of friendship and cooperation with Ethiopia and South Yemen. It was stated in all these documents that they were based "on the principles of Marxism-Leninism and proletarian internationalism," and were the first diplomatic instruments of this kind with African countries to be signed by Bulgaria. (Cf. Radio Free Europe Research, *Bulgarian Situation Report*, 7 November.) Libya's Mu'ammar al-Qadhafi had visited Sofia in June; the emphasis in his talks with the Bulgarians was put on trade and economic cooperation.

Relations with Middle Eastern countries remained active, as trade interests are of mutual benefit, especially after the Soviet Union indicated its preference for routing East European oil demands to Middle Eastern sources. Top-level exchanges included the visit of the Iranian shah to Sofia (16−20 May). Trade relations with Iran have shown considerable advances in recent years, as Iranian oil is exchanged for Bulgarian machinery, and Iranian credits are being used for agricultural imports and joint ventures. A dispute between an Egyptian tenant and the Bulgarian embassy in Cairo that led to public disturbances, ended on 5 December in the break of diplomatic relations between Egypt and Bulgaria (*The Washington Post*, 6 December).

Western Europe and the United States. Nothing of particular importance happened in Bulgarian relations with the Western European countries. The two major visits included that by Foreign Minister Mladenov to the Federal Republic of Germany on 3−4 July and Zhivkov's visit to Austria on 18−21 September. Mladenov's visit came at a time when the Bulgarian government had arrested and extradited to the Federal Republic four West German terrorists, and therefore, the atmosphere in Bonn was one of appreciation. But, in business terms, trade was stagnating because the enormous Bulgarian deficits forced contraction of its imports from the West in General and from its most important Western partner, Germany, in particular.

Zhivkov's visit to Austria confirmed the trend of expanded cultural, scientific, and, in some respects, economic relations. Austria occupies fourth place among Bulgaria's Western trade partners although trade has not increased much during the last few years due to the same problem of excessive Bulgarian deficits.

Bulgarian-U.S. relations in general reflect to a great degree the state of U.S.-Soviet relations, although bilateral issues have assumed a more businesslike character. Thus, at the National Party Conference Zhivkov identified as a major source of international difficulties "the actions of the reactionary and militarist forces, whose most powerful nucleus is the military-industrial complex in the U.S. and the other NATO countries" and argued that "the course adopted by the new U.S. administration retards and pushes backwards the development of the Soviet-American relations . . . and foments antisocialist propaganda." And the party daily echoed the line by accusing the United States of "escalating anti-Sovietism" and "initiating a new kind of cold war" (*RD*, 29 July).

In more concrete matters, however, the Bulgarian regime removed travel restrictions on U.S. diplomats, the last East European country to do so (except the USSR), showed a willingness to negotiate pre-World War II financial claims by U.S. citizens, and accepted the training in the U.S. of Bulgarian agents to reduce drug trafficking from Asia. Cultural and scholarly exchanges were also continued. At the same time, however, the jamming of Voice of America broadcasts from Greece was resumed and the regime's refusal to pledge free emigration as a precondition of qualifying for most-favored-nation treatment hampered the development of further trade relations.

The regime was also repeatedly critical of the Western attitude taken at the Belgrade conference on the Helsinki agreements, blaming the U.S. in particular for insisting on the defense of human rights "in a selective manner" (*RD*, 1 August).

In the field of trade with the West, the huge Bulgarian indebtedness, approaching $3 billion, not only led to a drastic reduction in imports from the West but also to a variety of other measures, including the encouraging tourism from the West through increasing the official exchange rates for tourists by 50 percent, and permitting Bulgarian citizens to shop at the special foreign-goods stores without justifying the possession of foreign currency in small amounts.

Publications. The official daily of the BCP is *Rabotnichesko delo* (Worker's cause), its monthly is *Partien zhivot* (Party life), and its theoretical journal is *Novo vreme* (New times). Other mass publications are *Politicheska prosveta* (Political education) and *Ikonomicheski zhivot* (Economic life). The official news agency is *Bulgarska telegrafna agentsiya* (BTA).

University of Vermont   L. A. D. Dellin

Czechoslovakia

The Communist Party of Czechoslovakia (Komunistická strana Československa; KSČ) was constituted in November 1921 from the left wing of the Social Democratic Party and a number of splinter groups, ethnic and other, in the socialist movement. It was shortly afterwards admitted to membership in the Communist International. In February 1948 the KSČ seized power by means of a coup d'etat and put an end to a pluralist system of long standing. The present Czechoslovak polity is a one-party regime despite formal existence of three other parties because the government is in the hands of the National Front of Working People, a formalized coalition in which the KSČ has assured itself a two-thirds majority. The three most important political functionaries—President of the Republic Gustav Husák, Federal Prime Minister Lubomír Štrougal, and Federal Assembly Chairman Alois Indra—are all members of the KSČ.

In October 1968 a constitutional reform which transformed the hitherto centralist-dualist state into a federation of two autonomous republics (the Czech Socialist Republic and the Slovak Socialist Republic) was enacted in Czechoslovakia. The federalization of Czechoslovakia was the work of the reformist leadership under Alexander Dubček, whose program included important changes in other aspects of political, economic, and social life, which could not be realized because of the military intervention by five Warsaw Pact countries in August 1968. The decentralization of the government, however, was not matched by any similar step on the part of the KSČ. This resulted in an incongruity where a federal polity is governed by a centralist-dualist party, the KSČ, with its "territorial organization" in Slovakia, the Communist Party of Slovakia, or the KSS. Party spokesmen and media had for a long time avoided explaining this paradox; only in 1978 did the official organ of the KSS admit that "even following the federal arrangement of the state, the KSČ remained a unified party" and justified the contradiction by concern for the unity of the working class (*Pravda, Bratislava*, 6 September).

In proportion to the population, the KSČ is the largest communist party in the world. On 1 January 1978 it had 1,473,000 members and candidates for membership. Some 92,000 new members had been admitted during the preceding two years. Since the population of Czechoslovakia had reached the fifteen million mark in 1977, this means that almost 10 percent of the entire population is in the KSČ. The leadership expressed its satisfaction about the fact that 62 percent of the newly admitted party card holders are workers (*WMR*, June 1978).

Leadership and Organization. The KSČ is administered by two supreme organs: the Central Committee and the Presidium. The latest party congress was held in April 1976. According to the official count, this was the Fifteenth Congress although it should have been the Sixteenth, but the present leadership does not recognize the legality of the congress convened in August 1968 after the entry of Soviet troops into Czechoslovakia. The next congress is scheduled for 1981.

The Central Committee is composed of 121 members and 52 candidates, and the Presidium has eleven members and two candidates. The executive body is the Central Committee Secretariat, headed by the secretary general and with eight secretaries and two secretariat members. The KSS has a structure similar to that of the KSČ, except that the head of the Central Committee Secretariat has the title of first secretary. The secretary general of the KSČ is Gustav Husák; the first secretary of the KSS is Jozef Lenárt.

Party Internal Affairs. For the party 1978 was a year of two important anniversaries: thirty years had elapsed since the seizure of power in February 1948, and ten years had passed since the Soviet-led military intervention against the reformist course of Alexander Dubček. The anniversary of the 1948 coup was celebrated with the customary pomp, but observers noted a certain lack of enthusiasm among the prominent guests and speakers. Secretary General Husák, in his address, seemed to adopt a rather defensive tone. Among other things, he denied that the government was preparing a new monetary reform and also labeled as untrue the rumors about a dispute among party leaders concerning the correctness of present policies. These remarks were later dropped from the text of his speech as it appeared in the press (*Rudé právo*, 25 February). Unofficial reports concerning a controversy between Husák and the representatives of the more dogmatic, as well as of the more pragmatic, current in the party had been circulating since the end of 1977. The transfer of the regional party secretary for South Bohemia, Jaroslav Hejna, allegedly the most outspoken critic of Husák, to another post was seen as being connected with the dispute (*Le Monde*, 6 January). It would seem that disagreements have plagued the KSČ since Husák took over the party secretariat from his predecessor, Dubček, in April 1969, but that he has thus far been able to maintain his power and influence.

The other anniversary, although more controversial than that of the 1948 coup, was given more attention in party circles and in the media. A concerted propaganda campaign was conducted with the goal of justifying the Soviet action in August 1968 and, by implication, the present regime. In this context, assertions were made that in 1968 "countless Communists and noncommunists had requested military intervention of fraternal nations to save socialism" (Husák's words of welcome to Brezhnev, as reported in *Rudé právo*, 28 May), but no proofs were offered. Regime spokesmen and the press also claimed that the reformist leadership had intended to establish a dictatorship and liquidate "loyal comrades and faithful Communists" physically (*Rudé právo*, 17 June) and that the whole reform program had been "a perfidious instrument for subverting socialism and restoring capitalism" (*Nové slovo*, 13 July). The campaign testified to the feelings of insecurity among the Husák team which faces a public that has never ceased questioning the legitimacy of the postinvasion course.

The plenary session of the Central Committee of the KSČ was held 15–16 March. The fact that its date had been twice postponed before the meeting actually took place rekindled speculations about possible conflicts among the top officeholders. The dealings and the decisions of the plenum, however, did not bring any surprises. Both from the report of the secretary general and the accompanying discussions it was evident that economic problems continued to keep the leadership busy and that it felt threatened by the criticism coming from the major West European communist parties.

Domestic Affairs. The two anniversaries, significant for party history, coincided with an important national anniversary: the sixtieth anniversary of the foundation of the Czechoslovak republic. Independence Day, celebrated on 28 October, has been observed in various ways under communist rule. In the years before 1968 it was remembered as the so-called Day of Nationalizations, recalling a minor event of 1945 when the takeover of key industries by the state had been promulgated, which obviously was intended as a substitute for an event connected with the traditions of Western liberal democracy. Later in the 1960s and especially during the Dubček era, the original meaning of this holiday was partly restored. The fact that the constitutional reform of 1968 had also been enacted on 28 October 1968 provided new significance for Independence Day. After the invasion, the official historiography began again to present 28 October as the anniversary of the 1945 nationalizations. This was how it was observed in 1978. The shyness of the regime's representatives about the Czechoslovak national holiday reflected their uncertainty in the matter of legitimacy of the order imposed by the Soviet intervention.

During the week of the tenth anniversary of the Soviet invasion, the statue of the last chairman of the KSČ, Klement Gottwald, was destroyed by unknown persons in the southwestern Bohemian town of Příbram (*Rudé právo*, 25 August). This act was an obvious political demonstration against the presence of Soviet troops in the country, but it may have also been provoked by the recent revival of the Gottwald cult in the party, as the ceremonies in commemoration of the thirtieth anniversary of the communist takeover had demonstrated (Radio Prague, 25 February). Dissent in Czechoslovakia in 1978 took various forms: protest letters to authorities and complaints about the suppression of civil and human rights lodged with international agencies and sometimes even with foreign communist parties.

Charter Movement in 1978. The most articulate expression of discontent with the state of affairs imposed after the invasion of 1968 has been the so-called Charter movement (named after the petition which its leaders had addressed to the Czechoslovak authorities in January 1977), which in the course of the last two years has grown and consolidated itself. At the close of 1978 it was clear that this group has provided a common platform for all protests against violations of civic liberties (as well as against foreign interference) whether the protests came from the opposition in the KSČ or from the public at large. On 2 January a prominent spokesman of the Charter group, former Foreign Minister Jirí Hájek gave an interview to the West German weekly *Der Spiegel*. A month later, the Austrian socialist daily *Arbeiterzeitung* published another interview with Hájek. On these occasions, Hájek explained the objectives of the Charter movement and assessed the results of its activities. Later in the year, the leadership of the group passed into the hands of a former communist philosopher and psychologist, Jaroslav Šabata (UPI, 6 April). In the spring the Chartists addressed a new petition to the president of the republic, exposing recent violations of human rights, some of them perpetrated against the signatories of the 1977 Charter. This petition was referred to in a part of the Western press as "Charter 1978" (*La Stampa,* Turin, 9 March; *Frankfurter Allgemeine Zeitung,* 11 April; hereafter *FAZ*). A similar letter was sent to the Czechoslovak Federal Assembly on 24 April (Reuters, 2 May). A prominent Chartist, playwright Pavel Kohout, made a declaration to the *Frankfurter Allgemeine Zeitung* (5 May) in which he denounced the spying and the persecution that he had to suffer from the police. Later in the year, Kohout was given permission to leave Czechoslovakia and work as a special adviser of the Burgtheater in Vienna (*San Francisco Chronicle,* 21 October). This indicated a more subtle handling of the Charter issue by the authorities. The same method applied in the case of two other members of the group, Vilém Hejl and Ivan Medek (Reuters, 17 August; UPI, 18 August). The permission to leave was actually an expulsion in disguise. Formally expelled from Czechoslovakia was Associated Press correspondent Robert Reid, for allegedly having "harmed the interests of the country" but in reality for having contacts with the Charter sponsors (Radio Prague, 5 May). During the visit of Leonid Brezhnev to Prague in May, the most active supporters of the Charter were temporarily interned (*NYT,* 30 May). In August and September the Chartists met in secret sessions with Polish human rights activists and exchanged information (*Washington Post,* 16 August). It was probably in response to the various protests stimulated by the Charter group that the official KSČ organ asserted in a lengthy editorial that Czechoslovakia scrupulously observed all commitments resulting from the Helsinki treaty (*Rudé právo,* 3 August).

Culture and Religion. Culture, a politically sensitive area since the 1950s and especially since the brief spell of the "Prague Spring," continued to be a matter of serious concern for the party leadership. More "streamlining" of cultural life was attempted by setting up a Union of Czechoslovak Musicians, which held its constituent congress at the end of 1977 (Radio Hvězda, 17 January) and by changing the 1957 Theatre Act (*Tvorba,* 22 February). Since literature in general had been subjected to stricter ideological controls, most literary creations appeared in a semiclandestine form in emulation of the example of "samizdat" practiced in the Soviet Union. The largest of these underground publishing undertakings appears to be "Edice Petlice" (Padlock editions), which brought out the novel *Dotazník* (Questionnaire) by Jiří Gruša in 1978. The author was arrested (*NYT,* 7 June), but the series continued. Early in 1978 a literary almanac entitled *The Twelve,* referring to the volume's twelve contributors and containing short stories by writers committed to the reform course of 1968, began to circulate in Prague (Radio Free Europe *Background Report,* no. 115, New York, 7 June). Regime reaction testified to a hardening of policies toward cultural nonconformists. Some of them, such as the Christian-oriented poet Zdeněk Rotrekl, were subjected to search warrants and police interrogation (*Die Welt,* Hamburg, 2 January).

Although the antireligious drive of the regime was not abandoned, some regularization of relations with the Catholic church was achieved. František Cardinal Tomášek was confirmed as archbishop of Prague, and the establishment of an independent metropolitan bishopric for Slovakia was discussed with Vatican authorities both during the visit of State Secretary for Church Affairs Karel Hrůza in Rome and again later in Prague (*FAZ,* 12 January). With the encouragement of the KSČ, the Fifth All-Christian Peace Congress was held in Prague in early summer (*Lidová demokracie,* 24 June). The second papal election in 1978 which made Cracow Archbishop Wojtyla Pope John Paul II was duly covered by Czechoslovak media, and after some hesitation the KSČ joined in the chorus of those who hailed this choice. President Husák sent the new pope a message of congratulations (Radio Prague, 18 October). Despite these formal improvements in relations between the state and the church, many believers felt that their rights and freedoms were not respected. Late in 1977 a letter of protest from a large group of priests and laymen was received by Cardinal Tomášek. The petitioners requested that the cardinal submit this protest to the president of the republic. They complained about continuing persecution of practicing Christians and obstacles to religious education in schools (*FAZ*, 23 December 1977).

Economy. According to the report presented by Husák to the plenary session of the Central Committee in March, the various sectors of the national economy had developed satisfactorily on the whole although not as "dynamically" as expected (*Rudé právo*, 23 March). The unfavorable balance of payments remained the single most difficult economic problem. It was partly due to an increase in the price of Soviet oil, which was consistent with the trend of oil prices in the world market (Radio Prague, 17 January). The overall energy problem persisted; coal output, for example, failed to meet demand (*Rudé právo*, 4 September). In order to meet future shortages, plans for the development of nuclear energy production were worked out in cooperation with the Soviet Union (Radio Prague, in English, 21 March). To remedy the poor quality of commodities, a three-year experiment was launched in twelve national corporations, comprising 150 industrial plants. The expectation is that better wages and bonuses will be the stimuli to improve consumer goods (ČETEKA, 14 February). Although the 1978 harvest was fairly good (*Zemedělské noviny*, 15 July), agricultural production fell over the last three years; hence a need for increased imports of food was anticipated (*Politická ekonomie*, December 1977). Sectors which could help offset this new expenditure of foreign currency, such as tourism, reached record figures in 1978 but have not yet been exploited to their full potential (*Statistické přehledy*, January). A serious obstacle to the development of tourism has been the rigid practice followed in granting visas to visitors from the West, mainly for political reasons. An important aspect of the agricultural sector during the year was the continuing merger of collective farms, the average size of which has reached more than 2,000 hectars (5,000 acres). But the new large cooperatives posed a problem—obtaining competent management (Radio Prague, 7 February).

Foreign Affairs. The most important event in Czechoslovak relations with the countries of the West was the visit of Gustav Husák to the Federal Republic of Germany, 10–13 April. This was Husák's first official trip to a West European country and actually the first official visit of a communist statesman from Czechoslovakia to the German federal capital. The results of his talks with Chancellor Schmidt were summed up in a joint declaration which, according to Husák, reflected "a substantial improvement of atmosphere" (Radio Prague, 13 April). A five-year cultural agreement signed on this occasion is to facilitate scientific and cultural cooperation between the two countries. The "atmospheric improvement" seen by the KSČ secretary general was soon afterwards imperiled by the expulsion from Czechoslovakia of a correspondent of the West German First Television Network, Helmut Clemens (Radio Prague, 4 July), which prompted an official protest from Bonn. Clemens had allegedly "damaged neighborly relations between Czechoslovakia and the FRG," but the impression of unbiased observers was that he had been perceived as an unwelcome witness of the tensions building up in the country around the tenth anniversary of the Soviet invasion. Another official contact with a Western country at a high governmental level was the visit of Foreign Minister Bohuslav Chňoupek to Austria, undertaken with the view of "further promoting the ever-improving relations between the two nations" (Radio Prague, 10 May).

The climate between the communist regime in Prague and the United States did not improve much in 1978; the unambiguous stand of President Carter on human rights did not endear him to the present KSČ leadership. Czechoslovak media recorded, with a good deal of malicious satisfaction, the controversial statement by the U.S. ambassador to the United Nations, Andrew Young, about the supposedly large number of political prisoners in American jails (Radio Prague, 7 August).

In matters of world politics, Czechoslovakia, as usual, faithfully followed the line set by the Soviet Union and supported, among others, Vietnam in its border dispute with Cambodia (Hanoi radio, in English, 5 January) and continued to denounce the Chinese Communists for "liberal use of lies, falsifications, and demagogy," as well as the "militarist course of the new Chinese government" (*Práce,* 17 August).

Foreign Trade. The foreign trade deficit, especially with Western countries, considerably hampered imports to Czechoslovakia of vital raw materials and quality products. Nevertheless, several contracts, treaties, and agreements were concluded with a number of Western nations. After the agreement with the Sperry Rand Corporation of the U.S. on scientific and technological cooperation (*Christian Science Monitor,* 30 May), which incidentally was not reported by Czechoslovak media, economic talks were held in Prague with American representatives (*Zemědělské noviny,* 13 September). Czechoslovak spokesmen occasionally complained about "discriminatory measures in regard to trade with socialist countries," which, they argued, were used by the U.S. as a means of political pressure (Radio Prague, 18 August). An agreement was also reached with the European Economic Community on the volume of sales and the prices of Czechoslovak steel exported to the nine countries of the Common Market (Reuters, 13 August). Reports which appeared in the press in summer suggested that a project of cooperation in the automobile industry with the Federal Republic of Germany was contemplated (Radio Hvězda, 31 August; *FAZ,* 1 September). The Czechoslovak minister of metallurgical industry visited India in February and discussed cooperation with Indian government officials (ISI Radio, New Delhi, English service, 3 February).

As for economic contacts with other communist countries, friendship, cooperation, and mutual assistance treaties were signed with East Germany, providing among other things for an exchange of goods worth two billion rubles per year (ČETEKA, 5 April), and with Cuba regarding purchase of Cuban sugar (at an especially favorable price for Cuba), and deliveries of Cuban mineral ores to Czechoslovakia (Radio Hvězda, 27 March). With respect to economic relations among communist nations, two meetings in 1978 were of particular importance: the CMEA Council session in September and the conference of the CMEA ministers of domestic trade in October. The Council discussed again a proposition by the Soviet delegation, which previously had been tabled, that would change the CMEA into a supranational organ and allow decisions by simple or qualified majority vote instead of the presently required unanimity. The proposition was not adopted because the smaller CMEA nations feared that it would give the USSR more control over their economies, but during the preparations for the Council session Czechoslovakia had lent full support to the Soviet initiative (Tanjug, 12 June).

International Party Contacts. The most important meeting of representatives of ruling communist parties loyal to and controlled by Moscow took place in the Crimea in June. The Czechoslovak party press noted that these talks had "already become a tradition" and stated "with joy and satisfaction" that the meeting between Brezhnev and Husák "was characterized—now, as always—by a profound unanimity of opinion" (*Rudé právo,* 27 July). Next in importance was the conference of Central Committee secretaries in Budapest from 27 February to 1 March (*WMR,* May). In 1978, too, Soviet party leader Brezhnev visited Prague. A "Joint Declaration on Further Development of Fraternal Friendship and All-round Cooperation between the KSČ and the CPSU, as well as between the CSSR and the USSR" was signed on this occasion (*Rudé právo,* 3 June).

Relations between the KSČ and the communist parties of the West, on the other hand, which have been strained since the military intervention of the Warsaw Pact countries in Czechoslovakia in 1968, suffered a new setback during the year. The deterioration was in large extent due to the disapproval by the Western parties of the way the Czech leadership handled the issue of dissidents. The sympathy shown in European communist circles for the Charter movement alarmed the Prague regime and stiffened in turn its position on issues concerning matters such as Eurocommunism. On 20 January the Italian Communist Party weekly *Rinascità* published an article by a former theoretician of the Communist Party of Slovakia, Professor Milan Huebl, in which he evaluated the 1968 reform movement positively and condemned Soviet interference. At about the same time a former Central Committee member and chairman of the National Front, František Kriegel, gave an interview to the Spanish communist weekly *Mundo Obrero,* defining the present regime in Czechoslovakia as "harsh and repressive" (18 January). On 24 January Zdeněk Mlynář and Jiří Pelikán, both former prominent officials of the KSČ, had talks in Madrid with the secretary of the Communist Party of Spain, Santiago Carrillo, and expressed their gratitude for the solidarity that his party had manifested towards the dissidents in Czechoslovakia (Agence France Presse, 25 January). The Italian party publishing house brought out the Italian translation of a book by Jiří Hájek on the "Prague Spring," which originally had appeared in French (Jiří Hájek: *Prague dix ans après,* Paris) and had received a warm reception in European left-wing circles (*France nouvelle,* Paris, 23 January). Later in the year a member of the Presidium of the Communist Party of Italy discussed in Belgrade with the representatives of the League of Communists of Yugoslavia the consequences for the world communist movement of the continuing Soviet interference in Czechoslovakia (*NYT,* 7 September). In July the communist-sponsored Gramsci Institute in Rome organized a seminar on the significance of the "Prague Spring." Czechoslovak media reacted angrily when the institute refused to invite officials of the KSČ to this seminar (*Rudé právo,* 1 July; *L'Unità* 6 July).

The frustrations of the Czechoslovak power holders fueled their animosity, perceptible since 1977, against the idea and the concept of Eurocommunism. This year the attack on Eurocommunist theories was launched by the party ideologist Jan Fojtík in an article in *Tribuna.* The article was later reprinted in Moscow *Pravda.* Fojtík asserted that Eurocommunism was "alien and unacceptable to all real socialists" and designed "to drive the workers' movement into the embrace of the bourgeoisie" (*Tribuna,* 19 April). A lively controversy broke out between the KSČ and its sister parties in the West before the tenth anniversary of the Soviet intervention. Repeated condemnations of the Soviet action in 1968, supported by a special declaration released by the Communist Party of China (*Washington Post,* 23 August), were countered in Prague by distribution via the Czechoslovak embassy in Paris of a list of communist parties which in August 1968 had approved the military intervention. Although the list was not quite accurate and omitted all parties, however large, which had not pledged their allegiance to Moscow, it was obvious that important communist parties had denied their endorsement to the "fraternal assistance" granted by the USSR to Czechoslovak socialism (Agence France Presse, 22 August).

At the international theoretical conference on "Construction of Socialism and Communism and World Progress," organized in Sofia by the Bulgarian CP and the *World Marxist Review* between 12 and 15 December, and attended by 73 communist and workers' parties, Vasil Bilák, a member of the KSČ Politburo, accused Peking of opposing peace and attempting to set up a "reactionary U.S.—China —Japan axis" directed against the Soviet Union and its allies (Reuters, 13 December).

Publications. The KSČ central daily is *Rudé pravó,* published in the Czech language in Prague. The Slovak edition of *Rudé právo* was discontinued several years ago. The main organ of the Communist Party of Slovakia is *Pravda,* appearing in Bratislava. Problems of theory and general policy are dealt with in the Czech weekly *Tribuna* and the Slovak periodical *Předvoj.* Organizational questions and daily party activities are treated in the fortnightly *Život strany.* The Central Trade Union Council publishes a daily, *Práce,* in Prague and a Slovak version of the same name in Bratislava. The Czechoslovak Socialist Youth Union publishes a Czech daily, *Mladá fronta,* and a Slovak paper, *Smena.* Questions of international politics, economics, and culture are discussed in the weekly review *Tvorba.* The official press agency is *Československá tisková kancelář,* abbreviated as *ČETEKA* or *ČTK.*

University of Pittsburgh   Zdenek Suda

Germany:
German Democratic Republic

Shortly after the Soviet Occupation Zone of Germany became operational, the Soviet Military Administration (SMA) issued Order No. 2 (10 June 1945) permitting the founding or reactivation of "antifascist" political parties in its zone. The Communist Party of Germany (Kommunistische Partei Deutschlands; KPD), an underground party during the Third Reich, was immediately reactivated by cadres who had arrived with the Red Army. The Social Democratic Party of Germany (Sozialdemokratische Partei Deutschlands; SPD) was next. The Christian Democratic Union of Germany (CDU) and the Liberal Party of Germany (LDPD) followed and were new political creations.

The SMA regarded the KPD as its indigenous instrument for implementing Soviet policies. Therefore, substantial material support was provided to the German Communists. However, the KPD did not succeed in gaining the confidence of the population, most likely because of the brutal behavior of the Soviet occupation forces and the German experience with the Nazi version of totalitarianism. The strongest competition to the Communists came from the Social Democrats. The SMA forced the merger of the KPD and SPD, thus creating a new party, the Socialist Unity Party of Germany (Sozialistische Einheitspartei Deutschlands; SED) at the "Unity Party Congress" (21–22 April 1946). Delegates of both parties "unanimously" agreed to the merger. Many Social Democrats strongly objected to the forced merger and continued to work underground with the result that many were arrested and some killed. In spite of the assertion of Walter Ulbricht, Moscow's trusted agent and SED deputy chairman, that from then on only Socialists, and not Social Democrats or Communists, existed, it was increasingly obvious from the very beginning that the SED considered itself a part of the international communist movement. Within the next two years the Communists gained control of the party apparatus and modeled the SED after the Communist Party of the Soviet Union (CPSU).

About one month after the establishment of the Federal Republic of Germany (FRG) in the three Western occupation zones, the "German People's Congress" met on 7 October 1949 and unanimously approved a proposal to create the German Democratic Republic (GDR). On 10 October the SMA transferred its administrative functions to the new GDR government and five days later extended diplomatic recognition to the "first German socialist state." The pro-Moscow SED leadership was in control of the GDR from its very beginning.

Moscow anticipated that its early political initiative would make its zone the nucleus for a reunited Germany under Soviet control. Consequently, the first constitution of the GDR consciously followed features of the Weimar Constitution, such as the federal system and the existence of several political parties. As soon as Moscow recognized that its initial assumption of extending Soviet control to the western parts of Germany in the immediate future no longer appeared likely, the federal system was replaced by a highly centralized unitary order. Moreover, the new GDR "socialist constitution" of 1968 was amended in 1974 in order to update the constitution in line with changed overall policies. For example, all references to the "German nation" and to "German reunification" were eliminated.

Within a few years, the SED succeeded in creating the political, social, and economic structure of a "people's democracy" by utilizing terror and various means of mass intimidation. Prior to the creation of the Berlin Wall and the massive border fortifications, about three million persons fled to the West.

Moscow's stringent control of the GDR, the largest single "trading partner" of the Soviet Union, has been achieved by various means. Only pro-Moscow SED officials are permitted to hold significant offices. The forced economic and military integration of the GDR with the Soviet Union and the other communist-ruled countries of Eastern Europe also serves the purpose of retaining control. In September 1950 the GDR joined the Council for Mutual Economic Assistance (CMEA). In May 1955 it became a full member of the Warsaw Pact. Instigated by SMA, the remilitarization of the GDR started as early as July 1948.

In 1977 the SED officially had 2,077,262 members and candidates. The population of GDR at the end of 1977 was 16,757,000 (*Frankfurter Allgemeine Zeitung,* 4 September; hereafter *FAZ*).

Leadership and Organization. As in other communist-ruled countries, the decision-making institutions in the GDR are the SED Politburo and Central Committee. The functions of government institutions are reduced to the execution and administration of decisions made by the top party organs. The most powerful position is the post of secretary general, held since 1971 by Erich Honecker, who is also chairman of the State Council.

The State Council and the Council of Ministers are appointed by the People's Chamber. (For a detailed discussion of government institutions, see *YICA, 1977,* p. 26.) Honecker assumed the position of chairman of the State Council in October 1976. This governmental organ, like the Soviet Presidium, manages the business of the People's Chamber between its infrequent sessions. Honecker also is chairman of the National Defense Council, the governmental institution which has practically unlimited powers in emergency situations resulting from domestic or external causes.

The present People's Chamber's 500 members were elected on 17 October 1976. The National Front (the SED-controlled alliance with the four "bloc parties"), the trade unions, and such "mass organizations" as the Free German Youth (Freie Deutsche Jugend; FDJ) presented to the voters a single list of candidates, which received 99.86 percent of the valid votes.

The purpose of the further existence of the formerly "bourgeois parties" — the [East] CDU, LPDP, the Democratic Peasant Party of Germany (DBD), and the National Democratic Party of Germany (NPDP) — is to appeal to specific segments of the population to support the SED program and to expedite political and social integration into a socialist society. (For membership figures and their congresses held in 1977, see *YICA, 1978,* pp. 23–24.)

The only change in the composition of the SED Politburo and Secretariat in 1978 came as a result of the death of Werner Lamberz in a helicopter accident on 6 March in Libya. Lamberz, who was in charge of "agitation" in the Secretariat, was considered by many observers as the most likely successor to Honecker. Candidate member of the Politburo and editor in chief of the official organ of the SED, *Neues Deutschland,* Joachim Herrmann was advanced to full membership in the Politburo at the eighth session of the SED Central Committee on 25 May and selected to succeed to the position formerly held by Lamberz. (Bundesminister für innerdeutsche Beziehungen, *Informationen,* no. 11, p. 3; hereafter *Informationen;* for names of the other members of the Politburo and Secretariat, see *YICA, 1976,* p. 27). For Herrmann, see Biographies, p. 451.

Auxiliary and Mass Organizations. Mass organizations in the GDR have at least four main functions: (*a*) to assist the SED in its control functions; (*b*) to provide manpower reserves for additional party members; (*c*) to supply the party with a mass basis for political indoctrination and premilitary training; and (*d*) to support the work of the party in both the domestic and international spheres. The most important recruiting ground for future party functionaries (Kampfreserve) of the party, is the FDJ, which also serves as the combat reserve. Its membership, which consists of youth between the ages of 14 and 25, numbered, in June 1977, 2,193,488. (*Rheinischer Merkur*, 25 November 1977.) The first secretary of the FDJ is Egon Krenz, a candidate member of the SED Politburo. The communist children's organization, the Ernest Thälmann Pioneers, is supervised by the FDJ.

The Free German Trade Union Federation (FDGB), which has over 8,300,000 members, is used by the party as an important organ to control workers. Its chairman is SED Politburo member Harry Tisch. FDGB members are forced to contribute to a "Solidarity Fund," which is used to support "liberation movements" and to provide material aid to socialist countries in the Third World. In 1977, the "solidarity expenditures of the FDGB amounted to 160 million marks, 60 percent of which came from monthly contributions by FDGB members (compared with a general budget of 880.2 million marks). (*Deutsche Lehrerzeitung*, East Berlin, no. 7; *Junge Welt*, East Berlin, 26 May.)

Another mass organization is the Society for German-Soviet Friendship (DSF), which held its Eleventh Congress in East Berlin (19–20 May), with 2,700 delegates attending. The DSF has over 5.5 million members. SED Politburo member Erich Mückenberger was elected as its new president. (*Informationen*, no. 10, p. 6) Even the GDR Red Cross, with a membership of 587,000, is utilized to support the GDR's activities in the Third World, providing material assistance to the struggle "against imperialism and colonialism," and for "national and social liberation." In the past 25 years more than 700 relief assignments, costing close to 70 million marks and financed from donations, have been dispatched. (Press Department, GDR Ministry of Foreign Affairs, *Foreign Affairs Bulletin*, vol. 18, no. 1, East Berlin, 11 January, p. 7; hereafter *Bulletin*; for other mass organizations, see *YICA, 1976*, p. 26 and *YICA, 1977*, p. 24.)

Party Internal Affairs. The glorification of the person (*Personenkult*) of the secretary general of the SED, Erich Honecker, continued during 1978. His photos can be found in all public places. Several books containing his speeches and articles have been published. An official Honecker biography is intended to enhance further Honecker's leadership position (*Rheinischer Merkur*, 12 May). It is possible that the apparent rehabilitation of former SED chief Walter Ulbricht, who since his death in 1973 has hardly been mentioned, is in direct relation to the present *Personenkult*. Honecker, accompanied by several party and government leaders, placed a wreath on Ulbricht's grave on the anniversary of his eighty-fifth birthday. The official SED paper, *Neues Deutschland*, also dedicated a whole page, celebrating his life struggle for socialism. (*FAZ*, 1 July.)

In a report to the eighth session of the Central Committee on 24 May, Honecker spoke about party efforts to intensify the work and effectiveness of its officials. As early as 17 February at a meeting with the first secretaries of the *Kreis* (county) committees, the party's tasks were expounded at length. In follow-up meetings at the *Kreis* level, over 106,000 party members participated. Another 300,000 took part in seminars. About 1.85 million members and candidates attended over 75,000 meetings held by the basic organizations. Honecker paid official tribute to the work of the approximately 7,000 unpaid party secretaries. (*Neues Deutschland*, 25 May.)

The same session of the Central Committee decided on the procedures to be followed for the 1978–79 party elections. On the basis of party statutes and electoral rules of the SED Central Committee, the presentation of accountability reports and the election of new leaders of the basic organizations at the *Kreis* and *Bezirk* (district) levels are scheduled between 1 November 1978 and 18 February 1979. (*Neues Deutschland*, 26 May.)

In January 1978 the Secretariat of the Central Committee decided the topics of instruction for party members for 1978–79. About three-fourths of the party members and about 200,000 nonparty members participated in the program. The topics dealt among others, with the founding of the GDR, the history of the SED, and basic issues of Marxism-Leninism and the revolutionary world process. (*Informationen*, no. 9, pp. 12–14.)

Apparently not all is well within the SED. Honecker and other party leaders criticized the lack of party discipline and the poor performance of workers in the production process, which in turn is held responsible for failure to achieve planned economic growth. (*Rheinischer Merkur,* 24 March; *Die Welt,* 26 and 29 May.)

SED leaders reacted violently to the "Manifesto" of an alleged opposition group within the GDR, which the West German weekly newsmagazine *Der Spiegel* (30 December 1977, 9 January) published in two parts (*Neues Deutschland,* 31 December 1977, 9 January). The opposition group, calling itself the League of Democratic Communists of Germany, is highly critical of the performance of SED leaders and accused them of betraying the cause of socialism. The document was dismissed by the SED leaders as a fabrication of the West German intelligence service.

Domestic Affairs. *Legal Reforms.* As of 1 January 1978 new traffic and labor laws were in force (*Informationen,* no. 26, 1977, pp. 8—9). With the beginning of the academic year 1977—78, new disciplinary rules replaced those of 1957. The new order is supposed to have educational functions. The provisions dealing with misbehavior and neglect of duties are considerably stricter than before. (Ibid., no. 1, pp. 9—11.) This change might possibly be the official reaction to restlessness among youth in the GDR.

On 13 October the People's Chamber passed a new law on defense of the country (*Landesverteidigung*), which does not substantially change the 1961 law, except that it increases the power and area of jurisdiction of the National Defense Council and reduces the power of the Council of State. The National Defense Council is now the most powerful organ in emergency situations. (*FAZ,* 14 October.)

Youth Indoctrination. About 600 delegates at the conference of SED students, meeting in May in East Berlin, decided to establish "schools of propaganda" at the universities and 240 vocational schools. These "schools" are supposed to train FDJ-students for political propaganda activities in factories and in the ninth and tenth grades of the vocational high schools. (*Informationen,* no. 30, pp. 7—8)

The SED places great emphasis on youth indoctrination. Erich Honecker stated that with "class-oriented education" all youngsters will act as "socialist patriots and proletarian internationalists and actively cooperate in the building of the developed socialist society" (*Neues Deutschland,* 18—19 February). The study of Marxism-Leninism is obligatory for all postsecondary students in the GDR. About 150 professors and 350 additional faculty of lower ranks serve as instructors.

As in previous years, the practice of youth consecration (*Jugendweihe*) was continued in 1978. More than 285,000 fourteen-year-old students participated in over 7,000 festivals and celebrations and pledged to fight for the "humanistic ideals of socialism," to practice "solidarity in the spirit of proletarian internationalism, and to defend socialism against any imperialistic interference" (*Die Welt,* 28 March).

In the fall of 1978, the GDR school system commenced a new required subject, "military education" (*Wehrerziehung*), for students in the ninth and tenth grades. Instructors are reserve officers of the National People's Army (*Nationale Volksarmee;* NVA). SED Central Committee member Herbert Scheibe, who is in charge of the Security Department of the Central Committee, declared that "socialist military education is an integral part of political work among the masses." As a result of strong opposition from all churches in the GDR, the content of the military instruction was somewhat altered for the first time. (*FAZ,* 19 and 20 August.)

State-Church Relations. The meeting on 6 March of the president of the Conference of the Protestant Churches, East Berlin Bishop Albrecht Schönherr, with Erich Honecker dealt with relations between state and church and was the first encounter of this kind in twenty years. The eight Protestant churches, which have about 8.4 million followers, assigned great significance to this meeting. Honecker stressed the clear separation of state and church but promised further state assistance for the education of Protestant ministers. He also paid tribute to the charitable work of the churches. (*Die Welt,* 8 March.) A Protestant clergyman explained that this meeting demonstrated that while the opposing life views of Christians and Marxists should not be belittled, they do not create insurmountable barriers (*Standpunkt* [a Protestant monthly], East Berlin, no. 4).

For the first time, on 24 March, an eight-minute sermon given by Bishop Schönherr was produced on GDR TV, a concession made by Honecker (*Die Welt,* 25 March). From 26 to 28 May, the Protestant Provincial church of Saxony held a church festival in Leipzig. The buildings for the meetings were provided by the local SED. About 4,100 church members participated in the congress, and about 10,000 attended the closing event. (*Washington Post,* 29 May.)

Approaches have also been made at a lower level toward the Roman Catholic church, which has about 1.3 million followers. The SED district chairman of Schwerin met with the Catholic administrator from Mecklenburg in order to improve contacts with the church. In contrast to the Protestant churches, the administrative organization of the Catholic church in the GDR does not coincide with the borders of the country. The seven districts, served by nine bishops, are administered by the Berlin Bishops' Conference, chaired by the Bishop of Berlin, who is directly subordinate to the Vatican. At present there are 1,342 Catholic priests in the GDR. (*Die Welt,* 3 April, 16 May.)

The announcement of military education for high school students brought strong protests from both Catholic and Protestant churches because according to their view it reduces the credibility of the alleged "peace policy" of the GDR (*Die Welt,* 26 June; *FAZ,* 10 July). Suddenly the old antagonism was revived (*FAZ,* 1 July). Earlier Bishop Schönherr had declared that the Protestant church in the GDR is not willing to be drawn into SED propaganda against the neutron bomb (*Die Welt,* 20 April).

Military Affairs. The estimated strength of the different components of the NVA showed a marked upward trend in 1978. Army personnel strength is given as 105,000 men on active duty and a ready reserve of 200,000. The army is comprised of two armored divisions, four motorized rifle divisions, two rocket brigades, two artillery brigades, two antiaircraft artillery regiments, one airborne battalion, and two antitank battalions. Organization and armament of the army indicated its offensive character. It has been reported that special units of battalion strength have been equipped with weapons and ammunition for chemical warfare. They are stationed in military districts III (Leipzig) and V (Neubrandenburg). (*FAZ,* 9 September.) Also, the training and the type of maneuvers conducted seem to confirm the intended offensive use of the military. For example, crossing of water obstacles similar to the canals found in West Germany and France is being practiced (*Bayernkurier,* 24 June).

The air force of the NVA consists of two divisions, two air defense regiments, and two parachute battalions. It possesses 416 combat planes, 61 training planes, and 46 helicopters. No new figures of its personnel strength have been obtained. In 1977, it had 28,000 men. The navy has increased its manpower from 17,000 to 25,000 and is equipped with seventeen submarine chasers, fifteen torpedo boats (equipped with rockets), and two frigates of the Riga class. (Ibid.) No new information concerning the border troops is available, but they had a known strength of 46,000.

Erich Honecker emphasized that political-ideological work within the NVA is of extreme importance because

> every member of the armed forces must obtain communist consciousness in order that he makes the decisions of our party his own, fulfills faithfully and consciously every command for the defense of socialism, and acquires the [knowledge] needed to be victorious in combat (*Neues Deutschland,* 9 June).

According to Defense Minister Army General Heinz Hoffmann, the NVA receives new weapons and equipment continuously from its "Soviet brothers-in-arms." He also thanked the Group of Soviet Armed Forces in Germany for training the NVA in the use of the new material. (Ibid.)

The GDR, like all Warsaw Pact countries, has compulsory military service. Nevertheless, the NVA needs more professional soldiers, who will volunteer to serve longer than the eighteen months of compulsory service. It was decided to intensify the propaganda for enlistment of officer and non-commissioned officer candidates, with the FDJ considered as the best recruiting ground. (*FAZ,* 22 September.)

Great emphasis is still placed on civil defense, which is directly under the Ministry of Defense. The active and noncommissioned officers of the civilian defense have had new uniforms since 1 January. Also on the same date, their new career regulations came into force. (*National-Zeitung,* East Berlin, 12 June.) The civilian population is also subjected to civil defense training.

The "combat groups of the working class," formerly known as "armed factory units," are estimated at 450,000 to 500,000 men, organized in over 400 battalions and armed with about 500 T54/55 tanks and other heavy weapons. They are a combat-ready force, intended to be used in conjunction with the NVA. (*Bayernkurier,* 30 June; *FAZ,* 18 September.) Up to 70 percent of its personnel are NVA reservists. The combat groups are the motorized infantry of the party. (*Die Welt,* 15 June.)

The GDR does not recognize "conscientious objectors"; however, there are alternative services with other military organs of the GDR, such as the Ministry for State Security, People's Police, Transport Police, construction units of the Ministry of Defense, and civil defense. The decision where a draftee is to serve rests with the military command and is based on the personnel requirements of the NVA and the other institutions. (*Neue Zeit,* East Berlin, 13 April.)

Nico Hübner, a resident of East Berlin, refused to comply with the universal military service law, claiming the demilitarized status of all of Berlin as his justification, and was arrested and eventually sentenced to five years for draft-dodging and illegal contacts with Western intelligence agents. The three Allied city commandants of West Berlin protested the violation of the Berlin Agreement by the GDR. The East Berlin city commandant stated that the declaration of his West Berlin counterparts concerning the validity of the Four Power Berlin Agreement has no significance. Berlin, the capital of the GDR, is according to the official position of the East German Communists, an integral part of the GDR where all laws of the GDR, including the military service law, are in force. (*Die Welt,* 5 May.)

Dissatisfaction and Repressive Measures. The "Manifesto" of the alleged communist opposition group within the GDR mentioned earlier is in all probability an authentic statement of several dissidents and therefore symptomatic of the restlessness of a large segment of the East German population. Regime critic Professor Robert Havemann, who for over two years has been kept under surveillance, declared that "in the eyes of 95 percent of the population, party and government have not the slightest respect. They do not even have the confidence of those who are supposed to execute their orders." (*Die Welt,* 19 May.)

Not only are the East German communist leaders concerned about the antiregime attitude of a part of the population; the generals of the approximately 400,000 Soviet troops stationed in East Germany have also indicated their displeasure. Their warnings were published in the SED party organ *Neues Deutschland.* (*NYT,* 29 January.) They declared that in "fraternal alliance" with the NVA, they would nip in the bud any aggressive act directed at the "achievements of the October Revolution." The Soviets are also highly critical of the work of the Department of Education of the SED Central Committee and of the Society for German-Soviet Friendship because they failed to deepen the commitment of GDR citizens, especially young people, to the Soviet Union and remained at times passive in the face of anti-Soviet slogans. (*Die Welt,* 19 January.) The president of the Academy of Pedagogical Science in East Berlin admitted that among GDR youth, a "potential of unrest" can be recognized (ibid., 1 February).

In spite of the Berlin Wall and the formidable border fortifications, East Germans are still attempting to escape. At least 173 persons have died in these efforts since the erection of the Wall in August 1961. Nevertheless, almost 175,000 East Germans have managed to leave the GDR. In the first five months of 1978, 1,325 refugees reached the West, including 137 who braved the border fortifications (*NYT*, 31 July). More automatic firing devices of the SM70 type have been installed, and other "improvements" along the 635-mile-long border have been made (*FAZ*, 30 August).

Only some of the cases of legal or physical repression of people in the GDR have become known through the news media. The Central Registry, a West German office attempting to register East German human rights violations, stated that since it began its work in 1961, 22,317 incidents or acts of violence were registered (*Die Welt*, 16 June). For example, on 7 April Rainer Bäurich was sentenced to five years and six months because he made use of his constitutional right of freedom of expression and wrote a "Manifesto of a Christian in Socialism" critical of the regime (*Rheinischer Merkur*, 21 July). On 16 August the married couple Harry and Renate Pohl were arrested in East Berlin because they opposed the introduction of "military education" for students in grades nine and ten (*FAZ*, 19 August). The practice of "forced adoption" of children of parents who attempt to flee the GDR and are apprehended continues. In the case of Gisela Mauritz, the court declared that she had forfeited the right to bring up her son because she intended to have him exposed to the "children-hostile" capitalist system (*Die Welt*, 20 February).

The estimated number of political prisoners held in GDR penal institutions varies between 5,000 and 7,000 (*Die Welt*, 29 June). West German Federal Minister for Intra-German Affairs Egon Franke stated that as of May 1978 there were about 1,300 known political prisoners in the GDR (*Informationen*, no. 11, p. 5). This figure appears too low on the basis of other available information. For example, in August 391 West Germans and West Berliners alone were in East German jails. (*FAZ*, 26 August.) In October it was reported that during the first nine months of 1978, East Berlin released about 1,000 political prisoners ransomed by the FRG (*International Herald Tribune*, 7–8 October). Since 1964 over 15,000 persons have been ransomed, at an estimated cost of $500 million (*Informationen*, no. 11, p. 5; *Washington Post*, 19 May).

The U.N. Human Rights Commission confronted on 31 January the representative of the GDR (Hans Heilborn) with more than 130 questions pertaining to the human rights situation in East Germany. Heilborn declared that East German law permits such restriction of civil rights as limitations on freedom of movement, forced exile, and revocation of citizenship. He denied the existence of political prisoners, assured the commission that churches are not disturbed, and claimed that discrimination in the educational field does not exist. According to him, human rights, within the principles of the East German constitution, are fully realized. (*Die Welt*, 1 February.)

A prisoner exchange between the U.S. and the GDR took place on 1 May. Soviet spy Robert Thompson was exchanged for a U.S. student, Alan van Normann, who had been sentenced in the GDR to 2.5 years for assisting in the attempt of an East German citizen to flee the country. (*Die Welt*, 2 May.)

The Economy. Honecker's report to the eighth session of the Central Committee (24–25 May) claimed that "in 1967–77, the proportional five-year plan goals with higher plan tasks were fulfilled and even exceeded. This was managed despite the price rises on the world market." (*Neues Deutschland*, 24 May.) He stated also that the goals for industrial goods production were fully achieved and the planned increase in labor productivity in industry was exceeded. Socialist intensification and greater efficiency in production are given credit for the increase in performance. (Ibid.) Also, a report of the Central Statistical Office of the GDR claimed that the targets set in the 1977 economic plan had been attained. The report stated that the "capitalist crisis and the resulting restrictive trade practices" adopted by several capitalist industrial nations complicated the foreign trade situation. (Ibid., 12 January.)

An analysis of this report reveals that the second year of the present five-year plan failed to reach its economic goals. Planned targets in the agricultural field were not reached, and the GDR was forced to import more than four million tons of grain. Foreign trade, which increased 7 percent, fell far short of the planned 8.7 percent. (*Informationen,* no. 2, pp. 11–13; no 3, pp. 10–11; *U. S. News and World Report,* 3 July, p. 37.)

According to the results achieved so far, the objectives of the five-year plan (1976–80) are almost impossible to reach. (This is the opinion of the German Institute for Economic Research (DIW) as reported in *FAZ,* 14 September.) Foreign trade with the Western industrialized countries went down from 24.2 to 21.8 billion marks. The foreign debt of the GDR with the CMEA countries was about 3 billion marks at the end of 1977, and with the West approximately $3.2 billion. (*Die Welt,* 20 February; *FAZ,* 14 July.)

At the eighth session of the Central Committee, Erich Honecker and Willi Stoph, chairman of the Council of Ministers, severely criticized the state of affairs in the economy and blamed the state apparatus for the failures (*Neues Deutschland,* 24 May).

Consequently, the goals for the 1978 plan, as adopted by the People's Chamber on 21 December 1977, were lowered. The economic results for the first half of 1978 indicate that in some areas the planned increases have been met, while in others they have not. For example, the increase in national income was 5 percent (planned 5.2 percent); industrial production, 5.2 percent (planned 5.7 percent); labor productivity, 5.1 percent (planned 5.0 percent); construction, 4.8 percent (planned 5.7 percent); and investments, 3.5 percent (planned 2.1 percent). It also was reported that exports to the CMEA countries increased by 11 percent and to the countries of the Third World by 30 percent. No figures for exports to the capitalist industrialized countries were given. The report merely stated that exports continued to increase. (Ibid., 15 July.)

The GDR trades with about 100 countries and has commercial treaties with more than 80. About 65 percent of the GDR's foreign trade is with CMEA countries, half of this with the Soviet Union and about 27 percent with Western countries, of which almost 9 percent is with the FRG. (*Informationen,* no. 4, p. 6.)

Prices of raw material imports on which the East German economy depends have tripled since 1970. The price of oil and gas from the Soviet Union went up on 1 January by 20 percent. Active foreign trade is essential to counteract these price increases and also to make up for the shortage of consumer goods production in the GDR. The price of basic food items, rents, and public transportation remained stable as a result of government subsidies, which are expected to amount to 44.3 billion marks (about $5 billion in 1978). (*Die Welt,* 14 January.) At the same time, incomes were permitted to rise. This policy of subsidies is a commitment of the SED leaders who are afraid of a further increase in the discontent of the people, who are aware that their real income, compared with that of the West Germans, has decreased from 76 percent at the time the Berlin Wall was built in 1961 to about half as much at present. (*U.S. News and World Report,* 3 July.)

As far as foreign trade is concerned, East Berlin succeeded in substantially increasing its trade with France. A contract with the Citroën branch of the P.S.A. Citroën-Peugeot was concluded for the building of a plant in the GDR (*Wall Street Journal,* 8 June). A new trade agreement covers the years 1978–85 and foresees various barter arrangements. The GDR is also greatly interested in intensifying trade with other Western countries. A number of agreements have been made with the U.S. firms. (*Die Welt,* 22 March.)

As a result of a decision of the FRG, East Germany is considered to some extent a part of the European Economic Community. Bonn maintains that intra-German trade is not foreign trade, and goods from the GDR frequently reach other European Common Market countries via the FRG. The financial advantage for East Berlin resulting from this assumption amounts to about $300 million per year (*Rheinischer Merkur,* 28 July). The GDR is short on hard currency. The East German mark is nonconvertible and is useless for foreign trade. Officially it is traded in East Berlin one to one against the West German mark. Actually it is worth less than 25 West German pfennig (13 U.S. cents). Foreign currency is obtained from the approximately eight million visitors, from the corps of diplomats, journalists, and businessmen in East Berlin, and from the West German government, which pays large sums for various services (*Calgary Herald,* 10 April). East Germany is also able to obtain credits in the West and loans from various sources. For example, East Berlin was rewarded for its strong pro-Arab policies with an Arab-financed loan of $22 million (*Christian Science Monitor,* 17 May). An especially significant source for the regime for obtaining hard currencies and for the citizens in acquiring high-quality consumer goods is some 100 so-called Intershops in which merchandise is available only to holders of West German marks, American dollars, and other solid currencies. Levi Strauss, for instance, sells more jeans to East Germany than to any other communist country, primarily through the Intershops network. The current sales of these shops are estimated at $40 million a year. There are also similar stores that sell western goods for East German marks. Such consumerism puts the GDR regime in an awkward situation—between the need for hard currency and its ideological dedication to socialist principles (*The Washington Post,* 3 December.)

The shortage of labor is supposed to be overcome with more 'socialist rationalization." By 1985, the intention is to increase the degree of mechanization from the current 42 to approximately 60 percent and release about 30,000 workers. (GDR radio, 22 April.) The 1978 economic plan emphasizes the intensification of research and development and new forms of organization which are designed to combine several related enterprises with large concerns (*Grosskombinate*). At present about 600,000 elderly pensioners are still employed. (*Die Welt,* 9 February, 20 May.) The 3.6 million working women represent 87 percent of the female population of the GDR between the ages of 15 and 60 (*Informationen,* no. 6, p. 7).

In order to improve services, the East German regime has permitted an increase in privately operating craftsmen. At the beginning of 1978, there were 86,560 private craftsmen enterprises compared with 1,420 production cooperatives of craftsmen. (*Die Welt,* 17 January.)

The GDR hopes that by the end of the century at least half of its energy requirements will be met by nuclear power plants. Two power stations are already in operation, and a third is reported under construction. (*NYT,* 30 May.)

Foreign Affairs. *Relations with the Federal Republic of Germany.* The year 1978 did not bring any fundamental changes in relations between the GDR and the FRG. The publication of the "Manifesto" of an alleged group of East German dissidents in the West German weekly *Der Spiegel,* however, caused an additional strain on relations. East Berlin through its permanent representative in Bonn, Dr. Michael Kohl, officially protested against "the newest fabrication in the defamation of the GDR" and emphasized that such "pamphlets . . . violate the rule of normal coexistence between states" (statement of the official East German news agency, ADN, reported in *Informationen,* no. 2, p. 2). The government of the FRG rejected the protest and explained that the federal government had nothing to do with the contents of the *Spiegel* report and that the constitutional guarantee of the freedom of the press precludes any government interference (ibid.).

The GDR Foreign Ministry announced that the East Berlin office of *Der Spiegel* was closed (ibid.). Erich Honecker accused other West German journalists of violating the spirit and letter of the Final Act of Helsinki, interfering in the internal affairs of the GDR, and disseminating lies, defamations, and malicious inventions. A number of them were warned and threatened with expulsion. (*Die Zeit,* 14 July.)

The East German government's refusal to permit the leader of the Christian Democratic Union, Helmut Kohl, and other CDU members of parliament to travel to East Berlin, as well as the numerous rejections of visitor visas, increased tensions. For example, at least 105 West German citizens were not allowed to travel to the Leipzig Trade Fair (*Die Welt*, 21 March). During the month of April alone, 47 West Berlin residents were refused entrance into East Berlin or the GDR, and eight persons were arrested (ibid., 5 May). GDR officials also continued to harass the transit traffic between the FRG and West Berlin. Numerous travelers underwent time-consuming body searches. During the first seven months of 1978, about 70 persons were arrested, 40 of them in connection with assisting East Germans to leave the GDR illegally. The government of the FRG and the three Western Allies protested the infringement of the transit agreements. (*Informationen*, no. 13, p. 2.) East Berlin's response to these protests was that all searches of persons in transit were permissible according to Article 16 of the Transit Agreement and necessary because of the "justified suspicion" of the misuse of transit roads (ibid., no. 3, p. 5). The GDR accused the FRG of violating the Four Power Agreement concerning Berlin (3 September 1971) by holding meetings there of prime ministers, ministers of various state (*Land*) governments, committees of the federal parliament (*Bundestag*), and bodies of the European parliament (*Neues Deutschland*, 11 April).

The East German government also protested against the surveillance of GDR citizens traveling in the FRG as "a gross interference in the internal affairs of the GDR . . . directed against the normalization of relations between the GDR and the FRG (*Bulletin*, vol. 18, no. 18, 21 June, p. 144). Conversely, the Federal Counterintelligence Agency (*Bundesverfassungschutz*) reported that during the first three months of 1978 the GDR Ministry for State Security approached at least 194 persons in order to recruit them for intelligence purposes (*Die Welt*, 14 June). The State Counterintelligence Service of North Rhine-Westphalia found that 90 percent of all Eastern intelligence activities were conducted by the GDR (ibid., 13 June).

Ewald Moldt was appointed as the new permanent representative in Bonn of the SED regime, replacing Michael Kohl, who had held this position since its inception in May 1974. Moldt was one of the deputy foreign ministers. (*Informationen*, no. 14, p. 18.)

The GDR government continues to express its desire to normalize relations with the FRG provided Bonn is willing to recognize certain realities. Erich Honecker's report to the eighth session of the Central Committee of the SED contained the following statement:

> We are prepared . . . to help clear away obstacles that are not of our doing.
> If the FRG, too, were always guided by the principles of recognition of the frontiers, respect for sovereignty, and noninterference in internal affairs as agreed in the Basic Treaty, progress would be possible. Relations between the GDR and the FRG are relations between two sovereign states which are independent of each other. This is ignored and assailed . . . by those who keep rehashing old formulas which have long since been discarded by history. (*Neues Deutschland*, 24 May.)

On the occasion of an address to the first secretaries of the party district executive committees, Honecker stated:

> It is only on the basis of the treaties concluded and of the Final Act of Helsinki that relations between the GDR and the FRG can develop in a meaningful way. Both the GDR and the FRG manifested in the Basic Treaty and by signing the Final Act of Helsinki that in the conduct of relations between them they would strictly apply the basic principles of international law and would be guided entirely by recognition of the sovereign equality and territorial integrity of states and by noninterference in the internal affairs of states.
> The GDR would like to see relations between the two German states expanded along these lines. This would also serve the European peace effort. (*Bulletin*, vol. 18, no. 8, 13 March, p. 59.)

Honecker's formulations did not preclude the SED regime's campaign against the FRG. At an 8 May rally in East Berlin to commemorate the thirty-third anniversary of the defeat of Nazi Germany, SED Central Committee member and Deputy Defense Minister Colonel General Heinz Kessler attacked the FRG (*Neues Deutschland,* 9 May). In July, SED propaganda centered on the subject of alleged human rights violations and the revival of nazism in the FRG. *Neues Deutschland* (15 July) charged that perpetrators of crimes against humanity occupy the highest offices and find safe haven in the FRG. The same paper (17 July) accused West Germany of harboring 200,000 war criminals and of indoctrinating its soldiers with fascist concepts.

Despite these attacks and polemics, negotiations concerning a number of joint traffic projects led to the conclusion on 16 November of a major traffic pact whose target is the construction of a four-lane highway between Berlin and Hamburg by 1984. For the GDR the building of the autobahn between the two largest German cities represents a major economic benefit because of the FRG's willingness to pay East Germany about $3.5 billion over the next 10 years. On his side, West Berlin's mayor, Dietrich Stobbe, told the city parliament that the "political price" was worthwhile because of the "positive psychological effects" of improving ties and facilitating transit. (*NYT* and *The Washington Post,* 17 November.)

The GDR receives substantial financial and economic benefits from the FRG. In the period from 1970 to 1977, about 6.58 billion marks (about $3.3 billion) were paid to East Berlin by Bonn, West Berlin, the Federal Post Office, the Federal Railroad, and by private offices. If the interest-free credit from the interzonal trade (SWING) is added to this sum, the benefits amount to a total of 11.32 billion marks ($5.7 billion). (*Die Welt,* 1 March.) Bonn also pays annually a lump sum for transit travel to West Berlin. During the first four years since the Transit Agreement of 1972, the Federal Government has paid yearly 234.9 million marks ($117.5 million). Based on the new agreement of 19 December 1975, the annual lump sum for the years 1976 to 1979 was raised to 400 million marks (about $200 million). (*Die Welt,* 5 April.)

Relations With The Soviet Bloc. At the same time Honecker continued the tradition of praising the increased integration of the GDR economy with those of the Soviet Union and the other countries of the CMEA:

> Our fraternal alliance with the Soviet Union, the fact that our state is firmly embedded in the socialist community, are the foundations of our successes. Thus, the German Democratic Republic belongs to the strongest and most influential force of our era, the world socialist system. (*Neues Deutschland,* 24 May.)

He also stated that the progress of specialization, division of labor, and cooperation between the GDR and the Soviet Union for the period of 1980 to 1990 is making further progress (ibid.). From 19 to 21 June the twenty-third session of the Governmental Commission for Economic and Scientific-technological Cooperation, composed of representatives of the GDR and the Soviet Union, dealt with the further intensification of the two countries' collaboration (*Informationen,* no. 13, p. 3).

About 450 Soviet research, development, and manufacturing enterprises are working together with 380 East German institutes and factories in various specific technical and scientific programs. Some outstanding results have already been achieved, including the MKF-6 multispectral camera used in space flights and the world's first 30-ton plasma-melting furnace for high-grade steel. There are presently over 100 bilateral agreements serving socialist economic integration (*Bulletin,* vol. 18, no. 14, 15 May, p. 112). On the basis of the long-term agreement between the GDR and the Soviet Union on cooperation in setting up industrial enterprises in the GDR and on delivery of equipment from the Soviet Union, a protocol on deliveries and services for 1979 was signed in East Berlin on 21 April. The imports will include equipment for nuclear and thermal power stations. (Ibid., no. 15, 24 May, p. 119.)

The Soviet-East German space enterprise saw the first German in outer space at the end of August. The SED-regime utilized this event in its propaganda as proof of the close scientific collaboration between the two countries. (Ibid., no. 25, 13 September, pp. 193−94.)

As in the preceding years, the SED regime supported Moscow's foreign policy, although Honecker was supposed to have carefully criticized Soviet foreign trade policies at the eighty-fourth session of the CMEA Executive Committee on 21−23 February (ibid., no. 8, 13 March, p. 63). Also, Peking reported that Honecker expressed concern about the process of specialization of production (*Die Welt,* 22 February). Highest GDR representatives attended the Warsaw Pact's Political Consultative Committee meeting, which took palce in Moscow in mid-November.

Official relations between the leaders of both countries remain as close as before. Honecker spent his vacation in the Soviet Union and visited with CPSU Secretary General Brezhnev (*FAZ,* 27 July). Soviet Foreign Minister Andrei Gromyko called on Honecker, briefed him about the results of Brezhnev's visit to the FRG, and assured him of the continuation of the common foreign policy of the "socialist fraternal states" (*Die Welt,* 13 May). Mikhail Suslov, a member of the Politburo and Secretariat of the CPSU, received East Germany's highest decoration, the Karl Marx Order, on the occasion of his seventy-fifth birthday (*Informationen,* no. 2, p. 4). East Germans were encouraged to subscribe to Soviet publications and to enroll in Russian language courses. About seven million persons are studying Russian at various clubs and educational institutions. About 800 teachers of Russian graduate every year. (*Bauern-Echo,* East Berlin, 10 May.) From the fifth school year on, Russian is a required subject (*Die Welt,* 11 March). "Moscow Days" held in East Berlin from 31 January to 5 February were probably a new device intended to influence the attitude of the East German population. The participating Soviet delegations included representatives of the CPSU, trade unions, and youth organizations. (*Bulletin,* vol. 18, no. 6, 22 February, p. 46.)

Mutual visits of SED leaders with their counterparts in the other socialist countries of Eastern Europe and in Cuba continued during 1978. Meetings of the Joint Economic Commissions of the GDR with each of these countries worked on the implementation of economic and scientific-technical collaboration. The president of the Socialist Republic of Romania, Nicolae Ceauşescu, received the Karl Marx Order (*Informationen,* no. 3, p. 3). East Berlin hosted the Fifth Conference of the Ministers of Justice of the Socialist States on 16−18 May (ibid., no. 10, p. 5). SED representatives participated in the Budapest meeting of the secretaries of the communist and workers' parties of ten socialist countries on 27 February−1 March. The central topics were "the strengthening of the common ideological work in the struggle for the consolidation of peace, for the continuation of the détente process, against the arms race fanned by the imperialists, and for disarmament." (*Neues Deutschland,* 7 March.) Hermann Axen, member of the SED Politburo and secretary of the Central Committee, attended and addressed the international theoretical conference on the "Construction of Socialism and Communism and World Progress," sponsored jointly by the Bulgarian CP and the *World Marxist Review*, and held in Sofia on 12−15 December. Seventy-three communist and workers' parties sent delegations to the conference.

The GDR, as a member of the CMEA, participated in the eighty-fourth session of the Executive Committee (21−23 February) which dealt with the implementation of the program decided at the thirty-first Council meeting (*Bulletin,* vol. 18, no. 8, 13 March, p. 63). Willi Stoph led the East German delegation to the thirty-second CMEA Council meeting in Bucharest on 26−28 June (*Informationen,* no. 13, p. 5). The member countries of the CMEA have jointly undertaken about 10,000 technological and scientific projects since the adoption of the program of socialist economic integration in 1971. Considerable headway has been made with regard to the utilization of nuclear energy. (*Bulletin,* vol. 18, no. 5, 13 February.) GDR officials attended the meeting of the foreign ministers of the Warsaw Pact countries in Sofia 24−25 April and the session of the Military Council in Budapest on 16−19 May (*Informationen,* no. 9, p. 4; *Neues Deutschland,* 20−21 May). The collaboration with other socialist countries was also manifested in the draft convention of the Warsaw Pact states addressed to the Geneva Disarmament Committee on 9 March regarding the prohibition of neutron weapons (*Bulletin,* vol. 18, no. 10, 4 April).

Relations with Capitalist Industrialized Countries. For the GDR, 1978 witnessed further improvement of relations with these nations. The SED regime based its efforts to a great extent on the results of its better understanding of the political and economic processes in these countries. In 1971 the Institute for International Politics and Economy was founded. It employs about 400 scientists. The Scientific Council for Imperialism Research, established in 1969, is charged with the coordination of the work of a number of additonal research institutes. (*FAZ,* 18 September.)

GDR Foreign Minister Oskar Fischer continued the practice of visiting his counterparts in other countries. Following his visit and discussions in Japan on 12—17 December 1977 (*Bulletin,* vol. 18, no. 3, 24 January, p. 20), he visited Belgium and Luxembourg in May. His efforts were directed towards greater cooperation, especially in the economic, scientific, and technological fields. His most important negotiations took place in June in the United States where he met with U.S. Secretary of State Cyrus Vance. He also met with members of the Committee on Foreign Relations of the House of Representatives and with David Rockefeller. (*Informationen,* no. 12, p. 3.) Fischer's diplomatic efforts centered on at least three items: concluding a consular agreement held up so far by East Berlin's insistence on a specific definition of East German nationality, which is considered extraordinary and unnecessary by U.S. officials and furthermore is strongly opposed by the FRG; obtaining "most-favored-nation" status in order to increase trade with the U.S., a difficult undertaking in the face of a $7 billion foreign debt; and finally, improving the image of the GDR in American opinion by denying East Germany's involvement in Angola and Ethiopia (*Informationen,* no. 12, p. 3; *Baltimore Sun,* 6 June). In 1977 trade between the two countries amounted to $350 million, but East Germany's exports to the U.S. accounted for a mere $16 million.

The East German art exhibition "Splendor of Dresden—Five Centuries of Art Collecting" in Washington (later exhibited in New York), opened by the GDR minister of culture on 31 May, was a great success (*Informationen,* no. 11, p. 7). From 9 to 16 May "Economic-Technical Days of the GDR" were organized in New York, pointing out that economic cooperation has developed favorably since diplomatic relations were established in September 1974, the U.S. being the 110th state to recognize the GDR (*Bulletin,* vol. 18, no. 19, 4 July, p. 151). Fischer also visited Italy and signed an agreement of cooperation on 27 October. Afterwards, he met with newly elected Pope John Paul II, the first minister of a communist-ruled country to come on official business to the Vatican. (*FAZ,* 28 October.)

East Berlin also attempted to improve relations and contacts on a nongovernmental level. For example, a delegation of the National Christian Council (NCC) visited the GDR in April. (*Informationen,* no. 8, p. 4.) The emphasis of GDR's relations with other capitalist industrialized nations was also placed on trade and improved contacts with the executive and legislative branches of their governments. Delegations of the People's Chamber visited Norway (3 April), Japan (17—25 May), and Sweden (5—10 June). Government representatives carried on negotiations in Australia (18—19 April), Belgium (20—23 May), France (21 April and 5—8 June), Great Britain (January and July), Iceland (2 June), New Zealand (21 April), and Turkey (16 June). The GDR played host to parliamentary delegations and government officials from Austria (29 May), Denmark (9 March), Finland (19 January), Great Britain (16—23 February), and Japan (30 June). Among the most significant visitors was Austrian Chancellor Bruno Kreisky (30 March—1 April). A long-term trade and payment agreement between the two countries and an agreement about economic, industrial, and technological cooperation were signed. (*Bulletin,* vol. 18, no. 12, 24 April, pp. 89—90.)

East Berlin continued the practice of utilizing or creating mixed government commissions charged with making agreements about scientific-technological cooperation with countries such as

Australia (18–19 April), Austria (3 March), France (21 April), Iceland (2 June), Norway (8–12 May), and Turkey (16 June). The long-term trade agreement between the GDR and New Zealand (21 April) is the first "most-favored-nation treaty" signed by East Berlin (*Calgary Herald,* 1 May).

Erich Honecker sent a telegram of condolence to the Italian president following the murder of former minister-president and president of the Italian Christian Democratic Party, Aldo Moro. He asserted that Moro was a victim of a crime committed by fascists. (*Neues Deutschland,* 10 May.) Prior to the murder, the SED had already claimed that the "Red Brigades" are a neofascist group supported by the CIA and NATO (ibid., 18–19 March; *Bauern-Echo,* 25 April).

Relations With the Third World. The GDR's support of Soviet policies in the Third World continued during 1978. For home consumption East Berlin's activities were declared to be part of the worldwide "anti-imperialist struggle." Honecker in his report to the Central Committee (24 May) stated:

> The Political Bureau has on various occasions dealt with matters relating to anti-imperialist cooperation with the nationally liberated states and the national liberation movements. We attach great importance to such cooperation, which is part of the international class conflict with imperialism. One focal point is Africa. . . .
> It is a well-known fact that we have joined the Soviet Union, Cuba, and the other fraternal socialist states in providing active support to the peoples of Ethiopia, Angola, and Mozambique and to the liberation movements in southern Africa. . . . We reconfirm our active solidarity with the Ethiopian revolution. (*Bulletin*, vol. 18, no. 17, 13 June, p. 131.)

It appears that Moscow has assigned an important role to the GDR in its overall African strategy. This coincided with the interests of the SED regime, which saw in Africa good prospects for its efforts to gain recognition. In 1978, 45 of the 49 African states maintained diplomatic relations with East Berlin. While economic and technological aid to the Moscow-oriented black African states plays a significant role, the main emphasis is placed on military support. The cost of weapons and military equipment shipped from the GDR to Africa amounts to at least $100 million. Military aid is accompanied by control over the police and secret services in the Marxist-oriented countries. (*Le Figaro,* Paris, 29–30 April.) It is estimated that the overall expenditures of East German "anti-imperialist solidarity" amounts to 500 million marks per year. Most of this aid goes to about a dozen countries, such as Ethiopia, the People's Republics of the Congo and Benin, and the five former Portuguese colonies, notably Angola and Mozambique. (*Die Welt*, 19 April.)

The number of East Germans in Africa is estimated to be more than 2,000, including military instructors, attachés, and specialists such as engineers, signal corpsmen, and artillery and armored personnel (*Die Welt*, 7 June). The Brookings Institution (Washington, D.C.) estimates that about 17,000 men of the NVA are operating in fifteen African states (reported in *Bayernkurier,* 17 June). The abortive invasion of Zaire by the National Liberation Front of the Congo (FLNC) was organized by NVA officers (*Die Welt*, 22 May). A military delegation, led by Politburo member and GDR Defense Minister Heinz Hoffmann, visited the Republic of Guinea, Angola, the People's Republic of the Congo, and Tunisia during May (*Neues Deutschland,* 15, 16, and 17 May).

Great importance is placed on the support of the "liberation movements" in those countries which are not yet under communist control, such as the South West African People's Organization (SWAPO), the African National Congress (ANC), and the Zimbabwe African People's Union (ZAPU). The leaders of these movements have been received by the SED regime.

Middle East. In this region East Berlin provided diplomatic and military assistance to the Arab states against Israel and criticized the U.S.-backed efforts for a peaceful settlement. For example, the GDR Solidarity Committee condemned Israel's "barbarous military aggression" against Lebanon and the backing of "other imperialist powers" designed to "destroy the patriotic forces of the sovereign state of Lebanon and the Palestinian resistance movement" (*Bulletin,* vol. 18, no. 9, 22 March, p. 67).

An estimated 2,000 men are involved in East Berlin's support of the People's Democratic Republic of Yemen. The East Germans are supposed to have organized and are administering the country's security system, which includes ten concentration camps. (*Die Welt,* 6 February.) GDR Defense Minister Heinz Hoffmann visited the country at the end of 1977 and initiated the reorganization of Yemen's military forces. These forces are to be increased from 22,000 to 40,000 men. (*Die Welt,* 8 December 1977.)

Also in the Middle East, the SED regime utilized the so-called "joint committees on economic and scientific-technological cooperation" to maintain its influence. Meetings of these committees took place in Syria (4—7 December 1977 and 4—7 June 1978) and in Iraq (4—10 February). A number of delegations from the Middle Eastern countries visited the GDR, and several East German delegations traveled to the Middle East. Yassir Arafat, leader of the PLO, was in East Berlin at least twice and also participated in the "Week of Solidarity with the Struggle of the Anti-imperialist Forces in the Middle East for Peace and Social Progress" (5—11 June).

The pragmatic approach of GDR foreign policy is exemplified by the visit of Foreign Minister Fischer to the shah of Iran (30 April) in an effort to lay the groundwork for normalization of relations between the two countries in spite of East Berlin's strong opposition to the Iranian political system.

Asia. East Germany's involvement in Asia in 1978 was primarily with communist-ruled Vietnam, Laos, and the People's Republic of Korea. However, there are also indications of attempts by East Berlin to increase its influence in India.

Joint committees for economic and scientific-technical cooperation were organized with Laos and North Korea. On 13 March a long-term agreement on friendship and cooperation with Vietnam was signed in East Berlin. Following Soviet policy, the SED regime supports Vietnam's stand on the border issue with Cambodia (Hanoi radio, in English, 5 January) and continues to provide substantial material aid to Hanoi through a Solidarity Committee, which also organized on 2 September a "National Day of the Socialist Republic of Vietnam" in the GDR. On 20 January the annual agreement on trade for 1978 was signed with North Korea.

An agreement of cooperation in science, education, and culture was concluded with India on 3 March. A People's Chamber delegation visited India (1—8 March), and the Indian defense minister came for discussions to East Berlin. East Germany's interest in Asia was also demonstrated by the trip Honecker undertook in December 1977 to Vietnam, North Korea, and the Philippines.

Latin America. The only significant contact of the GDR during 1978 in Latin America was with Mexico. The first session of the Joint Governmental Commission, which began on 6 March, was concerned with present and future prospects for relations and trade. (*Informationen,* no. 6, p. 2.) A consular agreement was signed on 28 March (ibid., no. 7, p. 4.)

Yugoslavia, China, Albania, and Eurocommunism. The SED regime continued it efforts during 1978 to improve Yugoslavia's relations with the Soviet bloc. A Yugoslav government delegation visited the GDR (6—11 February). An NVA delegation led by Lieutenant General Heinz Kessler, deputy defense minister, spent several days (May—June) in Yugoslavia and had talks with leading representatives of the Yugoslav People's Army. (Ibid., no. 11, pp. 4—5.)

East Berlin welcomed "the constructive efforts undertaken by the Soviet Union to normalize relations with the People's Republic of China" (*Neues Deutschland,* 17 April).

On 21 December 1977 the deputy foreign trade ministers of the GDR and Albania signed in East Berlin the annual agreement about trade and finances for 1978 (*Informationen,* no. 26, 1977, p. 4).

Eurocommunism is totally rejected by SED leaders because according to them Marxism does not provide for "national variations" or for "regionalization." The attempts of "so-called Euro-communism" lead toward the relativization of the fundamental findings of Marxism-Leninism, which are of a general, i.e., international, validity. (*Neues Deutschland,* 29—30 April.) A discussion in East Berlin with a delegation from the Communist Party of France apparently did not change the SED's attitude toward Eurocommunism. It is noteworthy, however, that the communiqué did not carry any reference to "proletarian internationalism." (*FAZ,* 20 October.)

Collaboration with International Organizations. In 1978 the GDR was successful in utilizing the United Nations and its specialized agencies in its effort to increase its role at the international level, thereby adding to its prestige. GDR representatives were particularly active in the U.N. Economic Commission for Europe in Geneva, UNESCO, and ILO. They invariably supported Soviet proposals prohibiting all nuclear tests, ending the nuclear arms race, and prohibiting new types of weapons of mass destruction. (*Bulletin,* vol. 18, no. 26, 21 September, p. 200.) Erich Honecker in a letter on 21 March to U.N. Secretary General Kurt Waldheim assured him of his country's support for the activities of the International Anti-apartheid Year (ibid., no. 10, 4 April, p. 75).

International Party Contacts. Honecker declared in May in his report on the occasion of the eighth session of the Central Committee that "since the seventh plenary session, 65 delegations from communist and workers' parties, national revolutionary parties and movements, as well as socialists of social democratic parties have been guests of the SED. During the same period, our party had sent 63 delegations for exchange of views and experiences with communist and workers' parties as well as with national revolutionary parties and movements. We are endeavoring to continually deepen internationalist cooperation between the fraternal parties in the common interest of socialism and peace." (*Neues Deutschland,* 25 May.)

A high level SED delegation, led by Hermann Axen and two other members of the party's Politburo, took part in the deliberations of the German Communist Party (DKP) congress in Mannheim, West Germany. In a message of greetings to the congress, Erich Honecker declared that the "SED will stand firmly by the side of the DKP in the spirit of proletarian solidarity" (East Berlin Radio, 20 October).

SED leaders received delegations and high functionaries of numerous communist and workers' parties. Among the delegates visiting the GDR were representatives from the Party of Labor of Switzerland as well as from the communist parties of Denmark, Austria, Paraguay, Lebanon, Chile, Great Britain, Portugal, FRG, U.S.A., and France.

SED delegations led by various Politburo members participated during the first half of 1978 in many congresses of fraternal parties and movements. Among them were in January the First Congress of the People's Movement for the Liberation of Angola (*Horizont,* East Berlin, no. 3), and the congresses of the communist parties of Sri Lanka, India, Norway, Spain, West Germany, Switzerland, Greece, Cyprus, Finland, and Yugoslavia.

Publications. According to the GDR constitution, the freedom of the press is guaranteed by Article 27, paragraph 2. Constitutional and political reality, however, indicates that the mass media are subject to severe party censorship and control. The newspapers implement the concept of "identity of party and mass media." The daily papers have a total circulation of 8.3 million. The proportion of newspapers to population is better than one to two despite the fact that all of them contain the same information that can be heard and seen the evening before on the TV program "Current Camera." The contents of the central organ of the SED, *Neues Deutschland* (circulation of more than one million), and of the district and county papers (circulation of four million), can also be found in other newspapers, such as the organs of the "bloc parties:" *Der Morgen,* central organ of the LDPD (50,000 copies); *Bauern-Echo,* the official newspaper of the DBD (100,000 copies); *Neue Zeit,* central organ of the CDU (50,000 copies); and *National Zeitung,* the organ of the NDPD (50,000 copies). The mass organizations also have their own dailies. The FDGB's paper is the *Tribüne* (400,000 copies), and the paper of the FDJ, *Junge Welt,* has a circulation of 900,000. (*Die Welt,* 20 January; for a listing of additional newspapers and periodicals, see *YICA, 1977,* pp. 43—44.)

The University of Calgary   Eric Waldman

Hungary

Hungarian Communists formed a party in November 1918 and were the dominant force in the Hungarian Soviet Republic that lasted from March to August 1919. Thereafter the party functioned as a minute and faction-ridden movement in domestic illegality and in exile. With the Soviet occupation at the end of World War II, the Hungarian Communist Party emerged as a partner in the coalition government, exercised an influence disproportionate to its modest electoral support, and gained effective control of the country in 1947. In 1948 it absorbed left-wing social democrats into the newly named Hungarian Workers' Party. On 1 November 1956 during the popular revolt that momentarily restored a multiparty government, the name was changed to Hungarian Socialist Workers' Party (Magyar Szocialista Munkáspárt; HSWP).

The HSWP rules unchallenged as the sole political party, firmly aligned with the Soviet Union. Its exclusive status is confirmed in the revised state constitution of 1972: "The Marxist-Leninist party of the working class is the leading force in society." Current party membership is 770,000 out of a population of 10,693,000. At the time of the HSWP's Eleventh Congress (March 1975), physical workers comprised 45.5 percent of the membership; "immediate supervisors of production," 6.1 percent; intellectual workers, 40 percent; and dependents and others, 8.4 percent. In the 1971—75 parliament, 71 percent of deputies were party members. About 47 percent of municipal and local council members belong to the HSWP as do about 90 percent of officers in the police forces.

Leadership and Organization. Ultimate political power in the HSWP, and therefore in Hungary, remains in the hands of the first secretary, János Kádár. The 66-year-old Kádár has been party leader longer (since November 1956) than any of his counterparts in the Soviet bloc. He holds no state office. Current Politburo members are Kádár, György Aczél, Antal Apró, Valéria Benke, Béla Biszku, Jenö Fock, Sándor Gáspár, István Huszár, György Lázár, Pál Losonczi, László Maróthy, Dezsö Nemes, Károly Németh, Miklós Óvári, and István Sarlós. In addition to Kádár, the Central Committee Secretariat includes Sándor Borbély, András Gyenes, Imre Györi, Ferenc Havasi, Mihály Korom, Németh, and Óvári. János Brutyó is chairman of the Central Control Committee. Óvári is chairman of the Agitprop Committee, Németh of the Economic Policy Committee, and

Arpád Pullai of the Youth Committee. Pál Romány, who is minister of agriculture, is chairman of the Central Committee's Cooperative Policy Team; Óvári, of the Cultural Policy Team; Németh, of the Economic Team; and Béla Biszku, of the Party Building Team (see *YICA, 1978,* p. 37 for discussion of party committees).

Losonczi is chairman of the Presidential Council and therefore nominal head of state. Lázár is prime minister, and Aczél and Huszár are among the five deputy premiers. Apró is chairman of the National Assembly. Gáspár is secretary general of the National Council of Trade Unions, Maróthy of the Communist Youth League, and Sarlós of the Patriotic People's Front.

At its 20 April meeting the Central Committee approved a major reshuffle of the party leadership. The most significant change was the dismissal of Béla Biszku from the Secretariat. A close associate of Kádár since before the 1956 revolution, Biszku had served as interior minister in 1957−61 and joined the Secretariat in 1962. He had enjoyed wide-ranging authority over the party apparat and the defense and security forces and was generally regarded as Kádár's deputy. His demise has been variously attributed to his penchant for authoritarianism; to administrative inadequacies highlighted in the Central Committee's resolution on the need to develop socialist democracy, curtail misuse of power by party organizations, and improve economic efficiency; to his opposition to further decentralization of the economic mechanism; and to his ambition to succeed Kádár. Biszku, who is only 57, remains a member of the Politburo.

Added to the Secretariat were Ferenc Havasi, formerly a deputy premier, and Mihály Korom, formerly justice minister. Havasi, a skilled proponent of the New Economic Mechanism, has assumed some of Németh's responsibilities for the economy, while Korom took over Biszku's jobs in the realm of defense and security. Németh inherited Biszku's responsibility for the party apparat and has become Kádár's new de facto deputy. The shift therefore redistributed the powers concentrated hitherto in Biszku's hands and enhanced the reformist complexion of the leadership.

József Marjai, a career diplomat and former ambassador to Moscow, was appointed deputy premier in place of Havasi, becoming the first foreign affairs specialist in that post. The justice portfolio was given to the career jurist Imre Markoja. In other changes, Lajos Méhes, a former first secretary of the Communist Youth Leage and secretary general of the Metalworkers' Union, was appointed first secretary of the important Budapest party committee in place of Imre Katona, who was named secretary of the Presidential Council; Imre Pardi was dismissed as head of the Central Committee's Economic Policy Department and replaced by his deputy, János Hoos.

Public reaction to Biszku's demotion was generally favorable. Media commentators reflected on the public's concern with personnel changes and with the secrecy surrounding these changes in contrast to Western practice and acknowledged that the shifts were prompted by certain unspecified shortcomings.

Auxiliary and Mass Organizations. The broadest umbrella organization for political mobilization, the Patriotic People's Front (PPF), is the agent of the party's alliance policy. Its domestic tasks include the organization of elections and various social projects as well as political education of the masses. It is also active in foreign relations; in 1978, for instance, the PPF sent a delegation to Vietnam and Laos (see below) and received a delegation from the "Lebanese National Movement." The PPF works through over 4,000 committees, with a membership of 112,400.

The National Peace Council is a member of the World Peace Council, a communist front organization. It participates in international conferences and maintains bilateral contacts. In March 1978, for instance, a delegation consisting of Gyula Sütö, its secretary general, and László Tolnai, vice-chairman of the Disarmament Subcommittee of its Science Commission, visited Stockholm for talks with Swedish peace organizations.

The Communist Youth League (Kommunista Ifjusági Szövetség; KISZ) is the youth branch of the HSWP. Its membership stands at over 800,000, in some 25,600 basic organizations. Thirty-one percent of working youths, 56 percent of secondary schools pupils, and 96 percent of postsecondary students belong to the KISZ; 7.5 percent of KISZ members also belong to the HSWP. The KISZ also directs the Pioneers, which has over one million members and accounts for 94 percent of the 6−14 age group. KISZ First Secretary Maróthy led a 450-member delegation to the Eleventh World Festival of Youth and Students in Havana in July−August. One task of the KISZ is the organization of summer labor camps, which have become a permanent institution designed to alleviate labor shortages. Participation is officially voluntary but is in fact a useful credit for access to higher education. Some 67,000 young people participated in 1978, mainly in agricultural projects. For the first time, school-age Pioneers also worked in summer labor camps.

The National Council of Trade Unions (NCTU) coordinates unions that include close to 4 million workers (94 percent of all salary and wage earners). It is also responsible for contacts with foreign trade union movements; in August, NCTU Secretary General Sándor Gáspár received a delegation from the Scottish Trade Union Congress.

Party Internal Affairs. The Central Committee's 20 April resolution reiterated the need for improvements in cadre work, including objective application of political, professional, and leadership criteria in the selection of cadres, better training of new cadres, and the systematic replacement of cadres in accordance with changing requirements (*Magyar Hirlap,* 23 April). In a subsequent interview, Central Control Committee Chairman János Brutyó indicated that party discipline was good but still in need of improvement. Closer relations with the West led to greater exposure to bourgeois views while greater enterprise autonomy led to abuses. Brutyó warned that party members had to offer active rather than merely passive support for party policy and that their failure to address mistakes was itself a dereliction of duty. At the same time, the principle that "we are fighting not against men but only against their errors" remained in force.

Brutyó denounced certain leaders' abuse of authority, e.g., failure to consult their collectives, willful contravention or neglect of party resolutions and government decrees, and the stifling or punishment of criticism. Since the Eleventh Congress, 102 members had been expelled for this "grave violation of communist conduct." (See in this connection the details of the 1976 party card exchange, *YICA, 1978,* p. 37). He also mentioned that there had been only a few recent cases of disciplinary action for the even graver crime of factionalism. Apart from abuses, party leaders who failed to use power properly should also be subjected to disciplinary action, warned Brutyó. (*Népszabadság,* 23 July.)

In a speech to the Central Committee on 20 April, Kádár warned certain cadres against being too hasty or vociferous in the promotion of Hungarian-Soviet friendship. That friendship had to be taken seriously, not preached with false words; Kádár observed that some say one thing and do another regarding relations with the Soviet Union. Another deviation among certain cadres was a "vulgar simplification" of the West's iniquities, of seeing only harm in the intensification of relations. This, said Kádár, was contrary to the policy of peaceful coexistence and to Hungary's economic interests (Tanjug, 26 May).

The Eleventh Congress had urged an increase in the proportion of workers, women, and young people in the party membership. Accordingly, Borbély has reported that in 1977 almost 60 percent of new recruits were workers and peasants, two-thirds were under 30 years of age, and over 32 percent were women (*Pravda,* 28 January).

Domestic Affairs. *Culture and Ideology.* The Central Committee's 20 April resolution deplored the remnants of bourgeois and petit bourgeois values as well as nationalism. It invited greater efforts in ideological indoctrination to strengthen patriotism, internationalism, and the work ethic and to ward off dogmatism and revisionism disguised as the "modernization of Marxism." The regime continues to seek some enduring compromise between ideological orthodoxy and intellectual freedom, particularly in the social sciences.

The question of qualifications for higher degrees has prompted some debate. The law requires that candidates support the building of a socialist society with their work and that their theses be compatible with Marxism-Leninism, but the argument has been advanced (without official contradiction) that the militant profession of Marxism-Leninism is mandatory only in the social sciences (*Népszabadság*, 21 February). The Central Committee's Agitprop Committee, headed by Óvári, has been grappling with the thorny problem of sociology. The official revival of this discipline in 1961 created serious ideological problems. An academic group led by András Hegedüs pursued a "critical sociology" that the party branded as deviating from Marxism and which it suppressed. The party is now attempting to create a new academic order by establishing university chairs of "general sociology" subordinated to existing chairs of Marxism-Leninism and designed to train ideologically compatible sociologists (*Szociológia*, no. 2, 1977). A Hungarian Society of Sociologists was founded on 15 May under the presidency of the distinguished scholar Sándor Szalai. Professor of sociology and an active social democrat prior to the communist takeover, Szalai was imprisoned from 1950 to 1956. Media commentaries focused on the scientific and political role of sociology, a dualism that is fraught with tension in a one-party system.

Four dissident Marxist intellectuals, the philosophers Ferenc Fehér, Ágnes Heller, and György Márkus and the sociologist Mária Márkus, were induced to emigrate at the beginning of 1978. Culture Minister Imre Pozsgay commented that although their work was "opposed to the foundations of the socialist system" and had to be banned, their departure was a loss to Hungary and he did not consider their exile permanent (*L'Unità*, 9 February). As active members of the "Lukács school," they had been censured for ideological transgressions. They had signed the Korčula (Yugoslavia) protest against the invasion of Czechoslovakia in 1968 as well as an endorsement of the Czechoslovakian Charter 77. In the meantime, they had been expelled from the party and prevented from publishing and holding academic office.

A book by two other dissidents, the urban sociologists György Konrád and Iván Szelényi, is about to be published in the West under the title *The Road of the Intellectuals to Class Power*. The book was written in 1974, but its publication was blocked. The authors were briefly detained, and Szelényi emigrated to the West. The work argues that in the post-Stalin era a burgeoning technocratic intelligentsia accepted the party elite's offer of alliance and now serves the regime in exchange for power and privilege. The authors suggest that the technocrats may be growing uneasy in this role, that a variety of marginal intellectuals are challenging the theory and practice of socialism, and that some new alliance might emerge which could liberalize the police state and advance the real interests of the working masses.

Normal book publishing in Hungary is subsidized. There is no formal system of prior censorship, and the bounds of the permissible are loosely defined and observed by editors as well as writers, the latter being expected to exercise self-censorship. Private publishing is technically permitted but is severely constrained by the difficulties of financing and distributing.

Illegal, "samizdat" publishing surfaced in the autumn of 1977. One work, *Marx in the Fourth Decade*, edited by András Kovács, is a collection of writings mainly by disillusioned Marxists who question the adequacy of Marxist ideology in relation to the problems of Eastern Europe. Another, *Profile*, edited by János Kenedi, is a collection of works rejected for official publication. The contributions are mainly from non-Marxists and indicate the range of politically sensitive subjects, such as criticism of the Soviet Union and certain social problems. The title of the collection is an allusion to the common editorial rationale that a certain manuscript does not fit the publishing house's "profile." In the introduction, Kenedi excoriates the prevailing control system which induces self-censorship by subtle forms of blackmail. A third samizdat work, dated January 1978, is entitled *One Tenth of One Percent* (an allusion to the proportion of Hungarians willing to take a public stand against the regime's policies). Produced at the request of Polish dissidents, it includes material from the previous two collections as well as some additional works, such as an account of the difficulties encountered by working-class Methodists. Overt intellectual dissent in Hungary has until recently been less evident than in Poland or Czechoslovakia, but these samizdat works indicate that it covers a broad ideological spectrum. The dissidents include members of the old Lukács school as well as younger ones farther removed from Marxism.

The Central Committee's 20 April resolution noted the settled state of church-state relations. In fact, severe restrictions exist on religious education and publication, but after consultations with the Vatican several new bishops were appointed in March, the eighth in a series of appointments since 1964.

In January the Politburo passed a resolution on ethnic minorities urging the fullest application of Marxist-Leninist principles to safeguard their cultural interests. Recent estimates indicate that minorities in Hungary include 200,000—220,000 Germans, 100,000—110,000 Slovaks, 80,000—100,000 Southern Slavs, and 20,000—25,000 Romanians. (The approximately 350,000 Gypsies are regarded as a culturally and linguistically heterodox group and therefore not a single ethnic minority.) The regime has been promoting bilingual schools and other cultural facilities for the minorities, partly to induce similarly liberal treatment of the large Hungarian minorities in the surrounding communist states. National congresses of the four minorities were held in November.

Other Social Issues. The theory of a socialist life-style and the reality of income differentiation and conspicuous consumption are recurring topics of debate in the party and the media. The party, observed Brutyó in an interview, was opposed to "petit bourgeois egalitarianism and a primitive interpretation of socialism." The differentiation of reward according to work is officially sanctioned, but certain types of material gain are undesirable. Thus, gratuities in the catering industry are regarded as normal, but the widespread practice of tipping doctors, lawyers, shop clerks, etc. is frowned upon (*Népszabadság*, 23 July).

A survey of workers' attitudes in a large enterprise found that most expend little energy on their job, preferring to concentrate on moonlighting and after-hours small-plot farming. The respondents exhibited little knowledge of or interest in Marxism. (*Christian Science Monitor*, 8 June.) Despite building programs and incentives for private construction, housing remains the major sociopolitical problem, particularly in Budapest and other urban areas. Rising alcoholism prompted new regulations and restrictions on consumption, and in July the price of spirits was raised by an average of 25 percent. Civil ceremonies for marriage and burial have long been promoted by the regime and are currently propagandized as important symbols of a socialist life-style (*Pártélet*, January). Despite much covert pressure, religious ceremonies remain very popular for aesthetic as well as religious reasons.

Economy. The tenth anniversary of the introduction of the New Economic Mechanism prompted numerous analyses of its achievements and shortcomings. Rezső Nyers, an architect of the reform who was subsequently demoted to the post of director of the Institute of Economic Science, evaluated positively the improvement in living standards and decentralization of authority engendered by the NEM but deplored such enduring inadequacies as excessive investment, low productivity, an unrealistic price system, and misallocation of manpower (*Közgazdász*, 9 March). The veteran Communist and economist István Friss also praised the reform while noting the shortage of competent enterprise managers and the difficulty of replacing incumbents, the unresolved tension between enterprise autonomy and central guidance, the drawbacks of domestic monopolies, and the excessive materialism induced in part by the NEM. It is noteworthy that a critique of the reform by the U.S. economist Béla Balassa was also published in Hungary (*Valoság,* July).

The Central Committee's resolution of 20 April concentrated on the economy and provided a realistic appraisal of the successes and failures of economic policy since the HSWP's Eleventh Congress. It noted many shortcomings and urged energetic remedies, notably a reform of the price system to reduce state subsidies. The resolution was generally regarded as a strong confirmation of the NEM (*Népszabadság,* 23 April). In a major speech in Debrecen, 8 June, Kádár confirmed that producer prices would have to be modified and that this would inevitably affect some consumer prices, but he insisted that the overall standard of living would not suffer (ibid., 9 June). Prime Minister Lázár told the National Assembly on 6 July that a carefully prepared reform of the price system was under way. He acknowledged deficiencies in the government's executive and administrative activities and promised that they would be remedied.

In a report to the Central Committee on 1 December 1977, Németh indicated that over the first two years (1976–77) of the current five-year plan most targets had been marginally exceeded. The economic regulation system was to be modified effective 1 January to make enterprises more efficient and responsive to external market forces. Certain producer prices, including electric power, were to be increased, central subsidies were to be reduced, and bank credits limited. Among the 1978 plan's targets are a 5 percent increase in national income, a 2.8–3.0 percent increase in average real wages, and a 4 percent rise in the consumer price level. Exports, reported Németh, had been increased, but the terms of trade continued to deteriorate. Among the reasons for this imbalance were a weak world wheat market and price increases that were greater for imported raw materials than for Hungarian exports. (Indeed, for 1978 the price of Soviet crude oil was increased by 21.3 percent over the 1977 level.) The 1978 budget provided for revenues of 385.9 billion forints and expenditures of 389.7 billion forints. Various subsidies account for 32.8 percent of expenditures, and international financial obligations for 7.9 percent. The budget indicated major increases in expenditures on cultural projects, public health, and welfare (*Magyar Közlöny,* 27 December 1977).

Foreign trade is a critical component of the economy because it generates over 40 percent of national income. The current deterioration in the terms of trade is therefore regarded as a crucial problem. On the export side, the need is seen to increase not only volume but also profitability; in 1977, some $200 million worth of exports did not receive a profitable price (*Magyar Hirlap,* 26 February). Foreign trade enterprises are being reorganized in order to effect closer links to producers, greater financial autonomy, and better flexibility in adjusting prices to capitalist competition. The Interag Foreign Trade Agency has set up a holding company, Globinvest A.G., in Luxembourg, whose purpose is to secure a controlling share in technologically advanced Western enterprises to the ultimate benefit of Hungarian industries; most of the funds for investment are borrowed in the West. The company has purchased majority interest in a financially troubled Danish television and radio firm. In other measures designed to boost trade and modernize industry, the Hungarian National Bank in late 1977 opened a branch in New York and raised $200 million on the U.S. money market; and in September, Japanese banks lent the equivalent of $205.3 million to Hungary for trade development. The Hungarian Chamber of Commerce meanwhile organized a number of "economic days" in U.S. centers to boost trade and cooperative ventures. One recent example of such ventures is an agreement with the Levi Strauss Company to produce denim clothes in Hungary, the technology and know-how being paid for with part of the output.

In intra-Comecon trade, the Hungarians continue to press for at least partial convertibility of the transferable ruble to facilitate multilateral settlement of accounts, but the Soviet Union favors instead more centralized planning. Joint Comecon raw material extraction projects located in the Soviet Union consume 4 percent of Hungary's total investment budget, the highest proportion among socialist countries, and some experts have suggested that this may not be in the nation's economic interest (Radio Budapest, 23 February). Commentators have pointed out that these low-interest credits, ultimately repayable in raw materials and energy in amounts reduced by price inflation, are more advantageous to the Soviet Union than to the East Europeans (*Külgazdaság*, April). At the thirty-second Comecon session, held in Bucharest 27—29 June, Prime Minister Lázár reflected on problems of product quality and variety and of late delivery in Comecon trade, and he drew a parallel between the massive investment program in raw materials and energy and the needs of agricultural modernization. He observed that Hungary had already invested heavily in agriculture and warned that agricultural trade could be increased "only if conditions are clarified by bilateral talks" (Radio Budapest, 27 and 28 June). The implication was that Hungary wanted a better price for its agricultural products and possibly also joint investment in the sector.

Agricultural production increased in 1977, and indeed the growing affluence of the rural population is reflected in the conspicuous consumption that has prompted cautious criticism by the media. In a report to the Central Committee on 15 March, Németh reiterated the regime's strong support for small-scale farming, most of which is a part-time activity (*Népszabadság*, 18 March). The private sector in agriculture supplies a large proportion of vegetables, meat, and milk, and the government is providing incentives to sustain and expand this production. New regulations on sharecropping are designed to expand agricultural production in areas not suited to large-scale farming. There is a continuing stress on the use of Western machinery and know-how and the export of agricultural products.

There is official concern at the declining rate of growth of tourism, an important source of hard currency. An acute shortage of modern hotel space is one obvious constraint. In a liberalizing measure, mandatory foreign currency exchange for tourists was lifted effective 1 January 1978.

Foreign Affairs. *Main Trends.* The general line of official concordance with Soviet policies and normalization of relations with the West continues to prevail in Hungary's foreign relations. In a report to the National Assembly on 24 March, Foreign Minister Frigyes Puja deplored the deceleration of the process of détente, which he attributed to the miscalculation of reactionary circles. He also bemoaned slow progress on disarmament and railed against the possible acquisition of neutron warheads by NATO. On specific world trouble spots, such as the Horn of Africa, the Middle East, and the Cambodian-Vietnamese conflict, he faithfully followed the Soviet line. Puja expressed satisfaction at Hungary's good relations with its socialist partners and with the West while deploring the latter's discriminatory economic measures, promised to help developing countries consolidate their political and economic independence, and praised the rapprochement with the Hungarian diaspora in the West (*Magyar Hirlap,* 25 March). The Central Committee's 20 April resolution took the same line on détente and its enemies and noted that Hungary's relations were improving with Finland, Austria, West Germany, Italy, and even the United States.

Hungarian-U.S. Relations. The normalization of Hungarian-American relations took several tangible forms in 1978. The crown of St. Stephen and other coronation regalia were returned on 6 January. The ancient crown, a sacred symbol of nationhood for Hungarians, had been in U.S. safekeeping since 1945. The Carter administration evidently judged that the relative domestic liberalism of the Kádár regime warranted this gesture and stressed that the crown was being returned to the "Hungarian people." Secretary of State Cyrus Vance led the American delegation for the ceremonial transfer in the parliament building in Budapest; Kádár was not present. The two parties agreed that the regalia would be put on permanent public display, and the return met with virtually unanimous approval in Hungary as well as some hostility among Hungarian emigrés in the West.

The liberalization of trade relations was held up for years by the congressional stipulation regarding unfettered emigration, but the Carter administration has come to the conclusion that

Hungary had an acceptable record on emigration and the reunification of families, while the Kádár regime has tacitly agreed to maintain its liberal policies in this respect. As a result, agreement was reached in March on mutual trade concessions, and following approval by Congress, most-favored-nation tariffs took effect 7 July. Hungarian-American trade amounted to less than $150 million in 1977, with the balance heavily in favor of the United States. One unnamed Central Committee member was quoted as saying that Hungary was taking advantage of the Carter-Brzezinski policy of treating the East European countries selectively and individually rather than as a bloc (*NYT*, 29 April). U.S. Secretary of Agriculture Bergland visited Budapest 20−23 May to confer with his counterpart Pál Romány on the expansion of economic cooperation. Also in May, János Berecz, head of the Central Committee's Foreign Affairs Department, visited the United States at the invitation of the State Department.

Relations with Romania. The problem of the Hungarian minority in Romania continues to exacerbate relations between the two countries and their parties, and the dispute has recently taken the form of public polemics. In November 1977 Károly Király, a former member of the Romanian party's Politburo, addressed a letter to the leadership protesting the official pursuit of discrimination and cultural assimilation against the two-million-strong Hungarian minority. His complaints were endorsed by several prominent Hungarian-Romanians, and the Ceauşescu regime has responded with some palliative measures as well as with an international propaganda campaign defending its minority policies and denouncing its critics. In the meantime, Hungary's greatest living writer and poet, Gyula Illyés, wrote a series of articles arguing that Hungarians formed the largest national minority in Europe and deploring cultural discrimination without actually naming Romania (*Magyar Nemzet,* 25 December 1977, 1 January). When the Romanian academician Mihnea Gheorghiu accused Illyés of having an anti-Romanian obsession and of being dissatsified with the results of two world wars (i.e., the loss of Transylvania), the vice-president of the Hungarian Academy of Sciences, historian Zsigmond Pál Pach, rose to the defense of Illyés and reminded his Romanian critic that "problems do not cease to exist if we do not talk about them" (Agerpres, 6 May; *Élet és Irodalom,* 8 July). The dispute also has a historiographic dimension, with Romanian scholars asserting the continuity of the Romanian state and its Dacian and Roman antecedents, and Hungarian historians maintaining that the Hungarians settled an unpopulated Transylvania in the tenth century (*Magyar Hirlap,* 25 December 1977, *Contemporaneul,* 10 February).

At the official level, the Hungarians have complained that the Debrecen-Oradea agreements concluded by Kádár and Ceauşescu in 1977 have not led to the authorization by the Romanians of new consular facilities. Ştefan Andrei, a Romanian Communist Party Central Committee secretary, visited Budapest 16−19 February for talks with Kádár and Gyenes, and he was followed by the Romanian education minister, Suzana Gadea. In an interview with the *New York Times* (10 June), Kádár observed that "certain progress" had been made in his 1977 talks with Ceauşescu and argued that the national minorities should serve to link, not to separate, Hungary and Romania. Ceauşescu, for his part, delivered a stern warning on 10 June against outside interference in Romania's nationality affairs.

Foreign Visits. Official foreign visits by Hungarian statesmen include that of President Losonczi to Mexico and Ecuador in November 1977, in the course of which agreements were signed on trade and economic cooperation. Foreign minister Puja made an African tour 10 January−2 February, visiting Ethiopia, Congo, Angola, Mozambique, Tanzania, and Nigeria. The trip was a demonstration of solidarity with the more socialist African states (apart from Nigeria) as well as a stimulus for commercial expansion. Puja endorsed the cause of independence for the peoples of Zimbabwe (Rhodesia) and Namibia (South-West Africa). He subsequently visited Belgium (6−8 February), the Netherlands (11−13 September), and Norway (18−20 September). The visits allowed for routine exchanges on détente as well as economics. In June, a Hungarian military delegation led by General István Oláh, chief of staff and deputy defense minister, visited France in the first such venture to a NATO country.

Visitors to Hungary included the West German Social Democratic leader Willy Brandt, 21–30 March, who had several interviews with Kádár and other HSWP figures and delivered a lecture on détente. The shah of Iran paid an official visit 19–22 May. The Libyan head of state, Colonel Qadhafi, passed through Budapest 23–26 June and was accorded a warm reception. Trade relations with Libya are currently unbalanced in favor of Hungary, but it is expected that with the opening of the Adria pipeline in early 1979 Hungary will begin to import Libyan crude oil.

Austrian Chancellor Bruno Kreisky paid an "informal working visit" to Hungary 22–24 September for discussions on economic relations. Hungary and Austria have agreed to abolish visas for travel between the two countries effective 1 January 1979. The measure will facilitate tourism from Austria, but Hungarians will still be restricted in their mobility by the need to have their passports validated for travel to the West. They are normally eligible for one tourist passport every three years and a visitor passport (without foreign currency entitlement) every two years.

International Party Contacts. In what has become an annual ritual, Kádár met Brezhnev in the Crimea in late July for discussions that apparently focused on economic issues and Comecon's cooperative programs. István Katona, a Central Committee member and chief of the Central Committee's bureau, led a party delegation to the Soviet Union 12–15 July to exchange information on party work with their Soviet counterparts.

A conference on ideological and international issues was attended by Central Committee secretaries of ten ruling communist parties in Budapest 27 February–1 March. The Hungarian delegation was led by Miklós Óvári. The conferees deplored the threat to détente from Western military-industrial complexes and bourgeois politicians, who allegedly had a stake in maintaining tensions and in sustaining the arms race as well as slander campaigns aimed at splitting progressive forces. The conference reaffirmed the unity of the three main revolutionary forces: the world socialist system, the international workers' movement, and the national liberation movement. It expressed solidarity with communist parties in capitalist countries and called for the clarification and synthesis of Marxist-Leninist theory and practical experience.

French Communist Party leader Georges Marchais visited Budapest 24–27 November 1977, less than two months after a similar visit by Enrico Berlinguer, for talks with Kádár, Berecz, and Gyenes on international questions. The discussions were apparently narrower in scope and less cordial than had been the case with the Italian party leader. The communiqué on the talks referred to respect for each other's opinions, normally a euphemism for disagreement, while Marchais in an interview indicated an "essential" identity of views (Magyar Távirati Iroda, 28 November 1977). Party and media commentators have taken to avoiding the term Eurocommunism, which is disparaged as a Western fabrication, and to stressing that common revolutionary goals can be pursued by differing means and conceivably more gradually in the developed capitalist countries. However, they expect the parties in those countries to respect certain general laws of revolutionary progression as well as the example of the East Europeans and to work toward voluntary coordination of action. They credit Kádár's influence with helping to foil Western efforts to split the communist movement.

A Youth Conference on European Disarmament was held in Budapest 20–22 January. The conference was opened by Prime Minister Lázár and addressed by Maróthy. The participants came from mainly leftist organizations, but some delegates challenged the Soviet bloc's selective denunciation of U.S. neutron warheads as well as Soviet-Cuban intervention in Africa, and some Western noncommunist delegations refrained from signing the final statement.

In Kádár's Debrecen speech, 8 June, he deplored Peking's anti-Sovietism and noted that Hungary had no party relations with the Chinese. However, he had "no wish to intensify the disputes" and hoped that diplomatic and commercial relations could be normalized. A Hungarian trade delegation had traveled to China in February and concluded a trade agreement. In late January an economic delegation led by Huszár visited Vietnam and signed an economic cooperation agreement. In February a PPF delegation headed by Secretary General István Sarlós also visited Hanoi and expressed full support for Vietnam's position on the border issue with Cambodia. Huszár's delegation also visited Laos.

In other Soviet bloc contacts, an East German party delegation headed by three Politburo members visited Budapest on 26 February, and the Cuban foreign minister paid an official visit to Hungary in August.

Miklos Óvári represented the HSWP at the international conference on "Construction of Socialism and Communism and World Progress" which took place in Sofia on 12—15 December, sponsored by the Bulgarian CP and the *World Marxist Review.* The conference was attended by the representatives of 73 communist and workers' parties.

Publications. The HSWP's principal daily newspaper is *Népszabadság* (People's freedom), edited by Dezsö Nemes, with a circulation of 750,000. The theoretical monthly *Társadalmi Szemle* (Social review) has a circulation of 40,700. The monthly organizational journal *Pártélet* (Party life) has a circulation of 130,000. In 1978 the Central Committee's Department of Agitation and Propaganda launched a new periodical, *Propagandista.* Other major newspapers are *Magyar Hirlap,* the "government" daily; *Magyar Nemzet,* published under the auspices of the Patriotic People's Front; and *Népszava,* the organ of the trade unions. The official news agency is Magyar Távirati Iroda (Hungarian Telegraphic Agency; MTI).

University of Toronto   Bennett Kovrig

Poland

The history of the communist movement in Poland goes back to the formation in December 1918 of the Communist Workers' Party of Poland; the name changed in 1925 to Communist Party of Poland. The party operated underground until its dissolution in 1938 by the Comintern.

In January 1942 the movement was revived by the Comintern under the name Polish Workers' Party. It seized power after the war and consolidated control through gradual elimination of potential competitors. In December 1948 the Communists forced a merger with the Polish Socialist Party to establish the Polish United Workers' Party (PUWP). Ever since, the PUWP has maintained a dominant position in political and economic life. Two other existing political organizations, the Democratic Party (DP) and the United Peasant Party (UPP), have been restricted to essentially supportive functions. The PUWP's leading role was legally formalized in 1976 through a constitutional amendment.

A crucial feature of this role has been the operational control over elective state organs and public institutions. The main instrument for coordination of electoral activity is the Front of National Unity, a formal coalition of all social and political groups, which has been chaired since February 1976 by PUWP Politburo member Henryk Jabłonski. No organized group capable of competing with the candidates proposed by the Front of National Unity has been allowed to exist. Since the last parliamentary election in March 1976, the communist party has had 262 out of 460 available seats in the Sejm; 112 are held by the United Peasant Party and 39 by the Democratic Party. The remaining 49 seats are filled with nonparty deputies, including thirteen from various Catholic groups (five PAX, five Znak, two Christian Social Association, one Caritas).

The most important governmental functions are in the hands of PUWP leaders. By the end of 1978, Politburo members occupied four out of seventeen positions on the Council of State (Henryk Jabłonski as chairman or titular head of state, Edward Babiuch and Władysław Kruczek as deputy chairmen, and Edward Gierek). They also held the office of the prime minister (Piotr Jaroszewicz) and five out of eleven deputies to the prime minister. Two other Politburo members, Stanisław Kowalczyk and Wojciech Jaruzelski, headed the ministries of Internal Affairs and National Defense, respectively.

The PUWP is the largest political organization in the country, with 2,885,729 members of whom 46.4 percent are workers, about 35 percent are white-collar employees, less than 10 percent are peasants, while the rest includes retirees, artisans and others. About 26 percent of party members are women (*Zycie partii,* April, p. 10 and December, p. 19). The UPP has about 420,000 and the DP approximately 95,000 members. The population of Poland is 35 million.

Leadership and Organization. There was stability in the PUWP leadership throughout the year. Edward Gierek continued as leader of the party, and the composition of both Politburo and Secretariat of the Central Committee remained the same as in 1977 (for the list of incumbents, see *YICA, 1978,* p. 50).

PUWP organization consists of 72,000 civilian and about 3,500 military primary units, 2,300 communal and town committees, and 49 provincial committees. The distribution of power is based on the principle of democratic centralism: each organizational unit elects its executive organs, which conduct party work in their respective spheres of competence and are accountable to their membership, while decisions taken by higher organs are binding on lower ones.

According to party rules, the highest authority within the organization is the congress, which is convened at least once every five years (the last one met during 8–12 December 1975). It elects the Central Committee and Central Control Commission. The Central Committee, presently composed of 141 full and 110 deputy members, directs and controls all party activities between congresses. To effectively perform this task, it elects from among its members the Politburo and the Secretariat. The Politburo acts as the main policy-making body between Central Committee plenary meetings (plenums). The Secretariat is the executive organ of the Central Committee and is charged with supervision over party work. The Party Control Commission watches over internal discipline and also serves as an appellate office from decisions made by lower units. Corresponding structures are maintained at lower organizational levels.

Auxiliary and Mass Organizations. The PUWP's relation with society revolves around the concert of a centrally directed coordination of all organized political and social activities in order to achieve a planned program of socioeconomic development. Foremost among the mass public organizations are the 23 trade unions, with a total membership of more than 12.5 million. Their activities are coordinated by the Central Council of Trade Unions, which, under the leadership of Politburo member Wladyslaw Kruczek, serves as a policy organ for the entire trade union movement. The legally defined scope of its work ranges from supervision over work safety standards to adminis- tration of social programs, such as health services and recreational facilities. The Central Council has an advisory role in formulation of government economic plans and policies on wages for employees. Its most important task, however, is to secure cooperation between workers and manage- ment to achieve economic targets. Unions attempt to prevent production slowdowns or work stoppages and act as arbitrators in disciplinary conflicts between workers and management. Official duties of unions and the 5,814 local Conferences of Workers' Self-management are restricted to cooperation with appropriate governmental bodies in preparing and implementing labor legislation (*Labor Code,* 1975, art. 19).

The party also maintains close links with the three youth organizations: Union of Polish Socialist Youth (ca. 2,000,000 members); Socialist Union of Polish Students (300,000); and Union of Polish Scouts (3,000,000). All three are united in the Federation of Socialist Unions of Polish Youth, chaired since April 1977 by Krzysztof Trebaczkiewicz, a PUWP Central Committee member.

Among other mass organizations are the Union of Fighters for Freedom and Democracy, a veteran's group (650,000); the League of Women, active in propagating a proper model of socialist family life (445,000); the Volunteer Citizens' Militia Reserve, a parapolice force frequently used in quelling social dissent and disturbances (325,000); and the League for Defense of the Country, a civil defense organization (1,850,000). All are headed by members of the party's Central Committee.

Party Internal Affairs. The most important party event in 1978 was the Second National Party Conference on 9–10 January. It was convened to take stock of the social and economic situation in the country, to sound out a wide circle of party activists on the issues of the day (2,152 delegates were present), and to map out national tasks for the next three years. The main emphasis was put on continuing economic development. In the opening address, Gierek called for the establishment of several special committees and other less specified government organs to develop "appropriate solu- tions" to the problems of old-age assistance and improvement of working conditions, as well as de- fining "comprehensive programs of modernization" and preparing a "national program for the devel- opment of fuels and the power economy" (*Trybuna ludu,* 10 January). No deadlines, however, were set for the completion of their work.

The conference also accepted reports of the five previously established (1976) party/government teams, which had been charged with suggesting solutions to a continuing crisis in agricultural production, market supply, and food shortages. None of these reports was made public, although Gierek acknowledged that their "findings showed a growing disproportion between food prices and the prices of industrial products, something that makes it difficult to achieve progressive transformation in the structure of consumption" (ibid.). Gradual food price increases were proposed as a means of improving the situation.

The PUWP Central Committee met four times during the year, with economic issues clearly dominating agendas. The tenth plenum, held during a break in the national conference, ratified the work of the conference and approved its resolutions. The eleventh plenum in March discussed agricultural problems and means of coping with persistent shortages of food, especially meat. In the keynote speech, subsequently adopted as a guideline for party policy, Gierek admitted that "the growing demand for meat could not be met" but also asserted that "we have good grounds to think that our agricultural policy serves the common interests of the peasants, the workers, and the whole society well" (ibid., 18–19 March). Consequently, no new decisions were taken, but an appeal was made to streamline the available means of agricultural production.

The twelfth plenum in June dealt with the problems of work organization, management of energy resources, and expansion of production. In the main address, Gierek called for closer links between scientists and production units. He also proposed a major project to regulate the flow of the Vistula river and its tributaries in order to develop Poland's water resources comprehensively. (Ibid., 16 June.) Preparatory works on mapping out future investments for the long-term project, which promises to facilitate transportation as well as expand agricultural and energy production, began soon after the plenum.

The thirteenth plenum in December debated ways to revitalize the conomy. In the main address, Gierek warned about the necessity of imposing far-reaching austerity measures in 1979. They would include freezing the growth of real wages to only 1.5—2.0 percent (the plan for 1978 envisaged an increase in the range of 1.8—3.0 percent), putting a ceiling on industrial investments, and curtailment of administrative expenses. He also announced that the main emphasis in economic activity in 1979 would be on development of food production, housing, and consumer goods. Major efforts would be made to increase exports, so as to improve the adverse balance of payments that Poland had with the Western countries during the last several years. Gierek also defended the proposal presented at the Warsaw Pact summit in late November that all East European communist countries increase their military expenditures in 1979. He saw the justification behind this proposal in what he called the "long-term program of intensification of armaments" among NATO states (Warsaw radio, 13 December).

In January signs of internal factional ferment came to public attention. In an open letter to Gierek, a group of older party notables, including former First Secretary Edward Ochab as well as past secretaries of the Central Committee Jerzy Albrecht, Władysław Matwin and Jerzy Morawksi, called for a public discussion on current political and economic difficulties. Charging that "the mood among broad circles of the population shows that the citizens' trust in the party and government has been shaken," they accused the leadership of conducting policies which "caused disruption and disorganization of the economic life of the country." They also demanded large-scale political reforms, pointing out that "preponderantly, the source of our main difficulties and failures is political, including undemocratic forms of government and, above all, a lack of democratic discussion to determine the objectives and choose the methods for solving sociopolitical problems" (*Der Spiegel,* 16 January). There was no direct official reaction to these accusations. Instead, Gierek rebuked them indirectly when he appealed in a speech to the Second National Party Conference for political "unity of the party around its Central Committee" in order "to consolidate what we have already achieved, to overcome difficulties, and to ensure the fulfillment of the basic socioeconomic tasks" (*Trybuna ludu,* 10 January).

But in November, Mieczysław Moczar, a former leader of a nationalistic faction of the party during the 1960s who was demoted from top party functions in 1971 and has since held the relatively obscure position of chairman of the Supreme Control Chamber, made a new bid to reenter the political arena. Writing in a national magazine in his capacity as head of an agency charged with supervision of government activities, Moczar complained about the continuing practices of preparing fraudulent statistical reports on the economy by low-level officials, attacked high economic and political functionaries for tolerating such abuses, and called for a "decisive purge from directing posts of those people who are dishonest, incapable, and negligent of their responsibilities and who therefore have no moral right to exercise such functions" (*Zycie literackie,* 19 November).

The health problems of Edward Gierek, who spent more than two weeks during November in Czechoslovak spas recuperating from acute attacks of lumbago, only added a new element to growing factional tensions.

Domestic Affairs. The main efforts of the party in its domestic activity concentrated on finding ways to overcome mounting economic difficulties and to revitalize the country. It is clear that an earlier attempt to improve the situation through a partial shift in emphasis from heavy industry to food production and services, described officially as a "new economic maneuver" (see *YICA, 1978,* pp. 52−53), has failed to bring the expected results. Few of the centrally defined directives were implemented, and industrial investment plans remained overfulfilled to the detriment of agriculture and the consumer sector, with the result that the gap between production and market demands increased. At the same time, the net monetary income of the population went up much faster than envisaged by the 1978 plan—the nominal wage in the socialized sector during the first six months of 1978 was 5.3 percent higher than in the same period of 1977 (*Contemporary Poland,* September, p. 25)—merely adding fuel to inflationary pressures. The resulting difficulties were further compounded by the continuing fear that any economically necessary increase in prices could be politically disastrous (the last attempt to increase prices led in 1976 to massive protests and public disturbances). The official prices for food, transportation, and housing were maintained artificially at 1975 levels through a massive program of government subsidies. They amounted in 1978 to 270 billion zlotys, which was about 61 percent more than in 1975 (*Trybuna ludu,* 18 April). To neutralize the economic impact of this situation and also to introduce an indirect form of price increase, the government expanded a network of special "commercial shops," which sell food, primarily meat products, at premium prices. By August there were 300 such shops in all large cities—a threefold increase over 1977— and another 150 were planned (ibid., 4 August).

Agriculture continued as the most troublesome area of the economy. Although the 1978 harvest appeared to have brought better results than the 1977 harvest, the output was not large enough to meet domestic demands for food; further imports of grain and other agricultural products are inevitable. Particular difficulties concerned the persistent shortage in meat supply on the market. While there was some improvement in livestock (cattle increased by about 100,000 head, pigs by 1.7 million, and sheep by 300,000), numbers were still below the plan. By October there were only 13.1 million cattle, 21.7 million pigs, and 4.2 million sheep. These numbers were close to the situation in 1974. In the meantime, however, the population grew by about 1.5 million people, and the market deteriorated considerably (*Zycie gospodarcze,* 29 October).

Much of the problem results from the structural character of the agricultural sector. About 76.6 percent of arable land belongs to small farms, of which 29.3 percent are less than four acres in size; only 13.5 percent exceed 20 acres (*Wies wspolczesna,* September, p. 25). These farms have little capability to increase production, and many farmers cannot even afford to raise cattle or pigs for market supply. Government efforts to induce some of the smaller farmers to sell land to the state or other, more prosperous farmers, initiated in 1977 (see *YICA, 1978,* p. 52), have largely failed. Of some 850,000 hectares currently available for sale, only 75,000 were sold in 1977, and the plan for 1978 envisaged a mere 50,000 to be sold. In part, the continuing reluctance of individual farmers to invest in land appears to have been determined by a lack of confidence in state policy toward private agriculture in general. But it also resulted from the unwillingness of local government authorities to facilitate transactions among private peasants and the persistent support given to cooperative farming. There were some 2,000 agricultural cooperatives in 1978, and their number as well as the area they cultivated (630,000 hectares) doubled since 1974 (*Trybuna ludu,* 18−19 November).

In the area of industrial development, the rate of investment during the first six months of 1978 declined by 1.8 percent and several projects were not completed. The joint session of the party Politburo and the government presidium on 19 October criticized "insufficient discipline in the implementation of [the investment] program as a result of the continuing underconcentration of efforts on projects nearing completion" (Warsaw radio, 19 October). At the same time, a list of priority projects was revised with several outlays canceled or postponed.

At the end of November, planning officials released partial information on the forthcoming 1979 plan. Its draft form called for considerable tightening of investments and economic activity. The increase in national income was set at 2.8 percent, compared with a planned growth of 5.4 percent in 1978. Industrial investments were to decline by 14 percent, while consumer goods production was to grow by 8 percent. The program of government subsidies of food prices was to be maintained, but the level of foreign trade was to be curtailed with considerable cuts in imports envisaged and emphasis put on export expansion. (*Trybuna ludu,* 1 December.)

Throughout the year, major efforts were undertaken to reduce adverse balance of payments in trade exchanges with Western countries. After the first nine months, the trade deficit was cut by some 42 percent in comparison with the same period of 1977. Imports from the West declined by 6 percent, while exports to noncommunist countries increased by 9 percent. Trade turnover with communist countries, conducted on a barter basis, showed a small surplus (Reuters, 21 November). Notwithstanding these efforts at improving its trade position, Poland's indebtedness to noncommunist, primarily Western countries, further increased. It was estimated to have reached about $15 billion by the end of the year (*NYT,* 28 November), with the interest rate approaching 30–40 percent per annum. To finance that debt, the government was seeking a new loan of at least $500 million from Western banks while promising to give detailed information on the state of economy and financial prospects (*Financial Times,* London, 1 December).

On 1 October a comprehensive program of energy savings, including power cuts in some 3,000 large industrial plants and restrictions on power use in the entire socialized sector of the economy, was introduced. It indicated the government's determination to avoid the repetition of severe power breakdowns, which took place in early months of 1978 and cost about 27.5 billion zloty in production waste. It also was an attempt to form some regulatory mechanism in the area of energy use and production.

Among more important political developments, there was a national election to 2,353 people's councils on 5 February. There were 157,458 candidates on a single list prepared by the Front of National Unity competing for 100,876 seats. Of the 24,267,950 votes cast (98.77 percent of all eligible voters), 99.69 percent went for the FNU list.

There were also numerous personnel changes in the government structure, primarily at the level of vice-ministers. Among senior ministers replaced, three—agriculture, transportation, and light industry—lost their jobs in December 1977. One major change, minister of culture, took place during spring and summer 1978. In January Politburo member Jozef Tejchma resigned as minister of culture and was replaced by acting minister Janusz Wilhelmi, who died in a plane crash in early March. He was followed by Jan Mietkowski, who was named a titular head of the ministry on 24 March but then suddenly died on 4 July. His successor since 20 July was Zygmunt Najdowski, a former party official in both regional and central party administration.

During 6–11 November Poland celebrated the sixtieth anniversary of independence. On 15 December there was also a massive celebration of the sixtieth anniversary of the organized communist movement as well as the thirtieth anniversary of the formation of the PUWP.

Political dissent. The year 1978 marked a further expansion in the active opposition to party and government policies. Since the formation of the Committee for Workers' Defense (KOR; the name changed subsequently to Committee for Social Self-defense) in September 1976, the dissident movement has grown in number of participating groups and has enlarged the scope of its work. Indeed, it could be said that during 1978 social dissent established itself as a permanent fixture of Poland's political scene (for details on earlier dissident activity, see *YICA, 1978,* pp. 53–55).

A new feature of dissident activity, which received considerable public support and recognition, was the formation in January of the Educational Courses Society. This organization, modeled on the underground educational societies active in partitioned Poland before the First World War, was formed by several separate groups of dissidents and numerous prominent intellectuals, but it officially registered its activity with proper government authorities. Its program of privately offered courses on humanities, Polish history, sociology, and philosophy was motivated "by the desire to satisfy the aspirations, which are growing stronger among the students and young intellectuals in Poland, to broaden, enrich, and supplement their knowledge" (Agence France Presse, 13 February). Despite periodic arrests of both lecturers and students, official harassment, and frequent attempts at intimidation, activity of the society or "Flying University," as its program of lectures has been called, continued unabated throughout the year.

Even more significant was the creation of several self-defense committees in the villages of the central, eastern, and southern provinces of the country to protest official agricultural policies. Until 1978 dissident activities were largely limited to intellectuals and students, but since summer they have expanded to other social groups. The unifying element of peasant dissent was dissatisfaction with basic provisions of a pension law of 1977 (for details, see *YICA, 1978,* p. 52) and the way it was imposed upon the farmers. Since the law links the size of a farmer's pension to the level of production delivered to the state and offers much lower benefits than those granted to other groups of the population, the peasants considered it discriminatory. Several petitions and memorandums opposing the law were sent to the authorities since the summer. No official response was registered.

But peasant dissatisfaction with government policy was gradually growing. During the first five months of the year, about 250,000 farmers failed to contribute to the pension fund. By October this number grew to about 480,000, or about 15 percent of the total number of peasants (*London Times,* 5 October). Several stoppages of the delivery of milk and other agricultural products were also reported.

In February an attempt was made to organize a "free trade union" among mining workers in Silesia. Similar action was subsequently taken in the coastal city of Gdansk. In both instances, however, the reaction of the government was swift and determined. The main organizers were promptly arrested (Agence France Presse, 28 February) and subsequently became victims of prolonged harassment by authorities. The continuing opposition of the party leaders to even a semblance of either occupational or political autonomy of workers' organizations became evident during a national conference of Workers' Self-management Councils, held on 3 July. In the keynote speech, Gierek affirmed that "the prime interest of workers' self-government should revolve around work effectiveness and productivity" while "the principle of one-man management remains unchanged" (*Trybuna ludu,* 4 July.)

The most significant political development in the area of dissident activity was the explicit rapprochement between Polish and Czechoslovak human rights activists. Representatives of Poland's Committee for Social Self-defense (KOR) and Czechoslovakia's Charter 77 met in August at the border of the two countries and decided to establish joint working groups as well as to coordinate their actions (*London Times,* 18 August). The second meeting was held in late September. But an attempt at another meeting on 23 September was broken up by police of both countries. Would-be Polish participants were temporarily detained, but a Czechoslovak delegate, Jaroslaw Šabata, was put in prison. Subsequent protest letters from Polish dissidents to the Polish and Czechoslovak parliaments against official harassment did not bring any response. In mid-October KOR issued an appeal addressed to "men of good will all over the world" to help in obtaining Šabata's release (Agence France Presse, 14 October).

On 11 November, the date of the sixtieth anniversary of Poland's independence in modern times, several dissident groups issued commemorative papers and appeals calling for greater national independence and respect for human and civil rights. On the same day, a spontaneous mass public rally took place at the Tomb of the Unknown Soldier in Warsaw. Similar manifestations took place in several other cities throughout the country. There was no official attempt to disperse those demonstrations.

In 1978 more than twenty separate, continuing underground periodicals were being published by different dissident groups. Numerous appeals for greater public involvement in political affairs were issued and several detailed reports on various aspects of Poland's social and economic life were released.

Relations with the Catholic Church. Throughout the year, the party's attitude toward the church remained ambiguous— cooperative in those aspects of the church's activity which could be considered as being either of marginal political importance or helpful for government operations and clearly adversary in refusing to grant any tangible concessions to Catholic demands.

Following a relative rapprochement between the church and the party at the end of 1977 when Gierek had met with Cardinal Wyszyński and subsequently was received by Pope Paul VI (see *YICA, 1978*, pp. 55—56), there were expectations that a more permanent normalization of church-state relations would be forthcoming. To some extent, certain steps were taken in that direction. Numerous permits for construction of new churches were granted in 1978. Catholic officials were invited by the government to take greater part in some national social programs, e.g., the fight against alcoholism. When Cardinals Wyszyński and Wojtyla visited West Germany during 20—25 September, the first official foreign visit of the head of the Polish episcopate since the Second World War, their trip was supported by the government and subsequently was positively evaluated in the party press. Even official negotiations between the church and the government resumed, after a pause of more than eleven years (an earlier series of meetings was broken off in 1966).

But the party remained firm in ignoring those demands of the church which could stabilize and institutionalize its position in society. Those demands, repeatedly presented to the government and publicized in periodic public statements and pastoral letters, included calls for a lifting of the censorship of and more newsprint for the Catholic press, for periodic television and radio broadcasts of religious services, for the right to form autonomous Catholic associations, and, above all, for full recognition by the state of the church's legal status as a public institution.

In voicing these demands, church leaders pointed to the traditional role of religion as a continuing basis for national spiritual and cultural values. But they also rationalized them in practical terms, i.e., the need for some institutional guarantee for maintenance of political and social equality between Catholics and nonbelievers within the framework of a militantly atheist state. This concern that Catholics must not be deprived of their essential civil rights was fully manifested in a sermon of Cardinal Wojtyla of Cracow, who pointed out during Corpus Christi celebrations in June that "being such a vast community, a community almost as great as the nation itself, we cannot be outside the law. Definition of the legal status of the church is at the same time definition of our place, of our rights, of everything which originates in the concept of the freedom of religion, which is recognized in the whole world and declared in international documents" (Reuters, 1 June).

The most important development, which is likely to affect church-state relations profoundly, was the election on 16 October of Cracow's former Cardinal Karol Wojtyla to the throne of Saint Peter. The new pope took the name of John Paul II. His inauguration was broadcast live by Polish radio and television, the first religious broadcast in Poland since 1945.

The immediate effect on Poland of the papal election was a massive outburst of national pride and satisfaction. But its more enduring consequences were the increase in influence and prestige of the church in Poland and the relative weakening of the party's political control over society. In Cardinal Wyszyński's first sermon after returning from Rome, he pointed out that as a result of John Paul II's election, "all critics [of the church] fell silent" (UPI, 7 November). He also decried the continuing government restrictions on church activity. Cardinal Wyszyński attacked particularly the state censorship of Catholic publications, but he also reminded that "we have no press, the church has no right to form Catholic associations and does not have complete freedom for social work, even that necessary for the moral life of the nation." He also announced that John Paul II would probably visit Poland in May 1979.

The complaints about state censorship were subsequently repeated in several public pronouncements by both Cardinal Wyszyński and other bishops. On 11 November the episcopate issued a pastoral letter, commemorating the anniversary of Poland's independence, in which it demanded that "conditions of social life must be created in which the people can fully feel that they are masters of their own land, which was given to us centuries ago by the father of all peoples" (*Tygodnik powszechny*, 12 November). On 30 November another communiqué from the episcopate confirmed John Paul II's intention to come to Poland in May 1979. At the same time, the bishops renewed their requests for "the increase in circulation of Catholic papers" and demanded "curbs [on] censor interference" (UPI, 30 November).

There was no direct response from the government. Its official statements omitted the problem of church grievances, and on the subject of the forthcoming papal visit, it was said that "since no official information from the Vatican" had been received, "the details of the visit and its itinerary were still to be determined" (*NYT*, 19 November). There is no doubt, however, that in the present situation, when the position of the church is perceived by both the public and the government as much stronger than ever before, some concessions by the state will be inevitable. What remains to be seen is the scope and the timing. As for the role of the new pope in shaping the future development of church-state relations in Poland, his continuing interest in Polish affairs was confirmed through a letter from John Paul II to Poland's head of state, Henryk Jabłonski, in which he affirmed his "conviction that the work of the church, in consonance with generally approved principles of freedom of religion, creed, and conscience, will continue to develop in our country" (Radio Warsaw, 23 November). However, the authorities censored the pope's Christmas message to his home diocese of Cracow, cutting out all references to Poland's patron, St. Stanislaus. A separate papal message to the entire nation was printed in full by the Cracow Catholic weekly (*NYT*, 22 December). On 30 December, Pope John Paul II selected his close friend and protégé, the 51-year-old Msgr. Franciszek Macharski, as his successor as Archbishop of Cracow (ibid., 1 January 1979).

Party International Affairs. During the year PUWP's representatives took part in several multilateral communist meetings. In February Jerzy Lukaszewicz and Ryszard Frelek participated, along with secretaries of nine other parties, in a conference on ideological problems in the field of international relations held in Budapest. The conference condemned the neutron bomb, developed by the United States, as a major impediment to the development of peaceful cooperation between nations. In September Warsaw hosted an international meeting of ten ruling communist parties on "development of democracy and implementation of human rights under the socialist system." In the keynote speech, Central Committee Secretary Jerzy Lukaszewicz stressed that the problems discussed at the meeting "are the centerpiece of the ideological confrontation between socialism and the forces of progress . . . and capitalism and the forces of social reaction." He also pointed out that "the socialist concept of democracy and human rights and the practical implementation of democracy are one of the many proofs that socialism is superior to capitalism and that our solutions, aimed at the good and happiness of the entire society and of each individual, are superior" (*Trybuna ludu*, 28 September).

In mid-October there was another international communist gathering in Warsaw, this time devoted to a discussion of the mass media and their role in educational work and in the ideological struggle. Its purpose was to coordinate propaganda work in all communist-ruled countries of Eastern Europe (Warsaw radio, 16 October). On 24–26 October PUWP representatives attended a conference on ideology and international relations in Prague. At the same time, other high party delegates went to Budapest to take part in a meeting on party organizational matters. In a communiqué issued at its conclusion, the participants proclaimed that inasmuch as "depending on the specific historic conditions and national peculiarities, one or more parties may operate in the specific socialist states . . . the leading power of the society and the core of its political system is always the Marxist-Leninist party. Essentially, this fact guarantees . . . its solidity and successful operation" (Magyar Távirati Iroda, in English, 25 October).

Ryszard Frelek, a member of the Secretariat of the PUWP's Central Committee, represented the Polish party at the international theoretical conference on "Construction of Socialism and Communism and World Progress," which took place in Sofia on 12–15 December, sponsored by the Bulgarian CP and the *World Marxist Review*. The conference was attended by 73 communist and workers' parties.

In the area of bilateral relations with other communist parties, PUWP received several high-ranking representatives of Western European communist organizations. Among them were Alvaro Cunhal, secretary general of the Portuguese Communist Party (in June), and a delegation from the Communist Party of Spain (in November).

The PUWP's relations with Western European parties were not free of occasional difficulties, however. In November a foreign affairs expert of the French Communist Party published a strong critical analysis of PUWP domestic policies. He accused the Polish leadership of a "lack of sensibility to the hopes of the population" and affirmed that "reestablishing permanent contact with the requirements and the preoccupations of the population is now of vital necessity for the authorities, especially for the success of the economic policy." The analysis also emphasized that the existence of a "militant Catholic church, which enjoys uncontestable prestige among the masses" could facilitate the opening of a "true debate" on internal political, social, and economic difficulties. (*Cahiers du communisme,* November.) This French criticism was reminiscent of a similar assessment of the situation in Poland presented by Italian Communists in December 1977 (*L'Unità,* 25 December 1977).

Foreign Affairs. In the area of Poland's foreign relations, the most important events were extensive contacts with Soviet party and state officials. Several Politburo members traveled to Moscow—Premier Jaroszewicz to coordinate economic policy in January and in November; Jagielski for economic consultations; Jaruzelski to streamline military coordination (both in June); and Lukaszewicz for ideological discussions in October. Gierek himself visited the USSR three times. On 17–19 April he went for detailed political and economic discussions with the highest Soviet leaders. The results of this meeting were later described as having had "immense significance for the deepening of internationalist ties between the Soviet and Polish parties, for the consolidation of friendship between both fraternal parties, and for the development of mutually advantageous economic cooperation" (Warsaw radio, 20 April). In July Gierek spent a short working holiday in the Crimea, visiting with Leonid Brezhnev, and in November he led the PUWP delegation to the summit meeting of the Warsaw Pact organization. At this meeting, PUWP representatives took a position of a full and unquestioned support for the Soviet political line.

Further expansion took place in economic cooperation between the USSR and Poland. Trade turnover between the two countries reached 6.7 billion rubles in 1978, a 19 percent increase over 1977 and more than in the entire five-year period of 1961–65. Just as it had done in several previous years, Poland registered a negative trade balance with the Soviet Union. Most of Poland's exports to the USSR were in seagoing vessels, shipbuilding equipment, chemical products, textiles, and clothing. Its imports concentrated on oil and petroleum products (70 percent of all of Poland's imports in this area), natural gas (100 percent), cotton (about 75 percent), iron ore, and other raw materials (Warsaw radio, 8 November). Because of its involvement in the building of the Orenburg gas pipeline, Poland was offered the right to participate in the construction of an oil pipeline which will be run from Surgut in western Siberia to Belorussia (Warsaw radio, 23 October). In return, some as yet unspecified shipments of oil will be guaranteed for Poland.

A long-term outline of future relations between Poland and the Soviet Union appeared in a special article by Politburo member Jagielski (*Nowe drogi,* November), where he pointed out that "the strengthening of our alliance is a guideline ensuing from the Marxist-Leninist policy pursued by the Soviet Union, the main line of this policy consistently aims to strengthen the links between Poland and the Soviet Union in their common striving for freedom and democracy, socialism and peace."

Among the highest level bilateral contacts with other East European communist states, the most important was Gierek's visit to Yugoslavia in June. Important visitors to Poland were János Kádár (June) and Bulgarian Premier Stanko Todorov (September). Gierek's planned visit to Bulgaria, which was to have taken place in October, was abruptly canceled because of the Polish leader's illness.

In its relations with Western countries, Poland continued strong efforts to expand economic cooperation and contacts. The Federal Republic of Germany (FRG) remained a primary area for Polish diplomatic activity and its most important trading partner. Throughout the year numerous official exchanges were held between the two countries. They included a second session of "Poland-FRG Forum," a semiofficial meeting of leading political, economic, and cultural personalities from both countries (October). Among the major subjects discussed were problems of economic cooperation (particularly ways to increase the level of Poland's exports to Germany), cultural coordination of history textbooks for schools, and long-term normalization of political relations. On 2−4 November FRG Foreign Minister and Vice-chancellor Hans-Dietrich Genscher came to Warsaw for a formal visit. Although no new departures were undertaken, the relations between Poland and the FRG were optimistically assessed by the Poles as indicating a developing "new spirit" of cooperation and mutual understanding (*Trybuna ludu,* 4−5 November).

Polish-American relations also expanded during the year. Following a visit by President Carter in December 1977, several U.S. officials came to Poland in 1978. They included Agriculture Secretary Robert Bergland in May and Health, Education, and Welfare Secretary Joseph A. Califano in November. While Bergland's trip was primarily exploratory, Califano signed an agreement on further cooperation between Poland and the U.S.A. in the area of health care. He also met with several important Polish officials and paid an informal visit to Cardinal Wyszyński.

In November vice-premier Jagielski went to Washington to attend the eighth session of the joint American-Polish Trade Commission. The trade turnover between the two countries after the first ten months of 1978 totaled $914 million with Polish imports exceeding exports by about $258 million. Most of the imports were grains and general agricultural products. During the financial year ending in September, Poland used $400 million worth of American credits, and it was offered another $200 million in additional credits for the next fiscal year. During the talks in Washington, Jagielski sought to obtain American assistance in eliminating persistent Polish deficits and to establish a long-term pattern of economic cooperation between the two countries. His visit culminated in signing a five-year agreement to facilitate expansion of trade between small and medium-sized U.S. and Polish enterprises.

Another important development in the area of Polish-American trade relations was a formal agreement in August between Poland and the Occidental Petroleum Company on exchange of minerals and chemicals, worth an estimated $1 billion.

Among other Western contacts, particularly noteworthy was the visit by French President Valery Giscard d'Estaing in September. During his two-day informal trip to Warsaw, he had extensive conversations with top Polish leaders, particularly on economic relations and trade. In November Premier Jaroszewicz went on a five-day trip to Japan to discuss economic and cultural cooperation.

It ended with the signing of several agreements aimed at facilitating economic exchanges between the two countries. At the same time, an announcement was made that a consortium of Japanese banks opened a $450 million credit line for Poland to finance Polish purchases of foundry and chemical equipment and textile products (*Financial Times*, 14 November).

Poland was also active in developing relations with numerous countries of Asia and Africa. During November and December, Polish Foreign Minister Emil Wojtaszek visited several states of Southeast Asia as well as Australia. Polish representatives also visited several African states. The most important was a trip by Poland's head of state, Henryk Jabłonski, to Angola in December. The purpose of his trip was not only to expand economic relations with Angola but also to provide political aid to Namibia's SWAPO revolutionary movement (Radio Warsaw, 6 December).

Publications. The official organ of the PUWP is the daily *Trybuna ludu;* the party also has daily newspapers in all 49 provinces. Its monthly theoretical journal is *Nowe drogi.* Another monthly, *Zycie partii* and the biweekly *Zagadnienia i materialy* are for party activists. Another biweekly, *Chlopska droga,* is for rural readers; the monthly *Ideologia i polityka* is for the general public. The most important weekly, *Polityka,* is closely linked to the party without, however, any official political identification.

Radio Free Europe   Jan B. de Weydenthal
Munich, Germany

Romania

The Communist Party of Romania (Partidul Comunist Român; CPR) was founded on 8 May 1921. Throughout most of the interwar period the CPR was outlawed. Factionalized and controlled by the Soviet-dominated Communist International, the party had little popular support. The Soviet occupation of Romania in 1944 ensured the emergence of a people's republic headed by the party, which was renamed the Romanian Workers' Party (Partidul Muncitoresc Romîn) in 1948. Under the leadership of Gheorghe Gheorghiu-Dej, the party gradually initiated in the 1960s a more nationalistic internal course and a more autonomous foreign policy. This orientation has been continued by Nicolae Ceauşescu, who succeeded Dej upon the latter's death in 1965. In that same year the Ninth Congress of the CPR proclaimed Romania a Socialist Republic, and the party reverted to its original name. Since 1948 the CPR has been the only party in Romania.

As of 31 December 1977 party membership was 2,747,110 (up from 2,655,000 as of 31 December 1976), of which 51 percent were workers, 19 percent were peasants, 22 percent were intellectuals and white-collar personnel, and 8 percent were in other categories. At the CPR's 22–23 March plenum, much stress was placed on the need to recruit more workers, women, and youth into the party (*Scînteia*, 24 and 30–31 March). The CPR's ethnic composition approximated that of the country as a whole—88.1 percent Romanian, 7.9 percent Hungarian, 1.6 percent German, and 2.4 percent other nationalities. Total population as of 5 January 1977 was 21,559,416 (ibid., 4 January 1977).

Organization and Leadership. The CPR is organized into basic units—at local working places—and into organizations at the communal, town, municipal, county, and national levels. There are 50,037 basic party units. Every five years the 39 county organizations and the Bucharest party organization elect deputies to a national party congress, which, according to party statutes, is the supreme authority of the CPR. In practice, congresses (the most recent was in 1974) have merely ratified personnel and policy decisions made by other party bodies: the Central Committee, the Secretariat, the Political Executive Committee, and the Permanent Bureau. Supplementing the work of these ongoing bodies is the national conference of the CPR, which meets two or three years after a party congress to review the progress made in implementing party decisions and to set policy guidelines for the next several years. The most recent conference was held 7—9 December 1977. Increasingly all these party organizations have been dominated by the CPR secretary general, Nicolae Ceauşescu.

Unlike most other communist parties, the CPR does not have a politburo. Decision-making is centered in two bodies: the Political Executive Committee and the Permanent Bureau. The Secretariat also exercises considerable influence on party policies and personnel. Ceauşescu's sweeping shake-up of the party and state leadership in March led to some 23 major personnel changes. The Political Executive Committee was expanded from 23 to 26 full members with the addition of Iosif Banc, Virgil Cazacu, and Constantin Dăscălescu. The Permanent Bureau was increased from nine to eleven members with the addition of Iosif Banc and Paul Niculescu. The Secretariat, on the other hand, was reduced from eleven to nine members with the removal and transfer of Ştefan Andrei, Cornel Burtică, and Ilie Verdeţ to key government positions, the removal of Aurel Duma and Ion Stanescu, and the addition of only three new secretaries: Virgil Cazacu, Vasile Musat, and Vasile Marin, all relatively unknown party functionaries (*Scînteia*, 8 and 24 March).

While the March shake-ups affected nearly all areas of the party-state apparat, the economic leadership was almost totally revamped, supposedly to provide new leadership for Ceauşescu's economic reform program. Ceauşescu fired several ministers, moved some of his key advisers to key governmental economic posts, and charged them with implementing the reforms. Thus, Ilie Verdeţ became chairman of the State Planning Commission and, along with Gheorghe Oprea, was assigned to the reestablished position of first deputy prime minister; Cornel Burtică was appointed minister of foreign trade; and Paul Niculescu made a comeback as minister of finance. Verdeţ and Burtică returned to positions they had held in the early 1970s.

Another area significantly affected was that of security affairs. Ceauşescu removed one of his key security advisers, Ion Stanescu, from the Secretariat, reassigned Deputy Minister of the Interior Nicolae Doicaru to be minister of tourism, and appointed several party people to major positions in the Ministry of the Interior. All of this indicated that Ceauşescu was highly displeased with the work being done in domestic surveillance and foreign intelligence. The situation was exacerbated by the defection of Lieutenant General Ion Pacepa, a high-ranking Interior official dealing with foreign intelligence, to the West in July (*Washington Post*, 9 August). Ceauşescu reacted with shock, denouncing "rotten and déclassé elements . . . who betray their country for a handful of silver" (*Scînteia*, 1 September) and called upon the party to exercise a "rigorous control" over the security area. Subsequently he fired Pacepa's former superior, Nicolae Doicaru, removed Minister of the Interior Teodor Coman, and appointed new people to most of the leading Interior posts. George Homostean, a provincial party functionary, replaced Coman (*Buletinul Oficial*, no. 81, 5 September; no. 88, 4 October). Rumors circulated that twelve senior Romanian army and security officers were under arrest (Reuters, 5 September).

Ceauşescu also recalled several foreign affairs officials from abroad, including Romania's ambassador to the United Nations, Ion Datcu, and its ambassador to the United States, Nicolae Nicolae. Despite the spillover into the foreign policy area, Ştefan Andrei, who had replaced George Macovescu as minister of foreign affairs in March and is generally recognized as one of Ceauşescu's most influential advisers, seemed to have survived the shake-up.

Mass and Auxiliary Organizations. There exists in Romania a large number of mass organizations involving nearly all major groups and activities in the society as a way of harnessing them to the party. The CPR's conception of democracy revolves around building up the mass organizations, which usually meet in plenary session at least once every few years. Most sessions begin with a keynote speech by Ceauşescu in which he outlines the problems, prospects, and directions of the group. Among the more important organizations are the Socialist Unity Front (a general political mobilization organization), the General Union of Trade Unions, and the Union of Communist Youth.

While the previous year had highlighted organizations of the working class as a response to workers' unrest, there was no particular emphasis in the 1978 gatherings. Ceauşescu, confronted with minority discontent in Transylvania, convened a joint session of the Councils of Working People of Hungarian Nationality and of German Nationality (*Scînteia*, 16 March). There was also a meeting of the National Women's Conference (ibid., 22 April). And, after being postponed twice, a Fine Arts Conference was held (ibid., 23—24 June).

Internal Party Affairs. For the CPR it was a year of leadership reshuffles, economic reforms, foreign policy spectaculars, and internal unrest. It was also a year which saw Ceauşescu's personality cult reach new heights. As a result of the 1978 shake-ups his personalization of power continued to grow at the expense of continuity within the bureaucracies. Even though he encountered unrest among the Hungarian minority and suffered a blow from the defection of Pacepa, Ceauşescu's personal position of primacy within the CPR seemed unaltered. Indeed, the year was ushered in by a campaign to boost Ceauşescu's already considerable personality cult.

In the weeks preceding his sixtieth birthday (26 January) and the anniversary of his forty-fifth year of "revolutionary activity," Ceauşescu became the object of an all-consuming media barrage. Poems were published, along with paintings and sculptures depicting Ceauşescu as a great leader. Exhibits of Ceauşescu-related memorabilia were opened. Ceauşescu received doctorates in political science and economics. The CPR Central Committee, the State Council, and the Council of Ministers sent him a lengthy, unabashed message of praise which asserted:

> It is an indisputable reality and a truth written eternally in Romania's history that the years since you have been at the head of the party and state have been the most fertile and fruitful period . . . in the entire millenary existence of the Romanian people (ibid., 26 January).

On the days surrounding January 26 all major dailies had nothing but such manifestations of praise.

The most significant aspect of all this was the attempts to portray Ceauşescu as a creative communist theoretician and political leader. His "thought" is now placed at the center of all Romanian accomplishments since 1965. The party-state congratulatory message asserted: "Your extensive activities in the area of sociopolitical thinking and of the theoretical generalization of revolutionary practice . . . have enriched with new ideas, theses, and conclusions the heritage of scientific socialism, of knowledge and historical insight of our era" (ibid.).

As if to underscore this point, Ceauşescu unveiled in the first quarter of the year an economic reform program which was ratified by the CPR Central Committee plenum of 22—23 March. The program's aim, in the words of Ceauşescu, is a restructuring of the economic mechanism, which is "too centralized, rigid, outdated, and very complicated." This is to be done by

> uniformly guiding and blending the activity of building the comprehensively developed socialist society on the basis of the uniform national plan, with the economic and financial autonomy of administrative and production units, with the principles of workers' self-management and with the self-administration of enterprises (ibid., 25 March).

While sweeping in its rhetoric, the reform is not an attempt at Yugoslav-style market socialism and workers' self-management. It seeks rather to give greater latitude to individual enterprises to coordinate their activity with the central authorities, who are still charged with drawing up a central economic plan. Enterprises, however, will have leeway to: (*a*), devise their own plans and annual budgets, which must be balanced; (*b*), institute a profit-sharing system among the workers; and (*c*), consult with workers (via the workers' councils) as to the best ways of achieving specified goals. Enterprises' productivity will be measured on the basis of net rather than gross output. Production will now be tied to domestic and foreign contracts. (Ibid., March 28.) Pricing, however, is still retained by the central authorities, and it is not clear how the enterprises will "coordinate" with the latter.

Ceauşescu has indicated that all reform measures will be instituted by 1 January 1979. Whether they will be remains to be seen, for even Ceauşescu admitted that there were individuals within the party who did not support these changes and preferred the more comfortable route of following orders handed down from above. In theory, however, the reform proposals constitute Ceauşescu's answer to the question of how Romania will become a developed state by 1985—a goal proclaimed by the CPR's national conference in December 1977.

Domestic Affairs. The internal domestic scene was dominated by the ongoing struggle to create a "multilaterally developed socialist society." This goal is pursued in the context of a developmental strategy which stresses rapid industrial growth at the expense of agriculture and consumption. Approximately one-third of the national income is reinvested in the economy—an unusually large percentage by world standards. Given this, and its original underdevelopment, Romania has registered one of the highest average annual rates of economic growth in the world and the highest in Eastern Europe in the 1970s. This rapid growth rate, however, is becoming harder to sustain. While the country is relatively rich in some raw materials (including oil), domestic supplies are becoming tighter. At the same time, the labor pool is expanding more slowly as the manpower reserves in the countryside dry up. The net hard-currency debt is around $4 billion as Romania continues to have problems penetrating international markets with industrial goods.

The difficulties in sustaining rapid growth have increasingly occupied the Romanian leadership. For example, Ceauşescu indicated that as of September the 1978 plan in industrial production was being "overfulfilled . . . but compared with last year this overfulfillment is small." He also cited "very serious lags" in investments; problems with material supplies; "lags" in exports; large inventories of products for which there are no domestic or foreign buyers; "serious lags" in housing construction; and consumer supplies which are "not up to planned levels." He gave few data, but the general picture suggested that it would be difficult to meet many of the objectives of the 1978 plan. (Ibid., 30 September).

The economic situation was complicated by worker unrest, especially the miners' strike of 1977. Although this discontent appeared to moderate in 1978, there were still problems with worker productivity. Ceauşescu felt it necessary to call for "firm measures to strengthen discipline, order and responsibility at the working place." (Ibid.)

More directly of concern to the regime, however, was the development of discontent in that part of Romania known as Transylvania, where some 2 million people of Hungarian background live. This minority—or at least segments thereof—have long perceived themselves to be second-class citizens in Ceaușescu's highly nationalistic Romania. The year witnessed major internal and external criticism of Romanian policy toward its Hungarian minority.

The first public salvo in the controversy over the Hungarians was fired in Budapest by the noted poet Gyula Illyés, who indirectly accused the Romanian regime of carrying out an apartheid-like policy toward the Transylvanians (*Magyar Nemzet*, 25 December 1977, and 1 January 1978). At the same time, a Hungarian academician, Antal Bartha, published an article in Hungary attacking the Romanian position on the historical continuity of Transylvania, annexed to Romania at the end of World War I (*Magyar Hirlap*, 25 December 1977). Bucharest issued a strong retort to the Bartha article in the 10 February issue of *Contemporanul* but did not rebut the Illyés critique until the 6 May issue of *Luceafarul*. In the latter journal, Mihnea Gheorghiu, head of the Romanian Academy of Political and Social Science and a Central Committee member, issued a slashing attack on Illyés, accusing him of an "anti-Romanian obsession" and "absolutely subjective reasonings grounded on imagined data from which he was drawing so crazy a conclusion."

The intensity of the Romanian response was, in part, stimulated by the fact that the issue was gaining international attention. Károly Király, a former high-ranking CPR official of Hungarian background, had released in the West several letters that he had sent to the CPR hierarchy protesting discrimination against Romania's minorities, especially the Hungarians. One of these letters appeared in the *New York Times* on 1 February. Király accused the regime of noble principles on the nationality question but poor performance because of the failure to increase educational opportunities in minority languages, various de facto prohibitions against the use of native languages, preferential treatment of Romanians for jobs, etc., and in general, "forcefully assimilating nationalities living in Romania." He attributed this not to the socialist system but to Ceaușescu, who was accused, albeit indirectly, of policies based on "demagogy, the personality cult, and the capricious application of Marxism." Király's critique jolted the regime because it was an unprecedented attack on Ceaușescu by a former leading party figure and, at the same time, gave encouragement to restive Hungarians who constitute a significant subgroup in Romanian society. Three other notables of Hungarian background were also reported to have sent lengthy memoranda to the regime offering their solutions to the minority problem (*Christian Science Monitor*, 2 May).

With the advent of Western attention the Romanian regime launched a concerted media effort to rebut charges of discrimination. On 14 March Ceaușescu himself joined the controversy with a major speech on the nationality question before the joint plenum of the Councils of Working People of Hungarian Nationality and of German Nationality. While generally defending his policies, Ceaușescu admitted that no part of life is perfect and that there had been "shortcomings and mistakes" regarding the nationalities and promised that these past errors would be "eliminated." Ceaușescu went on, however, to define the problem as one that had its roots outside of Romania and stated that the country's enemies sought to mobilize a few disoriented persons in order to weaken the Romanian state. And he warned these enemies:

> We will not permit anyone to interfere in our internal affairs. . . .There still exist plastic and morally weak elements who, for two pieces of gold or silver, for a bowl of lentils or goulash, go to serve foreign circles. . . . Those who defect to the enemy camp outright must be treated with all the scorn they deserve (*Scînteia*, 16 March).

Ceaușescu, who has always had a penchant for a conspiratorial view of politics, seemed to believe that the Hungarian unrest in Romania was primarily a product of collusion between Hungary and the

Soviet Union as a way of chastising Bucharest for its increased foreign policy independence. Ceauşescu reiterated his view on 10 June before a Bucharest rally of over 100,000 people: "The problems of the Hungarian, German, Serbian, and other nationalities are not solved in Budapest, Berlin or Bonn, Belgrade or elsewhere, but here in Bucharest, by our party. . . . I firmly state that we will not allow anybody to use the nationality problem to interfere in any way in Romania's internal affairs" (ibid., 11 June).

Convinced that Moscow's hand was involved in this issue, Bucharest retaliated by raising, implicitly but strongly, its historical claim to Bessarabia—the former Romanian province which was ceded to the Soviet Union in 1940. Long an indication of the state of Soviet-Romanian relations, Bessarabia has been a source of contention between the two countries for years. The Romanian position was articulated in an article which referred to Bessarabia as being Romanian (*Anale de Istorie,* no. 2).

While the minorities' issue seemed to taper off by the end of the year, it was clear that a new area of internal unrest, with international ramifications, had been added to the problems confronting Ceauşescu and the CPR.

International Affairs. Romania, known as the maverick of the Warsaw Pact and Council for Mutual Economic Aid, intensified its independent foreign policy in 1978. Ceauşescu heightened Bucharest's ties to Western Europe, the United States, the Eurocommunists, and the People's Republic of China as counters to Soviet leverage over Romania. This more provocative foreign policy stance was elaborated by Ceauşescu in a comprehensive speech before 7,000 party-state activists on 3 August (*Scînteia,* 4 August).

Belgrade Conference and Relations with the West. Romania, which had been very active in the deliberations of the review meeting in Belgrade of the Conference on Security and Cooperation in Europe, broke ranks with the Soviet Union and most other East European states in criticizing the results of the meeting. Working closely with neutral and nonaligned states, the Romanians had submitted proposals which would have placed greater curbs on NATO and Warsaw Pact military maneuvers in Europe. The failure of the Belgrade meeting to reach substantive decisions on this or any other area upset Bucharest, which labeled the results "poor, unsatisfactory," and a "regression" from the original conference in Helsinki (ibid., 11 March).

While critical of the Belgrade conference, Ceauşescu continued to seek political and economic support from major West European states. West German Chancellor Schmidt visited Romania 6—7 January. In what was probably a quid pro quo, Schmidt extended 700 million DM in foreign trade credit guarantees, while Ceauşescu agreed that "humanitarian problems" involving family reunifications would be "further dealt with in good will." The Schmidt visit also gave Ceauşescu an opportunity to point out again that by establishing relations with West Germany in 1967 Bucharest had been a precursor of détente (ibid., 7—8 January). On 13 June Ceauşescu traveled to the United Kingdom. Aside from the pomp and circumstance of being hosted by the queen, Ceauşescu authorized agreements whereby Romania, at the cost of 315 million pounds, would purchase licenses from British Aerospace and Rolls Royce leading to the phased production in Romania of 80 BAC 1—11 jets. Later in the year, Romania initialed an agreement to purchase two Canadian-designed nuclear reactors at a cost of $300 million (Montreal radio, 18 October). All of this was in keeping with Ceauşescu's injunction during his 3 August speech that Romania's "comprehensive relations" with the West "must continue and, in some fields, they must be expanded" (ibid., 4 August).

Ceauşescu's 11—17 April visit to the United States, however, was the high point of Romania's 1978 Western initiatives. The Romanians took pride in the fact that Ceauşescu, the first Warsaw Pact leader to be received by President Carter, was praised by the U.S. president as a "great leader of a great nation." Both sides seemed to consider the visit a success. Bucharest received a reaffirmation of U.S. political and economic support, a key element in Romania's cultivation of alternatives to Moscow, while the U.S. government got Romania to agree to "cooperate in the settlement of humanitarian issues," a key point for the administration's human rights policies. Although the visit mainly generated symbolic atmospherics, these were important to Ceauşescu as an indication that President Carter would maintain the positive relations with Romania forged under President Nixon and Secretary of State Kissinger. The Romanian media gave the trip in-depth coverage and evaluated its results highly (*Lumea,* 13 and 20 April).

It was symptomatic of Romania's good relations with the U.S., Egypt, and, to a lesser extent, Israel that the Camp David accords on the Middle East were given a cautious endorsement by Romania—unlike the Soviet Union and its allies. While noting that certain problem areas had been excluded from the accords, the Romanian media stressed "the significance of the agreements between Egypt and Israel . . . as an important step along the road of continuing negotiations for a comprehensive solution" of the Middle East crisis (Bucharest radio, 27 October). In this way Ceauşescu sought to keep open his good offices to all immediate parties in the conflict and thereby continue the intermediary efforts which in 1977 had contributed to Sadat's visit to Israel.

Eurocommunism. The Eurocommunist parties' right to chart their own independent course was strongly reaffirmed by Ceauşescu:

> We believe that their orientation is generally correct. . . . We understand that in Eurocommunism the respective parties desire to promote an independent policy, that in their revolutionary activity they want to act in accordance with the conditions in their respective countries. (*Scînteia,* 4 August.)

Relations with the Spanish Communist Party were given particular attention, perhaps because of the latter's more provocative challenge to the Soviet Union. Spanish party leader Carrillo visited Ceauşescu 11—12 March and vacationed in Romania in August. A CPR delegation held extensive talks with Spanish Communist Party leaders in Madrid from 14 to 21 October. Ceauşescu backed the Spanish party's decision to no longer call itself a Leninist party. Said Ceauşescu, "It is each party's right to choose its name as it thinks best" (ibid.). Ceauşescu also met on 23 July with French Communist Party leader Georges Marchais who was also vacationing in Romania.

Relations with Asian Communist States and the PRC. A dramatic development in Romanian foreign policy was the heightening of the already close relations between Bucharest and Peking—symbolized by Ceauşescu's visit to China during his 15—30 May tour of Asia and Hua Kuo-feng's unprecedented visit to Romania (and Yugoslavia) in August. Interestingly, Hua's Balkan visit was scheduled to coincide with the tenth anniversary of the Soviet invasion of Czechoslovakia.

The warmest receptions that Ceauşescu received during his Asian tour were in Peking (15—20 May), Pyongyang, North Korea (20—23 May) and Phnom Penh, Cambodia (28—30 May). His welcome in pro-Soviet Vietnam (23—26 May) and Laos (26—28 May) were correct but restrained, particularly in Vientiane where a final joint communiqué was not issued. Hua told Ceauşescu that China would fight with Romania against "imperialism, colonialism and hegemonism" (i.e., the Soviets), and Ceauşescu stated that Romania and China have long been united in the "struggle against foreign oppression and domination." Both sides agreed to expand their relations by signing a ten-year economic and technical cooperation agreement, a consular convention, and a cultural cooperation agreement (*Scînteia,* 16—21 May) Ceauşescu's visit to a Chinese tank unit hinted at what was publicly stated several months later—that Romania and China are cooperating in arms production (New China News Agency, Peking, 12 September).

In North Korea both Ceauşescu and Kim Il-song praised each other for resisting "dominationists"—a North Korean code word for big-power chauvinist behavior. Both sides indicated that they reached "complete identity of views" on the issues they discussed (Pyongyang radio, in English, 20 and 23 May). And in Cambodia, Ceauşescu and Pol Pot signed a friendship treaty stressing political independence, which implicitly supports Phnom Penh in its border conflict with Hanoi. This treaty was the first that Cambodia has signed. For Romania the treaty's main significance was that by giving strong support to Peking's main Southeast Asian ally, Bucharest had underscored its tilt toward China.

Hua reciprocated Ceauşescu's visit by traveling to Romania, 16—21 August, in what was the first Western visit by a Chinese party chairman. In so doing, Hua found a platform in the Soviets' backyard for attacking "hegemonism." By inviting Hua to Romania as Sino-Soviet relations were in a downward spiral, Ceauşescu sought to promote further Romanian ties to Peking, institutionalize them and, in the process, expand the boundaries of Romania's independent foreign policy. As a result of Hua's six-day stay, both sides signed an official joint statement which pledged them to "increasingly expand and deepen" bilateral ties and to oppose "all forms of domination." A Sino-Romanian Intergovernmental Committee on Economic and Technological Cooperation was established, and eight other agreements and protocols of cooperation were concluded (*Scînteia*, 17—22 August).

Relations with the Soviet Union. Romania's foreign policy activity had a cumulatively negative impact on its relations with the Soviet Union. This was apparent during Ceauşescu's August meeting with Brezhnev in the Crimea, in the Soviet reaction to Hua's visit, in the results of the Soviet-Romanian discussions in Bucharest during October, and especially in Romania's challenging the discipline of the Warsaw Pact in November.

Unlike Brezhnev's meetings with other Warsaw Pact leaders, the Ceauşescu-Brezhnev tête-à-tête was brief and discordant. Ceauşescu did not join in the Soviet-orchestrated anti-China campaign, and the official statement on the discussions described them as "frank and friendly"—a communist euphemism for disagreement. Ceauşescu had little reason for a cordial meeting with Brezhnev, having just delivered a 3 August speech filled with indirect criticism of Soviet policies toward the Third World, the nonaligned countries, China, and Eurocommunism.

The Soviet reaction to Hua's visit was one of predictable fury. Moscow blasted Hua for what was seen as an anti-Soviet foray into Eastern Europe. While not criticizing Romania directly, the Soviets used Western and Albanian editorials to chastise Bucharest for involving itself with Peking's anti-Soviet goals. Tass's commentary on the Sino-Romanian statement hinted that there was collusion between the two states in that the statement had "the purpose of veiling the essence and direction of the negotiations." Ceauşescu later criticized "the press from some socialist countries" for not reporting objectively on the visit and for repeating "tendentious" Western press accounts (ibid., 3 September).

The 12—15 October visit of a Soviet delegation to Romania failed to resolve the differences between the CPR and the Communist Party of the Soviet Union. The Soviets, headed by Foreign Minister Andrei Gromyko, met with Ceauşescu and a Romanian delegation led by Minister of Finance and Political Executive Committee member Paul Niculescu—Ceauşescu's old trouble-shooter in the late 1960s. It was announced that the two sides had "examined . . . a wide range of problems" between the two parties and that the talks had passed in a "frank, comradely working atmosphere" (ibid., 16 October).

The tensions within Soviet-Romanian relations culminated at the Warsaw Pact Political Consultative Committee (PCC) meeting held in Moscow in late November. There Ceauşescu's opposition to Soviet policies on China, the Middle East, Warsaw Pact military integration, and Vietnam apparently led to the issuance of a bland final communiqué on the meeting. Pact members, minus Romania, were forced to declare their opposition to the Camp David accords in a separate statement (*Pravda*, 25 November).

Upon returning to Bucharest, Ceauşescu launched another unprecedented public attack—in five major speeches between 25 November and 1 December—against what he implied were Soviet efforts at the PCC to have pact members increase their military expenditures and to institute more effective command and control procedures that would place members' pact forces directly under Moscow's direction (*Scînteia*, 26 November—2 December). The longest and the most comprehensive of these speeches was delivered in Bucharest on 1 December, at a solemn session of the RCP Central Committee, Grand National Assembly, and the Socialist Unity Front National Council, marking the sixtieth anniversary of Romania's unification. Ceauşescu pegged his criticisms around the military expenditures issue, which he rejected as unjustifiable, a point he said he also made in Moscow. He argued that "there is no imminent danger of war," the money is needed at home, and Romania has "good relations with all NATO member countries." He also asserted in highly emotional and nationalistic terms that "the Romanian army will only take orders from the supreme party and state bodies, and at the call of the people, and that it will never receive orders from outside." At the same time, however, Ceauşescu (in what some foreign correspondents saw as an apparent gesture to Moscow) stated that "Romania will fulfill its obligations under the Warsaw Pact in the event of imperialist aggressions in Europe directed against the socialist member-countries of this pact," and also pledged to work for "cooperation, friendship and solidarity" among the communist countries. The CPR's Political Executive Committee and Central Committee "unanimously" endorsed Ceauşescu's stand.

Ceauşescu's opposition at the PCC and his going public with his protests prompted the Soviets to issue a separate party-government statement arguing for the various issues which the Romanians opposed. And Brezhnev took the occasion of a toast to visiting Afghan Prime Minister Taraki 5 December to rebuke Ceauşescu indirectly: "We will never agree to the weakening of our defenses in face of the growing military might of imperialism, no matter by what demagogic arguments such calls are camouflaged" (*Washington Post*, 6 December). Likewise, *Pravda* (16 December) carried an attack on a speech by Dumitru Popescu, a member of the RCP's Political Executive Committee, for underestimating the military danger posed by the West and for opposing a denunciation of China. The speech was given at the occasion of the international theoretical conference on "Construction of Socialism, Communism and World Progress" held in Sofia 12—15 December, in the presence of representatives of 73 communist workers' parties.

The rapid downward spiral in Soviet-Romanian relations brought strong public press support from China and an endorsement of Romania's independence from the United States. U.S. Secretary of the Treasury Michael Blumenthal made a hastily arranged two-day visit to Bucharest where he delivered a letter from President Carter to Ceauşescu which, according to Blumenthal, stressed "how greatly" Carter values the relations that were established during Ceauşescu's April visit to Washington. Blumenthal had just been in Moscow for trade talks (*Washington Post*, 9 and 10 December).

Publications. *Scînteia* is the daily newspaper of the CPR, while *Era Socialista* is its theoretical journal. *Lumea* is a foreign affairs weekly. *Anale de Istorie* is the CPR's historical journal. *Revista de Economica* is devoted to economic policy and problems. Agerpres is the Romanian news agency.

Washington, D.C.   Robert L. Farlow

Union of Soviet Socialist Republics

The Communist Party of the Soviet Union (Kommunisticheskaia Partiia Sovetskogo Soiuza; CPSU) traces its origins to the founding of the Russian Social Democratic Labor Party in 1898. The party split into Bolshevik (claiming "majority") and Menshevik (alleged by the Bolsheviks to be the "minority") factions at the Second Congress, held at Brussels and London in 1903. The Bolshevik faction, led by Vladimir I. Lenin, was actually a minority after 1904 and, unable to regain the policy-making dominance attained at the Second Congress, broke away from the Mensheviks in 1912 at the Prague Conference to form a separate party. In March 1919, after the seizure of power, this party was renamed the "All-Russian Communist Party (Bolsheviks)." When "Union of Soviet Socialist Republics" was adopted as the name of the country in 1924, the party's designation was changed to "All-Union Communist Party (Bolsheviks)." The present CPSU name was adopted in 1952. The CPSU is the only legal political party in the USSR.

As of 1 January 1978, party membership approximated 16,300,000 (Moscow radio, 21 April). The party has sought to stabilize membership growth in recent years by various means, including more stringent admission requirements and an exchange of party cards conducted between 1973 and 1975. Between 1961 and 1966, the average annual increase in CPSU membership was 6.0 percent; between 1973 and 1976, 1.96 percent. In the years 1976 and 1977, the average increase declined further, to 1.85 percent. Present party membership is about 9.2 percent of the adult population and approximately 6.2 percent of the total USSR population of 261.2 million (*Izvestiia*, 22 July).

The recent deceleration in growth of the party reflects both a preference for maintaining the elite status associated with party membership and concern for the caliber of new Communists. The latter consideration was emphasized in a number of articles in the official press during the year. An editorial in *Krasnaya zvezda,* the army newspaper, on 14 March stated that "army and navy political organizers and party organizations have intensified their controlling influence on the makeup of those accepted into the CPSU. The most worthy of the servicemen with leading specialties are selected for the party." At the same time, the military paper accused unspecified civilian organizations of lack of vigilance: "It must be noted that in some places there is not a sufficiently serious approach to CPSU selection; undue haste is often shown in accepting people for the party; statements on acceptance into the CPSU are seldom examined at open party meetings."

A *Pravda* editorial on 1 August also emphasized the need for discussion of candidates' qualifications at open party meetings and denounced the alleged widespread "formal approach" to admitting party members. Primary party organizations were urged to exercise their responsibilities more carefully and to take into account not only the opinions of Communists but also those of "nonparty comrades." According to *Pravda*, the strengthening of rural party organizations is especially important and "demands paramount attention."

The comparative weakness of the party in the rural sector is reflected in the fact that only about 14 percent of the members are collective farmers, compared with worker membership of approximately 42 percent. The remainder of the membership is composed of professional people, white-collar employees, and military personnel. More than four million Communists are women, representing slightly less than one-fourth of total membership. The most recent data on educational levels show that 24.3 percent of party members have a higher education and 41 percent have an incomplete higher or secondary education. Great Russians constitute about 60 percent of the party membership, Ukrainians approximately 16 percent, Belorussians more than 3.5 percent, and remaining nationalities about 20 percent.

Organization and Leadership. The structure of the CPSU parallels the administrative organization of the Soviet state. There are approximately 390,000 primary party organizations. Above this lowest level are 2,857 rural *raion* committees, 815 city committees, 10 *okrug* (area) committees, 148 *oblast'* district committees, 6 *krai* (territorial) committees, and 14 union-republic committees. There is no separate subsidiary organization for the Russian republic (RSFSR), the largest constituent unit of the union. At the top, the All-Union Congress is, according to party rules, the supreme policy-making body. The Congress elects the Central Committee and the Central Auditing Commission. The Twenty-Fourth Congress, in 1971, set the maximal interval between congresses at five years. Between congresses, the highest representative organ is the Central Committee. At this level, power is concentrated in the Politburo, the Secretariat, and various departments of the Central Committee.

Two plenums of the Central Committee were held in 1978. The first, in July, was mainly devoted to matters of agriculture (see below) and only one organizational change was announced. Boris N. Pastukhov, first secretary of the Komsomol, was promoted from candidate member to full member of the Central Committee (Radio Moscow, 4 July).

The second plenum of the Central Committee, held in Moscow in November, inaugurated important leadership shifts. Konstantin Ustinovich Chernenko (see Biographies, p. 450), was promoted on 27 November from alternate to full membership in the Politburo. At the same session Kiril T. Mazurov was released from his functions as member of the Politburo "because of his health and in connection with his request." The plenum also decided to promote as candidate members of the Politburo, Nikolai Semenovich Tikhonov (b. 1896; first deputy chairman USSR Council of Ministers), and Eduard Ambrosievich Shevardnadze (b. 1928; first secretary, Georgia Central Committee). Finally, the plenum nominated Mikhail S. Gorbachev (b. 1931; first secretary of the Stavropol *krai* party committee, and member of the CPSU Central Committee) to the position of the new CC secretary for agriculture in place of the deceased Fedor Kulakov. (*Pravda*, 28 November; see also Radio Liberty Research, 28 November.)

Fedor D. Kulakov, member of the Politburo and party secretary for agriculture, died in Moscow on 17 July (*Pravda*, 18 July). Kulakov had been party secretary for agriculture since 1965 and a member of the Politburo since 1971.

Karl Vaino was named first secretary of the Estonian Communist party in July, replacing Ivan G. Kebin, who had headed the Estonian party for 28 years. Vaino, 55, had been a secretary of the Estonian party's Central Committee since 1960. Kebin, 72, was elected to the honorific position of president of the Presidium of the Supreme Soviet of Estonia. (*Pravda*, 27 July.)

Anastas I. Mikoyan, a once powerful figure in the CPSU who served as a member of the Politburo under Stalin, Khrushchev, and Brezhnev, died on 21 October at the age of 82 (Tass, 22 October). Best known as a trade expert, Mikoyan held many official positions during his long career and was president of the USSR from 1963 to 1965. Following his retirement from the presidency, he had continued to serve on the Central Committee until March 1976 when he concluded his political career at age 80 (see *YICA, 1977*, p. 71).

The present composition of the Politburo is shown in the accompanying list:

Members: **Politburo**

Brezhnev, Leonid I.   General Secretary, CPSU Central
                                    Committee; Chairman, Presidium
                                    of the USSR Supreme Soviet
Kosygin, Aleksei N.   Chairman, USSR Council of Ministers
Suslov, Mikhail A.   Secretary, CPSU Central Committee
Kirilenko, Andrei P.   Secretary, CPSU Central Committee
Pel'she, Arvid I.   Chairman, Party Control Commission
Chernenko, Konstantin U.   Secretary, CPSU Central Committee
Grishin, Viktor V.   First Secretary, Moscow City
                                    Party Committee
Kunaev, Dinmukhamed A.   First Secretary, Kazakh Central
                                    Committee
Shcherbitsky, Vladimir V.   First Secretary, Ukrainian Central
                                    Committee
Andropov, Yuri V.   Chairman, Committee of State
                                    Security (KGB)
Gromyko, Andrei A.   Minister of Foreign Affairs,
                                    USSR Council of Ministers
Romanov, Grigori V.   First Secretary, Leningrad
                                    Oblast' Party Committee
Ustinov, Dimitri F.   Minister of Defense,
                                    USSR Council of Ministers;
                                    Secretary, CPSU Central Committee

Candidate Members:

Demichev, Piotr N.   Minister of Culture,
                                    USSR Council of Ministers
Rashidov, Sharaf R.   First Secretary, Uzbek
                                    Central Committee
Masherov, Piotr M.   First Secretary
                                    Belorussian Central Committee
Solomentsev, Mikhail S.   Chairman, RSFSR Council of Ministers
Ponomarev, Boris N.   Secretary, CPSU Central Committee
Aliev, Geidar A.   First Secretary, Azerbaidzhan
                                    Central Committee
Kuznetsov, Vasily V.   Deputy Minister of Foreign Affairs,
                                    USSR Council of Ministers;
                                    First Deputy Chairman, Presidium
                                    of the USSR Supreme Soviet
Shevardnadze, Eduard A.   First Secretary, Georgia
                                    Central Committee
Tikhonov, Nikolai S.   First Deputy Chairman
                                    USSR Council of Ministers

The present Central Committee Secretariat is composed of twelve men. Their names and Secretariat functions are: Brezhnev (general secretary), Kirilenko (organizational affairs), Suslov (ideology), Gorbachev (agriculture), Ustinov (armed forces), Ponomarev (nonruling communist parties), Vladimir I. Dolgikh (heavy industry), Ivan V. Kapitonov (cadres), Konstantin U. Chernenko (General Department, Central Committee), Mikhail V. Zimianin (culture), Yakov P. Ryabov (defense industry), and Konstantin V. Rusakov (ruling communist parties). It is not definitely known what specific duties in the Secretariat, if any, have been performed by Ustinov since his elevation to defense minister in April 1976; the heavy demands of the armed forces post would seem to rule out a very active role for Ustinov in the Secretariat. There has been some speculation that Ustinov has retained supervisory responsibility for the Department of Administrative Organs, which, among its many functions, oversees the police.

Republic first secretaries are Karen S. Demichyan (Armenia), Geidar A. Aliev (Azerbaidzhan), Piotr M. Masherov (Belorussia), Karl Vaino (Estonia), Eduard A. Shevardnadze (Georgia), Dinmukhamed A. Kunaev (Kazakhstan), Turdakun V. Usbaliev (Kirghizia), August E. Voss (Latvia), Piatras P. Griskiavicus (Lithuania), Ivan I. Bodiul (Moldavia), Dzhabar R. Rasulov (Tadzhikistan), Mukhamednazar G. Gapurov (Turkmenia), Vladimir V. Shcherbitsky (Ukraine), and Sharaf R. Rashidov (Uzbekistan).

Auxiliary and Mass Organizations. The most important of the many "voluntary" organizations allied with the CPSU is the Communist Youth League (Kommunisticheskii Soyuz Molodezhi; Komsomol). The Eighteenth Congress of the Komsomol was held in Moscow, 25–27 April. The major address was delivered by CPSU General Secretary Leonid I. Brezhnev. The first plenum of the Komsomol Central Committee elected by the Eighteenth Congress met on 28 April and reelected Boris N. Pastukhov, 45, as first secretary of the youth organization. A. V. Fedulova was appointed chairman of the Central Committee of the All-Union Pioneers Organization (*Komsomolskaia pravda,* 29 April). The Komsomol has a membership of about 38 million.

Other large mass organizations include the All-Union Central Council of Trade Unions (AUCCTU), with more than 107 million members; the Soviet Voluntary Society for the Promotion of the Army, Aviation, and Navy (DOSAAF), whose members seek to "instill patriotism and pride" in the armed forces; the Union of Soviet Societies for Friendship and Cultural Relations with Foreign Countries; and the Soviet Committee of Women.

Party Internal Affairs. The aging CPSU leadership continued to hold on tenaciously to power and sought to reinvigorate a political system afflicted with signs of increasing apathy, inefficiency, and corruption. Admissions of the need for measures of organizational revitalization contrasted strikingly with the image of growing and menacing Soviet strength increasingly accepted by the outside world. The prevailing gerontocratic politics within the CPSU appeared to be an obvious obstacle to dynamic activism; as of October 1978, the thirteen full members of the Politburo averaged 67 years of age and 288 full members of the Central Committee averaged 62. There seemed to be a pressing need for an infusion of new and younger figures into party leadership ranks; yet the Central Committee plenum in early July virtually ignored organizational questions. Instead, the roles of older leaders were increasingly emphasized. Despite the pronounced media concentration upon activities of the elderly hierarchs, problems of age and health have made it necessary for some of them, notably Brezhnev, Kosygin, Suslov, and Kirilenko, to be supported by other personnel in the performance of their official duties.

Succession Politics. Much attention was devoted by Western observers during 1978 to the question of the succession to Brezhnev. Such speculation is, of course, muted within the Soviet

Union, but the approaching leadership transition is necessarily a concern to ranking CPSU elites. General Secretary Brezhnev has deftly avoided the development of an obvious candidate for the succession but events during the summer of 1978 pointed to a weakening of the party leader's political position. However, at the second Central Committee plenum of the year in November, he appeared to have largely succeeded in reasserting his authority.

The death of Fedor D. Kulakov, Politburo member and Central Committee secretary for agriculture, on 17 July, may have altered considerably the context of succession politics. Kulakov, a protégé of Brezhnev, had been frequently mentioned as a possible successor to the general secretary. One of the few Great Russians among those whose age and official rank entitled them to serious consideration, his chances had appeared to depend upon the strength of political forces allied to Brezhnev. A possible Kulakov candidacy had been shadowed, however, by his background, which featured almost exclusively assignments in the field of agriculture. In any case, the departure of Kulakov undoubtedly weakened the political position of Brezhnev within the ruling Politburo. The number of his protégés and close associates among the full membership was reduced to three—Kirilenko, Shcherbitsky, and Kunaev—and it appeared unlikely that Brezhnev could regain the dominance he had attained at the time of the Twenty-fifth CPSU Congress in February 1976 (see *YICA, 1977,* p. 73). However, the unexpected retirement of First Deputy Prime Minister Mazurov and the promotion of Brezhnev's protégé Chernenko in November changed the political balance within the Politburo considerably and apparently gave Brezhnev a stronger position among the hierarchs at year's end than he had held prior to Kulakov's death.

There were indications that at the time of his death Kulakov was in trouble politically and that his difficulties posed a serious problem for his patron Brezhnev. Kulakov had been party secretary for agriculture since 1965; during that period, Soviet agriculture experienced some severe reverses, but Brezhnev had always been able to protect his protégé from the political consequences. By July 1978, pressures for a confrontation of the problems on the agricultural front had evidently escalated to the point where they could not be ignored, and the Central Committee plenum was devoted almost entirely to agriculture. Perhaps the most interesting aspect of Brezhnev's lengthy report was an apparent attempt to deflect attention from Kulakov and himself by a severe attack upon governmental agricultural personnel and *Gosplan aparatchiks,* although he did name specific regions where agricultural performance was unsatisfactory, with an implied warning to party officials in those areas (*Pravda,* 4 July). Brezhnev renewed his attack upon *Gosplan* and governmental ministries at the November Central Committee plenum (*NYT,* 30 November).

There were some unusual events in the aftermath of Kulakov's death that puzzled Western observers and heightened speculation about the succession. Party Organizational Secretary Kirilenko delivered the main eulogy at Kulakov's funeral (*Pravda* and *Izvestiia,* 20 July); Brezhnev, who was on a state visit to Czechoslovakia, did not return from Prague for the funeral (*Pravda,* 21 July). Since Kulakov had been for years one of Brezhnev's closest associates, this was strange indeed, and there was no fully satisfactory explanation for it. However, Brezhnev's trip to Prague was followed by an extended vacation in the Crimea. Since Brezhnev normally takes his main vacation during the winter months, it seemed plausible that his absence from Kulakov's funeral was related to his health. Brezhnev returned to Moscow in late August (Moscow radio, 31 August).

Brezhnev had pursued a rigorous schedule of activities earlier in the year. Following a demanding tour of the Soviet Far East in April with Defense Minister Ustinov and several top generals, he traveled to Bonn for a meeting with West German leaders. An incident occurred during this visit which aroused intense Western speculation about Brezhnev's physical condition. Brezhnev was photographed being assisted from a chair by Foreign Secretary Gromyko and FRG Chancellor Helmut Schmidt. The resulting worldwide publicity must have been somewhat embarrassing to the Soviet leadership. The geriatric hazards posed by an aging leadership were further spotlighted when

Foreign Secretary Gromyko collapsed while addressing the U.N. General Assembly in New York in September (*Washington Post,* 27 September). While Western observers watched for signs of physical decline in all the aging hierarchs, most attention was, of course, devoted to Brezhnev. In July, portraits showing an aged Brezhnev began appearing in Moscow while pictures of a much younger Brezhnev continued to be displayed in Leningrad. Some observers noted that a similar phenomenon had occurred in Moscow in 1964 in the months immediately prior to Khrushchev's ouster.

The death of Kulakov was followed be a remarkable concentration by the Soviet media upon Party Organizational Secretary Kirilenko. The 72-year-old Kirilenko had been very much in the background in recent years. Since 1976, there had been repeated reports that many of his duties had been assumed by Central Committee Secretary Konstantin U. Chernenko, another protégé of Brezhnev, who has served the current leader in various organizational capacities most of the time since 1950. The Soviet press did report that Kirilenko attended the Komsomol Congress in April (*Pravda,* 27 April), but otherwise his political visibility was quite low during the first six months of 1978. By the summer of 1978, Chernenko had become so prominent in party affairs that he was widely assumed to be acting as de facto organizational secretary. This situation changed abruptly following the July Central Committee plenum. On 12 July Kirilenko was principal speaker at a meeting of regional secretaries and government officials (Moscow radio, 12 July). After serving as the main eulogist for Kulakov, Kirilenko was given close attention by the press during a busy round of activity in August. He was reported to have taken part in the meeting of the RSFSR Supreme Soviet in early August (ibid., 7, 8 August). Unusual publicity was accorded his meeting with a group of Soviet miners on 25 August (*Pravda,* 26 August). On 31 August, Moscow radio reported that Kirilenko had inspected factories and met with *oblast'* party officials in Rostov 29–31 August and, in a separate broadcast, noted that Kirilenko had also been among the party leaders who met Brezhnev upon his return to Moscow on the morning of 31 August.

In the weeks following Kulakov's death, Kirilenko was clearly given more media attention than any other Soviet official with the exception of Brezhnev. This naturally led to Western speculation that Kirilenko was being built up as the potential successor to Brezhnev. It seems more likely, however, that the tensions surrounding the July Central Committee plenum and the new political balance in the Politburo resulting from Kulakov's demise forced Brezhnev and his close associates to take immediate action to prevent further erosion of Brezhnev's influence on matters of both policy and personnel. Brezhnev has probably been under pressure to do something about the succession problem; the most obvious action would be the appointment of a new, younger, more vigorous organizational secretary who might qualify as a successor to the present general secretary. But such a solution would undermine Brezhnev's leadership position; moreover, under prevailing political circumstances he probably could not dictate the choice. Thus, the reassertion of Kirilenko's authority serves to dampen any demands for a portentous appointment of a new number-two man in the party.

Chernenko's promotion prompted another round of speculation among Western observers about the succession, with the veteran *aparatchik* now the focus of attention. However, Chernenko has never held a major position of command in the field, having been for the past 30 years or so strictly a staff man. His deficiencies of experience would seem likely to rule him out as a possible successor. Chernenko's promotion appears to represent a successful move by Brezhnev to strengthen his political position within the Politburo and another stopgap measure to stave off pressures for a decision on the succession.

Other Politburo members who have been mentioned as possible successors to Brezhnev include Romanov, Shcherbitsky, and Grishin. Romanov and Shcherbitsky both lack experience in Moscow. Moreover, Shcherbitsky has the handicap of being an ethnic Ukrainian. The career background of

Moscow party chieftain Grishin is not particularly impressive. Under the circumstances, it seemed probable that the leadership would try to postpone the succession decision as long as possible; but the physical condition of Brezhnev could force a decision at an early date. The general secretary appeared rather feeble at the signing of the Soviet-Vietnamese treaty in early November and at the Central Committee plenum in late November. At the end of the year, further changes in party and government that might be portentous for the succession seemed imminent.

Collective Leadership. It is generally assumed by Western students of Soviet politics that the next succession will be accompanied by a marked reversion to emphasis upon "collective leadership" since the new party leader will not possess the authority attained by Brezhnev over many years of leadership. Various party spokesmen stressed the concept of "collective leadership" during 1978, perhaps in anticipation of a forthcoming leadership change. During the year 1976, there had been striking manifestations of the growth of a "personality cult" around party leader Brezhnev, and in 1977 he had added the chief of state role to that of party leader. In 1978, there was evidently an attempt to redress the balance in intraparty politics and contain the media's adulation of Brezhnev.

Party Secretary Mikhail A. Suslov, following receipt of an award in a Kremlin ceremony on 5 January, delivered a speech in which he characterized the work of the Politburo since October 1964 as "creative collectiveness"; the credit for this, said Suslov, "belongs primarily" to General Secretary Brezhnev (Moscow radio, 5 January). This reference seemed somewhat ironical in view of the well-known fact that Suslov has been the principal force opposing development of a Brezhnevian "personality cult."

Alternate Politburo member Mikhail S. Solomentsev, in his Lenin Anniversary speech in the Kremlin Palace of Congresses on 21 April, emphasized "the Leninist norms of party life" and "the collective nature of the leadership" (ibid., 21 April). A lengthy article on democratic centralism by N. Petrovichev, which appeared in *Pravda* in August less than a week before Brezhnev's return from the Crimea, stressed the allegedly democratic character of party decision-making. Petrovichev stated that decisions of the party's higher organs are the result of "collective discussion" and noted that adherence to CPSU rules strengthens "the collective bases of party leadership" (*Pravda,* 25 August).

Other Organizational Matters. A meeting of regional party secretaries and heads of ministries and departments was held in Moscow on 12 July in the wake of the Central Committee plenum dealing with agriculture. Participants discussed means of implementing the decisions of the Central Committee plenum (Moscow radio, 12 July).

The party has been plagued in recent years by revelations of corruption, inefficiency, and disorder in several areas, particularly the republics of Belorussia, Georgia, and Azerbaidzhan. All three of these republics have witnessed organizational shake-ups since 1975, and they continued to be trouble spots during 1978. In Georgia, Tsulukidzeveskiy *raikom* First Secretary V. S. Kurtskhalia was fired and replaced by V. A. Kuaratskheliya (*Zarya vostoka,* 6 August). Azerbaidzhan First Secretary and alternate Politburo member Geidar A. Aliev was reported to have resumed his former duties as minister of state security for Azerbaidzhan after the outbreak of a scandal of mass bribery, in the course of which five high Azerbaidzhan officials were sentenced to be shot (*Christian Science Monitor,* 7 July).

Azerbaidzhan was also the scene of a bizarre incident in July involving the assassination of a ranking official, a rarity in recent Soviet history. According to Soviet sources, a 29-year-old prison official named Muratov shot and killed Lieutenant General Arif Nazar Geidarov, Azerbaidzhan minister of the interior, and two of his aides in the minister's office (*NYT,* 5 July). No motive for the assassination was disclosed, and according to the official account, Muratov committed suicide.

Western correspondents noted that the assassin was Russian and the minister an Azerbaidzhani, raising the possibility that ethnic tensions may have figured in the murder-suicide.

Ideology and Propaganda. Party spokesmen continued to emphasize the major themes that have dominated the regime's approach to domestic ideological questions during the Brezhnev era—the growing role of the party, "the party and state of all the people," and the homogenization of Soviet society in terms of class and culture. All of these themes were featured in Solomentsev's Lenin Anniversary address. Solomentsev particularly emphasized the claim that Soviet society is becoming more homogeneous:

> Under the determining influence of the working class, a steady convergence is taking place of all classes and social groups. Appreciable differences between urban and rural, between intellectual and physical work are gradually being overcome. The features of a classless structure of society—our great programmatic aim—are visibly taking shape. (Moscow Domestic Service, 21 April.)

Another recurring theme was the defense of the Soviet system against criticisms from the outside world, especially those originating in the world communist movement. In a hard-hitting speech against "revisionism" in Kiev in July, Ukrainian party chief Shcherbitsky charged the critics, especially "Euro-communists," with "liquidationism," "opportunist opinions and arrangements," and desertion of revolutionary action (*Pravda ukrainy*, 28 July).

A problem of some importance for the party in recent years has been the apparent apathy of the masses and even a large proportion of party members toward ideological indoctrination. The appointment of Yevgeny N. Tyazhelnikov as head of the Propaganda Department of the Central Committee in May 1977, after a seven-year vacancy in that position (see *YICA, 1978*, p. 71), had signaled the party's intention to upgrade propaganda work. Since that time, the party has emphasized the ideological responsibility of both party workers and the media, with uncertain results.

In December 1977, the editors of *Novy mir* were sharply criticized on ideological grounds and were admonished by the writers' union to do better in contrasting the "deep processes" of communist thought with the "inhuman essence" of imperialism (*Christian Science Monitor,* 29 December 1977).

Alternate Politburo member Solomentsev, in his Lenin Anniversary speech, noted that in the field of "ideological-political" education "a considerable number of complex problems remain to be solved" and reiterated the "Leninist formula" that "all propaganda must be built on the political experience of economic construction" (Moscow Domestic Service, 21 April). A Central Committee resolution in March had pointed to shortcomings in the work of party lecturers and set out specific measures to be employed by various party organizations in the improvement of propaganda work (*Pravda,* 5 March).

In August, a meeting of representatives of all the mass media was held in Moscow to discuss the role of the "mass information and propaganda media" in building support for party decisions. The main speech at the media conference was delivered by CPSU Cadres Secretary Ivan V. Kapitonov (ibid., 22 August).

The party's approach to propaganda is incompatible with the existence of counterchannels of communication. Here a special problem has been created by the operation of thousands of unlicensed radio operators. The broadcasts have little political content but are considered dangerous because the party does not control them. Despite severe regulations against unauthorized broadcasts, the number of such transmitters has grown steadily. The frustration of CPSU officials over this matter was reflected in a *Komsomolskaia pravda* article which denounced the operators as "radio hooligans" (*Christian Science Monitor,* 20 June).

Domestic Affairs. On the domestic front, the CPSU's major concerns during 1978 included constitutional matters, nationalities tensions, dissent, and economic problems, especially in agriculture.

Law and Constitution. Adoption of the new USSR constitution in 1977 inspired considerable activity aimed toward bringing other laws into line with the basic charter of the regime. A resolution adopted by the CPSU Central Committee, the Supreme Soviet Presidium, and the Council of Ministers in April provided for preparation of a new code of laws for the USSR and for its publication between 1981 and 1985 (*Izvestiia,* 25 April).

A new law defining the role of the Council of Ministers was adopted by the Supreme Soviet at its July session. Premier Kosygin said that the draft law was "new evidence of the concern shown by the CPSU and the party's Central Committee headed by Leonid Brezhnev for the further consolidation of the legal basis of state and public life" (Tass, 5 July).

The major activity related to the new USSR constitution was the drafting and adoption of new constitutions for the union republics. The USSR constitution promulgated in October 1977 had stipulated that the republican constitutions should conform to the national basic document, and whole chapters of the USSR constitution were incorporated into the new constitutions of the republics with the names of the republics substituted for that of the USSR.

In the new constitutions, the formal right of the republics to have their own military formations has been eliminated, and there is an increasing emphasis upon the oneness (*edinstvo*) of the USSR. In the drafts of the constitutions for the RSFSR, the Ukraine, and Azerbaidzhan there is a statement that the people (*narod*) of the republic concerned recognize themselves "as an inalienable part of the whole Soviet people," which seems to vitiate the provision concerning the right of secession (Radio Liberty, 18 April).

The drafts of the new constitutions were more uniform in content than the old documents, and comments in the Soviet media indicated that this was a reflection of the regime's goal of homogenization of Soviet society and the *sliianie* (amalgamation) approach to nationalities questions. The *sliianie* approach was particularly evident in the original drafts of the new constitutions for Georgia, Armenia, and Azerbaidzhan. These had been the only three republics whose national languages had been recognized as state languages; this provision was not included in the original drafts of the new constitutions. However, this omission set off a wave of national sentiment in these republics, and the central authorities were forced to retreat.

A demonstration against the dropping of any reference to Georgian as a state language was held in Tbilisi on 14 April, coinciding with a meeting of the Georgian party Central Committee to consider the constitutional draft (Radio Liberty, 16 April). This spontaneous demonstration, something most unusual in the USSR, produced quick results. On 17 April, Georgian was restored as the official state language (*NYT,* 18 April). Armenia won its language fight on the same day, and on 24 April, Azerbaidzhan had its national language guaranteed in the new constitution (ibid., 25 April).

In an unusual development triggered by the process of constitution making, the autonomous republic of Abkhazia sought to secede from Georgia, which has effective administrative control over the Abkhazians. The incident occurred in May on the heels of Georgia's successful resistance, and the central authorities were in no mood to further antagonize the Georgians by concessions to the less powerful Abkhazians. CPSU Cadres Secretary Ivan V. Kapitonov was dispatched to Sukhumi where he laid down the law to the rebellious Abkhazians (*Zarya vostoka,* 26 May). In June, the new Abkhaz constitution was adopted, with no significant changes (ibid., 7 June).

Nationalities. The Abkhazians had feared that their national culture was being smothered by the Georgians and had in effect appealed to the Russians to protect them against another subordinate nationality. Elsewhere, the issues were less complex, with subordinate nationalities clearly confronting

Great Russian pressures for conformity. The KGB continued its relentless pressure against prominent nationalists and was particularly concerned with what is apparently the greatest nightmare of the secret police—the threat of linkage between nationalist groups and the general dissent movement.

The Ukraine has been a special target in the regime's drive against nationalism, particularly since Vladimir V. Shcherbitsky, an ardent proponent of the *sliianie* approach although himself an ethnic Ukrainian, took over as Ukrainian Communist Party first secretary in 1972. Nationalist and human rights activists in the Ukraine have been mostly silenced, but repressive measures continued during 1978. Two Ukrainian nationalists who had joined the Ukrainian Helsinki monitoring group were sentenced in March for "anti-Soviet agitation and propaganda." Mykola Matusevych and Myrostov Marynovych received identical sentences of seven years in strict-regime camps followed by five years in exile (Radio Liberty, 12 April). In December 1975, Matusevych had been sentenced to fifteen days of imprisonment for "hooliganism"; reportedly, this earlier arrest had been occasioned by his participation in traditional Ukrainian Christmas caroling (ibid., 29 March).

Another member of the monitoring group, Piotr Vins, was sentenced on 6 April to a one-year term on charges of "parasitism" (*Intercontinental Press,* 8 May). Vins is the son of Georgi Vins, a prominent leader of dissident Baptists who is now serving a ten-year term because of his role in an officially unregistered religious group. Two other monitors, Mykola Rudenko and Aleksei Tykhy, had been sentenced to terms of twelve and fifteen years respectively in July 1977 for "anti-Soviet agitation and propaganda."

In Georgia, nationalists have also formed a group to monitor compliance with the Helsinki accords. One of its members, Viktor Rtskhiladze, was arrested in January. Rtskhiladze was editor of an underground journal and had led a campaign to save an ancient monastery from gradual destruction by the Soviet army (*NYT,* 27 January). Another member of the monitoring group, Grigori Goldshstein, a physicist who had sought to emigrate to Israel, was sentenced on 20 March to a year in a labor camp for "parasitism" (Radio Liberty, 25 March). Two other members, Zviad Gamsakhurdia and Merab Kostava, were sentenced on 19 May to three years of imprisonment plus two years of exile for "anti-Soviet agitation." Gamsakhurdia, who had openly advocated Georgia's secession from the Soviet Union, appeared on Moscow television on 19 May and recanted his actions (*NYT,* 20 May; Radio Liberty, 22 May). The genuineness of Gamsakhurdia's television confession was challenged by American correspondents; the sequel was a new source of tension between the U.S. and the USSR (see below).

Other groups to monitor compliance with the Helsinki accords have been set up in Armenia and Lithuania. In Armenia, a nationalist organization has reportedly been formed recently under the name Armenian National United Party. According to documents received in the West in early 1978, this group demands a referendum on self-determination under U.S. auspices and U.N. guarantees for an independent Armenian state (*Observer,* London, 8 January).

Lithuanian human rights activist Balys Gajauskas was sentenced in April to ten years of "the most severe prison regime" and an additional five years of internal exile (Radio Liberty, 23 April). Gajauskas had served a 25-year term between 1948 and 1973 for participation in the post-World War II anti-Soviet resistance movement in Lithuania. In July, prominent nationalist and human rights activist Viktoras Petkus was also sentenced to a lengthy imprisonment (*Sovetskaya Litva,* 16 July). In both cases, the interest of the KGB seemed to be largely focused on their activities related to the Catholic church. Petkus was also a member of the Lithuanian Helsinki monitoring group (*NYT,* 13 July).

Despite official efforts to suppress it, the *Chronicle of the Lithuanian Church,* an underground Catholic newspaper, continued to appear (Radio Liberty, 12 April). This "samizdat" periodical records the persecution of religious and political activists in Lithuania. The underground nationalist journal *Ausra* also survived. Its ninth issue, appearing in January, reported three recent demonstrations in Vilnius and the harassment of ethnic groups.

Latvian dissident Gunars Rode went into exile in Sweden in May (Radio Liberty, 29 May). Rode had reportedly been constantly harassed by the KGB since his release in May 1977 following a fifteen-year term in prisons and labor camps for "anti-Soviet activity."

Several thousand Tatars exiled to Soviet Central Asia reportedly sent a petition to General Secretary Brezhnev seeking permission to return to the Crimea (*L'Unità,* 24 August). The Tatars were deported from the Crimea in 1944 on Stalin's orders for alleged collaboration with the Nazis. The charge of collaboration was officially annulled in 1967, but only 1,600 families have been allowed to return to the Crimea.

Jews who had not participated in public protests reportedly were finding it easier to emigrate during the first half of 1978. Official commentary on matters pertaining to Soviet Jews also seemed to be somewhat restrained during this period, but in August the Soviet media vigorously renewed their verbal assaults against dissident Jews and Zionism (*Christian Science Monitor,* 16 August).

Dissent-Democratic Movement. The regime's concerted drive against dissidents, which dates back at least to 1966, seemed to reach a point of culmination in 1978 with severe punitive measures against some of the leaders of the Democratic Movement, the loosely structured human rights group headed by Andrei D. Sakharov that has taken several organizational forms. Harassment of Westerners also intensified, darkening U.S.-Soviet relations. By midsummer, repressive activities had become so unrestrained that some Western observers in Moscow described the KGB as "out of control." It did indeed appear that the political police had attained a greater degree of independence than it had possessed at any time since the purging of Lavrenti Beria in 1953. In August, the campaign of repression slackened.

Former Major General Piotr G. Grigorenko, perhaps the most prominent member of the Democratic Movement next to Sakharov, was deprived of his Soviet citizenship by a decree of the Supreme Soviet Presidium on 10 March. The decree, signed by Leonid I. Brezhnev in his capacity as chief of state, accused Grigorenko of having "inflicted damage to Soviet prestige" and barred his return to the USSR (*NYT,* 11 March). Grigorenko, who had spent more than five years in prisons and psychiatric hospitals because of his dissident activities, was in New York for medical treatment when the decree was announced. He subsequently made formal application for political asylum in the United States (ibid., 19 April).

Yuri F. Orlov, a physicist and chief organizer of the main Helsinki monitoring group, was sentenced in May to seven years in prison followed by five years of exile or enforced residence after a tumultuous trial in Moscow (ibid., 18 May). Orlov, who is also credited with organization of the Georgian monitoring group, was charged under Article 70 of the RSFSR Criminal Code with "anti-Soviet agitation and propaganda" (Radio Liberty, 18 May). A key element of the charge was Orlov's conveyance of reports on rights violations to foreign correspondents and to Western governments that signed the Helsinki accords. At the time of Orlov's conviction, at least 22 members of various Helsinki monitoring committees had been arrested.

A number of Orlov's supporters maintained a vigil outside the courthouse during the proceedings. Tensions ran high, and seven dissidents, including Andrei D. Sakharov and his wife, were arrested after a scuffle with police. The Sakharovs were charged with striking policemen but were later released.

Aleksandr Ginzburg, another dissident leader, was sentenced in July to eight years in a strict-regime labor camp for "anti-Soviet agitation and propaganda." Ginzburg had administered a fund established by Aleksandr Solzhenitsyn with royalties from *The Gulag Archipelago* to aid families of political prisoners. The trial, like that of Orlov closed to the public, was held in Kaluga, 100 miles southwest of Moscow (*NYT,* 13 July).

Amid a storm of protest from the West, Anatoli B. Shcharansky, a leader of the Jewish monitoring group, was also convicted in July. He was sentenced to three years in prison and ten years in a strict-regime labor camp for treason, espionage, and "anti-Soviet agitation." Shcharansky was accused of passing state secrets to the U.S. Central Intelligence Agency through *Los Angeles Times* reporter Robert C. Toth. U.S. President Carter personally intervened in the case, issuing an assurance to Soviet leaders that the 30-year-old computer specialist had no links with American intelligence, but to no avail (ibid., 14 July).

The trial was closed except to Shcharansky's brother, Leonid, and for five days relatives and supporters of the defendant, including his mother and Andrei D. Sakharov, maintained a vigil outside the Moscow courthouse. At the trial's conclusion, Sakharov denounced the police as "fascists." After sentencing, Shcharansky was sent to the tsarist-era Vladimir Prison, one of the USSR's harshest places of confinement (ibid., 19 July).

Aleksandr Podrabinek, a 25-year-old member of the monitoring group who had investigated Soviet use of psychiatric hospitals as punishment for political dissidents, was sentenced on 15 August to five years of internal exile (*Christian Science Monitor*, 16 August). The trial was held in Elektrostal, an industrial city 40 miles east of Moscow and was off limits to foreigners and Western correspondents.

Despite overwhelming pressures from the regime, the dissident movement continued to enlist recruits. In July, Sergei M. Polikanov, 51, announced to Western correspondents that he had joined the Helsinki monitoring group. Polikanov, a prominent atomic physicist, is a corresponding member of the Soviet Academy of Sciences. He was awarded the Lenin Prize in 1967 and also holds the Order of Lenin decoration (Hamburg DPA, 15 July).

Dissident Feliks Serebrov was freed in August after completing one year of detention in a camp in Mordovia. Serebrov had been sentenced for "using false documents" (*L'Unità*, 24 August).

Perhaps the most embarrassing recent act of dissidence from the standpoint of the regime was the attempted formation of an unofficial labor union in the "workers' state." Vladimir A. Klebanov, a former Ukrainian coal-mine foreman, and four other workers announced in January the formation of a union to protect workers' interests. All the spokesmen had been dismissed from their jobs after complaining about corruption or safety violations. They claimed that at least 200 workers were ready to join the union and stated their intention to apply to the International Labor Organization in Geneva for recognition (*NYT,* 26 January).

A spokesman for the group reported in February that five of its members, including Klebanov, had disappeared after being arrested and that two others had been committed to psychiatric hospitals. But the spokesman, Valentin T. Poplavsky, affirmed the group's intention to continue its activities. At a February human rights meeting, Yelena Bonner, wife of Andrei D. Sakharov, expressed support for the principle of free unions (*NYT,* 27 February).

Economy. The CPSU and the government of the USSR continued in 1978 to wrestle with persistent economic problems—technological backwardness compared with the West, low labor productivity, inferior quantity and quality of consumer goods, uneven development of economic sectors and geographical regions, corruption, and perhaps most important of all, deficiencies in agriculture. The latter problem was spotlighted by reports that China, which has food rationing, has more fresh meat, fruits, and vegetables available in shops and restaurants in its big cities than Russia (*Newsweek,* 30 October). As indicated above, agricultural shortfalls appeared to generate new tensions during 1978 between party and government and within the CPSU leadership.

Data on 1977 national economic performance, released in late January, showed the usual quantitative increases in most indices but pointed up serious shortcomings. Industrial output was reportedly up 5.7 percent and agricultural production, 3 percent. Labor productivity was claimed to have risen 4.1 percent in industry and 4.3 percent in agriculture. However, there were significant differences in labor productivity achievement between different sectors of the economy; power and electrification and ferrous and nonferrous metallurgy barely topped the figures for the previous year. As usual, most of the outlying union-republics scored poorly on labor productivity, although Georgia recorded a 5.4 percent increase. In Turkmenia, labor productivity actually declined during 1977.

Grain production was down from 223.8 million tons in 1976 to 195.5 million tons in 1977. Production of sugar beets, potatoes, and vegetables also declined. The volume of consumer services reportedly increased 8 percent, including 6 percent in rural localities. The Central Statistical Administration admitted that "despite the growth in commodity turnover, the public demand for certain commodities was still not fully satisfied." As a percentage of 1976 sales, the 1977 sales of bread products were 99 percent; butter, 98 percent; and confectionary products, 99 percent. Continuing postponement of consumer satisfaction was reflected in the overall indices of production, which showed a 6 percent rise in manufacture of the means of production, against a 5 percent increase in the manufacture of consumer goods (*Pravda,* 28 January).

The annual appeal on "socialist competition" issued by the CPSU Central Committee, the USSR Council of Ministers, the AUCCTU, and the Komsomol Central Committee was unusually critical of economic performance and particularly scored low labor productivity. The jointly issued "letter" singled out the primary party organizations as having a special "combat task" to create "an atmosphere of public intolerance toward bad workmen, loafers, and violators of labor, planning, and technological discipline" (*Sovetskaia rossiia,* 25 January). According to the "letter," tens of millions of man-days are wasted because of absenteeism and idleness. In 1977, this resulted in the loss of more than three billion rubles' worth of production in industry (Radio Liberty, 18 January).

Price increases announced at the beginning of March brought home to the Soviet consumer the reality of new economic pressures confronting the USSR. The price of regular gasoline was increased to the equivalent of 83 cents per gallon and of high-octane fuel to $1.10. The price of coffee, which reappeared in stores after having been unattainable for several months, quadrupled. Cocoa and chocolates went up about 30 percent, and gold and platinum jewelry prices were raised 60 percent. These price increases were attributed to the rising cost of developing energy sources at home and the difficulty in obtaining foreign currency to buy goods abroad. The cost of repair work and spare parts for automobiles was also raised 35 percent, but prices were cut on some Soviet-made commodities, including some items of clothing, detergents, small refrigerators, and black and white television sets (*NYT,* 1 March).

The Central Committee plenum in July was devoted almost entirely to agricultural problems. Brezhnev's lengthy report was sharply critical of performance in this sector of the economy, detailing specific areas of serious shortcomings. According to Brezhnev, plans for development of the non-black-soil zone, a major goal of current agricultural policy, were not being adequately fulfilled. In 1976 and 1977, Brezhnev said, gross farm production was less than planned in a number of regions of the Russian Federation, the Ukraine and Kazakhstan, and in Moldavia, Latvia, and Kirghizia. Overall, Brezhnev stated, "returns in agriculture are not yet sufficient compared with investment." "Increasing the efficiency of agricultural production," he said, "should be given top priority." The party leader stressed the need for increasing the capacity of industries serving the countryside and set goals of an average annual grain harvest of 238 to 243 million tons for the years 1981–1985 and meat production of 19.5 million tons by the end of that period (Tass, 3 July). The Central Committee passed a resolution embodying Brezhnev's criticisms and suggestions; the resolution admitted that "the general level of development of this vitally important branch does not yet accord with the rapidly growing requirements of society" (Tass, 4 July).

Early reports on the 1978 harvest indicated that good weather and intensive efforts to overcome harvesting bottlenecks were likely to lead to a satisfactory grain yield; official optimism seemed to be considerably higher than usual (Moscow radio, 3 August). This optimism proved to be fully justified; in November the government reported a record harvest of 235 million tons (*NYT*, 30 November).

The severe problems in agriculture have caused the leadership to de-emphasize the preferred organization of the farms on the basis of massive "factories in the field" and to upgrade the peasants' private plots; the new constitution includes a provision guaranteeing the peasants' right to a measure of private plot farming. The regime's more favorable approach to the private plots was emphasized in a January article in *Trud* by agricultural economist G. Shmelev. According to Shmelev, in 1976, 25.5 percent of everything grown in agriculture, including 18.5 percent of farm produce and 32 percent of livestock produce, came from private plots. Shmelev argued that the private plots are not incompatible with socialism: "Private plot farming is not a remnant of private, peasant farming, but a new type of agriculture brought to life by the socialist transformation of the countryside. It is a component part of socialist agriculture." (*Trud*, 8 January.)

Economic crime, or the "misappropriation of socialist property," has been an increasingly worrisome problem for party and government in recent years. It was reported in 1978 that new measures have been devised to combat it. Special departments have been formed at factories and in the republican ministries for light industry to conduct economic analyses of documents and production processes to establish "what makes possible misappropriation of socialist property" (Radio Liberty, 23 May).

The midyear economic report showed increases in production in most sectors of the economy but continuing unsatisfactory results in labor productivity and agricultural production. Less electricity was produced than in the corresponding period of 1977, and productivity was down in the coal and fish industries. Labor productivity continued to be a severe problem in certain areas, with only slight increases recorded for Kirghizia, Tadzhikistan, and Moldavia. Production of livestock and poultry reportedly increased, but output of butter and canned goods was down from the previous year. Average wages increased by 3.4 percent (*Izvestiia*, 22 July). *Gosplan* head Nikolai K. Baibakov announced in late November plans for a substantial increase in consumer goods and food supplies in 1979. The promises came two days after Brezhnev's speech to the Central Committee in which he accused *Gosplan* and government ministries of not fulfilling promises on consumer goods (Tass, 27 November). Preliminary reports on industrial performance for 1978 showed mixed results. Overall industrial output was reportedly up 5 percent, against a planned 4.5 percent. However, oil output was 572.5 million tons and coal output 729 million tons; the planned targets had been 575 million and 746 million tons. Labor productivity was up 3.6 percent, against a planned increase of 3.8 percent (*NYT*, 30 November).

Foreign Affairs. CPSU spokesmen continued the rhetorical offensive that has marked the Soviet approach to world politics in recent years. Support for "proletarian internationalism" and the "restructuring of international relations" again tended to dominate official pronouncements about the USSR's foreign relations. Under the former rubric, Soviet leadership of world revolutionary forces was claimed; this involved especially a basic hositility to "Eurocommunism," although a measure of tactical flexibility was maintained in regard to the increasingly independent European communist parties. The "restructuring of international relations" postulates a decisive change in the world "correlation of forces" favorable to the USSR. On the practical level, Moscow sought to exploit perceptions of rising Soviet strategic power and to outflank its major competitors, China in the Far East and the U.S. in Africa and Europe.

Despite the confident assertions of Soviet strength, there were notable indications of growing fears in the leadership's assessment of world affairs. The possibility of new weapons development by the U.S., efforts toward the revitalization of NATO, and the vigorous diplomatic activity of the new Chinese leadership all seemed to arouse extreme nervousness in Moscow. Strong pressures were exerted to prevent new linkages between China and Japan, but to no avail. Evidently aiming to demonstrate that American support for human rights in the USSR was fruitless, the Soviet authorities carried out a heavy-handed campaign of repression that affected Americans in Moscow as well as native dissidents. As a result, in July Soviet-American relations reached the lowest point since the inception of détente. Despite rising tensions, both sides seemed genuinely interested in agreement on strategic arms limitations. Negotiations were vigorously pursued amid frequent expressions of optimism. But the final agreement proved elusive, and SALT II talks bogged down in December.

Soviet influence in the Middle East suffered another setback as the U.S. resumed the role of principal mediator between Egypt and Israel. In the aftermath of the Camp David summit, the USSR appeared unable to affect the course of developments pointing toward a settlement of the great issues in the eastern Mediterreanean area. However, the Soviets maintained a capacity for stirring up trouble in the Middle East through its ties with radical Arab "rejectionist" forces, its connections with anti-Western elements in the Horn of Africa and the Arabian peninsula, and its new foothold in Afghanistan.

The election of Karol Cardinal Wojtyla as pope of the Roman Catholic church in October was an unsettling reminder of Soviet control problems in Eastern Europe. However, the practical effect upon Soviet foreign policy was uncertain.

Soviet-American Relations. Much Soviet effort during the year was devoted to the disarming of American critics of the USSR through protestations of peaceful Soviet intentions and encouragement of those groups and political figures in the U.S. who were inclined to take Moscow's assertions of pacific aims at face value. The Soviet media poured scorn on prominent Americans who emphasized growing Soviet military capabilities rather than intentions and denounced critics of internal repression in the USSR for unwarranted interference in Soviet internal affairs. In its campaign to convey the image of a peacefully inclined USSR, Moscow evoked a degree of sympathetic reaction among some Americans. Despite the USSR's recent reputation in Western leftist cricles as an essentially nonrevolutionary society, it appeared that Moscow could still recruit a measure of at least indirect support for some of its foreign policy goals from noncommunist elements in the U.S. Nevertheless, the Soviet leadership had to take account of sharp controversy between the so-called "hawks" and "doves" in the U.S., particularly within the ranks of the ruling Democratic party and the Carter administration, and this appeared to be a factor in Soviet avoidance of "linkage" politics.

A ten-man delegation of the Supreme Soviet, headed by Central Committee Secretary Boris N. Ponomarev—an old hand at coordinating ideological offensives—toured the U.S. in January and early February (AP, 22 January). The delegation included Georgi A. Arbatov, director of the Institute for the U.S.A. and Canada. Ponomarev delivered a speech to the U.S. Congress, in which he asserted Soviet peaceful aims and warned that if the U.S. produced the neutron bomb, the USSR would follow suit (Tass, 23 January). Senator Edward Kennedy and other members of Congress were quoted by Soviet reporters as being delighted with the visit of the delegation and the reception accorded it (*Pravda,* 29 January). However, Senator Daniel P. Moynihan denounced Ponomarev, claiming that his job was the subversion of Western parliamentary democracy (*NYT,* 27 January).

The delegation also visited Houston, Los Angeles, Detroit, Arkansas, and New York. In Los Angeles, they were greeted by Governor Jerry Brown, who spoke in favor of détente and U.S.-USSR trade (Tass, 27 January). In New York, Ponomarev gave a speech at the United Nations, and the delegation was received by the Soviet-American Trade and Economic Council (*Pravda,* 2 February). The welcoming speech was delivered by Pepsico president Donald Kendall; this, however, did not prevent his subsequent loss of the exclusive soft-drink concession for the 1980 Olympics to Coca-Cola.

Encouraged by the generally favorable reception of the Ponomarev group, Soviet leaders welcomed Senator George McGovern, representing the U.S. Senate Foreign Relations Committee

(Tass, 11 March). McGovern's subsequent report to the committee criticized the U.S. human rights campaign against the Soviets and trade discrimination toward the USSR; the senator expressed the view that the Soviet bloc represented no real threat and that the U.S. should not try to seek military superiority. The report was warmly received in Moscow (*Pravda*, 24 March). Similar views were expressed in an interview by disarmament negotiator Paul Warnke, McGovern's former foreign-policy adviser. However, Warnke's views and past association with McGovern complicated President Carter's political problems in obtaining Senate approval of the projected SALT II agreement.

Mindful of Senator Kennedy's role in the Ponomarev visit and, more importantly, of his domestic political power in the U.S., Brezhnev and other Soviet leaders welcomed him to Moscow in September. Brezhnev made a conciliatory gesture during the visit by arranging exit visas for eighteen Soviet families at Kennedy's request (*Washington Post*, 12 September).

Soviet efforts to influence American public opinion in general were clearly secondary to the specific goal of checking new U.S. weapons development. Early in the year, the Soviet propaganda apparatus was cranked up for a wide-ranging offensive against the neutron bomb. The USSR Academy of Sciences unanimously condemned U.S. plans to build the neutron bomb (*Pravda*, 5 March), and called upon President Carter to scrap the project (Tass, 14 March). After U.S. Defense Secretary Harold Brown said that the U.S. might use the neutron bomb as a bargaining counter in arms limitations negotiations, Moscow issued a statement indicating that the USSR would accept such a challenge but called upon the U.S. to agree to a joint renunciation of the neutron bomb (ibid., 11 March). The Soviets expressed displeasure over reports that the Pentagon would begin producing a modified version of the U-2 plane (ibid., 12 February) and also criticized Carter for failing to keep his election promise to reduce arms expenditures (*Pravda*, 4 March). However, when Carter announced a decision to postpone production of the neutron bomb (much to the consternation of West German Chancellor Helmut Schmidt who had braved domestic political pressures to support American plans for the weapon), Soviet spokesmen dismissed the decision as not representing "a significant renunciation of the neutron weapon" (Tass, 8 April).

When President Carter, in a major foreign policy speech at Wake Forest University in March, warned that the U.S. would match Soviet military force levels and denounced Soviet and Cuban activities in the Horn of Africa (*NYT*, 18 March), the Soviet press responded by blaming Carter for the rising level of U.S.-USSR tensions (Tass, 17 March). Georgi A. Arbatov, in a lengthy *Pravda* article, placed the entire blame for deterioration of relations upon the U.S. and warned that further worsening would result if the Americans did not accept a new strategic arms limitation agreement (*Pravda*, 28 March). When Carter voiced similar warnings in a speech at Annapolis in June, the Soviet press responded with another attack upon the American president's policies (ibid., 17 June). Further, in a televised speech in Minsk, Brezhnev charged that Carter was pursuing a "short-sighted policy" of trying to "play the Chinese card" against the USSR (Tass, 25 June).

In an address to the Supreme Soviet in early July, Premier Kosygin blamed the U.S. for the sharp decline in Soviet-American trade in 1977 and said that the U.S. was unwilling to establish normal trade relations (Associated Press, 5 July).

American press reportage of the repression of internal dissidents produced another source of tension in May. After Georgian human rights activist Zviad Gamsakhurdia appeared on Moscow television to apologize for his actions, *New York Times* reporter Craig Whitney and *Baltimore Sun* correspondent Harold Piper filed stories casting doubt on the authenticity of the recantation. The Soviet authorities reacted by bringing formal legal charges againsty the American newsmen, accusing them of libeling the Soviet state television. In July, a Soviet court found Whitney and Piper guilty, fined each $1,647, and ordered them to publish retractions (*Washington Post*, 19 July). Two weeks later, the court fined the reporters $72.50 each for failing to publish the retractions.

The action of the Soviet authorities was unprecedented, involving in effect the claim of authority for a Moscow city court to censor the content of newspapers published in the United States. Official American reaction was mild, hardly conducive to prevention of such incidents in the future.

Washington seemed more disturbed by the trials of prominent dissidents within the USSR, particularly the Shcharansky case, which directly involved the American government since Shcharansky was accused of espionage on behalf of U.S. intelligence. Carter's response to the Shcharansky affair was a ban on the sale of a Sperry-Univac computer and restrictions on delivery of oil-drilling equipment to the USSR. The Soviet leadership could hardly have been gravely concerned by this minor sanction, but *Pravda* did take note of it, calling the action "blackmail" (*Pravda,* 20 July).

Two Soviet diplomats were arrested for espionage in the United States on 20 May but were not released and deported in accord with usual practices. Instead, formal charges were brought. Apparently in reprisal, American businessman Francis J. Crawford was seized by KGB plainclothesmen in Moscow, being forcibly ejected from his car on a Moscow street, and was held in prison for fifteen days. The Soviet authorities were evidently uncertain what charges to bring, but when Crawford was released from custody in early July, he had been formally charged with currency violations. In September, Crawford was convicted and given a suspended five-year labor camp sentence (*Washington Post,* 8 September). The two Soviet diplomats, Valdik A. Enger and Rudolf P. Chernyayev, were sentenced to 50 years of imprisonment for espionage but were allowed to remain free pending appeal (Associated Press, 30 October).

Amid this upsurge of tensions, officials on both sides attempted to keep strategic arms limitation talks on an even course. The negotiators continued their attempts to narrow differences, and U.S. Secretary of State Cyrus Vance and Soviet Foreign Minister Andrei Gromyko held several conferences on SALT matters in Moscow, Washington, New York, and Geneva. In April, negotiator Warnke reported that both sides had agreed to a joint draft treaty that "resolves well over 90 percent of the issues" (UPI, 4 April). Following an October round of negotiations in Moscow in which Soviet leader Brezhnev played an active role, it was reported that at least 95 percent of the treaty had been completed. State Department spokesman Hodding Carter said that "we continue to hope an agreement is possible by the end of the year" (Associated Press, 23 October). Vance and Gromyko agreed that further progress had been made in the Moscow talks (Tass, 23 October). They met again in Geneva for three days in December, but despite agreement on "most" issues concerning a treaty on the limitation of strategic arms, failed to conclude the accord (*NYT,* 24 December). The Soviet last-minute proposals calling on the United States to curb new generations of advanced missiles caused — according to some U.S. officials— the failure of the Geneva talks (ibid., 28 December). The other explanation for the Soviet reticence was the U.S. decision to establish diplomatic relations with the PRC, despite President Carter's pledge not to use the new relationship against the Soviet Union. According to the aides of Secretary Vance, Soviet delay in signing the SALT II treaty was tied to the U.S.-China links (ibid., 25 December).

Soviet-Chinese Relations. Tensions continued to run high during 1978 along the Soviet-Chinese border, and the USSR made several efforts to improve relations. Radio Peking reported two border incidents in early February (*Japan Times,* 8 February). Moscow denied the report (UPI, 8 February) and made two conciliatory gestures toward Peking. Brezhnev and Kosygin sent congratulatory messages to their Chinese counterparts, Yeh Chien-ying and Hua Kuo-feng, upon their reappointments (New China News Agency, Peking, 11 March, in *FBIS,* 13 March). The Soviet government also proposed immediate talks on a statement of principles to govern overall relations. According to Tass, China answered on 9 March with "unacceptable preliminary conditions" (Tass, 20 March).

Finding Peking inflexible, the Soviets resorted to rather unsubtle pressure. Brezhnev and Defense Minister Ustinov visited the Soviet Far East in early April, conspicuously observing military exercises and emphasizing Soviet armed might (*Pravda* and *Izvestiia,* 29 March–7 April). Peking viewed the tour as a provocation; a PRC spokesman vowed that China would not be intimidated (*Hsin Wan Pao,* Hong Kong, 30 March, in *FBIS,* 3 April). Moscow reponded with a *Pravda* editorial assailing China on the border question and accusing Peking of "obvious distortions" and "deliberately misinforming the world public" (*Pravda,* 1 April).

During April and May, Moscow made several diplomatic moves to defuse tensions, but USSR-PRC relations continued to deteriorate. I. T. Grishin, vice-minister of foreign trade, led a Soviet delegation to Peking and signed an agreement on goods exchange and payments (New China News Agency, Peking, 19 April, in *FBIS,* 20 April). Deputy Foreign Minister Leonid Ilichev returned to Peking for another round of talks on the frontier dispute (Hong Kong AFP, 26 April, in *FBIS,* 26 April). Ilichev had barely got the discussions underway when a new border incident erupted.

Yu Chan, PRC deputy foreign minister, lodged a strong protest over an "organized military provocation" that allegedly took place on 9 May. According to Yu Chan, Soviet military forces had penetrated four kilometers into Chinese territory in Heilungkian and assaulted Chinese civilians. A helicopter, 18 military boats, and about 30 troops were said to be involved in the incursion. (New China News Agency, Peking, 11 May, in *FBIS.*) Obviously anxious to avoid a breakdown of negotiations, Soviet officials described the penetration of Chinese territory as "inadvertent" and issued a formal apology to the PRC (*Izvestiia,* 14 May).

Peking's anger over the latest border incident had not been dissipated when the two nations became embroiled in controversy over Vietnam. Chinese spokesmen blamed the USSR for Vietnam's expulsion of Chinese (*Wen Wei Po,* Hong Kong, 22 May, in *FBIS,* 25 May). The Chinese charged that the Soviets had built a guided missile base in Vietnam directed at China (*NYT,* 1 June). Chinese sources also reported construction of a Soviet naval base to protect the Huangsha islands, held by Vietnam and claimed by China (*Wen Wei Po,* 14 June, in *FBIS,* 16 June). In the developing border clashes between Vietnam and Cambodia, the USSR sided with Vietnam and the PRC with Cambodia; the Soviet and Chinese media engaged in heated exchanges over the issue. With tensions mounting and the talks apparently stalled, Ilichev left Peking in late June (Hong Kong AFP, 29 June, in *FBIS,* 29 June).

Unable to make diplomatic headway with the Chinese, Moscow kept up a steady drumbeat of verbal attacks upon the PRC's policies and leadership. Moscow radio charged that the PRC's "anti-Sovietism" was a means of diverting the Chinese public's attention from domestic crises (Moscow radio, 1 August, in *FBIS,* 3 August). Peking was accused of forming an alliance with the United States against progressive regimes in Africa (Moscow radio, International Service, 3 August, in *FBIS,* 4 August). An "I. Aleksandrov" article in *Pravda* on 4 August accused the PRC of "militarist hysteria" and of "ganging up with the most aggressive forces of imperialism and reaction." *Krasnaya zvezda* attacked the PRC's alleged "falsification of history" in the interest of "Great Han chauvinism" and China's "great-power hegemonist course" (Tass, 4 August). The PRC was also accused of attempting to subjugate Cambodia in order to put pressure on Vietnam and achieve its goal of dominating Southeast Asia (Moscow radio, 3 August).

Moscow expressed intense concern over negotiations between the PRC and Japan on a treaty of peace and friendship. Following completion of the treaty drafting, Soviet spokesmen saw the pact as a Japanese capitulation to "Great Han chauvinism" and charged that the "antihegemony" clause in the treaty was "directed against the Soviet Union" (Moscow radio, 12 August). The Soviets exerted strong diplomatic pressure on the Japanese to prevent ratification of the treaty (*Christian Science Monitor,* 15 August), but Japan refused to yield and the treaty was formally sealed in Tokyo in

October. The establishment of normal U.S.—PRC diplomatic relations on 15 December, caused an obvious concern in Moscow. Although President Carter declared on 19 December that a message received from Leonid Brezhnev conveyed the Soviet leader's understanding of the U.S. policy and was "very positive in tone" (*NYT*, 20 December), a Tass communication published two days later presented the matter differently. According to the Soviet press agency, Brezhnev expressed concern about a passage in the joint Chinese—American communiqué opposing "hegemony," a term perceived as anti-Soviet and already attacked with regard to the PRC—Japanese treaty. The first comments of the Soviet press conveyed Soviet worries in much more direct terms. *Pravda* (19 December) vented its skepticism about President Carter's pledge not to use the new relationship against the Soviet Union, but reserved its strongest disapproval to Chinese leaders:

> Bluntly speaking, this belated act by the United States followed as a result of changes in the orientation of the Peking leadership, which embarked upon a road of open antagonism toward the world of socialism and an alliance with the most bellicose circles of the West.

> We must be wary of Peking's desire to enlist Western support for its hegemonistic plans. This refers particularly to the unusual interest now evinced in some Western countries for Chinese orders of weaponry and technology, the readiness to satisfy Peking's big military appetite.

East Asia. Recently beset by sagging influence in this area, the USSR made vigorous efforts in 1978 aimed at the creation of a new balance of power unfavorable to China. In Southeast Asia, the Soviets offered strong support to Vietnam in its conflict with Cambodia and sought to strengthen ties with Laos. General Ivan G. Pavlovsky, USSR deputy defense minister, headed a Soviet military delegation on a five-day mission to Laos in February (Vientiane radio, 4 February). In a reversal of policy, the USSR gave its support to the Association of Southeast Asian Nations (ASEAN), which includes Thailand, Malaysia, Indonesia, Singapore, and the Philippines (Hong Kong AFP, 7 July). However, Thailand resisted pressures from the USSR for the signing of a cultural agreement (*Nation Review*, Bangkok, 7 July). Soviet President Brezhnev and Vietnamese party Secretary General Le Duan signed a "treaty of friendship and cooperation" between the USSR and the Socialist Republic of Vietnam at the conclusion of a three-day visit by Le Duan to Moscow in early November (Tass, 4 November).

In northeast Asia, the USSR sustained efforts to draw Mongolia and North Korea more fully into the Soviet orbit. But Japan proved intractable and drew further away from the proffered Soviet embrace. At the outset of the year, Moscow called for increased trade between the USSR and Japan (Tass, 5 January) and welcomed Japanese Foreign Minister Sonoda Sunao for a three-day visit (UPI, 12 January). Confronted with Soviet unwillingness to compromise on long-standing territorial disputes, Sonoda refused a Soviet draft of a peace treaty. Thereafter, the USSR concentrated on efforts to prevent signing of the PRC—Japanese treaty, but without success. In August, the projected visit of Deputy Foreign Minister Nikolai Firyubin to Japan was cancelled (*Washington Post*, 24 August).

Europe. V. A. Kirillin, deputy prime minister, headed the USSR delegation at the May meeting of the Anglo-Soviet Permanent Intergovernmental Commission on Scientific, Technical, Trade, and Economic Cooperation in London. The delegation met with Prime Minister James Callaghan, Energy Minister Tony Benn, and other officials. Soviet spokesmen reported "substantial progress" in trade and technical cooperation (*Sotzialisticheskaia industria,* 31 May); *Pravda* called for further development of "all-round Soviet-British cooperation" (*Pravda,* 31 May).

The CPSU continued to oppose strongly the phenomenon of "Eurocommunism," particularly in its Spanish version (Tass, 14 March). However, Moscow supported efforts by the Italian Communist

Party to gain admission to Italy's government and stabilize that country in the wake of Red Brigade terrorism (Moscow radio, 13 March).

Soviet relations with France oscillated considerably during the year. The CPSU and Soviet government assumed a hands-off attitude toward the French parliamentary elections in the spring, but Moscow was sharply critical of French intervention in Zaire to protect European nationals. Brezhnev's visit to Bonn in May was widely viewed not only as a move designed to weaken the FRG's commitment to the anticommunist NATO front but also as a warning to Paris that West Germany might supplant France as Moscow's favored candidate for a "special relationship" in Western Europe. Subsequently, *Pravda* spoke glowingly of Moscow's good relations with Bonn, and Soviet television showed a flattering documentary on West Germany (*Christian Science Monitor,* 8 August.)

Apparently moved by Chinese efforts to establish broad ties with the West, the USSR acted later in the year to thaw cool relations with France. Foreign Minister Gromyko made a three-day visit to Paris in October. At its conclusion, Gromyko stressed the "privileged rleations" between France and the USSR (*Washington Post,* 29 October).

At the invitation of the CPSU Central Committee, a delegation of the Center Party of Finland visited Moscow and Armenia in January (*Pravda,* 1 February). In the same month, Soviet and Swedish cultural societies signed an agreement on cultural exchange in Stockholm (Tass, 29 January). In August, a two-year agreement on cultural exchange was signed by the USSR and the Republic of Cyprus (ibid., 14 August).

Near and Middle East. As Egyptian President Anwar Sadat moved toward a settlement with Israel and established even closer relations with the United States, the USSR stepped up its support for Arab "rejectionist" forces. In June, a delegation of the Democratic Popular Front for the Liberation of Palestine headed by the group's secretary general, Nayif Hawatimah, was given an exceptionally warm reception in Moscow (Moscow radio, 4 June). Meanwhile a coup in Afghanistan had brought a pro-Soviet regime to power in that country, posing a threat to the pro-Western government of the shah in Iran. Despite massive evidence to the contrary, Soviet spokesmen vigorously denied USSR interference in Afghanistan (Tass, 8 August). Widespread antigovernment rioting in Iran produced fears among American officials that the shah's downfall would lead to a pro-Soviet regime in Iran, with "ripple" effect upon Arabic and other Persian Gulf states (AP, 1 November). On 5 December a 20-year "treaty of friendship, good neighborliness and cooperation" was signed in Moscow between the USSR and Afghanistan. It pledges the countries to mutual economic, military and technical aid (*The Washington Post,* 6 December).

India. Anxious to restore the former "special relationship" between the USSR and India, Moscow sent a delegation to New Delhi in August headed by Antenas Bankauskas, deputy chairman of the Supreme Soviet Presidium. The delegation took part in festivities commemorating the thirty-first anniversary of India's independence and the seventh anniversary of the treaty of peace, friendship, and cooperation between India and the USSR (Moscow radio, 7 August).

Africa. The USSR continued to press its drive for expanded influence in various areas of sub-Saharan Africa. In January, CPSU Central Committee Secretary Boris N. Ponomarev met in Moscow with Joshua Nkomo, president of the Zimbabwe African People's Union (Tass, 6 January). Talks between a CPSU delegation and FRELIMO leaders were held in Mozambique in February (Maputo radio, 21 February). Strong support for rebel forces and opposition to "NATO's armed intervention" in Zaire was expressed by the Soviet press in June (Tass, 1 June). Aiming to consolidate its foothold in the Horn of Africa, the USSR further strengthened its ties with Ethiopia. A medical detachment of the Soviet Red Cross was dispatched to Ethiopia in August to provide assistance for victims of that country's protracted drought (ibid., 10 August). The Soviets also signed an agreement to promote merchant shipping between Ethiopia and the USSR (ibid., 9 August). An agreement on cultural and scientific cooperation between Kenya and the USSR was signed in Nairobi in August (Moscow radio, 20 August).

Latin America. In January, Soviet news media strongly encouraged a strike that had practically paralyzed Colombia (*Pravda,* 30 January). However, later in the year, Moscow sought to improve state relations with a visit by a Soviet delegation headed by USSR deputy president Kuznetsov to attend the inauguration of Colombia's new president, Julio César Turbay Ayala (Moscow Domestic Service, 5 August). Kuznetsov also visited Venezuela and Panama, where he conferred with Venezuelan President Carlos Andres Pérez and Panamanian President Omar Torrijos (Tass, 8 August). Moscow continued to be sharply critical of the military dictatorships in Chile and Argentina but during the year displayed a more conciliatory attitude toward the authoritarian regimes in Bolivia and Brazil.

International Party Contacts. The CPSU continued its efforts to maintain and expand contacts with communist movements of varied ideological persuasions. Coordination of these activities was mainly the responsibility of Boris N. Ponomarev, Central Committee secretary for nonruling communist parties, and Konstantin V. Rusakov, CPSU Central Committee secretary for ruling communist parties. These CPSU officials were required to perform a real balancing act in view of the obvious contradictions between "proletarian internationalism" and world communist unity, between Moscow's opposition to "Eurocommunism" and the electoral interests of European communist parties, and between Moscow's hegemony in Eastern Europe and the domestic political pressures confronting communist leaders in that area.

A meeting of secretaries of ten ruling communist parties was held in Budapest from 27 February to 1 March. In addition to the CPSU, the parties of Bulgaria, Cuba, Czechoslovakia, the GDR, Hungary, Mongolia, Poland, and Romania were officially represented. A secretary of the Vietnamese Communist Party attended as an observer. Attention was focused on "the role of the mass media in present-day international policy." The participants pledged solidarity with "the just struggle of the communist, progressive, revolutionary, and national-liberation forces" (*WMR,* May). Boris Ponomarev led a CPSU delegation to the international theoretical conference on the theme "Construction of Socialism and Communism and World Progress." It was held in Sofia on 12–15 December, attended by seventy-three communist and workers parties, and sponsored jointly by the Bulgarian CP and the *World Marxist Review* (Radio Sofia, 12 December).

CPSU Central Committee Secretary Mikhail A. Suslov was awarded the Order of Karl Marx at a ceremony in Moscow in January attended by CPSU and East German officials. The ceremony was initiated by the German party Politburo and the State Council of the GDR (Moscow Domestic Service, 11 January). Also in January, Nacho Papazov, a member of the secretariat of the Bulgarian party, discussed furthering of USSR-Bulgarian cultural ties in a meeting with CPSU Secretary Rusakov in Moscow (*Pravda,* 26 January).

CPSU General Secretary Brezhnev made a lengthy visit to Czechoslovakia in June for discussions with Czechoslovak party leader Gustav Husák and other officials. The visit reportedly strengthened the ties between the Soviet and Czechoslovak parties and governments (*Pravda* and *Izvestiia,* 1 and 3 June).

CPSU Central Committee Secretary and Politburo member Fedor D. Kulakov headed the Soviet delegation to the congress of the League of Yugoslav Communists in Belgrade in June (Tass, 20 June). Kulakov delivered a major speech at a rally in Smederevo (Moscow radio, 21 June) and was received by Yugoslav President Tito. Soviet spokesmen described the talk with Tito as "cordial and friendly" (Tass, 20 June).

USSR Defense Minister Dimitri F. Ustinov sent greetings to the Polish armed forces on the thirty-fourth anniversary of the liberation of Poland (*Krasnaya zvezda,* 22 July). Moscow City CPSU secretary and V. F. Promyslov, Moscow's mayor, also dispatched congratulations to their Warsaw counterparts (*Moskovskaya pravda,* 22 July).

Brezhnev conferred with Romanian party leader and chief of state Nicolae Ceauşescu in the Crimea on 7 August. The meeting was reportedly devoted to discussion of "the prospects for developing the diverse ties between the CPSU and the RCP, between the Soviet and Romanian peoples" and to "foreign-policy questions." Tass said that the meeting passed in a "frank and friendly atmosphere" (Tass, 7 August). Visits of the PRC chairman Hua Kuo-feng to Romania and Yugoslavia in August elicited strong criticism in the Soviet press. In mid-October, Andrei Gromyko paid a three-day visit to Bucharest in an apparent attempt to influence Romania's foreign policy. However, by the end of November Romania challenged the discipline of the Warsaw Pact Alliance by refusing, at the Moscow meeting of the leaders of the Warsaw Pact, the proposed increase in military spending and tighter unification of the Pact's military command. (*Associated Press,* 29 November.) In several public speeches in Romania, Ceauşescu reiterated Romania's position, explaining that increased military expenditures would threaten the implementation of domestic programs devised to raise the living standard. He also declared that "the Romanian army will only take orders from the supreme party and state bodies, and at the call of the people, and that it will never receive orders from outside" (Radio Bucharest, 1 December). At the same time, in an apparent gesture to Moscow, Ceauşescu appealed for "socialist unity" and pledged to work for "collaboration, friendship, and solidarity" among the communist countries. Soviet initial reaction to Romania's behavior was restrained. Still, *Pravda* (16 December) attacked a Romanian speaker at Sofia's conference of the communist parties of 73 countries, accusing him of "underestimating the military danger posed by the West and for opposing a denunciation of China."

Armando Hart Dávalos, member of the Cuban party Politburo and Cuban minister of culture, conferred with Piotr N. Demichev, alternate member of the CPSU Politburo and USSR minister of culture, in Moscow in January (*Pravda,* 27 January). Hart also addressed a group of Soviet intellectuals (Havana radio, 6 February). Isidore M. Peoli, member of the Cuban party Politburo and Cuban foreign minister, visited Moscow 18−24 April (*Pravda,* 25 April). A Soviet delegation headed by Belorussian Party chief Piotr M. Masherov took part in festivities commemorating the twenty-fifth anniversary of the beginning of the Cuban revolution in Havana in July (Moscow radio, 31 July).

Pedro Antonio Saad, secretary general of the Ecuadorian Communist Party, toured Armenia in April at the invitation of the Armenian Communist Party (*Yerevan kommunist,* 14 April).

A delegation of the Vietnamese Communist Party visited Moscow in August to participate in activities commemorating the twentieth anniversary of the Soviet-Vietnamese Friendship Society (*Krasnaya zvezda,* 2 August). A Laotian delegation headed by Lao People's Revolutionary Party Politburo member Sisomphon Lovansai visited Moscow in August (Tass, 3 August). Amid growing Soviet-Cambodian hostility, the Supreme Soviet, instead of the CPSU, dispatched a congratulatory message to Phnom Penh on Cambodia's National Day; the message was brief and highly formal (Phnom Penh Domestic Service, 22 April).

Mongolia awarded its Order of Victory to CPSU General Secretary Brezhnev in February (MONTSAME, Ulan Bator, 22 February, in *FBIS,* 23 February). Mongolian party chief Yumzhagin Tsedenbal sent a congratulatory message to Brezhnev, Kosygin, and Ustinov on the occasion of the sixtieth anniversary of the Soviet armed forces (ibid.)

Dinmukhamed A. Kunaev, Kazakhstan party first secretary, headed a Soviet delegation to Pyongyang in January. The delegation was received by Korean party leader Kim Il-sung, who was awarded the Order of Lenin by Kunaev (*FBIS,* 23 January).

CPSU Central Committee Secretary Vladimir I. Dolgikh headed a delegation which visited Portugal for conversations with Portuguese party leader Alvaro Cunhal and other officials in May (Tass, 7 May). Viktor G. Afanasyev, editor of *Pravda* and a member of the CPSU Central Committee, led a Soviet delegation which attended the Ninth Congress of the Spanish Communist Party (PCE) in Madrid in April (*Le Monde*, 25 April). Enrico Berlinguer, secretary general of the Italian CP, visited Moscow on 6–9 October at the invitation of the CPSU Central Committee. He had talks with Brezhnev, Suslov, and Ponomarev, which Radio Moscow (9 October) qualified as "friendly, comradely." The communiqué, issued at the end of his visit, emphasized "a joint concern over the slowing down of détente and international cooperation" (blaming this on "certain imperialist, militarist and reactionary circles"), advocated "real measures aimed at preventing an intensification of the arms race," and pledged "full solidarity with the struggle of the peoples of Asia, Africa and Latin America for national and social emancipation." Referring to the situation in Western Europe, the communiqué approved "cooperation between the communists, the socialists and the social democrats, and other democratic forces, including Christian ones" aiming at "strengthening the processes of détente and cooperation between states with different social systems" (Tass in English, 9 October).

The Tenth Congress of the Communist Party of Greece in May was attended by a Soviet delegation headed by CPSU Central Committee Secretary Konstantin U. Chernenko, who delivered an address to the congress (Tass, 16 May).

Leningrad party First Secretary Grigori V. Romanov led the Soviet delegation at the Eighteenth Congress of the Finnish Communist Party, held in Helsinki in June (Moscow Domestic Service, 4 June).

The Eleventh Congress of the Communist Party of India in March was attended by a CPSU delegation headed by Geidar A. Aliev, alternate Politburo member and first secretary of the Azerbaidzhan party (Tass, 28 March).

Publications. The main CPSU organs are the daily newspaper *Pravda* (circulation more than eleven million), the theoretical and ideological journal *Kommunist* (appearing seventeen times a year, circulation more than one million), and the twice-monthly *Partiinaia zhizn',* a journal of internal party affairs and organizational matters (circulation more than 1.16 million). *Kommunist vooruzhennikh sil* is the party theoretical journal for the armed forces, and *Agitator* is the journal for party propagandists; both appear twice a month. The Komsomol has a newspaper, *Komsomolskaia pravda* (six days a week), a monthly theoretical journal, *Molodoi kommunist,* and a monthly literary journal, *Molodaia gvardia.* Each USSR republic prints similar party newspapers in local languages and usually also in Russian. Specialized publications issued under supervision of the CPSU Central Committee include the newspapers *Sovetskaia rossiia, Selskaia zhizn', Sotzialisticheskaia industria, Sovetskaia kultura,* and *Ekonomicheskaia gazeta* and the journal *Politicheskoye samoobrazovaniie.*

University of New Orleans   R. Judson Mitchell

Yugoslavia

Yugoslav Communists date the beginning of their party back to April 1919 when a "unification congress" in Belgrade established a Socialist Workers' Party of Yugoslavia (Communists), including both communist and noncommunist elements. This party was disbanded in June 1920, and a Communist Party of Yugoslavia (CPY) was formed. At its Sixth Congress, in November 1952, the name was changed to the League of Communists of Yugoslavia (Savez komunista Jugoslavije; LCY). The LCY is the only political party in the Socialist Federal Republic of Yugoslavia (SFRY) and exercises power through its leading role in the Socialist Alliance of the Working People of Yugoslavia (Socijalistički savez radnog naroda Jugoslavije; SAWPY), a front organization that includes all the mass political organizations as well as individuals representing various social groups.

On 1 January 1978 the LCY claimed a membership of 1,629,082 (*Borba,* 10 February) whose nationality composition was as follows: Serbs, 790,344 (or 48.68 percent); Croats, 244,046 (15.04 percent); Muslims, 105,589 (6.51 percent); Macedonians, 101,547 (6.26 percent); Slovenes, 95,305 (5.88 percent); Montenegrins, 94,620 (5.84 percent); "Yugoslavs" 90,732 (5.59 percent); Albanians, 59,501 (3.67 percent); Hungarians, 21,280 (1.31 percent). (*Večernji list,* Zagreb, 14 August.)

According to an official estimate of 1 July 1978, Yugoslavia had 21,968,000 inhabitants (*Večernje novosti,* Belgrade, 30 July), which means that 7.42 percent were LCY members.

Leadership and Organization. The supreme bodies of the LCY are the 166-member Central Committee and its 24-member Presidium (23 plus Tito, LCY president for life). The Eleventh Congress of the LCY (see below) abolished the twelve-member Executive Committee. Instead, nine members of the Central Committee were elected executive secretaries without belonging to the party Presidium.

Auxiliary and Mass Organizations. The SAWPY has 13,000,000 members (*Komunist,* 6 February), compared with the 8,000,000 recorded in 1975 (*Politika,* 20 November 1975). The supreme body of the SAWPY is the Federal Conference (FC), the president of which is the Serb Todo Kurtović (b. 1919) elected in May (*Borba,* 27 May). The executive branch of the FC is the 51-member Presidium. The SAWPY's main publication is the daily *Borba.*

The Confederation of Trade Unions of Yugoslavia (Savez sindikata Jugoslavije; CTUY) held its Eighth Congress in Belgrade on 21−23 November, attended by 1,363 delegates. In 1978 the CTUY had a total membership of about 6,000,000 (ibid., 26 August). The Croat Mika Špiljak (b. 1916) was reelected president of the CTUY, while Rade Galeb (b. 1927), a Serb, and Janez Braborič (b. 1931), a Slovene, were elected vice-presidents (*Vjesnik,* 25 November). The new CTUY Presidium includes 31 members. The new CTUY statutes provide for a "new concept of the political and organizational structure of trade unions" (ibid.). The daily *Rad* (Labor) is the CTUY's official publication.

The League of Socialist Youth of Yugoslavia (Savez socijalističke omladine Jugoslavije; LSYY) has, according to the latest official statistics, "about 3,610,000 members organized in 35,500 basic organizations of the LSYY" (*Borba,* 8 December). Of 3,610,000 members of the LSYY only 608,369 were party members in the first half of this year (ibid.). Between 13 and 15 December, the Tenth Congress of the LSYY took place in Belgrade. Azem Vlasi, a student of Albanian origin and president of the LSYY, opened the congress, which was attended by 1,450 delegates, 250 guests from Yugoslavia, and 160 guests from abroad. In his message of greetings, Tito called upon young people to develop "the love for freedom and independence, socialism and self-management" (*Borba,* 14 December). In his speech, Vlasi proposed that Tito's idea of a "collective leadership" at all levels in Yugoslavia should be adopted also into the LSYY, which means that presidents of the organization should rotate annually. A Slovene, Lev Kreft (b. 1951), professor of philosophy at Ljubljana, was elected the new LSYY president. His deputy is a Macedonian, Vasil Tupurkovski (b. 1951), an assistant professor at the Skoplje Law Faculty. The Presidium of the LSYY is composed of 41 members, while the secretariat has 10 members elected from among the Presidium members. The secretary is Darko Myrvoš (b. 1953) of Croatia, who gave his nationality as Yugoslav (*Politika,* 16 December). The main LSYY publication is the weekly *Mladost* (Youth).

Party Internal Affairs. Between 3 April and 31 May, six republican party congresses and two provincial party conferences were held in Yugoslavia, while from 20–23 June the Eleventh Congress of the LCY took place in Belgrade.

Congresses of Republics and Provinces. The Slovenian LC held its congress 3–5 April; the Croatian LC and the Montenegrin LC 24–26 April; the Macedonian LC 25–27 April; the Vojvodina LC 26–28 April; the Bosnian-Herzegovinan LC and the Kosovo LC 9–11 May; and the Serbian LC 29–31 May.

Even though the party congresses and conferences in the republics and autonomous provinces concentrated primarily on local issues, their chief concern was with preparations for the Eleventh LCY Congress. In all the main reports read by the presidents of the central and provincial committees, loyalty to President Tito and to the central party in Belgrade was emphasized, as were pledges that everything would be done to help the central party authorities in their efforts to bring about a full-fledged stabilization of party ranks at all levels.

As far as personnel changes are concerned, the republican and provincial party organizations have been rejuvenated to a certain extent. In Slovenia, both the president of the Central Committee (Franc Popit; b. 1921) and the secretary of the Central Committee Presidium (Franc Šetinc; b. 1929) were reelected; in Croatia, Mme. Milka Planinc (b. 1924) was reelected president of the Central Committee, and Milutin Baltić (a Serb; b. 1910) was elected secretary; in Montenegro, Vojo Srzentić b. 1934) was reelected president of the Central Committee, and Vuko Vukadinović (b. 1937) was elected secretary of the Central Committee Presidium; in Macedonia, both Angel Čemerski (b. 1923; president of the Central Committee) and Boro Denkov (b. 1937; secretary of the Central Committee Presidium) were reelected; in Vojvodina, Dušan Alimpić (b. 1921) was reelected president of the Central Committee, while Boško Krunić (b. 1929) was elected secretary; in Bosnia-Herzegovina, both the president and the secretary are new—Nikola Stojanović (a Serb; b. 1933) was elected the new president of the Central Committee, while Hrvoje Ištuk (a Croat; b. 1935) was elected secretary; in Kosovo, Mahmut Bakalli (b. 1936) was reelected president of the Central Committee, while Petar Matić (a Serb) was elected the new secretary; finally, in Serbia, Dr. Tihomir Vlaškalić (b. 1923) was reelected president of the Central Committee, while Špiro Galović (b. 1938) was elected the new secretary. All these persons are known to be loyal to Tito and the central party apparatus.

The Eleventh LCY Congress. Tito opened the Eleventh LCY Congress in the presence of 2,283 delegates with voting rights (eight were reported sick), 119 foreign delegates, and several hundred guests from Yugoslavia. The Eastern European communist parties (with the exception of the Albanian) sent representatives; the Soviet party's delegation was headed by Fedor D. Kulakov, a member of the Politburo and a secretary of the Central Committee of the Communist Party of the Soviet Union (CPSU). The Chinese Communist Party sent only official greetings, which were received enthusiastically; Vietnam did not send either a delegation or greetings. The greatest applause at the congress was accorded to Enrico Berlinguer, leader of the Italian Communist Party.

In his one-hour speech, a phonographic record of which was distributed to all delegates (*NYT,* 24 June), Tito praised the stability of Yugoslavia over the past 30 years. He talked about the "deep crisis of capitalism" and of the irrepressible advance of socialism. Immediately afterwards he extolled the different roads to socialism and deplored conflicts between various socialist forces. Tito praised the policy of nonalignment highly and complained that attempts were being made to incite conflicts between nonaligned countries. In this connection, he mentioned the situation in Africa. Discussing the state of the international communist movement, Tito stressed that a respect for independence and equality has to be observed and criticized what he called attempts to reimpose "old and obsolete relations" on other communist parties. He hailed the results of the June 1976 East Berlin conference of European communist parties at which "a free exchange of opinion" had taken place. (*Borba,* 21 June.)

Tito commended highly the "great foreign political successes" of Yugoslavia and stressed that Belgrade had maintained relations with all the countries of the world. As far as Yugoslavia's future is concerned, he said that speculation about this was "nonsensical" and pledged that the country and party would continue their present political course. In the country itself, there had been some "technocratic resistance" and mistakes had been made, especially in the economic sphere. He mentioned an unfavorable foreign trade balance as one of the most important problems and also spoke about unemployment and the need for young people to be helped in finding jobs. Tito also hailed the country's armed forces, which are now better prepared "than ever before" to confront any aggressor and defend the country's independence and sovereignty. Concerning party life, Tito stressed the importance of the teachings of Marxism and the necessity that democratic centralism remain the basis for all party activities, especially in view of the fact that 71 percent of the party members were young people. He suggested that "a greater number of candidates" should compete for party offices, this being the only way to prevent a specific number of individuals keeping party jobs longer than necessary. Finally, he spoke about party unity, which he claimed to have been an element contributing to its "naked survival." (Ibid.)

Proceedings at the Congress. After the opening session the congress continued its work in six commissions: (a), Development of Self-managing Socioeconomic Relationships and Material and Social Development; (b), Development of the Political System of the Socialist Self-managing Democracy; (c), Ideological-Political and Organizational Development, the Cadre and Action Training of the LCY, and Statutory Questions; (d), Questions of Socialist Transformation of Education, Science, and Culture; (e), Questions of International Relations and Yugoslavia's Foreign Policy; and (f), Questions of Nationwide Defense and Social Self-protection (*Politika,* Belgrade, 21 June). None of the speeches delivered at the commissions' sessions revealed anything new about the attitudes of the Yugoslav party as a whole.

Unlike the May 1974 Tenth Congress, at which a dozen resolutions were adopted, the Eleventh Congress approved only two: The Role of the Tasks of the LCY in the Struggle for the Development of Socialist Self-management and for the Material and Social Progress of the Country; and the LCY in the Struggle for Peace, Equal International Cooperation, and Socialism in the World (*Vjesnik,* Zagreb, 24 June). Both resolutions were explained by Stane Dolanc. He spoke especially about "various roads to socialism" and stressed that the Yugoslav party would continue to oppose all attempts designed "to proclaim one's own experiences in constructing socialism as universally valid." In the second resolution itself it was emphasized that everything must be done to prevent "the imposition of somebody else's experience as generally valid, as well as somebody else's nationalistic tendencies." (*Borba,* 24 June.) The second resolution had special praise for "the role and the influence of some communist parties in Western Europe and Japan" and emphasized that the LCY considered it "urgent to have a discussion among communist parties concerning all essential problems in the struggle for socialism." According to the resolution, the LCY will support "only those meetings [of communist parties and movements] which make it possible for all progressive forces to take part in them and conduct a free democratic exchange of opinions, without issuing any obligatory documents; no meetings will be recognized whose aim is to institutionalize the [international communist] movement and to restrict it into small narrow groups." (Ibid.)

Both resolutions as well as Dolanc's interpretations of them attracted the particular interest of the CPSU delegation to the congress. A speech delivered by Fedor Kulakov in a Serbian town on 21 June revealed at least four points over which there have been differences between Moscow and Belgrade: (a), the interpretation of the idea of "proletarian solidarity"; (b), the interpretation of "democratic centralism"; (c), the role of nonaligned countries; and (d), the status of Yugoslav-Soviet relations in general (Tass, in Russian, 21 June).

The second resolution of the congress, in which "the denial of the rights of the Macedonian national minority in Bulgaria" was attacked as being contrary "to the United Nations Charter and the Helsinki European Security Conference's Final Act," led to strong Bulgarian objections. The head of the Bulgarian party delegation to the LCY congress declared that his group had complained to Yugoslav leaders that the allegations were contrary to history because in Bulgaria "there has never been and there is not at present a Macedonian national minority." He also said that apart from "tendentious evaluations and unfounded accusations" made from the rostrum of the congress, the Yugoslav press had reached what he described as "the absurd conclusion" that Bulgaria aspired to appropriate parts of Yugoslav territory. He said that the 15 June speech of Bulgarian party leader Todor Zhivkov should be recalled. Zhivkov had stated in a speech delivered in Blagoevgrad, the capital of Pirin Macedonia, that Sofia was ready to sign a treaty with Yugoslavia renouncing territorial claims and proclaiming the inviolability of frontiers. Belgrade, according to the Bulgarian delegate, had so far not responded or even told the public of Zhivkov's offer (Bulgarian Telegraphic Agency, in English, 24 June).

New Party Bodies. Before the congress closed, the delegates approved the election of a new 165-member Central Committee (Tito being the 166th), 96 of whom are newcomers to the top party leadership. The six republican parties were entitled to twenty members each; the two provincial parties to fifteen members each; and the remaining fifteen came from the LCY organization in the army.

At its first session on 23 June, the new Central Committee confirmed the election of 23 (Tito being the 24th) members of the new Central Committee Presidium (*Borba,* 24 June) with the following composition: for the Slovenian LC, Edvard Kardelj (b. 1910), Stane Dolanc (b. 1925), and Franc Popit; for the Serbian LC, Petar Stambolić (b. 1912), Miloš Minić (b. 1914), and Dr. Tihomir Vlaškalić; for the Montenegrin LC, Vidoje Žarković (b. 1927), Veselin Djuranović (b. 1925), and Vojo Srzentić; for the Macedonian LC, Lazar Koliševski (b. 1914), Aleksandar Grličkov (b. 1923), and Angel Čemerski; for the Croatian LC, Dr. Vladimir Bakarić (b. 1912), Dr. Dušan Dragosavac (b. 1919), and Mme. Milka Planinc; for the Bosnian-Herzegovinan LC, Branko Mikulić (b. 1928), Cvijetin Mijatović (b. 1913), and Nikola Stojanović; for the Vojvodina LC, Stevan Doronjski (b. 1919) and Dušan Alimpić; for the Kosovo LC, Fadil Hodža (b.1910) and Mahmut Bakalli; and for the army, General Nikola Ljubičić (b. 1914).

The streamlining of the Central Committee Presidium, i.e., the reduction of its size from 48 to 24 members, reflects a conscious effort to keep the supreme policy-making power, on both the state and party levels, in the same hands. In fact all nine members of the SFRY presidency are also members of the LCY Presidium. These collective arrangements were made in order to ensure a smooth succession, as Tito himself explained even before the Eleventh LCY Congress: "We have established the Presidency so that we may insure ourselves against trouble even when I no longer hold that post. . . . We are doing all we can that nothing will change" (from an interview with James Reston, *NYT*, 3 March). With an identical intention, the new Central Committee Presidium was designed to form "a central core of authority in a highly diffuse system and . . . a kind of collective leadership to guarantee continuity in the eventual post-Tito period" (*Financial Times*, London, 23 June). Moreover, "all but four members of the Presidium are former Partisans, and President Tito continues to rely exclusively on this group to fill the positions closest to him" (*NYT*, 24 June).

The nationality composition of the Central Committee Presidium is as follows: nine Serbs, four Croats, three Slovenes, three Montenegrins, three Macedonians, and two Albanians. No changes were made in the list approved in advance by Tito, which means that for the next four years the Slav Muslims (1,500,000 of whom live in the Socialist Republic of Bosnia-Herzegovina as a separate nationality) will not be represented in the supreme party body even though they have almost 87,000 party members. In comparison, some 400,000 Montenegrins with only 60,000 party members have three full members in the Yugoslav Presidium.

Stane Dolanc (see Biographies, p. 450) was elected secretary of the Presidium, while the following nine members of the LCY Central Committee were elected executive secretaries: Milojko Drulović (b. 1924, Serbian LC); Pavle Gaži (b. 1927; Croatian LC); Trpe Jakovlevski (b. 1925; Macedonian LC); Vlado Janžič (b. 1936, Slovenian LC); Marko Orlandić, (Montenegrin LC); Ferhad Kotorić (b. 1934; Bosnian-Herzegovinan LC); Nandor Major (b. 1931; Vojvodina LC); Djuro Trbović (b. 1931; Kosovo LC); and General Milan Daljević (b. 1925; Army LC). These are not members of the Presidium but will work under Stane Dolanc and be "liaison officers" between the top Yugoslav party body and the republican and provincial parties.

The New LCY Statutes. The new party statutes adopted at the Eleventh Congress provide party members "who have remained in a minority" with the right to defend their views but at the same time point out their obligation "to accept and carry out decisions adopted by the majority." According to Section 15 of the new statutes, such members are not permitted to engage in any "factional activity," even though they are allowed to present their views regarding the decisions adopted "in the organizations and agencies whose members they are, rather than outside them" (*Komunist*, Belgrade, special supplement, 27 March).

Even though the position of the LCY president has always been extremely strong, the new statutes strengthen that position even more. This is reflected in the order in which the party organs are listed: (a), Congress of the LCY; (b), LCY President; (c) LCY Central Committee; (d), Central Committee Presidium; (e), Statutory Commission; and (f), Control Commission. In the old party statutes the LCY president was placed fourth after the Congress, the Central Committee, and the Central Committee Presidium. The president of the LCY is also given greater rights over political activities, which can only refer to Tito's successor rather than to Tito himself, since his authority has always been unchallenged. Finally, the party statutes provide for Tito's party chairmanship for life. (Ibid.)

The New Standing Rules of the Presidium. In October the Presidium adopted its standing rules (SR) concerning "the organization" of this supreme body of the party. The SR contain 69 articles, based on Article 85 of the party statutes. According to Article 1 of the SR, "the Presidium is a collective, democratic, and political body in which all its members have the same rights and responsibility for its entire work in all areas of its activities" (ibid., 10 November). In addition to the LCY president, who is the unchallenged ruler of the party, the SR provide for a new office:

"chairman of the Presidium," who is authorized "to prepare and convoke the Presidium's sessions following an agreement with, and authorization by, the LCY president and in cooperation with the secretary and other members of the Presidium." The SR also make it possible for "the Presidium to meet with a restricted number of members" [uži sastanci], which means that not all 24 members must necessarily be present at every session. After such meetings, however, the full session of the Presidium must be informed of the subjects they discussed. The number two person is the secretary of the Presidium (now Stane Dolanc), who "shall devote himself to executing the decisions made by the Presidium." The first chairman of the Presidium, elected on 19 October, is Branko Mikulić, a Croat party functionary from Bosnia-Herzegovina. He is going to deputize for President Tito for a period of one year. After that, the chairman of the Presidium will be elected annually, always in rotation from another republic or autonomous province. (Ibid.)

On 19 December the Central Committee of the LCY held its second session in Belgrade under the chairmanship of Mikulić. The major report was read by Vladimir Bakarić who attacked the "opposition groups from the past with which we have had open and public conflicts." In this connection, he mentioned Milovan Djilas and some "nationalistic groups" in Croatia who were attempting to establish contacts and find a common language. Bakarić also attacked "anti-Yugoslav émigré terrorists" being helped by "certain reactionary circles" in the West. (See also "Hostile Forces" and Political Trials section, below.) Mikulić also delivered a speech that was then followed by a general debate during which the Kosovo leader Mahmut Bakalli discussed "a number of new and very harsh attacks on Yugoslavia by most responsible leaders of Albania" (Politika, 20 December). The Central Committee approved the recent decisions passed by the CC Presidium, especially the idea of "collective leadership" at all levels.

LCY's Ideological Problems. As indicated previously (see *YICA, 1978,* pp. 94−95), it was Edvard Kardelj's book *Roads of Development of the Socialist Self-management Political System* which served as the basis for the discussion—both prior to and after the Eleventh Congress—about the "new role" to be played by the party. In Kardelj's book one finds so many of the theses which Milovan Djilas advanced in 1952−54 (i.e., before he was purged in January 1954) that one might also regard Kardelj's book as a kind of ideological rehabilitation of Djilas. In his book Kardelj writes: "The LCY is less able than ever to hold any political monopoly or to govern society by itself . . . Therefore, the LCY must not be a kind of commanding force outside the system of self-management, nor should it pull the strings operating the system without taking responsibility for it, although there are many in this country who would like to see it do so." (pp. 180−181.)

Kardelj writes that the LCY has reached a turning point: "Either the party will act as a motive force for the great majority of people, who directly control their own and social labor . . . or else the party will be a small bureaucratic minority, divorced from the masses, which, while ruling ostensibly on behalf of the working class, would actually be ruling over this class and over the entire nation by controlling the government apparatus and technocratic structures" (p. 180). At this point Kardelj comes to the conclusion that the party "is less able than ever to hold any political monopoly or to govern society by itself" (ibid.). For this reason Kardelj returned to the idea, included in the Yugoslav party program of April 1958, that instead of a one-party system or a multiparty system "a nonparty system" should develop (*Socijalizam,* Belgrade, no. 11, November 1966). All this should happen "via the Socialist Alliance as its political framework." In his major speech at the Eleventh Congress, Tito required "greater independence" for the Socialist Alliance and other organizations" (*Socialist Thought and Practice,* Belgrade, no. 6, June), while Kardelj, although also insisting on front organizations being "autonomous in their activities and responsible to their membership," immediately stressed that this did not mean that "they can be independent of other guiding factors of socialist consciousness," i.e., of the party (Kardelj, op. cit., p. 184). This is how Kardelj and other

Yugoslav theoreticians contradict themselves by claiming that the party is both to rule and yet not be dominant. Consequently, the main argument of Kardelj's book appears to be that "pluralism of interests" must exist but that the existence of different parties is prohibited. Instead of different political parties, the various "mass organizations" should be given greater independence but remain under the control of the party.

The Thirteenth Anniversary of the Cominform: 1948—78. The failure to mention the 1948 conflict with the Cominform at either the party congress or during Hua Kuo-feng's visit to Yugoslavia in August (see below) was a surprise, indicating that the Yugoslav leaders were trying to avoid any new deterioration in their relations with Moscow. Still, in a speech on 7 September before Slovenian party officials in Ljubljana, Tito dealt with the Cominform affair, this time in connection with Hua's visit to Belgrade. Criticizing the Soviet media for their hostile attitude toward Hua's visit, Tito said he was told by the Chinese leader that in 1973 Mao, in a statement made "to an inner circle," had emphasized "that Yugoslavia was right in 1948," but at that time Mao did not want to state this publicly, "out of regard for the prevailing atmosphere between China and the Soviet Union" (*Vjesnik,* 9 September).

Domestic Affairs. *Elections— The "System of Delegations."* With the convocation of the new Assembly of the SFRY on 15 May and the presentation of a new federal government (officially called the Federal Executive Council) on 16 May, a five-month electoral procedure drew to an end. About one million delegates were elected to communal assemblies, to assemblies of intermunicipal communities, to assemblies in the republics and autonomous provinces, as well as to the two chambers of the Federal Assembly in Belgrade. In addition, during March and April millions of Yugoslav citizens were called on to elect delegations to and delegates for about 21,000 basic organizations of associated labor (BOAL) which include enterprises and institutions, local communities, social organizations (such as the LCY, the Socialist Alliance of the Working People, and trade unions), the armed forces, private artisans, and private farmers. The BOAL encompasses about 5.5 million people (*Politika,* 4 March).

The elections began in January when Yugoslav citizens were invited to register the names of people who, in their opinion, deserved to be included in the lists of candidates for various delegations. About 2.5 million people were registered. From these about one million delegates for more than 100,000 delegations at all levels were elected. The trade unions in BOAL and the Socialist Alliance in the citizens' communities were in charge of organizing nomination and election meetings.

In February 1974 the Yugoslav Federal Assembly adopted a new constitution which provided for a new electoral system called the "system of delegations." This unique system replaced the old "bourgeois-type" parliamentary system. The new electoral system enables party officials to dominate completely the elected representatives, who are now called delegates.

The communal, intermunicipal, provincial, and republican assemblies are divided into three chambers: chamber of associated labor, chamber of local communities, and sociopolitical chamber. The Assembly of the SFRY has only two chambers—the Federal Chamber with 220 delegates (30 delegates from each of the six republics and 20 delegates from each of the two autonomous provinces, all elected by communal assemblies) and the Chamber of Republics and Autonomous Provinces with 88 delegates (12 delegates sent to Belgrade by each of the six republics and eight from each of the two autonomous provinces).

The basis for the delegations' activities has been the idea of "imperative mandate," i.e., the rule that individual delegates or complete delegations are obliged to follow the instructions given to them by "their basic organizations" rather than being allowed to make their own decisions. In this way, the authors of the electoral law anticipated that the party could easily recall people trying to march along their own road. All the delegates to the SFRY Assembly were known in advance. The same was the case with the "election" of members to the Assembly's presidency, as well as those chosen to be members of the government. Thus, for instance, it was known many weeks in advance that the Serb Dragoslav Marković (b. 1920) would be elected the new president of the SFRY Assembly. The new president of the Federal Chamber of the Assembly is the Montenegrin Dobroslav Ćulafić (b. 1926), while the Slovene Zoran Polič (b. 1912) was reelected to the post of president of the Chamber of the Republics and Autonomous Provinces.

The post of Yugoslav prime minister is retained by Veselin Djuranović (b. 1925), a Montenegrin, who one year earlier replaced Džemal Bijedić, who had died in an airplane crash in Bosnia. Yugoslavia's new foreign minister is the Croat Josip Vrhovec (b. 1926) while General Nikola Ljubičić (a Serb) was reappointed the country's defense minister. The Croat general, Franjo Herljević (b. 1915), was reappointed Yugoslavia's minister for internal affairs and chief of all the police forces (*Borba,* 17 May).

"Hostile forces" and Political Trials. Despite the stability that characterized Yugoslavia's political life in 1978, the activities of "hostile forces" were strongly attacked by the top LCY leaders. The most specific attacker was the secretary of the Croatian LC Central Committee, Milutin Baltić, who in a public speech in Zagreb warned against "the continued, very aggressive activities of certain nationalist elements." He assailed in particular Milovan Djilas, accusing him of traveling to Zagreb and meeting there with Croatian "nationalist protagonists," i.e., the people who have recently been released from jails after serving sentences in connection with the 1971 events in Croatia (ibid., 24 September). The existence of such an "oppositional rail Zagreb-Belgrade" (*see Süddeutsche Zeitung,* Munich, 26 July) was confirmed in an interview which the well-known Yugoslav dissident, Mihajlo Mihajlov, gave in Paris to the daily *Le Matin* (4–5 November). Mihajlov stated that "since last spring, unity has been effected between the Serbian and Croatian dissidents. Opposition to the dictatorship is their cementing element. The understanding [was] reached among the opposition around Djilas, who himself comes from Montenegro."

Displeasure of Croatian authorities was also manifest after the publication of the 15 June issue of the organ of Croatian university students, *Studentski list,* commemorating in a favorable and nostalgic manner the anniversary of the 1968 student unrest. An editorial in the same paper was entitled "Ten Years of Manipulation." Baltić characterized it as "a hostile position toward this society, toward the League of Communists and its policy" (ibid.).

Besides being linked to Djilas, the most prominent living Serbian novelist (and former high-level party official), Dobrica Ćosić, was criticized in strong terms after the publication of his address on the occasion of his admission to the Serbian Academy of Arts and Sciences. He was accused for writing from the position of "greater Serbian nationalism," for falsely depicting the essence of the Partisan-Chetnik conflict during the last war, and for mystifying Serbian history by interpreting it in a "bourgeois manner" (*Politika,* 12 November). Another noted Serbian poet, Tanasije Mladenović, a party member since before the war, addressed on 4 April a bitter letter of criticism to Josip Vrhovec (who on 16 May became Yugoslavia's foreign minister), complaining about being persecuted because of his alleged "greater Serbian nationalism" (*Radio Free Europe Research,* 30 May).

Throughout the year the Yugoslav press devoted much space and used harsh terms to attack the political emigrés and their activities abroad. The issue of terrorism soured relations between Yugoslavia and the Federal Republic of Germany. In September, the West German government refused extradition to Yugoslavia of Stjepan Bilandžić, a leader of the anti-Yugoslav Croat nationalist movement in West Germany. Two months later, in a move perceived as a retaliation, a Yugoslav court refused to extradite four of West Germany's most wanted alleged terrorists. Lack of evidence was invoked in both cases (*Christian Science Monitor,* 21 November). On 2 November the District Court of Zagreb passed sentences ranging from one to five years on five defendants found guilty of organizing a group "with the intention of endangering the Yugoslav social order from a counter-revolutionary position." The group was also accused of "maintaining contact with Ustashi terrorist organizations abroad" (Tanjug, 2 November).

In April came the denouement of the case of "Cominformist" leaders, i.e., apparent chiefs of the violently anti-Titoist and pro-Soviet "Communist Party of Yugoslavia" (see *YICA, 1977,* pp. 111−20). According to a Belgrade lawyer, Dr. Mileta Perović, the leader of that group was kidnapped in Switzerland in July 1977 and in April 1978 brought to trial in Belgrade (*Neue Zürcher Zeitung,* 25−26 March). On 13 April the Belgrade District Court sentenced him to twenty years' imprisonment "for plotting against the state" and other political crimes (*Vjesnik,* 15 April). On 7 June Tanjug reported that Professor Bogdan Jovović, Perović's closest collaborator, was in Yugoslavia after having "voluntarily" returned from abroad. According to Tanjug, Jovović had confessed his sins, saw the "absurdity" of the anti-Titoist struggle, and had consequently been pardoned.

Economy. There was a "powerful increase in industrial production (8.3 percent)" accompanied by "a high increase in employment (5 percent)" (*Borba,* 12 September), while at the same time huge losses in hundreds of the country's enterprises were reported, which in the first six months of 1978 amounted to about $600 million (*Ekonomska politika,* 18 September). A government report said that "a dynamic growth in material production, with the exception of agriculture, was realized in nearly all other spheres" of the economy (*Borba,* 12 September). According to some other reports, a sharp rise in the Yugoslav money supply reinforced concern that the economy was becoming severely overheated and that measures were overdue to cut back the level of domestic demand and investment (*Financial Times,* 11 October). The official October figures showed a 28 percent rise in the money supply in July, against the background of the previously mentioned 8.3 percent rise in industrial production over the first eight months of the year, and inflation was running at 14 percent on an annual basis (ibid.).

In the first nine months of the year, Yugoslavia's exports amounted to 73.1 billion dinars (about U.S. $4.1 billion; $1=18 dinars) and imports to 130.5 billion dinars (about $7.25 billion), which means that the trade deficit in the first nine months was 57.4 billion dinars (about $3.2 billion) (Tanjug, in English, Belgrade, 16 October). The overall balance of payments was improved, however, by record tourist receipts, "netting over $1 billion" this year (*Borba,* 21 September). Emigrant remittances and transit fees, the other main items of the invisible balance, were also reported to have been running at a satisfactory level.

In 1978 there were 5,274,000 employed persons in Yugoslavia (ibid., 20 May); if the 755,000 unemployed in the country and the 825,000 people working abroad (with no chance of getting jobs in Yugoslavia) are taken together, it appears that 1,580,000 persons must be considered unemployed, which makes for an unemployment rate of almost 30 percent. (If only the 755,000 are counted, the rate is 14.3 percent). The average monthly salary of Yugoslav workers in the first three months of 1978 amounted to 4,672 dinars (about $260) (*Ekonomska politika,* 7 August). Workers in Yugoslav enterprises "producing losses" received the so-called "guaranteed minimal wage" amounting to between 55 and 75 percent of the average wage (*Večernje novosti,* 21 September).

Workers' Strikes. Yugoslavia is the only communist country in which workers' strikes are neither forbidden nor permitted; they are tolerated. Neca Jovanov, a senior Yugoslav trade union official, whose doctoral dissertation dealt with a study of strikes between 1958 and 1969, revealed that during the preparation of the Law of Associated Labor in 1976, two groups within the party opposed each other to such an extent that finally the decision that strikes should not be mentioned in the law, either in a negative or in a positive sense, was made: "We checked each other!" Jovanov said

(*Vjesnik,* 2 September). According to Jovanov, there were several thousand strikes in Yugoslavia, whose main cause was not only "bureaucratized technocratic forces" but also the party organizations and trade unions, who were also responsible for the dissatisfaction that the workers had been voicing. Party and trade union officials have, Jovanov stressed, simply turned the self-management system into an institution out of the control of the working class. He added that the "workers' influence" had decreased at all levels, from workers' councils to trade unions. The chief causes of strikes are low wages and violations of self-management rules. (Ibid.)

In another interview Jovanov insisted that leading people in Yugoslavia were against workers' strikes because both in the past and today, "especially among the generation which took part in the war," there are people "who regard socialism as an idyllic system" and who are not ready to recognize hard facts. "For this reason not a few very influential people—and this is the case even today—have regarded strikes as a political disgrace," Jovanov said. He did not try to conceal the fact that the party apparatus has drifted away from the working class because of its "social composition." In other words, people who were previously workers and later became party leaders have practically ceased to be part of working class to which they once belonged. This has led to conflicts between the workers and party leaders, the latter "becoming alienated from the working class and, in the end, turning against the workers." Theoretically, said Jovanov, workers are promised freedom in disposing "of their entire income, while instead they practically have to fight to get their own wages." He criticized trade union officials for not trying to fight such abuses. "In analyzing the political aspects of strikes," Jovanov said, "I have come to the conclusion that attitudes toward strikes bear a close relation to the status of individuals in the structure of social power—the higher the position, the more rare, cautious, or even negative is any opinion about strikes; people occupying lower positions are readier to recognize the right of workers to strike." Jovanov insisted that "if you do not open vents" to allow workers to genuinely demonstrate their "pluralistic interests," then strikes would become more frequent and it would be a major question whether the system in general would be capable of surviving. (*Start,* Zagreb, 6 September.)

Foreign Affairs. *The Soviet Union.* In comparison with 1977 when Tito (in August) paid an official visit to the Soviet Union, Yugoslav-Soviet relations in 1978 seem to have stagnated if not even slightly deteriorated. Fedor Kulakov's speech during the LCY's Eleventh Congress (see above) indicated that despite the official statements concerning the "favorable development" of relations, the main ideological differences remained. The Soviet attitude has been to make it clear that Moscow is not ready to make ideological (or any other) concessions to Tito while making efforts not to go too far in criticizing Yugoslavia in general and Tito in particular. On the other hand, the Yugoslav media have been full of various reports criticizing, in most cases indirectly, Soviet ideas about a "centrally managed" international communist movement. The Yugoslav authors especially criticized the Soviet "falsification of history," concerning both the international communist movement and Yugoslavia and its party. Yugoslav radio's star commentator, Milika Šundić, said in a commentary: "We cannot remember Soviet historians having ever told the truth about the Yugoslav socialist revolution" (Tanjug, 12 January). Yugoslav newspaper correspondents in Moscow published many articles in connection with Moscow's attacks on Eurocommunism and on Yugoslavia (*Vjesnik,* 14 and 20 January, 19 February; *Borba,* 23 January). Also Soviet schoolbooks dealing with Yugoslavia in a "distorted manner" were sharply criticized (*Večernje novosti,* 16 March; *Politika,* 16 March). Some Yugoslav correspondents saw "ideological troubles" as plaguing the Soviet leaders, especially the problem of "how to analyze changes both in internal and international life" (*Politika,* 20 March). The Yugoslav press reacted spiritedly against what it perceived as anti-Yugoslav attitudes in the Soviet media, as was the case when the leading Belgrade daily, *Politika* (19 July), and the weekly *NIN*

(23 July) criticized the Moscow daily *Novoe vremia* for taking the Bulgarian side in connection with the Macedonian question.

In an important speech before Slovenian party activists on 7 September largely devoted to Chairman Hua's visit to Yugoslavia the preceding month (see below), Tito was both critical and conciliatory vis-à-vis the Soviet Union. He expressed his surprise that Hua's visit evoked an unfavorable reaction in the Soviet Union and complained that "the Soviet information media took at face value and persistently quoted the speculations in various Western countries designed to make us quarrel with the Soviet Union." He denied that Hua had criticized the Soviet Union while on Yugoslav soil and stated that there was no sin committed in Yugoslavia's establishing relations with China. To make the point stick, Tito asserted that "we have done nothing directed against the Soviet Union. . . . On the contrary, we are doing and shall do everything to avoid conflicts and the worsening of relations" (Tanjug, 8 September).

Later in the fall some Western newspapers claimed that relations between Yugoslavia and the Soviet Union "have reached their lowest ebb for years" (*Manchester Guardian,* 4 October; *Daily Telegraph,* 4 October). On the other hand, the *Daily Telegraph* (27 October) reported that Soviet submarines were "being repaired and refitted in Yugoslavia on a regular basis."

On 18 December Mikhail Solomentsev, chairman, RSFSR Council of Ministers and a CPSU Politburo candidate, arrived in Belgrade for an official visit to Yugoslavia's constituent republics of Serbia and Montenegro (*Borba,* 19 December). Originally Solomentsev was scheduled to come in August, but Moscow cancelled his visit (as Yugoslav commentators told Western correspondents privately) as a kind of "punishment" for Tito's too great friendship for China (*NYT,* 30 September). At the same time Leonid Brezhnev's son, Yuri Leonidovich Brezhnev, the Soviet deputy minister of foreign trade, had been in Belgrade discussing ways of improving transport links between Yugoslavia and the Soviet Union (Tanjug, 18 December). These two highly placed Soviet officials are believed to have come to Belgrade to honor Tito's restrained attitude toward Romania's stand vis-à-vis the Warsaw Pact in general and the Soviet Union in particular.

Yugoslav-Soviet economic relations should be evaluated within the framework of a long-term (1976–80) agreement on trade between the two countries. The overall value of trade in both directions should total $14.2 billion. The value of trade has grown on the average by 12 percent per year—$2.4 billion in 1976; $2.7 billion in 1977; $3.05 billion in 1978. Some 50 percent of Yugoslav exports to the Soviet Union consist of machinery and industrial equipment—more specifically, products of the shipbuilding industry, metallurgical equipment, electrical engineering products, special equipment for nuclear power plants, and automobile part and gears. About 30 percent of Yugoslav exports are consumer goods, such as textiles, leather footwear, etc. Yugoslav imports from the Soviet Union include machinery and equipment for power generation and mining, machine tools, construction industry equipment, tractors, fuels, and aluminum (Tanjug, 24 October). On 20–24 November the Yugoslav-Soviet Committee for Economic and Scientific-Technical Cooperation met in Moscow to devise long-term cooperation plans (*Borba,* 25 November).

The United States. A high degree of official cordiality marked relations between the U.S. and Yugoslavia in 1978, disturbed occasionally by the terrorist activities of extremist Croatian exiles. The culminating point in relations between the two countries was Tito's visit to Washington on 6–10 March. In February a U.S. State Department report on human rights said that Yugoslavia's citizens, unlike those in other Eastern European countries, enjoyed broad freedom of movement and access to foreign publications and broadcasts. The report did, however, add that restrictions on freedom of speech do exist: "The regime tends to interpret written, and even oral criticism, as political 'crimes.' " In other human rights areas, according to the report, there was no evidence of the use of torture in Yugoslavia, although there have been occasional allegations of cruel and inhuman treatment or degrading punishment (*NYT,* 10 February).

In an interview with James Reston of the *New York Times,* Tito stated that U.S.-Yugoslav relations were "good, friendly," and he even indicated that differences over transferring nuclear technology and fuel from the United States had been resolved. He was, however, "worried very much" about the disagreements between the U.S. and the Soviet Union. Concerning the situation in the Middle East, Tito made his first public criticism of President Sadat over the latter's trip to Jerusalem and complained that he had not been informed about it. As far as Yugoslavia's future is concerned, Tito declared, nobody should be worried about his country's departing from its policy of independence and detachment from any political bloc. Speaking about his wife Jovanka, Tito said that their differences had nothing to do with politics (ibid., 3 March). In an interview with the CBS Television Network, Tito told Walter Cronkite that Yugoslavia sought no guarantees from President Carter for Yugoslavia's security because "Yugoslavia is itself a guarantee of its own security" (Radio Belgrade, 8 March).

A joint Yugoslav-U.S. statement issued on 9 March said that "the two presidents held extensive and useful talks in a spirit of mutual regard, candor, and friendship." They also affirmed "that the right of all states to determine their own social systems without outside interference must be respected" and that "nonalignment is a very significant factor in world affairs." After having expressed their "special concern" about the situation in several parts of the world (especially in the Middle East), "the two presidents discussed a variety of aspects of the human rights problem in the contemporary world." Two points of the joint statement drew particular attention. One was President Carter's commitment to "take firm measures to prevent and to prosecute" criminal terrorist activities by anti-Tito Yugoslav emigré groups in the United States, which "went further than any previous American policy statements on Yugoslavia and was particularly gratifying to President Tito" (*NYT,* 10 March). The other was the proclamation of "continuing support of the United States for the independence, territorial integrity, and unity of Yugoslavia." The insertion of the word *unity* "carried this beyond previous American policy statements over the last 30 years" (ibid.).

During 1978 several high-level U.S. congressional and military delegations paid official visits to Yugoslavia. The U.S. ambassador to the United Nations, Andrew Young, spent two days in Belgrade (17−18 July) discussing international problems with Yugoslav Foreign Minister Josip Vrhovec. Yugoslav Finance Minister Petar Kostić, accompanied by high representatives of the Yugoslav Chamber of the Economy and the National Bank of Yugoslavia, had "extensive talks" in Washington with U.S. Secretary of the Treasury Michael Blumenthal and the chairman of the U.S. Overseas Private Investments Corporation (Tanjug, 22 September; *Vjesnik,* 23 September).

Yugoslav Defense Minister General Nikola Ljubičić traveled to Washington (24−30 September) on his first visit to the U.S. He came at the invitation of U.S. Defense Secretary Harold Brown, who had visited Yugoslavia in October 1977. Besides his encounters in Washington, General Ljubičić was taken to Norfolk, Virginia, and Colorado Springs, Colorado, to see U.S. military installations (*Borba,* 1 October). According to the *Washington Post* (29 September), one result of General Ljubičić's visit to the U.S. will be "a substantial increase in U.S. arms sales to Yugoslavia over the next few years." An official spokesman of the Yugoslav Foreign Ministry put it somewhat differently: "Yugoslavia gets its arms and military equipment from more than one country, on a purely commercial basis and without any strings attached or concessions made, the chief criteria being price and quality" (Tanjug, 28 September).

In the first four months of 1978 Yugoslav exports to the United States totaled over $120 million, while Yugoslavia's imports from the United States totaled $185 million. On 4−7 June a group of 120 U.S. businessmen conferred with 200 Yugoslav economic functionaries in Dubrovnik (*Politika,* 5 June). On 7 November the World Bank in Washington granted a loan to Yugoslavia amounting to $55 million to be used for the development of agriculture and agro-industry in Bosanska Krajina (Tanjug, 7 November).

Yugoslav-Chinese Relations. Chairman Hua Kuo-feng paid an official visit to Yugoslavia from 21 to 29 August. He was returning Tito's visit to China of 30 August—8 September 1977 (see *YICA, 1978,* pp. 98—99). His visit marked the final reconciliation not only between China and Yugoslavia as states but also between the Chinese and Yugoslav parties. While in Yugoslavia, Hua had talks with Tito both in Belgrade and on the resort island of Brioni and visited three of Yugoslavia's six constituent republics—Serbia, Macedonia, and Croatia. He was enthusiastically greeted everywhere he went. The Yugoslavs had been doing their best—although in a subtle way—to tell both their own people and the world at large that it was the Chinese who had to change their mind about Yugoslavia and Tito rather than the reverse. In 1958 Peking may have called Tito "worse than Judas" who "betrayed a single Jesus, while Tito is betraying the entire Yugoslav people" and the whole international communist movement (*Red Flag,* Peking, 14 June 1958), but on his arrival in Belgrade, Chairman Hua said: "You, President Tito, enjoy great prestige among the Chinese people; your visit to China [in 1977] left a deep impression on them" (New China News Agency, in English, 21 August).

For his part, Tito, in a toast delivered during a dinner in Belgrade on 21 August, rejected "the imposition of any models or prescriptions" from outside and instead insisted on the need for "constant observation and application" of the principles "of independence, autonomy, equality, sovereignty, territorial integrity, noninterference, respect for indigenous paths of development, international cooperation and solidarity on a voluntary basis, and acknowledgment of the difference existing between countries and parties" (*Borba,* 22 August). He also mentioned "understandable differences" between Belgrade and Peking. In his toast, Hua extended his "great respect" not only to the Yugoslav government and people but also "to the League of Communists of Yugoslavia." He described Tito's visit to China as "a historic event" and said that "in the past year" mutual Yugoslav-Chinese understanding "has greatly increased." He avoided saying anything about past conflicts and did not apologize for Mao's mistakes (as Khruschev had in May 1955 for Stalin). He did, however, say that "the Chinese are deeply impressed by the long and courageous struggles waged by the Yugoslav people," which they had followed "with great admiration," and because of which "Comrade Mao Tse-tung had called Yugoslavia a heroic country." He then added: "Your victory has been a source of inspiration for us."

Hua admitted that the Yugoslav party had been developing "the socialist system of self-management," proceeding "from the scientific theory of Marxism." He lavishly praised Yugoslavia's nationwide defense system, which makes the country ready "at all times to repulse any enemy who dares to intrude." Hua also hailed Yugoslavia's policy of nonalignment as a "very important force in the struggle of the world's people against imperialism, colonialism, and hegemony." After having mentioned the smashing of the "antiparty clique" in China, Hua turned to Yugoslav-Chinese relations and stressed that they were based "on Marxism-Leninism" both at the state and party levels. "We are linked by a similar past and united in a joint struggle," he said. (Ibid.).

Nonalignment. The Coordinating Bureau of the nonaligned movement met in Havana on 15 May on the ambasssadorial-expert level and adopted a proposal for the nonaligned foreign ministers' meeting, which took place 18—21 May. On the agenda was the movement's ministerial conference in Belgrade and the sixth summit conference in Havana next year (Tanjug, 18 May). Yugoslav Foreign Minister Josip Vrhovec urged the nonaligned nations to prevent mutual conflicts (*Borba,* 20 May). A document attacking oppression and colonialism but smoothing over the movement's own differences was published on 21 May. The Yugoslav information media admitted that differences do exist among the nonaligned states (*Vjesnik,* 18 May; *Politika* 28 May). On 28 May Yugoslavia's assistant foreign minister criticized the intervention of Cuban troops in Eritrea and said he did not exclude the possibility of a further sharpening of confrontation within the nonaligned movement (Reuters, 28 May). The Yugoslavs listed at least five reasons why the nonaligned countries have been fighting each other: (a), ideological issues ("different socioeconomic systems"); (b), political affiliations (individual nonaligned countries linked "with this or that power"); (c), economic interests; (d), conflicts over international political problems (some countries supported the U.S. in Vietnam, others did not; some condemned the Soviet military intervention in Czechoslovakia in August 1968, some did not); and (e), bilateral conflicts, e.g., Arab disagreements (*Vjesnik,* 24 June). Between 25 and 30 July the nonaligned ministerial conference was held in Belgrade. It was attended by 86 full members, ten observers, seven guests (Austria, the Philippines, Finland, Portugal, Romania, Switzerland, and Sweden), and the representatives of ten liberation movements and organizations (*Borba,* 24 July). Tito greeted the participants and warned against new forms of domination in major nonaligned regions, particularly Africa. He said that the nonaligned countries should unite in resisting efforts at foreign domination. He told the delegates that the movement had arrived at a "dangerous crossroads" and that nonaligned policy was directed against imperialism, neocolonialism, racism, power politics, political and economic hegemony, and every kind of external interference and dependence (*Politika,* 26 July). The facade of unity cracked very soon, and differences came out into the open, especially over Cuba's presence in Africa. A long declaration, issued after the conference had ended, omitted anything that might demonstrate differences among nonaligned countries, especially between the pro-Moscow minority group and a vocal anti-Moscow minority. Still, the Yugoslav information media hailed the Belgrade conference as a "huge success" (*Borba,* 31 July).

Eurocommunism. *Edvard Kardelj's Views.* The Yugoslav party leaders have followed the development of Eurocommunism, and especially the conflict between Moscow and the Western European communist parties (in Italy, France, and Spain) with keen interest. In the original version of Kardelj's book, the author dealt with Eurocommunism more or less in passing. In the revised version of the book, which has an additional 24 pages, a whole chapter, " 'Eurocommunism' and Yugoslavia's Self-management Democracy," is devoted to Eurocommunism. While repeating his initial statement that " 'Eurocommunism' should not be subject to any dogmatic 'anathema,' " Kardelj emphasized that (a), Eurocommunism was "a special product of current conditions in Western Europe" and thus could not be adopted "as universal policy for all countries in the world"; (b), Eurocommunist ideas could not serve "as the domestic policy of a socialist country in which the working class has won power by force of arms because it would inject sharp antagonisms into the struggle for power and open the doors to counterrevolution"; and (c), Eurocommunism fits only the Western European capitalist countries "and countries having a similar social structure and position in world affairs" (p. 50).

The LCY and Relations with the Italian, French, and Spanish Communist Parties. Throughout the year LCY leaders had a very extensive exchange of visits with top Italian party functionaries. A member of the Secretariat and Directorate of the Italian Central Committee, Giancarlo Pajetta, was twice interviewed by the Yugoslav press (*NIN,* 12 February; *Delo,* Ljubljana, 12 August). In the latter interview, reproduced in all major Yugoslav newspapers, Pajetta defended "real internationalism" which recognizes "the differences between parties and the independence of each communist party." In yet another interview, published by an Italian-language periodical in Rijeka, Pajetta praised Tito's 1977 trips to Moscow and Peking highly (Tanjug, 28 September). The greatest significance, however, was attached to Enrico Berlinguer's trips to Moscow (6–10 October) and Yugoslavia (10–11 October) where he met with Brezhnev and Tito, respectively. A joint communiqué following the Berlinguer-Tito talks stressed "the spirit of mutual understanding which characterizes LCY-PCI relations," and hailed the results of the 1976 Berlin conference of communist and workers' parties of Europe, which called for "broad, open, and constructive bilateral dialogues between parties and movements" (ibid., 11 October). This rather innocuous communiqué did not, however, reveal anything about the substance and the deeper meaning concerning the triangular Tito-Berlinguer-Brezhnev relationship.

While the closeness between the Yugoslav and Italian parties was no surprise to anyone, it is noteworthy that relations between the Yugoslav and the French communist parties warmed considerably during the year. On 6–8 November Stane Dolanc paid an official visit to the French Communist Party in Paris where he met with Georges Marchais, the secretary of the French party. In a joint statement published on 8 November, the LCY and the French party agreed that "voluntary cooperation among communist parties and internationalist solidarity require strict respect for equality and independence and noninterference into others' internal affairs while honoring the orientation of each party" (ibid., 8 November). While in Paris, Dolanc delivered a lecture at the French party's Central Party School about Yugoslavia's self-management system (*Borba,* 9 November). Marchais told a press conference that "relations between our two parties are good since we have corrected past errors, but they will now take on a new breadth." On the same occasion, Marchais announced that he had accepted an invitation from Tito to visit Yugoslavia some time next year (Reuters, 8 November).

Aleksandar Grličkov, the chief LCY liaison with other communist parties, headed the Yugoslav party delegation to the Ninth Congress of the Spanish Communist Party, held in Madrid on 19–23 April. In his speech at the congress, Grličkov recalled "the traditional and friendly relations existing between the LCY and the Spanish Communist Party" (Tanjug, 20 April). He also met with Spanish party leader Santiago Carrillo.

Contacts with Other Ruling Communist Parties. While Yugoslav-Albanian relations continued to improve in the trade and cultural fields, the LCY did not maintain any contact with the Albanian Party of Labor. Yugoslav commentators carefully pondered the future orientation of Albanian policies in view of the severance of relations between Albania and China and expressed the hope that Albania will maintain an independent position, i.e., will not be tempted to reestablish closer ties with the USSR and the countries of the Warsaw Pact (Radio Zagreb, 13 November). In October Albanian leader Enver Hoxha published a book entitled *Yugoslav Self-government: A Capitalist Theory and Practice.* The book not only assailed Yugoslav economic and social systems but was considered an ostensible reply to Edvard Kardelj's book (see *Radio Free Europe Background Report*, 28 November).

The Macedonian issue (see above) troubled Yugoslav-Bulgarian relations throughout the year despite the frequent exchange of high party and diplomatic delegations. The Yugoslav press constantly polemicized with its Bulgarian counterparts, and the polemics covered not only the Macedonian problem but also conflicting interpretations of national and party histories. In an extremely blunt interview with the West German daily *Die Welt* (22–23 July), Milovan Djilas asserted that "behind [the Macedonian] issue most certainly stands the Soviet Union because this is one of its methods—to work through Bulgaria to shatter Yugoslavia."

On 20 May Fidel Castro received Yugoslav Foreign Minister Josip Vrhovec. Relations between Yugoslavia and Cuba lacked cordiality, without leading however to an open conflict.

On 3–4 March Stane Dolanc paid a visit to Czechoslovakia and conferred with the communist party secretary and the president of the republic, Gustav Husák.

On 20 June the East German press published a Central Committee message to the LCY Eleventh Congress referring to traditions of cooperation between German and Yugoslav Communists dating back to before World War II. The message also said that it is vital for Communists today to strengthen "the internationalist, comradely, and voluntary cooperation and solidarity of communist and workers' parties on the basis of equality and the foundations of Marxism-Leninism" (*Neues Deutschland,* 20 June).

At the end of February Stane Dolanc visited Hungary and Poland for high-level political talks. On 2–3 June Polish Communist Party leader Edward Gierek paid an official visit to Yugoslavia and met Tito at the latter's retreat on the island of Brioni. Originally Gierek was to have arrived in Belgrade on 11 May, but on 10 May that visit was canceled at Tito's request. From 6 to 9 December Stane Dolanc paid a sudden "friendly and working" visit to Poland where he had talks with Gierek and Politburo member Edward Babiuch (*Borba,* 11 December). Upon his return to Belgrade Dolanc said that even though Yugoslav-Polish relations were good, there were also differences, especially arising from the fact that Poland is a member of the Warsaw Pact and Yugoslavia is a nonaligned country (Radio Belgrade, 10 December).

In mid-May, an LCY study delegation visited Mongolia. Throughout the year, high-level party delegations were exchanged between the LCY and North Korea.

Relations between Yugoslavia and Romania continued to be close at all levels. On 16 and 17 November Nicolae Ceaușescu paid an official visit to Belgrade as the head of a top state-party delegation. This was the first meeting between Ceaușescu and Tito since the August visit to Romania and Yugoslavia of Chinese party leader Hua Kuo-feng. The two leaders discussed international topics, as well as the situation in the Balkans.

Publications. The main publications of the LCY are *Komunist* (weekly) and *Socijalizam* (monthly). The most important weeklies are *NIN* (*Nedeljne informativne novine*; Belgrade) and *Ekonomska politika* (Belgrade). The most important daily newspapers are *Borba* (with Belgrade and Zagreb editions), *Vjesnik* (Zagreb), *Oslobodjenje* (Sarajevo), *Politika* (Belgrade), *Nova Makedonija* (Skoplje), and *Delo* (Ljubljana). Tanjug is the official news agency.

Radio Free Europe   Slobodan Stanković
Munich

Council for
Mutual Economic Assistance

Organized in January 1949 as a response to the Marshall Plan, the Council for Mutual Economic Assistance (CMEA) remained dormant for more than five years. Not until 1954 did the organization recommend that all member states coordinate national economic plans. Initially encompassing only the Eastern European bloc, without Yugoslavia, the CMEA has since admitted other countries: Mongolia (1962), Cuba (1972), and Vietnam (1978). Albania left the CMEA in 1961, but Yugoslavia applied for and received limited-participant status four years later.

All the above countries have ruling communist parties in power. Cambodia, Laos, and North Korea are not CMEA members, although the latter two did send observers to the Council session held at East Berlin in July 1976. In addition, several noncommunist regimes have signed cooperation agreements with the CMEA: Finland (1973), Mexico (1975), and Iraq (1976). Guyana reportedly has applied for affiliation (Kingston radio, 3 May).

During the year under review, about 59 percent of the Soviet Union's foreign trade was to be conducted with its East European allies. In billions of rubles, the following had been planned: East Germany (7.3), Poland (6.7), Hungary (6.4), Bulgaria (5.6), Czechoslovakia (5.5), and Romania (2.1), according to Moscow radio (9 January). That same month the USSR increased the price of oil it sells to these countries by 21 percent, from $9.66 to $11.72 per barrel, which is still slightly below the world market price of $12 to $14 (*Wall Street Journal*, 2 February).

The thirty-second Council session took place during 27—29 June at Bucharest, where coordination of economic plans until 1990 was discussed. Angola, Ethiopia, Laos, and North Korea sent deputy premiers as observers. The USSR proposed to supply the East European states with raw materials, energy, some industrial products, and even food in return for manpower, hard currency, and even credits for joint projects like the Orenberg gas pipeline that will link the Soviet Union with Czechoslovakia and Hungary. Targets were established for nuclear power development (up to 37 million KWH in capacity), agriculture, and machine building (communiqué in *Pravda*, 30 June).

Admission of Vietnam as tenth member at this time may have serious repercussions for the CMEA. That country requires about three billion dollars in developmental aid over the next three years. Most, if not all of these funds, will come from the CMEA, which already subsidizes the economies of Mongolia and Cuba. In addition, the total current CMEA debt to Western Europe and the United States already amounts to almost $50 billion in hard currency. Admitting Vietnam also may represent a first step in opening membership to other Third World countries, especially those in Africa which describe themselves as Marxist.

Closer to its own borders, during the current five-year plan (1976—1980), the USSR has obligated itself to supply Eastern Europe with some 364 million tons of oil, about 90 billion cubic meters of natural gas, and 67 billion KWH of electricity. Whether these large amounts can be sustained after 1980 is questionable, and recipients are being urged by the Soviet Union to arrange bilateral deals with the Middle East and North African states that export oil. It is probably inevitable that USSR prices for this fuel will be increased each year, as they have been for some time now.

The CMEA's Executive Committee met at Ulan Bator between 27 September and 1 October for discussions on how to implement the Council decisions made in Bucharest. Agreement was reached on reconstruction of the Hanoi—Ho Chi Minh City (Saigon) railroad line and completion of projects abandoned in Vietnam by China. Applications for developmental assistance from Ethiopia and Angola were acted upon positively, according to the communiqué in *Pravda* (4 October).

Finally, negotiations took place during the year between the CMEA and the European Economic Community (EEC) in Moscow as well as in Brussels. Work has proceeded on drawing up an agreement for cooperation between the two organizations, after five years of talks. The main difficulty appears to lie in Western Europe's insistence that trade relations must be conducted by the EEC with individual Eastern European states and not with the CMEA, due to the fact that these economic blocs differ in structure. By year end no agreement had been reached.

Hoover Institution   Richard F. Staar

Warsaw Treaty Organization

Established as a multilateral military alliance on 14 May 1955, the Warsaw Treaty Organization (WTO) came into being one day before the state treaty in Vienna which restored sovereignty to Austria and obligated the USSR to evacuate its armed forces from Hungary and Romania. The WTO provided a legal basis for Soviet troops stationed in Poland and East Germany.

Status-of-forces agreements with Poland (1956), East Germany, Romania, Hungary (all 1957), and Czechoslovakia (1968) remain in effect except for Romania, which lapsed in 1958 upon withdrawal of USSR troops from that country. Albania de facto left the WTO in 1961, although it did not announce withdrawal until 13 September 1968. Yugoslavia never became a pact member, although there were reports that during November 1976 Brezhnev's attempts in Belgrade to affiliate that country with the WTO had been rejected by Tito (see *YICA, 1977*, p. 105).

During the year under review, an eight-day command post map exercise took place in Romania, with staff officers from Bulgaria and the USSR (*Scînteia*, 22 March). WTO commander in chief Marshal Viktor Kulikov and the two other defense ministers participated. Three weeks later Soviet troops in the German Democratic Republic (GDR) conducted maneuvers under simulated conditions of a nuclear attack (*Krasnaya zvezda*, 13 April). That same month GDR, Polish, and USSR navies conducted exercises in the Baltic Sea (*Neues Deutschland*, 24 April).

The Military Council of the WTO met at Budapest during 16–19 May and "discussed timely issues . . . and adopted relevant recommendations." No other information came out in the brief communiqué, although on 8 June a new proposal was offered NATO at mutual force reduction talks: a common ceiling of 900,000 troops on both sides. However, the WTO asserts that it has 150,000 fewer men in uniform than the NATO assessment. The Soviet Union refused to admit Western military observers to attend ground/air maneuvers with 30,000 troops in East Germany during early July, even though the Helsinki accords pledged each side to invite the other when 25,000 or more troops were involved. The International Institute for Strategic Studies in London reported in September that the U.S. has deployed 3,600 nuclear missiles in Europe compared with 5,609 for the USSR, with an even greater inferiority in tanks: 25,373 in NATO versus 65,525 for the WTO (*The Military Balance, 1978–1979*, pp. 3–5).

A second conference of the pact Military Council took place in East Berlin and ended with an almost identical communiqué which revealed nothing other than that "sessions passed in a friendly atmosphere, in the spirit of close cooperation and mutual understanding" (*Pravda*, 20 October). However the sixteenth consecutive meeting of the WTO Political Consultative Committee, held in Moscow, did not end with unanimity.

Nicolae Ceauşescu refused to raise Romania's military expenditures. Upon returning to Bucharest, he stated on 25 November that he saw no reason to increase the defense budget but would raise wages instead. Two days later ambassadors from the USSR, Hungary, and Bulgaria left the country on the eve of the sixtieth anniversary of Romanian acquisition of territory from those countries. A special session of the communist party Central Committee gave its support to Ceauşescu (*NYT*, 30 November).

It is also interesting that the Romanian delegation to the WTO refused to sign a statement condemning the Israeli-Egyptian peace talks. Ceauşescu did, however, add his name to a much longer declaration, which had been published the previous day. It called for an early SALT agreement and an end to "all vestiges of the cold war." A development of equal importance would be conclusion of a treaty "to which the other nuclear powers should also accede." The declaration supported steps to "resolutely advance the cause of military détente in Europe, lowering the level of military confrontation on the European continent, while safeguarding equal security of all European states." (*Pravda*, 24 November.)

The WTO defense ministers' committee, with Romanian participation, met in East Berlin during 4–7 December. A communiqué stated that "The committee had discussed questions relating to the status and current activity of the Joint Armed Forces and adopted appropriate decisions." It added that "the meeting took place in a friendly atmosphere, in the spirit of mutual understanding." (Moscow radio, 7 December.)

Hoover Institution   Richard F. Staar

WARSAW PACT COMMUNIQUE

On 22–23 November in Moscow a meeting of the Political Consultative Committee of the Warsaw Pact member-states took place on friendship, cooperation, and mutual aid.

Participating in the conference were: from the People's Republic of Bulgaria a delegation headed by Todor Zhivkov; from the Hungarian People's Republic a delegation headed by János Kádár; from the German Democratic Republic a delegation headed by Erich Honecker; from the Polish People's Republic a delegation headed by Edward Gierek; from the Socialist Republic of Romania a delegation headed by Nicolae Ceauşescu; from the USSR a delegation headed by Leonid Ilich Brezhnev; and from the Czechoslovak Socialist Republic a delegation headed by Gustav Husák.

Also taking part in the meeting were Marshal of the Soviet Union Kulikov, commander in chief of the Joint Armed Forces of the Warsaw Pact states, and Firyubin, secretary general of the Warsaw Pact Political Consultative Committee.

The Political Consultative Committee meeting examined topical questions of the development of the European situation, and there was an exchange of opinions on certain questions of the international situation as a whole. A central place in the discussion was occupied by further steps in the struggle for the development of the process of the relaxation of tension and for disarmament.

The meeting participants set forth their assessments of the situation, their conclusions, and their proposals in a unanimously adopted declaration of the Warsaw Pact states.

It was agreed that the Soviet Union, as the host country of the meeting, would disseminate the declaration as an official document in the United Nations and would inform all the states which took part in the Conference on Security and Cooperation in Europe of its contents. The participants in the meeting, true to the principled course drawn up at the congresses of the communist and workers' parties in their countries, once again affirmed their firm resolve to continue their consistent struggle for universal peace, freedom, and independence of peoples, an end to the arms race, disarmament, relaxation of international tension, and strengthening of trust and friendship among peoples. They will spare no effort to find a practical solution to these most topical tasks of our time.

Agreement was reached to the effect that the Committee of Foreign Ministers will, at its meeting at a later date, taking into account the development of the situation, further examine measures toward fulfilling the tasks set out in the declaration and that its participants will report to their governments on the results of the work done. The Political Consultative Committee heard a report by Marshal of the Soviet Union Kulikov on practical work done by the joint command.

The meeting of the Political Consultative Committee took place in an atmosphere of fraternal friendship and comradely cooperation.

The declaration by the Warsaw Pact states, which was passed at the meeting, will be published in the central press.

Text of Declaration. The People's Republic of Bulgaria, the Hungarian People's Republic, the German Democratic Republic, the Polish People's Republic, the Socialist Republic of Romania, the Union of the Soviet Socialist Republics, and the Czechoslovak Socialist Republic, represented at the conference of the Political Consultative Committee of the Warsaw Treaty member-countries in Moscow on 22–23 November 1978, considered topical questions of the development of the situation in Europe and exchanged opinions on some questions of the international situation as a whole.

The discussion centered around further steps in the struggle for the development of the process of détente and disarmament.

The participants in the conference pointed out that in recent years the determination of the peoples, all progressive and peace forces, to put an end to the aggressive and oppressive policy of imperialism, colonialism, and neocolonialism has become ever more stronger. Unfolding ever more widely is the struggle for peace, for détente, for an end to the arms race, for freedom and social progress, for peaceful equal international cooperation, resting on mutual respect of national independence, sovereignty, and nonintervention in internal affairs.

Source: Moscow radio, 23 November 1978.

Austria

The Communist Party of Austria (Kommunistische Partei Österreichs; KPÖ) was founded 3 November 1918 and quietly celebrated its sixtieth birthday in 1978. A legal party throughout Austria's democratic history, the KPÖ was represented in Austria's parliament in 1945–59 and in its government, 1945–47. Between the wars, the party's significance was constrained by the leftist orientation of the Social Democratic Party. Since 1945 its increasing insignificance has been due to the memory of Soviet occupation of northeastern Austria (1945–55) and to Soviet military intervention in neighboring Hungary and Czechoslovakia.

There were no newly reported estimates of KPÖ membership in 1978, and one can still assume that about 25,000 of Austria's 7.5 million people are party members. The KPÖ continued its rigid adherence to a pro-Moscow position.

During the period under review, public opinion polls showed a range of support for the KPÖ of 1.7 percent to 0.7 percent of Austria's population; the low figure is the most recent, for September 1978 (*Kurier*, Vienna, 21 October). The level of support is similar to that of the two previous years.

The party fielded lists of candidates in a number of elections, but with little success. In the provincial elections in Vienna and Styria, both held on 8 October, the KPÖ began with no seats and gained none. Its Styrian vote percentage was 1.34 (*Arbeiter-Zeitung*, Vienna, 9 October). In Vienna, the party is still represented in 5 of the 23 borough councils (one seat each), all in the former Soviet zone of occupation (ibid., 10 October). In the municipal election in Graz, the capital of Styria, on 29 January, the KPÖ received its lowest share of the vote since 1945 (2 percent) but retained its one seat on the city council (*Kleine Zeitung*, Graz, 30 January).

There were several other elections. On 30 November and 1 December 1977, Austria's railway workers and employees elected representatives. While the communist vote declined from 8 to less than 6 percent, the Communists retained one of eighteen seats on the central committee (*Wiener Zeitung*, 2 December 1977). On 5 and 6 April, the majority of Austria's municipal employees elected their representatives. Communists competed in Vienna and Upper Austria. Their vote share declined from 3 to 2 percent, their number of seats from four to two (ibid., 8 April). On 10 and 11 October 1978, the workers of VÖEST-Alpine, Austria's largest (nationalized) steelwork, elected their shop stewards. Probably because of a strong decline in the heretofore overwhelming majority of the Socialists, the KPÖ increased its number of seats from two to three (*Arbeiter-Zeitung*, 13 October), despite the fact that the first man on its Styrian list had been arrested while stealing in a store (*Die Presse*, Vienna, 10 October).

Leadership and Organization. The major organizational event was the KPÖ's Twenty-third (now triennial) Party Congress, held in Vienna 8–11 December 1977. In a critical review of the organizational work done preparatory to the congress, Wolfgang Oberleitner painted this realistic picture in *Die Presse* (7 December 1977):

> The balance sheet of the past 3 years which will have to be dealt with by the party congress is decidedly dismal. . . . It has been pushed out of all the provincial assemblies, and even . . . onetime bastions among the plants (such as Glanzstoff in St. Poelten) have been lost . . . and in only three municipal councils (Linz, Graz and Klagenfurt) is the KPOe still represented by one person each. . . . While the veteran fighters of past decades continue to be loyal to the party, their sons have long since turned away from it, regarding the KPOe as a sterile cadre party without any effect on the working class, turned bourgeois and now only capable of gathering signatures against the new taxation burdens. . . .
>
> Nevertheless it is being asserted boldly that there has been progress since the last party congress in the KPOe efforts of politicization and consolidation. Apparently not even the party members believe this . . . in the . . . *Volksstimme*, Kurt Palm states without embellishment that "this is an erroneous assessment." Consolidation, he points out, means greater influence among the "masses," good election results and an extra-parliamentary movement. "I think we have again reached the point we started from—our party's organizational weakness."
>
> . . . [T]he Politburo [is] being reproached for having acted too little or too late. . . . [T]he practical party work should be conducted by the district secretaries, who . . . are paid to do just that. In the party assemblies the comrades maintain silence, but outside they "gripe" all the more . . . and an eminently dangerous tendency of "you up there, and we down here" is spreading. . . .
>
> [Former Central Committee member Jenoe] Kostmann is . . . not afraid to speak the truth about the present hopeless situation of the KPOe, which has forgotten the vaunted communist self-criticism. He thinks that the leadership's negative view of the improved situation of the Austrian working class contradicts outright the experience of wage earners. Thus, he states, the KPOe with its gloomy predictions has increasingly lost its credibility and has become isolated from the workers.

In contrast to this well-researched account by a conservative newspaper based on material from the KPÖ's own paper, the *Volksstimme*, the report of the KPÖ Central Committee to the party congress, presented by Chairman Franz Muhri, contained only little in the way of organizational information (*Volksstimme*, Vienna, 10 december 1977). It stated that 2,448 new members had been recruited since 1974, two-thirds of them "young people," resulting in a "slight" increase of the percentage of the members below the age of forty. The following sentence is telling: "Individual organizations have already managed fully to offset natural attrition through new recruitment, but a greater number of organizations have not recruited any new members." The *Volksstimme* acquired 5,400 new subscribers since 1974 (cancellations or expired subscriptions were not reported). Since 1974, 1,457 persons participated in seminars and courses, more than twice as many as for the period 1971–74.

The new Central Committee met on 10 December 1977 to elect officers. Not surprisingly, the *Volksstimme* (13 December) reported all of them as having been unanimously elected. The results were chairman, Franz Muhri; Politburo members, Franz Hager, Anton Hofer, Hans Kalt, Franz Karger, Gustav Loistl, Franz Muhri, Josef Progsch, Karl Reiter, Erwin Scharf, Ernst Wimmer, and Karl Zenker; secretary of the Central Committee, Erwin Scharf; secretary for organization, Karl Reiter; chairman of the Finance Commission, Walter Wachs; and for the *Volksstimme*, chief editor, Hans Kalt, deputy editor, Otto Janecek. In April, Friedl Fuernberg, one of the senior leaders of the KPÖ, died at the age of 75 (*FBIS*, 28 April).

Domestic Attitudes and Activities. In regard to domestic policy, Muhri's report to the party congress dealt with two special Austrian peculiarities in the face of an international economic crisis: (*a*), there is not (as yet) mass unemployment in Austria; and (*b*), in Austria, the class struggles of the workers have not increased. These two developments, pleasing as they are to most Austrians, were characterized by Muhri as "this crisis and its particular features in the past few years." (*Volksstimme*,

10 December 1977.) Muhri characterized the policy of Kreisky's Social Democratic government as a "policy of taxation, of insecurity, of increased exploitation, of antidemocratic methods." Muhri's proposed answer to this alleged policy was a regional and structural policy of production and employment within the nationalized sector, a moving away from trade with the European community, and an increase of purchasing power through wage and tax reform (*Wiener Zeitung,* 10 December 1977). Specific demands included the nationalization of the pharmaceutical industry, equal rights for women, and the democratization of the media and education. Muhri claimed that the communist program for the economy would create 400,000 jobs (*WMR,* March 1978, pp. 33—40).

In March, Muhri warned against the increasingly nationalist direction of the Austrian Freedom Party under its new leader, Mayor Götz of Graz. He underscored his warning by referring to the impending fortieth anniversary of the *Anschluss* (*IB,* no. 8, 30 April). Muhri's May Day address was a synopsis of his presentation to the party congress (*Wiener Zeitung,* 2 May).

International Views and Positions. At the very beginning of the period under review, Moscow celebrated the sixtieth anniversary of the October Revolution. For the occasion, Muhri wrote "Inspiring Force of Example" for the *World Marxist Review* (November 1977, pp. 37—45).

Muhri's report to the party congress contained attacks on Eurocommunism, nationalism, Western armaments, Maoist activities in Austria, and Austria's adaptation to the economics of the European community (*Volksstimme,* 10 December 1977). The congress affirmed Israel's right to exist and attacked Sadat's then impending peace move (*NYT,* 15 December 1977). The KPÖ took an unusual step when it exchanged letters with the Communist Party of the Soviet Union (CPSU) on the subject of the expansion of trade relations between Austria and the USSR (*Volksstimme,* 5 February).

On 15 February, Johann Steiner, member of the Secretariat of the Central Committee of the KPÖ, published an article in *Pravda* commemorating the sixtieth anniversary of the Austrian Republic and of the KPÖ (*FBIS,* 16 February). In this article, Steiner wrote:

> When the Communist Party of Austria . . . came into being sixty years ago bourgeois propaganda often labelled us as "a hand of Moscow". . . . Today, just as sixty years ago, we reply to such statements that Austrian communists have always come out for the national interests of Austria and its working people. Throughout the past sixty years relations between the Communist Party of Austria and the CPSU have been truly fraternal, comradely relations. Contrary to what is alleged sometimes, never throughout this period did the CPSU try even once to impose on the Austrian party any positions or points of view of its own.

KPÖ endorsement of the "Marxist-Leninist, internationalist positions" firmly supported by the Soviet Union and the communist parties of Eastern Europe was also emphasized during Franz Muhri's visit to East Berlin in June. In a toast to Muhri, the secretary general of the East German communist party, Erich Honecker, said: "Comrade Franz Muhri quite justifiably stated at yesterday's rally that the further development of the developed socialist society in the GDR represents the most efficient assistance for the Austrian Communists in their struggle for noble goals" (*FBIS,* 7 June). Support was also given the Soviet government on the question of human rights. In the 15 July edition of *Volksstimme,* editor Hans Kalt condemned the Western media, including Vienna's socialist *Arbeiter-Zeitung,* for slandering the Soviet Union in the Shcharansky case.

International Activities and Party Contacts. In this area, 1978 was a busy year for the KPÖ. Late in 1977, the sixtieth anniversary of the Russian Revolution was the occasion of an exchange of delegations between the CPSU and the KPÖ. Muhri, Scharf, and Salzburg chairman Josef Wodradzka flew to Moscow, while Alexey Smirnov and Valeriy Mantsev came to Vienna. The festive reception given in Vienna on 7 November by Ambassador Yefremov was attended by President Kirchschläger, Chancellor Kreisky, Nationalrat President Benya, several ministers, Muhri, and several members of the Politburo. Scharf and Steiner visited Budapest on 19 November. Czechoslovak Premier Lubomír Štrougal on a visit to Vienna (his first) had a friendly meeting with Muhri, Scharf, and Hofer.

The party congress was, of course, the occasion for many talks between KPÖ leaders and functionaries of other communist parties, including Eurocommunists. The head of the CPSU delegation, Ivan Kapitonov, secretary of the CPSU Central Committee, was received by Chancellor Kreisky on 7 December (Tass, 7 December 1977).

In late 1977, Murhi visited Katowice in Poland, Johann Steiner visited Prague in February, and in March, Karl Reiter, Joseph Progsch, and Erich Zagler, a prominent member of the Vienna KPÖ, visited the leaders of the West German communist party in Düsseldorf.

June was also an important travel month. First, Muhri met Todor Zhivkov, the leader of the Bulgarian Communists, during his visit to Vienna; then a Vienna KPÖ delegation headed by Franz Karger visited Moscow; and Scharf traveled to Ulan Bator to visit the Mongolian party. In August, Muhri returned Zhivkov's visit and went to Sofia.

When Günter Mittag, secretary of the East German party's Central Committee, visited Vienna, he not only met with Muhri and other KPÖ leaders, but he was also received by Kreisky and Staribacher, Austria's minister of commerce (*FBIS,* 21 September).

Kreisky's visits in 1978 to Moscow and East Berlin did have a temporary influence on international policy pronouncements of the KPÖ. In fact, Kalt praised Kreisky's visit to the USSR in the *Volksstimme* (*FBIS,* 10 February). Austrian social democracy, so roundly attacked up to and including the Twenty-third Party Congress, was now de-emphasized as a foe, and prime attention was devoted to the threats posed by China and Eurocommunism.

Publications. The KPÖ continues to publish the daily *Volksstimme* and the theoretical monthly *Weg und Ziel.*

Other Marxist Groups. The Communist League of Austria held its First National Congress in Vienna on 6—8 January. Walter Lindner was elected secretary of the Central Committee. The congress resolved that Austrian Communists "should struggle against the attempt of the two superpowers to place Austria under their economic, political or military control" (*Peking Review,* 10 February). On 3 February, the Austria-China Association was founded. Its officers are Edith Kent, Erwin Landrichter, and Rita Zeller (*FBIS,* 24 March). On 11 September, the Communist League of Austria and the Worker-Peasant Party of Turkey issued a joint statement in defense of Kampuchea, which "is being attacked by Vietnamese leaders at the instigation of the social-imperialists" (*FBIS,* 15 September).

The Communist League of Austria continues to publish the daily *Klassenkampf* and the monthly *Kommunist.*

University of Alberta   Frederick C. Engelmann

Belgium

The Communist Party of Belgium (Parti communiste de Belgique/Kommunistische Partij van België; PCB/KPB), founded in 1921, has an estimated 10,000 members in a population of 9,840,000 (1 January). Since its peak years as a member of the postwar government coalition (1945-1947), the PCB/KPB's influence in Belgian politics has declined.

In the April 1977 legislative elections, it acquired 151,000 votes, or 2.7 percent of the total (1974: 170,000 votes; 3.2 percent), losing 2 of its 4 seats in the 212-member Chamber of Representatives and retaining its single seat in the 181-member Senate (only 106 seats are elected). The PCP/KPB has insignificant representation in three of the nine provincial councils.

National elections were held 17 December. In the 212-seat Belgian parliament the Liberal Party gained four seats for a total of 37. Prime Minister Paul Vanden Boeynant's Christian Social Party gained 2 seats for a total of 82, and the Socialists lost 4 for a total of 58 seats. As a consequence, the PCB was able to gain 2 seats for a total of 4 (the PCB received between 3 and 4 percent of the vote) [in the 1974 parliamentary elections the PCB won 4 seats, and lost 2 of these in the elections held in 1977].

The PCB/KPB has in part been weakened since the mid-sixties by the emergence of three competing groups (see below), of which the Maoist AMADA/TPO and Trotskyite LRT/RAL polled 40,000 votes in the 1977 elections, representing 26 percent of the PCB/KPB total. The PCB/KPB does not have its own labor organization but exercises influence in the two principal federations: the Walloon-dominated Belgian General Confederation of Workers (FGTB), tied with the Socialist Party (PS); and the larger, Flemish-dominated Confederation of Christian Trade Unions (CSC), tenuously linked with the Christian Socialist Party (CVP). In 1977, the two federations formed a common front (Front commun syndical; FCS). The PCB/KPB is also active in various front organizations.

Leadership and Organization. In December 1977 the PCB/KPB Central Committee reelected Louis Van Geyt as chairman and Claude Renard, Jef Turf, and Jean Terfve as vice-chairmen. (Terfve, a party veteran and former cabinet minister, died in April 1978 at age 71.) There is a four-member National Secretariat and thirteen-member Politburo. (*Drapeau rouge,* 20 December).

These central organs maintain the unity of a party otherwise split since 1974 into Flemish (Dutch-speaking), Walloon (French-speaking), and Brussels (bilingual) regional councils. PCB/KPB vice-chairman Renard and Turf head the Walloon and Flemish federations respectively. In recent years, the Flemings have sharply increased their representation in a party that had traditionally been 80 percent Walloon.

The PCB/KPB's auxiliary organizations, limited to the Communist Youth of Belgium, the National Union of Communist Students, and the children's Union of Belgian Pioneers, are not mass organizations but serve primarily as party training and socialization outlets. More important outlets for influencing public opinion and political alignments are the strong Christian Workers' Movement (MOC/ACW), a united front of Christian workers and cooperative associations which has, since

1974, been radicalized from within by the Communists and other leftists; the Belgian Union for the Defense of Peace; the National Action Committee for Peace and Development; the International Committee for European Security and Cooperation, a Soviet front organization; and an active Belgian-Soviet Friendship Association.

The PCB/KPB's Twenty-third Congress, scheduled for 15–17 December, was postponed to early 1979 following the announcement of the 17 December general election. Nearly 40 percent of the 12,000-word preparatory discussion document for the congress is devoted to internal party problems. The document outlines steps to build a stronger party but states that "our membership, sales of our newspaper, and our election results show that the active forces of the workers' movement are far from aware of this need" (ibid., supplement, 24 August).

The sources of the PCB/KPB's difficulties are in part the strain between its liberal leadership supported by the Brussels and Flemish federations and a traditional, neo-Stalinist base centered in the Walloon (especially Liège and Verviers) federations and the awareness by both factions that a precipitous pro-Soviet defection would most likely lead to the disintegration of the party. Unlike the other Belgian parties and newspapers, the PCB/KPB and its organs receive no state subsidies. It relies for its income on membership dues, subscriptions (the bulk of which is absorbed by Soviet bloc states), and revenues obtained from its indirect control of import-export firms and tourist and publicity agencies doing business with Eastern European countries. Thus, a split, on these grounds alone, is to be avoided at all costs. (See Willy Estersohn, *Le Parti communiste de Belgique devant la dissidence et l'* "eurocommunisme" [*1968–1978*]. Brussels, 1978, p. 25).

Domestic Attitudes and Activities. In spite of only a marginal base of support in the working class, the PCB/KPB continued to stress its policy of forming "large alliances" of "progressive and democratic forces" to "limit the power of monopolies and impose structural reforms." (*Drapeau rouge,* 21 January, 24 August). This appeal has been directed without result at the Socialist Party (which split into the French-speaking PS and the Flemish BSP in October 1978), as well as to the left wing of the Christian Socialists and the para-political MOC/CW. The Socialists, however, after three years in opposition (1974–1977), have remained in the government's center-right coalition and continued in the coalition following the resignation of Prime Minister Leo Tindeman's government in October 1978 and the formation of the more rightist interim government headed by the former Defense Minister Paul van den Boeynants.

In May the PCB/KPB, through the National Action Committee for Peace and Development and other fronts, helped organize a demonstration-march to "Disarm for Survival," part of a more widespread international protest against the neutron bomb. The march of an estimated 10,000 demonstrators was disrupted at several points by about 200 AMADA/TPO militants (ibid., 8 May).

In domestic policy, the PCB/KPB rejects the government's so-called "anticrisis law," whose budgetary restrictions are seen as injurious to workers and favorable to monopoly capital. In its place, the party favors a 36-hour workweek coupled with the creation of 100,000 new jobs; the progressive taxation of large fortunes; and antimonopolistic structural reforms, i.e., nationalization of heavy industry and energy (ibid., 13 October).

The PCB/KPB also opposes the greater regionalization foreseen in the government's community pact as not going far enough. Van Geyt, in a Chamber speech, said the pact "does not provide real powers for the regions" (ibid., 4/5 March). The party advocates the direct election by universal suffrage of regional (Wallonia, Flanders, Brussels) assemblies and executives as well as strengthening the two cultural communities (Flemish, Walloon) by granting the right of autonomous financing (ibid., 21 December 1977, 25 April). Under this system, the current provinces and the Senate would be abolished while communal powers would be reinforced (ibid., supplement, 24 August).

International Views and Positions. The PCB/KPB's prudent adhesion to Eurocommunism and bolder criticism of repressive features in the Soviet systems were the highlights of the party's international positions in 1978. Beneath these gestures, however, the PCB/KPB remains a loyalist party (i.e., pro-Soviet), and this ambiguity reflects the tensions within the party.

Of central concern is vice-chairman Claude Renard's 21 January report to the Central Committee on the PCB/KPB's role in the international communist movement, excerpts of which were published in an eight-page supplement in the 26 January issue of *Drapeau rouge*. Renard began by emphasizing the PCB/KPB's "international solidarity" with the socialist camp and the Soviet Union in particular, while pointing out that the quality of this internationalism depended on the quality of its national roots. He also added, as a further rejoinder, that "Soviet society today has faults that help the bourgeoisie conduct extremely efficacious propaganda campaigns against the *whole* communist movement." He also criticized the persecutions in Czechoslovakia of the Charter 77 signatories.

The party spoke out on other occasions against human rights violations in the Eastern European countries. It expressed its "anxiety and censure" at the trial of so-called Soviet dissidents (ibid., 17 July), and Renard, writing in the metropolitan *Le Soir* (18 July), said the trials "profoundly shock Belgian democratic opinion."

Until Renard's January report, the PCB/KPB had made no attempt to come to grips with Eurocommunism. Heretofore, the attitude of the party toward Eurocommunism was, using Van Geyt's and Renard's own words, "confused and ambiguous" (see *YICA, 1978*, p. 110). Renard's reassessment began with the assertion that the world communist movement was on the threshold of a new, fifth phase of international relations, whose distinguishing characteristic was "diversification." This diversification is what "underlies the new notion of international solidarity upheld by the 1976 Berlin conference [of European communist parties]" and which translates itself in "the convergence and conjunction, for specific objectives . . . of independent revolutionary forces (who) freely confront their experiences, often from situations that present similarities and analogies."

Renard pointed out that "the idea of 'Eurocommunism' [was] born in and of this diversity," that it represented "a *specific* solidarity dictated by an evident community of interests" among the communist parties of Western Europe. "There is no doubt," asserted Renard, "that the development and crisis of contemporary capitalism has created a general common framework for the struggle [of these parties] and for the pursuit of political objectives that participate in the same general antimonopolistic orientation, the same vision of the democratic road to socialism." Finally, Renard stipulated that the Eurocommunism which he had in mind reflected more the Italian and French variety than the Spanish.

The report was adopted unanimously by the Central Committee except for abstentions from the two members of the Liège federation. Following the debate on the report, a resolution was adopted (with one dissenting vote) that retained the tone and character of Renard's remarks on Eurocommunism (*Le Soir*, 25 January). It cited the common struggle among the communist parties of Western Europe against "the policy of the monopolies" and underscored the "convergent" views shared by these parties with regard to a democratic and "pluralist" path to socialism. "*Understood in this way,*" the resolution concluded, "*the idea of Eurocommunism reflects a positive reality.*" (*Drapeau rouge,* 23 January).

The PCB/KPB's preparatory document for its Twenty-third Congress reaffirmed these views while adding that the Eurocommunist idea did not imply "a concerted strategy" that pointed to a "new bloc ideology," much less a diminution of the national struggle (ibid., supplement, 26 August).

Nonetheless, a step was taken in the direction of a "regionalist" approach to socialism in Western Europe. This is also reflected to some degree in the PCB/KPB's positions with regard to the EEC and NATO. In April Van Geyt described the EEC as a "reality" that "merits a positive approach on the part of the workers' and democratic forces," who were urged to act within it (ibid., 28 April). On another occasion, Van Geyt pointed out that the PCB/KPB favored enlargement of the powers of the European Parliament, though at the expense of the executive and not to the detriment of national parliaments (ibid., 6 November). In brief, the PCB/KPB has adopted the slogan, "For Europe of the people against Europe of the monopolies" (ibid., 23 January).

While condemning NATO's promotion of the neutron bomb, the PCB/KPB does not "advocate either a unilateral withdrawal [of Belgium] from NATO or a unilateral dissolution of the Atlantic alliance," said Van Geyt in his April speech. Rather, it favors "the parallel and simultaneous dissolution of the military blocs" through "progressive and balanced measures of reducing the military forces" (ibid., 28 April), a view analogous to that of the French Communist Party.

International Activities and Party Contacts. Compared with the previous year, the PCB/KPB maintained a lower active international profile in 1978. Bilateral party contacts included Chairman Van Geyt's New Year Budapest talks with Hungarian party Secretary János Kádár; the Belgian visit of Luis Corvalán and a Chilean CP delegation (ibid., 19 April); and Central Committee-level talks with the Communist Party of Netherlands (ibid., 4/5 November). A delegation of secretaries and activists of the Flemish federations visited the USSR 4−15 July at the invitation of the Communist Party of the Soviet Union (Tass, 15 July).

Finally, Vice-chairman Jef Turf led a PCB/KPB delegation to the Ninth Congress of the Spanish Communist Party in April and reported back on the youth and grass-roots character of the Spanish Communists. Vice-chairman Renard was accompanied by a Central Committee member to the July congress of the Yugoslav League of Communists.

Publications. The PCB/KPB's French daily, *Le Drapeau rouge,* is the party's main organ with a claimed printing of some 25,000 copies. The Flemish weekly, *De Rode Vaan,* of which Jef Turf is political director, is of a slightly higher literary standard. The party's monthly theoretical journal, *Cahiers marxistes,* has a Flemish counterpart, *Vlaams Marxistisch Tijdschrif,* which appears in Ghent three to four times annually. Local and provincial organizations publish some twenty newspapers, the majority consisting of six issues annually, which are distributed free of charge.

The publications are in part financed by the Joseph Jacquemotte Fund created in 1961 and the more recent Masereel Fund. The former has begun a book series, of which the French translation of Jef Turf's *A Political Identity for the Communists* (originally published in 1977 in Dutch) appeared in September.

Other Communist Groups. The Marxist-Leninist Communist Party of Belgium (Parti Communiste marxiste-leniniste de Belgique; PCMLB) split from the PCB/KPB in 1963 to become the first official Peking-line party in Western Europe. Its membership is estimated to be not more than several hundred, although it maintains an effective propaganda apparatus. Its leader, First Secretary Fernand Lefebvre, headed a party delegation to China in August. The party's organ is *Clarté et l'exploité.*

Competing with and to the left of the PCMLB is the Antwerp-centered All Power to the Workers (Alle Macht Aan De Arbeiders/Tout le pouvoir aux ouvriers; AMADA/TPO), a militant Maoist organization not recognized by China. It polled some 24,000 votes in the April 1977 elections.

The Trotskyite Revolutionary Workers' League (Ligue revolutionnaire des travailleurs/ revolutionaire Arbeiders Liga; LRT/RAL) represents the Belgian section of the Fourth International and appeals primarily to students and intellectuals, of whom the most prominent is Ernest Mandel. It held its Fifth (Extraordinary) National Congress on 12 November.

Of the three groupings, LRT/RAL is the most politically influential and has the largest share of members in a combined estimated total membership of 4,000.

International Academy of Manternach
Luxemburg

Peter Gyallay-Pap

Cyprus

The original Communist Party of Cyprus (Kommonistikon Komma Kiprou; KKK) was secretly founded by Greek-trained Cypriots in 1922. Four years later, the party openly held its first congress after the island became a British Crown Colony. Finally outlawed in 1933, it survived underground until it appeared again in April 1941 under the name of the Progressive Party of the Working People (Anorthotikon Komma Laou tis Kiprou; AKEL). The party was again proscribed by the British in 1955, along with all political organizations during the EOKA insurgency. AKEL has had legal status since the proclamation of the Republic of Cyprus in 1960.

As the oldest and best-organized political party in Cyprus, AKEL commands a following far larger than its estimated 12,000 members. (*Cyprus Mail,* 26 May). Virtually all of its overt support comes from the Greek Cypriot majority, about 80 pecent of the island's estimated 640,000 population. The proportion of party members to national adult populace probably ranks AKEL second only to its Italian counterpart among nonruling communist parties. Despite its overall potential, AKEL has played down its strength in both parliamentary and presidential elections, and it has never been represented in any cabinet of the republic.

Since the Turkish invasion and subsequent occupation of some 40 percent of the island in July 1974, the sociopolitical setting in Cyprus has been a fragile calm. Pending a final resolution of the constitutional problems in the government, Turkish Cypriots have formed a "Turkish Federated State of Cyprus" and have held separate elections within their own community for the past fourteen years. Within the Greek Cypriot community, AKEL leaders claim that their party is "the most influential political force" (*WMR,* February). In the elections of September 1976, "the three cooperating parties—AKEL, the Democratic Front, led by Spyros Kyprianou, and the United Democratic Union of the Center (EDEK)—won about 75 percent of the vote" (ibid.). AKEL contested only its nine previously held seats and received a minimum of 30 percent of the coalition vote. (For the election results, see *YICA, 1976,* pp. 127–128.)

The February presidential election was both the first since the Turkish invasion and the first since the death of President Makarios in 1977. It was seen by AKEL as being "of crucial importance for the future of the liberation struggle of our people and country" (*IB,* 15 March). To preserve the coalition formed following the last parliamentary elections, AKEL backed the incumbent Spyros Kyprianou, who won easily over token opposition. While intentionally never seeking any presidential posts in past elections, AKEL boasted that it could have "put forward an able presidential candidate" (ibid.).

AKEL's reluctance to show its true potential is still based upon two fundamental realities: (*a*) the fact that the 1959 Zurich and London Agreements—which gave Cyprus its original and ultimately unworkable form of independence—includes a rationale for the three guarantor powers (the United Kingdom, Greece, and Turkey) to intervene against an illegal subversion of the republic; and (*b*), the probability that a legal push for power by AKEL would surely unite the nationalists and the rightists against the Left. Thus, the main reason why AKEL did not enter a candidate in the presidential election was based upon "the assumption that his victory in the elections could create a situation bordering on civil war," which the Communists "wish to avoid" (*WMR,* Feburary).

AKEL maintains that Cyprus has not yet reached the stage which would enable the party to follow its "more distant goal—the socialist transformation of society" (*IB,* 15 March). Hence, AKEL claims it is a "Marxist-Leninist party, a party of the working class and of the other working people, whose goal is socialism and communism" (*WMR,* June). The party considers its tactics effective as they have evolved "on the basis of scientific analysis of the specific situation in our country and its international position."

While AKEL continues to minimize its friction with the noncommunist Greek Cypriots, its most consistent tactic in recent years has been the open endorsement of the domestic and foreign policies of the late president, Archbishop Makarios. The party feels that "of necessity there exist crucial common points" with "all the patriotic democratic forces" upon which a "minimum program could be constructed" (*IB,* 15 March). It believes that for the time being "not only general democratic but also socialist goals" can be reached by "democratic means" (*WMR,* June). As a result, "parliamentary activity is an important aspect" of AKEL's work. Therefore, "the participation by AKEL deputies in the work of all the parliamentary committees and the party's very presence in parliament have an effect on the adoption of important decisions and laws" (ibid.). In 1974, AKEL first put forward its demand for a "coalition government of anti-imperialist parties and a seat in the Cabinet of Ministers." When this met with little success, it shifted its focus to

> the establishment of a government of national unity with a clear cut anti-imperialist orientation on the basis of a minimum program envisaging, in accordance with the decisions of the recent 14th Congress of AKEL, the solution of the working people's urgent economic and social problems (ibid.).

AKEL has played down its differences with the Orthodox church of Cyprus, particularly over the redistribution of church-owned land to tenant farmers. AKEL has learned from bitter experience that the church in Cyprus is influential in secular politics and the Communists cannot appeal to Greek Cypriots by attacking their Orthodox faith.

While AKEL is the only professed Marxist-Leninist party, there seems to be more and more agreement on current issues with the much smaller socialist party, the Democratic Union of the Center (EDEK). This political grouping is led by a 58-year-old physician, Dr. Vassos Lyssarides, who at one time was the personal medical adviser to President Makarios. The socialists were part of the coalition with the Communists and the Kyprianou forces in both the last parliamentary and the last presidential elections and as a result now hold four seats in the House of Rperesentatives. EDEK and AKEL have had their differences in the past, but as both are leftist parties and their leaders try to avoid any open feuding. Instead they usually refer to one another as part of "the progressive forces in Cyprus."

Leadership and Organization. The leading figures in AKEL are the general secretary, Ezekias Papaioannou, in office since 1949, and his deputy, Andreas Fantis. Both were reelected in May at the party's Fourteenth Congress, which is the supreme authority and meets every four years. In addition to the two top leaders, the following were elected to the four-man Central Committee: Dinos Konstandinou, organizational secretary; and Yiannis Katsouridhis. In addition to these four, the congress also elected the following to be members of the Political Bureau: K. Mikhailidhis, A. Ziartidhis, K. Petas, M. Poumbouris, Y. Khristodoulidhis, A. Mikhailidhis, K. Khristou, and Y. Sofoklis. A new Central Control Committee, chaired by incumbent Yeoryios Savvidhis, was also elected by the congress (*Dhimokratia,* 29 May). A "Bureau of Vigilance" headed by Y. Katsouridhis, assisted by a Mr. Zambas, also exists to check on the loyalty of party members (*I Simerini,* 11 November 1977).

The leadership structure follows the usual pattern of communist party organization—from the primary party groups at members' places of work through the elected town committees and then up to the six provincial committees. It is estimated that 30 percent of the AKEL membership is under the age of 30 and that women make up about 24 percent. A communist source gives the social composition of AKEL as "workers 65.3 percent; peasants 17.7 percent; artisans and small businessmen 11.9 percent; professional and others 5.1 percent" (*Communists of the World and Their Parties,* Prague, 1976, p. 118). The Party leadership is notable for stability and comparatively advanced age, as most are sixty years or older.

Party Internal Affairs. There have been reports of serious disagreement in the party between the "hard-core" leaders and some younger cadres over such issues as Eurocommunism, the party's support of the Soviet intervention in Czechoslovakia, and the need for more "independence" from Moscow (*I Simerini,* 21 October 1977). There is also criticism of "nepotism" within the party (ibid.). Special reference was given to Central Committee member Katsouridhis, who has a son, a daughter, a daughter-in-law, and wife all on the AKEL payroll (ibid., 11 November 1977).

At the opening of the Fourteenth Party Congress in May, General Secretary Papaioannou stressed the need to draft "new cadres to the party" after "careful selection of individuals from schools and universities" (*Cyprus Mail,* 26 May). He also noted, in reference to his "careerist" position, that "care should be taken not to push them up the hierarchy too suddenly" (ibid.).

Each September AKEL holds a fund-raising campaign, which in 1977 produced the sum of 82,000 Cypriot pounds. This was a record amount in the annals of communist fund-raising, for in past years the usual target was 25,000 Cypriot pounds. The Central Committee issued a statement saying that this large amount represents the

> expression of the people's deep love and appreciation for AKEL, a concrete as well as an ostentatious approval of its political line and tactics, and a recompense for its long struggles for the political, economic, and social interests of the working people (*Kharavyi,* 17 November 1977).

Additional operating capital is provided from at least two industrial enterprises: the People's Spirits Manufacturing Co., Ltd. (LOEL), which produces brandies and wines; and the People's Coffee Grinding Co., Ltd.

Auxiliary and Mass Organizations. The total membership for all elements within the AKEL apparatus, including various front groups and allowing for overlapping memberships, is estimated at over 60,000. The most important front is the island's largest labor union, the Pan-Cypriot Workers' Confederation (PEO), which has about 45 percent of the 100,000 organized workers and is an affiliate of the communist front World Federation of Trade Unions. Andreas Ziartidhes, a labor leader for over 35 years, was reelected as PEO general secretary in April 1975, with Pavlos Dinglis as his deputy. Both are influential in AKEL affairs, and Ziartidhis is a member of the House of Representatives from Nicosia.

The AKEL-sponsored United Democratic Youth Organization (EDON) is headed by a 31-year-old London-trained lawyer, Mikhail Papapetrou, elected in 1975. EDON claims to have over 10,000 active members on the island and also has a branch in England, where more than 125,000 Cypriots live. Through a popular sports and social program and a secondary school organization called PEOM, it extends its influence to more than three times its membership. EDON holds a seat on the Executive Committee of the communist front World Federation of Democratic Youth. In addition, the Pan-Cypriot Federation of Students and Young Professionals (POFNE) is composed of students and graduates of institutions of higher learning in the Soviet Union or other East European countries. They constitute about 8 percent of Cypriots studying abroad.

Other AKEL-dominated organizations include a farmers' union (EKA); the Confederation of Women's Organizations (POGO); the Pan-Cyprian Peace Council (PEI), a member of the communist front World Peace Council; and a number of friendship clubs sponsored by East European countries. The AKEL-sponsored Union of Greek Cypriots in England has about 1,200 members.

While AKEL has claimed to have had "hundreds of Turkish Cypriot members in the past," many of these have been allegedly murdered by the right-wing Turkish resistance organization in Cyprus (TMT) (*Kharavyi,* 12 December 1976). Papaioannou claims AKEL is in "contact with its Turkish Cypriot members and progressive Turkish Cypriots in general," but he noted there are "immense difficulties in keeping in touch with them" (ibid.). At the Fourteenth Party Congress, the Turkish Cypriots were represented by one Muzafer Ahmet, who spoke about "the close cooperation between Turkish and Greek Cypriots in the past" (Nicosia radio, 27 May). Papaioannou said in his opening remarks at the congress: "It is high time we turned to our Turkish Cypriot fellow countrymen, to help them in every way to uproot their mistrust and suspicions toward the Greek Cypriots" (*Cyprus Mail,* 26 May).

Domestic Attitudes and Activities. AKEL's line and tactics on domestic issues facing Cyprus have been consistent in recent years. They exploit anticolonialist sentiment by continual attacks on the 1959 Zurich-London agreements which created the dyarchy government. The presence of British Sovereign Base Areas and troops in Cyprus, under terms of the same agreements, provides a fruitful target for communist propaganda since they claim the bases are used for NATO purposes. The crash of an American U-2 reconnaissance plane on takeoff from one of the bases reinforced this notion and inspired AKEL to demand a halt of all such flights from the island (*NYT,* 10 December 1977). This position is consistent with prior demands for "withdrawal of all foreign troops," including the Turkish troops in the North, as "an indispensable condition of a just settlement of the Cyprus problem" (Tass, 19 November 1977). At the party congress AKEL reaffirmed its stand that Cyprus should be "truly independent, sovereign, territorially integral, nonaligned and demilitarized" (*Kharavyi,* 28 May).

An important congress resolution, directed to the president of Cyprus, stressed "the government's imperative duty to strengthen our domestic front on all sides and, primarily, the unity of our people's patriotic and democratic forces" (ibid.). The text of the resolution stated that the "essential prerequisites" are

(*a*), the forging of a firm and solid unity of the patriotic forces of the Cypriot people on the basis of a minimum program and one common line and strategy; (*b*), the cleansing and purging of the security forces—army and police—of the state machinery, and of the quasi-state organizations; (*c*), the dissolution of all illegal organizations and the confiscation of all illegal weapons; (*d*), the solution of the basic refugee problems and especially of the housing problem as well as the solution of the people's primary economic problems such as the equitable distribution and redistribution of the economic burdens and the fairer distribution of the national income for the benefit of the working masses; (*e*), the democratization of the political and social life of the country through communal, municipal, and other elections, the democratization and modernization of the law on cooperatives and institutions, the implementation of the simple proportion (electoral) system and other measures; (*f*), the elimination of discrimination at the expense of AKEL members and of the leftist progressive elements in general as concerns the appointments and promotions in government positions and in quasi-state and other organizations; (*g*), the formation of a political government representative of the patriotic, democratic forces on the basis of a simple platform (*Kharavyi*, 8 June).

Concerning the intercommunal talks between the Cypriot Greeks and Turks, AKEL has usually been pessimistic because of what it terms the "intransigent stand of the Turkish Cypriots." Specifically, the party's position is as follows:

> We are always ready for talks with the Turkish Cypriot side, and life has proved that we have done whatever we could for constructive, fruitful, intercommunal talks. However, the other side brings forward unreasonable demands which . . . [called for] the actual dissolution of the Cyprus republic as a unitary economic-political entity. If the Turkish side truly wants the intercommunal dialogue to be resumed, it has only to submit reasonable proposals within the framework of an independent, federal Cyprus on the basis of the procedure which has been agreed upon with U.N. Secretary General Dr. Waldheim. (*Kharavyi*, 29 August.)

AKEL acknowledges, regardless of years of disappointment, that "the UN remains, despite its shortcomings, a powerful instrument in waging a struggle for a peaceful, democratic solution of the Cyprus issue (*IB*, 15 June). The goal would be to use diplomatic sources "aimed at utilizing valuable international support and solidarity—particularly that of the Soviet Union—for the convocation of a special international conference" (*Kharavyi*, 28 May). The "international conference" theme is an old slogan, which AKEL has promoted unsuccessfully for the last four years.

International Views and Positions. The direction of AKEL's views on foreign affairs was "decided by President Makarios." The election of Spyros Kyprianou, "a loyal and consistent adherent of the line of deceased Archbishop Makarios, will ensure the unhampered and steadfast continuation of the policy of nonalignment, inspired by the deceased president" (*IB*, November 1977). The AKEL Central Committee passed this resolution before the election of Kyprianou as president in February, since he was a man who "has won international repute in the UN and among nonaligned countries" (ibid.). Thus, a resolution at the party's Fourteenth Congress emphasized that the government of Cyprus must pursue in the future "its policy of nonalignment" (*Kharavyi*, 8 June).

The political resolution of AKEL's Fourteenth Congress regarding the international situation contained a comprehensive analysis of the past year with particular reference to

> the achievements of the struggle for international detente; to the final Helsinki agreement and the victories of the people in Afghanistan, Angola, Ethiopia, and Indochina; to the fall of the dictatorial regimes in Greece, Spain, and Portugal; to the struggles of the people in the Middle East, Africa, Latin America, and elsewhere for freedom, democracy, and progress; and finally, for the definite change in the relationship among the world powers for the benefit of socialism (ibid.).

Concerning the issue of "so-called Eurocommunism," AKEL rejects it as something "launched by bourgeois propaganda" (*WMR*, February). AKEL acknowledges that in the communist movement, "there are different views of this matter, and it is being discussed." But the bourgeoisie, "seeking to divide communism into several parts on the geopolitical principle," gives the term a "peculiarly biased anticommunist slant and use it as a way of fighting communist parties." What particularly interests bourgeois politicians "is that the simple insertion of particle 'Euro' turns communism into reformism" (ibid.). AKEL concludes that encouraging "reformism in the working-class movement" is the objective of the bourgeoisie and that is why the term was invented in the first place. Thus, AKEL regards "any forms of anti-Sovietism as a manifestation of anticommunism." (Tass, 20 May.)

When the United States proposed to end the three-year-old arms embargo against Turkey, AKEL's general secretary saw this as having "negative effects on Greek-Turkish relations and on developments in the Eastern Mediterranean and the Middle East in general." He claimed that "the battle of the embargo" made it clear "that there is no barrier at all in the way of the interests of U.S. imperialism when it comes to serving them—there are no principles of morality, justice, or human rights." He further noted that the decision to lift the embargo shows that "the responsible circles of U.S. imperialism favor Turkey, which they want to use as their main base and springboard for their more strategic plans in the area . . . a fact that will lead to new tension in Greek-Turkish relations" (*I Dhimokratiki,* 7 August).

In April an unconfirmed news report in the Turkish press and Reuters news service that the Soviet Union had offered military aid to Turkey caused considerable alarm in Cyprus. Without necessarily authenticating the report or waiting for an official confirmation, Cypriot President Kyprianou sent a strong protest to the Soviet government. This was seen by the communist paper in Cyprus "as a hasty and awkward move" because notice of such a serious demarche could not be based upon news sources. Moreover, AKEL stressed that "it would be impossible and inconceivable for the Soviet Union to grant arms to Turkey, a member of NATO and CENTO" (*Kharavyi,* 28 April). AKEL was not "disturbed" by the news report because "everyone knows that the Soviet Union follows a principled policy and not an opportunistic one in matters of international relations, and particularly in the Cyprus issue" (ibid., 29 April). AKEL believed that Kyprianou's "strong protest" will have "negative effects on the Cyprus republic's international relations at a most critical period when Cyprus has the duty to promote and develop its ties with its friends and supporters throughout the world" (ibid.).

AKEL continued its criticism of China and maintained that the "successes of the socialist community countries" would be ever greater "had not the unity of the communist movement" been undermined by "the dogmatic, nationalistic, sectarian policy and tactics followed by the new leadership of the Chinese Communist Party and the People's Republic of China (PRC)" (ibid., 19 March). In an attempt to improve relations following this criticism, the head of the party's International Department, Dr. Christofinis, hand delivered a letter of friendship to the Chinese embassy in Nicosia. It was returned to him unopened by a PRC representative, who was quoted as saying: "We have no relations with you" (ibid., 11 April).

International Activities and Party Contacts. AKEL maintains extensive and frequent contact with both ruling and nonruling communist parties, as well as with all the various international communist front groups. The party's Fourteenth Congress was attended by "representatives of more than 30 fraternal communist and workers' parties and national liberation movements" (Tass, 28 May). The Soviet Union's delegation was led by Central Committee Secretary Yakov Ryabov, who emphasized at his departure that AKEL's "prestige is growing constantly" because of its "consistent loyalty to the principles of Marxism-Leninism and proletarian internationalism" (ibid., 31 May).

In addition to "the great friend and ally of the Cypriots," the Soviet Union, the other countries in attendance included Greece, Bulgaria, Italy, Cuba, and some unspecified parties from "Asia, Africa, and Latin America" (ibid., 28 May). The Cuban delegation was headed by Jorge Enrique Mendoza, a newspaper publisher and a member of the Central Committee. All of the communist delegations were received in the office of the president of Cyprus, and Mendoza expressed "his thanks for the solidarity shown to the Cuban delegation" (Havana radio, 30 May). Greetings were also sent to the AKEL Congress from, among others, the Communist Party of Vietnam and the Communist Party of Turkey (Nicosia radio, 26 May).

During the fall of 1977, Papaioannou chose to go to Moscow—"instead of attending the Cyprus debate in the United Nations"—in order to celebrate the sixtieth anniversary of the October Russian Revolution, which was occurring at the same time (*Cyprus Mail,* 22 October 1977). The AKEL delegation was received by Chairman Brezhnev, and both sides "expressed themselves in favor of the further development of fraternal relations between the CPSU and AKEL" (Moscow radio, 9 November

1977). During the same visit, the AKEL delegation met with the delegation of the Israeli Communist Party (RAKAH). The Israeli leader, M. Wilner, said that "the problems of Cyprus and the Middle East are linked" with "imperialism and Zionism against the Palestinians, the Arabs, and the Cypriots" (*Kharavyi*, 5 November 1977).

Other trips during the year included one in July to Hungary, where a three-member AKEL delegation got "acquainted with the life and activities of the sister party as well as with its achievements in building socialism" (ibid., 15 July). In August Papaioannou vacationed in Bulgaria and took the opportunity to meet with Todor Zhivkov, head of the Bulgarian Communist Party (Sofia radio, 21 August).

Greetings were exchanged between AKEL and the First Secretary of the Greek Communist Party (KKE), E. K. Florakis, who noted his party's "solidarity with the Cypriot people for the sake of a just solution of their problem" (*Kharavyi*, 29 November 1977). At about the same time, AKEL sent congratulations to Yugoslavia's President Tito on the occasion of that country's national anniversary (ibid., 29 November 1977). In July AKEL sent a greeting to the Workers' Party of North Korea to bid them support in their "struggle to force U.S. forces to withdraw from South Korea and for attaining the country's peaceful reunification" (Phyongyan radio, 27 July).

AKEL's general secretary addressed the Second World Congress of Overseas Cypriots which was held in Nicosia in August. This group, which "represents the Cypriots living abroad" was lauded for continuing "the struggle of Cyprus in the countries where you live, and as our motherland's true ambassadors to these countries, you will preserve the flame of Cyprus's battle for freedom" (*Kharavyi*, 29 August). It cannot be determined at this time to what extent AKEL has infiltrated this organization, but it is of the type which has been beneficially exploited by AKEL in the past.

Publications. AKEL has long enjoyed influential press channels in Cyprus. AKEL's central organ is the large-circulation daily *Kharavyi* (Dawn), but there are also sympathetic writers and editors on most of the island's periodicals. AKEL also publishes a weekly newspaper, *Dhimokratia* (Democracy), and a weekly magazine, *Neoi Kairoi* (New times). Its *Theoritikos Dhimokratis* (Theoretical democrat) is a scholarly journal. The PEO publishes a weekly newspaper, *Ergatiko Vima* (Workers' stride), and EDON a weekly called *Neolaia* (Youth). In London, a weekly called *Ta Vima* (The stride) has been published by Greek Cypriot Communists for the past 37 years.

Puebla, Pue., Mexico   T. W. Adams

Denmark

The Communist Party of Denmark (Danmarks Kommunistiske Parti; DKP) sprang from the left-wing faction of the Social Democratic Party (SDP) in the turbulent aftermath of World War I. The DKP was organized on 9 November 1919, and except for the German occupation during World War II, it has always been a legal party.

The DKP draws most of its support from among urban industrial workers, together with some leftist intellectuals in Copenhagen and other urban centers. Membership has edged upward during the mid-1970s after a decade of stagnation and is now estimated between 7,500 and 8,500. The population of Denmark is about 5,120,000.

The continuing discontent of Danish wage earners and taxpayers—first expressed by a high protest vote in the national election of 4 December 1973—has benefited the DKP and other leftist groups. A sudden parliamentary election on 15 February 1977 saw twelve parties vying for representation, and all but one of these parties gained entrance to the new parliament. Despite the continuing political turmoil, the governing Social Democrats significantly increased their mandates and continue to govern, and in August 1978 the SDP formed a coalition with the right-of-center Venstre (Liberal) Party. The new government is still short of a parliamentary majority and must seek support from center and moderate right parties. In 1977 the DKP received 114,022 (3.7 percent) votes, a loss of 0.5 percentage points from 1975. The DKP seems to have stabilized its electoral strength at around 4 percent during the past three elections, but this is a stronger performance than during the period 1953—73, when the DKP typically polled only 1 percent. Frequent public opinion polls during 1978 have indicated a slight decline in support, which could jeopardize one of the party's seven seats in the 179-member Folketing (parliament). In the March municipal and county elections, the DKP made slight gains, particularly in Copenhagen, where a Communist, Ivan Hansen, became an administrative magistrate.

The DKP would appear to be the strongest of several socialist parties to the left of the reformist Social Democrats. The Left Socialists (Venstresocialisterne; VS), who had fallen below the 2 percent threshold for parliamentary representation in the 1971 and 1973 elections, returned to parliament in 1975 and gained an additional seat in February 1977 for a total of five mandates (2.7 percent of the vote). The Socialist People's Party (Socialistisk Folkeparti; SF) received seven seats (3.9 percent of the vote), a loss of two seats from 1975. Intermittent intraparty strife in the SF during 1976 resulted in a large turnover of elected representatives, with gains for the party's more radical wing. Internal disagreements (inter alia, about the extent of SF cooperation with the DKP and VS) have reappeared at times since the disappointing electoral showing and have cost the party some support in public opinion polls during the year.

Leadership and Organization. Supreme party authority is the DKP's triennial congress, which held its twenty-fifth meeting in September 1976. It discussed the report of the Central Committee, adopted the party program and rules, and elected the leading party bodies, consisting of the Central Committee (41 members, 11 alternates), a 5-member Control Commission, and 2 party auditors. The Central Committee elects the party chairman, the Executive Committee (15 members), and the Secretariat (5).

Knud Jespersen, who had been DKP chairman since 1958, died unexpectedly on 1 December 1977. Meeting on 10 December, the DKP Central Committee chose DKP member of parliament Jørgen Jensen as its new chairman. Jensen, 59, is a veteran of many years of DKP activity and has been a member of the Central Committee since 1952. Jensen is active in trade union affairs and is a member of the Danish Metalworkers' Union (Dansk Metalarbejderforbund) Executive Committee, despite the fact that the union is controlled by Social Democrats. He has also been chairman of a union local in Lyngby (a Copenhagen suburb). Ib Nørlund, who was briefly acting DKP chairman during Jespersen's illness, is the party's parliamentary leader and its chief theoretician. Paul Emanuel is party secretary.

The DKP has been unique among the several Marxist parties in Denmark in that personality conflicts and policy differences, if any, have not been discussed in public (since 1958). Late in 1977 an exception to this was party criticism of Central Committee member Preben Møller Hansen for his autocratic behavior as chairman of the communist-dominated Seamen's Union (Dansk Sømaendenes-forbund). (*Berlingsk Tidende,* 28 November 1977.) Party continuity has been typified not only by the late Knud Jespersen's long chairmanship but also by the reelection in February 1977 of the same seven parliamentary representatives who had sat in the previous session. It is felt that Jensen's election demonstrates the DKP's conservatism in internal affairs. Jensen is tried and true but without the personal popularity that Jespersen used to good advantage.

Not much is known about party finances other than that they seem to be adequate and that there are frequent collection campaigns for the party's daily newspaper, *Land og Folk.* Like other parties represented in the Folketing, the DKP receives a monthly subvention from the public treasury. It is currently D. Kr. 25,837 per month (equivalent to about $57,952 per year).

The party's two main auxiliary organizations are the Communist Youth of Denmark (Danmarks Kommunistiske Ungdom; DKU) and the Communist Students of Denmark (Danmarks Kommunis-tiske Studenter; DKS). The latter is quite well organized and has won a substantial number of seats on university councils, on which students are entitled to representation. The autonomous Faroese Communist Party (FKP), which is active on the Faroe Islands, was formed in 1975 and is headed by Egon Thomsen. The FKP did not participate, however, in the 1977 parliamentary elections and failed to gather even the few hundred signatures necessary to appear on the ballot during the November 1978 local elections. The DKP is not active in Greenland, where the leftist Siumut Party has elected Lars Emil Johansen as one of the island's two parliamentary representatives. Johansen has been affiliated with the SF parliamentary group.

Domestic Attitudes and Activities. Again in 1978 the Danish economy suffered from high unemployment, large deficits in trade and in the state budget, and only minimal economic growth. The underlying rate of inflation declined to about 7 percent. These issues dominated internal Danish politics and were the focus of DKP comments during the past year. The industrial crisis was especially acute at most of the shipyards, a sector where communist trade union strength is especially strong. The August 1976 and September 1977 agreements between the Social Democrats and several center-right parties eased the rate of inflation and the size of the nation's trade deficit at the cost of rising unemployment. The DKP had violently opposed these measures, and the party reiterated its opposiiton throughout 1978. The DKP remains committed to its demands for sizable wage increases, a 35-hour work week, and 35 days of paid vacation per year.

The formation of the Social Democratic−Liberal coalition government on 30 August 1978 sparked strong protests not only among the three left-socialist parties but also in the trade union movement and among some left-wing Social Democrats as well. This alliance between the Social Democrats and the main opposition party confirmed the swing to the right of the Social Democratic leadership under premier Anker Jørgensen. The Social Democratic chairman of the Trade Union Confederation (Landsorganisationen; LO), Thomas Nielsen, called the coalition a break with all of the principles of the workers' movement (*Nordisk Kontakt,* no. 12). Thousands of trade unionists demonstrated outside the parliament, while DKP Chairman Jensen denounced the new government and vowed total opposition (ibid., no. 13). The first action of the new government was to raise the value-added tax to 20.25 percent; the measure passed by only two votes with the three left-socialist parties, as well as the right and center parties, generally opposed. Although several centrist parties have promised pragmatic support for the minority coalition government, there remains the danger of defections within the Social Democratic parliamentary group.

Dissatisfaction among trade unionists could provide an opportunity for increased DKP activity because the party has long been stronger in the trade union movement than in electoral politics. Although the LO is firmly controlled by unionists previously quite loyal to the SDP, some communist and other Marxist activists are prominent in union locals. Mention has already been made of communist strength in the Seaman's Union and the Metalworkers' Union. In contrast with 1977, labor peace prevailed during the past year, except for several short wildcat strikes in protest against the new SDP-Liberal government in August and September. National industrial labor contracts are due to expire in March 1979, and the government is committed to a tight incomes policy and seeks only to maintain real disposable income. The government passed a law in September freezing prices, rents, and wages except for previously signed contracts. (Ibid. no. 13.) Moreover, the Social Democrats are encouraging unions to introduce "economic democracy" demands in current contract talks, which would specify worker rights to participation in management, investment decisions, and profits. The likelihood of severe labor disputes early in 1979 is additionally increased by the militant position of the DKP and other leftist forces. An important instrument of leftist trade unionists has been the Shop Stewards' Initiative Group (Formandsinitiativet), in which unionists sympathetic to the DKP compete with SF, VS, and other activists for control. Communist Metalworkers steward Jan Andersen is considered the dominant figure in the Initiative Group, but following unsuccessful actions in 1977, there is doubt about the group's continuing unity and effectiveness (*Berlingske Tidende*, 3 March).

Another important trade union goal of the DKP leadership, and other left-socialist forces as well, is to undermine the extensive Danish labor court and labor law system, which provides for substantial penalties for unlawful strikes and lockouts. The DKP sees the increased use of the labor court against militant actions as an effort to hurt workers (*Land og Folk*, 1 January).

International Views and Positions. The Twenty-fifth Congress (1976) and more recent statements by the DKP leadership reaffirmed the party's established international views. Primary attention is given to denouncing Danish participation in the EEC, NATO, and other Western organizations. During 1978 the DKP focused upon the direct elections to the parliament of the EEC scheduled for June 1979. The DKP has been prominent in the Popular Movement against the EEC (Folkebevaegelsen mod EF), which was formed in the early 1970s as a nonpartisan alliance to keep Denmark out of the EEC. A dispute arose within the movement early in 1978 as to whether there should be a single anti-EEC list of parliamentary candidates or whether each constituent anti-EEC party should present its own list. The DKP has favored the former course, while the SF prefers the latter (*Berlingske Tidende*, 26 January). The DKP leadership has indicated that it will give the highest priority to the election of anti-EEC candidates in the upcoming election.

The traditional DKP anti-NATO line focused on Danish defense expenditures (already among the lowest in NATO), Denmark's commitment to purchase the F-16 fighter, and American plans to deploy the neutron bomb. On the latter issue, the DKP has sought to promote an anti-neutron bomb movement among noncommunist opponents of NATO (*Land og Folk*, 20 October 1977). More generally, DKP publications and statements echo such Soviet security concerns as the growing West German role in NATO and the Soviet positions on the Middle East, Africa, and Southeast Asia.

International Activities and Party Contacts. Danish Communists continue to participate in frequent contacts with their counterparts in other European communist parties, and loyalty to the Soviet party remains the sine qua non of DKP international activity. The Berlin conference of European communist parties in June 1976 has become the symbol of DKP interparty standards (*Tiden*, no. 8, 1976). DKP admiration for its Soviet comrades was demonstrated on the occasion of the sixtieth anniversary of the Bolshevik Revolution in November 1977. As Ib Nørlund expressed it, "the October Revolution stands out as a tower of inspiration and strength" (*WMR*, September 1977).

With the change in DKP leadership following Knud Jespersen's death, visits to and by Danish Communists were more numerous than usual in 1977–78. A delegation of Bulgarian Communists visited Copenhagen in September 1977 (*Rabotnichesko delo*, Sofia, 28 September 1977), and a

Romanian delegation visited in January (Bucharest domestic radio, 10 January). DKP Chairman Jensen visited Poland in April (Tass, 13 April), East Germany in May (Allgemeiner Deutscher Nachrichtendienst, 19 May), Moscow in June (*Pravda*, 17 June), Romania, Bulgaria, and Hungary in July (Bucharest domestic radio, 3 July; Bulgarska telegrafna agentsiya, 11 July; Magyar Távirati Iroda, 14 July).

There were a number of substantive demonstrations of DKP support for other communist parties and regimes during 1978. The DKP expressed unqualified support for the Vietnamese government's position in that country's border war with Cambodia (Vietnam News Agency, 19 March). Danish Communists also defended the conviction of dissidents Ginzburg and Shcharansky in the Soviet Union. Jørgen Jensen claimed that "human rights are even more extensive in socialist countries than elsewhere; but, naturally, the laws must be observed" (*Berlingske Tidende*, 19 July).

Publications. *Land og Folk* (Nation and people), a daily newspaper, is the DKP central organ. Its circulation of some 10,000 increases on weekends to about 12–14,000. *Tiden-Verden Rund* (Times around the world) is the party's theoretical monthly journal. The DKU publication is *Fremad* (Forward).

Other Marxist Groups. Mention has already been made of the two principal competitors with the DKP for left-socialist support. In domestic politics, both the VS and SF try to maintain independent profiles. Since 1958 the SF has been the most pragmatic of the various left-socialist groups, and in 1966–67 and 1971–73 it provided parliamentary support for minority SDP governments in domestic matters. One consequence of this has been internal party splits and power struggles. Most severe were the splits in 1967 over support of SDP economic policy and in 1976–77 over general party orientation. Although the SF is a purely Danish party, it has had close ties to an analogous party in Norway (Sosialistisk Venstreparti; SV) and expresses enthusiasm for the leading advocates of Eurocommunism.

The VS is also a native party without institutional ties to foreign movements. It stresses the limitations of parliamentary action in its program and has been vocal in its support for student activists and minority elements in the trade union movement. Although not uncritical of events in communist countries, the VS, like the SF, directs most of its foreign policy criticism against the United States, NATO, and the EEC. The VS has been anxious to avoid strongly institutionalized leadership and demands continuous activity by its members. A result has been recurrent intraparty policy struggles. It is estimated that the VS has at present between 2,500 and 3,000 active members (*Berlingske Tidende*, 13 July). Like the SF, the VS was extremely critical of the new SDP-Liberal coalition government. Recent public opinion polls have indicated some increase in support for the VS at the expense of the SF and the DKP. The party also increased its support in urban areas in the March municipal elections.

In addition to these two small parties, there are a myriad of "parties," cultural groups, and publications reflecting various Marxist viewpoints. The former Communist League of Marxist-Leninists (Kommunistforbund Marxister-Leninister), which is now known as the Communist Workers' Party of Denmark (Kommunist-Arbeiderparti; KAP), is headed by Copenhagen University lecturer Benito Scocozza. The KAP has remained loyal to its pro-Peking line on foreign policy and also supports the positions of North Korea and Cambodia. It has also been active in student protest movements and in the most radical factions of the trade union movement. The Trotskyist Revolutionary League (Revolutionaere Socialisters Forbund; RSF) is critical of all foreign powers and domestic competitors.

Among the many non-DKP leftist publications are the SF's daily *Socialistisk Dagblad* (Socialist daily), formerly *Minavisen*; the KAP's *Arbejderavisen* (Worker's news), formerly *Kommunist*;

the RSF's *Klassekampen* (Class struggle); and the independent and radical socialist *Politisk Revy* (Political review).

University of Massachusetts   Eric S. Einhorn
Amherst

Finland

Consistently attracting nearly a fifth of the electorate, the Communist Party of Finland (Suomen Kommunistinen Puolue; SKP) continued in 1978 to hold the distinction of being the only European communist party (except for the special case of Iceland) participating in a democratic parliamentary government. Given the strains facing any Finnish government, the SKP's distinction was perhaps a mixed pleasure. Nevertheless, the history of the Finnish communist movement has been one of dramatic changes in fate reflecting the country's special history and geographic position. The SKP was established in Moscow on 29 August 1918 by "reds"—dissident Social Democrats—escaping from Finland's bloody civil war. Until 1930, the SKP operated through a variety of front organizations, but during the 1930s the party was forced underground by a government ban on its operations. It became legal in 1944, as stipulated by the Finnish-Soviet armistice. During the years of Soviet-Finnish armed conflict (1939-40 and 1941-44), nearly all Finnish Communists remained loyal to their country.

The SKP draws most of its members from either the industrialized urban areas of southern Finland or the small farming communities of the northern and eastern districts, where a "northland" radical tradition thrives. SKP membership is estimated at about 45-48,000, while the Finnish population totals 4,770,000.

The economic difficulties which had first appeared in 1974-75 (inflation, balance of payment difficulties, and rising unemployment) preoccupied the multiparty coalition government headed by Social Democrat Kalevi Sorsa during the past year. Although the rate of inflation fell, partly in response to governmental price controls, the level of unemployment reached 9.1 percent of the labor force early in 1978. The Communists participated in center-left governments in the late 1960s, and in November 1975 they joined the center-left coalition formed by centrist Martti Miettunen. Ten months later the coalition collapsed over economic crisis measures, and the SKP was vigorous in opposition to the now-minority Miettunen government's economic stabilization measures. Again, in May 1977, the SKP leadership was persuaded to join a five-party majority coalition headed by the Social Democratic leader Sorsa. Finland's 60th government in as many years of national independence is a coalition of the Social Democrats (Finland's largest party with 54 of the Parliament's 200 seats); the SKP through its traditional electoral and parliamentary front organization, the Finnish People's Democratic League (Suomen Kansan Demokraatinen Liitto; SKDL) with 40 seats; the Center Party (formerly the Agrarians) with 41 seats; the Liberal Party with 8 seats; and the Swedish People's Party (center-right) holding 10 parliamentary seats. In February 1978, the Sorsa government was modified by the withdrawal of the Swedish People's Party.

Three Communists hold cabinet posts in the Sorsa government: the vice-minister of education, the minister of labor, and the traffic minister. Labor Minister Arvo Aalto has been secretary-general of the SKP for ten years.

Leadership and Organization. Aarne Saarinen, aged 65, a "liberal" Communist and popular former union leader, has been SKP chairman since 1966 and has supported SKDL participation in center-left governments. The 1978 party congress which reelected him also reelected the so-called "Stalinist" (hardline, particularly in parliamentary and cabinet issues) Taisto Sinisalo and liberal Olavi Hänninen as vice-chairmen, and liberal Arvo Aalto as secretary-general. The Eighteenth Party Congress confirmed the relative strength between the two factions, which has remained relatively constant since 1970. The 50-member Central Committee has 29 majority (liberal) and 21 minority (Stalinist) members, and the ratio in the party's Executive Committee (politburo) is 9 majority—6 minority. The SKDL Executive Committee maintains similar proportions (with some variation on different issues), and the current SKDL chairman is the liberal Socialist (not formally a Communist) Ele Alenius. For the SKP the Central Committee is the highest decision-making body between the triennial congresses (*Land og Folk*, Copenhagen, 29 June; *Nordisk Kontakt*. no. 11).

Party Internal Affairs. It is not easy to define the issues that split the two SKP factions, even though their disagreements over day-to-day political tactics are argued in public. The division can be traced back at least to the ideological turmoil following the 1956 "de-Stalinization" congress of the Soviet Communist Party. Among the issues widening the split have been different reactions to the Warsaw Pact invasion of Czechoslovakia in 1968, domestic political tactics (especially the question of political collaboration with the Social Democrats), and interpretations of Moscow's preferences. Personality issues have undoubtedly also played a role. With a majority of the SKP supporting governmental responsibility and political pragmatism and the always vigorous public discussion between the two factions, Finland may rightfully claim to have a "working model" of Eurocommunism, a phrase that chairman Saarinen does not disown. So far the party has not been hurt by such activity, and as one editorial writer put it, "the Saarinen-Sinisalo show will continue to receive good ratings" (i.e., attract public interest in the party) (*Uusi Suomi*, 30 January).

Mutual toleration between the two factions is not easy. At a meeting of the SKP Central Committee in December 1977, chairman Saarinen strongly attacked the Stalinists and threatened them with expulsion (*Helsingin Sanomat*, 17 December 1977). Sinisalo's position was defended by the minority's paper, and Saarinen was denounced (*Tiedonantaja*, 20 December 1977). The SKP Central Committee met in February to prepare for the election of delegates to the Eighteenth Party Congress but it proved impossible to work out a compromise. Hence, contested delegate elections were held in March with the liberal candidates outpolling the Stalinists in most urban areas. The actual breakdown of congress delegates was 278 liberals and 215 Stalinists (*Kansan Uutiset*, 18 March; *Helsingin Sanomat*, 13 April).

At the Eighteenth Congress itself, the two factions avoided direct confrontations by formulating statements in rather general terms and avoiding votes (by previous agreement). Chairman Saarinen remarked that an open split in the party would only make matters worse; two competing parties would each fare less well in parliamentary elections, there would be problems of political coalitions and cooperation (especially within the SKDL), and as Saarinen put it, "in considering international relations alone the division of the party into two is impossible" (i.e., the Soviet Union wants to maintain party unity) (*Helsingin Sanomat*, 28 May).

Relations between the SKP and its political front organization, SKDL, have received less attention. As previously mentioned, SKDL chairman Ele Alenius has been very positive about SKP/SKDL participation in the coalition government and about prospects for "Eurocommunism" in Western Europe. During the spring of 1978 these normally placid relations were severely disrupted by the frank remarks of SKDL parliamentarian Ilkka-Christian Björklund, who directly condemned bureaucratic Communists in the Soviet Union and East Germany for their suppression of dissidents. The imprisonment of Rudolf Bahro in East Germany was directly denounced. Björklund drew analogies to "petty bureaucrats" among Finnish Socialists and Communists (*Suomen Kuvalehti,* 16 June). The reaction to Björklund's remarks was violent protest from both wings of the SKP, with demands that the SKDL discipline its outspoken politician (*Helsingin Sanomat,* 16 July). Finnish Communists clearly draw a line between their own internal debates and criticism directed at neighboring communist regimes.

Domestic Attitudes and Activities. Finland's continuing economic problems, noted above, preoccupied the coalition government in which the SKP participated during the past year. The presidential elections in January provided an additional focus of attention, although there was never any doubt as to who the winner would be. The Sorsa government proposed several new economic measures aimed at slowing inflation, strengthening Finland's international economic position, and preventing increasing unemployment. The SKP was opposed to wage freezes and currency devaluations, but the majority of the SKP, including its three ministers, accepted the December 1977 economic stimulation package. Prior to Kekkonen's new presidential term, the Sorsa government tendered its resignation (a formality), but real political difficulties suddenly appeared. First, the Swedish People's Party no longer wished to continue in the government. Second, the Bank of Finland forced an 8 percent devaluation of the Finnish markka in February, a similar devaluation took place in Norway, and there was a prolonged downward float of the Swedish krona. The SKP Politburo and communist trade unionists protested this decision vehemently (*Nordisk Kontakt,* no. 4). At President Kekkonen's request, Premier Sorsa was able to reconstruct his government on a four-party basis. Continued SKP support was secured by promising compensation for the devaluation. When the trade unions threatened "warning strikes" for 31 March-2 April, the government was able to offer an acceptable series of modifications of the economic package (ibid., nos. 5-7).

Despite these crises, the Sorsa government continues to search for pragmatic solutions to Finland's economic difficulties. The latest trend has been to encourage modest wage demands by reducing state social security taxation. Since part of these taxes are paid directly by employers, the overall effect is to lower costs and encourage employment. The "liberals" within the SKP have accepted these measures despite criticism from the Stalinist wing, which regularly votes against the government. Despite its accommodating performance in the government, the SKP still advocates much more radical measures, such as: (1) expansion of the state sector in industry and services, along with better parliamentary control of such activity, (2) nationalization of all banks and major financial institutions, and (3) dismantling of Finnish economic and trade ties with the West and increased economic and technological ties to the Soviet bloc (*WMR,* January 1977). Sharing power and responsibility has muted the SKP program.

Consensus also dominated the presidential elections of January-February 1978. The five governing parties along with the Conservative, the main opposition party, all endorsed U.K. Kekkonen for reelection. President since 1956, Kekkonen is the symbol of Finland's careful relations with her eastern neighbor. Despite his advanced age, Kekkonen faced only token opposition. He received 82 percent of the popular vote and 259 of the 300 electoral votes. Despite their participation in the government, the SKDL vote declined only slightly (Kekkonen was technically the candidate of several parties) (*Nordisk Kontakt.* no. 2).

Despite domestic political détente, the SKP still competes against the Social Democrats for positions and influence in the powerful Finnish labor movement. Although the SAK (Finnish Confederation of Trade Unions) is run by Social Democrats, Communists currently lead several of the constituent unions including the Construction Workers, Food Distributors, Rubber and Leather Workers, and Maintenance (real estate) Workers. The Social Democrats enjoy only a slight majority in the Metal Workers' and Paper Workers' unions. Communists are not powerful in most white-collar organizations or among state and municipal workers (*Helsingin Sanomat*, 28 May).

As the coalition government moved into its second year, the approaching parliamentary elections (scheduled for March 1979) received greater attention. With unemployment looming as a major election issue, SKP Minister of Labor Aalto called for an even larger deficit state budget in order to relieve unemployment (ibid., 10 July). The government's response in September was more moderate, however, calling for continued tax reductions to cheapen the cost of labor (*Nordisk Kontakt*, no. 12). Public opinion polls taken in October 1978 showed slight gains for the Social Democrats and slight losses for the SKDL. A continuation of the Sorsa coalition is likely after March, unless there are some last minute upsets.

International Views and Positions. The intraparty schism in the SKP is least evident in foreign policy. The Helsinki Accords of 1975 remain the keystone of SKP foreign policy views along with the party's traditional opposition to NATO, the EEC, and other ties with the Western community. Finland's special relationship with the Soviet Union is symbolized by the 1948 Treaty of Friendship, Cooperation, and Mutual Assistance. The 30th anniversary of the FCMA treaty provided an opportunity for the SKP to reaffirm its foreign policy views. The SKP position is that the treaty guarantees the independence and security of Finland. President Kekkonen's special foreign policy responsibilities have led him to declare that Finland is not neutral on the issue of war and peace. The SKP believes that Finland must show even greater consistency on this issue (*WMR*, no. 10).

On the same occasion chairman Saarinen attacked China for its failure to accept Soviet moves toward reconciliation, and he specifically attacked the Chinese embassy in Helsinki for publishing and spreading anti-Soviet propaganda (*Nordisk Kontakt*, no. 7). Thus the SKP remains resolutely in the pro-Soviet camp—whether in advocacy of specific economic programs or general loyalty to the pro-Soviet international communist movement. This position was demonstrated by the SKP leadership at the June 1976 European communist summit in East Berlin.

Foreign policy issues frequently are tied to domestic politics. The SKP minority Sinisalo wing differs from the majority in its especially passionate denunciation of Finland's economic and political ties to the West. Sinisalo observed that the true political color of every Communist was unstinting loyalty to the foreign policy goals of the Soviet Union (*Pravda*, 4 September). Such remarks are unusual among contemporary Western European communist leaders. The Stalinists created a major foreign policy episode for Finland when their daily newspaper *Tiedonantaja* called several times for joint maneuvers between Soviet and Finnish military units. Coming after the visit of Soviet Defense Minister Ustinov in the summer of 1978, the articles created serious concern inside and outside of Finland. On 10 October centrist Defense Minister Tänkämaa responded to questions in the Finnish parliament and denied that the Soviet defense minister or government had demanded joint maneuvers. *Tiedonantaja* editor Urho Jokinen claimed that his paper's editorials had been misinterpreted and that only social and friendship contacts between the two countries' armed forces had been intended (*Nordisk Kontakt*, no. 13; *New York Times*, 15 November).

Such flaps notwithstanding, the basic principles of Finnish foreign policy, especially good relations with the USSR, are not contested by any significant political group in Finland. President Kekkonen's reelection campaign demonstrated this: one widely displayed campaign poster pictured the president and his initials, and stated, "Confidence beyond our borders." Typically the USSR takes 20 percent of Finland's exports and provides 18 percent of imports (*Yearbook of Nordic Statistics*, 1977). In November 1977, a fifteen-year plan for Finnish-Soviet economic cooperation was concluded. Foreign Minister Väyrynen noted that current Finnish-Soviet trade provides at least 120,000 jobs and that the new trade agreement calls for significant expansion of trade, energy supplies, and joint projects, including nuclear power plants (*Nordisk Kontakt*, no. 15, 1977).

International Party Contacts. The SKP maintains close relations with the communist parties of both Western and Eastern Europe. As in recent years, visits between Finnish and Eastern European and Soviet communist leaders are quite regular. The 60th anniversary of Finnish independence in December 1977, brought Soviet Premier Kosygin to Helsinki along with other Soviet dignitaries, and another large Soviet delegation was present at the SKP party congress in June. SKP chairman Saarinen led a substantial delegation on a ten-day visit to Cuba in November 1977 (*Granma*, Havana, 25 November 1977).

Mention has already been made of the controversial visit of Soviet Defense Minister Dimitri Ustinov to Helsinki in July. Soviet contacts with noncommunist Finnish leaders, especially President Kekkonen, are also quite intense. Premier Sorsa received a delegation of Soviet Central Committee members for a joint meeting between the CPSU and the Finnish Social Democratic party in March. Agreement about the direction of bilateral relations as well as general world views was noted. This is historically interesting given the traditional suspicion between the two parties (*WMR*, no. 10).

Finnish Communists visited few other Eastern European countries in 1977-78, but a large number of delegations came to Finland: Czechs and Romanians in December 1977, and many delegations to the Eighteenth Party Congress. At the invitation of the Portuguese Communist Party, an SKP delegation visited Portugal in April (*Avante!*, Lisbon, 4 May).

Other Marxist Parties. The only noteworthy Marxist-Leninist group outside of the two factions is the pro-Chinese "Marxist-Leninist Group of Finland," whose activities are regularly reported in the Chinese press. Despite visits to Peking and occasional demonstrations against Soviet "social imperialism," the group remains without political significance. Nevertheless, as noted above, the SKP is quite critical of the propaganda activities of the Chinese embassy in Helsinki and its Finnish contacts.

Publications. The SKP/SKDL's *Kansan Uutiset* (People's News), published daily in Helsinki, is the main organ of the liberal majority of the SKP (circulation 55,600). *Kommunisti* is the monthly theoretical journal. *Tiedonantaja* (Herald) and *Hämeen Yhteistyö* speak for the SKP's orthodox minority faction. The weekly *Folktidningen* (People's News) is the communist newspaper for Finland's small Swedish-speaking minority. The Finnish "Maoists" circulate several publications including *Lakakuu* (October) and *Aamulehti*, which are perhaps the only violently anti-Soviet publications in the country.

University of Massachuetts   Eric S. Einhorn
Amherst

France

A currently fashionable interpretation of French Communist Party (Parti communiste français; PCF) history places the real birth of the party at the Congress of Villeurbanne in 1936 rather than at the Congress of Tours in 1920. The rationale for this view is that since the Popular Front of the 1930s—excepting the sectarian years of 1939—41 and 1947—52—the PCF has continuously adhered to a policy of unity on the Left. These two exceptions might be attributed to the unusual circumstances surrounding the origins of the Second World War, when the party was repressed following the signing of the Nazi-Soviet pact, and to the coming of the Cold War, when the founding congress of the Cominform, after the exclusion of the party from the French government in May 1947, forced a return to a harder, if not a revolutionary, line.

The PCF has otherwise faithfully pursued a policy aimed at rebuilding the Popular Front of old; it collaborated loyally in the French governments of the Liberation era; it backed Mendès-France in 1954 and Guy Mollet in 1956 in its eagerness to bring an end to the Vietnam and Algerian Wars; and it doggedly refused any opening to the revolutionary romanticism of the New Left in the 1960s, opting instead to reunite with what appeared a thoroughly discredited and outworn Socialist Party (Parti socialiste; PS). The PCF thus instructed its followers to back François Mitterand against de Gaulle's reelection bid in 1965, and it pushed the PS into the signing of the Common Program of 1972.

Simultaneously the party embarked upon a gradual policy of liberalization and measured differentiation from the USSR, the direction of which was set during the brief tenure of Waldeck-Rochet from 1964—69 and which culminated in the Twenty-second Congress of 1976. At that historic congress the PCF recommitted itself to an original French path to socialism, characterized by peaceful transition, political pluralism, freedom, and democracy. It formally abandoned, to the consternation of its orthodox Marxist wing, the much maligned and misunderstood phrase of "dictatorship of the proletariat."

These policies successfully brought the party, widely billed as the "New Communists," to the very edge of power. The dynamic of left-wing unity, manifested in the stunning success in the municipal elections of 1977, promised to carry the PCF and its rejuvenated ally to victory in the legislative elections of 1978—a prognosis which the polls, up to the very last and despite preelection difficulties between the two parties, continued to confirm. But the March 1978 elections did not bring the victory for which so many party militants had hoped, and their concerns became apparent in a post-election crisis, the depth and significance of which, at this writing, are impossible to determine.

Leadership and Organization. There have been no substantive changes in leadership since the Twenty-second Congress in 1976 (see *YICA, 1977*, p. 146) except for the death of Political Bureau member Jean Kanapa on 7 September. Kanapa had once played a significant role in intellectual matters, particularly during the cult-of-Stalin years, and had been head of the party's Committee on

Foreign Policy since 1959. A confirmed Stalinist, Kanapa had refused to admit the existence of political repression in the USSR publicly until 1976, although he had confided his misgivings some years earlier in private. In recent years, however, Kanapa was thought to have been the principal adviser pushing Marchais into a more radical opposition to the USSR. He was succeeded as head of the Foreign Affairs Committee by Maxime Gremetz, who has been a member of the Political Bureau since 1976. (See *Le Monde,* 10 and 11 September.)

There were signs of a crisis in PCF organization during 1978 as democratic centralism came under attack from all sides and was openly flouted by prominent party intellectuals and dissidents (see below), who no longer hesitated to publish their critiques and polemicize against the party leadership and one another in the "bourgeois" press and especially in *Le Monde.* Marchais stuck by his promise that the era of exclusions from the party was closed, but a veiled threat remained in his reminder that expulsion was still permitted by party statutes. The leadership was held to its interpretation of democratic centralism, keeping the pages of the party organ *L'Humanité* closed to dissidents.

In the course of the year there was a good deal of criticism of leadership policies expressed in the cells. Many of the cells function democratically and give full freedom of expression to their members. The absence of horizontal contacts between protesting individuals or groups, however, renders much of this dissent ineffectual unless a whole cell, or in rarer cases, an entire section of the party, can be persuaded to take a position contrary to that of the leadership. At the end of May Marchais announced that only 65 out of a total of 27,000 cells and 5 out of 2,724 sections had thus far challenged the leadership's policies, and he estimated the total number of dissidents at 1,000 out of 630,000 members. (*L'Humanité,* 30 May.) At the September meeting of the Central Committee, however, the party tacitly admitted the existence of a crisis in the cells by calling for "exceptional efforts for the [regular] meeting of all cells." At the time of this writing, there were reports that the party's Political Bureau was paralyzed by divided opinion on how to deal with the crisis (Thierry Pfister, *Le Monde,* 19 October).

There were signs of stagnation in the PCF's membership drive during 1978. In 1977 the party said it had achieved its goal of 600,000 members by October, and announced a goal of 632,000 by the end of the year. The latter figure remained in use for most of the year, but the party hoped to have one million members within a few more years. PCF member Charles Fiterman announced on 6 July that 7,000 new members had joined in June and that the midyear total was 80,000 higher than it had been a year before. Marchais said in August that 700 more had joined during the first week in that month, and he expressed confidence that the figure of 700,000 would be reached by December 1978. (*L'Humanité,* 6 July, 11 August.)

On the other hand, by 29 September the PCF was able to announce a figure of only 650,000, which indicated some slowing. At the same time the General Confederation of Labor (CGT) admitted its own inability to make further progress toward its membership goal of 3,000,000 and estimated its membership at 2,300,000 in October. Of these members, CGT leader and PCF Political Bureau member Georges Séguy said that 500,000 were members of the Communist Party, while 1,600,000 were apolitical, and he estimated that as few as 60 percent of CGT members vote Communist, while 30 percent vote Socialist (*Le Monde,* 21 October).

The Mouvement de la jeunesse communiste de France, the party's youth auxiliary, announced a decline in membership from 113,000 to 109,000, which its secretary attributed to post-election disenchantment among youth (ibid., 17 October). There were some publicly announced resignations from the party with attendant publicity, but Marchais said in June that only the normal annual loss of 7 percent was being observed. The PCF is notorious for being a *parti-passoire,* a kind of sieve, through which a good part of the country's electorate has already passed, since ex-Communists are now the largest group in France.

Domestic Attitudes and Activities. It is with the failure of negotiations to update the Common Program on 22 September 1977 (Programme commun de gouvernement; signed by the PCF and PS in June 1972) that one must begin an analysis of French domestic affairs. It is difficult to speculate concerning which party was at fault since each party appeared to have a good deal to gain from taking a relative distance from the other. Despite their claims to the contrary, neither party observed the Common Program to the letter.

In a formal sense the PCF initially and unilaterally altered the Common Program by reversing its position on nuclear policy in May 1977 and by declaring its support for the *force de frappe.* It also focused attention on the issue of nationalization by adding Peugeot-Citroen, the oil conglomerate Total, and the ailing steel industry to the list of companies to be nationalized agreed on in 1972 and insisted that subsidiaries of the nine industrial groups mentioned in the Common Program would have to be nationalized along with the parent companies. But neither of these issues needed to be spoilers in themselves since the Socialists were undoubtedly moving toward acceptance of a French nuclear deterrent in any case and the PCF showed some willingness to compromise on nationalizaton. It ultimately pared down its list from over 1,400 to slightly in excess of 700 companies but insisted this was a minimum threshold essential to achieve real change in France. This figure, however, might have been further negotiable. Despite the PCF's claims that it had made every concession possible, emphasis in its subsequent public statements and in the Central Committee resolution of 11 November 1977 clearly suggested that the PS should take the next step and should increase its maximum figure of 250 companies to be nationalized.

In effect, given the increasing electoral strength the PS had been showing since the signing of the Common Program, the PCF was seeking to compensate for its weakened position vis-à-vis its partner by securing certain guarantees of its own power in the French sociopolitical structure. The PCF scheme for control of nationalized enterprises varied little from that put forward during the Liberation. It was a tripartite formula in which councils of administration would be composed in equal parts of representatives of management, workers, and consumers of the businesses concerned. The Socialists did not contest this structure despite its capability for favoring the communist-affiliated labor union, the General Confederation of Labor (Confédération générale du travail; CGT). The PS did, however, adamantly refuse to surrender the government's power to name the directors of nationalized enterprises to these same councils. It is on this issue that real control over the enterprises promised to hinge, and it was an issue little susceptible to compromise since the issue of control appeared so clear-cut.

Parallel concerns were manifest in negotiations for a division of ministries between the two parties, despite the fact that if communist weight in a future coalition were reduced as a result of the election in 1978, the old Gaullist stricture against communist occupation of the "key" ministries—Interior, Foreign Affairs, and Defense (one could also add Finance)—would likely remain in force. Marchais appeared to accept this possibility tacitly in a reply to a journalist's question on 2 September 1977. He claimed that the ministries concerned with economics, social affairs, and national development were of greater concern to him in any case. But the PCF sought to counter such a development by advocating a change in the powers of the crucial Interior and Finance ministries, depriving the former of its controls over local government and the latter of its powers of inquisition over other areas of economic activity. These changes threatened to strengthen communist positions both in municipalities and in socioeconomic structures and were therefore categorically rejected by the Socialists.

Since the negotiations to revise the Common Program failed in the autumn of 1977, the PCF leadership then sought to justify its position by arguing that the PS had in fact made a turn to the right. PCF Secretary General Georges Marchais charged that the Socialists, seeking new votes from centrist voters disaffected by the austerity policies of the regime but fearful of communist influence in the left coalition, had every reason to want to contest the first ballot with "free hands." The PCF did, however, appear to have tried to force the Socialists back into an agreement. This would, at any rate, appear to be the reasoning behind the implicit threats by Marchais that in the absence of an updated Common Program, communist support for Socialist candidates on the second ballot could not be assumed. On 21 November 1977 Marchais stated that any question relating to an electoral agreement was "premature" and on 9 December 1977 warned that if the PS continued to refuse to return to the Common Program, the PCF would draw the "appropriate conclusions" at its scheduled January conference. (See *L'Humanité,* 8 and 22 November 1977.)

At the January party conference the PCF raised the level of its rhetoric by declaring that without a sufficiently large vote in its favor on the first ballot, any real policy of change would be impossible, given the formidable pressures being exerted by the bourgeoisie to win the PS over to a policy of class collaboration. If the March ballot were to tip the scales in favor of change, Marchais warned, a 21 percent vote for the PCF would not be good enough. On the other hand, he believed that 25 percent would be sufficient. In the absence of 25 percent, Marchais stressed, there could be no guarantee of what the PCF would do on the second ballot. This threat was consistently repeated up to the election itself. (Ibid., 7 January.)

For its part the PS professed complete indifference to PCF threats regarding the second ballot, stating simply that mutual withdrawal of the two parties had predated the existence of the Common Program and was not, as far as the PS was concerned, a subject for negotiation. This policy of calling the PCF's bluff worked, and the PS stood firm in the last weeks before the balloting, rejecting Marchais's repeated call for negotiations and ignoring the PCF's assumption of a much milder stance just prior to the balloting (in particular the PCF's declaration that it would be satisfied with only seven ministries in a coalition government and its positive reception of a new compromise proposal on the nationalization issue proposed by the Socialist-oriented labor union (CFDT). Indeed, in the immediate aftermath of the narrow defeat suffered by the Left on the first ballot on 12 March, all critical differences of the previous September were suddenly forgotten or glossed over as the two parties scrambled to secure maximum representation in parliament by agreeing to support on the second ballot whichever candidate (from the two parties) had received the largest percentage on the first ballot.

Although Marchais expressed his disappointment that the Left had failed to get a majority, he claimed a measure of satisfaction with the communist showing. The PCF received an increase of some 800,000 votes over the legislative elections of 1973 for a total of 5,870,402 and a net gain of twelve seats in the National Assembly, which increased the PCF total from 74 to 86. But the electorate was much larger than in 1973 owing to the enfranchisement of those age 18−21, as well as normal population increases; despite the proportionately large share of the youth vote enjoyed by the PCF−28 percent according to the polls−the PCF total had actually declined almost a point since 1973, from 21.41 to 20.55 percent. This latter figure was the lowest percentage the PCF had received since the Liberation with the exception of the elections of 1958.

There was almost no change in the contours of PCF electoral geography, although there was a noticeable decline in party strength in its traditional bastions surrounding Paris: the PCF declined 4.5 percent in Paris, 3.5 percent in Seine-Saint-Denis, 3.3 percent in Val-de-Marne, 5 percent in Essonne, and 3.88 percent in Yvelines (see Jean Elleinstein, *Le Monde,* 13 April). The fact that the Socialists, for the first time since the war, outdistanced the PCF by two points, garnering 22.58 percent and laying claim to the title of "first party of France," only underscored the picture of a PCF confined within a gradually shrinking set of political and social parameters at a time of general resurgence of the Left in France.

This trend became much more dramatic in a series of five by-elections in September, necessitated by election annulments by the Constitutional Council. The Left had narrowly won three of the contested seats in March, the majority two; in the by-elections the Left swept all five, dramatically bettering its showing over March. It was a striking confirmation of a widespread current of hostility to the austerity policies practiced by President Giscard d'Estaing and Prime Minister Raymond Barre since the elections. It could also be construed as a demonstration that many Frenchmen generally want to vote for the Left but refrain from doing so when it appears that the Left might really win. The PS received 32 percent of the September totals, the PCF 18 percent; the PCF was thus declining in the face of spectacular PS gains. Thus, the communist votes have been in steady decline since the 1962 high of 28.7 percent; i.e., 1968, 25.3 percent; 1973, 22.16 percent; March 1978, 20.61 percent; September 1978, 19.33 percent. (Ibid., 26 September.)

Elections for workers' committees within French industrial enterprises following the March balloting also showed some erosion in the position of the communist-affiliated CGT. These very serious election losses occured amid the general resumption of the party's internal problems with its dissidents and amid the general post-election malaise after a summer lull.

International Views and Positions and Party Contacts. One of the major complaints of a leading critic within the party, historian and PCF member Jean Elleinstein, has been the unwillingness of the PCF to sever the ties that continue, in his view, to bind it to the Soviet Union. The party leadership has angrily denied Elleinstein's charges, noting that the PCF has long since rejected the idea that there can be any "model" of socialism and stressing that the building of socialism in France will be unique, in accordance with French creative genius, and infused with freedom and democracy. In accordance with this conception Jean Kanapa noted in December 1977 a clear divergence between the PCF's and the Communist Party of the Soviet Union's (CPSU) concepts of socialism and recalled that for the PCF "proletarian internationalism" rather than "internationalist solidarity" characterized its relations with the Soviet camp (*L'Humanité*, 12 December 1977).

In practice this has meant a steadily increasing chorus of protests in *L'Humanité* about the denial of freedoms in the USSR (and in Czechoslovakia), while the party shows a continued reluctance to criticize any aspect of Soviet foreign policy openly. Thus, on 19 October *L'Humanité* charged that Czech treatment of the Charter 77 group "disfigures the face of socialism." On 1 January it found "inadmissible" the Soviet denial of dissident Shcharansky's right to a defense. On 1 April the PCF condemned the Soviet refusal to allow Leningrad artist Yuri Lyubimov to produce a play in Paris and used the occasion to proclaim its own commitment to artistic freedom. On 18 May it characterized the Orlov trial as a "denial of justice," and on 1 July *L'Humanité* noted with unease a proliferation of trials in the USSR involving Jews. A high point was reached in the Shcharansky and Ginzburg cases in July, during which the PCF formally delivered a note of protest to the Soviet embassy in Paris, and for the first time an official party delegation headed by Paris Deputy Henri Fiszbin joined a delegation of PCF students and participated in a public street demonstration against Soviet repression along with a variety of organizations, not all of them of the Left. The CGT also became involved when it withdrew its candidate's nomination for the presidency of the World Federation of Trade Unions and called for a critical analysis of the situation of trade unions in all socialist countries.

On the other hand, these protests did not prevent a continued exchange of relatively high-level delegations between the CPSU and the PCF. On 24–30 April a PCF delegation visited the USSR, and on 22 June a Soviet "study delegation" headed by Viktor Afanasyev of *Pravda* was hosted by the PCF in Paris. If Georges Marchais remained personna non grata to the CPSU, contacts remained assured by Political Bureau member Gaston Plissonier. Thus, during the election campaign a propaganda brochure entitled *Vivre* was prepared, showing the PCF's commitment to human rights and depicting, among other incidents, a 1977 party meeting in support of Soviet dissident Leonid

Plyushch. According to the account subsequently published by Jacques Fremontier, who resigned his party functions over the incident, the brochure had been approved by Marchais, Fiterman, Paul Laurent, and Kanapa before it was printed in over one million copies. Yet Plissonier's objections were vociferous enough to force it, along with a second, revised edition, to be shredded prior to circulation, at a total cost of some two million francs (*Le Monde,* 30 April).

At the April Central Committee meeting Marchais returned to the theme of the PCF's differences with the CPSU over democracy and declared that the situation in the socialist countries had deteriorated since the PCF's Twenty-second Congress (*L'Humanité,* 21 April). Marchais appeared to promise further evolution within the PCF as well by admitting that the PCF had been slow to draw the necessry lessons in the past following the de-Stalinization campaign of 1956. On 27 July *L'Humanité* violated a Soviet taboo by publishing selections from the memoirs of Mexican communist Valentin Campa, relating how Stalin ordered the Mexican Communist Party to arrange the assassination of Trotsky in 1940. A turning point appears, indeed, to have been reached with the publication of a book, under the general editorship of Francis Cohen, entitled *The USSR and Us,* which, if it was not commissioned by the Political Bureau, received the latter's unanimous endorsement in September. In his preface (see ibid., 4 September) Cohen undertook to explain why the USSR now appears less and less to the French as an appropriate model of socialism; he confessed to the adoption of "gross simplifications" of Marxism by French Communists during the cult-of-Stalin years; he complained that blemishes and imperfections in Soviet society had too often been viewed as an alien disease which had somehow invaded a basically healthy body; and he caused a minor sensation by referring to both Trotsky and Bukharin as "great personalities who have not been rehabilitated in the USSR" and to their currents of thought as authentic components of the working-class movement. Although observers generally found little that was startling and much that was ambiguous in Cohen's analysis of Soviet society, the Soviets themselves attacked the book for its "anti-Soviet" potential.

The PCF was very active in its relations with other communist parties, and much of its action can be seen in the light of its differentiation from the CPSU and its attempt to gain support for its own version of "Eurocommunism." Spokesman Jacques Denis characterized Eurocommunism as the rejection of any model of socialism, the assimilation of the "lessons" of Stalinism and the Soviet invasion of Czechoslovakia, an autonomous national form of socialism infused with freedom and democracy, and the rejection of a monopoly by any party in power or the identification of any single party with the machinery of the state (*Cahiers du communisme,* April).

Of particular significance were Marchais's choices of Hungary and Romania for personal visits. In November 1977 he was met personally at the airport by János Kádár, and the final communiqué referred to "identical views" between the Hungarian and French parties on problems of the international communist movement. Marchais vacationed in Romania in July and conducted talks with Ceauşescu, which were carried on in an atmosphere of "friendship and mutual esteem." A discordant note was struck, however, by a joint declaration of the East German and French parties in October. It affirmed the commitment of the two parties to the Helsinki accords while pointedly ignoring the repression of dissidents in the GDR. Notable extracontinental visits were made by Charles Fiterman to Japan in October and by Marchais to Mexico in June.

The PCF appeared more troubled in its relations with its Eurocommunist neighbors. Delegations met with the Belgian party (14 April), the West German party (18 May), the Danish party (9 June), and the Dutch party (9 August). The Danes joined the PCF in a repudiation of any model of socialism and an affirmation of the commitment of both parties to freedom and democracy. The others sounded the more usual note of equality, autonomy of each party, and mutual respect and understanding. The PCF sent a warm congratulatory message to the congress of the Spanish party (PCE) in April, lauding the mutual commitment of each party to freedom, cooperation, and independence. It also declined to take exception to the PCE's abandonment of the appellation of

"Leninism," and PCF member Paul Laurent noted in an interview in Madrid that Lenin had been dead for 54 years and the PCF was opposed to all dogmatism (*L'Humanité,* 21 April).

On 1 August PCE member Manuel Azcárate attacked the PCF, accusing it of electoral demagoguery and chauvinism, which brought a stinging reply from *L'Humanité.* The Spanish party also openly drew closer to PCF dissidents, and an official representative appeared at a weekend symposium organized by French Trotskyites and featuring PCF dissenting intellectuals Elleinstein and Rony along with ex-Communist Roger Garaudy. There were also more muted criticisms of PCF election tactics from the Italian Communists, and Elleinstein's critique of the PCF leadership was widely featured in the Italian communist press. The Italians, moreover, appeared to be deliberately bolstering Elleinstein's position by awarding him the Gramsci prize for the study of history on 9 November. The two parties were also divided over the enlargement of the Common Market, which the Italian party favors, and the powers of the future European Assembly, which the PCF wants to see restricted to the greatest extent possible. However, Berlinguer, Carrillo, and Marchais published a joint declaration on 7 October in Rome declaring, despite their differences, their joint commitment to democracy, pluralism, and the principles enunciated in the tripartite Madrid declaration on Eurocommunism of March 1977.

The PCF continued to offer a radical alternative to French foreign policy—not so much in Europe, where it supports détente, disarmament, and application of the Helsinki accords, but in Africa, where Marchais even appeared at times to be conducting his own external relations. Thus, on 19 November 1977 a PCF delegation returned from Mozambique, declaring that an alliance with the FRELIMO had been concluded. On 24 November a PCF delegation went to Algiers with the stated intention of securing the release of French hostages held by the Polisario Front in the former Spanish Sahara. Marchais followed this by a personal visit to Algiers to announce the success of the mission despite what he characterized as the "inefficiency" of a clearly irritated French government. Marchais went on to condemn French support for the reactionary Moroccan and Mauritanian regimes in the Sahara and to score France for its "abandonment" of Algeria, while announcing increased PCF—FLN cooperation (ibid., 3 January). Meanwhile, in December 1977, Gaston Plissonier completed a voyage to Angola where he condemned the French role as an arms supplier to South Africa and saluted the birth of a "vanguard party" in the former Portuguese colony. The PCF unreservedly condemned the French intervention in Zaire in June, complaining that France had become a colonial policeman for the Atlantic alliance in order to enable the multinationals to dominate Africa.

In Asia the PCF aligned itself with Soviet policy, expressing official support for Vietnam in its border dispute with Cambodia, and supported Vietnamese government denials of the existence of concentration camps in that country. *L'Humanité* also expressed reservations about the Sino-Japanese treaty, noting that the antihegemony clause was clearly directed at the USSR. With regard to the Middle East, Marchais expressed the opinion that the visit of President Sadat to Jerusalem had not "advanced the fundamental questions one iota," but he refused to comment on *Pravda's* condemnation of the trip as an imperialist trick. The PCF does not hesitate to couple its support for the PLO with declarations of its belief in the right of Israel to exist within secure and recognized borders. (Ibid., 11 December 1977.)

In Europe the PCF prepared to participate in the campaign for direct elections to the European Assembly, but it continued to appear thoroughly Gaullist in its suspicion of supranationality and its distinction between the Atlantic alliance, which it supports, and the integrated NATO military command, which it firmly rejects. The PCF joined the rest of the French political community in expressing its "indignation and horror" at the kidnapping and murder of Aldo Moro (ibid., 11 May).

Dissidence within the PCF. The electoral defeat gave rise to an unprecedented outburst of public criticism of the party leadership by PCF intellectuals. Much of it was stimulated by the apparent cynicsim with which the 13 March accord with the Socialists was negotiated and by the post-election statement of the Political Bureau squarely dumping all responsibility for the defeat on the Socialists. It bears noting that none of the dissidents questioned the view that the PS had effected a "turn to the right"; it was rather the PCF's handling of this turn of affairs that was at issue. Thus, Raymond Jean observed in *Le Monde* (31 March) that if an accord with the PS was possible on 13 March, then it had also been possible earlier. Jean Rony criticized the Political Bureau statement attributing responsibility for the defeat to the Socialists and expressed fears that the PCF leadership was returning to the old "united front from below" strategy, which he argued was associated with the Comintern's worst defeats.

The greatest effect was created by the prominent PCF members Elleinstein and Louis Althusser. In the past Althusser and Elleinstein had criticized from the left and the right—the former notably rejecting the Twenty-second Congress, while the latter advocated a further, more rapid evolution in its spirit. Their post-election critiques dovetailed on a number of crucial points. But it was clear that Althusser represented a smaller group than Elleinstein, whose support was broad based and, according to many reliable sources, extended to a significant minority on the Central Committee itself. Elleinstein noted the electoral costs of the PCF's strategy, argued that responsibility for the defeat was shared more or less equally by the two left-wing parties, and insisted that the PCF must accelerate its evolution away from the USSR, which he claimed was in reality not a model but rather an "antimodel" of socialism. Both Althusser and Elleinstein criticized the outmoded procedures of democratic centralism as practiced by the PCF and called for a thorough democratization of party ranks—Elleinstein going so far as to demand the rehabilitation of historic party figures who were victims of Stalinist purge trials, such as Charles Tillon and André Marty.

The high point in the dissident campaign was reached with the publication of a letter of protest with 300 signatures in *Le Monde* on 30 May. Its author, Michel Barak, accused Marchais of having caricatured the views of party intellectuals in his Central Committee speech of April, argued that a clear "regression" had taken place in terms of the party's historic policy of alliance between intellectuals and the working class, and called for an end to a policy that treated party militants like children.

Immediately after the publication of Barak's letter, which its author denied represented any challenge to the leadership, the Political Bureau expressed its "surprise and severe disapproval" of what it claimed was an obvious violation of the principles and rules governing the party and called upon the petition's signers to reconsider their position. (See *L'Humanité*, 12 May.) Throughout June readers of *L'Humanité* were treated to an apparently orchestrated series of resolutions from party cells and sections condemning the views of dissidents (of which they could not, however, have known without reading the "bourgeois" press).

In September the PCF leadership appeared to have taken another turn—on the one hand with the publication of *The USSR and Us* and on the other with Marchais's welcome of Elleinstein at a fête for *L'Humanité* as a "good Communist with whom one discusses" and not a dissident (ibid., 12 September). Elleinstein did not moderate his position, however, and attacked the USSR for its anti-Semitism, stating that he was being personally attacked by the Soviets as a Jew, that recent Soviet articles were of "fascist inspiration," and that the Russians had smeared the names of Marx and Lenin with those of Goebbels and Rosenberg. He also criticized the French party leadership for not defending him against the Soviet attacks. (*Le Monde,* 6 October.)

For its part, a beleaguered leadership seemed unable to devise a response to the crisis among militants, the election defeats of September, or the continued criticism by intellectuals. A frustrated Marchais lashed out at Premier Raymond Barre in the National Assembly on 14 October, vowing that he would do everything to prevent policies that were moving even further toward austerity and clearly aggravating unemployment in the country. If Marchais was to achieve this challenge to Barre's policies, alliance with the Socialists seemed the only way. Yet the Central Committee meeting of 29–30 September denounced the PS for its "slide to the right," and the PCF described the whole of the Socialist International as "an essential pillar against which big capital can lean with certainty in its effort to block the progress of democracy." In all countries where socialists held power, Marchais said, they were "a recourse of the grand bourgeoisie permitting it to preserve its policies and its domination." (Ibid., 30 September.)

These new attacks on the role of social democracy occurred amid reports that the PCF Political Bureau remained divided between divergent views of what strategy to follow toward the French Socialists in the future. A group of hard-liners centered around Roland Leroy and Gaston Plissonier have allegedly concluded that the PS has hopelessly compromised with the bourgeoisie and that the PCF must therefore rely on its own devices, even if this means a new period of isolation or "crossing of the desert." A more moderate group whose views are generally recognized to be expressed by Paul Laurent remains closer to the dissidents in believing that the drift to the right of the Socialists is reversible and that unity on the Left can be once again achieved. (See articles by T. Pfister, ibid., 19 and 23 October.)

Such divergent analysis has occurred before in party history, the most notable example having been the controversy over Gaullism in 1960–61. But the present confrontation would appear to be conducted for the moment on a live-and-let-live basis with the party's Twenty-third Congress in 1979 now cast in an arbitrating role. If this analysis is correct, given the promised reexamination of the functioning of democratic centralism at the upcoming congress and the unwillingness thus far to take any disciplinary action against the unprecedented actions of the dissidents, not to mention the publication of *The USSR and Us,* it would seem that the PCF is currently undergoing one of the most profound upheavals in its history.

Publications. Roland Leroy remained director of *L'Humanité*, and René Andrieu remained its editor in chief. Circulation is estimated at 650,000–670,000 (a 35 percent increase from 1976). Similarly, the popular weekend magazine *L'Humanité dimanche* was reported to have increased its readership. The party's provincial newspapers include three dailies: *La Liberté* (Nord), *L'Echo du centre,* and *La Marseillaise.* Plans to add a new regional daily in the fall, serving Lyons, Grenoble, and Saint-Etienne, were announced by Leroy on 26 March 1977. In October 1976 the Paris federation began to publish a new weekly popular magazine, *Paris-Hebdo,* and in March-April 1977 the first issues of publications geared specifically to the police forces and the army, *Police et Nation* and *Armée-Nation*, appeared.

The regular party press also includes the weekly, *France nouvelle;* the monthly theoretical journal, *Cahiers du communisme;* a rural weekly, *La Terre;* an intellectual monthly, *La Nouvelle critique;* a literary monthly, *Europe;* a philosophically oriented bimonthly, *La Pensée;* a bimonthly economic journal, *Economie et politique;* a historical bimonthly, *Cahiers d'histoire de l'Institute Maurice Thorez;* and a monthly review for teachers, *L'Ecole et la nation.* For interparty communication, the Central Committee publishes *La Vie du parti.*

In the early 1970s there were approximately 5,000 cell newspapers or periodicals, about a tenth printed, the others mimeographed, and this figure has undoubtedly increased in recent years. The press of the youth movement was reorganized at the national conference of the Communist Youth Movement (MJCF) of 22–23 October 1977; *Avante-Garde* (previously bimonthly) is to become a weekly, with the goal of reaching 150,000 young readers, and *Clarté* (previously also a bimonthly) becomes the monthly theoretical, ideological, political, and cultural review of the Union of Communist

Students (UECF). The major communist publishing houses, Editions sociales and Editeurs français réunis, put out a considerable number and variety of books and pamphlets.

University of California, Riverside   Irwin Wall

Germany: Federal Republic of Germany

The Communist Party of Germany (Kommunistische Partei Deutschlands; KPD) was founded on 31 December 1918 by the Spartacist League, a revolutionary group which emerged during World War I within the Social Democratic Party of Germany (Sozialdemokratische Partei Deutschlands; SPD). During the period of the Weimar Republic, the KPD obtained substantial support in elections, but the party was outlawed in 1933 after Hitler came to power. After the end of hostilities in 1945, the KPD was reconstituted in the four Allied occupation zones of Germany and in the area of Greater Berlin. Pressured by Soviet authorities, the KPD merged with the larger SPD in the Soviet Zone and in the Soviet Sector of Berlin, creating the Socialist Unity Party of Germany (Sozialistische Einheitspartei Deutschlands; SED). In the other parts of occupied Germany, the SPD rejected the merger, and the two parties remained separate. In the first election following the establishment of the Federal Republic of Germany (FRG) in 1949, the KPD received 5.7 percent of the vote, giving the Communists fifteen seats in the Bundestag. The communist vote at the next elections, held in 1953, fell to 2.2 percent, i.e., below the 5 percent required to qualify for representation in the legislature. On 17 August 1956 the Federal Constitutional Court found the KPD's objectives and methods in violation of Article 21/2 of the FRG's Basic Law and outlawed the party.

The KPD lost a substantial part of its members as a result of being outlawed but continued to operate as an underground organization. Its chairman, Max Reimann, directed the party's activities from East Berlin.

In 1965 Communists, former socialists, and pacifists founded the German Peace Union (Deutsche Friedensunion; DFU), a communist front organization. The DFU participated in federal elections that year and polled 1.3 percent of the vote. The DFU is still in existence, merged with the International of War Resisters (IDK) and the Association of War Service Resisters (VK), but its efforts to organize communist-controlled "unity of action" activities in line with the world peace movement have enjoyed only limited success.

The DFU held its Eighth Congress in Cologne 15—16 April, attended by over 200 delegates who elected the seven-member Directorate. The statements made and resolutions passed at this congress clearly identified the DFU as a member of the communist-controlled World Peace Council. (*Radical-Info*, no. 2, March/May, p. 1.)

In September 1968 another communist party, the present German Communist Party (Deutsche Kommunistische Partei; DKP), was established. At that time the underground KPD had about 7,000 members. All of them were ordered to join the new DKP, and most of its leadership consisted of KPD members. Because of the identity of personalities and the same unconstitutional objectives of both parties, the DKP is clearly a successor organization to the KPD and could be outlawed by a decree of the federal minister of the interior. (See *YICA, 1975*, p. 174.) The outlawed KDP is still in existence although its importance to Moscow has substantially decreased as a result of the legal DKP. (See *YICA, 1977*, p. 158.)

The DKP is part of the pro-Moscow communist world movement. Its membership, as reported at the Fifth Party Congress (October), is 46,380—an increase of 3,927 since the Fourth Party Congress held in March 1976. Thus, in spite of great efforts to increase membership, the party has not had great success. If *Pravda*'s (16 January) reported increase of 5,100 new DKP members is correct, then over 1,000 old members must have dropped out if the figures presented at the Fifth Party Congress are accurate. (*Frankfurter Allgemeine Zeitung*, 19 and 21 October; hereafter cited as *FAZ*.) The population of the Federal Republic of Germany is about 61,520,000.

The following tabulation from the annual report of the Federal Security Service (*Bundesverfassungsschutz*) provides an overview of the left-extremist organizations in the FRG at the end of 1977.

Type of Organization	Number of Organizations	Membership	
Orthodox Communist:			
Basic organizations	2	49,000	
Affiliated organizations	11	28,400	
Organizations influenced by Communists	58		52,600[a]
Maoist:			
Basic organizations	15	6,600	
Affiliated organizations	28	9,700	
Organizations influenced by Maoists	12		3,900[a]
Trotskyist	12	900	
"New Left"	68	5,500	
Anarchists	19	200	
TOTAL	225	100,300	56,500[a]
Deduction for membership in more than one organization		25,100	14,100
		75,200	42,400
Total membership		117,600	

Source: Bundesminister des Innern, Bonn, *Verfassungsschutz* 1977, September 1978, p. 62.

Note: The membership of 117,600 for 1977 is 7,600 more than the membership given for 1976.

[a] Among them are also non-Communists.

Leadership and Organization. The Fifth Party Congress at Mannheim (20—22 October) confirmed the existing leadership of Chairman Herbert Mies and his deputy Hermann Gautier. The Presidium also remained unchanged. Only Rolf Priemer, who in the meantime had become chairman of the Saar party district, left the Secretariat; however, he kept his seat in the Presidium. The Party Directorate remains at 91 members. The percentage of women members increased from 14 to 23 percent. (*FAZ*, 23 October.)

Close cooperation of the DKP with the SED in the German Democratic Republic (GDR) continued during 1978. For example, three members of the SED Politburo attended the Fifth Party Congress (*FAZ*, 21 October). The SED was, as heretofore, the major source of financial support and provided direct supervision of DKP activities, including the political schooling of DKP functionaries in SED schools in the GDR. The Federal Security Service (Bundesverfassungsschutz; BVS) reported that in 1977 the DKP and its affiliated organizations received more than 50 million marks from the SED, compared with 30 million marks in 1976 (*FAZ*, 26 July). The DKP receives additional income from extensive advertisements in the Leipzig Trade Fair magazine, which is printed by the DKP's publishing firm. (*Deutscher Informationsdienst*, Bonn, 29, no. 1487, 14 September 1978, p. 7; hereafter cited as *DI.*) The Association for Furthering East-West Trade solicits advertisements from Western firms and passes the fees to the DKP for the financing of political activities. There are also more than 25 communist-owned economic organizations in the FRG dealing in East-West trade which channel their profits to the DKP. These firms are primarily shipping companies, printing plants, trade firms, travel agencies, and advertising agencies. They are controlled by the commercial apparatus of the Central Committee of the SED. Most of the persons in charge of these firms have been members of the outlawed KPD. (*Focus on Germany*, Bonn, March, p. 4.)

The most important affiliated organizations of the DKP are the Socialist German Workers' Youth (SDAJ), Marxist Student Union—Spartakus (MSB-Spartakus), and Young Pioneers (JP).

The SDAJ, modeled after the Free German Youth (FDJ) of the GDR, has 15,000 active members according to the latest report of the Federal Security Service (*FAZ*, 26 July). On 4 May the SDAJ celebrated its tenth anniversary. Its chairman is Wolfgang Gehrcke. (*Unsere Zeit*, 4–5 May; hereafter cited as *UZ.*) In North Rhine—Westphalia, SDAJ membership is about 6,000, organized in 178 local groups, which publish 80 group newspapers, 47 factory papers, 14 vocational school papers and 19 papers for high school students. (*DI*, 29, no. 1485, 15 August, p. 7.)

The MSB-Spartakus, founded in May 1971, has a membership of 5,800 and is represented at most German institutions of higher learning (*FAZ*, 26 July). Its coalition with the Socialist Student League (SHB), the former official SPD student organization, and frequently with the Young Socialist University Groups (or "Jusos") gives these groups decisive influence and control of student governments in postsecondary schools (*DI*, 29, no. 1485, 15 August, p. 7). Forty-five out of 75 student representative bodies at universities in the FRG are dominated by members of left-wing groups (*DI*, ibid.; *Die Welt*, 26 July; for additional information, see *YICA, 1978*, p. 143).

The Young Pioneers claimed to have increased their local groups from 200 (1976) to 332, with a membership of about 6,000. (Bundesminister des Innern, *Innere Sicherheit*, no. 45, Bonn, 29 September, p. 5.)

In addition to these organizations, there exist several comunist-led groups that seek support among the population for DKP activities and objectives. Membership in these groups is not exclusively reserved for Communists, although they usually occupy the key positions in these organizations.

The German Peace Society/United War Service Resisters (DFG-VK) is the largest of these organizations. It held its federal congress in Nuremberg (16—17 September), which was attended by 255 voting delegates representing 97 local groups. The congress decided to intensify the creation of youth clubs, called "Courage," and to establish a coordinating working group of all youth clubs in the FRG. (*DI*, 29, no. 1488, 30 September, pp. 8–9.) The DFG-VK has about 19,500 members. (*Radical-Info*, Bonn, no. 3/4, June/August 1978, p. 10.)

The Committee for Peace, Disarmament, and Cooperation (KFAZ) was most active during 1978 in promoting "unity of action" among Communists, socialists, Protestant churches, and public figures for propaganda purposes in support of "peace" and "disarmament." While most of the members are noncommunist, the KFAZ leadership is composed primarily of members of the DKP or affiliated organizations. (Bundesminister des Innern, *Innere Sicherheit*, no. 43, Bonn, 12 May, pp. 8–9.)

Other organizations of this type include the Association of Victims of the Nazi Regime—League of Antifascists (VVN-BdA), which held its federal congress at Mannheim (20–22 May). More than half the members of its Presidium are known Communists. The Association of Democratic Jurists (VDJ) and the Socialist Bureau (SB) with headquarters in Offenbach are also communist-infiltrated organizations. (*Radical-Info*, no. 3/4, June/August, p. 10; *DI*, 29, no. 1485, p. 9.) The Anti-Apartheid Movement (AAB), with headquarters in Bonn, is also a recently founded communist-inspired front organization. Its propaganda aim is the immediate termination of nuclear energy collaboration between the FRG and South Africa. The AAB sponsored an international congress in Bonn (11–12 November). Among the supporters were the Anti-Imperialist Solidarity Committee (ASK), the Working Group of the Catholic Students' Society, the Federal Association of Citizen Initiatives for the Protection of the Environment (DFG/VK), the Young Democrats, Jusos, the Communist League, the Falken, the Socialist Bureau, and the United German Students' League (VDS). (*DI*, 29, no. 1489, 14 October, p.3; for additional communist front organizations, see *YICA, 1978*, p. 144.)

Party Internal Affairs. The main internal event of the DKP in 1978 was the Fifth Party Congress held in Mannheim 20–22 October. The seventh session of the Party Directorate (19–20 November 1977) adopted the draft for a new party program, which was published in the official party newspaper, *Unsere Zeit*, on 9 December 1977 and widely distributed. Members were encouraged to discuss the program and to forward to the party leadership proposals for changes. (*UZ*, 25 November, 9 December 1977.) At the traditional meeting honoring V. I. Lenin, Karl Liebknecht, and Rosa Luxemburg on 15 January, Kurt Bachmann, one of the most senior West German Communists and a member of the DKP Presidium, emphasized that the focus of work for 1978 would be the discussion of the DKP's draft program (*Pravda*, 16 January). At the eighth, ninth, and tenth sessions of the DKP Directorate (1 April, 17 June, and 18 September), the main agenda item was approval of the organizational preparations and the timetable for the party congress (*DI*, 29, no. 1477, 13 April, p. 10; *Neues Deutschland*, 18 September).

In spite of all the propaganda surrounding the draft proposal of the new program, no significant changes emerged. Marxism-Leninism, as interpreted by the SED and the Communist Party of the Soviet Union (CPSU), remains the theoretical basis for the party. The DKP designates itself "the revolutionary party of the working class of the FRG" and seeks to establish "real socialism" as it is practiced in the GDR. The program reaffirms the DKP's claim that it operates within the framework of the Basic Law but simultaneously emphasizes that the teachings of Marx, Engels, and Lenin serve as the "political compass" for its policies. The DKP is strongly pro-Soviet and opposes right-wing opportunism (i.e., Eurocommunism), left-opportunism, including pseudo-revolutionary adventurism, as well as the activities of Maoists, Trotskyites, and anarchists who divide the labor movement.

A number of proposed changes of minor consequence were adopted in the final draft of the new party program. Those changes which would have weakened the positive relationship with the Soviet Union, as well as those expressing opposition to nuclear energy and to the concept of marriage and family, were rejected or disregarded. The final draft was unanimously approved by the party congress. (*FAZ*, 23 October.)

Deputy DKP Chairman Hermann Gautier related at a press conference in Bonn on 5 October that 1,290 proposals dealing with the draft program were submitted and that 42 proposals concerned current political problems. DKP members in more than 5,000 meetings at different party levels discussed the draft program prior to the congress. District conferences of delegates elected 648 voting and 174 guest delegates to the congress. About 80 percent of the delegates were blue- or white-collar workers. Thirty percent were women, and almost half of the delegates were between the ages of 20 and 40. The average age was about 35. (*DI*, 29, no. 1489, 14 October, p. 8.)

The year also witnessed the tenth anniversary of the founding of the DKP. Chairman Mies declared on the occasion of this anniversary: "The founding of the DKP . . . was a declaration to fight against the attempts to prevent the emergence of the class struggle in the Federal Republic and banish from public life the idea of basic social changes in our country. It was a blow against the extreme right-wing forces of German imperialism, against all the reactionary forces gathered around the banner of anticommunism." (*DI*, 29, no. 1489, 14 October, p. 11.)

The ideological schooling of party members continued to be a high-priority item. In the beginning of March, a course of the Marxist Factory Workers' School commenced in Mannheim. The course, of ten months' duration, was attended by young DKP members from various large industrial enterprises and met twice a week. (*DI*, 29, no. 1475, 15 March, p. 2.) Weekend seminars are conducted regularly and are designed especially for new party members (*DI*, 29, no. 1476, 31 March, p. 2). The Party Directorate developed a plan for "Marxist educational work" for the period from September 1978 to May 1979, which is to be carried out in the Marxist factory workers' schools at the level of the party district directorates. These schools are considered a permanent part of the party educational system. Courses are of one year's duration. (*DI*, 29, no. 1486, 30 August, pp. 3–4.)

Domestic Attitudes and Activities. DKP Chairman Mies declared in his New Year's message that the party's tasks for 1978 would focus on the folowing issues:

> . . . the right to work, against unemployment, the dilemma in education and vocational training. For the defense of democratic rights, against the right-wing forces, against neo-Nazism and the prohibition to carry on one's profession [Berufsverbot]. For the end of the arms race, against the neutron bomb and the disregard of the rights of those who refuse to serve in the military. For the unity of action of Communists and Social Democrats, for democratic alliances and common actions of the democratic forces. For further strengthening the DKP and the distribution of its newspaper in the "year of the *UZ*." (*DI*, 29, no. 1471, 14 January, p. 3.)

Party activities were thus centered on continuous efforts to gain influence among the masses through "unity of action," extensive work within the trade unions in support of trade union objectives, and mobilization of party members to propagate those objectives in local and state elections.

The short-range objective of "unity of action" was to overcome the isolation of the party and to establish alliances with noncommunist parties and organizations in support of specific goals and thereby obtain a "mass basis." The DKP and its affiliated organizations were quite successful in a number of cases. For example, the fight against the *Berufsverbot* has continued for six years, and the DKP, with the assistance of "citizens initiatives" and sympathizers abroad, was able to "internationalize" opposition to this policy of not employing Communists in civil service jobs. The DKP obtained the support of trade unionists, Social Democrats, and several left-oriented organizations in their propaganda against the *Berufsverbot*. (*DI*, 29, no. 1474, 24 February, p. 7; no. 1484, 31 July, p. 10.)

In the beginning of September, the Party Directorate decided to broaden its efforts to establish "unity of action" and to include foreign laborers employed in the FRG in the struggle for social and economic improvements and in the fight for peace, détente, and disarmament (*DI*, 29, no. 1487, 14 September, p. 6). The academic community, including university and high school students, was also considered to be a good prospect for "unity of action" efforts. For example, on 27 January about 600 university professors and scientists participated in a demonstration in Hanover against the *Berufsverbot*. The League of Democratic Scientists (BdWi), which is strongly influenced by the DKP, played a leading role in this event, which also had the support of the Trade Union for Education and Science (GEW). (*DI*, 29, no. 1472, 31 January, p. 2.) However, the "unity of action of the working class" (i.e., the collaboration of Communists, Social Democrats, and socialists) represented only the first of three phases of DKP strategy. The second phase included additional elements of the working population and broadened participation in a so-called "united front" (*Einheitsfront*), which is eventually to lead to a "popular front" (*Volksfront*) through alliance with non-left oriented groups, Christians, liberals, and persons without any party affiliation. (*Bayernkurier*, 24 December 1977.)

In spite of strong efforts to increase the vote of the DKP in local and state (*Land*) elections, the outcome proved again disastrous. In the last four *Land* elections in 1978, the DKP lost about 40 percent of its voters. (*FAZ*, 19 October.) The results were as follows:

Land elections	1978 votes	percentage	1974 percentage
Lower Saxony	12,708	0.3	0.4
Hamburg	9,378	0.1	2.2
Hesse	14,531	0.4	0.9
Bavaria	33,148	0.3	0.4

DKP leaders expressed disappointment over the poor election results and blamed them on the "undemocratic 5 percent clause," which requires a party to obtain at least 5 percent of one vote to receive representation in state legislatures. The DKP rationalized that many communist sympathizers voted for the SPD in order to prevent a victory of the "reactionary" CDU/CSU (*DI*, 29, no. 1489, 14 October, p. 10).

In addition to its "unity of action" and election efforts, the DKP carried on a number of other activities designed to improve its image in the FRG and to increase its membership. As in previous years, the "Week of the DKP" (14–22 January) was supposed to facilitate contact with the "masses" through distribution of literature at information booths in cities and at factories, meetings, demonstrations, and discussion groups and through sales of the party newspaper, *Unsere Zeit*.

The traditional May Day celebration provided the opportunity to propagandize the objectives of the DKP. The party newspaper listed 128 events scheduled throughout the FRG. The Party Directorate declared 1 May as the "day of struggle for the right to work" and in its May Day slogans urged protection of "democratic rights and freedoms," supported the fight against lockouts and the *Berufsverbot*, and opposed the neutron bomb. (*UZ*, 7 and 21 April.)

The "Festival of Youth" in Dortmund on 13–14 May, organized by the SDAJ and MSB-Spartakus, drew 200,000 participants (*UZ*, 19 May). In addition to communist attacks against the *Berufsverbot* and neutron bomb, the festival was dedicated to "international solidarity." Participants included representatives from African liberation movements, from countries suffering under "fascist dictatorships," and from over 80 organizations and youth groups in the FRG.

A mass meeting of the DKP was held in Cologne on the occasion of the visit of Leonid Brezhnev to the FRG in May. Herbert Mies welcomed the Soviet leader and emphasized the "strong fraternal relations" between the DKP and CPSU (Tass, 4 May).

International Views and Party Contacts. The international views of the DKP are in every respect identical to those held by East Berlin and Moscow. For example, the DKP's explanation of the division of Germany follows the concepts expressed by the GDR. According to the DKP, the fight between "reaction and progress" led to two independent and sovereign German states recognized by international law and marked by different social orders. The FRG developed as a result of the restoration of the power of monopoly capitalism. The GDR emerged as a consequence of the antifascist and socialist revolution. (DKP, *Entwurf Programm der Deutschen Kommunistischen Partei*, Beilage zu *UZ*, 9 December 1977, p. 15.)

As part of the international communist movement, the DKP maintained close contact with fraternal parties and movements. In 1978 DKP functionaries and delegations visited the Soviet Union, the GDR, and the Mongolian People's Republic and received at its headquarters in Düsseldorf delegations from the CPSU, the Hungarian Socialist Workers' Party, the Communist Party of Austria, and the PLO. Chairman Herbert Mies met with Leonid Brezhnev and Erich Honecker. On the occasion of the visit to the Mongolian People's Republic, Mies received the "Order of Friendship" (*UZ*, 13 June).

The international communist periodical *Problems of Peace and Socialism* organized a symposium in Prague to analyze the topic "Dialectic of Economics and Politics in the Period of the Struggle for a Revolutionary Change in Society." The DKP was one of the 45 communist parties represented at the symposium. (*DI*, 29, no. 1476, 31 March, p. 5.) Representatives of the DKP and the Communist Party of Luxembourg met at a conference in Saarbrücken and noted the need for "unity of action" among steelworkers of the Common Market countries (*IB*, 15 April, p. 52). On 22 September a meeting of representatives of the communist parties of the nine countries of the European Community met in Brussels. The main topic was the direct election to the European Parliament. (*DI*, 29, no. 1489, 14 October, p. 9.) The Party Directorate of the DKP announced that a conference of delegates will meet in Saarbrücken on 17 February 1979 to select its candidates for this election (*DI*, 29, no. 1488, 30 September, p. 3).

The DKP condemned the FRG government's stand on the production and possible deployment of the American neutron bomb in the FRG and appealed to the "peace-loving and democratic forces" to continue their struggle against the neutron bomb (East Berlin radio, 10 February, 14 April). The DKP supported the Soviet Union's "realistic and constructive proposals for concrete measures to limit arms and achieve disarmament" (Allgemeiner Deutscher Nachrichtendienst, East Berlin, 18 June) and demanded an end to the "dangerous and reckless anti-Soviet propaganda" carried on by "reactionary circles" in the FRG (Tass, 2 March).

Publications. The official DKP organ, *Unsere Zeit*, appears six times a week. Its daily circulation is about 30,000. The Friday edition has between 60,000 and 70,000 copies. The newspaper seeks to report on the interests of readers in various occupations and considers it essential to report "the truth about the class struggle" (*DI*, 29, no. 1477, 13 April, p. 8). The DKP publishes 600 factory and 800 residence and local newspapers. Most of the editors are volunteers well-versed in party ideology. In order to assist the amateur editors, the Party Directorate publishes a "handbook" providing guidance in producing different publications (Bundesverband Deutscher Zeitungsverleger, *BDZV Intern*, no. 26, Bonn, 18 May, pp. 4–5).

The *Berliner Extra-Dienst*, a Berlin newspaper closely aligned with the communist viewpoint, announced that starting in February 1979 a new "independent, left-oriented" daily newspaper will be published for the FRG and West Berlin under the title *Die Neue*. On 22 September the first issue appeared and contained advertisements of left-wing publishing houses and the SPD weekly *Vorwärts*. Articles by the chairman of the "Jusos," Gerhard Schröder, concerning the *Berufsverbot* and by other left-oriented authors criticizing the security agencies of the FRG indicate the general orientation of the paper. (*DI*, 29, no. 1488, 30 September, pp. 6–7.) On 7 October another DKP-oriented newspaper, "*Revier*," was introduced at a press festival at the University of Bonn. The main articles in the second edition of *Revier* dealt with lockouts and the shortening of the workweek. (*DI*, 29, no. 1489, 14 October, p. 4.) (For other DKP and leftist publications, see *YICA, 1978*, pp. 147–48.)

Other Leftist Groups—Rival Communist Organizations. The "New Left" is the collective term for the left extremists who are opposed to the pro-Moscow or "orthodox" Communists and who claim to follow the correct Marxist-Leninist line. The political spectrum of the New Left reaches from the many different Maoist-oriented groups to the antidogmatists, "spontis," and anarchists. Some consider themselves to be political parties. One of them, the Communist League of West Germany (Kommunistischer Bund Westdeutschlands; KBW) participated in all four *Land* elections held during 1978. The Communist Party of Germany/Marxist-Leninist (KPD/ML) ran candidates in the *Land* elections in Hamburg, polling a total of 911 votes (less than 0.1 percent). The KPD/ML declined to take part in the three elections subsequently scheduled in Lower Saxony, Hesse, and Bavaria.

It is very difficult to monitor the activities of the organizations of the New Left because they are in a continuous state of flux. They emerge, publish a newspaper, sometimes combine with other groups or form splinter groups, and frequently disappear as rapidly as they are formed. Maoist groups and other left extremists cooperate in special projects, such as protest demonstrations, only to feud again and attack each other because of their incompatible ideological positions.

The doctrinaire Maoists, Trotskyites, and antidogmatist groups subscribe to the use of violence in their attempts to revolutionize the people although they acknowledge that conditions must be ripe for the revolution. The terrorist groups, which also have their origins in revolutionary Marxism, maintain that the armed struggle, including assassinations, murders, kidnappings, bombings, and bank robberies, serve to intensify the revolutionary situation and sumultaneously demonstrate the vulnerability of the state.

The groups of the antidogmatic New Left combine their objective of the revolutionary destruction of the existing social and political order with the intent to revolutionize personal life-styles. A number of them collaborated during 1978 within a larger geographic area. For example, the "Red Cells" in Munich gave birth to nineteen "Marxist groups" in the FRG, which together published the *Marxist Student Newspaper* (MSZ) and the *Marxist Workers' Paper* (MAZ). The Gruppe *Rheinische Zeitung Bonn* (Group *Rheinish Newspaper Bonn*) coordinates its work with groups in Bielefeld, Berlin, Bochum, Duisburg, Cologne, and Münster. They distribute their publications *Rheinische Zeitung Bonn, Sozialistische Hochschulpolitik, Zeitschrift für internationale Solidarität* (ZAFRA), and the monthly *Rheinische Arbeiter-Zeitschrift*. A number of so-called "self-help groups" in various locations worked together and published, starting in November 1977, the newspaper *Wir wollen's anders* (We want it differently). Other instances of mergers within the antidogmatic New Left are the Verband des linken Buchhandels (Union of the Left Book Business) and Arbeitsgemeinschaft alternativer Verlage und Authoren (Working Group of Alternative Publishers and Authors; AGAV). (*DI*, 29, no. 1479, 31 March, pp. 8−10.)

The "K-groups" retained about the same overall membership and are considered to some extent a reservoir of members for terrorist organizations (*Rheinischer Merkur*, 4 August). The anti-nuclear power movement provided one of the best opportunities for members of the K-groups, anarchists, and sympathizers with terrorists to employ violent methods. A nineteen-page pamphlet, *Das tapfere Schneiderlein* (The courageous tailor; a title of a well-known German children's story), proposes "new forms of resistance," such as acts of sabotage on the roads leading to nuclear power plants, destruction of ticket automats serving public transportation, and bombing of court buildings. Some of these suggestions were implemented in 1978. (*Die Welt*, 16 February; Bundesminister des Innern, *Innere Sicherheit*, no. 43, 12 May, pp. 15−16. "K-groups" explained in *YICA, 1978*, p. 149.)

An anarcho-syndicalist organization, Freie Arbeiterunion (Free Workers' Union; FAU), attempted to infiltrate German trade unions. This "initiative" was begun in 1977, and presently there are about ten to twelve groups organized in three regions and led by a national committee. Their main activity is to carry propaganda into the factories. Eventually, they plan to organize an anarcho-syndicalist trade union following the Spanish model as a counterweight to the German Trade Union League (DGB). The FAU held its Third Congress in Cologne at Whitsuntide and decided that the time is ripe to coordinate the various leftist factory groups. The anarcho-syndicalists consider themselves an anti-parliamentary action organization and publish *Direkte Aktion* (Direct action). (*DI*, no. 1486, 30 August, pp. 11–14.)

The strongest Maoist "party" is the Communist League of West Germany (Kommunistischer Bund Westdeutschlands; KBW), founded in 1973. Its membership is about 3,500. (Some sources claim that the membership remained at 2,500, e.g., *FAZ*, 26 July.) The KBW polled the following number of votes in the four *Land* elections in 1978: Hamburg, 686 (0.1 percent); Lower Saxony, 2,803 (0.1 percent); Hesse, 2,710 (0.1 percent); and Bavaria, 3,042 (0.1 percent). Members of affiliated organizations, such as the Communist Youth League (Kommunistischer Jugendverband; KJV), the Communist University Group (Kommunistische Hochschulgruppe; KHG), the Society for Support of People's Struggles (Gesellschaft zur Unterstützung der Volkskämpfe; (GUV), and the very active Soldiers' and Reservists' Committees (Soldaten- und Reservistenkomitees; SRK) amount to an additional 3,000 persons (*DI*, 29, no. 1480, 26 May, p. 4). The KBW's finances are the strongest of the left extremists. In 1976 the KBW had a budget of seven million DM. In the spring of 1977, the KBW paid 2.7 million DM cash for their new headquarters building in Frankfurt-am-Main. In May 1978 the KBW forwarded 600,000 DM to the ZANU liberation movement, which is fighting against the Rhodesian internal solution. Most KBW income is from membership fees (3.5 million DM), gifts from "mass organizations" (1 million DM), and sales of literature (2 million DM). The members pay a high percentage of their income to the party and are requested to transfer their savings, inheritances, etc., to the KBW treasury (*FAZ*, 2 October).

One of the main efforts of the KBW is the struggle against the Bundeswehr (Federal armed forces). The antimilitary activity is based on the "Directives for Military Problems" and consists of two phases. The first is the creation of conspiratorial units within the military and other security organs of the FRG, such as the police. The second phase is disruption by KBW groups of military activities when the military is employed on behalf of the "bourgeois class." (*Die Welt*, 31 January.) On 30 May the Permanent Committee of the KBW Central Committee unanimously adopted the "Tactical Resolution." According to this document, the KBW considers itself a part of the proletarian world army and participates in the worldwide fight against imperialism. Furthermore, the KBW is dedicated to fight against the "occupation powers" in the FRG. (*Radical-Info*, no. 3/4, June/August, pp. 1–6; for additional information on the KBW, see *YICA, 1978*, p. 149.)

The Communist Party of Germany (Kommunistische Partei Deutschlands; KPD), with about 700 members, carries the same name as the pro-Moscow and illegal KPD but should not be taken as a successor organization. (For background, see *YICA, 1975*, pp. 183–84.) The outstanding event was the visit to China by a party delegation led by the chairman of its Central Committee, Christian Semler (*FBIS*, 22 June). The KPD supports Cambodia in its struggle against foreign domination (i.e., Vietnam) and maintains contact with Maoist parties in Turkey and Belgium. Its affiliated organizations are the Communist Youth League of Germany (KJVD), with about 450 members, the Communist Student League (KSV), the League against Imperialism, the Red Help (Rote Hilfe), the Union of Socialist Contributors to Culture, and the Association of Socialist Teachers and Educators. (*DI*, 29, no. 1485, 15 August, pp. 7–8.) The KPD's organ, *Rote Fahne*, has appeared since October as a weekly. The KJVD publishes a monthly paper, *Kämpfende Jugend*, and the KSV publishes *Dem Volke dienen*. The other affiliated organizations also have their own organs: the League against Imperialism publishes *Internationale Solidarität*; the Rote Hilfe publishes *Rote Hilfe*; the Union of Socialist Contributors to Culture publishes *Kämpfende Kunst*; and the Association of Socialist Teachers and Educators publishes *Info*.

The KPD/ML follows the ideological concepts of the Albanian Communist Party. Its membership is about 700 (*FAZ*, 26 July). Its chairman, Ernst Aust, visited Albania in July. He condemned the hostile acts of the Chinese leadership and assured Enver Hoxha of his party's solidarity and friendship. (*FBIS*, 31 July.) The KPD/ML advocates violent socialist revolution and destruction of the bourgeois state apparatus, followed by the dictatorship of the proletariat. KPD/ML members served as candidates for the Revolutionary Trade Union Opposition (RGO) in elections for shop stewards throughout the FRG and West Berlin. Its central organ is the weekly *Roter Morgen* (about 10,000 copies). The organ of the youth organization Rote Garde (Red Guard) is *Die Rote Garde.* The first and founding congress of the Rote Garde took place in Düsseldorf (13–15 May). (*DI*, 29, no. 1478, 28 April, p. 6.) A miniature edition of *Roter Morgen* is mailed into the GDR, and Radio Tirana broadcasts Maoist propaganda in German on behalf of the KPD/ML (*Rheinischer Merkur*, 5 May; *DI*, 29, no. 1479, 8 May, pp. 7–10).

Other Maoist organizations are the Communist League (KB), with about 1700 members, and the Communist Workers' League of Germany (KABD). (For additional information on the KB, KABD, and Trotskyite groups, see *YICA, 1977*, p. 167 and *YICA, 1978*, p. 150.)

West Berlin. West Berlin is still an "occupied" city. The U.S., Britain, and France maintain troops in their respective sectors and have suspended that part of the Basic Law of the FRG which included West Berlin as one of the *Länder*. The Four Power Agreement concerning Berlin of 3 September 1971 confirmed the fact that West Berlin is not a part of the FRG and retains its "special status" as a result of Allied agreements dating from 1944 and 1945. These agreements apply to the area of "Greater Berlin," the former German capital. However, the GDR has for all practical purposes incorporated the Soviet Sector and declared "Berlin" its capital. Western protests against the remilitarization of East Berlin in violation of the agreements signed by the Soviet Union and the Western Allies have been without effect, and the GDR, with Soviet support, continues policies intended to isolate West Berlin from the FRG as the first phase of an eventual absorption of the three Western sectors into the GDR. On the other hand, the FRG, encouraged by the Western Allies, maintains close ties with West Berlin, a situation reaffirmed by the Four Power Agreement in 1971.

The SEW. The special status of Berlin, though only observed completely in the Western sectors, made it possible for the SED to organize a West Berlin subsidiary. Thus, the present Socialist Unity Party of West Berlin (Sozialistische Einheitspartei Westberlins; SEW) is the creation of the East German SED and was not the work of Communists in West Berlin. Initially, it was the SED organization located in the three Western sectors of Berlin. Therefore, up to the time of the artificial "separation" from the "mother party," the communist organization in West Berlin had the same history as the SED.

The first change occurred as a result of Khrushchev's demand in the spring of 1959 that West Berlin be made a "free city." This resulted for the first time in the appointment of a separate leadership for the SED in the Western sectors in order to give the impression of the existence of an indigenous and independent communist party. The next step came in November 1962 when a "Conference of Delegates" changed the name of the party to Socialist Unity Party of Germany—West Berlin (SED–W). This change was necessary as a result of the erection of the Berlin Wall (13 August 1961), which physically divided East and West Berlin. A special congress changed the name in February 1969 to the present SEW. The removal of "Germany" was done to support the assertion that West Berlin is an "independent political entity." Only the ruling communist party in the GDR carries "Germany" in its name, implying that the other German communist parties (DKP and SEW) are mere subsidiaries of the SED and are of a transitory nature.

Leadership, Organization, and Domestic Activities. The sudden death of the chairman of the SEW, Gerhard Danelius, on 18 May necessitated convening an extraordinary party congress on 18 July. The former deputy chairman, Horst Schmitt, was elected by the 388 delegates as the new chairman. Inge Kopp, since 1970 a member of the SEW Bureau of the Party Directorate (identical to the politburo of other communist parties), was appointed to succeed Schmitt as deputy chairman. Dietmar Ahrens remains the second deputy chairman with equal standing. (*FBIS*, 19 July.)

Horst Schmitt declared at the congress that the death of Danelius did not create a crisis for the SEW and that the party will remain "the champion for the unity of action with Social Democrats and Christian workers and those without party affiliation" (*FAZ*, 20 July). In his speech he also referred to the current state of international affairs and the situation in West Berlin. He promised that the SEW will continue the struggle to strengthen peace and to safeguard the social and democratic rights of the working people. The party's task in the domestic sphere is to fight unemployment and political discrimination of "democrats," and it is dedicated to proletarian internationalism. (*FBIS*, 20 July.) (For a discussion of the organization, structure and leadership personnel, and affiliated organizations, such as the Free German Youth—West Berlin and other "mass organizations," see *YICA, 1976*, p. 157.)

The impact of the SEW is minimal. At the last elections in 1975, the party obtained 1.9 pecent of the vote. Its membership is about 7,500.

International Views and Party Contacts. The SEW's international views, including its position on West Berlin's relations with East and West Germany, are identical with those expressed by Moscow and East Berlin. The SEW maintains close relations with fraternal communist parties, especially with the SED from which the party receives most of its financial support and political guidance. In January Chairman Danelius visited the chairman of the DKP, Herbert Mies (*FBIS*, 13 January). On the occasion of Danelius' 65th birthday, he received from Erich Honecker the order "Star of International Friendship" in gold (*FBIS*, 6 April). Following the death of Danelius, the party received expressions of condolence from many fraternal parties (*FBIS*, 19 May).

Publications. Die Wahrheit, the official organ of the SEW, appears six times weekly, with about 16,000 copies. (For publications of the "mass organizations" affiliated with the SEW, see *YICA, 1975*, p. 191.)

Other Leftist Groups—Rival Communists. West Berlin remained one of the major areas of activity for left extremist groups which also operate in the FRG. Their influence among the working population is minimal. The institutions of higher learning provide them with most of their members. For example, a "National Congress of Resistance" met in West Berlin (27—29 January) and was attended by about 6,000 followers of the antidogmatist "New Left." The main topic was the destruction of the political system of the FRG. After the conclusion of the congress at the Technical University in Berlin, there was violence between approximately 4,500 demonstrators and the police. (Bundesminister des Innern, *Innere Sicherheit*, no. 42, Bonn, 8 March, pp. 5—6; for further details, see *YICA, 1977*, p. 169.)

The University of Calgary   Eric Waldman

Great Britain

The Communist Party of Great Britain (CPGB) was founded in 1920. It remains Britain's most significant Marxist party by virtue of the influence it can exercise in many trade unions. A recognized political party, the CPGB contests both local and national elections without conspicuous success. It currently has no members in the House of Commons, Britain's principal legislative assembly, and has had none since 1950 when it had two. Ironically (the party is committed to the abolition of the nonelected Upper House), the CPGB has one member in the House of Lords, Lord Milford. It has eight members in local councils plus a ninth who, although not a member of the party, campaigned as a "Communist."

Membership is still officially given as 25,938 but is probably less. The population of Great Britain is estimated at just below 56 million.

Leadership and Organization. The National Congress is constitutionally the supreme authority in the party. It meets once every two years; the last meeting was held in November 1977. It is responsible for electing the forty-two member Executive, discussing and considering documents on policies and activities, and listening to reports on the party's activities since the previous meeting. Delegates to the Congress are composed of representatives from both branches and districts. Serious opposition does not occur, and the Congress serves largely as a rubber stamp for the Political Committee, although amendments are made on occasion.

The Executive Committee, which meets once every two months, has overall responsibility for the party's activities on specific issues. It also chooses members for special committees, the full-time heads of departments, and the sixteen-member Political Committee. The Political Committee is the party's innermost conclave and therefore the effective controlling body. It meets every week, and as the occasion requires.

During 1978 leading officers and heads of departments were Gordon McLennan (general secretary), Mick Costello (industrial organizer), Jack Woddis (international department), Dave Cook (organization), George Matthews (press and publicity), Jean Styles (women), Betty Matthews (education), Malcolm Cowle (election agent), Dennis Ellwand (treasurer), and Martin Jacques (editor of *Marxism Today*).

The Young Communist League (YCL), the CPGB's youth organization, is in a parlous condition with membership now down to about 1,500. It held a *Challenge* festival on 13 May in a bid to raise money for its newspaper of that name. It has also been active in supporting ventures, such as the Anti-Nazi League, which has attracted large numbers of demonstrators. The YCL general secretary is Tom Bell.

Granted its lack of general support, the CPGB enjoys an extraordinary degree of strength in the trade unions. Low polls in union elections and the fact that the CPGB is the only effective organization trying to control election results have resulted in the CPGB having a member on almost every union executve in Great Britain. This strength is of considerable significance in British political life. Aside from the direct role of unions in the political process, some 80 percent of Labour Party funds are based on trade union contributions, and 88 percent of votes at the annual Labour Party conference are controlled by trade unions. The CPGB's influence in political life cannot therefore be discounted, although the party's former industrial organizer, Bert Ramelson, doubtless overstated the case when he said: "The party [CPGB] can float an idea early in the year and it can become official Labour policy by the autumn."

In general the CPGB fared badly in union elections in 1978. It was particularly disappointed in the voting for prominent positions in the influential Amalgamated Union of Engineering Workers (AUEW) which in April elected Terry Duffy as president, confirming a rightward shift virtually all down the line in the union's elections. Bill Benson, a communist shop stewards' convener at London Airport, was, however, elected president of the National Union of Sheet Metal Workers, Coppersmiths, Heating and Domestic Engineers.

In addition to the election of card-carrying Communists, a prominent Labour Party personality has alleged that 16 of the TUC General Council's 39 members have been actively pursuing associations with communist organizations (*Daily Telegraph*, 11 January). None of the facts used to substantiate his argument have been disputed.

The Communists work through the Liaison Committee for the Defence of Trade Unions (LCDTU), which is headed by Secretary Kevin Halpin. The party held a conference of workplace delegates on 9 April. Attendance was lower than the previous year, but representatives included delegates from Ford, Rolls Royce, British Leyland, Firth Brown Tools, NCB Workshops, GEC, the shipyards, printing workers, British Rail, local government, Post Office, power and building industry branches, and full-time union and party officials. The CPGB has about 200 workplace branches, but the main emphasis of debate was on the need to build more workplace branches.

Party Internal Affairs. The debate in the CPGB on its program, *The British Road to Socialism*, adopted in November 1977, continued in 1978. The program envisages a broad democratic alliance of left-wing forces leading to the election of a communist-influenced Labour government. Such a government would pave the way for socialism by a combination of mass extraparliamentary struggles (i.e., strikes and demonstrations) and a legislative program designed at wholesale nationalization, the control of the media, the abolition of the monarchy and the House of Lords, and the removal of hostile elements from the civil service, armed forces, and judiciary.

The governing Labour Party itself refused the communist invitation to cooperate with it at the national level, but there were several requests at local levels for communist speakers and copies of *The British Road to Socialism*. However, many Communists feel uneasy at the role the party has cast for itself. This uneasiness is most strikingly illustrated in membership figures, which are declining at a rate of about 7 percent a year. Ideologically, the party's long-standing ban on factions makes it difficult to assess the strength of opposition currents. However, the party has set up a sixteen-member commission on inner-party democracy. One opposition group is based around a pamphlet entitled *Out of the Ghetto*. This is sometimes called the "Manchester School" on account of its strength in that city. It also has the support of some academics on the party's economic advisory committee. It advocates a greater emphasis on reformist over revolutionary politics. Another group centers on Jon Blomfield, the Birmingham CPGB organizer, and advocates a more active role for overt rather than industrial CPGB campaigning. In general the party is undergoing a phase of self-examination, and its future is unclear. Writing in *Socialist Challenge*, Michael Prior, a CPGB member since 1961, said that the party had collapsed and that "it has been outflanked and bypassed both to its left and right."

This picture of decline was underlined in the fate of the party's daily newspaper, the *Morning Star*, which now has a sale of only 21,000 copies daily. This paper is heavily dependent on its sales to Eastern Europe, and finance remains a big issue for the paper and for the party.

The CPGB retains a significant interest in many business concerns, including Central Books Ltd., Lawrence and Wishart, publishers, Farleigh Press and London Caledonian, printers, the Labour Research Department, and the Marx Memorial Library.

Domestic Attitudes and Activities. As usual the CPGB fared badly in local government elections. It retains eight councillors including Annie Powell, who was appointed deputy mayor of Rhondda, Mid-Glamorgan, in May 1978.

The Communists continued to campaign against the government on a number of issues, most notably concerning income policies. The party has not done this with great success, and the TUC continued to support government policies until late in the year.

The Communists tried to exploit various campaigns against racism in the course of the year but were pushed well out of the forefront by the Socialist Workers' Party (SWP). Most antiracist campaigns were conducted by the Anti-Nazi League (ANL), which is heavily influenced by the SWP, but which the Communists felt obliged to support. A special week of activity against the development of the neutron bomb was sponsored from 15 to 21 May. On 16 January a campaign against the West German *Berufsverbot* was launched that later resulted in organized meetings in London. Southhampton, Reading, Birmingham, Liverpool, Manchester, Leeds, and Bradford. Opposition to the renewal of the Prevention of Terrorism (Temporary Provisions) Act was also a keynote campaign of the year.

The successful People's Festival launched the previous year was held again on 18 June at Alexandra Palace, North London. Consisting largely of popular music, radical plays, games, and various newsstands, it attracted people from a large spectrum. Significantly, the CPGB itself barely succeeded in retaining control as various Trotskyite bodies played a significant role. A People's Festival was also held in Bell Vue in the greater Manchester area on 26 November.

The *Morning Star* garnered a little notoriety when it published the name of Colonel 'B', a key figure in an Official Secrets case whose anonymity was to be preserved, after a left-wing Labour MP using parliamentary immunity had named him. In April a "personal and in confidence" letter was sent by the prime minister's press secretary to the *Morning Star* editor, Tony Chater, asking him to join with others in keeping a change of leadership at MI5 and MI6 quiet. The paper published the letter in full and announced that it would not take part in a "cover up charade," although it did not in fact disclose the identities of the new intelligence chiefs.

On 4 April a postal bomb was delivered to the CPGB headquarters and injured the caretaker. It was presumed to be the work of a right-wing extremist group, although the initial claim that it was the work of Column 88, a neo-Nazi group, seemed less likely on closer examination.

The tenth Communist University of London (CUL) was held at the Polytechnic of Central London from 15 to 23 July. It was well attended with some 1,000 full-time and about 500 part-time participants. General courses included the British Labour Movement, Culture and Ideology, Racism and State Monopoly Capitalism, while specialist courses included the Factory and the City, the Future of Health Care, and Literature and Industrial Relations.

International Views and Party Contacts. Internationally, the CPGB expressed criticism of the Soviet Union on the occasion of the tenth anniversary of the Soviet invasion of Czechoslovakia and over the trials of dissidents in the USSR. On 18 May the CPGB Political Committee issued a statement urging the Soviet authorities to rescind the sentence passed on Soviet dissident Dr. Yuri Orlov: "We cannot agree that public disagreement or even misrepresentation of the policies of the Soviet government should be the subject of court action and heavy punishment as in this case." This was followed in July by a call from the Political Committee for the release of Aleksandr Ginzburg, Viktoras Petkus, and Anatoli Shcharansky. The party's industrial organizer, Mick Costello, signed an appeal in July calling for the rehabilitation of an old Bolshevik, Nikolai Bukharin.

In general, however, the party pursued a line of support for the Soviet Union. The CPGB denounced the intervention of French forces in Shaba province of Zaire as "imperialist." It lent active propaganda support to Vietnam in its war with Cambodia. It condemned the internal settlement in Rhodesia, and gave its support to the Patriotic Front. It advocated British withdrawal from the European Economic Community (EEC). Chile and South Africa remained leading targets for communist propaganda. Indeed, the CPGB is affiliated with the Chile Solidarity Campaign.

The Communists showed their disdain for acts of terrorism on the occasion of the murder in Italy of Aldo Moro by the Red Brigades. A CPGB statement said: "Communists believe that political advance can only be won by mass democratic struggle of the people. We are therefore totally opposed to such foul acts of terrorism as that which resulted in the death of Aldo Moro."

Various international contacts were made in 1978. Tom Bell, general secretary of the YCL, visited Romania in January and was received by the secretary of the Central Committee of the Romanian Communist Party, Stefan Andrei. On 23 January General Secretary Gordon McLennan and Jack Woddis had talks in East Berlin with the head of the East German party, Erich Honecker. In April Mishov Mishev, chairman of the Central Council of Bulgarian Trade Unions, had talks with Gordon McLennan on the development of bilateral relations and cooperation between the two countries' communist parties. On 16 May Jack Woddis had talks in Hungary with András Gyenes, secretary of the Hungarian Socialst Workers' Party's Central Committee. Two days later Woddis was received by Petur Dyulgerov, secretary of the Bulgarian Communist Party's Central Committee. On 24 May Gordon McLennan met Enrico Berlinguer, Italian Communist Party general secretary, and Sergio Segré, head of that party's International Department, in Italy. In Romania on 16 June McLennan was received by Nicolae Ceauşescu. On 2 October Dimitur Stanishev, Bulgarian party Central Committee secretary, received Mick McGahey, chairman of the CPGB, in Sofia. The same month Mick Costello attended the congress of the West German communist party as a fraternal delegate. The YCL was also an important constituent element in the British delegation to the World Youth Festival held in Cuba in the summer.

Publications. The chief CPGB organ is the daily *Morning Star.* Other leading papers are *Comment* (fortnightly) and *Marxism Today* (a monthly theoretical journal). The YCL publishes *Challenge* and *Cogito.*

In addition the Communists publish several magazines of specialized interest. The quarterlies include *Science Bulletin, Red Letters, Country Standard, Medicine and Society,* and *Eurored,* a periodical devoted to Western communist parties. Irregular publications are *Socialist Europe* (on Eastern Europe), *Economic Bulletin,* and *Music and Life. Socialist Europe* has from time to time published genuinely critical articles, but a woman's magazine, *Link,* had to be withdrawn because it was taking too independent a line.

Other Principal Marxist groups. Britain's leading Trotskyite organization is the Socialist Workers' Party (SWP). It has a membership of about 5,000 but a significantly larger number of sympathizers. It has at last had some success in making the transition from being a largely middle-class student body into a group with some working-class connections, albeit largely among white-collar workers and schoolteachers. This achievement is largely due to the success of two campaigns: one against unemployment and the other against racism.

Among the unemployed the SWP's rank-and-file movement has succeeded in garnering the party some support. In 1978, however, there is no doubt that it was the success of the Anti-Nazi League (ANL) which succeeded in mobilizing large numbers of young people into a cause which the SWP felt well able to exploit.

Britain's Anti-Nazi League was founded explicitly to combat the growth of the National Front, a right-wing extremist organization. Founded in November 1977 the ANL soon acquired a membership of 30,000, organized in some 250 branches. It was a windfall for the far Left, which had been seeking a mass mobilization campaign since the end of the Vietnam War. It attracted a significant degree of wholesome broad-based support, including such noted celebrities as Prof. Ralf Dahrendorf, actor Warren Mitchell, and renowned football players.

Yet it soon became clear that the ANL was deeply penetrated by the SWP, which sought to promote wider radicalization among ANL rank and file. Much ANL literature, notably that concerning trade union activity, is almost word for word the same as corresponding SWP leaflets. SWP posters ostensibly concerned with other causes have tried to link their campaigns with popular anti-Nazi propaganda, as in the curious slogan: "No Nazis and No Dole Queues." The ANL is headed by Paul Holborrow, a member of the SWP.

The SWP has groups of militants in the auto industry, the docks, the railways, the National Union of Mineworkers, the National Union of Teachers, and the National Association of Local Government Officers. Many of these sections produce their own paper, but the principal SWP paper is the weekly *Socialist Worker*, with a claimed circulation of about 25,000. Recruitment of Asians and West Indians continues, and there is a SWP section called Chingari (Spark), which produces papers in Bengali, Punjabi, and Gujerati. The SWP also has an active publishing press, the Pluto Press, associated with it.

The SWP has a full-time Central Committee of ten members, paid out of party funds. The party is centrally organized and has about 70 districts and branches. It claims that its main support is in Glasgow and the north of England. The SWP chairman is Duncan Hallas.

Ideologically, the SWP is Trotskyite but also holds the USSR to be "state capitalist." The party favors abolishing the wage structure and replacing it with a form of social benefits. The SWP does not seek to model society on any existing country but believes that the country could be governed by representative bodies spontaneously created during the armed struggle which it thinks will be necessary to destroy the present capitalist society.

The International Marxist Group (IMG) is the British section of the Trotskyist United Secretariat of the Fourth International, with a membership of about 1,500. IMG's national secretary is Bob Pennington, but its most prominent personalities are Tariq Ali and Robin Blackburn. The IMG held its conference, which is the highest decision-making body of the IMG, in London on 15−18 April. It adopted a five-point tactical program: (*a*) building up IMG cells in trade unions and other mass organizations; (*b*) gaining support in the Labour Party; (*c*) supporting the socialist unity electoral alliance; (*d*) building unity among all revolutionary forces; (*e*) continuing to sponsor *Socialist Challenge*.

Socialist Challenge, launched by the IMG, seeks to provide the basis for a united revolutionary movement in Britain. There are more than twenty Trotskyite groups in Britain, and *Socialist Challenge* has been trying to unite these groups on the basis of principled unity rather than tactical differences. At the first national conference of supporters of *Socialist Challenge,* held in London on 27 May, its editorial board therefore put forward a set of theses—"Our Common Ground"—which the IMG believes should unite all revolutionaries in the country. It attracted some interest from the International Socialist Alliance (ISA), the newest breakaway from the SWP, and from Big Flame. These organizations are about 150 and 100 strong respectively. *Socialist Challenge* currently has paid sales of about 6,000 and has ambitions of expanding this to 10,000.

The IMG specialty tends to be single-issue campaigns, such as solidarity with the working classes and colored peoples of Chile, Rhodesia, and South Africa; racism; and unemployment. It is also closely involved with solidarity campaigns on behalf of convicted IRA prisoners in Northern Ireland. In this connection it has begun to work more closely with the SWP. A joint IMG/SWP appeal for solidarity with IRA prisoners was issued for a demonstration to be held on 26 November. A conference of Sinn Fein, the political wing of the Provisional IRA, which was held in Dublin, appeared to have an IMG observer present. A group calling itself "Friends of Astrid Proll" attempted to prevent the extradition from London to West Germany of a convicted terrorist and received considerable publicity in *Socialist Challenge.*

The other principal Trotskyite group in Great Britain is the Workers' Revolutionary Party (WRP), an affiliate of the Fourth International (International Secretariat). It publishes a daily newspaper, *Newsline,* and an irregular journal, *Fourth International.* It has a large youth section, the Young Socialists. The WRP operates in an atmosphere of great secrecy, but it is known to have small groups in the docks and in engineering, mining, the theater, and the auto industry. It also operates the All Trade Union Alliance (ATUA), its principal arm for industrial campaigns. Membership is about 1,000 and its best known personalities are Corin and Vanessa Redgrave. Its chief publicity in 1978 came from a libel action the party brought against the *Observer,* which it finally lost in November. The party is disdained by most other Trotskyite groups because of its alleged sectarian attitudes. The WRP has frequently refused to cooperate with other left-wing extremist groups even on popular single-issue campaigns. It has, for example, shunned the Anti-Nazi League movement on the grounds that such campaigns only lead to greater sophistication and more effective techniques of riot control.

Other small Trotskyite groups include the International Communist League, the Revolutionary Communist Group, the Workers' League, Workers' Action, Big Flame, the Workers' Socialist League and the Spartacist League.

The small New Communist Party (NCP)—a Stalinist breakaway from the mainstream CPGB—made little impact on the national scene in 1978. Its banners were frequently seen in trade union and antiracist demonstrations, but little else appeared to have been effected, although its weekly, *New Worker,* is better produced than those of some of the other small parties. Membership is below 1,000, and the NCP's rigid pro-Soviet attitudes make it unlikely that it will attract many new adherents from the young.

There are now only two Maoist groups with visible organizations. The newly formed Revolutionary Communist League of Britain was created by the merger of the Communist Federation of Britain (Marxist-Leninist) and the Communist Unity Association of Britain (Marxist-Leninist). The other is the Communist Party of Great Britain—Marxist-Leninist, headed by Reg Birch. Both have avoided taking sides in the split between China and Albania.

London   Richard Sim

Greece

The Communist Party of Greece (Kommunistikon Komma Ellados; KKE) evolved from the Socialist Workers' Party of Greece, organized by a small group of leftist intellectuals in November 1918. Outlawed in 1936 by the Metaxas dictatorship, the KKE emerged as a major political force in the early 1940s while Greece was under the Axis occupation. Its attempts to seize power by force in December 1944 and later in 1946–49 failed, and the party remained outlawed between 1947 and 1974. The United Democratic Left (EDA) was organized in 1951 to act as a substitute for the KKE during those years.

During the military dictatorship of 1967–74, the party split into two factions, which became known as the KKE (Interior) and the KKE (Exterior). With the collapse of the military regime in July 1974, the KKE was legalized, but the split remained unbridged. In the 1977 parliamentary election, the KKE (Interior), which echoed the moderate line of Eurocommunism, received only 2.72 percent of the popular vote, while the KKE (Exterior), which follows a pro-Soviet, traditional Marxist-Leninist line, received 9.29 percent and eleven seats in the 300-seat legislature. The EDA joined the KKE (Interior) in an electoral coalition and managed to elect its longtime leader Elias Iliou.

The 12.01 percent received by the three principal parties of the Communist Left is less than the support given the EDA during the years it acted as a surrogate for the KKE. However, this should not be taken as an indication that the Communist Left has lost ground. The elections of 20 November 1977 revealed strong support for municipal candidates supported by the KKE (Exterior). It must also be noted that the growing Marxist influence in Greece is reflected in the continuing expansion of support for the Marxist-nationalist party of Andreas Papandreou, the Panhellenic Socialist Movement (PASOK), which received 25.33 percent of the popular vote in the parliamentary election of 1977 and emerged as the major opposition party with 92 seats in the 300-seat legislature.

The growing influence of the PASOK was manifested in the municipal elections of October 1978. The professed goals of the PASOK (total withdrawal from NATO, rejection of membership in the European Economic Community, total elimination of American and NATO military installations in Greece, and a socialist-communal organization of the economy) do not differ much from those of the Communist Left—in fact, they are more radical than those of the KKE (Interior) or the EDA. Hence, a realistic appraisal of Marxist-Leninist influence in Greece must include not only the following of the parties of the Communist Left but also that of PASOK. This means, on the basis of the electoral results of the 1977 parliamentary election and those of the municipal elections of 1978, that between 37.34 and 40.00 percent of the voters reflect a basically anti-American, anti-Western, anti-NATO, pro-socialist, pro-Marxist (though not necessarily pro-Soviet) orientation. This is a significant increase compared with the traditional 10–13 percent received by the Marxist-Leninist Left in the postwar years.

If the influence of the Marxist Left continues to expand in the coming years—as is likely—Andreas Papandreou may well emerge as Greece's prime minister after the next parliamentary election, which is to take place no later than November 1981.

Leadership and Organization. The Tenth Congress of the KKE (Exterior), which convened in May 1978 in Athens, elected a new Central Committee, which in turn elected the Politburo, composed of Kharilaos Florakis, Nikos Kaloudhis, Andonios Ambatielos, Grigoris Farakos, Mina Giannou, Roula Koukoulou, Kostas Loules, and Kostas Tsolakis, all members of the previous Politburo. Added to these were three others: Loula Logara, formerly an alternate member; Dimitrios Gondikas, secretary of the Communist Youth Organization (KNE) and member of parliament; and Stratis Tsambis, seaman. The alternate members are Dionysios Georgatos, Nikolaos Kyriakidis, Takis Mamatsis, and D. Sarlis. Kharilaos Florakis, the party's first secretary, was reelected, and his post retitled "secretary general." The Central Committee also created a Secretariat, which will assist the Politburo.

The other communist party, the KKE (Interior), held its Second (Tenth) Congress in April 1978. The new Central Committee elected the Executive Office, which has replaced the traditional Politburo. The new Executive Office is composed of B. Drakopoulos, B. Georgoulas, G. Giannaros, P. Dimitriou, L. Kyrkos, G. Banias, T. Benas, I. Straveris, and K. Filinis. Andonis Brillakis, one of the leading members since the split, was not elected to the Central Committee and is no longer a member of the Executive Office. L. Tzerronis and B. Theodoridis were not reelected to the Executive Office and were replaced by B. Georgoulas, a member of the Central Council of the youth organization "Rigas Feraios"; P. Dimitriou, a member of the KKE Central Committee at the time of the 1968 split; and Giannis Banias. Babis Drakopoulos continues as the party's leading official, the secretary general.

The EDA had its Third Conference in early April 1978 in Athens. The conference revealed the internal dissensions within this party. One hundred of the participating 234 delegates refused to be candidates for election to a new Central Committee, and of these 27 were members of the outgoing Central Committee. Such party luminaries as S. Iliopoulos, M. Glezos, Mikis Theodorakis, and T. Katrivanos are no longer members of the 50-member Central Committee. Nevertheless, Elias Iliou, the party's leader since the 1950s and its only deputy in the legislature, was reelected chairman of the eleven-member Executive Committee.

The PASOK is directed by an Executive Office led by Andreas Papandreou as its chairman. Papandreou is the founder of the party, which came into being in 1974 following the collapse of the dictatorial regime. Other members of the Executive Office are Giannis Alevras (a deputy in the legislature), Paraskevas Avgerinos, Giorgos Gennimatas, Kostas Laliotis, Kostas Simits, Akis Tsokhatzopoulos, Giannis Kharalambopoulos (also a deputy), and Andreas Khristodoulidis. The Central Committee is the supreme organ of the party between congresses and is composed of 80 party members. Twenty of these are deputies in the legislature. Andreas Papandreou is the president of the Central Committee and, for all practical purposes, the personification of the party, which, in spite of its Marxist ideology, has a highly personalized character.

Party Internal Affairs. The major event of the year for the Communist Left was the convening of the Tenth Congress in May by the KKE (Exterior). (Note: The KKE (Exterior) no longer uses the word "Exterior," and in fact the use of the adjective is being dropped by most others in referring to this party, which is becoming generally accepted as *the* communist party of Greece by most other communist parties in the world.) The congress lasted from 15 to 20 May and was attended by delegates representing more than 40 foreign communist parties. The congress was dominated by Florakis, the party's secretary general, and by Grigoris Farakos, generally considerd the second in command and a known hard-liner in ideological matters.

The KKE (Interior) held its congress 16–19 April in Athens. The congress was attended by representatives from the communist parties of Italy, Spain, Romania, Korea, and Yugoslavia. The presence of these foreign delegations reflected the Eurocommunist orientation of the KKE (Interior).

The Third Conference of the EDA, held in the first part of April, was intended to solidify its ranks and culminate the campaign for the party's renaissance. Instead, it revealed the failure of this effort. The EDA is no longer a significant political force.

Domestic and International Views and Positions. The Tenth Congress of the KKE (Exterior) did not reveal any spectacular changes in the party's ideological line or in its strategy and tactics. The Ninth Congress, held in East Germany in 1973 while Greece was ruled by the military dictatorship, had posed an intermediate stage on the "road to socialism," namely the passing to a "genuinely new democracy." The Tenth Congress concluded that this intermediate step had been largely bypassed and that the "revolutionary transformation" would or should go through the traditional two stages advocated by Marxism-Leninism. At the first stage, "democratic objectives will be resolved, and certain socialist tasks will also be tackled . . . by regrouping the forces favoring socialism . . . adopting a new, democratic constitution . . . freeing the country from imperialist dependency, including the abrogation of all agreements that violate its sovereign rights, withdrawal from NATO and the EEC, and dismantling of all foreign bases . . . an independent, peace-loving foreign policy . . . nationalization of foreign and domestic monopolies of national significance . . . a planned restructuring and development of the national economy." (See the "Political Resolution" of the Tenth Congress as translated by the author, *Rizopastis,* May.)

The end result of this first stage, according to the KKE, will be an "anti-imperialist, antimonopoly democracy of the people led by the working class. This system will be a democracy of a new type, a transitional system, which, as the revolutionary process acquires a more profound democratic character, will grow into a socialist democracy." The passing of the "popular democratic state into a socialist state" will be effected "by methods and at a rate corresponding to the balance of forces and the intensity of the class struggle." (Ibid.)

Grigoris Farakos explained in his report that the "people's democracy" will lead to the "socialist state," which "is another name for the dictatorship of the proletariat." The congress also condemned the KKE (Interior) for "rejecting all forms of armed struggle and supporting only a peaceful road to socialism." The congress, in fact, included in its main resolution a warning to "the workers to be prepared ideologically and politically for the case when the oligarchy of the monopolies and of imperialism will make it necessary to resort to the nonpeaceful road." (Ibid.)

The KKE (Interior) declared at its congress that the party's primary objective at this stage is the formation of "a government of democratic cooperation" and called for an "alliance" with the EDA and other socialist groups in the country. A great part of the time was devoted to the internal dissension raging through the ranks of the party's youth organization, "Rigas Feraios," and to the objections voiced by many delegates to the Eurocommunist policy followed by the party. In the end, the Eurocommunist orientation, supported by Drakopoulos, was approved but at the price of having several leading members excluded from the Central Committee. One may predict that several of these dissenting cadres will join the KKE (Exterior).

The Central Committee of the PASOK held a two-day plenary meeting in Athens on 25–26 February. The meeting approved a lengthy resolution dealing mostly with current issues but at times outlining some of the party's basic views. The resolution reiterated the party's main contention that "the country manifests the main characteristics of capitalist dependency under foreign economic, political, and military domination" and called for "the broadest alliance of all workers and underprivileged Greeks . . . for the speedy and peaceful assumption of power by the people's forces through democratic means." This reference to "democratic means," however, does not seem to relate to the Western idea of democracy. The PASOK seems to favor a one-party system: "The two-party system of alternating in power is not viable in a regional country with a dependent economy." The Central Committee also reaffirmed the party's commitment to an anti-imperialist, anti-Western, anti-NATO, anti-EEC, anti-military bases, and anti-monopoly line, and to a "socialist change." (See the reports on the plenary session published in the Greek daily *Vima* and translated here by the author.)

Andreas Papandreou is convinced that the PASOK can muster sufficient electoral support at the polls to gain a majority in the legislature and then proceed through legislation to fashion his own brand of a socialist system, which seems to reflect traces of Yugoslav "self-management," Chinese "communes," and Soviet-style "central planning." He is critical of the KKE (Exterior) but not for its "anti-imperialist, anti-monopolistic line which are [sic] a positive point of reference"; the PASOK rather sees the KKE (Exterior) as a rival organization with similar goals, which can only split the popular support PASOK would otherwise attract. (Ibid.)

The municipal elections of October 1978 showed that the PASOK is correct in this assessment. Nevertheless, one may expect that in the event the PASOK becomes the dominant party in the legislature, the KKE (Exterior) will support the PASOK program of transition to socialism, unless the PASOK takes the drastic step of putting into effect its notion of a "one-party" system. While both the KKE (Exterior) and the PASOK are fiercely anti-American and anti-Western, the PASOK does not share the KKE's commitment to the Soviet Union. The PASOK, with its strongly national-istic orientation, seems to favor a nonaligned foreign policy, choosing friends as circumstances dictate. (Ibid.)

Other Marxist-Leninist Organizations. Although several organizations continued to publish an occasional brochure or pamphlet, their significance should not be exaggerated. In both the parliamentary and the municipal elections, the Revolutionary Communist Movement of Greece (EKKE), relatively the most important among them, was ignored by the voters. For the record, one may mention the Organization of Marxist-Leninists of Greece (OMLE) with a pro-Chinese orientation, the Greek Revolutionary Liberation Front (EEAM), and the Greek Communist Party/Marxist-Leninist (KKE/ML), both of which are Stalinist in their views.

Publications. The KKE's official daily is *Rizospastis.* The KKE (Interior) and the EDA publicize their views through the daily *Avgi.* The KKE publishes a monthly theoretical review, *Kommunistiki Epitheorisi.* The OMLE publishes rather irregularly the tabloid *Laikos Dromos;* the EKKE, *Laikoi Agones;* and the KKE/ML, *Kokkini Simaia.* The PASOK does not have an exclusive daily organ, but its views are reflected in such noncommunist publications of wide circulation as the daily *Eleftherotypia,* the afternoon daily *Ta Nea,* the weekly *Oikonomikos Takhydromos* (occasionally), and at times the weekly *Politica Themata.* The leftist, anti-American, anti-NATO, and pro-socialist orientation of these noncommunist publications is a legacy of the 1967–74 military dictatorship, which brought together in joint opposition many groups from liberal to Marxist-Leninist and legitimized socialism and anti-imperialism and turned the United States and NATO into hostile forces in the eyes of most Greeks. The writings that appear in these noncommunist publications are more influential in shaping public views than those of the Marxist publications, which have much smaller circulations.

Howard University   D. G. Kousoulas

Iceland

Iceland's political culture, with its emphasis on personalities, egalitarianism, and fervent nationalism, has produced various left-socialist and communist movements over the years. Although analogies can be made with other Western European countries, Icelandic political institutions retain certain unique styles and characteristics. For the past decade the main left-socialist party has been the People's Alliance (Altydubandalagid; AB), which, while advocating fairly radical alternatives to current domestic and foreign policies, nevertheless does so without any reference to communist pronouncements and clichés from abroad. The AB is thus the latest form of a solidly established native radical tradition, but one that is quite concerned about international and foreign policy questions. The AB is supported by a heterogeneous collection of trade union members, radical teachers and students, extreme nationalists, and disenchanted Social Democrats. Until the 1978 parliamentary elections, the AB was considerably stronger than the reformist Social Democratic Party (Altyduflokkurinn; SDP); Iceland is the only Nordic country in which the Social Democrats are not the largest political party, but that trend may be changing. The People's Alliance has an estimated 3,000 members, out of a total population of about 224,000. Its main strength rests in the Reykjavik area (where half the population lives) and in the smaller fishing and processing towns along the eastern and northern coasts.

Communism has had a rather confusing and maverick history in Iceland. Its first organizational form was a secessionist left-wing splinter from the SDP in 1930. There have never been any legal prohibitions against the Communists. In 1938 the communist party withdrew from the Third International (Comintern), reconstituted itself to include more radical Social Democrats, and took the name of United People's Party—Socialist Party (Sameiningar flokkur altydu-Sosialista flokkurinn; UPP-SP). Even before this realignment, the Icelandic Communist Party (Kommunistaflokkur Islands; ICP) had actively sought a "popular front" with the Social Democrats. The new UPP-SP based their ideology on "scientific socialism—Marxism," and although there were no longer organizational ties to Moscow, the UPP-SP generally echoed Moscow's viewpoint on international affairs. In 1956 an electoral alliance was formed between most of the UPP-SP, the National Preservation Party, and dissident Social Democrats. This "People's Alliance" of 1956 strengthened the electoral position of the socialist Left and paved the way for the UPP-SP's participation in a broad national coalition (1956—58). Moreover, the merger with the National Preservation Party (formed in 1953 to protest NATO membership and the NATO air base at Keflavik and to promote a return to neutrality in foreign policy) made the AB the principal opponent of NATO membership. The AB became an avowed "Marxist political party" in November 1968 and so replaced the UPP-SP. Several elements in the National Preservation Party objected and under the leadership of Hannibal Valdimarsson formed the Organization of Liberals and Leftists (Samtök frjalslyndra og vinstri manna; OLL). In domestic policy the OLL has been more pragmatically socialist than the AB's leading elements. There is also a pro-Soviet Marxist faction, the Organization of Icelandic Socialists, and a Trotskyite Revolutionary Communist League (Fylking Byltingarsinnadhra Kommunista; FBK). The Icelandic Communist Party—Marxist-Leninist (ICP-ML) was formed in April 1976, and its chairman, Gunnar Andresson, claimed that the new party was the rightful heir to the original ICP. With its warnings against modern revisionism and Soviet "social imperialism," the ICP-ML has close ties to the Chinese Communist Party and is mentioned frequently in the *Peking Review* (e.g., 4 August).

The main left-socialist/communist group, currently represented by the People's Alliance, has consistently polled between 12 and 22 percent of the popular vote in postwar elections. Between 1971 and 1974 the AB participated in a coalition government formed by the Progressive (agrarian centrist) leader, Olafur Johannesson, along with the OLL (Trond Gilberg, "Patterns of Nordic Communism," *Problems of Communism,* Washington, May/June 1975).

The AB gained substantially in the June 1978 elections to the 60-member Althing (parliament). Polling 22.9 percent of the vote (up 4.6 percentage points from 1974), the AB won 14 mandates (a gain of 3). Their advance was overshadowed by the dramatic gains of the Social Democrats, who polled 22 percent (a gain of 12.9 percentage points) and won 14 seats (a gain of 5). The OLL polled only 3.3 percent (a loss of 1.3 percentage points) and lost both of its parliamentary seats. The governing Independence Party (moderate conserative) lost 5 of their 25 seats, and their coalition partners, the Progressives, also lost 5 of their 17 seats (*Nordisk Kontakt,* no. 12).

In the wake of this strong swing to the left, the government of Geir Hallgrimsson resigned, and there ensued a lengthy period of political negotiations. SDP leader Benedikt Gröndal was the first to try to form a government; then Independence Premier Hallgrimsson tried unsuccessfully. When the leader of the AB, Ludvik Josefsson, was given a chance, Iceland attracted considerable attention from other NATO countries. Would Iceland be the first NATO country to have a Marxist premier, who had campaigned vigorously against the alliance? Josefsson failed when the SDP refused to accept him as premier, and the AB leader later blamed politicians in Norway, Washington, and Brussels for this decision (ibid.). The fourth and successful effort was made by the former Progressive Premier Olafur Johannesson in August. The new coalition consisted of the Progressives, the Social Democrats, and the People's Alliance. Social Democrat Gröndal became foreign minister with his strong pro-NATO stand, while three AB leaders received cabinet posts: former AB Chairman Ragnar Arnalds became minister of education and communications, Hjörleifur Guttormsson became minister of industry, and Svavar Gestsson became minister of commerce. The new center-left government issued a lengthy declaration, and on the sensitive issue of foreign and NATO affairs it was noted that the AB maintained its position against NATO membership and the stationing of American forces in Iceland but that this would not affect the government's policies (ibid.). Compromise is also a virtue in Iceland.

Leadership and Organization. The AB limits leadership positions to one term, and so in November 1977 former Fisheries Minister Ludvik Josefsson replaced Ragnar Arnalds as party chairman. The new vice-chairman is Kjartan Olafsson, editor of the party daily, *Thjodhviljinn* (*Nordisk Kontakt,* no. 15, 1977). Josefsson is also leader of the AB parliamentary group. The Management Council is the party's highest authority between meetings of the 32-member Central Committee.

Personalities weigh heavily in Icelandic politics, and over the years the Communists have had their full share of factionalism, splits, and realignments. This has been especially true of the AB, whose parliamentary strength has fluctuated more because of internal strife than from changing public support. The 1968 formation of the OLL cost the AB several parliamentary seats. In recent years such turmoil has declined, but with the AB participating in a three-party coalition, there are bound to be intraparty frustrations.

Domestic Attitudes and Activities. The Icelandic economy in 1977—78 exhibited its unique strengths and weaknesses to an unusual extent. The consolidation of a 200-mile coastal economic zone with nearly exclusive fishing rights after years of intermittent disputes with Great Britain contributed to the country's prosperity. At the end of 1977 the center-right government could announce prospects for significant growth in real incomes, continued full employment, and a reduction in the inflation rate to 26 percent. During the year, however, labor unrest, wage drifts, and the complex wage-indexing system caused inflation to soar at an annual rate of 43 percent, the country's balance of payments to deteriorate, and several currency devaluations, with predictable political consequences. These economic questions were the focus of AB political activity and dominated the election campaign (*NYT,* 24 November). Efforts by the government to contain the increasing inflation by reducing indexation resulted in recurrent illegal strikes by both industrial and public employee unions in the spring of 1978. The AB demanded the government's resignation in bitter parliamentary exchanges (*Nordisk Kontakt,* no. 4).

Labor strife is a frequent phenomenon in highly unionized Iceland. Until the 1968 split in the People's Alliance, communist influence in the Icelandic Trade Union Federation (Altydusamband Islands; ASI) was significant. Direct control has been less during the past decade, but the AB consistently supports the more radical demands of organized labor. The private sector collective agreement of June 1977 provided for wage increases of up to 45 percent, and similar demands were then made by public sector employees. Labor unrest in 1978 was sporadic, with short stoppages targeted against exports (excepting fresh fish products) and oil imports. None of these actions was prolonged or totally effective. (Ibid., nos. 4, 5, 7, and 10.)

Worker discontent and the approaching municipal and parliamentary elections provided the focus of AB statements and proposals. AB statements called for direct price negotiations between farmers and the state, publication of the names of recipients of bank loans, and public ownership and control of all economic resources in the seas, on and under Icelandic land, or otherwise part of the country's resources (ibid., no. 6). This proposal reflects certain AB objections to large-scale foreign investments in joint ventures to use Iceland's abundant energy supplies. Although the new coalition government's program calls for increased planning and regulation of investment, it does not reflect the extreme AB position. Although participation in the coalition undoubtedly gives the AB increased influence, it does make the party responsible for the country's perennial economic and trade problems. The sensitive collective bargaining agreement of 1977 has now been extended by the government to December 1979. They should allow the coalition ample time to work out economic policy issues among themselves and with union and management representatives. (Ibid., no. 12.)

International Views and Positions. No Icelandic party is more consistently suspicious of things foreign than the People's Alliance. This has meant continuing opposition to Icelandic membership in NATO and to retention of the U.S.-Icelandic Defense Force (the Keflavik Base) in any form. There are currently some 3,000 American troops stationed at the base, and their main missions are reconnaissance, antisubmarine warfare, and air interception (*NYT,* 1 December). The AB's long-term objective has been and is an unarmed (except for the Coast Guard) and neutral Iceland.

The AB, when last in the government (1971−74), forced the United States to reopen negotiations with Iceland over the Keflavik NATO Base. The AB advance in the 1974 elections may have been promoted by anti-NATO feelings, but the even larger gains of the Independence Party and the mass "Defend Our Land" petition campaign indicated that most Icelanders favor a more moderate security policy. The NATO base continues, however, to give the Icelandic government considerable leverage in political and economic dealings with other Western states. This occurred during the 1975−76 "Cod War" between Iceland and Great Britain, which ended with an agreement greatly favoring the Icelandic position. The use of the British navy to protect British fishing trawlers provided the context of an attack on NATO membership by AB foreign policy spokesman Gils Gudmundsson, who characterized the connection as a "political swindle" (*Nordisk Kontakt,* no. 15, 1976).

Nearly 80 percent of Icelandic exports are fish or fish-related products, which explains the broad national consensus that Iceland must have exclusive control of its coastal waters. For years Iceland has had substantial trade with the USSR, and the AB has been among the most enthusiastic for increasing trade with non-Western nations. About 10 percent of Iceland's foreign trade is with the USSR, while nearly 30 percent is with the United States. During 1977 Iceland signed a large contract with China for the purchase of 11,000 tons of Icelandic aluminum, and an important sale of powdered fish protein was made to Cuba. (Ibid., nos. 13, 16, 1977.)

International Party Contacts. Icelandic Communists connected with the AB have been consistently absent from international communist meetings and have avoided contacts with foreign communist movements. In fact, no other Western European communist party has maintained such an isolationist position (see Gilberg, op. cit., pp. 34−35).

The AB maintains no formal ties with the Communist Party of the Soviet Union (CPSU), and it condemned the Warsaw Pact invasion of Czechoslovakia in 1968. Accordingly, there have been no AB representatives present at periodic gatherings of pro-Soviet parties, such as the Twenty-fifth Congress of the CPSU in February 1976 or the meeting of European communist parties in East Berlin in June 1976. In the past the AB has offered moral support for communist parties, most notably those of Romania and Yugoslavia, which are known for their independent or nationalistic views. The AB has also maintained periodic contacts with the Italian Communist Party (PCI), including a visit to Rome by then party chairman, Ragnar Arnalds, in 1976.

Publications. The AB's central organ is *Thjodhviljinn* (Will of the nation), a daily newspaper in Reykjavik. It has a national circulation of some 10,000. The party also publishes a biweekly theoretical journal, *Ny Utsyn.* Outside the capital, there are at least two pro-communist weeklies: *Verkamadhurinn* in Akureyri and *Mjolnir* in Siglufjördhur.

Other Marxist Groups. Mention has been made of the Organization of Liberals and Leftists which split from the AB in 1968, as well as two smaller Maoist and Trotskyite groups formed in the mid-1970s. The OLL's parliamentary support steadily declined through the 1974 elections. In October 1976, the OLL Executive Committee decided to cancel the party's National Congress and dissolve itself in favor of the two-man parliamentary group. In some regions of the country OLL activists seemed anxious to support the AB, in others the SDP, and in still others to continue an independent political organization. Although candidates were run in all electoral districts in June 1978, the OLL polled only 3.3 percent of the vote and failed to elect any members. With this setback the party seems likely to continue to disintegrate.

The Icelandic Communist Party−Marxist-Leninist drew little voter support but continued its active support of Chinese foreign policy goals. An ICP-ML delegation headed by Chairman Andresson visited Peking in May (New China News Agency, 24 May). The party's main publication is *Stettabarattan* (Class struggle).

The Trotskyite FBK ran parliamentary candidates in 24 electoral districts, but none received any significant number of votes. Although active in most leftist activities, the FBK is critical of the AB and most other competitors for support on the left. Its publication is *Neisti* (The spark). (*Intercontinental Press,* 10 April 1978.)

University of Massachusetts
Amherst   Eric S. Einhorn

Ireland

The first Irish Communist Party was founded on 14 October 1921 as a result of a schism in the existing Socialist Party. It swiftly became irrelevant during the ensuing Civil War (1922–23) and became extinct. Small cells of Marxist-Leninists remained, known collectively as Revolutionary Workers' Groups. In June 1933 a conference of these groups led to the formation of the Communist Party of Ireland (CPI). This is now the date adopted by the Irish Communists for the party's formation.

The Second World War, known as the "emergency" in the South, severely disrupted the communist organizational structure, largely because of the belligerent status of Northern Ireland and the neutrality of the South. In 1941 the southern organization suspended its activities and the present-day general secretary of the party, Michael O'Riordan, was interned. Two separate Irish communist groups then emerged: the Irish Workers' League, later renamed the Irish Workers' Party in the South, and the Communist Party of Northern Ireland in the North. At a special "Unity Congress" held in Belfast on 15 March 1970, the two factions reunited to form a unified CPI.

Today the CPI has a membership of about 600, based mainly in Dublin and Northern Ireland. Members in the North are usually of a Protestant background. In the South there are numerous Marxist groups, and it is more usual for left-wing militants to join either the Socialist Labour Party or Sinn Fein–Workers' Party. The population of the Republic of Ireland is 3,288,000 and of Northern Ireland, 1,537,000.

Leadership and Organization. The CPI is divided into two area branches, Northern and Southern, corresponding to the political division of the country. The Congress is the supreme constitutional authority of the party, but overall direction is otherwise upheld by the twenty-three-member National Executive. The innermost and effective controlling body is the National Political Committee, which includes Andrew Barr (chairman), Michel O'Riordan (general secretary), and James Stewart (assistant general secretary).

The CPI holds no seats in any legislative assembly in either North or South and has little prospect of doing so. The Communists do, however, have some influence in the trade unions and in the Northern Ireland Civil Rights Association. The CPI also controls a small youth organization, the Connolly Youth Movement.

Domestic Attitudes and Activities. Since an earlier schism when the more liberal-minded part of the membership left to form the Irish Marxist Society, the CPI has had no further serious disruption. It remains a hard-line pro-Moscow party.

The central ambition of the CPI is a unified socialist republic of Ireland created through the efforts of a broad democratic movement. This strategy received a setback in the breakdown of the Liaison Group of the Left, a loose grouping of far-left organizations. The official Sinn Fein–Workers' Party (SFWP) and the newly formed Socialist Labour Party (SLP) are now making a determined bid to become major working-class parties.

The CPI urges the unification of the efforts of the CPI, SLP, and SWFP and the construction of a wider "national alternative" which would include other left-wing and mass organizations. The CPI suggests its own draft program for discussion by such a national alternative. This consists of—

1. A job creation scheme by state industrial development
2. Opposition to direct elections for a European parliament
3. Support for Irish neutrality
4. A campaign to secure British withdrawal from Northern Ireland together with an IRA (Irish Republican Army) ceasefire
5. Support for small farmers' organizations
6. The repeal of all repressive legislation.

In the North the CPI seeks the withdrawal of British troops but itself eschews violence and condemns the activities of the Provisional IRA. It has continued to campaign for the adoption of a bill of rights as expounded by the Irish trade unions in their "Better Life for All" campaign. Although hostile to the IRA, the CPI wishes IRA prisoners to be granted political-prisoner status. In a surprise article on 19 August in *Unity*, editor Brian Roe stated that the CPI was not necessarily against an independent six-county state. Indeed such a state based on a "Bill of Rights, with a progressive, democratic government, would be a massive advance."

The CPI remained very hostile to Ireland's continuing membership in the EEC and feared that key decisions affecting Ireland would be increasingly dependent on German financial strength. The CPI was also opposed to Ireland's joining the proposed European Monetary System (EMS). The Communists felt that the Irish currency should not be tied to any other, whether the British pound or the German mark. "Its international exchange rate should in general find its level according to the proportions of our foreign trade, subject to the power to adjust it as necessary in relation to the volume of our production and creation of real values." (Ibid.)

In general CPI policies remained largely unchanged from previous years, but additional emphasis is now being given to job creation schemes. Banks, mines, and oil companies should be nationalized, according to the CPI, in order to make more rational use of investment.

International Views, Positions, and Party Contacts. The CPI is completely loyal to Moscow and is not associated with the Eurocommunist phenomenon. The major heretical work of Santiago Carrillo, *Eurocommunism and the State*, was condemned by the CPI before it had even appeared in Ireland.

CPI statements on foreign policy were generally predictable—emphasizing the advance of peoples living under socialism; castigating the EEC and the U.S.A.; condemning French intervention in Zaire; calling for solidarity with the peoples of Chile, Rhodesia, and South Africa; attacking Iran; and lauding the Soviet Union.

In recognition of General Secretary Michael O'Riordan's "struggle for peace, democracy, and social progress" he was awarded the Order of the October Revolution in November 1977. On 21 July James Stewart, deputy general secretary of the CPI, had a meeting in East Berlin with Hermann Axen, a member of the East German Politburo and a secretary of the Central Committee.

Publications. The CPI publishes a weekly, *Unity*, and the *Young Worker*, in Belfast. In Dublin it also publishes the monthly *Irish Socialist*. This also carries Irish-language reports in addition to those in the English language. *Irish Socialist Review*, a theoretical quarterly, is also produced in Dublin.

Other Marxist Groups. There are numerous small Marxist groups in Ireland. The leading one is Sinn Fein—Workers' Party, the political wing of the official IRA, which is pro-Moscow. It produces the monthly *United Irishman.* Other groups include the Movement for a Socialist Republic, which is the Irish section of the Fourth International; the League for a Workers' Republic; and the Irish Republican Socialist Party (IRSP).

The Irish Marxist Society, a Eurocommunist splinter from the CPI, has not acquired a significant membership but reflects a more open atmosphere in its *Socialist Quarterly*.

London   Richard Sim

Italy

The Italian Communist Party was founded in January 1921 when a radical faction of the Italian Socialist Party (PSI) led by Amedeo Bordiga, Antonio Gramsci, Palmiro Togliatti, and others seceded from the PSI and formed the Partito Comunista d'Italia, later renamed Partito Comunista Italiano (PCI). Declared illegal under the fascist regime, the PCI reappeared on the political scene in 1944, and it participated in governmental coalitions in the early postwar years. Excluded from office in 1947, it has remained in opposition at the national level until very recently. At the local level, however, the PCI has been in power in a number of municipalities since the 1950s, particularly in the regions of Emilia-Romagna, Tuscany, Umbria, and Marches. Following the municipal elections of 1975, the PCI gained control of an even larger number of local governments, and at the present time it shares power, generally, with the PSI in all major urban centers of the country (Rome, Milan, Turin, Bologna, Florence, Naples, Venice, and others).

Equally important changes have occurred in the role of the party in national politics in recent years. The returns of the parliamentary elections of 1976 gave the PCI 34.4 percent of the vote, a sizable increase over the 27.1 percent received in 1972. As a result, the party's strength in parliament grew to 228 seats out of 630 in the House of Deputies and to 116 out of 315 in the Senate. The altered balance of strength and the refusal of the Socialists to support another center-left coalition with the Christian Democrats (DC) led to a political deadlock. The impasse was resolved in the summer of 1976 with the inauguration of a minority cabinet led by Giulio Andreotti, indirectly supported by several parties including the PCI. To stress the new position of influence achieved by the PCI, party Secretary Enrico Berlinguer stated: "Everybody knows by now that if we voted against the government, it would fall immediately" (*L'Unità*, 11 August 1976).

This step broke a 30-year confinement of the PCI in the role of permanent opposition and was followed in the spring of 1977 by another round of negotiations among the parties that led to the adoption of a common program. The agreement dealing with domestic affairs was signed in July of 1977, and a joint statement on foreign policy was made in September of that year. Thus, by the fall of 1977 the PCI had acquired a measure of influence in Italian national politics that was unprecedented. Yet later in the year the party began to express dissatisfaction with the arrangement, arguing that the emergency situation required a more explicit and formal recognition of the role of the party as a governmental force.

Leadership and Organization. The basic unit of the party organization is the section. The smaller units which existed in the past (the cells) are no longer functioning. PCI members belong to one of the 11,000 sections organized in neighborhoods, villages, or places of work. Activities of the sections are coordinated through plant, town, and area committees. Sections are grouped into federations, which usually coincide with the area of a province. In turn, federations are grouped into regional committees. The national organization includes a Central Committee (177 members), a Central Control Commission (53), a Directorate (33), and a Secretariat (8). In addition, there are several bureaus, or departments, staffed by experts in different policy areas (labor, economic affairs, local government, interior, etc.).

Officers at the different levels are selected through section, federation, and national congresses. The last national congress (the fourteenth) was held in 1975, and the next is scheduled for early 1979. It is expected that the Fifteenth National Congress will be devoted to assessing the results of the policy pursued by the party since 1975. Other issues to be discussed include the possible modification of the bylaws, especially the article referring to "Marxism-Leninism." It also seems likely that the congress will discuss the theory and practice of "democratic centralism," which still regulates internal party affairs and has been the target of attacks by other political groups.

No significant changes in the composition of the leadership occurred in 1978. Party president is Luigi Longo, who represents continuity with the past and whose role is largely, but not entirely, a symbolic one. General Secretary Berlinguer has been subjected to some criticism, but for the moment his leadership has not been challenged. Other important leaders, constituting a "shadow cabinet" of sorts, include Giancarlo Pajetta and Emilio Segre (foreign affairs), Giorgio Napolitano (economic affairs), Armando Cossutta (local government), Achille Ochetto (education), Luca Pavolini (press and information), Ugo Pecchioli (interior affairs), as well as Giovanni Cervetti, Gerardo Chiaromonte, and Paolo Bufalini.

Membership remained unchanged in 1978, at approximately 1.8 million members (*Corriere della Sera,* 9 September).

Young Communists are organized in the Youth Federation (FGCI), led by Massimo D'Alema. The federation, which has approximately 150,000 members, held its national congress in April 1978. It was decided to replace the Central Committee with a National Council in which members of the apparat would be joined by representatives of different groups, such as workers, young women, students, etc. It was also decided that in addition to territorial districts, grass-root activities of the federation should be organized by "collectives" focusing upon themes and problems important for young people, such as housing, energy, environmental protection, and the like. (*Rinascita,* 28 April.)

The volume of the activities carried out by the party can be gauged in part by the PCI balance sheet. In 1977 revenues amounted to 39.9 billion lire and expenses to 40.4 billion. The three largest entries on the revenue side were the annual membership dues (35.1 percent of total income), the contribution by the Italian state (13.4 billion lire or 33.4 percent of the total), and the sums collected through the Unità festivals and subscriptions to the party's press (29.5 percent). On the expenditure side, the largest item was the 26.2 billion lire distributed by the party's central headquarters to peripheral offices and organizations. Expenditures related to the party's publications amounted to over 21 percent of the total. Approximately 14 percent of the expenses incurred went for staff salaries and general expenditures. In the statement that accompanied the release of the balance sheet, the PCI Directorate stressed that public contributions amounted to only one-third of the total revenue and that income from self-financing activities had increased considerably: "Between 1976 and 1977 the yield from membership contributions increased by 52.8 percent, and the yield from press subscriptions increased by 47.3 percent and hence rose at a rate incomparably higher than the depreciation of money." The Directorate also pointed out that the party can count "on incalculable contributions in terms of the voluntary work of thousands and thousands of comrades and on the contribution of other comrades who work exclusively for the party for a wage equivalent to that of a skilled worker." (*L'Unità*, 27 January.) The projected budget for 1978 was 46.4 billion lire, with an increase of 6.7 billion in annual membership dues and other self-financing income.

Other activities of the party are likely to be financed directly with funds generated by the Cooperative League (Lega delle Cooperative), which is controlled by the PCI although formally independent from it. The league is a federation of some 11,000 production and service cooperatives, which employ 170,000 people and account for 2.8 percent of the total Italian GNP. Activities carried out by cooperatives affiliated with the league include agriculture, fishing, milling, baking, insurance, food distribution, travel, and supermarkets. The strongest segment of the cooperatives is in construction and housing, and many lucrative contracts have been secured, particularly in African countries. The growing profits of the league have been used recently to acquire a stake in various private enterprises. (*NYT,* 18 June.)

Domestic Views and Activities. At the beginning of 1978 the PCI made further progress on its march toward participation in the government. Speculation about an impending governmental crisis had been circulating in the late fall of 1977, and it grew in early January. The PCI Directorate met on 12 January and in a communiqué stressed "the pressing need for a thorough change which will lead to the formation of an emergency government" (*L'Unità*, 14 January). Two days later Premier Andreotti resigned. The position and the demands of the PCI were made clear in a number of statements, including an article written for the *New York Times* by Gerardo Chiaromonte, a member of the PCI Secretariat. Chiaromonte spoke of a "glaring contradiction" between the fact that "the agreement to support the government involved six parties" while "the government was made up only of Christian Democrats" (*NYT,* 17 January). Since the DC was unwilling to accede to the demands of the PCI, a deadlock ensued. After almost two months of negotiations, a compromise was reached in early March. The Communists obtained explicit recognition of their role as members of the parliamentary majority supporting the new Andreotti government. But they did not receive posts in the cabinet and thus had to settle for a solution that was short of their goal. In assessing the agreement, Berlinguer stressed the "climate of deeper and broader convergence" and "solidarity among the five democratic and people's parties" which had led to the "innovation of our clear and explicit entry into the parliamentary majority." However, he added that the agreement was only partially satisfactory: "We did not achieve the solution that we considered and still consider the surest and the best in order to meet the country's needs." (*L'Unità*, 18 March.)

The solution of the governmental crisis coincided with the beginning of what was later to become the "Moro affair." The president of the DC was kidnapped on the day that the new cabinet was to receive a vote of confidence. The reaction of the PCI to the escalation of terrorist activities included expressions of solidarity for Moro's family and a strong condemnation of the Red Brigades and of other groups described as "gangs of fanatics with sticks and guns" (ibid., 19 March). The abduction of Moro and the other acts of terrorism were seen by the PCI as a threat for the country, and the source of this threat was identified as "powerful internal and international forces controlling this ruthless attack on the state and on republican freedoms." The aim of terrorism, continued Berlinguer, is "to replace the people's increasing presence, initiative, and participation." (Ibid.) And a few days later he added: "Terrorism serves the enemies of democracy. And democracy in Italy is essentially the result of the gains and of the struggles of the working masses, of the Communists, of the socialists, and of all those struggling for democratic progress in our country" (ibid., 7 April). The strong reaction by the PCI and the denunciation of the Red Brigades are understandable in view of the attacks that the terrorists and other radical leftist groups had been leveling against the communist party. The PCI was variously defined as "the watchdog of the imperialist bourgeoisie," as an apparatus of spies and informers, and as an "accomplice of the bourgeois regime" (Agenzia Nazionale Stampa Associata, 8 April, hereafter ANSA; 6 May). Consequently, the PCI viewed the problem of responding appropriately to this threat as one of mobilizing the masses in public demonstrations against violence and isolating the terrorists from the radical, but not openly violent, elements of the Left. This required that the party respond to the accusation that it had betrayed the cause of revolution. Addressing this point PCI Senator and member of the Directorate Ugo Pecchioli said: "What is meant by 'revolution'? We Italian Communists are working in a developed capitalist state with democratic traditions. We can achieve a 'revolution,' that is, a profound change of society toward socialism, only through the strictest observance of the democratic rules. Many extremists believe that such a change can be achieved only by force. . . . In our opinion these brigade people, even though they purport to be fighting for the proletariat, are clearly the enemies of the workers' movement. They are completely isolated from the masses." (*Der Spiegel,* 3 April.)

When the Red Brigades made it known that they would spare Moro's life in exchange for the freedom of a number of jailed terrorists, the PCI took a very firm position against any kind of negotiation. On 23 April Berlinguer spoke at the closing session of the Italian Communist Youth Federation Congress and said: "Regarding the fate of Moro, we repeat that we have always shared not only the anguished concern for his life but also every appeal and every humanitarian activity aimed at restoring him to his loved ones. . . . At the same time we have always maintained and we still maintain that there could be no yielding to the blackmail, to the ultimatums, or to the exchange demands of the Red Brigades." This firmness was required, explained Berlinguer, "not in order to comply with an abstract and dispassionate reason of state, but because if we yield, democratic institutions will be subjected to a suicidal logic. . . . There would certainly be no truce. . . . On the contrary, life in society would become a jungle with a continuous spiral of terrorist exploits. . . . Encouragement would be given to the formation of other 'armed parties' in opposition to the one that describes itself as 'red.' . . . There would be widespread guerrilla fighting and civil warfare, which would inevitably result in a regime of evil tyranny and fierce reaction." (*L'Unità*, 24 April.)

When Socialist leaders argued in favor of taking a more flexible posture toward the terrorists and suggested that judicial pardon or stay of sentence be used to obtain the release of Moro, the PCI maintained its negative stand: "Apart from the fact that pardon is governed by precise circumstances defined by law, a pardon granted to anyone as a terrorist would add a further element of virtual impunity and thus would be an incentive to political crime and even to the political conversion of common criminals" (ibid., 28 April). As to the proposed revision of the regulations concerning "special prisons," another proposal to deal with the terrorists, the PCI observed "There is nothing 'special' about any Italian prison, if that means a discriminatory limitation of the prisoners' rights. What exists in some prisons are special security measures designed to put an end to the serious phenomenon of escape." (Ibid.) After the Red Brigades carried out their threat to kill Moro, Berlinguer declared in a television interview that the governmental majority had on the whole withstood the test to which it had been put and that "all the conditions for more solid relations between the DC, the PCI, and the PSI had been created" (ANSA, 12 May).

A few days after the assassination and the release of the body of Moro, approximately 10 percent of the Italian electorate was called to the polls to elect municipal councillors and other officers in a number of communities. Although these elections were local in nature, many observers and politicians looked upon them as an important political test. The returns showed that the PCI had maintained its ground compared with the results of previous municipal elections but that the party had suffered considerable and unprecedented losses in comparison with the returns of the parliamentary election of 1976. In the 255 communes for which this second comparison is meaningful, the PCI lost approximately 9 percent of the vote. In the elections for the provincial council of Viterbo and Pavia, the PCI lost 1 percent compared with the provincial election of 1972 and 5 percent compared with the parliamentary election of 1976. In assessing the results, PCI commentators pointed out that the party generally does less well in local than in national elections and that these returns were not a genuine test of the party's strength. Communist politicians, however, admitted that there were also other factors. In an interview given two days after the election, Gerardo Chiaromonte said that the poor showing had its roots in the terrorist wave, which had caused a "moderate backlash" (ibid., 18 May). Asked whether the electoral defeat could be attributed to the "historic compromise" line pursued by the party in recent years, Secretariat member Armando Cossutta said: "We are looking at the facts and at the real situation of the country. . . . Without our assumption of responsibility it would not have been possible to deal with a serious crisis. Indeed, by now the crisis would have plunged the country out of control, dragging the country, and thus also the workers and the people, into a disastrous and irremediable situation." (*L'Unità,* 17 May.) The PCI Directorate discussed the results of the election on 19 May and in its analysis stressed the importance of the "emotive repercussions" generated by the kidnapping of Moro. The document approved by the Directorate stated that "terrorism, violence, and disorders have as one of their fundamental objectives damaging the communist party and obstructing its line, and these have been put to advantage by those on various sides who have taken the opportunity for a shameful and underhanded campaign" (ibid., 20 May).

The electoral difficulties experienced by the party in mid-May were destined to continue. On 11 June two nationwide referenda were held. The electorate was asked to vote for or against the repeal of two laws: one concerning the public financing of political parties and the second a 1975 law that gave the police and the courts greater powers (limitation of bail, preventive detention, etc.). Of the two, it was the second that gave the PCI more trouble, for since 1975 the party had reversed its position and was now asking its followers to vote in favor of a law that it had originally opposed. Thus, the referenda represented a test of the party's ability to control and influence the rank and file. The results seemed to indicate that part of the electorate, including communist voters, had not heeded the party's plea. Commenting on the results of the referenda, Berlinguer stressed that "the vast majority of the electorate had demonstrated its support for a strict and rigorous policy in defense of the democratic order." He admitted, however, that the results could be construed as a criticism, as lack of popular support. (Ibid., 13 June.)

Another round of elections took place toward the end of June (regional elections in Aosta, Friuli-Venezia Giulia, and communal elections in Trieste and a score of other communities). Once again the returns showed that popular support for the PCI was somewhat down as compared with the 1976 levels. Commenting on the success obtained by some local lists, which had attracted a substantial percentage of the vote away from the national parties, Senator Cossutta said: "The results are a sign of a crisis in the relationship between the citizens and the parties" (*Corriere della Sera,* 27 June).

The somewhat negative electoral results did not, however, lessen to any significant degree the influence of the PCI in national politics. This fact was demonstrated very clearly by the events that led to the resignation of President of the Republic Giovanni Leone and to the subsequent election to this office of Socialist leader Sandro Pertini. Charges of tax fraud and unsavory real estate dealings had been hurled against Leone and his family for some time. While other political groups had openly suggested that Leone should step down, the PCI had been very cautious on this issue, asserting that such delicate matters required careful examination (ANSA, 15 June). On the very day on which this statement appeared, the PCI Directorate met, and upon learning that Leone intended to stay on and was preparing a self-defense, the PCI Directorate called for the immediate resignation of the head of state (*Corriere della Sera,* 17 June).

Leone's fall was later described by the PCI as "an event of great political significance. . . . which we Communists agreed to bring about. . . . the resignation took place because such a solution was requested by the PCI" (*L'Unità*, 17 June). Equally important was the role of the PCI in the selection of the new president of the republic. In this respect, the primary goal of the party was to make sure that the choice of the new head of state would not create conflict among the parties and thus shatter the parliamentary majority. Hence, it was argued that "the appointment should be the result of the broadest possible consensus among the democratic and antifascist forces" (ibid.).

The search for such an agreement was not, however, easy, and a deadlock developed when the PSI insisted that the new president be a Socialist. On 27 June, two days before the first ballot, the PCI endorsed the choice of a Socialist for the position. In the first four ballots, which were fated to be inconclusive since no agreement among the major parties had been reached, the Communist senators, deputies, and regional representatives cast their votes for senior PCI leader Giovanni Amendola. Finally, on 8 July the Christian Democrats gave in, and Sandro Pertini was elected with a large majority of the vote. The "broadest possible consensus" had been achieved, and Berlinguer voiced the "great satisfaction" of his party (ANSA, 8 July). Speaking at a Central Committee meeting two weeks later, Berlinguer argued that the election of Pertini made possible a continuation of the cooperation among the parties composing the parliamentary majority, and this was viewed as a success for the PCI (ibid., 24 July).

During the summer a polemic flared up between the PCI and the Socialist Party. Some tension between the two parties had developed in the previous months, but the exchanges among party leaders had been subdued. The spark that ignited the controversy was an interview given by PSI Deputy Secretary Signorile. The Socialist leader argued that the PCI was still a Leninist party, that it had a nonpluralistic view of democracy, and that it was still linked to the USSR, and he concluded that the Communists were not yet ready for assuming a governmental role. After an initial, angry reply by *L'Unità* which accused the Socialists of having become "an instrument of anticommunist agitation" (29 July), Berlinguer joined the issue with an interview published in the daily *La Repubblica* on 2 August. The PCI secretary stated that the party had no intention of repudiating Lenin since "the lesson which Lenin taught us in elaborating a truly revolutionary theory is still living and valid." Berlinguer added that Leninism was not "a manual of doctrinal rules, or bloc of theories, statically considered, which has hardened into scholastic formulas to be applied uncritically at all times and in all places." Lenin's theory, Berlinguer argued, helps in overcoming the tendencies toward "reformist evolution" and in fighting against "positivism, vulgar materialism, and the messianic wait-and-see attitudes." He added: "Valid too is the lesson of the Lenin who smashed the domination and world unity of the capitalist, imperialist, and colonialist systems." Asked whether the PCI still wanted to abolish capitalism, Berlinguer replied: "The answer is yes. We do eventually want to establish here in Western Europe an economic, social, and state order which is no longer capitalist but which does not copy any model or repeat any of the socialist experiences realized so far. At the same time the goal is not simply to resurrect social democratic types of experiences which have restricted themselves to administering capitalism. We want a third solution which is determined precisely by the impossibility of being satisfied with the current world situation."

The publication in August of an article entitled "The Socialist Gospel" by PSI Secretary Bettino Craxi gave new impetus to the ideological dispute between the two parties. The PCI answer was articulated more explicitly in a long speech made by Berlinguer on 17 September at the closing of the Unità Festival in Genoa. In response to Craxi's critical assessment of the fruits of Leninism, Berlinguer said: "I am not and never will be among those who start with a legitimate and necessary critical reconsideration of the history of existing socialist societies and end by rejecting or losing sight of the worldwide value of Lenin's work, of the October Revolution and its developments, of the greatest historical event of this century, and of what it represented and still represents—with all of its dark and oppressive sides—to the struggle of revolutionary, democratic, progressive forces in the world today" (*L'Unità*, 18 September). He then proceeded to argue that the PCI, while rejecting the social democratic model, intended to move toward socialism "in an entirely different way than that followed in the Soviet Union and in other Eastern bloc countries" and that the party would guarantee full political democracy and stay away from general collectivization. In response to those intellectuals and politicans who had argued that there was no third way between social democracy and the Soviet model, Berlinguer said: "Why should it be impossible to follow a different path than that pursued by social democracy or by the Soviet Union? Why should it be obligatory to imitate and closely follow paths that were traced in very different historical, social, and political circumstances?" (Ibid.)

By the fall of 1978 the PCI appeared to be on the defensive. The party press spoke of a "vast, multiform, and partly orchestrated campaign aimed at pushing back the process of democratic unity, splitting the majority, and therefore hitting and isolating the PCI" (ibid., 1 October). A number of disagreements developed among the parties composing the parliamentary majority. Issues such as the strike of hospital workers, the renewal of contracts for public employees, and legislation to abolish sharecropping contracts provided fuel for the controversy among parties. The PCI interpreted these difficulties as an indication of the willingness of other parties to seek a new type of coalition formula that might result in the exclusion of the PCI from the majority. Rumors about the possibility of anticipated parliamentary elections began to circulate.

An additional source of worry for the PCI leadership came from its own ranks. Debates and meetings held in preparation for the Fifteenth National Congress revealed a certain amount of dissatisfaction on the part of the rank and file and intermediate-level cadres with the results of communist participation in the majority supporting the Andreotti cabinet. Not surprisingly, the PCI looked with considerable interest and some anxiety at the outcome of the regional election held on 19 November in the region of Trentino-Alto Adige. Although the election involved only 600,000 voters, the returns represented an important test for the PCI, since in this region the party had made great strides in 1976 (almost doubling the percentage of the vote it had received in the regional election of 1973).

The PCI mounted a vigorous campaign but the results were disappointing. The party did improve marginally its position compared with 1973 (up 1.4 percent of the vote) but lost a significant 4.3 percent compared with 1976 (*Corriere della Sera,* 21 November). Partly as a result of this test, the PCI renewed its pressure on Andreotti as 1978 drew to a close for more decisive action and let it be known that it would leave the coalition if it did not obtain satisfaction on a number of issues.

International Views and Positions. No major changes took place in 1978 as far as the PCI's stands on international affairs are concerned. The PCI repeatedly stressed its position in favor of détente and the necessity to increase the dialogue across blocs as well as within them. The party expressed alarm at the increase in U.S. military spending (*L'Unità*, 3 February). It first welcomed President Carter's decision to postpone manufacturing of the neutron bomb (ibid., 8 April), but later in the year it denounced the U.S. decision to go ahead with the manufacturing of components for that weapon. The PCI also expressed concern for the possible consequences of the USSR-Cuba intervention in the Horn of Africa. On the Middle East and the agreement reached at Camp David, the PCI maintained that "it was a dangerous and partially limited solution" and stated: "As far as we are concerned, our international solidarity still commits us to friendship with the Arabs in the occupied territories and with the PLO" (ibid., 19 September).

In spite of a fair amount of references to aggressive, militarist, imperialist, capitalist forces, communist analyses of the U.S. role in world affairs were somewhat more balanced and cautious than in the past. Dispatches filed from the U.S. by *L'Unità* correspondent, Alberto Jacoviello, while containing occasionally negative evaluations of American society and criticism of American foreign policy, tended to project a somewhat more objective view of the U.S. The harshest criticism of the U.S. was expressed prior to and during the Italian cabinet crisis of January when the PCI accused the U.S. of "open and coarse interference in Italian affairs" (*Washington Post,* 14 January). On the subject of the U.S. "human rights" policy, the PCI stressed the contradiction between the posture taken by Washington and "what is happening in Iran and Nicaragua" (*L'Unità,* 2 October).

Critical evaluations of the Soviet Union and of other communist regimes of Eastern Europe made by PCI leaders and intellectuals were more common and explicit in 1978 than in previous years. In January senior party maverick and Directorate member Umberto Terracini referred to Soviet reality as being "totally deprived of any trace of civil or political freedom of thought or action" (*Corriere della Sera,* 23 January). A few days before *L'Unità* had published a long and favorable review of a satirical "samizdat," *Yawning Heights,* by Aleksandr Zinoviev. The reviewer stressed the parallels between the imaginary country of the novel and the Soviet Union, referring to "the privileges, the informers, the careerists, the promotion of mediocrity, the mortification of the intellect" (*L'Unità,* 11 January). Additional criticism surfaced in a book review of a volume by Adriano Guerra which dealt with Cominform activities and the Soviet attempt to control the communist parties of other countries. A three-day seminar on "Problems of the History of the USSR" provided another opportunity for criticism of some of the developments that had occurred in the Soviet Union (ibid., 13 January).

But it was the trial of dissident Yuri Orlov in the spring and of Rudolf Bahro (in the GDR), Shcharansky, Ginzburg, and others that provoked the most explicit criticism. Commenting on the first case, *L'Unità* wrote: "Our paper has not failed in the past to express explicitly and clearly its disagreement and condemnation, and it is therefore natural on this occasion to reassert our stand. The Moscow verdict against Orlov certainly does not help to improve the current image of the Soviet Union in world public opinion. It does not contribute to the cause of détente either" (ibid., 24 May). While the trials against other dissidents were in progress, the PCI Secretariat published a communiqué stating: "The Italian Communists, who have always opposed manifestations of anti-Sovietism, felt a duty to express a deep concern and their full censure of the current trials in Soviet courts. The absence of publicity at the hearings and the absence of adequate monitoring by the public do not provide a guarantee of the correct administration of justice." (Ibid., 13 July.) The PCI's position was summed up two days later by Berlinguer in the statement: "We see the trials as events that contradict the ideals and practices of freedom, which, according to us, must constitute the essential and inalienable part in the life of a socialist society" (ANSA, 17 July).

The anniversary of the Soviet-led intervention in Czechoslovakia in 1968 provided the PCI with another opportunity for expressing its views toward the Eastern bloc. In July the Federation of Trade Unions (including the PCI-influenced General Confederation of Italian Labor) wrote a letter to its counterpart in Czechoslovakia expressing concern about rumors that "Czechoslovak workers and citizens were allegedly subjected to arbitrary firing practices, discrimination, and other forms of reprisals because of their political ideas during the well-known events of ten years ago." The letter also asked that a delegation of Italian trade unionists be allowed to visit Czechoslovakia and meet with the appropriate authorities. (ANSA, 22 July.)

In August, *L'Unità* engaged in a polemic with Vasil Bil'ák of the Communist Party of Czechoslovakia and rejected the notion that the Soviet intervention was only meant to thwart "imperialist plans": "In view of the problems existing in Czechoslovakia," wrote *L'Unità,* "we find unacceptable the statement by Bil'ák that every citizen is guaranteed fundamental rights in that country" (10 August). On the anniversary of the Soviet-led invasion, the PCI proclaimed its "resolute condemnation of the event" and stated that Czechoslovakia was still "an open wound" (ibid., 20 August). Finally, in September the publishing house of the PCI (Editori Riuniti) brought out the essay *Prague 1968* by Jiri

Hájek, foreign minister of Czechoslovakia during the Spring period and spokesman for the Charter 77 movement. The book was very positively reviewed (ibid., 21 September).

International Party Contacts. During 1978 the PCI maintained contacts with a large number of communist parties around the world. In January a PCI delegation went to the Soviet Union, and another visited PLO leader Yassir Arafat. Giancarlo Pajetta, widely regarded as the PCI "foreign minister," visited the Arab Socialst Ba'ath Party and held conversations with President Hafiz al-Asad (Baghdad radio, 20 January; Damascus Sana, 23 January). In the same period delegations of the Mozambique Liberation Front (FRELIMO) and the Eritrean Liberation Front (ELF) visited PCI headquarters in Rome (L'Unità, 12 and 14 January). In February and March PCI delegations traveled to East Germany, Somalia, and Aden where a meeting with representatives of the Yemen National Front took place (ibid., 9, 10, and 24 February).

In the same period PCI officials conferred in Rome with a delegation of the Bulgarian Communist Party, with Ethiopian Foreign Minister Feleke Geddle Giorgis, and with the exiled leader of the Chilean Communist Party, Luis Corvalán (ibid., 10 February, 3 and 19 March). Delegations of the Korean Workers' Party and the Brazilian Communist Party were received by Berlinguer on 11 April and 15 May. A few days later the PCI secretary attended a meeting of the Catalan Communists (PSUC) in Barcelona (ibid., 29 May). In June and July Italian delegations attended the congresses of the communist parties of Greece and Finland and the celebration of the anniversary of the Cuban Revolution (ibid., 6 June, 26 July). PCI President Luigi Longo traveled to Bucharest for a visit with Ceauşescu. In the same period PCI officials conferred in Rome with delegations of the communist parties of Belgium, Argentina, and Morocco (ibid., 18 June, 6 and 11 July). Other exchanges took place later in the year with Ethiopia, Algeria, Spain, and the United Kingdom.

PCI contacts were not limited to communist parties. In February Pajetta met in London with representatives of the British Labour Party (ibid., 24 February), and in October he attended the congress of the Labour Party. In June a delegation of the Australian Labour Party visited PCI headquarters in Rome. In April Secretariat member Giorgio Napolitano traveled to the United States and gave talks at Princeton, Harvard, Yale, and other universities (ibid., 9 April). An academic forum was also provided for Pajetta at St. Catherine College in Oxford (ibid., 26 February). Other PCI intellectuals traveled to the U.S. to attend a seminar on Eurocommunism held in Rochester, N.Y., in October.

Of particular significance was the trip to Paris, Moscow, and Belgrade made in October by Berlinguer and Antonio Rubbi, deputy chief of the Foreign Section of the party. In Paris the Italian visitors met with the secretary of the French party, Georges Marchais. The communiqué released by the two parties after the visit reaffirmed "the validity of the Eurocommunist line," but it also stressed the "full independence of the activities of both parties" and recognized "the diversity of the conditions under which the parties pursue their policies and the differences existing with respect to certain aspects of the European community" (ibid., 6 October). A few days later Berlinguer was greeted at the Moscow airport by Boris Ponomarev of the Soviet Central Committee, and later he spoke with Mikhail Suslov, a member of the Soviet Politburo (Tass, 7 October). The joint communiqué spoke of a "joint concern over the slowing down of détente and international cooperation, which was the result of the activities of certain imperialist, militarist, and reactionary forces."

The communiqué also included a statement that could be interpreted as an endorsement of the domestic strategy of the PCI: "Cooperation between the Communists and socialists, social democrats, and other democratic forces—including Christian ones—can make its own contribution to strengthening the process of détente and cooperation between states with different social systems" (ibid., 9 October). The third leg of Berlinguer's trip took him to Belgrade. There the subjects discussed were "the recent international activities of the League of Communists of Yugoslavia (LCY) and of the

PCI," that is, the visit of the Chinese leader Hua Kuo-feng to Belgrade and Berlinguer's talks in Moscow. The joint PCI-LCY communiqué touched upon the theme of the parties' autonomy, stressing the "need for developing cooperation coupled with full respect for the independence of every party." The communiqué made an indirect reference to the USSR-China conflict, and it was stated that "the existence of different concepts and interests in the world workers' movement is not and must not represent an obstacle to developing dialogues, mutual understanding, and equal cooperation" (Tanjug, 11 October).

The PCI also supported restoration of interparty relations with the Chinese Communist Party, with which it has had no contact since the early 1960s. In an interview published in September, Giancarlo Pajetta argued that a restoration of the relationship between the two parties would be "a natural event in the development of the workers' movement, within which there should be no guiding party and no guiding state. . . . and neither should there be anyone who is the enemy of others." (L'Unità, 1 September). Asked whether a rapprochement with the Chinese would affect the PCI's relationship with Moscow, Pajetta replied: "No one should think that a restoration of the relationship with Peking can be regarded as a sort of plot against Moscow. Having said that, my reply is clear and brief: It is our business and we certainly shall not go and ask permission of anyone." (Ibid.)

In line with this position, the PCI later expressed a positive evaluation of Hua Kuo-feng's visit to Romania and Yugoslavia (ibid., 9 September). The party also expressed its disappointment when it was learned that women representing the PCI in the Italian parliament had not been included as members of a delegation visiting China, while women from other parties had been invited (Corriere della Sera, 20 September).

Publications. PCI party newspapers, magazines, and journals, as well as the publishing house, Editori Riuniti, are administered under the direction of Renato Zangheri, mayor of Bologna, who also supervises the ideological and cadre schools. The major PCI newspaper is L'Unità, appearing daily in both Milan and Rome, edited by Central Committee member Luca Pavolini. The weekly Rinascita, a popular culture journal, is aimed at intellectuals. The bimonthly Critica Marxista is the theoretical journal. La Nuova Rivista Internazionale is a journal of international affairs, while Politica ed Economia deals with economics, and Studi Storici with history. In addition, each PCI auxiliary has a journal; e.g., the women's federation publishes Donne e Politica, a political magazine for women.

Other Communist Groups. A number of Marxist groups operate to the left of the PCI. They are small, politically insignificant, poorly organized, and constantly torn by internal disputes that lead to fragmentation. Some of these groups are radical but opposed to violence; others openly advocate and carry out terrorist activities. Among the former are Democrazia Proletaria (DP), Partito Democratico di Unità per il Comunismo, (PDUP), Lotta Continua (LC), the Unified Communist Party of Italy (strongly pro-China), and the Marxist-Leninist Communist Party of Italy (strongly pro-Albania).

In addition to the Red Brigades (BR), a number of other groups have claimed credit for terrorist activities. They include Nuclei Armati Proletari (NAP), Prima Linea (PL), Autonomia Operaia (AO), and others.

Ohio State University   Giacomo Sani

Luxembourg

The Communist Party of Luxembourg (Parti communiste de Luxembourg; PCL) was founded in January 1921. Until World War II the party played an insignificant role in Luxembourg politics but increased its influence to some degree following the war, in part because of the enhanced prestige of the Soviet Union. The PCL has been represented in parliament since 1945, as well as in town councils of Luxembourg City and several industrial centers of the South. During 1945–47 the cabinet included one communist minister. The party's influence decreased thereafter but increased again following the elections of 1964. It reached a new climax in the elections of 1968 and decreased again in the elections of 1974. Estimated party membership is between 500 and 600. The population of Luxembourg is 358,000.

For many years the PCL recruited its members from among industrial workers but has been able to broaden its membership gradually to include other segments of the population. In the most recent parliamentary elections, held in 1974, the PCL received 9 percent of the vote and won 5 of the 59 seats. The next elections are scheduled for May 1979.

On the municipal level, the PCL increased its influence as a result of the decision of the Luxembourg Socialist Workers' Party (Parti ouvrier socialiste luxembourgeois; LSAP) to form a coalition government with the PCL after the municipal elections of October 1969. This occurred in Esch-sur-Alzette, the second largest town of the country, where PCL Secretariat member Arthur Useldinger (also a member of parliament) continued as mayor following the municipal elections of 12 October 1975.

In 1945 the PCL formed its own trade union, which merged in 1965 with the far stronger LSAP-oriented workers' association. This merger permitted the PCL to influence the union in a Marxist direction significantly and paved the way for the opening of relations with Eastern European labor unions. The policy of the LSAP to cooperate more and more with the PCL engendered strong tensions among LSAP members and resulted in a party split in 1970.

Leadership and Organization. The PCL, strongly pro-Soviet, presents the image of a united party. Differences of opinion are not made public. Party members vote as a bloc in parliament. The decisions of the party's congress and of its leading bodies are usually passed unanimously. The congress itself meets once every three years, most recently at Luxembourg City in December 1976. At that time the Central Committee was extended to 31 members and four candidates (formerly 28 members and no candidates). The Executive Committee remained at ten members. The Secretariat consists of the new party chairman, René Urbany, and his father, the honorary chairman, Dominique Urbany. The party treasurer, Arthur Useldinger, died in March, and his seat in the Secretariat apparently has remained vacant. The party leadership is strongly centralized. This point is emphasized by the complete absence of regional party organizations, although local party sections do exist.

Members of the Urbany family occupy key party positions. In addition to Dominique and René Urbany, the "Réveil de la résistance" is directed by François Frisch, brother-in-law of René Urbany and a member of the Central Committee. René Urbany's sister, Yvonne Frisch-Urbany, leads the Soviet-sponsored Cultural Center Pushkin. His father-in-law, Jacques Hoffmann, is a member of the Central Committee and the Executive Committee, and his brother-in-law, François Hoffmann, is a member of the Central Committee and is assistant editor of the party press. The PCL moved into new party headquarters at the beginning of 1977.

The party leads the League of Luxembourg Women (Union des femmes luxembourgeoises) and has a youth auxiliary (Jeunesse progressiste). In addition, it dominates a group of former resistance members (Le Réveil de la résistance) and various societies which cultivate good relations with Eastern European organizations.

Domestic Attitudes and Activities. The PCL sharply criticizes the social, economic, and political situation in Luxembourg and in the course of the year reconfirmed its policy of strict adherence to and support for the international solidarity of the communist movement. The PCL asserts that the interests of the working class and of the nation are best served by close association and cooperation with the Communist Party of the Soviet Union (CPSU), as well as with other pro-Soviet communist parties.While there do exist small leftist groups in Luxembourg, their influence is of minor significance for Luxembourgian political life, and their activities are only incidentally disruptive to those of the PCL.

International Views and Positions. The international views of the PCL reflect those of the CPSU, and the Soviet Union's diplomatic representation in Luxembourg far exceeds the number of persons normally assigned to a small country. There are also strong indications that the PCL is financially dependent on the CPSU. PCL members travel frequently to the Soviet Union and Eastern Europe and often spend their vacations in these countries.

Publications. The *Zeitung zum Letzeburger Vollek* is the party organ and has a daily distribution of between 1,000 and 1,500 copies. The party also publishes the weekly *Wochenzeitung*. The party's publishing company, Co-opérative ouvrière de presse et d'éditions, publishes these two papers and also distributes foreign communist publications. The PCL distributes its publications periodically to households and also participates in the political programs of Radio Luxembourg. The value it places on the remarks of PCL members in parliament is illustrated by the gratis door-to-door distribution of parliamentary reports.

Luxemburger Wort   Leon Zeches
Luxembourg

Netherlands

The Communist Party of the Netherlands (Communistische Partij van Nederland; CPN) was founded as the Communist Party of Holland in 1918, but the official founding date is that of affiliation with the Comintern, 10 April 1919. The present name dates from December 1935. The party has always been legal (with the exception of the World War II period).

CPN policy was based for more than ten years on the "new orientation" proclaimed at its 1964 congress. It gave primary importance to domestic political goals; relations with international communism were subordinated to the goal of creating a united front in which Communists and Socialists should play the leading role. Since 1975, however, increasing involvement in the international communist movement was noticeable and led to the normalization of relations with the Communist Party of the Soviet Union (CPSU), which in fact meant the end of the "new orientation policy."

From 1959 (when the party was split) until 1972, the CPN share in elections steadily increased (from 2.4 to 4.5 percent of the vote). Elections for the Lower House of the parliament in May 1977 brought a considerable loss. Compared with 1972, CPN votes declined from 329,973 to 143,420 (from 2.41 to 1.73 percent). CPN seats in the Lower House dropped from 7 to 2 (out of 150).

Provincial and municipal elections in the spring of 1978 confirmed this decline. CPN seats in provincial governing bodies dropped from 19 to 5 and in municipal governing bodies from 129 to 85.

In spite of considerable losses in the elections, CPN membership increased from 10,000 to 14,000–15,000 in the last few years. Its followers are scattered over the country, with centers of activity in the provinces of North-Holland and Groningen. The population of the Netherlands is approaching fourteen million.

Leadership and Organization. The CPN's Twenty-Sixth Congress, on 21 January 1978, elected a new Central Committee of 60 members, and abolished honorary membership in the Central Committee. This decision was directed against Paul de Groot, former CPN chairman and signified the end of his influence in the party.

On 11 February the Central Committee elected a sixteen-member Executive Committee of the Central Committee, the principal policy-making body. It includes Henk Hoekstra (chairman), Rinus Haks (organization secretary), Harry Kleuver (general treasurer), Joop IJisberg (propaganda), Marcus Bakker (chairman of the CPN faction in parliament), and Gijs Schreuders (editor-in-chief of *De Waarheid*). The secretariat, consisting of three members of the Executive Committee and one general member of the Central Committee, is the organizational and administrative center of the party.

The most active of the CPN front organizations is the General Netherlands Youth Organization (Algemeen Nederlands Jeugd Verbond; ANJV). The Netherlands Women's Movement (Nederlandse Vrouwen Beweging; NVB), like the NJV, works to support CPN demands.

Party Internal Affairs. The CPN's Twenty-Sixth Congress drew 485 delegates of whom 130 were industrial workers (the largest group). The principal appeal of the congress was directed against the

Van Agt—Wiegel government, which was accused of undermining the standard of living and the rights and security of the population. Therefore, the CPN urged the population to unite in a new coalition of struggle against the "right-wing" government. In this regard high priority was given to intensifying efforts to recruit industrial workers and to organizing the training of party cadres.

Domestic Attitudes and Activities. The poor election results and successful extra-parliamentary action have changed the attitude of the CPN leadership toward representation in governing bodies. The CPN has adopted a new line, the so-called "new coalition" policy, directed not only at the social-economic struggle but also at the struggle against rearmament and for peace (in accordance with Soviet peace policy).

The CPN's major focus of activity during 1978 was mobilization of Dutch public opinion against the neutron bomb. This absorbed so much time that little was left for other activities, including necessary election campaigns. Apart from taking part in various demonstrations, the only other noteworthy activity was increasing participation in associations working for the "interests" of the unemployed.

CPN opposition to the neutron bomb operated with the slogan "Stop the Neutron Bomb" and was organized as a CPN front organization. More than a million signatures opposing the bomb were obtained and were presented to parliament as a "poll of the people." Although it is difficult to estimate the influence of this movement on molding public opinion, it did contribute to growing aversion in the Netherlands to the neutron bomb.

International Views and Positions and Party Contacts. The opposition of the CPN to the neutron bomb resulted in the party's involvement in international opposition to the bomb's development. As a consequence an "International Forum," supported by the Communist Party of the Soviet Union, was held in Amsterdam on 18 March. Participating in the forum were prominent representatives of Eastern European countries, who joined CPN members on 19 March in a demonstration of 50,000 people held in Amsterdam. CPN participation in the forum also promoted, as a side effect, extensive travel of CPN members throughout Eastern and Western Europe.

The party attitude concerning the international communist movement was most clearly visible in its reaction to the dissident movement in Eastern Europe. In past years Soviet treatment of dissidents has been criticized as an "evil." During 1978, however, such criticism diminished, and harsh treatment of dissidents was increasingly described as representing "cosmetic imperfections." This change in criticism of Soviet policy was also reflected in CPN judgment of the Soviet invasion of Czechoslovakia of 1968. At that time Soviet intervention was unequivocally condemned, but during 1978 the CPN party organ, *De Waarheid*, carried a series of three articles analyzing the events of 1968 in which all condemnation was absent. This return to complete support of Soviet foreign policy positions represented a definite break with previous CPN policy.

Publications. The CPN daily, *De Waarheid* (The truth), has a circulation of about 20,000. The theoretical bimonthly, *Politiek en Cultuur*, is used for training purposes. The ANJV and NVB publish monthly newspapers. The CPN's Instituut voor Politiek en Sociaal Onderzoek (IPSO) issues a quarterly, *Info*, which draws attention to articles published by other communist parties on problems of present-day communism. The CPN maintains its own publishing house and bookshop, Pegasus, and operates two commercial printing plants, one for *De Waarheid* and one for other printed matter.

Pro-Soviet Groups. The pro-Soviet groups of the years 1964—75 can, because of the CPN's change in policy toward the Soviet Union, no longer be regarded as dissident groups. Nor can they be regarded as CPN front organizations because of their independent activity. The main group is the "Nederland-USSR" friendship society, which promotes cultural relations between the Netherlands and the Soviet

Union. Its monthly paper is *NU* (Netherlands-USSR). The travel agency Vernu BV organizes tourist visits to the Soviet Union.

In 1973 young members of the Nederland-USSR founded a new organization, Jongeren Kontakt voor Internationale Solidariteit en Uitwisseling (Youth Contact for International Solidarity and Exchange; JKU), which issues a paper, *Nieuwsbrief*. The JKU also established a travel agency (Kontakt B.V.) in 1973 which has developed into a full and independent body in the meantime. The JKU maintains contact with similar organizations in other West European countries and with the coordinating Soviet youth organization. JKU is a member of the World Federation of Democratic Youth.

Pro-Chinese Groups. The emergency of pro-Chinese groups was the result of the autonomous policy of the CPN in the Sino-Soviet dispute. There were eight of these small groups in the Netherlands, all ostensibly governed by Marxist-Leninist principles. Although they often competed with each other, there is a marked tendency now, encouraged by the Communist Party of China, for them to act in a more unified fashion. In May 1978 three of these organizations decided to discontinue independent operation and to establish a new organization, Communist Workers Organization—Marxist-Leninist (KAO-ML). The KAO-ML publishes the paper *Red Flag*.

Apart from this organization, the three other main groups are: the Netherlands Communist Unity Movement—Marxist-Leninist (KEN-ML); the Marxist-Leninist Party of the Netherlands (MLPN); and the Socialist Party (SP).

Oost-West Instituut   C. C. van den Heuvel
The Hague

Norway

The Norwegian Communist Party (Norges Kommunistiske Parti; NKP) remains small and isolated following its decision in 1975 not to merge with several left-socialist parties and factions. This decision split the party and caused its then-chairman, Reidar T. Larsen, and several other leaders to leave the NKP for the new Socialist Left Party (Sosialistisk Venstreparti; SV). The NKP is now the weakest of three main parties to the left of the powerful and ruling Norwegian Labor Party (Det Norske Arbeiderparti; DNA), which is a reformist social-democratic movement. In addition to the SV and NKP, current Marxist activity in Norway includes the Maoist (and consistently pro-Chinese) Workers' Communist Party (Arbeidernes Kommunistiske Parti; AKP), which has run in the last two parliamentary elections as the Red Electoral Alliance (Rød Valgallianse; RV).

The NKP was organized on 4 November 1923 by a few radical politicians and trade unionists who split from the DNA, as the latter was ending its brief membership in the Third International. The NKP first demonstrated electoral strength in 1945, when it won 11 of the 150 Storting (parliament) seats, thanks to communist participation during World War II in the Norwegian resistance movement and the Soviet liberation of northern Norway. The Cold War quickly eroded NKP strength, and by 1957 the Communists held only a single seat in parliament. In 1961 dissident Laborites started the Socialist People's Party (Sosialistisk Folkeparti; SF), and the NKP lost its last mandate. Not until the formation of the Socialist Electoral Alliance (Sosialistisk Valgforbund—a forerunner of the SV) in 1973 by the SF, NKP, and dissident left Laborites did Communists once again sit in the Storting. Standing alone in the 1977 elections, the postschism NKP polled 8,448 votes (0.4 percent of the total), far short of what was necessary to gain a parliamentary mandate and even down from the party's 1.0 percent in 1969.

NKP membership currently is considerably below the 2,000 to 5,000 estimate before the 1975 schism. The population of Norway is just over four million.

Although the SV was initially an electoral alliance with a common platform, the 1975 decision to merge and form a regular party has not created a stronger left-socialist wing. Its spectacular parliamentary gains in 1973 (11.2 percent of the vote, 16 out of 155 seats) proved to be a singular phenomenon. In the 1975 municipal and county elections, SV electoral strength was down, and in the September 1977 parliamentary elections, the party drew only 4.2 percent of the vote and held only 2 seats in the new Storting.

The SV's surprising strength in 1973 resulted from the emotional national campaign against Norwegian membership in the expanded European Economic Community (EEC). Supported by many nonsocialist parties and groups, the National Movement Against the EEC was victorious in the September 1972 referendum. Parliamentary elections a year later showed severe losses for those parties (especially the DNA) which had supported EEC membership. By 1975 the EEC issue was closed, and surveys showed that the SV was losing strength mainly because of its anti-NATO line and the internal turmoil connected with the merger efforts. With the results of the 1977 elections and the gains made by the Labor Party (DNA), the situation resembles that prior to 1970 before the EEC issue arose. Nevertheless, the governing Labor Party is dependent upon the two SV parliamentary votes for a majority in any socialist/nonsocialist confrontation. With the announcement of an economic austerity program in September 1978, the Labor government was moving to the right and was unlikely to seek SV support (*Nordisk Kontakt*, no. 12). The Marxist Left is thus not only divided into three competing factions but is electorally weak—sharing 5.2 percent of the vote among them (*see* Henry Valen, "The Storting Elections of 1977; Realignment or Return to Normalcy?" *Scandinavian Political Studies*, new series, vol. 1, no. 2/3, pp. 83—107).

Leadership and Organization. Personalities are important in a small democracy, and there is considerable continuity among the three left-socialist parties. Current NKP Chairman Martin Gunnar Knudsen emerged as leader of the rump-NKP after the party's divisive Fifteenth Congress (November 1975), which voted 117 to 30 against merger with the SV. Knudsen was unanimously reelected as chairman at the NKP's harmonious Sixteenth Congress in April 1978, as were Rolf Nettum, organizational vice-chairman; Hans Kleven, political vice-chairman; and Arne Jørgensen, editor of the party's twice-weekly *Friheten* (*Friheten*, 18 April). The Norwegian Communist Youth League (Kommunistisk Ungdom; KU) is the party's most important affiliate.

The SV can be most easily traced as an evolution of the SF group which emerged among anti-NATO Laborites in the early 1960s. Nevertheless, the party has a more overt radical and Marxist image, which was confirmed by its preelection congress in Oslo in March 1977. Tromsø University historian Berge Furre was reelected as chairman, and Otto Hauglin, Berit Ås, and Bjørgulv Froyn as vice-chairmen. Former SF founder and leader Finn Gustavsen, who became a prominent SV parliamentarian and played an important role in the party's development, retired in 1977. Of the SV's leaders and prominent MPs, only Berit Ås (by a narrow margin) held her parliamentary seat in the September 1977 election (*Aftenposten*, September issues, 1977).

Less is known about the organization of the Norwegian Workers' Communist Party, which polled 0.6 percent of the vote in 1977 (a gain of 0.2 percentage points from 1973). An amalgam of various Maoist groups that arose in the late 1960s, mainly as splinter groups from the SF and NKP youth organizations, the AKP was formally organized in late 1972. Its Second Congress, November 1976, reelected Paal Steigan as chairman. Ideologically, politically, and presumably organizationally and financially, the AKP maintains very close ties with the Chinese Communist Party and stresses Maoist thought in a variety of situations (New China News Agency, 17 November 1976). These ties were not diminished by Chinese domestic political developments during 1978.

Domestic Attitudes and Activities. Nineteen seventy-eight was the year Norway rejoined the world. North Sea oil activities and investments along with petroleum export revenues have spared Norway the economic stagnation and unemployment prevalent in most of Western Europe. Oil revenues have increased more slowly than planned, while production costs have soared. Moreover, Norwegian prosperity stemmed partly from large foreign loans, whose carrying costs have become massive. Hence, following its strong showing in the 1977 Storting elections, the Labor government has applied increasingly stronger controls on the economy. These measures have drawn increasingly virulent criticism from the Left, and the SV's parliamentary delegation declared that they would not support the Labor government's budget (*Nordisk Kontakt*, no. 12). SV support had been crucial to the government's bills in December 1977 to provide for employee and public representation on the boards of banks (*Aftenposten*, 2 December 1977) and in June 1978 to liberalize abortions.

The NKP's platform was reiterated at the party's Sixteenth Congress. Chairman Knudsen stressed that Norway's class struggle could not be waged according to a pattern from the Soviet Union or from other socialist countries. Nor could it be waged according to an Italian, French, or Portuguese formula. Even the other Scandinavian countries could not provide a model for political action. The party leadership defended the decision not to merge with other socialist groups except in ad hoc electoral alliances (*Arbeiderbladet*, 15 April). The NKP remained committed to its 24-point election manifesto issued prior to the September 1977 parliamentary elections. These proposals stressed traditional NKP views: heavier taxes on higher incomes; replacement of the 20 percent value-added tax (on all items) with luxury taxes; improved working conditions through shorter working hours; greater worker participation in enterprise management; better employment security; and specific promises for special groups—more day-care centers, higher minimum old-age pensions, etc. These issues had not allowed the party to attract a significant number of votes.

The SV blamed its electoral disaster on divisions among the socialist parties and the adverse propaganda from the revelations during the summer of 1977 that certain NATO installations in Norway (particularly Loran-C transmitters) were exclusively for use by American nuclear missile submarines. The disclosure of secret defense information led to threats of legal action against two leading SV MPs (neither of whom was reelected in September 1977) and to legal action against a journalist attached to the SV weekly *Ny Tid* (*Berlingske Tidende*, Copenhagen, 5 September 1977). The small SV delegation in the new Storting continued the party's strong anti-NATO line by demanding a categorical condemnation by the government of U.S. plans to develop and deploy neutron bombs. Increasing Norwegian defense expenditures were likewise denounced, but without effect.

The Maoist AKP is less interested in electoral campaigns, even though the party participates through the RV. Committed to "extraparliamentary" tactics, the AKP has succeeded in gaining influential positions in several issue-oriented and special interest organizations. Members have dominated the Oslo University Student Association for several years and have gained some important positions in trade union locals, although the larger unions as well as the Norwegian Trade Union Confederation (Landsorganisasjonen; LO) is firmly controlled by Laborites. With the growing importance of issue organizations in Norwegian politics, the strength and influence of the AKP may be far greater than TV's meager electoral results.

Norwegian Communists have traditionally been stronger in the trade union movement than in electoral politics, but neither they nor other small left-socialist groups have been able to challenge the DNA-LO links. This could change if the government's income policy continues to provoke discontent within the unions. Neither the Communists nor the SV have representation in the LO national executive or control any national labor union. At the local level, the NKP is most significant in the construction worker's union, and to a lesser extent in the metal, wood, transport, and electrochemical fields.

International Views and Positions. The 1975 split in the NKP has not significantly changed the party's views on international issues. This was confirmed in the party manifesto issued at the conclusion of the party's Sixteenth Congress in April. The Final Act of the 1975 Conference on Security and Cooperation in Europe (Helsinki accords) was stressed as a prelude to an attack on NATO and Norway's role in the Western alliance. The United States, NATO, and particularly West Germany were seen as forcing Norway to increase its military activity. The stationing of heavy NATO military equipment in Norway and the participation of West German troops in NATO maneuvers held in Norway were denounced. The neutron bomb and its possible deployment in Europe were attacked. In the continuing Norwegian-Soviet disagreements over demarcation of territorial limits in the Barents Sea, the NKP advocated compromise and cooperation. Parallel reduction and dissolution of NATO and the Warsaw Pact were advocated. Outside Europe, the NKP reiterated its support of "national and social liberation movements." In short, the NKP reaffirmed its adherence to Soviet international policies (*WMR*, no. 14).

This manifesto is the latest evidence that following the 1975 party schism, the NKP has lost most of its "nonaligned" orientation and has become more strongly supportive of Soviet foreign policy views. As the independent socialist periodical *Kontrast* pointed out, NKP Vice-chairman Hans Kleven, writing in his book *Vår Strategi* (Our strategy), praised the constructive role of Soviet troops in Eastern Europe.

The SV has continued to make its anti-NATO, antimilitary, and antifunctional economic cooperation position a central plank of its party platform. Public statements devote far more attention to cataloging the evils of American monopoly capital and the CIA than to regretting Soviet civil rights violations. A somewhat more balanced view of the Soviet Union appeared in the SV weekly *Ny Tid* (10 November 1977) on the occasion of the sixtieth anniversary of the October Revolution. While calling the revolution "a victory for the working class of every country," the editorial noted the many shortcomings of the Soviet Union today and classified it as a transitional society between capitalism and socialism.

On civil right issues the NKP has taken a low profile. NKP officials have refused to regard the trial of dissidents in the Soviet Union as contrary to the Helsinki principles. When asked about the convictions of Soviet dissidents Ginzburg and Shcharansky, NKP editor Arne Jørgensen commented: "Every country has its laws, and they must be observed" (*Aftenposten*, 18 July).

The AKP remained the exception to the general line of the Norwegian socialist Left. Reflecting its ties to China, the AKP denounced the military programs of both the United States and the Soviet Union. Particular attention was given to Soviet threats to Norway in the Barents Sea boundary dispute. The AKP feared that Svalbard might become a Soviet base (*Arbejderavisen*, Copenhagen, 18–24 August 1977).

The AKP took a strong pro-Cambodia line during the hearings held in Oslo in April 1978 under official Norwegian sponsorship. The AKP also supported closer Norwegian political and economic ties with China during Foreign Minister Frydenlund's visit to Peking in March 1978. Despite the changes in Chinese positions since the death of Mao in 1976, the AKP has remained loyal.

International Party Contacts. The international position of the NKP is reflected by close ties to the communist parties of Eastern Europe and the Soviet Union. Visits by NKP officials to the East and return visits symbolize these bonds. In November 1977 Vice-chairman Kleven led a NKP delegation to Romania. In the same month an Italian communist delegation visited Norway and held talks with NKP officials but also met with Foreign Minister Frydenlund and Labor Party leaders as well as the leaders of the SV. In December 1977 a NKP delegation headed by Vice-chairman Nettum visited party leaders in Czechoslovakia. Party Chairman Knudsen led a delegation to the German Democratic Republic in early February and met with leading East German party officials, including Secretary Honecker and Politburo member Herman Axen, who has special responsibilities for East German relations with the Scandinavian Left. An East German delegation headed by Politburo member Horst Sindermann visited Oslo in April.

Representatives of nine foreign communist parties attended the Sixteenth Congress of the NKP in April. The Soviet delegation was headed by Sizov, which together with the relatively small number of international representatives, reflects the NKP's limited importance (*Arbeiderbladet*, 15 April; Moscow radio, 11 April).

As mentioned above, the NKP has frequently had to address the topic of Eurocommunism. Official party statements have been ambivalent. While stressing that different national circumstances dictate varying tactics, the NKP has been critical of the moderate line on specific issues followed by French and especially Italian Communists. The dangers of "revisionism" are frequently cited. While emphasizing human rights and national independence, the NKP refused to distinguish between the so-called Eurocommunist parties of France, Italy, and Spain and other more orthodox movements. The NKP is anxious not to be driven to criticism of the Spanish, Italian, and, to a lesser extent, French parties for which there is substantial sympathy in Norway, and the orthodox Eastern European and Soviet parties for which there is little support outside of NKP ranks (*Friheten*, 20 April; *WMR*, no. 11, 1977).

The SV belongs to no formal network of international contacts but maintains close informal ties with the Socialist People's Party in Denmark, the Left Party Communists in Sweden, and the People's Alliance in Iceland. As evidenced by the meeting with Italian communist visitors in November 1977, the SV is enthusiastic about Eurocommunism, which may be said to have appeared in the Norwegian SF party in the early 1960s.

The AKP continued its close attention to events in China and its regular communications with the Chinese Communist Party (CCP). The latter congratulated the AKP on the occasion of its fifth anniversary in February 1978 (*Peking Review*, 24 February). In the late spring a delegation of AKP youth and student leaders paid an official visit to China and met with Chinese officials in several cities (New China News Agency, 10 May). In addition, the AKP communicated regularly with the communist parties of Albania and Cambodia.

Publications. The main NKP organ is *Friheten* (Freedom), first published as an underground paper during World War II. Dwindling circulation caused its transition from daily to weekly publication in 1967. Fund raising to keep the paper going is a continuous NKP preoccupation. During the fall of 1977, *Friheten* increased publication to twice a week. The KU publishes a youth bulletin, *Fremad* (Forward). The SV newspaper is *Ny Tid* (New times), which was intended to absorb the readership of the SF publication *Orientering*. The latter was respected by many readers outside the SF party circle. In addition to continuous financial difficulties, the SV weekly was involved in the "espionage" scandal of the election campaign in 1977. Nevertheless, given the sharp reduction in the SV parliamentary delegation, *Ny Tid* assumes greater importance as the SV mouthpiece. Finally, there is the AKP weekly *Klassekampen* (Class struggle) and the party's theoretical journal *Rǿd Fane* (Red flag).

University of Massachusetts   Eric S. Einhorn
Amherst

Portugal

The dominant left-wing organization in Portugal is the Portuguese Communist Party (Partido Comunista Portugûes; PCP). Its membership has grown from 115,000 at the time of its Eighth Congress in November 1976 to a claimed 142,000 (*IB,* no. 3). The population of Portugal is estimated at 9.7 million. The PCP has operated since 1921 but was proscribed between 1927 and 1974. Though now less influential politically than during the first two years following the 1974 revolution, the party has further solidified its supremacy in the trade union movement. The Socialists are said to have abandoned any notion of challenging the PCP's total control of the General Confederation of Portuguese Workers (Intersindical Nacional; CGTP-IN), which the Socialists claim "is preventing any democratic life." Because of the further deterioration of the economy under the Socialist government, the Socialists have been losing trade union support (*Manchester Guardian,* 14 May).

The far left parties, most of them organized since 1974, exercise little impact today. The strongest radical group appears to be the Maoist Popular Democratic Union (União Democrática do Povo; UDP); its claimed membership of 10,000 − 15,000 is represented in parliament by one deputy. Handicapped by a lack of funds and poor leadership, the remaining radical parties are mostly limited to issuing manifestos. Some have changed their names, and others have regrouped in an effort to resolve internal rivalries and to concentrate their efforts more effectively. For instance, the Maoist Movement for the Reorganization of the Proletariat (Movimiento Reorganizativo do Partido do Proletariado; MRPP) changed its name to the Communist Party of Portuguese Workers (Partido Comunista de Trabalhadores Portugueses; PCTP). The Trotskyite Workers' Socialist Organization (Organização Socialista de Trabalhadores; OST) was set up in October by the Internationalist Communist League (Liga Comunista Internacionalista; LCI) and by the Revolutionary Party of Workers (Partido Revolucionário de Trabalhadores; PRT). (*FBIS,* 15 May.) The United Workers' Organization (Organização Unida de Trabalhadores; OUT), formed in April, was an outgrowth of the Popular Socialist Front (Frente Socialista Popular; FSP) and of the Revolutionary Party of the Proletariat (Partido Revolucionário do Proletariado; PRP). One of OUT's organizers was Major Otelo Saraiva de Carvalho, second-place candidate for president in 1976 and one of the officers implicated in the leftist attempt to overthrow the government in November 1975 (*Keesing's Contemporary Archives,* 28 July).

Other far left parties reported to be operating in 1978 included the League for Revolutionary Union and Action (Liga para a Unidade e Ação Revolucionário; LUAR), the Communist Party of Portuguese Workers (Partido Comunista de Trabalhadores Portugueses; PCTP), the Portuguese Communist Party, Marxist-Leninist (Partido Comunista do Portugal—Marxista Leninista; PCP-ML), and the Party of the Democratic and Social Center (Partido do Centro Democrático y Social; PCDS).

Leadership and Organization. The PCP operates through some 7,000 small cells in business and educational organizations, on rural estates, and in the armed forces. Some horizontal "street cells" include members of different enterprises and institutions. The highest authority is the party congress, which selects the 90-member Central Committee to direct activities between congresses and to organize the Secretariat and other executive organs. Eight congresses have been held since the party was founded.

The secretary general since 1961 has been Alvaro Cunhal, who quickly became one of Portugal's most influential and charismatic politicians following the 1974 revolution and occupied a portfolio in every cabinet for almost two years. He was elected to parliament in 1976 but resigned the following year to devote more time to administering the party. A loyal supporter of the Soviet Union and accused of being a rigorous Stalinist, Cunhal is a frequent critic of Eurocommunism.

Domestic Attitudes and Activities. What Socialist leader Mário Soares described as "guerrilla war" waged in parliament by the opposition parties brought continued political instability and three changes of government during 1978. In attempts to form a new cabinet early in the year following his ouster by a no-confidence vote in December 1977, Soares steadfastly refused coalition with the Right or the Left. He feared that either alliance would precipitate an explosive "radicalization in the country," with the Communists polarizing discontent in their favor if the Socialists tied themselves to the Right. He did accept a compromise formula in January by which three ministries would be filled by "personalities" of the conservative Social Democratic Center (Centro Democrático Social; CDS), but he denied that this was a formal "coalition." To the appalled Communists, it was a "scandalous marriage" to which they refused to give their blessing. (*CSM,* 12 December 1977, 10 January; *NYT,* 20, 27 January; *Diário de Notícias,* Lisbon, 20 February; *Keesing's Contemporary Archives,* 24 March.)

The new government lasted only six months, doomed from the beginning by what critics called the "political" appointment of incompetents. Particularly opposed by the CDS was Minister of Agriculture Luís Saias because of his lack of experience and his "sympathy" for the Communists. When Prime Minister Soares refused a CDS ultimatum in July that Saias be fired, the Center Democrats withdrew from the cabinet. They accused the Socialists of having made a secret deal with the Communists to halt the reversal of communist gains in the Alentejo farm areas in exchange for peace in the PCP-controlled labor unions (*Christian Science Monitor,* 6 February, 12, 25 and 26 July).

Astonished that the prime minister did not resign after losing his parliamentary support, President António Ramalho Eanes dismissed him. In August after the parties failed to reach agreement on a cabinet, Eanes appointed a nonpartisan government of technocrats under Alfredo Nobre da Costa, a prominent industrial administrator from Portugal's former right-wing regime (*NYT,* 28 July; *Christian Science Monitor,* 11 August). The collapse of that government in September was precipitated by Soares' refusal to cooperate with what he denounced as a "constitutionally illegal" government and by CDS opposition to what that party called a pro-leftist cabinet—including three "known Communist sympathizers" (*Washington Post,* 15 September, 26 October). The PCP for its part had reservations about the support Nobre da Costa received from "reactionary political forces" and about speculation that he proposed to continue overhauling nationalized industries and the collective farms (Lisbon domestic radio, 22 August). Finally, in October parliament accepted Eanes' appointment of another political independent, Carlos da Mota Pinto, as prime minister, though Soares later described his cabinet as the most conservative since 1974. The PCP gave notice in November that it would seek to oust the new government. (*Washington Post,* 26 October; *NYT,* 23 November.)

Throughout the year the PCP repeatedly stressed that only an understanding between Socialists and Communists could bring about a democratic solution to the government crisis. Rather than having direct representation in the government, they said, their primary aim was to have a say in the government's policies—mainly those related to agrarian reform, the nationalized firms, and the labor sector (*Christian Science Monitor,* 4 January; *FBIS,* 17 October). They accused Prime Minister Soares of presiding over a policy of "capitalist recovery," thereby "betraying the April 25 revolution" while demanding intolerable sacrifices from workers and the general population. Alvaro Cunhal said that Portuguese workers were prepared to involve themselves actively in an austerity policy designed to make possible economic recovery but opposed compensation to capitalists and big landowners whose lands had been expropriated (*El País,* Madrid, 2 February; *Díario de Notícias,* 16 May).

Calling for the "socialism of the possible," Soares responded that the building of socialism now was less important than economic recovery "if we are to save Portuguese democracy" (*Christian Science Monitor,* 6 February; *NYT,* 27 May). "Disintervention"—withdrawal of state-appointed managers of many businesses and their return to former owners—was considered necessary because productivity had been dismal in the post-revolutionary years (*Wall Street Journal,* 13 January). Soares boasted that he had returned almost 600 firms to their original owners during his two years in office (*NYT,* 27 May).

Communists warned in April of a vast politico-military destabilization conspiracy under way to restore a reactionary dictatorship (*Avante,* 20 April). The Council of the Revolution, a military advisory body to the president, also expressed concern about "a dangerous escalation" in attempts to destroy democracy in Portugal "with abusive and systematic use of techniques of verbal terrorism." No groups were specified, but the condemnation of "frontal atacks" against the constitution and demands for its early revision appeared to be directed at the Social Democrats (Partido Social-Democrático; PSD) and Center Democrats. These parties are opposed to the constitutional provision for a transition to socialism (*NYT,* 10 December 1977, 23 April; Lisbon domestic radio, 21 April).

It was reported that even though President Eanes' shifts and demotions of officers had given the military an increasingly conservative complexion, there were still many Communists and other leftists among the officers. It is allegedly an open secret that NATO headquarters refrains from showing the Portuguese Defense Ministry any documents with a security classification higher than confidential (*NYT,* 28 May, 30 July). In October President Eanes announced that the time would soon come for the armed forces to give up altogether their political role in national affairs (*Christian Science Monitor,* 13 October).

An Eanes decision criticized as "profoundly shocking" by the CGTP-Intersindical, the PCP, and the Socialists was to allow the former right-wing president, Admiral Américo Rodrigues Tomaz, to return freely to Portugal in May. The CGTP-Indersindical declared that this would further encourage reactionary and fascist forces in their campaign of destabilization (Lisbon domestic radio, 12 May; *Christian Science Monitor,* 24 May).

In spite of such complaints by the PCP, Cunhal was circumspect in his relations with the military president. Although the latter became increasingly impatient with the politicians in parliament because of the government crises produced by their wranglings, he was said to be relaxed with

Cunhal and full of compliments for the Communists. Grateful that the party "no longer tries to impose its ideology but rather to offer solutions to problems," he noted that it projected "an image of capability, of cohesion and of organization that leaves a good impression" (*Washington Post*, 26 September).

Socialists and Communists expressed alarm at a growing swing of public opinion in Portugal to the right, a "veritable counterrevolution," especially in schools, the press, and the church. Young supporters of the PSD and CDS were said to be dominating student councils, even in such communist strongholds as southern Beja. Some neo-Nazi youth movements were also making headway, especially in Lisbon and Oporto schools. Communists blamed this trend on the Ministry of Education as well as on the CDS, the PSD, and the Independent Movement for National Reconstruction (MIRN). (The latter is an anti-Marxist organization that seeks to be a "catalyst" for democratic forces ranging from the extreme Right to "non-Marxist socialists.") Other analysts concluded that students were simply "fed up with politics," with the "totalitarianism" and "demagoguery" of the Left, and with "seeing facilities constantly damaged by confrontations between factions." (*Expresso*, Lisbon, 17 December 1977; *Christian Science Monitor*, 27 February, 20 March; *Manchester Guardian*, 14 May; *Keesing's Contemporary Archives*, 28 July.)

International Views and Positions. According to Cunhal, a major objective of the separatist movement in the Azores was to strengthen the position of "international imperialism." He charged that the United States financed Azorean right-wing forces to assure the U.S. military presence in the archipelago. He also protested U.S. Senate "support" for the independence of the Azores as well as talks held with regional government leaders by U.S. Vice-president Walter Mondale, "encouraging reaction and its separatist trends" (*Díario de Notícias*, 10 July).

French instigation of "intervention and imperialist military aggression in Africa" was also denounced by the PCP secretary general. He warned that a planned visit to Portugal by French President Giscard d'Estaing would not be welcome if its purpose was to sway Portugal from its "correct foreign policy of friendship and cooperation with Portugal's former African colonies" and to secure support for current French policy toward Africa. He said it was time "to make the big imperialists understand that Portugal, although a small country, is adult and revaccinated and does not accept attempts . . . to map out its destiny from abroad" (ibid.).

Seeking to avoid the impression of intervening in the affairs of the Spanish Communist Party, which dropped "Leninism" from its party definition at its Ninth Congress in April, Cunhal said it was up to that party to define its own line. At the same time, he said it was "difficult to understand how a communist party could abandon principles which are an integral part of the ideology of the working class and which constitute a sure guide for feeling one's way over the troubled waters of revolutionary processes" (*Corriere della Sera*, Milan, 11 February; *Avante*, 27 April).

Cunhal criticzed the Chinese Communist Party for its "hostile attitude" toward the revolution in Portugal and for its support, "along with the American imperialists," of elements hostile to the Angolan people's independence and social progress (*Kyodo*, Tokyo, 21 October 1977).

International Activities and Party Contacts. In trips taken abroad by Cunhal to the Soviet Union, Poland, Czechoslovakia, and East Germany, a dominant theme of joint statements was a condemnation of Eurocommunism as "misleading both geographically and politically." Determination was expressed to strengthen further the unity and cohesion of the world communist working-class movement. Cunhal stressed to a visiting Soviet delegation visiting Lisbon that both countries' parties were on the same political course because they were following the same compass provided by Marxism-Leninism. Another major concern of joint statements were activities designed to step up the arms race and to develop new instruments of mass destruction, such as the neutron bomb.

(Allgemeiner Deutscher Nachrichtendienst, East Berlin, 27 February; Tass, 1 March; Polska Agencja Prasowa, Warsaw, 13 June.) A PCP delegation visited Moscow in August to study Soviet agrarian policy (Tass, 17 August).

The PCP was visited in October by an envoy of the Communist Party of Vietnam's Central Committee (*Avante,* 19 October).

Publications. The PCP's principal publications include the daily *Avante,* which has been publishing since 1931, and *O Militante,* the theoretical bulletin of the Central Committee. A semiofficial PCP daily newspaper is the *Díario de Notícias.*

Rival Far Left Organizations. At its constituent assembly in April, the new radical-left United Workers' Organization (OUT) called for the use of force to oppose the rebirth of fascism and to achieve socialism. It exhorted workers "in every phase of the class struggle" to take over the nation's political and military leadership through a mass movement. Major Otelo Saraiva de Carvalho, chief organizer of the group, saw the need for action because the revolution had been "abandoned by just about everyone." There was "total passivity" in the army, and the Communists were a "completely bourgeois party, sunk in this parliamentary business." The PCP denounced Carvalho's "divisive and adventurist" organization for its "slanderous attacks." Carvalho had still not been tried for his role in the 1975 attempted coup, but in February he was declared eligible for reinstatement in the armed forces. All decrees suspending him and other involved officers were declared unconstitutional by the Council of the Revolution. He indicated that he may run again for president in 1981 if he is not in jail. (*Avante,* 8 April; *Pravda,* 13 April; *NYT,* 2 June; *Keesing's Contemporary Archives,* 28 July.)

Other far left parties also bewailed the country's loss of revolutionary zeal. Hundreds of pamphlets signed by the League for Revolutionary Union and Action (LUAR) were disseminated in Coimbra in September accusing the government of "not fulfilling the constitution and its own program and of ordering the National Guard to beat up Alentejo workers." LUAR's arms were declared "at the service of the people" (*Díario de Notícias,* 12 September). In April police seized fourteen machine guns in a raid on the headquarters of the Communist Party of Portuguese Workers (*Keesing's Contemporary Archives,* 28 July). In October a newly formed Workers' Socialist Organization issued a manifesto declaring that three years of the Portuguese revolution had demonstrated that the working masses and young people were the only force capable of moving the country out of the chaos brought on by capitalists and big landowners (*FBIS,* 13 October). The Popular Democratic Union (UDP) called for a one-day national strike to protest the return to Portugal of former President Tomaz. Here was further evidence, it said, that right-wingers were regrouping in Portugal (*NYT,* 24 July).

"Soviet imperialism" was the major concern of the Maoist parties. Several PCP-ML delegations visited China during 1978, and numerous messages were sent to the Communist Party of China extolling its progress and activities. The publication of volume 5 of the *Selected Works of Mao Tsetung* was hailed as "an event of major importance" (ibid., 3 September). The PCP-ML joined the Spanish Workers' Revolutionary Organization in a Madrid statement of "full support for Chairman Mao's scientific theory of the differentiation of the three worlds" (*Peking Review,* 31 March). Messages of support were also sent by the PCP-ML to the Cambodian Communist Party.

Elbert Covell College
University of the Pacific

H. Leslie Robinson

San Marino

The Communist Party of San Marino (CPS) was founded in 1921 as a section of the Italian Communist Party (PCI). Although the CPS has independent status vis-à-vis the PCI, its political positions over the years have been affected by the presence and the policy of its Italian counterpart. This is not surprising since San Marino is located in the "Red Belt" of Italy and the small republic is surrounded by Italian communities in which the Left has traditionally been very strong. Following World War II, the CPS formed a coalition government with the Socialist Party. Excluded from office in 1957, the CPS has remained in opposition until very recently. Umberto Barulli is general secretary.

At the Ninth Party Congress held in 1976, CPS delegates voted to strengthen their relationship with the PCI and adopted a strategy similar to the "Historic Compromise" line pursued by the Italian Communists since the early 1970s. Thus, when a governmental crisis developed in San Marino in the fall of 1977, the CPS attempted to foster creation of a "government of national solidarity" that would have included Communists, Socialists, and Christian Democrats. In December 1977 CPS leaders failed to form a coalition government.

The persistence of a political deadlock in the first months of 1978 led to new elections for the General Council, the country's unicameral legislature. The tiny electorate of less than 20,000 voters was called to the polls on May 28. The returns gave the CPS 25 percent of the vote, a slight increase over the 23.7 percent received in the election of 1974. However, the strength of the CPS in the General Council remained unaltered at 16 out of 60 seats. (*Corriere della sera*, 29 May.)

The election did not resolve the deadlock. After an unsuccessful attempt by the Christian Democrats to form a government in June, the mandate was offered the CPS. Negotiations with other leftist parties led to the formation of a government of "democratic collaboration" backed by the CPS, the Socialist Party, and the left-wing component of the Social Democrats ("Socialist Unity"). In the Congress of State (the cabinet), the Communists received four of ten positions: Internal Affairs (Alvaro Selva), the Department of Industry and Crafts (Fausta Simona Morgante), the Department of Health (Adalmiro Bartolini), and the Department of Education (Umberto Barulli). (*Corriere della Sera*, 18 July.)

The formation of a leftist cabinet during the summer was followed in September by the election of a Socialist and a Communist to the positions of Captains-Regent, who act as "heads of state" and serve a six-month term. The Communist chosen for the post was CPS chairman Ermenegildo Gasperoni. (*Corriere della Sera*, 16 September.)

The return to positions of power in 1978 after twenty years of opposition represented a success for the CPS. The present cabinet rests on a slim majority of one vote, and its formula—a government by parties of the Left—is not favored by the CPS. It is, thus, to be expected that the CPS will continue to pursue a strategy focusing on the establishment of a "broad coalition" government in San Marino.

Ohio State University   Giacomo Sani

Spain

Among the various leftist organizations in Spain, the largest communist group is the Communist Party of Spain (Partido Comunista de España; PCE). It is also the most moderate, representing itself as a communist party of a new kind. Since it was founded in 1920, it has evolved from a hard-line Marxist-Leninist force to the foremost exponent of Eurocommunism. This movement of European Communists professes independence from Moscow and absolute respect for parliamentary democracy. Legalized in April 1977, the PCE claims to have increased its membership tenfold to more than 200,000 since its underground period under the Franco dictatorship. The population of Spain is estimated at over 36 million. Actually, the PCE is far more influential than its membership figures or its 9 percent share of the vote in the 1977 legislative elections would indicate. Its leverage derives primarily from its hegemony in the trade union movement and the charisma of its secretary general.

The most active terrorist organizations of the radical left in Spain are the guerrilla faction of the Basque separatist movement called ETA (Euzkadi ta Askatasuna, "Basque Homeland and Liberty") and the October First Antifascist Resistance Group (Grupo de Resistencia Antifascista Primero de Octubre; GRAPO), which receives its name from the date in 1975 when it killed a number of policemen in Madrid. Also avowing responsibility for some violent acts during 1978 were the International Communist Party (Partido Comunista Internacional; PCI), a small revolutionary splinter group, and the previously unknown Armed Proletariat Group (Grupo Armado del Proletariado; GAP). The Revolutionary Antifascist and Patriotic Front (Frente Revolucionaria Antifascista y Patriota; FRAP), actively terrorist in some recent years, is said now to be practically defunct (*Christian Science Monitor*, 18 April; hereafter *CSM*).

The ETA guerrillas have been active since 1959, when the organization was formed by radical youths disenchanted with the "bourgeois" Basque Nationalist Party (PNV). Numerous divisions into splinter groups since 1970 resulted from conflicts over whether to continue military extremism. By the end of 1977 most of the antiterrorist factions had abandoned the ETA label in favor of new names or affiliations, leaving the militant ETA with no more than an estimated 100–150 activists. The most important antiterrorist and Marxist faction is now called EIA (Party of the Basque Revolution). Another, originally called ETA-VI, fused with the Trotskyite Revolutionary Communist League (Liga Comunista Revolucionaria; LCR), which claims 10,000 members. Only a minority of Basques are said to be consistent ETA supporters, but sympathy for the group waxes when it clashes with police. (*Mundo Obrero*, 17–23 November 1977; *Intercontinental Press*, 16 January; *NYT*, 15 July; *CSM*, 24 August.) According to Spanish police, ETA militants have received three months of guerrilla training in Algeria from Cuban military experts (*NYT*, 7 July).

GRAPO is a Maoist movement said to be the armed wing of the Reconstituted Communist Party (Partido Comunista Reconstituido; PCR). Spanish police thought GRAPO had been extinguished in 1977, but it reappeared in 1978 after reportedly changing to a tactic of operating as "legal commandos," i.e., its members lead normal lives with their families while practicing terrorism on the side (*CSM*, 18 April; Madrid domestic radio, 6 September). GRAPO is said to have ties with Algeria and with the Canary Islands liberation movement (*NYT*, 20 April).

The remaining radical-left parties in Spain are mainly Maoist, Trotskyite, Marxist-Leninist, and anarchist. They include the Spanish Communist Workers' Party (Partido Comunista de Obreros Españoles; PCOE), led by Enrique Líster, who was expelled from the PCE in 1970; the Communist Party of Spain, Marxist-Leninist (Partido Comunista de España, PCE-ML); the Spanish Workers' Revolutionary Organization (Organización Revolucionaria de los Trabajadores Españoles; ORTE); and the Spanish Labor Party (Partido de Trabajo Español; PTE).

Organization and Leadership. Quite unprecedented in the history of the PCE was its Ninth Congress, which met in Madrid in April. This first legal congress inside Spain in 46 years was convened essentially to "modernize" the party and make it more attractive to new members and to diminish public distrust. It was conducted in such a way as to project an image of an open, "thoroughgoing Eurocommunist" party, no longer intent on armed insurrection or the dictatorship of the proletariat (*Mundo Obrero,* 26 January – 1 February; *Radio Free Europe Research Report*, 25 April).

At sessions open to the Spanish and foreign press, the 1,494 delegates chose leaders by secret ballot for the first time in the party's history. Santiago Carrillo, secretary general since 1960, was re-elected to that post, and Dolores Ibarruri was again voted president, primarily a figurehead position. The Central Committee, which acts for the congress between sessions, was increased from 142 to 160 members, and the Executive Committee from 33 to 45. The declared aim was to give more voice to newer and younger members, to Catalan Communists—who constitute nearly a quarter of the party's nationwide membership and who are represented in the Cortes by eight of the PCE's twenty deputies—and to the PCE-organized Workers' Commissions (Comisiones Obreras, or "CC OO"). (*Radio Free Europe Research Report*, 11 April; *Mundo Obrero*, 23 April.) The latter had prevailed in trade union elections held from January to March, winning over 35 percent of the union delegates throughout Spain. The second-place Socialist-dominated General Workers' Union (Unión General de Trabajadores; UGT) garnered only 22 percent of the vote. The latter represented an estimated one million workers after the two largest Socialist unions merged in December 1977, against 1.1 million believed to be in the CC OO. (*NYT*, 19 December 1977; *Keesing's Contemporary Archives*, 28 July.)

PCE pronouncements boasted especially of the "democratic atmosphere of the Ninth Congress, which permitted dissension and open debate. Opposing arguments on controversial proposals were published in the PCE's *Nuestra Bandera* (March-April). Even though Carrillo's proposed changes were supported by comfortable majorities, he faced a barrage of criticism at preliminary regional party conferences—especially from Catalan Communists. On the one hand, traditionalists attacked his "Eurocommunist" divergencies, and on the other, new recruits accused him of not being liberal enough and of using authoritarian, Leninist methods to forge the much-touted democratic image. (*Radio Free Europe Research Reports*, 3 and 25 April; *Washington Post*, 23 April; *NYT*, 29 April.)

The congress rejected a proposal calling for party governance by "democratic centralism," but centralized control by the higher committees was actually retained while "factional activity" continued to be banned (*Manchester Guardian*, 30 April). Carrillo assured those who could not accept discipline that they had chosen the wrong party (*NYT*, 20 April) and insisted that no party, whether on the Left or the Right, would tolerate "internal separate trends" (*Le Figaro*, Paris, 26 April). The congress created a six-man watchdog tribunal, the Central Guarantees and Control Commission, to "guarantee the rights of members and assure the internal democracy of the party, as well as the observance of discipline on the part of all committees and members." Party authorities were authorized, if this committee concurred, to expel wayward militants. While apparently no dissidents were purged from the PCE, many were said to have been excluded from positions of authority. (*NYT*, 28 April; *Mundo Obrero*, 8 – 14 June.)

Clearly it was still considered necessary to "homogenize" PCE thought, which meant, as one PCE spokesman had emphasized in March, "adjusting" new and old members "who do not fully understand the party" to PCE policy (*El País*, Madrid, 18 March). Even so, the party trod gingerly around the dissident Catalans and promoted their regional party to independent status "fraternally united to the PCE." Demands by other regional affiliates for greater organizational independence were shelved (*Manchester Guardian*, 30 April). The congress voted in favor of regional autonomy in Spain but opposed "separatist vanities" (*Economist*, 29 April).

Controversy at the congress centered around the adoption of some new statutes and "theses" proposed by Carrillo and approved earlier in the year by the Central Committee. The theses are official statements of ideology and policy. The one arousing the most spirited debate was Thesis 15, which proposed altering the party label from "Marxist-Leninist" to "Marxist, revolutionary, and democratic." The "sensationalist" press reaction that the party was "abandoning Leninism" was dismissed as inadequate and false by those advancing the Carrillo line; it was not a case of renouncing Lenin, "the greatest revolutionary in the history of mankind," but of recognizing that his fundamental precepts no longer represent the "Marxism of our epoch" since conditions now are totally different. Carrillo contended in fact that his own position was really "more faithful to the style of Lenin, who knew how to get rid of academic Marxism in order to make revolution in Russia." For the PCE, he said, "revolution" today meant putting an end to capitalism within the confines of parliamentary democracy. (*Mundo Obrero*, 26 January–1 February; *NYT*, 20 April; *Radio Free Europe Research Report*, 25 April.)

A fifth of the delegates voted against Thesis 15, but Carrillo denied that this represented a break in party unity; the discordant noises were in fact hailed as "the normal signs of democratic debate in open democratic parties" (*Washington Star*, 24 April). Lest the hierarchy be accused of stifling those noises on such an important issue, a departure from party rules permitted the opposition views on Thesis 15 to be aired before the open session of the congress. Normally a minority position can be presented only if it wins more than a third of the votes in a committee hearing, which Thesis 15 failed to do (*Washington Post*, 6 May).

Domestic Attitudes and Activities. The PCE continued in 1978 its ardent support of "national consensus" and collaboration with the government of Prime Minister Adolfo Suárez. Especially useful to the latter was the party's cooperation in the defense of wage and price controls, a key element of an economic recovery package accepted by the major opposition parties in the "Moncloa Pact" of October 1977 (see *YICA, 1978*, p. 200). Santiago Carrillo's affable relations with Suárez were somewhat ruffled, however, by a concern that much of the pact was not being precisely implemented. Carrillo cited the official refusal to consider a more thorough examination of a code of workers' rights and duties, "agreed to in principle at the Moncloa Palace," and the labor minister's announcement of a plan to give greater "flexibility" to the labor force. (*Mundo Obrero*, 16–22 February.)

The PCE Central Committee noted in June that the Moncloa Pact had yielded positive results in a number of fields but had not resolved the fundamental issue of unemployment. The jobless rate was variously estimated at 5–7 percent of a labor force of some 13.2 million, with youth making up some 40 to 50 percent of the unemployed. The PCE proposed alleviation of the problem through sharp increases in capital investment by the government. (*Wall Street Journal*, 5 June.) There was success in reducing inflation from the 25 percent rate of 1977 to what was expected to be the targeted 15 percent by the end of 1978; however, Suárez was not perceived by the Spanish public to be overcoming the nation's economic malaise. (*NYT*, 10 March; *Wall Street Journal*, 5 June.)

A fascinating relationship appeared to have developed during the year between Carrillo and Suárez, providing mutual benefits to each. An Italian reporter quoted the prime minister as praising the "exceptional capabilities" of Carrillo—"one of the most able and farsighted politicians I have ever met." Suárez was said to have confided that he often met with Carrillo in the evening, after which he could never sleep "because he always brings me plenty of ideas and also because I have to consider what lies behind his proposals. (*La Stampa*, Turin 23 March.)

While Suárez is using the Communists to ensure labor peace, Carrillo seeks to influence government policies and to enhance his party's image in Spain and abroad. Both had some success in advancing their aims. Labor was restless but relatively quiet. Communist labor leader Marcelino Camacho explained CC OO backing for the government's austerity measures by saying it was difficult for the working class to progress if the country itself was "going down the drain." None of the major unions made the economic recovery policy a big campaign issue in union elections (*Wall Street Journal*, 8 June).

Because of PCE collaboration with the government, public hesitation about the Communists was widely thought to have been erased or greatly reduced. The party's electoral pull was not significant, but Carrillo boasted that there was no doubt that the Communists would one day enter the government. For the present, however, conditions following a long right-wing dictatorship did not favor a government of the Left, he said, even if it had enough votes. This was an obvious reference to the danger of provoking a united right-wing reaction from the "economic bunker" and the armed forces. It was generally accepted that King Juan Carlos had the support of the Communists and Socialists because they saw him as the guarantor of the army's good behavior. (*Washington Post*, 8 February, 25 June; *El País*, 18 March.)

Carrillo's concern about a possible leftist government imperiling the democratic process at this time was particularly directed against the Socialist Workers' Party (Partido Socialista Obrero Español; PSOE), which began to predict an expected victory in 1979 legislative elections. The PCE leader assailed the "extraordinary partisan ambition" to "pass the ball" between the center and the PSOE in each election so as to continue playing practically "the same game as the Labourites and Conservatives in Britain" (*El País*, 31 January). He did not see a Socialist government as a viable alternative, however, because "no party can achieve an absolute majority" (*FBIS*, 4 February).

Smarting from criticism from extremists within the party because of its moderate consensus policies, the PSOE turned in March to a more belligerent stance. It denounced the government's rightist gyrations, threatening to "go to the streets" for popular action. It also temporarily withdrew from the committee drafting a new constitution, a move denounced by Santiago Carrillo as demagogic. The PCE, though opposed to a number of clauses, called the document "fully acceptable" because it represented a successful compromise among the principal political parties and because it recognized a wide range of fundamental social rights. (*Mundo Obrero*, 22—28 June; *American Universities Field Staff Reports*, no. 16.) The document was finally ratified by the Cortes at the end of October and approved in a national referendum in early December by 88 percent of those voting. A third of the eligible voters stayed away from the polls (*Christian Science Monitor*, 1 November, 8 December).

Though the Socialists were confident of winning forthcoming municipal and legislative elections, there were indications that their public support was waning and that the Communists' was on the rise. May by-elections for two Senate seats representing the traditionally leftist provinces of Alicante and Oviedo gave clear majorities to the Socialists, but their share of the vote—as well as that of Suárez's Democratic Center Union (Unión del Centro Democrática; UCD)—was smaller than in the June 1977 elections. The Communists, on the other hand, roughly doubled their showing. Some questioned how meaningful these results were, since there was a 50 percent abstention rate at the polls. The UCD maintained that militant leftists were more apt to vote in a minor by-election than centrists and conservatives. (*Los Angeles Times*, 19 May; *Keesing's Contemporary Archives*, 28 July.)

As a "logical consequence" of the elections, Santiago Carrillo proposed the formulation of a tripartite policy by the UCD, the PSOE, and the PCE, with the cooperation of Basques and Catalans. The new agreement, he said, should improve upon the Moncloa Pact by outlining an in-depth program to be implemented over a period of two or three years (*El País*, 23 May). On 29 December Premier Suarez dissolved parliament and called general elections for 1 March 1979 in an effort to strengthen the position of his "center" government.

Public acceptance of the PCE was seen to be growing despite the appearance of books by two former PCE militants damning Carrillo as a ruthless, authoritarian opportunist. The authors, Jorge Semprún and Fernando Claudín, had been expelled from the party in 1964. The former, a well-known novelist and screenwriter, alleged in his *Autobiography of Federico Sánchez* that he had been ousted for opposing Carrillo's "Stalinist" policies and for urging the party to adopt a new policy similar to the Eurocommunism advanced by Carrillo today. In *Documents of a Communist Divergence*, Claudín charged Carrillo with behaving in the party "like Juan Carlos in the country," that is, "like a monarch who bestows democracy on his subjects." He acknowledged, however, that even his critics within the PCE considered Carrillo irreplaceable since the party had not produced any other outstanding figures. (Ibid., 4 January; *Washington Post*, 14 January; *CSM*, 16 January; *NYT*, 24 February; *Radio Free Europe Research Report*, 3 April.)

Initially Carrillo ignored Semprún's attack, refusing to give publicity to what was "beneath contempt." Other party members wrote extensive rebuttals, and the secretary general himself was compelled to discuss the book as it turned into a best-seller. However, Carrillo still soft-pedaled his response, calling attention to the need for national reconciliation based on not stirring up the past. He said that the forthcoming PCE Ninth Congress would be the "best answer" to Semprún and that the party's archives would be opened to historians for clarification of a "confused period in Spain's history." (*El País*, 2 and 22 January; *Mundo Obrero*, 123–18 and 19–25 January; *La Vanguardia*, Barcelona, 18 January).

International Views and Positions. PCE officials continued in 1978 what the Soviets characterized as "crude attacks" against the USSR. A West German magazine quoted Manuel Azcárate, a deputy of Carrillo, as asserting that the Soviet Union was "not really a socialist state" and that "the characteristic feature of Eurocommunism is its rejection of the Soviet model." This provoked the official Moscow foreign affairs weekly, *Novoye vremya*, to renew in January its assault on Eurocommunism. (For an account of the controversy it unleashed in 1977, see *YICA, 1978*, pp. 200–201.) It explained, as it had similarly done in 1977, that it was attacking Azcárate personally, not the policies of the PCE or any other western party. It insisted that the Soviet Union had never sought to impose its "model" on anyone but pointed out that one could not "effectively fight for freedom and democracy in one's own country . . . while discrediting existing socialism." It further asserted that some of the most active proponents of Eurocommunism in effect brought "grist to the mill of imperialism." (Tass, 11 January, 1 February; *NYT*, 12 January; *IB*, no. 5, 15 March.) Later in the year, Carrillo provided additional "grist" by expressing indignation at the sentencing of several dissidents in the Soviet Union. He said that the practice of attempting to stamp out dissenting opinions was "contrary to our conception of what a socialist society should be" (*Mundo Obrero*, 13–19 July).

Eurocommunism was attacked by both Soviet and American leaders, Carrillo claimed, because for different reasons they prefer to have in Western Europe sectarian parties rather than parties capable of becoming governmental parties (*Radio Free Europe Research Report*, 6 February). The reference to "American leaders" was provoked by President Carter's January remark that the United States did not favor communist political influence or participation in governments of European countries. This "inadmissible interference in European internal affairs," said Carrillo, demonstrated that NATO "more than an instrument of European strategical balance, is an instrument of control of European policies" (*CSM*, 16 and 27 January; *Mundo Obrero*, 19–25 January).

The PCE also found itself in conflict with the French Communist Party because of the latter's resistance to Spain's entry into the Common Market. This position was denounced by the PCE as "parochial chauvinism" designed to win the sympathy of French farmers whose unprofitable agriculture would be hurt by the increased competition. The impasse was not resolved in subsequent discussions among Spanish, French, and Italian party leaders, although the Italian Communists were said to have a "sensible attitude" in the matter (*La Vanguardia*, 1 August; *Mundo Obrero*, 7−13 September; *L'Unità*, Rome, 27 September).

On two separate but related issues, the PCE simultaneously supported and opposed Algerian foreign policy. On the one hand, the party urged Spanish recognition of the "Polisario Front," an Algerian-backed guerrilla group in the former Spanish Sahara that opposed the 1975 partition of Spain's colony between Morocco and Mauritania (*Mundo Obrero*, 9-15 March). As leverage to secure Spanish government support for the Polisario Front, Algeria also sheltered Canarian liberation leader, Antonio Cubillo, and gave him free radio time for his anti-Spanish broadcasts. The latter's Movement for Self-determination and Independence of the Canarian Archipelago (MPAIAC) was opposed by most islanders and by the Communists (*NYT*, 20 April). When Algeria prodded the Organization of African Unity's Council of Ministers into branding the islands "unliberated African territory," the PCE called the move "scandalous" and "intolerable." The Canaries Communist Party stressed the Spanish character of the islands and denied the existence of any colonialism there. (*Mundo Obrero*, 23 February−1 March.)

International Activities and Party Contacts. The PCE's Ninth Congress in April was attended by 36 foreign delegations, with most Communist parties generally following the Soviet example in sending smaller-than-usual delegations headed by a central committee member. Yugoslavia had a strong representation. The Czechoslovak and Albanian parties, which have been particularly hostile to the PCE's "revisionism," were not invited. A Soviet party member in attendance was restrained in his reactions, commenting tersely that "Eurocommunism does not exist; only scientific Marxism exists." (*Radio Free Europe Research Report*, 25 April; *NYT*, 2 April.)

The PCE gave a warm reception to a probable new recruit to the Eurocommunist trend, the Greek Communist Party (interior). On a visit to Carrillo in October 1977, a delegation of that new party was "impressed" with measures taken in Spain to unite "progressive and leftist forces" in a policy of national consensus (*El País*, 29 October 1977). A PCE group attending the Eleventh Congress of the League of Communists of Yugoslavia also welcomed that party's expression of support for Eurocommunism and praised its policy of "dialogue and cooperation with all democratic and progressive forces" (*Mundo Obrero*, 29 June−5 July). A Carrillo-led delegation to Pyongyang in September to attend celebrations of the thirtieth anniversary of the founding of the Democratic People's Republic of Korea held talks that emphasized the "spirit of independence" of the two parties (ibid., 14−20 September).

There were numerous meetings with Romanian Communists, both in Spain, where the Romanian minister of foreign affairs held economic talks with the Spanish government in December 1977, and in Bucharest. During a month's vacation in August in Romania, Carrillo had ample opportunity to confer with Nicolae Ceauşescu, secretary general of the Romanian Communist Party. There were also contacts with the Soviets by Dolores Ibarruri, who spent a few days of "rest" in Moscow in July, and by three PCE delegations that visited the USSR in August.

In November 1977, the Spanish Communists hosted a delegation of the Palestinian Liberation Organization (PLO). The PCE expressed its solidarity with the struggle and rights of the PLO and promised to try to "sensitize" Spanish public opinion to the "just cause" of the Palestinian people (ibid., 24−30 November 1977).

Publications. The PCE's principal publications are the weekly *Mundo Obrero*; the bimonthly *Nuestra Bandera*, a theoretical and political journal; and various small regional newspapers.

Activities of Basque and Rival Communist Organizations. Terrorist bombings and killings, especially in the simmering Basque region, continued to convulse Spain in 1978. The chief assailants were militants of the extremist ETA, who claimed credit or were blamed for more than 50 murders, especially of policemen, as well as numerous bombings of rail lines, roads, police barracks and a nuclear plant under construction near Bilbao. Scores of others were killed or wounded by riot police in clashes with Basque demonstrators. (*NYT*, 15 July; *Keesing's Contemporary Archives*, 28 July; *CSM*, 9 November.)

The ETA was said to be seeking to polarize Basque political forces, undermine moderates, and ignite police repression to prove that "nothing has changed" and to exacerbate further Basque resentment. The group still insisted it would halt its "armed struggle" only after the Basque region had secured complete autonomy, with its own police force and military replacing the government "oppressors" and with all political parties legalized. (*CSM*, 2 June.)

The Basque population grew progressively more critical of the organization. One moderate said that ETA could thrive under a tough regime like Franco's, but that its leaders realized democracy would "kill them" (ibid., 7 August). The Communist Party of Euzkadi suggested that what most annoyed the present ETA mentors was that even the Left had now taken up battle against their armed action (Madrid domestic radio, 15 May). An indication of this irritation was provided by the June murder of a prominent Bilbao newspaper editor because of a critical article in his publication. ETA warned that other "insulting" journalists could be its next targets.

Responsibility for numerous other terrorist acts in Madrid and Barcelona were claimed by the ETA, the leftist GRAPO, the PCI, the GAP, and the ultraright Triple A (Anticommunist Apostolic Alliance) and Warriors of Christ the King. Those murdered included a former mayor of Barcelona, a reform-minded Spanish prison director, a judge and two army generals. A bomb intended for the editor of *El País*, an influential and outspoken Madrid daily, went off prematurely in its mailroom. (*NYT*, 26 January, 22 July; *CSM*, 28 March, 24 July, 2 November.) The LCR reported that its headquarters had been assaulted by hooded Warriors of Christ the King, but that police only arrested the Trotskyite victims (*Intercontinental Press*, 27 May, 19 June).

The government strategy was to try to isolate the terrorists with concessions designed to win over the moderate Basque mainstream. Provisional, limited autonomy was granted to the Basque provinces at the end of 1977—and, during 1978, to Andalusia, Galicia, Valencia, the Canary Islands, and various other regions as well (*CSM*, 20 January, 22 August; *Keesing's Contemporary Archives*, 28 July). To encourage continuing defections from the ETA, the government legalized the organization's political offshoot, the EIA, and even pardoned several convicted guerrillas, including the 1973 murderers of Prime Minister Luis Carrero Blanco. The minister of interior stressed, however, that there would be positively no more amnesties (*NYT*, 22 January).

At the same time that the government was seeking to appeal to moderate Basques, it proceeded to strengthen its security forces. An antiterrorism law decreed in June and approved by the Cortes in July set up special West German—style commandos and a special judicial police unit to investigate terrorist crimes. Police powers were broadened to permit the suspension of habeas corpus and the monitoring of telephones, mail, and telegraph services. The PCE agreed to support the law provided it was not abused with infringements on human rights. Some observers feared the government clampdown would merely reinforce the ETA, noting that "every time ETA has blundered, the government has blown it by overreacting," thereby assuring more Basque resentment and solidarity. (*CSM*, 7 July; *NYT*, 15 and 28 July.)

Meanwhile, Spaniards grew increasingly weary of the mounting violence. In October an estimated 35,000 Basques conducted a "peace march" in Bilbao, and in November hundreds of thousands of Spaniards took part in over 140 demonstrations throughout the country calling for an end to terrorism (*CSM*, 9 and 13 November). Even so, the Basque mainstream continued to be leery of the Madrid government and resentful that the new constitution slighted Basque demands for autonomy. At the

December constitutional referendum, some 50 percent of Basque voters abstained and over 19 percent of those voting cast negative ballots. Much of the abstention was apparently provoked by ETA terrorist threats (*NYT*, 8 December).

Elbert Covell College
University of the Pacific

H. Leslie Robinson

Sweden

The forerunner of Sweden's communist party (Sveriges Kommunistiska Parti; SKP) was founded in May 1917, and joined the Communist International in July 1919. During the 1920s and the 1930s inner tensions plagued the SKP until World War II. Following a period of relative insignificance during the 1950s, the party profited from the rise of the New Left in the 1960s. In 1967 it absorbed new groups from the radical Left and changed its name to Left Party—Communists (Vänsterpartiet Kommunisterna; VPK). A large minority within the party criticized the VPK for being "reformist" and founded the Communist League, Marxist-Leninist (Kommunistiska Förbundet Marxist-Leninisterna; KFML), which is pro-Chinese in orientation. In 1973 the KFML changed its name to SKP.

During the period from 1970 to 1976 the VPK exerted an influence on Swedish politics disproportionate to its number of seats in parliament. In the 1970 elections Prime Minister Olof Palme and the Social Democratic Party, with 163 seats in the 350-seat parliament, relied on the VPK for the survival of their government. During no other period in Sweden's postwar history has the communist party exerted such influence on parliamentary life. During the 1970—73 period it participated in such important parliamentary committees as defense and taxes. Following the 1973 elections, however, Palme frequently compromised to the right with the Liberal Party, thus weakening VPK participation in Swedish parliamentary life. The fall of the Social Democratic government in 1976, however, marked the beginning once more of political insignificance for the Communist party, of the kind it had experienced during the 1950s and 1960s.

In October 1978 the nonsocialist coalition government (Conservative, Liberal, and Center parties) resigned because it failed to reach agreement on Sweden's nuclear policy, and a minority government was formed by Liberal Party leader Ola Ullsten. It is generally speculated in Sweden that the resignation of the coalition government in October will result in the return of the Social Democratic Party to power after the elections of September 1979. This may in turn mean a renewal of the importance of the VPK in Swedish parliamentary life.

The latest VPK membership figure is reported to be 17,000. The population of Sweden is about 8,273,000.

Leadership and Organization. The party congress is theoretically the highest organ of the VPK. It elects the 35-member Central Committee, known since 1964 as the Party Board. The Board selects in turn an eight-member Executive Committee (Verkställande Utskott) which directs party work. There are 28 party districts, corresponding to Sweden's electoral regions, and 395 local organizations. The Communist Youth (Kommunistisk Ungdom) is the party youth organization. Party chairman is Lars Werner from Stockholm, who is generally regarded as less colorful than his predecessor, Carl-Henrik Hermansson.

Werner failed to put an end to the factional fighting within the VPK in 1976, and in February 1977 a long-expected split took place within the party. Three party districts left the VPK to form a new party, the Communist Workers' Party (Arbetarpartiet Kommunisterna; APK). The APK comprises 5,000 former members of the VPK and holds two of the seventeen parliamentary seats won by the VPK in the most recent national elections, held in 1976. The main strength of the APK is in northern Sweden, and it receives support from the daily newspaper *Norrskenflamman* published in Luleå. The leader of the revolt was a VPK member of parliament, Rolf Hagel. On 26–27 March 1977 the new party held its first conference, and Hagel was elected chairman.

The reaction to the emergence of the APK by the Communist Party of the Soviet Union (CPSU) and by the other communist parties of Eastern Europe was neutral. In April 1977 the Polish news agency PAP reported the formation of the APK in favorable terms. Both the VPK and the APK were invited to the sixtieth anniversary celebration of the Russian Revolution held in Moscow in November 1977. The VPK protested the invitation extended the APK and claimed that to invite the "small sectarian group" violated the principles of interparty relations approved at the East Berlin conference of European communist parties, held in June 1976. In an interview during the anniversary celebrations in Moscow, APK Chairman Hagel stated that "our party is pursuing Marxist-Leninist principles in a far better way and is holding high the banner of proletarian internationalism. The CPSU does not, however, show any preference, but treats us alike . . . our delegations are of the same size." (*Dagens Nyheter,* 3 November 1977.) Following the Moscow invitation, a new conflict was reported between the two parties. It concerned an invitation extended by the VPK of northern Sweden to the Murmansk district of the CPSU to visit Sweden. The response of the CPSU was that the delegation would accept the invitation, but it desired both the VPK and the APK to act as hosts. During the visit the delegation carefully avoided criticism of either party.

During 1978 the feud between the communist parties continued, and special attention was given the human rights issue. The APK attacked Soviet dissidents in June, accusing them of being "terrorists" and "fascists." The VPK, on the other hand, severely criticized the sentencing of Rudolf Bahro in the German Democratic Republic to eight years' imprisonment and concluded: "Free and open debate, even on complicated and controversial questions, is an indispensable part of socialist democracy. If the Bahro verdict has any connection with his severe and public criticism of conditions in the GDR, it is a scandalous verdict. If that is the case, he should be set free immediately." (*Ny Dag,* 7–13 July.)

Party Internal Affairs. In January the VPK held its twenty-fifth party congress. The major goals for the immediate future were declared to be creation of a new party platform and greater participation in Swedish political life. This would require an increase in party membership to 25,000 members by 1979 and "to fully break the role as a 4–5 percent party and take at least 7–10 percent of the votes" in the September 1979 national elections (*Socialistisk Debatt,* no. 30, p. 86). In an address to the congress, Lars Werner stated it was time to campaign offensively for wage negotiations and against inflation, unemployment, and the closure of companies. Werner also called for unity of action: "These tasks can be performed only in collaboration with other sections of the organized working class and other left forces outside the party." (*Dagens Nyheter,* 5 January.) Lars Werner was reelected as party chairman, and six new members were elected to the Executive Commitee. A plan was also adopted to publish the party newspaper *Ny Dag* five days a week as opposed to its previous publication twice weekly.

Domestic Attitudes and Activities. The most important domestic event for the VPK during 1978 was the Twenty-fifth Party Congress. During the meeting new cultural and energy programs were adopted as well as a crisis program to deal with the Swedish economy. An interest in cooperation with the Social Democratic Party was also expressed: "We would welcome an initiative for discussion of those questions that a majority of Social Democrats and Communists would pursue after an election in which the nonsocialist government lost" (*Svenska Dagbladet,* 21 February). In this regard, Gunnar Ågren, VPK chairman for Stockholm, emphasized to the congress that there are two main groups on the Left that the VPK should approach: (*a*) the independent radicals to be found in labor unions, other mass organizations, and radical front organizations; and (*b*) the growing but hard-to-define group of radical Social Democrats who do not accept that party's official policy.

The VPK's energy program opposed the use of nuclear power in Sweden. An adequate energy supply can, according to the VPK, be maintained without the use of nuclear energy. The party's "anticapitalist" economic program maintains that the Swedish economy is in a deep crisis. Among the ten main points of the program are, therefore, the nationalization of heavy industry, banks, and insurance companies. Export trade should be controlled by the state, and a six-hour workday should be introduced.

In September an appeal was issued in the main ideological organ of VPK for a "socialist offensive" to be initiated during the autumn of 1978: "The political platform in which political goals are established and the importance of unity on the Left is stressed is the crisis program of the party. Under the main slogan 'Socialist Offensive,' the problems of employment, energy, prices, and rents will be raised." (*Socialistisk Debatt,* no. 34–35, p. 8.)

International Views and Positions. In January VPK Chairman Lars Werner expressed the party's position on Eurocommunism in an interview with the French newspaper *France nouvelle* as follows:

When communist parties from Western Europe and from highly industrialized capitalist countries claim to approach socialism on the basis of their respective countries' traditions and the very traditions and experience of these countries' workers' movements, instead of mechanically following existing countries' socialist experiences, then we agree with the term of Eurocommunism. We have great affinities with the French, Italian, Spanish, and Finnish communist parties when they stress the need to develop and defend democratic freedoms and rights in the transition to socialism, in regard to plurality of opinions and parties founded on the long-standing traditions of West European workers' movements. In this respect, we are Eurocommunists, even though we do not accept the Eurocommunist concept. As far as we are concerned, the issue is not the creation of a new International or of a new association of communist parties; it is the exchange and comparison of common experiences in countries whose living conditions are comparable. One needs to stress that the issue is one of working-class experiences in each country and that it is above all in respect to this very class that our responsibility is committed." (16 January.)

In June the VPK participated in a Scandinavian seminar held in Norway on "Czechoslovakia, Ten Years Later." One of the speakers at the seminar was "Listy" member Zdenek Hejzlar, who now lives in exile in Sweden. His views were published in *Socialistisk Debatt,* thereby confirming the VPK's critical position on the Soviet invasion of Czechoslovakia.

International Activities and Party Contacts. Chairman Lars Werner and Bo Hammar of the Executive Committee visited the Italian Communist Party (PCI) in October 1977. Talks were held at the PCI Directorate's headquarters. They included exchange of information and opinions regarding the situation in both countries. Later in the month a four-member delegation from the VPK, led by Deputy Chairman Eivor Marklund, visited Hungary at the invitation of the Central Committee of the Hungarian Socialist Workers' Party. There was agreement that relations between the parties were to be furthered on the basis of Marxism-Leninism and proletarian internationalism.

In June 1978 a delegation of the VPK, led by Chairman Lars Werner, visited Romania. The delegation was received by the Romanian party Secretary General Nicolai Ceauşescu. According to a statement released by the Bucharest Domestic Service, views were exchanged concerning the independent policies of Europe's communist parties: "Since communist and workers' parties are carrying out their activity in very diverse situations and circumstances determined by historical, socioeconomic, and national conditions which differ from country to country, a key prerequisite for the success of their historical missions is the creative application of scientific socialism to concrete realities prevailing in each respective country" (22 June).

Communist parties and labor parties from twenty countries were represented at the twenty-fifth VPK congress in January. Among them were delegations from the Soviet Union, Italy, and France. The communist parties of Czechoslovakia and Bulgaria were not represented.

Other Leftist Groups — Rival Communist Organizations. There are a large number of extreme leftist groups in Sweden. The Maoists are represented by two parties. The SKP, as noted earlier, grew out of the KFML. Its membership is secret but believed to be around 2,000. According to reports in 1978, the circulation of the party newspaper has been falling, and party membership declining. There also seems to be factional fighting within the SKP. The SKP has a newly created anti-Soviet front organization, Socialistiska Östeuropagruppen (Socialist East Europe Group). It publishes the *East European Bulletin* and reports on dissident activities in Eastern Europe. The SKP has also published a number of anti-Soviet pamphlets.

In September the SKP and its Norwegian counterpart issued a joint communiqué denouncing the Soviet Union: "The Soviet Union is the latecomer superpower, the primary source of war, and the most dangerous enemy of the world's people. . . . Therefore, the front against the superpowers should first of all direct its spearhead at Soviet social-imperialism. . . . The Soviet Union is using Cuban mercenaries to serve its social-imperialist expansion and backs Vietnam against Kampuchea." (New China News Agency, Peking, 15 September.)

The Communist Party of Marxist-Leninist Revolutionaries (Kommunistiska Partiet Marxist-Leninisterna [revolutionärerna]; KPML[r]) grew out of the association of the same name which broke away from the KFML in 1970. Party Chairman is Frank Baude. The main strength of the party is in Sweden's second largest city, Göteborg. The party is active in almost 90 localities throughout the country. Membership is believed to be around 1,500, and the party does not seem to lack financial support. (It owns a large administrative building in the center of Göteborg.)

The Swedish section of the Fourth International is called the Communist Workers' League (Kommunistiska Arbetareförbundet; KAF). The KAF plays an insignificant role in Sweden's political life.

Publications. *Ny Dag* (New day) is the VPK central organ published twice weekly. The main organ of the APK is the daily newspaper *Norrskensflamman* (Northern lights), published in Luleå. The theoretical organ of the VPK is *Socialistisk Debatt* (Socialist debate). The SKP central organ is *Gnistan* (Spark). KPLM(r) publishes *Proletären* (Proletarian) twice weekly. The Trotskyite KAF publishes *Internationalen* (International).

Ängelholm, Sweden   Bertil Häggman

Switzerland

The oldest and most pro-Soviet communist party in Switzerland is the Swiss Labor Party (Partei der Arbeit; PdA/Parti du travail; PdT/Partito del Lavoro; PdL). The PdA was established as the Swiss Communist Party on 5—6 March 1921, was banned during the Second World War on 27 November 1940, and was reconstituted under its present name on 14 October 1944.

Three other communist organizations also warrant mention, although their influence on Swiss political life is marginal. The Marxist Revolutionary League (Ligue marxiste révolutionnaire; LMR/Marxistische Revolutionäre Liga/ MRL; here referred to as LMR) was established in 1969 by dissident members of the PdA in Geneva and Lausanne. The LMR is a member of the Trotskyite Fourth International and advocates violent overthrow of the Swiss political and economic system. The Swiss Progressive Organizations (Progressive Organisationen, Schweiz; POCH), founded in 1972, is composed primarily of younger intellectuals. Eduard Hafner is general secretary, and party headquarters are located in Bern. A pro-Chinese group, the Communist Party of Switzerland/Marxist-Leninist (CPS/ML), was organized in 1972. (See *YICA, 1977*, pp. 234—38, *1976*, pp. 222—27, and *1973*, pp. 227—29.) The Second Congress of the CPS/ML was held in December 1977 and was highlighted by the adoption of the first formal party program. The communiqué issued at the conclusion of the congress stressed that the party program "demonstrates the progress of the party in the application of Marxism-Leninism to the situation of our country, in the analysis of the domestic and international situation and in the strategy and tactics of the revolutionary struggle for socialism and a red Switzerland." The communiqué noted further that the CPS/ML "considers the struggle against revisionism as its principal ideological task . . . We see in the two superpowers, the Soviet Union and the U.S.A., the principal enemies of our revolution." (*Peking Review*, 20 January.)

PdA membership numbers about 5,000. In the most recent elections in 1975, the PdA captured 2.5 percent of the vote and elected 5 members to the 200-member Swiss parliament. The party's greatest strength is in the cantons of Basel, Vaud, Neuchâtel, and Geneva. The population of Switzerland is 6,500,000.

Leadership and Organization. At the Eleventh Congress of the PdA, held in Geneva at the Palace of Exhibitions from 13—15 May (the Tenth Congress was held in Basel in June 1974), a major change in leadership occurred. Longtime party chairman and Geneva lawyer, Jean Vincent, was elected honorary chairman at the age of 72. Political Bureau member and secretary of the party's Central Committee, Armand Magnin (Geneva; age 58), was elected general secretary of the PdA—a title especially created to replace that of "chairman."

Since the PdA has decreased in size over the past twenty years, party headquarters have been shifted from Zurich to Geneva, where the party enjoys its greatest strength. The party's new general secretary is supported by two German-speaking members, Hansjorg Hofer and Karl Odermatt, who serve as permanent secretaries of the Central Committee. The composition of the Political Bureau remains virtually unchanged; it has no woman members. The Central Committee, composed of members from Switzerland's German-speaking, French-speaking, and Italian-speaking cantons, elected only two new members, Claude Contini (Vaud) and Benjamin Degen (Basel). (*Neue Zürcher Zeitung*, 17 May.)

The congress, attended by more than 150 delegates representing all cantonal party organizations, discussed a major problem confronting the PdA—the advanced age of the leading cadres. The age group between 45 and 55 years is weakly represented, a consequence of the losses the party suffered in the 1950s following the denunciation of Stalin. The party has, in addition, not recovered from the losses suffered in 1968—69 when almost 100 younger intellectuals founded the LMR (ibid.). A number of them had been expected to succeed the present party leadership (ibid., 12 April).

Domestic Attitudes and Activities. The Eleventh Congress was the highlight of the year. A number of domestic issues were discussed, and the congress devoted considerable time to discussing the main directions of domestic activity for the "forthcoming" period. It was declared that the major focus would be on the "crisis" afflicting "the capitalist world . . . which is not only economic, but also ideological, political and moral, [and which] continually intensifies, bringing with it a general deterioration of the living conditions of workers and the entire people." (Tass, 13 May.)

Thus, the congress, open to members of the press for the first time, advocated increased support for the environmental protection movement, urged extension of holiday periods, supported a referendum opposing the federal security police, recommended the employment of stronger efforts to gain influence among the country's trade unions, and opposed "infringements of civil rights." The congress further proclaimed the need to renew efforts to attract younger intellectuals to the party, although it did note that the Swiss government was widely supported by the Swiss populace and that therefore, this task would be difficult. (*Neue Zürcher Zeitung*, 17 May.) The congress also singled out the issue of unemployment as a major problem. In early April at a cantonal meeting in Geneva, the PdA had given special emphasis to the claim that "in less than three years approximately 340,000 jobs have been lost. As a result, 210,000 foreign workers were forced to leave Switzerland. Major capital is trying to put the whole weight of the consequences of the economic crisis onto the shoulders of the working people." (*Pravda*, 2 April.)

While the PdA is playing a decreasing role in Swiss political life, it is also seeking to strengthen its position in Geneva, where it is strongest. Since 1973 the PdA has pursued an election campaign alliance with the Socialist Party in Geneva, although the party congress did accuse the Socialist Party of "tactical electioneering, party egoism and anticommunism." It is expected, however, that prior to the Geneva municipal elections in spring 1979, the PdA will seek to form a common platform and favor joint tickets with the Socialist Party in the hope of winning the uncertain liberal seat on the capital's five-member Administrative Council. There is also one Christian Democratic Party seat that the PdA maintains could be captured. Should this occur, it is possible that the office of mayor would be filled by the one PdA member already elected to the Administrative Council, Roger Dafflon, in accordance with the seniority principle. (*Neue Zürcher Zeitung*, 12 April.)

International Views and Positions, and Party Contacts. The Eleventh Congress was attended by representatives of fourteen foreign communist parties, including a delegation from the Communist Party of the Soviet Union (CPSU) led by a secretary of the CPSU Central Committee, Ivan Kapitonov. In his address to the congress, Kapitonov stressed common goals shared by all communist parties as well as the necessity for individual communist parties to pursue specific goals in their respective ways:

> The international situation . . . is at present characterized, first of all, by the confrontation between the forces of progress and peace and the forces of reaction and war. It is distinguished also by an unprecedented diversity of social development in different areas of the globe, in different countries. The communist

parties take all this into account and, naturally, this largely determines the concrete character and specific features in the activities of each of them.

Along with this, the communist and workers' parties have great common needs. And the most paramount and urgent among them is to arrest the arms race, to preserve and strengthen peace on earth. . . .

Of particular importance . . . is to keep in view all the time that reliable beacon which is called Marxism-Leninism, the general law-bound regularities and principles of revolutionary action and the socialist reshaping of the world, the life-giving ideas of proletarian internationalism. (Tass, Moscow, in English, 14 May.)

In the course of the congress, the CPSU delegation met with new PdA General Secretary Armand Magnin, Honorary Chairman Jean Vincent, member of the Political Bureau and Central Committee Secretary Hansjorg Hofer, and Political Bureau member Jakob Lechleiter. The CPSU representatives emphasized that the party would "continue to do everything possible to strengthen fraternal relations" with the PdA. (*Pravda*, 14 May.)

The foreign policy views of the PdA were presented in detail at the party's congress, and particular emphasis was given the importance of Switzerland's traditional neutrality. Notably the PdA does not support "Eurocommunism," but it did stress the necessity for "the special national road to socialism" and the need for the "independence of each party." (*Neue Zürcher Zeitung*, 17 May.) It remained, however, strongly pro-Soviet in orientation. In the congress's resolution, "Peace, Security, and Disarmament," the PdA endorsed détente and peaceful coexistence and the ten principles of peace and security set forth in the Final Act of the Helsinki Conference on Security and Cooperation in Europe:

The [PdA] will continue actively to further the struggle of the masses to:
—stop the arms race, particularly the nuclear arms race;
—ban the neutron bomb, a weapon of mass destruction;
—speed up the disarmament talks and the systematic reduction of military budgets;
—liquidate foreign bases and dissolve military blocs.

Our aims likewise presuppose:
—refusal to employ, or threat to employ nuclear weapons;
—a ban on all nuclear testing;
—removal of all nuclear weaponry from the territories of foreign states, stopping their dissemination and creating nuclear-free zones.

We are also working to:
—ban and destroy bacteriological and chemical weapons of mass annihilation and all means of using the climate for military purposes;
—mobilize all forces in Europe and the United Nations to fulfill these goals in Europe and on other continents. (*IB*, no. 14, 31 July.)

In the course of the year PdA representatives made a number of visits abroad and received a number of foreign delegations as well. In addition to the contacts which took place at the party's congress, a delegation of the party's Central Committee visited East Berlin in February. The delegation, headed by then Political Bureau member and Central Committee Secretary Armand Magnin, exchanged views with a delegation headed by Political Bureau member Herman Axen of the Socialist Unity Party (SED) of the German Democratic Republic. The PdA delegation also visited Leipzig and Dresden and included Political Bureau member Hansjorg Hofer and Central Committee member Jean Steiger. At the conclusion of the visit, the representatives of both parties declared their support for "the disarmament proposals submitted by the Soviet Union and the other socialist states . . .

[and] emphatically condemned the inhuman plans of U.S. imperialism to manufacture the neutron bomb." (Allgemeiner Deutscher Nachrichtendienst, East Berlin, 12 February.)

Publications. The PdA publishes newspapers in three languages: *Voix ouvrière*, Geneva, daily (7,000—8,000 circulation), in French; *Vorwärts*, Basel, weekly (6,000 circulation), in German; *Il Lavoratore*, Lugano, weekly (3,000 circulation), in Italian.

La Brèche is the twice-monthly French-language publication of the LMR, published in Lausanne. The monthly organ of the CPS/ML is *Octobre*, published in French. The POCH publishes in German the weeklies *POCH-Zeitung* (circulation 5,000—6,000) and *Emanzipation*, for "progressive" women's groups. It also publishes the weekly *Tribune ouvrière*, the French counterpart of the *POCH-Zeitung*, and *Positionen*, a periodical in German for university groups.

Hoover Institution   Dennis L. Bark
Stanford University

Turkey

During 1978 a new government came to power in Turkey, promising concerted efforts to deal with the major problems confronting the country, particularly political polarization and violence, a deepening crisis in foreign-exchange balances, and strained relations with the United States and Greece concerning the status of military cooperation and the future of the island republic of Cyprus. By the end of the year, the government's record in dealing with these problems was, at best, mixed. The status of the fragmented political Left, both inside and outside the country, remained basically unchanged throughout the year as well.

The new government, headed by Bulent Ecevit, leader of the Republican People's Party (RPP), came to power in January. Ecevit received the support of a bare majority of the parliament, including his own party (roughly 214 seats), some dozen independents who had deserted the Justice Party (JP) during the preceding months (most of them became ministers in the new cabinet), and two political fragments (the Reliance Party |RP| with two seats and the Democratic Party |DP| with one seat). The Central Committee of the clandestine Communist Party of Turkey (TCP) greeted the new government with skepticism, noting that it included such ardent anticommunists as Faruk Sukan (DP) and Turhan Feyzioglu (RP) as well as "figures acting as the Justice Party's Trojan horse" and that it was dominated by "the rightward leaning top leadership of the Republican People's Party." In short, said the TCP, "instead of uniting the forces that fought the reactionary fascist coalition [i.e., the National Front coalition of the Justice Party, National Salvation Party, and National Action Party] with the workers, the working people and all progressive forces, the leaders of the Republican People's Party embarked on a road of cooperation with the collaborationist bourgeoisie and internal reaction in the interests of the imperialistic circles." The party advocated withdrawing from NATO, CENTO, and the European Community, dismantling of foreign military bases, withdrawing troops from Cyprus, purging fascist elements and influences from the government and society, annulling the long-standing ban on the communist party, ensuring labor's right to organize a general strike, guaranteeing equal rights to the Kurds, nationalizing "imperialist and collaborationist capital" as well as heavy industry, and land reform. "A government that refuses to implement such a program cannot count on a long life," warned the TCP. (*WMR, Information Bulletin*, No. 8, 30 April.)

A noteworthy development on the fragmented extreme Left was the formation of a Workers' and Peasants' Party late in January 1978. The new party, which made official application for legal recognition by the government, was headed by Dogu Perincek, a former university assistant who had led an extreme Revolutionary Proletarian Enlightenment group within the umbrella Dev Genc organization in the mid-1970s (see Landau, *Radical Politics in Modern Turkey*). At a press conference on 30 January, Perincek described his party's program as opposing American imperialism and Soviet social imperialism as well as terrorism, as favoring stronger ties with Greece and Third World countries, and as ultimately aiming at the creation of a classless society, Radio Moscow denounced the new group as Maoist and anti-Soviet, accused it of covert alliance with extreme rightists, and denied that it was a true workers' and peasants' party.

The Ecevit government had some success in dealing with foreign-exchange problems and in improving relations with the United States. It devalued the Turkish currency rather drastically, imposed strict import regulations, and managed to secure support from the International Monetary Fund. It also persuaded the Carter administration to undertake a determined effort to bring an end to the congressionally imposed arms embargo. This effort ultimately succeeded and was shortly followed by Turkish agreement to reopen four U.S. military bases which had been closed in retaliation against the embargo. All this occurred in the wake of threats by Ecevit to seek arms supplies elsewhere, a much publicized visit to Moscow on his part, and an offer by the Soviet Union to supply the desired arms. Although all parties denied any connection, the Ecevit government also undertook a new initiative regarding Cyprus; but by the year's end this had not yet led to a resumption of active negotiations with the Greek community on the island.

The new government was less successful in dealing with political violence. The scope and frequency of incidents continued to increase. Official estimates indicated that approximately 300 had been killed, 3,000 wounded, and close to 6,000 detained during 1977. Early in May of 1978, the minister of the interior announced that during the first four months of the year, 159 had been killed; of these, 51 were believed to be right-wing extremists and 73 left-wingers; 83 were students whose average age was 22. Clearly, however, violent attacks and confrontations were spreading beyond the universities, in particular to smaller towns and cities in the East. Among the more serious incidents was a bomb attack on 17 April which killed the mayor of the provincial capital of Malatya and several members of his family. This was followed by three days of rioting involving confrontations between Turks and Kurds and between Shi'ite and Sunni Muslims. Another incident suggested that military authorities were now also becoming targets of terrorism. In June, a military judge was the victim of a bomb attack. Press reports attributed this incident to the Turkish Workers' and Peasants' Liberation Army (TIKKO), which had been the subject of the judge's investigatory activities. At about the same time press reports described a major clash among Kurdish groups in the far southeastern province of Hakkari. Hundreds were allegedly killed or wounded. These press reports cited a series of alleged links between the warring Kurdish factions and Savak, the American CIA, Armenian and Greek elements in Europe and the United States, and TIKKO within Turkey (*Milliyet,* 24 April; *Hurriyet,* 11 and 18 June; *Pulse,* 12, 14 and 19 June).

Since it is admittedly difficult to verify much of this information, the accuracy of these reports must remain in doubt. It seems certain, however, that political violence in Turkey in 1978 spread from large cities and university campuses to outlying provincial towns, particularly in the remote and undeveloped East, and that the flames of conflict have been fanned by traditional ethnic and religious animosities. Given these conditions, it is impossible to say what role ideological factors or leftist (or for that matter, rightist) groups are playing in this type of conflict.

Under these circumstances, even the best efforts of the Ecevit government to adopt a strict line on political terrorism and to enforce the law with an even hand may well be insufficient. That such efforts are underway is clear—witness complaints by former Deputy Prime Minister Alparslan Turkes that his followers have been subjected by government officials to torture; charges by the exiled TCP that the stability of governmental leadership depends on collaborationist bourgeois elements; and press reports that the RPP engaged in large-scale purges of its own membership in order to weed out possible communist infiltrators from its ranks. At the end of the year, it was impossible to predict the outcome of Turkey's volatile political processes.

University of Illinois at
Chicago Circle   Frank Tachau

ASIA AND THE PACIFIC

Afghanistan

On 27 April tanks appeared in the streets of Kabul and began firing on the presidential palace. After two days of fighting, the government of Mohammed Daoud was overthrown in a coup engineered by Colonel Abdul Qadir, leader of the Armed Forces Revolutionary Council. Almost immediately the military turned the reins of government over to civilians. A new government was created called the Revolutionary Council of the Democratic Republic of Afghanistan. This government is controlled by the People's Democratic Party (PDP) and includes only a few military people.

The government is headed by Nur Mohammed Taraki, who is not only prime minister but also president and chairman of the PDP. Taraki is 61 and comes from a peasant-herdsman background. He learned to read and write at home and received primary education in Afghanistan. Later he went to India where he worked and furthered his education, particularly in the area of literature and language. In the mid-1940s he was involved in a youth movement concerned with literary and social issues and participated in the publication of a newspaper called *Burning Coals*. In 1952 Taraki found employment in the Press Department of the government. As a result of his work there, he was appointed press attaché in the Ministry of Information and Broadcasting and assigned to the Afghanistan embassy in Washington. It was here that Taraki's revolutionary career may be considered to have begun formally. He published a letter in an American newspaper critical of the regime of King Zahir Shah. This ended his connection with the government, and he returned to Afghanistan to open a private translation service. (*FBIS*, 23 May.) See Biographies, p. 452.

At the time of his dismissal as press attaché, Taraki founded the People's Democratic Party. In 1967 he began publishing a weekly newspaper called *Khalq* (Masses). During the same year, the PDP split into two factions, one called Khalq under Taraki, and the other called Parcham (flag) under Aqbar Qabir. Parcham is considered to have been more radically leftist and pro-Soviet than the Taraki branch of the party. The two factions reunited in 1977. (*NYT*, 2 May.) Qabir's murder on 17 April was one of the incidents leading to the coup. The PDP has claimed a membership of approximately 50,000 in a population of some 14,381,600.

A power struggle within the PDP has resulted in the purge of several prominent Parcham members. Babrak Karmal, number two man in the regime, has been sent to Prague as ambassador. In August Abdul Qabir, leader of the coup and later defense minister, was arrested and accused of plotting to overthrow the new government. Taraki added the defense portfolio to his list of official duties. Several Parcham members have been removed from office, and others have been jailed. The officer corps of the military has been extensively purged as the government seeks to ensure the complete loyalty of the army. The number of Soviet military advisers has increased and includes some who are now in command positions (*Daily Telegraph*, 7 August).

There is not now and never has been an official communist party in Afghanistan (*NYT*, 20 May). On 9 June Taraki denied that his is a communist party. He claimed that the People's Democratic Party respects the principles of Islam, the positive customs and traditions of the people, and the principle of private property and has a nonaligned foreign policy. His government is willing to accept foreign aid from any country so long as there are no strings attached. He even denied his party is Marxist: "We consider ourselves to be radical reformers and progressive democrats. Marxist-Leninism is not a formula which we apply or claim." (*FBIS*, 9 June.)

But there is some evidence from the past to suggest that Taraki and his associates are at least not hostile toward communism. In November 1976 Babrak Karmal, then general secretary of the People's Democratic Party, in a letter to the Socialist Party of Australia said: "We hope that the leaderships of the fraternal communist and workers parties will avail themselves of all existing possibilities to defend the democratic working class movement in Afghanistan and its vanguard the PDP. . . . No difficulty can break the spirit and will of the communists in our party." (*Socialist*, 24 November 1976.) As recently as 9 April Taraki himself said in a letter to the Communist Party of India on the occasion of its Eleventh Party Congress: "May the unity of international communism and workers movement flourish on the basis of Marxism-Leninism and proletarian internationalism!" (*New Age*, 9 April.)

In a speech on 9 May, Prime Minister Taraki outlined the basic objectives of the new regime. Among the more important of these and first on the list is land reform. This includes both reclamation of barren or submarginal land and an effort to "abolish antiquated relations." Another significant goal, and an indication of the ideology of the new regime, is a commitment to consolidate the state sector of the national economy. There is concern about economic development and the need to expand internal and external trade. In the area of social reforms, the government is committed to the realization of equality of the sexes in all social, political, and cultural fields. Previous Afghan governments dating back to the early part of the twentieth century have been committed to a similar goal but, because of the rigid and highly traditional nature of Afghan social customs, have enjoyed relatively little success. There is also a commitment to establish educational opportunities for the million or so nomads in Afghanistan, a group that the new government feels has been ignored in the past. Educational facilities in general are to be expanded to combat illiteracy (Afghanistan has one of the highest rates in the world). (*FBIS*, 10 May.)

In order to achieve these goals, the PDP is confronted with the need to mobilize social resources. Afghanistan has virtually no modern political and economic organizations. Such organizations will have to be created, and it is probable that new organizational efforts will come into conflict with traditional, tribal, and family loyalties. The government thus far has undertaken three major organizational projects. First, "democratic youth groups" are being formed throughout the country. These groups are intended to educate school-age populations in the ideology and skills necessary for major social changes. Secondly, participation in trade unions is now being encouraged, and the government is making an effort to organize the working population, small as it is, into some sort of trade union system. Thirdly, in order to retain control over the new youth groups and trade unions, the PDP is undertaking a campaign to establish party committees in all settlements in the country, even in the remote parts that are largely inaccessible except on foot. (*FBIS*, 22 May; *Intercontinental Press*, 17 July.)

In July the Taraki government suppressed an alleged conspiracy in which Minister of Defense Abdul Quadir had been implicated. Taraki then assured the army that he would crush both the "lunatics" of the Right and the Left, and that the People's Democratic Party would remain in full control of the army (*Keesing's Contemporary Archives*, 20 October, p. 29264).

International Contacts. The Soviet Union has favored close relations with Afghanistan since 1919 when Lenin offered military assistance to King Amanullah. In 1921 a treaty of friendship was signed between the two countries. A pact of neutrality and nonaggression was approved in 1931 and renewed in 1975. Since World War II the Soviets have provided Afghanistan with a variety of aid projects and have developed an especially close relationship with the military. In 1956 the Afghans obtained military equipment from Czechoslovakia; later the Soviet Union assumed full responsibility for all Afghan military requirements. The Afghan military is modest in size and power but, as the 27 April coup indicates, is sufficient for political purposes. Various estimates of the size of the army range from 70,000 to 100,000. Heavy equipment consists of approximately 800 tanks of the T34 and T54−55 variety, which are antiquated by modern standards and are similar to the ones sent to Peking in the late 1950s. The air force, which played a role in the April coup, consists of 200 aircraft, including Mig 17s and a few Mig 21s. There are helicopters, reconnaissance, and transport aircraft as well, including a number of ancient biplanes. (*Daily Telegraph*, 8 May.)

The Russians have given $1.5 billion in aid to Afghanistan. Apart from military assistance, this has included funds for major highways, agricultural development, purchase of natural gas, technical education, and waterpower projects. One of the most dramatic Russian-sponsored efforts is the construction of the world's highest tunnel. Afghanistan is divided by the imposing mountains of the Hindu Kush, which makes movement from the northern to the southern part of the country extremely difficult even during the summer season. The Russians have constructed an all-weather road and the Salang Pass tunnel. It is now possible to travel back and forth across the Hindu Kush during all seasons. This tunnel, which is three kilometers long and is at 11,000 feet, required a prodigious effort. The Russians took ten years and spent $600 million to build it. (*Washington Post*, 8 May.)

Since the coup there has been a flood of agreements between the Soviet Union and Afghanistan. Hydroelectric-power development projects that had been in the planning stages prior to the coup have now been formalized and accelerated. The Russians are sponsoring construction of transmission lines and are building new substations in the southern part of the country near the Pakistan border. An agreement has been reached for technical and economic feasibility studies of the rich Aynak copper deposits in central Afghanistan. This agreement includes exploration, mining, and smelting. An agreement was reached concerning a major agricultural development project in Nangarhar province in central Afghanistan. The Soviets have agreed to provide the supplies, materials, and equipment necessary for exploration and development of oil and gas in the northern part of the country. They are to provide training facilities for Afghan political cadres at various Soviet educational establishments. Russian is to be taught as a second language to all students at Kabul University and at other schools around the country. The two countries reached agreement on the equivalency of degrees, thus expediting the employment of graduates of Soviet educational institutions (*FBIS*, 18 May).

A trade protocol calls for increased volume of trade. The Soviets agreed to send machines, equipment, petrochemicals, ferrous metals, cars, cement, sugar, borax, and cultural and consumer goods. In return the Afghans will send the Soviet Union natural gas, cotton, wool, dried fruit, citrus fruit, carpet articles, rawhides, and olives. There is to be radio and television cooperation, including the broad exchange of materials devoted to the lives of Soviet and Afghan people. The Soviets undertook a five-year commitment to provide assistance in the area of higher education. Two months after the coup, the Soviets had agreed to 25 specific assistance projects (*FBIS*, 24 May).

On 6 December 1978 Afghanistan signed a 20-year treaty of friendship and cooperation with the Soviet Union. This treaty pledged the Soviet Union to economic cooperation with Afghanistan, but it also extended to military cooperation. Mr. Taraki is reported to have publicly stated his country's willingness to develop friendly relations with China.

Other communist-bloc countries have offered assistance. The East Germans agreed to construct a 200-bed hospital and housing for 600 personnel in Kunduz in northern Afghanistan. They also agreed to build a facility to house a blood bank with a capacity of 4,000 to 6,000 liters in Kabul. Czechoslovakia and Poland have also offered help. Middle Eastern countries that are politically sympathetic to the new government have extended credit. Iraq and Libya were among the first to come forward. (*FBIS*, 28 June.)

University of Montana   Louis D. Hayes

Australia

The Communist Party of Australia (CPA), founded in October 1920, attained its highest membership when it reached 23,000. By 1978 this figure had dropped to about 1,500−2,000, and the party had split twice. The pro-Peking Communist Party of Australia (Marxist-Leninist)−CPA(M-L)−was established in 1964 as a response to CPA rejection of China in the Sino-Soviet dispute. It is pro-Peking and numbers 200−300 members. The Socialist Party of Australia (SPA) was formed in 1971 after the CPA had adopted a critical attitude toward the Soviet Union. It is pro-Moscow and has a current membership of about 650. The population of Australia is 14,227,000.

The CPA is headed by Laurie Carmichael as president, Bernie Taft as vice-president, and Mavis Robertson, Eric Aarons, and Joe Palmada as national secretaries. These and five others constitute the National Executive (see *YICA, 1977*, pp. 244−45). E. F. "Ted" Hill is chairman of the CPA(M-L); A. E. Bull and Clarrie O'Shea are the vice-chairmen. Pat Clancy is president of the SPA, and Peter Symon is general secretary.

Other left-wing groups include the Socialist Workers' League (SWL), the Spartacist League (SL), the Socialist Workers' Party (SWP), and the International Socialists (IS). The SWP is the Australian section of the Trotskyite Fourth International and publishes a weekly, *Direct Action*. The SL, based in Melbourne, has a monthly, *Australian Spartacist*, and attacks all other radical groups for not being sufficiently revolutionary. The SWL is a breakaway Trotskyite group which follows the line of an Englishman, Gerry Healey, and prints the fortnightly *Workers' News*. It has recently adopted the cause of Libya, rejecting Cuba as capitalist. Members of the group are active in various trade union and workers' educational groups and associations. The IS publishes a monthly, *The Battler*, and disagrees with the Fourth International's analysis of the USSR as "state capitalist."

Closely associated with the CPA(M−L) is the Australian Independence Movement (AIM), which has a glossy monthly, *The Independent Australian*, laying claim to the Australian folk tradition, and a weekly newspaper called *Independent Voice*. The AIM came out of the Student Worker Alliance, which, in turn, was formed by pro-Peking factions in the old CPA Eureka Youth League. These smaller groupings are not significant in numbers, popular appeal, or political effect. Their strongest support comes from student and trade union movements. There also exists a breakaway Maoist organization under the leadership of two former student activists from the 1960s, Albert Langer and Harry Van Moorst. Langer's group has attacked the present leadership in the People's Republic of China and the CPA(M-L) (*National Times*, 29 August).

All these movements within the far left spectrum dispose of considerable money for propaganda against uranium mining (in the case of the CPA[M-L] this occurs despite the fact that Peking might favor Australian nuclear independence as antihegemonistic), federalism, Western security organizations, Australia's relations with the West and with noncommunist regimes in Asia, capitalism, multinationals, and the like, but in support of women's, gay and national liberation, and nationalization of the economy and of the labor force.

During the year the CPA has been in the process of drafting a new party program, with planned approval late in the year (*Tribune*, 30 August). During a meeting in Sydney in January, the CPA's National Committee announced that the next party congress would be held in June 1979 and its major task will be the "construction of a general party program" (ibid., 1 February).

Communists and Labor Unions. According to a leading official of both the New South Wales Trades and Labor Council (NSW TLC) and of the Australian Labour Party (ALP), "approximately 25 percent of the membership of the NSW TLC is directly communist, belonging to one or other of the parties, with another 30−40 percent being under either CPA or SPA voting control." Therefore, states this official, "there is a constant and exhausting battle to prevent the council from becoming completely dominated by various Communists and their left-wing ALP allies, some of whom are secret Communists, others being former Communists who resigned after Hungary [1956] and Czechoslovakia [1968] but never lost their basic ideological commitments." (Interview with author, August.)

At the June conference of the New South Wales branch of the ALP, State Secretary John Ducker repudiated Senator Gietzelt's call for a union of the Left, spoke out strongly against the activities of the socialist Left/communist ambience, and opposed in the strongest possible terms plans for nationalization of banks and major industries. Ducker's address was accepted by 382 votes to 300, thus indicating the voting strength of the left-wing bloc in what is generally perceived as being the strongest state for right-wing labor in Australia. (For the CPA's analysis, see *Tribune*, 7 June.)

The Maoist unions, although remaining under the control of the New South Wales' Builders' Labourers' Federation, are not an important factor in labor politics. They are strongest in Victoria throughout the building, maritime, and waterside unions. Political battles, which sometimes become physical, are being waged for control among CPA, SPA, and CPA(M-L) union officials. In union terms, the CPA is the strongest in New South Wales, although there it is losing ground to the SPA and the socialist Left. This is partly because the CPA has become more issue-oriented than the other parties, but principally it is due to the fact that over the years it has lost the majority of its most effective industrial unionists and organizers to either the SPA, CPA(M-L), or ALP (ibid.).

The leader of the Labour opposition in Parliament, Ron Davies, attacked the activities of Maoist and other non-ALP union leaders and described them as "scabs." He said that such "people never help the ALP, often hinder it, and in fact have a vested interest in seeing the party out of office." (*Daily News*, Perth, 10 May.)

The president of the pro-Moscow SPA has warned Communists not to split the ALP and thereby endanger the successful "united front" strategy being conducted jointly by Communists and the socialist Left of the ALP (*News Weekly*, 1 July).

Attitudes toward Indochina, the USSR, and the People's Republic of China. In January the CPA wrote to the communist parties of both Cambodia and Vietnam, expressing deep regret at the border conflict and proposing comradely negotiations (*Tribune*, 18 January). Eric Aarons wrote as follows:

> Generations of the Australian left and peace movements have a special affection for Vietnam and Cambodia and their roles in defeating aggressive war in Indo-China. The present conflict saddens socialists and national liberation supporters while heartening those who favour Western domination of Asia. . . . China's latest public statements . . . offer a glimmer of hope. . . . The Soviet Union has already supported Vietnam's offer of negotiations. (Ibid.)

As the year progressed and the Cambodian-Vietnamese war intensified, along with the propaganda barrage between the Chinese and the Soviet communist parties, the CPA position (though still in search of reconciliation) increasingly favored the Vietnamese and Russian positions (ibid., 19 July, 27 September, and 11 November). The constant expressions of regret over world communist disunity is in accord with the CPA line of seeking a united front among all leftist forces in the Southeast Asian region, including Australia, regarding interparty relations.

The CPA's growing uncertainty about the USSR was revealed in an article applauding the victory of the socialist Left at the November conference of the ALP Victoria branch. A *Tribune* correspondent welcomed the defeat of a motion condemning Soviet repression of dissenters in these terms:

> The rejection of the motion of condemnation of the Soviet Union was an interesting aspect of the conference. The red-baiting tactics [of the proposers] made many delegates feel that they would not join the present anti-Soviet chorus initiated in the West. (Ibid., 22 November.)

Earlier, however, the CPA had condemned the trials in Moscow of Shcharansky and Ginzburg, asserting that they "represent a further concerted move against minority and dissenting opinions" (ibid., 19 July).

On the other hand, the CPA(M-L) opposes just about everything concerning the USSR whenever the latter's statements and activities come into conflict with the Chinese line. Its publications warn Australians of the Soviet "imperialist" threat (*Vanguard*, 21 September and 19 October). Cuba, Vietnam, and Angola are cited as bastions for expansionist activities of Soviet social-imperialism (ibid., 26 October). However, in areas where the Chinese and Soviet interests are not immediately in conflict, the CPA(M-L) still supports the USSR against Western "imperial" interests (ibid., 20 July).

Although the CPA has called for the rehabilitation by Soviet authorities of Nikolai Bukharin (*Tribune*, 18 October), it does not condemn the means being employed in Cambodia, Vietnam, and Angola to build socialism, involving as they do in each case the imprisonment and execution of local "Bukharins." In this regard, it is especially noteworthy that the CPA has not objected to the reported execution and imprisonment of former Viet Cong and NLF officials in Vietnam. The CPA has condemned the majority of South Vietnamese refugees as worthless beings escaping from paradise, bringing their evil intentions with them to Australia: "Who are these refugees? They are ex-police, high-ranking soldiers and spies. . . . Others don't like the rigours of a new regime which actually makes them work for a living . . . sharing their lot with ordinary Vietnamese. They come to Australia with diamonds hidden on their bodies." (Ibid., 5 April.)

Perhaps the most sensational revelation about the past activities of Australian Communists was the recent admission by a former CPA activist that his comrades had rigged ballots in union elections. This, according to the former activist, has occurred most blatantly in the Iron Workers' Federation, which had been controlled by the CPA through one of its officials, Ernie Thornton (who had bestowed on himself the title "Stalin of Newcastle"), until the Communists lost control to a Labour moderate, Laurie Short, after he had been physically beaten and successfully appealed for a court-controlled ballot (*Bulletin*, 12 May).

Publications. The CPA publishes a weekly newspaper, *Tribune*, a monthly theoretical journal, *The Australian Left Review*, and an occasional internal publication, *Praxis*. The SPA has a fortnightly newspaper, *The Socialist*, and a monthly digest, *Survey*. The CPA(M-L) prints a weekly newspaper, *Vanguard*, and a monthly theoretical journal, *The Australian Communist.* During the year the CPA published *Communist Party Documents of the Seventies* and *A New Course for Australia.*

University of Western Australia   Patrick J. O'Brien

Bangladesh

Following the attempted coup in Dacca in early October 1977 President Ziaur Rahman announced that the Bangladesh Communist Party (BCP), the largest communist party in the country and pro-Moscow, and the Socialist National Party (JSD), a left wing socialist party, were banned along with several other left wing and even right wing parties. President Ziaur accused these parties of "terrorism, foreign infiltration and conspiracy." Shortly after, he amended the Political Parties Regulation of 1976 in order to "dissolve" these parties. The pro-Peking Communist Party of Bangladesh (Marxist-Leninist) (CBP-ML) was not affected by the ban as its leader, Mohammad Toaha, supported the president. In December China formally recognized the CBP-ML, marking the first time that Peking had formally recognized any communist party on the sub-continent since Lin Piao's death. China continued to maintain ties with the CPB-ML, but gave a higher priority to its official contacts with Dacca because of the minor role of the CPB-ML in Bangladesh politics.

Party Activities. In April Moni Singh (chairman) and Mohammed Farhad (secretary general) of the pro-Moscow BCP were released from jail. The government gave no reason for their release, but it coincided with the departure of the foreign secretary for Moscow and the announcement of presidential elections in June. The BCP, however, was not legalized. In June the National People's Party, at a plenum meeting of the Central Organization Committee, called for the lifting of restrictions on the activities of political parties and specifically asked for cancellation of the ban on the BCP. In September a campaign began to collect signatures for legalizing the BCP, and in early December the BCP and other opposition parties were given legal status. The Central Committee of the BCP, however, issued a statement that the party would not participate in the 27 January 1979 parliamentary elections, because the atmosphere was not favorable for the holding of free elections (*FBIS*, 11 December). Subsequently, the government announced that martial law was being suspended and promised to release all political prisoners, actions which apparently were needed to persuade fifteen opposition parties to participate in the elections, but it was not clear if the BCP was among these (*San Francisco Chronicle*, 25 December).

In April the JSD was legalized, but apparently not before a number of its leaders were imprisoned and some of them, according to some reports, executed. Amnesty International reported that a number of the top leaders of the JSD who had already been tried were being tried again. Another source reported that most of the 10,000 to 15,000 political prisoners in Bangladesh were members of the JSD, the largest leftist party in the country prior to 1977. (*Intercontinental Press*, 1 May.)

These trials might have been a reaction to U.S. human rights campaigns and specific American efforts to get the Bangladesh government to account for its political prisoners. Or they can be interpreted as part of the government's preparations for its up-coming elections.

In March President Ziaur announced the formation of a new political party, apparently to expand his political power base from the army and to pave the way for an end to martial law. Ziaur's party, the Nationalist Democratic Party (BNDP) was to be formed from other political parties already in existence. Soon six parties joined the BNDP: the pro-Peking National Awami Party led by Mashiur Rahman, the Bangladesh Muslim League, led by Khan Abdus Sabur Khan, the leftist United Party, led by Kazi Zafar Ahmed, the rightist Labor Party of Moulana Matin and the Tapshili Federation led by Rashoraj Mandol. The CPB-ML did not join, apparently because it did not want to sacrifice its independent status. Furthermore, the National Awami Party had good relations with China.

General Ataul Ghani Osmani, who prepared to run against Ziaur after the announcement in April of elections in June, formed the Democratic Unity Front of four existing parties: the Awami League headed by Abdul Malek Unil, the pro-Moscow National Awami Party of Muzaffar Ahmed, the Jatiya Janata Party of General Osman, the Gonoazadi League of Moulana A. R. Tarkabagish, and the People's League of Dr. Alim al-Razee. Nine other lesser candidates also ran in the election. President Ziaur received 78 percent of the vote, thus strengthening his position and probably paving the way for a return to civilian rule with Ziaur remaining in power.

The election encouraged some splinter communist and other leftist groups that had been operating underground to emerge, some under new names. These included the Eastern Region Communist Party, Bangladesh Biplabi (Revolutionary) Communist Party, Bangladesh Communist Party—Leninist, and the East Bengal Proletariat Party.

The CPB-ML and two other parties, Jatiya Gonomukti Union Jagmui), and the Bangladesh National Awami Party, subsequently coalesced under the People's Democratic Front (PDF). The "front," which was announced on August 19, stated that its purpose was to "unite all patriotic democratic forces to launch a democratic movement in the country" (*FBIS*, 28 August). The PDF subsequently demanded the annulment of the U.S.-Bangladesh peace corps agreement, the India-Bangladesh friendship treaty, and the Berubara agreement. It also demanded the release of political prisoners and the withdrawal of all cases and warrants of arrest for political leaders and workers, the repeal of the constitution enacted during Sheikh Mujib's rule, and the formation of a national government to struggle against imperialism, expansionism and hegemonism. Referring to President Ziaur's call for unity, they stated that they would not support the president or join his party.

Relations with Foreign Countries. The CPB-ML maintained ties with Peking, but China dealt with the government of Bangladesh primarily on an official government-to-government basis and has maintained good relations with the military regime of President Ziaur. Ziaur visited China during the year, and China provided economic aid to Bangladesh. It is uncertain at this time how the merger of the CPB-ML with the PDF will influence relations with China. It is unlikely, however, to have much impact on the already friendly ties between Dacca and Peking.

Early in the year the Soviet Union complained that the BCP was banned and that its leader, Moni Singh, was in jail. Bangladesh's relations with Moscow have been proper but not especially cordial.

Southwestern at Memphis   John F. Copper

Burma

The Burma Communist Party (BCP) dates back its origins to 15 August 1939. At the end of March 1948, the "White Flag" Communists, always the most important communist group in Burma, went underground and have been fighting the central government until today. Reliable figures on the membership of the BCP are not available. The party probably has between 10,000 and 12,000 men under arms. Besides the BCP there is an "Arakan Communist Party" with only a few followers; it allegedly operates in the mountains of Arakan State, western Burma.

Leadership and Organization. No changes in the top ranks of the BCP occurred in 1978. Thakin Ba Thein Tin (probably residing in Peking) continues as chairman and Thakin Pe Tint as vice-chairman; (for Politburo and Central Committee members see *YICA, 1977*, p. 254). The government did not claim the death of any BCP leader except "Major-General" Saw Mun Na, chief of staff of the BCP-allied "Karenni National Progressive Party," who was killed on 16 April ten miles east of Ke-hsi Mansam while traveling "to the northeastern border area to establish contacts with the BCP" (*The Guardian*, Rangoon, 29 April).

Party Internal Affairs and Alliances. In his 1978 New Year speech Chairman Thakin Ba Thein Tin continued to praise the successes of the BCP without mentioning interparty struggles and rivalries: "Our Party and revolution won numerous victories in all spheres in 1977. The Party and Army grew in size, while old bases were strengthened and new ones established. More allied forces were organized and consolidated as the Party and Army gained strength." At the same time he emphasized once more the BCP's ideological dependence on Peking by "attacking the errors of Soviet social-imperialism" (radio, Voice of the People of Burma [VPB], 3 January; *SWB*, 7 January). In its proclamation on the "30th Armed Revolution Anniversary" (28 March), the Central Committee of the BCP urged "protracted armed struggle" based on three main weapons:

> "(1) A Communist Party which is well-disciplined, equipped with the weapon of Marxism-Leninism-Mao Tse-tung thought, self-criticizing and in touch with the people; (2) a people's army under the complete leadership of the Communist Party; and (3) a united front comprising the revolutionary classes and revolutionary groups and headed by the Communist Party." (VPB, 28 March; *SWB*, 31 March.)

A radio article exhorted the members "to further consolidate and unify the ranks in rallying around the party Central Committee" (VPB, 15 August; *FBIS*, 16 August). Other articles indicated the existence of groups with differing views and called for inner-party unity. The leadership also demanded party discipline on the part of members and conformance with "the democratic centralist principles of organization: the individual is subordinate to the organization; the minority is subordinate to the majority; the lower level is subordinate to the higher level; and the entire party is subordinate to the party Central Committee" (VPB, 22 August; *FBIS*, 25 August).

Because of intraparty quarrels, the BCP could not announce any alliances with minority groups—in spite of its call that "any organization or individual that opposes imperialism and the Ne

Win-San Yu military clique and that is not against the communist party must be united with us" (VPB, 24 August; *FBIS*, 29 August). From the 1978 government press it appears that the BCP had alliances with the Kachin Independence Army (KIA); the Shan State Progressive Party (which may have changed its name to Shan State Communist Party during the year; see VPB, 16 July; *SWB*, 28 July) and its military organization, the Shan State Army (SSA); the Shan State Nationalities Liberation Organization (SSNLO; see *YICA, 1978*, p. 220); and with the Kayah New Land Party (probably identical with the previously mentioned Karenni National Progressive Party). The KIA's strength is estimated at 1,500 men, the SSA's at 2,500 men (*Far Eastern Economic Review*, 28 April, p. 26).

Domestic Activities. As in the past, the BCP's underground activities against the Rangoon government took the form of armed struggle (see below). The party's "Voice of the People of Burma" (VPB) criticized the economic situation of the country, particularly the rice situation. The BCP predicted an insufficient harvest due to drought and warned that the government would try to purchase more paddy for export to benefit the ruling "military clique," thus aggravating the rice shortage inside Burma (VPB, 14 May; *FBIS*, 16 May).

To promote confusion and fear, the BCP also warned that the peasants "are usually robbed of all their paddy including the amount stored for their consumption . . ." (VPB, 22 January; *FBIS*, 26 January).

To support its struggle, the BCP called for the workers to "grasp the armed struggle as the key link and combine it with other forms of struggle to fight" (VPB, 30 April; *FBIS*, 3 May). The BCP also tried to embarrass the government by alluding to several high treason cases and to the purges in the Central Committee of the ruling "Burma Socialist Programme Party" (BSPP). The BCP propaganda also included allegations that "the government mercenaries had been robbing, oppressing and murdering the people" (VPB, 25 July; *SWB*, 28 July).

In the anti-rebel mass rallies arranged by the government, the speakers complained that "the BCP traitors also robbed the people and burnt down monasteries, schools, markets and dwellings" (*The Guardian*, 12 April). A more detailed account of the "atrocities and destructive activities of the BCP insurgents" was given at a rally in Kengtung. At the Kengtung rally the BCP's recruitment practices were described: "they kidnapped children from towns and sold them over to another country" (*The Guardian*, 1 March).

Armed Struggle. The tactics of the BCP can be described best in the party's own words:

> The people's army adopts and practices the following guideline: Make wiping out the enemy's strength our main objective. Do not make holding or seizing a city or place our main objective. Holding or seizing a city or place is the outcome of wiping out the enemy's strength. After destroying the enemy's strength, our forces work according to prearranged plans. After the objective is achieved according to plan, the people's army moves out systematically to a new place, taking along with it the prisoners, weapons and supplies seized in the battle. Much later, only after the people's army has moved, would the military government send reinforcements into the battle site. The new mercenaries would be drunk and wide-eyed, looking around everywhere in fear (VPB, 14 April; *FBIS*, 19 April).

In the northeast communist guerrilla activities declined after October 1977, probably due to a regional shift in fighting. Kunlong, also known as Northern Wa-State, must be regarded as a communist stronghold where government troops hardly ever leave the towns. In February and March there were major battles with BCP contingents of 1,300 and 600 men. The government claimed that "in the course of the Operation Ye Min Aung, 135 Tatmadaw [army] men gave up their lives for the country; 124 were listed as missing and 229 wounded" whereas the troops, supported by air force, "wiped out over 800 BCP rebels, 335 bodies of whom were captured by the troops" (*The*

Guardian, 27 March). The BCP, however, challenged the government's claimed losses as too low: "Actually, the number of mercenaries, including officers, crushed by the people's army in these battles totals more than 780" (VPB, 14 April; *FBIS*, 19 April) of whom 353 were killed, around 320 wounded and 108 taken prisoner (VPB, 13 April; *SWB*, 28 April). The heavy fighting even caused General Ne Win to visit Mong Hsat, Kengtung and Lashio from 17 to 23 March and hold discussions with the military commanders "on operational matters and the regional situation" (*The Guardian*, 24 March).

In all of northeastern Burma the government lost during the period from 1 January to 30 June 1978, according to BCP reports, "a total of 170 engagements, including eight large-scale battles," altogether 1,426 soldiers of whom 693 were killed, 613 wounded, 119 taken prisoner, and 1 defected to the BCP (VPB, 9 July; *FBIS, SWB*, 12 July). This means a decrease in casualties compared to 1977 when, in the whole year, "the people and the people's army fought a total of 562 large and small battles against the enemy in northeast Burma, killing 1,318 enemy soldiers, wounding 1,995 others and capturing 78. Eight others defected to the people's side. Thus, a total of 3,399 enemy soldiers were put out of action." Two fighter planes were also shot down. (VPB, 10 January; *SWB*, 13 January.) That the situation became altogether more critical for the government may be seen from the fact that the commander of the Northeastern Military Command, Col. Min Naung, was transferred to the post of director-general of the Fire Services Department (*Botataung*, 19 May; *SWB*, 31 May).

The other combat area in the Shan State is Kengtung region, where the front line runs approximately from Mong Yawng through Mong Yang to Mong Hsu. An extension of this area is not very likely because the southern part of Kengtung district is a stronghold of some Kuomintang remnants, especially rightist Shan separatists dealing in opium. The Shans, who also hold the west bank of the Salween river, were reenforced in the spring by several Burmese rebel groups who were expelled from Thai territory. Among them was Khun Sa, a dominant figure in the opium trade, whose base had been the Hin Taek area of Mae Chan district and who supposedly has rejoined the 4,000-strong "Shan United Army" (*FEER*, 28 April and 2 June).

A further stronghold of the Burmese Communists lies in Kachin State where they are allied with the KIA. Compared to 1977, activities have increased. The most important event during 1978 was the attack at Shwegu town on 15 April "by about 300 Kachin insurgents who were forced to retreat that evening"; about ten soldiers died on each side in this fight (*Botataung*, 23 April; *FBIS*, 27 April).

The treaty with the SSNLO (*YICA, 1978*, p. 220) led to the building up of another communist area around Hsi-hseng. Control of this new area enables the BCP to encircle more and more of the central Shan State. The central Shan State has become an attractive target for the BCP, since domination of this area will allow the party to control the land supply routes to the northeastern and eastern battle grounds.

In the rest of Burma the BCP appears less active. In Mindon township 138 Chin families, "who have been helping the BCP insurgents engaged in various subversive activities in the western mountain range, surrendered without arms" (*Myanma Alin*, 23 April; *FBIS*, 28 April). Here and in other parts of Arakan, communist activities were probably restricted to the Arakan Communist Party, which still seems to be independent of the BCP.

International Views and Contacts. The close relations between the BCP and the Chinese Communist Party continued through 1978. In an article celebrating the fifty-seventh founding anniversary of the CCP, a BCP broadcast praised the "courageous and acute leadership of Comrade Hua Kuo-feng" and the new party line and stressed: "Our parties, armies and peoples have the [noblest] tradition of consistently joining hands in struggle" (VPB, 4 July; *FBIS*, 3 August).

According to the German *Frankfurter Allgemeine Zeitung* (17 January) U Saw Oo, Central Committee member of the BSPP, made it clear to journalists that Peking continues its material support of the BCP and that there is no longer any hope in Rangoon that Peking will reduce its aid to only "moral support."

Saw Oo made his remark just a few days before Teng Hsiao-ping's six-day official visit to Burma (26–31 January). President U Ne Win went out of his way to welcome the Chinese vice-premier at the airport and to see him off as well. Burmese newspaper editorials recalled Ne Win's visit to China in November 1975 and indicated that the BCP still was a stain on this friendship (Burma Broadcasting Service, 27 January; *FBIS*, 30 January). In the official speeches, however, nothing was mentioned of the BCP. The reasons for this might be the following:

China's continuing influence with the BCP gives Peking additional leverage to ensure that Ne Win does not move Burma closer to the Soviet Union. . . . Analysts also believe that China does not want to commit itself too strongly to Ne Win who is 67 and known to be in ill-health. Should anything happen to the President, with no charismatic successor waiting in the wings, Burma's fragile political balance would be shattered. The BCP, one of the largest (10,000–15,000 men) and best organized insurgencies in Southeast Asia, could well emerge from the ensuing political chaos as a strong contender for power.

In addition, any major cutback in Chinese aid to the insurgents might prompt Moscow to fill the vacuum, creating a situation where the rebel groups would be operating with Soviet assistance along the Chinese border. Finally, due to its geo-political location, Burma is virtually compelled to have close relations with China, whatever policies Peking chooses to follow. (*FEER*, 3 March, p. 20.)

There are no indications that Teng Hsiao-ping's visit led to any cutback of Chinese support for the BCP. As in 1976 and 1977, the BCP started its offensive in the Kunlong area (see above) on 2 February. This may have been a case of "exercising power" to show BCP independence. The USSR has always pointed out that Chinese involvement in the BCP's activities was a "threat to Burma's sovereignty, independence and territorial integrity" (*Pravda*, 5 June; *FBIS*, 12 June). It even predicted the offensive (Moscow Radio, 20 January; *FBIS*, 23 January). Similar BCP reactions did not take place after the visit of a government military delegation under chief of staff and Minister of Defense General Kyaw Htin to Peking, Shanghai, and Kunming between 5 and 10 June and the visit of Foreign Minister Brigadier-General Myint Maung to Peking in September.

The government's changed attitude may be prompted by its failure to reach an accord with Peking. Teng Hsiao-ping confirmed in Singapore during his ASEAN-tour that Peking does not consider ending its support to underground communist parties in Southeast Asia. The BCP's other international contacts were evidently restricted to an exchange of greetings between the communist parties of Thailand and Malaysia on their respective anniversaries.

Publications. The only first-hand information on the BCP comes from the broadcasts of its clandestine radio station, the "Voice of the People of Burma," inaugurated on 28 March 1971 and supposedly located in southwest Yunnan Province in China.

Köln-Weiss   Klaus Fleischmann
Federal Republic of Germany

Cambodia

On the basis of refugee reports and government radio broadcasts, the ruling Khmer Communist Party (KCP) in Cambodia remained stable during 1978. (See *YICA, 1978*, p. 225, for a history of the KCP.) But the regime engaged in a severe conflict with Vietnam and mild clashes with Thailand; at the same time it tried to promote trade and other contacts with other Asian nations.

Leadership and Organization. The KCP is run by a Central Committee, which acts as the collective leadership of Cambodia. Although its membership is secret, press speculation has focused on a few individuals long active in Cambodian left-wing political circles. Saloth Sar has been variously described as chairman, secretary general, and secretary of the KCP. Pol Pot, who was named premier in April 1976, is probably a pseudonym for Saloth Sar. (The names are similar in the Khmer script. See also Biographies, p. 451.) Khieu Samphan, Ieng Sary, and Son Sen—who were named deputy premiers in August 1975—are believed to be members of the KCP Central Committee and dominant political personalities in Phnom Penh. All are in their late forties. Since 17 April 1975 Khieu Samphan has played a prominent but not preeminent role in the new regime. In the April 1976 government reshuffle, he was named head of the Presidium, replacing Prince Sihanouk as chief of state.

National Political Leadership.

State Presidium

Chairman	Khieu Samphan
First deputy chairman	So Phim
Second deputy chairman	Nhim Ros

Cambodian People's Representative Assembly, Standing Committee

Chairman	Nuon Chea
First deputy chairman	Nguon Kang
Second deputy chairman	Peou Sou

Members: Ros Nim, Sor Sean, Mey Chham, Kheng Sok, Mat Ly, Thang Si, Ros Preap

Government of Democratic Cambodia

Premier	Pol Pot
Deputy premier, foreign affairs	Ieng Sary
Deputy premier, national defense	Son Sen
Deputy premier, economy	Vorn Vet
Minister, information and propaganda	Hu Nim (purged)
Minister, public health	Thiounn Thioeunn
Minister, social affairs	Khieu Thirith (Mrs. Ieng Sary)
Minister, public works	Toch Phoeun (purged)
Minister, culture, education, and learning	Yun Yat (Mrs. Son Sen)

Auxiliary and Mass Organizations. During the 1970—75 war, refugee reports indicated that the usual mass organizations (e.g., for peasants, women, students, and Buddhist monks) were created by the KCP to rehabilitate Cambodian society. This was the central nonmilitary goal of the KCP during the war and still is of main concern after its military victory. We know little about these mass organizations in the postwar reconstruction. Many refugees have reported that their only contact with the new regime was with gun-wielding guerrillas and anonymous cadres, who lectured them on political subjects or on practical matters, such as farming.

Domestic Party Affairs. An attempted coup in May 1978 (attributed to Vietnam by Radio Phnom Penh) failed to produce any change in the top KCP leadership. However, refugees have reported a purge of mid-level KCP cadres in the western provinces. Refugees reaching Thailand are more likely to be informed about the western region than about other parts of Cambodia.

Prince Norodom Sihanouk, the former chief of state, is believed to be living in Phnom Penh under close guard by the KCP regime since he was forced to "retire" in 1976. He was last seen by the Yugoslav ambassador in early 1977. During his travels to noncommunist countries in 1978, Ieng Sary, deputy premier for foreign affairs, displayed photos of Sihanouk with members of the KCP regime, evidently to win favor with Sihanouk's admirers abroad.

On 29 December reports filtered out of Cambodia of a top official purge of cabinet officials who had opposed the nation's stringent economic and internal political programs. Although Pol Pot and Ieng Sary remained the principal leaders of the Phnom Penh government—and apparently remained in secure control, Hu Nim, minister of information and propaganda, and Toch Phoeun, public works minister, had been purged. This expulsion of top party members indicates some tension and discord within the Kampuchean regime (*San Jose Mercury*, 29 December).

International Views and Policies. Events during the past year indicate no change in party policy toward foreign states. The deputy premier for foreign affairs, Ieng Sary, showed greater visibility in meeting with foreign officials and traveling, in an obvious effort to gain support or sympathy for Cambodia in its conflict with Vietnam. For the first time since it came to power, the KCP maintained a delegation at the U.N. during the whole session of the General Assembly. Ieng Sary also had a successful visit to Tokyo. The Japanese government, reportedly at the urging of Peking, agreed to establish diplomatic relations with Cambodia (although not with a resident ambassador). Japan and Singapore now have a modest amount of trade with Cambodia, which previously traded almost exclusively with China.

Cambodia continued to receive Chinese diplomatic and military support in its conflict with Vietnam. Partly because of Chinese urging, it was expected that Thailand and Cambodia would eventually reopen their embassies in each other's capitals in early 1979. Indonesia formally exchanged recognition with Cambodia during 1979 (although there is no known plan to reopen embassies). Aside from Ieng Sary's travels, at least two other Cambodian leaders visited Peking during the year: Nuon Chea, chairman of the Standing Committee of the People's Representative Assembly, and Son Sen, deputy premier for national defense. Western diplomats believe that China has used Thailand's airspace to ship military aid to Cambodia for the expected intensification of the Khmer-Vietnamese conflict when the late-1978 rainy season ends.

In early December the Vietnamese news agency reported that an organization, the Kampuchean National Front for National Salvation, had been formed, held a congress, and elected a fourteen-member Central Committee headed by Heng Samrin. The news agency also reported that the National Front through its military arm, the Kampuchean Revolutionary Armed Forces, had as its goal the overthrow of the Pol Pot regime (*Palo Alto Times*, 4 December).

In the last week of December observers in Bangkok reported the North Vietnamese had mounted an all-out drive to overthrow the Cambodian communist government. They claimed that with the loss of Kratie, the Vietnamese 5th Division was now 100 miles northeast of the capital. Cambodia's president also accused Vietnam of a "large-scale aggressive offensive" deep into eastern Cambodia. There is now speculation that the North Vietnamese-sponsored United Front for National Salvation formed in November will proclaim Kratie its capital. Cambodian President Khieu Samphan has charged that North Vietnam is using a "huge number" of infantry, tanks, artillery and planes, and he has appealed to the United Nations and countries in Asia and elsewhere for help (*Palo Alto Times*, January 2, 1979).

Publications. Radio broadcasts by the two weak transmitters of Radio Phnom Penh are the only means the KCP has to communicate news and commentary on internal developments to the outside world—and to the Khmer people. No printed publications are known to circulate in the country. The Ministry of Information sometimes responds to requests from abroad for propaganda films and documents.

Old Dominion University   Peter A. Poole
Norfolk, Virginia

China

The Chinese Communist Party (CCP) claimed "more than 35 million" members at its Eleventh Party Congress in August 1977.

Organization and Leadership. According to the party constitution, the "highest leading body" of the CCP is the Party National Congress, which is to be convened every five years. Between congresses the Central Committee and the Politburo exercise party authority.

The Eleventh Central Committee (elected in August 1977) has 201 full members and 132 alternate members. The committee is dominated by older, experienced cadres, many of whom (76) had been purged in the Cultural Revolution, and many more of whom had been criticized at that time. The first secretaries of all 29 of China's major administrative divisions—provinces, autonomous regions, and municipalities—are full members. There is strong military presence in the committee as a whole, and this was reinforced in the Eleventh Central Committee's Politburo.

The officers, members, and alternate members of the Politburo are:

Chairman: Hua Kuo-feng

Vice-chairmen: Yeh Chien-ying, Teng Hsiao-ping
                  Li Hsien-nien, Wang Tung-hsing

                  (These five comprise the Standing Committee
                  of the Politburo.)

Members of the Politburo (22), in the order of the
number of strokes in their surnames:

Wei Kuo-ching   Wu Teh
Ulanfu   Yu Chiu-li
Fang Yi   Wang Tung-hsing
Teng Hsiao-ping   Chang Ting-fa
Yeh Chien-ying   Chen Yung-kuei
Liu Po-cheng   Chen Hsi-lien
Hsu Shih-yu   Keng Piao
Chi Teng-kuei   Nieh Jung-chen
Su Chen-Hua   Ni Chih-fu
Li Hsien-nien   Hsu Hsiang-chien
Li Teh-sheng   Peng Chung

Alternate Members of the Politburo (3), similarly listed:

Chen Mu-hua
Chao Tzu-yang
Saifudin

   Below the Central Committee and its Politburo extends a network of party committees at the provincial, special district, county, and municipal levels. A similar network exists within the PLA, from the level of the military region down to that of the regiment. According to the party constitution, primary party organizations or party branches are located in factories, mines, other enterprises, people's communes, offices, schools, shops, neighborhoods, PLA companies, and elsewhere as required.
   According to the state constitution adopted 5 March, the highest organ of state power in the PRC is the National People's Congress (NPC). The NPC is elected for a term of five years and holds one session each year, although both of these stipulations are subject to alteration. The Fifth NPC was held 24 February to 8 March 1978.

The officers and members of the Fifth NPC Standing Committee were elected on 5 March 1978. The officers are—

Chairman: Yeh Chien-ying

Vice-chairmen:
Soong Ching Ling   Chang Ting-cheng
Nieh Jung-chen   Tsai Chang
Liu Po-cheng   Teng Ying-chao
Ulanfu   Saifudin
Wu Teh   Liao Cheng-chih
Wei Kuo-ching   Chi Peng-fei
Chen Yun   Ngapo Ngawang-Jigme
Kuo Mo-jo
    (died 12 June)   Chou Chien-jen
Tan Chen-lin   Hsu Teh-heng
Li Ching-chuan   Hu Chuan-wen

Secretary-General: Chi Peng-fei (concurrently)

There are also 175 regular members of the NPC Standing Committee.

On 5 March 1978 the Fifth NPC decided on the following State Council appointments:

Premier: Hua Kuo-feng

Vice-premiers:
Teng Hsiao-ping   Chen Yung-kuei
Li Hsien-nien   Fang Yi
Hsu Hsiang-chien   Wang Chen
Chi Teng-kuei   Ku Mu
Yu Chiu-li   Kang Shih-en
Chen Hsi-lien   Chen Mu-hua
Keng Piao

Minister of Foreign Affairs: Huang Hua
Minister of National Defense: Hsu Hsiang-chien
Minister in Charge of the State Planning Commission: Yu Chiu-li
Minister in Charge of the State Economic Commission: Kang Shih-en
Minister in Charge of the State Capital Construction Commission: Ku Mu
Minister in Charge of the State Scientific and Technological Commission: Fang Yi
Minister in Charge of the State Nationalities Affairs Commission: Yang Ching-jen
Minister of Public Security: Chao Tsang-pi
Minister of Civil Affairs: Cheng Tzu-hua
Minister of Foreign Trade: Li Chiang
Minister of Economic Relations with Foreign Countries: Chen Mu-hua
Minister of Agriculture and Forestry: Yang Li-kung
Minister of Metallurgical Industry: Tang Ke
Minister of the First Ministry of Machine-Building: Chou Tzu-chien

Minister of the Second Ministry of Machine-Building: Liu Wei

Minister of the Third Ministry of Machine-Building: Lu Tung

Minister of the Fourth Ministry of Machine-Building: Wang Cheng (subsequently died,
   replaced by Chien Min, *NCNA*, 18 August)

Minister of the Fifth Ministry of Machine-Building: Chang Chen

Minister of the Sixth Ministry of Machine-Building: Chai Shu-fan

Minister of the Seventh Ministry of Machine-Building: Sung Jen-chiung

Minister of Coal Industry: Hsiao Han

Minister of Petroleum Industry: Sung Chen-ming

Minister of Chemical Industry: Sun Ching-wen

Minister of Water Conservancy and Power: Chien Cheng-ying

Minister of Textile Industry: Chien Chih-kuang

Minister of Light Industry: Liang Ling-kuang

Minister of Railways: Tuan Chun-yi

Minister of Communications: Yeh Fei

Minister of Posts and Telecommunications: Chung Fu-hsiang

Minister of Finance: Chang Ching-fu

President of the People's Bank of China: Li Pao-hua

Minister of Commerce: Wang Lei (subsequently "relieved of post," replaced by Yao Yi-lin,
   NCNA, 18 August)

Director of the All-China Federation of Supply and Marketing Cooperatives: Chen Kuo-tung

Minister of Culture: Huang Chen

Minister of Education: Liu Hsi-yao

Minister of Public Health: Chiang Yi-chen

Minister in Charge of the State Physical Culture and Sports Commission: Wang Meng

According to the 1978 state constitution, the people's congresses and revolutionary committees
in the communes are organizations of political power at the grass-roots level and are also leading
organs of the collective economy. Local revolutionary committees at various levels are the executive
organs of local people's congresses at the corresponding levels, and they are also local organs of state
administration. The local people's congresses elect and may recall members of revolutionary committees
at the corresponding levels.

The Supreme People's Court is the highest judicial organ. Its president, reelected at the Fifth
NPC, is Chiang Hua.

The Chief Procurator of the Supreme People's Procuratorate is Huang Huo-ching, also elected at
the Fifth NPC. The Procuratorate was reestablished by the Fifth NPC in March, after having been
abolished by the Fourth NPC in January 1975.

The Fifth National Committee of the People's Political Consultative Congress (CPPCC) held its
first session concurrently with the Fifth NPC in February-March. This was the first plenary session of
the CPPCC since the first session of the Fourth CPPCC National Committee in December 1964. Teng
Hsiao-ping was executive chairman of the February-March meeting (*Peking Review*, 3 March). Article
10 of the CPPCC 1978 constitution spells out the tasks of the organization:

1. Organize and encourage the patriotic democratic parties, people's organizations, and people from all
walks of life to study hard, on a voluntary basis, Marxism-Leninism—Mao Tse-tung thought, current affairs,
and politics and, through various feasible ways and in connection with practice, learn from the workers,
peasants, and soldiers, carry out criticism and self-criticism, and remould their ideology.

2. Hold report meetings and forums, organize visits and tours for investigation and study so as to gather and supply information on the actual situation, give advisory opinions or suggestions, assist the state organs in publicizing and implementing policies and in improving their work.

3. Conduct activities in the political, economic, cultural, educational, scientific, and technological fields in coordination with the departments concerned and extensively solicit the people's opinions and spot talented people for the benefit of national construction. Put into practice the policy of letting a hundred flowers blossom and a hundred schools of thought contend so as to facilitate the thriving of socialist culture and the progress of science.

4. Collect, collate, and edit materials for the writing of books on such subjects as modern Chinese history and history of the Chinese revolution.

5. Carry out work in connection with the liberation of Taiwan.

6. Study international affairs, propagate and implement the government's foreign policy, and in accordance with a unified arrangement, engage in activities for the development of the international united front.

7. Treat seriously the letters the people send in and the complaints they make when they call.

The CPPCC is organized into a National Committee (The Fifth National Committee has 1,988 members, two-thirds more than did the Fourth National Committee), which holds plenary sessions and elects its Standing Committee. The CPPCC also has local committees at the provincial, autonomous region, municipal, and other levels (ibid., 24 March).

The People's Liberation Army (PLA), which includes the Chinese navy and air force, is over 3.9 million strong. According to the 1978 state constitution, the command of this military organization continues to be the responsibility of the chairman of the CCP—Hua Kuo-feng. The chief of the general staff is Teng Hsiao-ping. The new defense minister is Hsu Hsiang-chien. The PLA remains influential in CCP affairs, as suggested by its heavy presence in the Central Committee and Politburo. It is apparent that the years of military austerity under the late Mao Tse-tung are soon to be changed. The PLA is at present professionalizing itself and divesting itself of the "people's army" image it had recultivated since the early 1960s. Plans are underfoot to modernize its weaponry. Several Chinese military delegations continued to examine possible foreign sources of arms supply during 1978, but decisions on major purchases have been delayed for the most part. It is believed that a debate continues among the Chinese leadership on the matter. The dominant line seems to be that China with its limited resources must first establish an adequate general industrial base, but it is expected that the PLA will be provided for in its turn. Meanwhile the Chinese remain anxious. In May deputy chief of staff Wu Hsiu-chuan told Japanese military specialists that "China is at least 20 years behind the Americans and the Soviets in weaponry" (*Los Angeles Times*, 11 June).

China has also begun to accelerate the training and arming of its huge militia, which may consist of between 60 million to 100 million persons. The 1978 state constitution specifically called for strengthening PLA control over the militia. Both of these developments underscore the decision to reform and to make properly controlled military use of the militia rather than to dismantle it out of fear that it may be manipulated as an independent political force, as was allegedly attempted by radical elements in 1975—76. The militia ostensibly is still seen to have a role to play in maintaining civil order. (Washington Post Service, 9 June.)

Mass organizations have played an important role in the organizational life of China, although they have for certain periods of time fallen into desuetude. Such was the case during the Great Proletarian Cultural Revolution. Following a period of resurgence which began just before the Tenth Party Congress in 1973, they again declined along with the fall of the "Gang of Four" in 1976. However, in 1978 they have once again been reactivated. All three of the major mass organizations held congresses late in the year. The All-China Women's Federation, founded in 1949, held its Fourth National

Women's Congress 8—17 September, its first since 1957. Nearly 2,000 delegates attended the congress, which adopted a new constitution for the federation and elected a new executive committee composed of 300 full and alternate members, with Kang Ke-ching (the wife of the late Chu Teh) as chairwoman. (*Peking Review*, 29 September.)

The Communist Youth League of China, which has 48 million members selected from the 300 million children of the country, held its Tenth National Congress in Peking in October. Two thousand delegates attended (NCNA, 16 October). The league, which was founded in 1922, held its last congress in 1964. This year's congress adopted a new constitution for the organization (ibid., 27 October). The Red Guard youth organization, founded during the Cultural Revolution in 1966, was formally abolished. A new charter was adopted for the Chinese Young Pioneers organization. The age limit for Young Pioneers was set at seven to fourteen instead of the nine to fifteen previously established (ibid., 28 October). Han Ying, a member of the CCP Central Committee, was elected first secretary of the Tenth Central Committee of the league at its first meeting (ibid., 28 October).

The All-China Federation of Trade Unions held its Ninth National Trade Union Congress in Peking on 11—21 October. It elected the new Ninth Executive Committee, composed of 278 members, and adopted a new trade union constitution (ibid., 21 October). Ni Chih-fu, a former bench worker and now a member of the Politburo, was elected president at the first meeting of the new Executive Committee (ibid., 23 October).

Domestic Party Affairs. The year 1978 was marked by several important large-scale meetings of party, state, military, and mass organizations, as well as of various groupings of intellectuals. It was a year for the election of new officers for state and mass organizations and for the adoption of new organizational charters, most prominent of which is the new state constitution. The theme of modernizing China quickly was repeatedly reaffirmed, and plans to that end were devised and refined. Teng Hsiao-ping continued to even scores with old opponents.

The second plenary session of the Eleventh Central Committee met 18—23 February in order to complete preparations for the convocation of both the Fifth NPC and the concurrent session of the Fifth National Committee of the CPPCC. The preparations included approval of all agenda items which were to be submitted to the two impending major meetings.

The 3,460 deputies of the Fifth NPC met in Peking from 26 February to 5 March. A preliminary meeting was held on 25 February, presided over by Soong Ching Ling (Madame Sun Yat-sen), who was vice-chairperson of the Fourth NPC's Standing Committee. The preliminary meeting elected the Presidium and the secretary general of the first session of the Fifth NPC and endorsed the agenda to be followed. Twenty-three executive chairmen of the Presidium were elected, including Hua Kuo-feng and the four CCP vice-chairmen.

The Fifth NPC was formally opened by Yeh Chien-ying; it was declared closed at the completion of its business by Teng Hsiao-ping. During its meetings it adopted a new state constitution; passed a resolution on the report on the work of the government (delivered by Hua Kuo-feng); elected Yeh Chien-ying chairman of the NPC's Standing Committee, along with vice-chairmen, the secretary general, and members of that body; appointed Hua Kuo-feng—on the proposal of the CCP's Central Committee—as premier of the State Council; elected the president of the Supreme People's Court and the chief procurator of the Supreme People's Procuratorate; decided—on the proposal of the premier—the other leading members of the State Council; appointed Kuo Mo-jo (who subsequently died on 12 June) as president of the Chinese Academy of Sciences and Hu Chiao-mu as president of the Chinese Academy of Social Sciences; and adopted new lyrics for the national anthem.

Premier Hua Kuo-feng delivered the lengthy 3½-hour report on the work of the government entitled "Unite and Strive to Build a Modern Powerful Socialist Country!" on 26 February. The report was divided into six parts: (*a*) the struggle over the first three years and the general task for the new period; (*b*) carry through to the end the struggle to expose and criticize the Gang of Four; (*c*) speed up socialist economic construction; (*d*) develop socialist science, education, and culture; (*e*) consolidate our political power and strengthen the great unity of the people of all nationalities; and (*f*) the international situation and China's foreign policy.

Hua disclosed that the revolutionary committees which had been established during the Cultural Revolution were to be abolished in schools, factories, and communes and at the provincial level, although they would be retained at the local government level. He mentioned some of the goals of the ten-year economic plan, which is to cover the years 1976–85 and which now incorporates a revision of the earlier 1976–80 Fifth Five-year Plan. China will strive to raise farm output at an average rate of 4 to 5 percent and industrial output at a rate of 10 percent. Grain production is to reach 400 million tons, while steel output is to almost triple to 60 million tons. (The unofficial estimate figure for 1977's harvest was 275 million tons, and 1977's steel output is estimated at 23 million tons.)

Premier Hua claimed that "sabotage and interference in 1974–76" by the radicals resulted in a loss of 100 billion yuan (U.S. $60 billion) in industrial output. He announced that China plans to build 120 large industrial complexes, including ten iron and steel plants, nine nonferrous metals centers, eight coal mines, ten oil and gas fields, 30 power stations, six main-line railroads, and five ports. These are to create fourteen "fairly strong and fairly rationally located industrial areas." The rate of population grown (which currently is thought to be about 1.6 percent) is to be reduced to less than 1 percent per year within a period of three years. China is to mechanize 85 percent of the major processes of farmwork by 1985; this goal supersedes the earlier target of 70 percent mechanization by 1980. Also, cultivated land will expand to an average of 0.16 acre per rural resident. This compares with the current estimated cultivated area of 33 million hectares and 700 million peasants. Six major economic regions—apparently similar to the administrative system abolished in 1954—are to be developed by 1985. Factory workers and managers are to receive gradual wage increases if the production plan is fulfilled, and 90 percent of the peasants are to receive larger incomes if harvests are normal. Hua affirmed that agriculture will continue to be the foundation of the economy, but he indicated that more consumer goods are to be produced and that more attention must be given to foreign trade. In education, the premier said that by 1985 eight years of schooling should be made universal for rural children and ten years for urban children. He foresaw that in the "wake of the new upsurge in economic construction a new upsurge of construction in the cultural sphere will follow" and acknowledged that it was important that the abilities of intellectuals be given "full scope" in order to accelerate the development of science, education, and other cultural undertakings. (*Peking Review*, 10 March; *China Record*, March.)

Yeh Chien-ying delivered to the Fifth NPC the "Report on the Revision of the Constitution." The new state constitution of 1978 was adopted by the Fifth NPC on 5 March. Its Preamble defines the general task in the "new period"—"to persevere in continuing the revolution under the dictatorship of the proletariat, carry forward the three great revolutionary movements of class struggle, the struggle for production and scientific experiment, and make China a great and powerful socialist country with modern agriculture, industry, national defense, and science and technology by the end of the century." Thus, the constitution itself expresses the goal of the "four modernizations." The Preamble also reaffirms the objective to "consolidate and expand the revolutionary united front," which is so prominently manifested currently.

There are a number of additions and deletions in the newly changed constitution, which is about twice as long as the 1975 constitution which it supplants, and a number of provisions in it are restored from the 1954 constitution. Among the notable additions are the following: In Article 7 it is now stipulated that a production brigade may become the basic accounting unit when its conditions are ripe.

Article 8 now declares that "the state prohibits any person from using any means whatsoever to disrupt the economic order of the society." Article 10 stipulates that "the policy of combining moral encouragement with material reward" is applied. Article 14 includes the slogan "letting a hundred flowers blossom and a hundred schools of thought contend," stating that this is to be applied to state policy. Article 18 now adds the category "newborn bourgeois elements" to the list of elements to be punished. Article 28 gives deputies to the NPC "the right to address inquiries to the State Council, the Supreme People's Court, the Supreme People's Procuratorate, and the ministries and commissions of the State Council, which are all under obligation to answer." The new constitution restores the function of representatives of the masses serving as assessors (members of a panel of judges) in the people's courts (Article 41). Also restored are the people's procuratorates as the organs with authority to ensure compliance with the constitution. The previous constitution had delegated this power to the public security organs. Article 47 stipulates: "No citizen may be arrested except by decision of a people's court or with the sanction of a people's procuratorate, and the arrest must be made by a public security organ." Article 41 restores an earlier stipulation that an accused person has the right to a defense, and that all cases, except those involving special circumstances, are to be heard in public. In general, the fundamental rights and duties of citizens are spelled out in much greater detail than in the previous constitution.

A National Science Conference, the first of its kind, was held 18–31 March and was attended by almost 6,000 representatives. To emphasize the theme of the conference, a nuclear device was detonated just three days before it was convened. Teng Hsiao-ping gave the opening address, declaring that the realizations of the "four modernizations" depends upon the mastery of modern science and technology. The aim of the conference was to mobilize the entire CCP and the entire country to attach importance to science and technology, draw up plans, commend advanced units and individuals, and study ways and means to accelerate the development of science and technology. He noted that since science and technology are productive forces, persons engaged in these essential pursuits are to be considered workers, thus blurring somewhat the distinction between manual and mental labor but taking pressure off teachers. (*Peking Review*, 24 March.) Vice-premier Fang Yi reported on an ambitious "Draft Outline National Plan for the Development of Science and Technology, 1978–85" and acknowledged that China still lagged fifteen to twenty years behind the developed world in many scientific areas and "more still in some others." Hence the goal is to reach by 1985 advanced world levels of the 1970s. To facilitate this, the number of scientific researchers will be increased to 800,000, a number of up-to-date scientific experiment centers are to be built, and a nationwide system of research is to be completed. Priority is to be given to agriculture, energy, materials, electronic computers, lasers, space, high-energy physics, and genetic engineering. Among the measures to be implemented for realizing this program is the strengthening of international academic exchange programs. (Ibid., 7 April.)

Hua Kuo-feng's speech to the science conference on 24 March appeared to take issue with three points made by Teng Hsiao-ping. Teng had sanctioned the training of an elite group of scientists and educators, had indicated that scientists and technicians should be given even more than than the five-sixths of worktime now guaranteed free from political meetings and other nonscientific obligations, and held that more autonomy should be given to scientists in running their laboratories. Hua, on the other hand, warned against elitism, emphasized the importance of politics, and said that science and technology should not be "left to a few people in research institutions or universities." In spite of these differences, both leaders agreed on the need for rapid modernization, including the need for studying foreign scientific advances and the purchase of some foreign technology. (Ibid., 31 March; *Washington Post*, 31 March.)

On 22 April, 6,000 persons attended the opening of a National Conference on Educational Work. The conferees, who met until 16 May, heard major reports by Teng Hsiao-ping, Fang Yi, and Liu Hsi-

yao. In his address, Teng Hsiao-ping said that China could not meet its goal to become a modern industrial power by the end of the century unless strict standards are imposed in schools and rigid discipline
is enforced. The speech appeared to challenge yet further the late Mao Tse-tung's views on education
and many of the experiments of the revolution in education in the decade following 1966. Teng asserted that the main task of students is to study and that examinations are as needed in schools as quality
control is in factories. Teng said that the political and social status of teachers had to be raised and that
they are to command respect. To this end, students were urged to respect their teachers, and com-
mendations and rewards are to be extended "with wide publicity to outstanding educational workers."
The wage scale of teachers (initially primary and secondary teachers) is to be studied, and "particularly
outstanding teachers may be designated as teachers of a special grade." Teng noted that because of
the "limited economic strength of the country, we cannot bring about a very marked improvement in
the material life of teachers and other schoolworkers for the time being, but we must actively create
the conditions that can bring this about." (*Peking Review*, 5 May.) A draft eight-year National Education
Program announced principles of (*a*) revolutionizing education by making education serve proletarian
politics and combining education with productive labor; (*b*) developing education in conformance with
general economic development in a planned, proportionate way; (*c*) modernizing teaching content and
teaching materials—including the use of television, radio, and newly compiled textbooks—to conform to
the needs of developing science and technology; and (*d*) (but primarily) raising the quality of education
and particularly attaching great importance to higher education (*China Exchange Newsletter*, June/August).

The Second National Petroleum and Chemical Industries Conference on Learning from Teaching
in Industry, attended by 4,300 conferees including 721 heroes and model workers, was held in Peking
in May (*FBIS*, 26 May).

An important All-Army Political Work Conference met in Peking from 27 April to June 6 and was
addressed by Hua Kuo-feng, Yeh Chien-ying, and Teng Hsiao-ping. Teng used the occasion to ex-
pound "Mao's concept of seeking truth from the facts" and enjoined his listeners "to proceed from
reality and integrate theory with practice." (*Peking Review*, 23 June.)

The largest conference on finance and trade since 1949 was held from 20 June to 9 July in Peking.
The more than 5,000 delegates heard speeches by Hua Kuo-feng, Li Hsien-nien, and Yu Chiu-li. (Ibid.,
28 July.)

On 18 May it was disclosed that the many thousands of persons who had been labeled "rightists"
twenty years previously were now rehabilitated, and the term "rightist" itself was reportedly banned
(*FBIS*, 19 May).

On 1 July, the fifty-seventh anniversary of the founding of the CCP, Chinese newspapers printed
the first official publication of a speech made by Mao Tse-tung on 30 January 1962 at an Enlarged
Working Conference convened by the Central Committee. The speech extolled democratic practices
and contained some self-criticism (text in *Peking Review*, 7 July). Such publication served more than
one purpose, but one of these appears to accord with a trend throughout the year to diminish by
degrees the late chairman's stature, although many of his achievements continue to be admired.
Nevertheless, the current public reevaluation of the Cultural Revolution, although it has not yet specified Mao's crucial role in it, has raised many indirect criticisms that are obvious to the general Chinese
audience (*NYT*, 16 May). Mao's personality cult has similarly been openly criticized (*Christian
Science Monitor*, 11 October).

The All-China Federation of Literary and Art Circles held an enlarged meeting of its national
committee after a twelve-year interruption in its work (*Peking Review*, 11 August). It was attended by
340 well-known writers, actors and actresses, and artists and critics.

As a follow-up to the renewed emphasis on higher education, it was announced in September that
twenty institutes of higher learning which earlier had been forced to close down or to merge by Lin
Piao and the Gang of Four have been reopened and that 44 new institutes of higher learning have been

established. The People's University of China in Peking, which had been established in 1950 and closed in 1970, has now been reopened. (Ibid., 15 September.)

National Day (the twenty-ninth since 1949) on 1 October was not celebrated this year with specially arranged activities in public parks. However, at a reception in Peking on the previous evening, Chairman Hua issued a call to speed up China's socialist modernization program, saying: "We must further emancipate our minds, be bolder, devise more measures and quicken our steps" (ibid., 6 October).

By October Teng Hsiao-ping appeared to be consolidating his position of strength within the political leadership, and he continued to deal with those who had incurred his enmity. After many months of sporadic wall poster criticism, most recently attacking alleged inefficient management of the city of Peking's services and high food prices, Wu Teh was finally removed as mayor of the capital city. Wu had incurred Teng's wrath for his role in putting down the Tien An Men demonstrations in 1976 and for having participated in the anti-Teng campaign which followed. Apparently, however, Wu Teh has retained his position in the Politburo. Earlier in October another Teng opponent, Tseng Shao-shan, who had been first party secretary of Liaoning province, was also removed from his post. (Time-Life News Service, Hong Kong, 11 October.) The new mayor of Peking is Lin Hu-chia, a planner who had been a popular mayor of Tientsin for a few months and before that, in 1977, a member of the Shanghai administration. (*Far Eastern Economic Review*, 20 October.)

The Peking Municipal Committee's decision to call the Tien An Men incident of April 1976 a "completely revolutionary action" apparently triggered a lively wall-poster campaign in November. This campaign, probably orchestrated by supporters of Teng Hsiao-ping, made new criticisms and raised many significant questions. There were denunciations of the Cultural Revolution, pointed comments about Chairman Mao's role in it, and outspoken charges against party vice-chairman Wang Tung-hsing. Intriguing questions also were raised about electoral processes and human rights. By late November large groups of Chinese held impromptu street discussion sessions and Chinese queried foreigners on a range of fascinating topics. This lively activity ceased suddenly on 1 December when a central document was circulated warning that if a state of confusion arose it would have adverse international implications for China's economic growth. Specifically, Chinese were cautioned not to discuss the wall posters with visiting foreigners, and this appears to have been complied with immediately and universally (author's personal observations in Peking).

Concurrently with the wall-poster campaign there began in mid-November a central leadership meeting either of the Politburo or a working conference of the Central Committee. This meeting, lasting for many days, was probably preparatory to the convening of the Third Plenum of the Eleventh Central Committee, which many observers expected by the end of the year. Economic matters were apparently discussed, and time was also taken to rehabilitate more old cadres including Peng Teh-huai and Tao Chu, both of whom are now deceased, and 61 others who had been declared renegades during the Cultural Revolution. Among the latter was prominent economist Po I-po. By year's end there was talk that former Peking mayor Peng Chen and even Liu Shao-chi, the principal victim of the Cultural Revolution, might eventually be rehabilitated. These developments, coupled with an earlier report that Cultural Revolution student leaders, Nieh Yuan-tze and Kuai Ta-fu, along with three others, had been executed (George Biannic, AFP, Peking, 16 November), showed how dramatically verdicts have been reversed since the death of Mao.

On 23 December 1978 Hsinhua press agency reported decisions made in Peking at a five-day session of the party's Central Committee. The party pledged to devote itself largely to economic development beginning next year and expanded its ruling Politburo by adding four members associated with the moderate wing aligned with Teng Hsiao-ping. These members are Chen Yun, a top economic administrator of the 1950s, named to be deputy chairman of the party and member of the Politburo's Standing Committee; Teng Ying-chao, Chou En-lai's widow; Hu Yao-pang, a former youth leader purged during the Cultural Revolution and now to head the Central Committee's Party Organization Department; and Wang Chen, a deputy prime minister in charge of industry. (*NYT*, 24 December.)

International Views and Positions. China's foreign relations remained very active and successful in 1978. Both Hua Kuo-feng and Teng Hsiao-ping made important trips abroad, as did various other Chinese leaders. Peking continued to receive a steady stream of important visitors and foreign delegations. Relations with the Soviet Union remained cool and perhaps further deteriorated as measured by mutually abusive rhetoric, but border talks did again resume. On the other hand, relations with Japan reached a new high following new long-term trade agreements and the ratification of the Sino-Japanese Peace and Friendship Treaty. Relations with the United States improved, particularly after successful visits to Peking by Zbigniew Brzezinski and James Schlesinger. Long smoldering differences with Vietnam suddenly erupted, bringing the two nations to the brink of war. Overall trade and academic exchange programs expanded greatly, mirroring the seriousness of Peking's intent to modernize rapidly. China's imports of technology and complete plants for the first half of 1978 were 70 percent above the same period in 1977. China's imports were 60 percent higher and her exports were 28.5 percent higher in the first six months of 1978 than the same period's figures in 1977 (*Current Scene*, August/September). Two more countries exchanged diplomatic recognition with the PRC: Oman on 25 May and Libya on 9 August. This brings the total of countries with which the PRC has formal diplomatic ties to 114. Only 21 countries continue to have diplomatic relations with Taiwan. (For a complete list, exclusive of changes made in 1977 and 1978, see *YICA, 1977*, pp. 277−78.)

Relations with the Soviet Union. Sino-Soviet relations, despite a renewed effort by the Russians in February to begin a constructive dialogue, deteriorated to a new low in 1978—at least in terms of mutually abusive rhetoric. Both sides scored diplomatic successes which were discomfiting to the other, although the Chinese diplomatic offensive appeared to be the more dramatic overall. China's fast-paced anti-Soviet diplomacy, its new no-nonsense determination to modernize quickly—with the implications this suggests for military modernization—and the Chinese shopping trips for modern Western military technology have surely caused consternation in Moscow.

Just three days before the beginning of the Fifth NPC in Peking, the Russians proposed that China and the Soviet Union begin a constructive dialogue. Tass subsequently disclosed on 20 March that on 9 March the Chinese reply had repeated unacceptable preliminary conditions (*NYT*, 20 March). On 23 March Teng Hsiao-ping confirmed the Chinese position on the Soviet proposal, saying furthermore that while war was inevitable, "the Russians can never win it because even if they occupy the whole of northeast China, including Peking, they will have occupied only 200 milion people and we will still have 700 million left." (Reported by West German parliamentarian Friedrich Zimmermann, ibid., 24 March.)

On 1 April a *Pravda* editorial accused Peking of trying to force the Russians to conduct a unilateral withdrawal of forces from the border that would leave open to Chinese invasion "a front stretching for thousands of kilometers" (*Washington Post*, 2 April). That theSoviet Union was disinclined to do so was then underscored by Soviet leader Leonid Brezhnev's several-day visit in early April to the border area, during which he watched war maneuvers in Khabarovsk.

These exchanges and the border visit by Brezhnev did not, however, deter the signing of a Sino-Soviet trade agreement on 17 April (*FBIS*, 18 April). Nor did it adversely affect the arrival in Peking on 26 April of Leonid Ilichev to renew border talks that had been suspended for fourteen months, since February 1977 (ibid., 26 April).

On 9 May Soviet frontier guards penetrated Chinese territory on the Ussuri River in a shooting incident which involved the wounding and manhandling of several Chinese citizens. The Soviet Union apologized for what it termed a "mistake" by the guards as they pursued fleeing criminals. But this explanation was severely questioned by the Chinese in a rebuttal delivered by Deputy Foreign Minister Yu Chan to Soviet ambassador U. S. Tolstikov on 17 May. (*Christian Science Monitor*, 19 May.) The incident apparently did not disrupt the border talks.

At the U.N. General Assembly's Special Session on Disarmament, Foreign Minister Huang Hua repeated the charge that the Soviet Union was the principal source of a new world war and detailed instances of worldwide Soviet military threats and expansionism. On 9 June Russian and East European guests walked out during a speech given by Teng Hsiao-ping at a dinner in Peking for the visiting president of Rwanda.

On 13 June an article by I. Aleksandrov appeared in *Pravda* (the fourth of the post-Mao period) and vehemently criticized China's foreign policy, accusing the Chinese of "intensifying war preparations" by means of "instigation, deceit, armed provocations, subversive activity, organization of 'fifth columns,' covert and overt interference in the affairs of other countries, and threats of force." On 7 July the Chinese replied in a *People's Daily* editorial asserting that the Soviet charges were groundless and that such myths as China's designs to "conquer the world" were invented "to cover up the facts of frenzied Soviet military buildup and expansion" and "are particularly funny" (*FBIS*, 17 July).

Chairman Hua Kuo-feng's trip to Romania, Yugoslavia, and Iran in August obviously upset Moscow. Hua attacked Soviet policy during talks in both Bucharest and Belgrade. Tass protested Hua's behavior (*London Times*, 18 August; *Manchester Guardian*, 26 August). This was followed by a very tough *Pravda* "observer" article on 24 August which warned that if China's leaders plunged the country into war, China would suffer mass annihilation.

During his visit to North Korea in September, Teng Hsiao-ping announced that China would not continue the 1950 Sino-Soviet Peace Treaty when it came up for renewal in 1979 (*Manchester Guardian*, 9 September).

Foreign Minister Huang Hua again denounced the Soviet Union in his address to the U.N. General Assembly in October. This elicited yet another authoritative article by I. Aleksandrov in *Pravda* claiming that China's policies were "fundamentally alien" to the rest of the world (*Christian Science Monitor*, 11 October).

Relations between the two countries were, of course, adversely affected by the conclusion of friendship treaties between China and Japan on the one hand and the Soviet Union and Vietnam on the other. Along the border—despite the resumption of border talks in April—both sides continued to build up military forces. However, it appeared unlikely that either side seriously contemplates an actual significant attack (ibid., 18 September). Furthermore, despite the mutually abusive rhetoric, the resumption of border talks in April implies the desire to achieve something significantly positive in the relationship.

Relations with the United States. The year 1978 began with the same optimistic caution that had come to characterize relations for many months as the delay in the completion of normalization of diplomatic relations continued. From January through April many prominent congressional leaders visited Peking without any progress toward normalization. Washington's decision in early May to reject the sale to China of airborne scanning equipment (which is not sold to the USSR either) was received by Peking's leaders in silence (ibid., 9 May).

But a turning point came on 16 May with the decision to reverse the ban on airborne scanning equipment. This decision was communicated to the Chinese by President Carter's national security adviser, Zbigniew Brzezinski, during his visit to Peking in late May (*NYT*, 9, 24 June).

The Brzezinski visit to China seems to have improved relations. The presidential adviser said: "The basic significance of the trip was to underline the long-term strategic nature of the United States relationship to China." Brzezinski gave Chinese leaders an unprecedented briefing on the Soviet-

American strategic arms talks and also explained in detail the contents of some secret White House documents (reportdly Presidential Review Memorandum 10 and Presidential Directive 18) on American security goals. The discussions were reportedly the most extensive consultations with the Chinese since 1971 (*NYT*, 27 May).

The improved atmosphere was further reflected in the visit to China in July by Dr. Frank Press, President Carter's science adviser. Teng Hsiao-ping described this visit as "very important." Science and Technology Minister Fang Yi said that it "opened up new prospects for Sino-American relations" (*Manchester Guardian*, 11 July). By September details were being worked out for the first six graduate students to arrive in the United States in October, and hundreds were scheduled to arrive in 1979. As many as 20,000 students are to study abroad by 1985 (*Asian Wall Street Journal*, 22 September).

Public opinion in the United States also reflected the improving atmosphere. A Harris Survey indicated that a great majority of Americans (74 to 17 percent) favored friendlier relations with the PRC. Specifically, a 66 to 25 percent majority supported full diplomatic relations with Peking. Interestingly, by 71 to 20 percent, a majority opposed the notion that the "United States work together [with China] as a force against Russia," and by 81 to 11 percent, a commanding majority opposed the "sale of U.S. electronic military defense systems" to China (*Honolulu Advertiser*, 11 September).

According to Dr. Ross Terrill, who spoke with Deputy Foreign Minister Wang Jai-jung in early October, Hua Kuo-feng has written to President Carter outlining Peking's position on normalizing relations with the United States. The letter allegedly stressed that U.S.-China relations are not a diplomatic, but a political issue. Echoing what was said during the Brzezinski visit in May, the Chinese wish the Americans to take a long-term view of the relationship, to view it politically and in strategic terms, and not just diplomatically (AP, Hong Kong, 15 October). Teng Hsiao-ping, speaking to reporters in Tokyo, also suggested patience in resolving U.S.-China normalization, saying: "We will continue prearranged talks with the U.S. government with a confident but not a hasty attitude." He also said that China might take over the island of Taiwan peacefully in the long-term future (UPI, Tokyo, 3 November).

Among the commercial arrangements pursued in 1978 was a reported agreement by China to buy three Boeing 747 jumbo jets (UPI, Tokyo, 14 August). The Ford Motor Company reportedly reached a preliminary agreement to set up an assembly plant in Shumchun, Kwangtung (UPI, Hong Kong, 14 August). In October preliminary negotiations began for the sale of a communications satellite (Los Angeles Times Service, 4 October). In November it was announced that Pan American's Intercontinental Hotels Corp. would construct several modern luxury hotels in China (ibid., 10 November). In early November the United States reversed its long-standing policy of discouraging Western arms sales to China, indicating it would no longer veto NATO members' military sales (ibid., 7 November). Following his fall visit to China, American Secretary of Energy James Schlesinger said that the United States has offered to help China mine coal and build a giant dam on the upper Yangtze River. He reached an agreement with Chinese officials for cooperating in five fields of energy development: coal, hydroelectric power, renewable energy, oil and gas, and high-energy physics. Schlesinger said that American oil companies may play a major role in developing China's petroleum resources.

In August Chai Tse-min took up his post as the new head of the Liaison Office in Washington, D.C.

Relations Elsewhere. China's relations with Japan improved remarkably in 1978. On 16 February the two countries signed a trade agreement that provides for an exchange of goods worth U.S. $20 billion over the next eight years. This significant breakthrough committed both countries to purchase specified quantities of goods within a given period of time; such a commitment had previously been avoided. The Chinese quickly apologized for a bizarre incident on 13 April in which a number of Chinese fishing boats patrolled the Tiao Yu T'ai or Senkaku Islands and displayed signs claiming China's right to these disputed islands. On 12 August in Peking both countries finally signed the long-awaited Peace and Friendship Treaty, much to the chagrin of the Soviet Union, whose ambassador in Tokyo was summoned home for consultations. The Japanese finally decided to accept the antihegemony clause which the Chinese had for so long insisted upon, although they inserted another clause stating that the treaty does not affect either country's relations with third countries. Teng Hsiao-ping went to Tokyo for the exchange of the instruments of ratification on 23 October. In September there were estimates that China would purchase about U.S. $30 billion in complete plants from Japanese businessmen. Sino-Japanese trade is expected to double in three years' time, and crude oil imports from China will increase six times in the next twelve years (Christian Science Monitor Service, Hong Kong, 18 September).

Relations with Vietnam plummeted sharply in 1978. These relations, already strained because of the dispute over the Paracel and Spratly islands, were greatly exacerbated as a consequence of the 27 March nationalization of wholesale trade in southern Vietnam. This measure had tremendous effect on the Chinese community in Vietnam, and ethnic differences and disputes quickly worsened. Many thousands of Chinese (as many as 160,000 by July according to NCNA on 17 July) fled into China, amid official Chinese charges of Vietnamese persecution. Hanoi retorted that Peking instigated dissatisfaction among Vietnam's Chinese minority in order to wreck its fragile economy. There were even armed clashes with loss of life along the border. Sino-Vietnamese tensions increased when China sided with Cambodia in its war with Vietnam. By November Vietnam claimed that China had sent 100,000 troops to Cambodia and was continuing to send men and weapons to be used against Vietnam (UPI, Bangkok, 2 November). Most alarming to China has been the Soviet Union's strengthened position vis-à-vis Vietnam. Vietnam was admitted to the Council of Mutual Economic Assistance as its tenth member state in Bucharest on 3 June (*Peking Review*, 14 July). On 3 July China ended its economic and technical aid to Vietnam and announced the closing of three Vietnamese consulates in China on 16 June (*Current Scene*, August/September). In early November Vietnam and the Soviet Union signed a treaty of friendship and cooperation.

China's top leaders traveled throughout the world. Teng Hsiao-ping visited Burma and then Nepal in January and February. Li Hsien-nien and Huang Hua visited Manila in March. Later the same month Li Hsien-nien visited Bangladesh. Vice-premier Ku Mu visited France, Switzerland, Belgium, Denmark, and West Germany in May. Hua Kuo-feng visited North Korea in May. Huang Hua visited Zaire, the Netherlands, and Turkey in June, following his participation in the U.N. General Assembly's Special Session on Disarmament in New York. Vice-premier Keng Piao visited Pakistan in June and then Trinidad and Tobago, Jamaica, and Guyana in July. Chi Peng-fei, vice-chairman of the NPC's Standing Committee, visited Syria that same month. Vice-premier Chen Mu-hua visited Somalia, Gabon, and Cameroon in July and August. Hua Kuo-feng made a much-publicized visit to Romania, Yugoslavia, and Iran in August and September. Teng Hsiao-ping visited Japan in October and subsequently visited Thailand, Malaysia, and Singapore in November.

Cordial relations with Albania, which since 1954 has received about $5 billion in assistance from China, have been a notable casualty of the foreign policy of this "New Period of the Long March" toward modernization. Reacting to continued Albanian criticism of Peking's three worlds thesis and other policies, the Chinese government on 7 July finally cut off its aid. Reasons given for this action were Albania's alleged anti-Chinese slander and sabotage and criticism of the late Chairman Mao Tse-tung (Washington Post Service, Hong Kong, 14 July).

Comprehensive statements of Chinese foreign policy are to be found in Hua Kuo-feng's major address to the Fifth NPC in February and Huang Hua's address on 28 September at the thirty-third session of the U.N. General Assembly in New York. A notable theme introduced in 1978 is that even though "War is inevitable and—independent of man's will . . . the possibility does exist of putting off its outbreak" (*Peking Review*, 6 October).

In November, limited hydrofoil and air travel between Hong Kong and China began for the first time.

Publications. The official and most authoritative publication of the CCP is the newspaper *Jen-min jih-pao* (People's daily), published in Peking. The theoretical journal of the Central Committee, *Hung Chi* (Red flag) is published approximately once a month. The daily paper of the PLA is *Chieh-fang-chun-pao* (Liberation Army daily). The weekly *Peking Review*, published in English and several other languages, carries translations of important articles, editorials, and documents from the three aforementioned publications. The official news agency of the party and government is the New China News Agency (Hsinhua; NCNA).

University of Hawaii   Stephen Uhalley, Jr.

India

The Communist Party of India was formed in 1928 and from the beginning was divided in social character, base of support, and ideological stance. These factional cleavages were difficult to contain, and the party split in 1964. The Communist Party of India (CPI) laid claim to the party's heritage and charged that the secessionist party, the Communist Party of India—Marxist (CPM), was heretical. Moreover, the Sino-Soviet split and the 1962 border clashes between India and China helped to precipitate the split. The CIP remained loyal to the international goals of the Soviet Union, while the CPM adopted a position of "equidistance" between the two communist powers.

The Setting in 1978. The March 1977 national elections and the two subsequent rounds of state elections in 1977—78 resulted in profound changes in the pattern of Indian politics. The Janata Party, supported by the CPM, displaced the Congress Party from power at the center, thus breaking the Congress's 30-year hold on the levers of power in New Delhi. The CPM, with 22 parliamentary seats and 4.3 percent of the popular vote, replaced the CPI, which won 7 seats and 2.82 percent of the popular vote, as the major representative of Indian communism.

Three months later the Janata and its allies took control of the state governments in the North; the CPM won a solid majority in West Bengal. In December the CPM and its left-front allies won 56 of the 60 legislative assembly seats in the northeastern state of Tripura. However, the results showed that with the exception of the southwestern state of Kerala, the CPM had very little drawing power outside of West Bengal and Tripura. The party's relatively poor showing in the February 1978 state elections again underscored its regional base of support. Nevertheless, its backing was essential for the Janata-backed governments in Assam and Maharashtra. The CPI, still discredited for backing the Emergency, did very poorly in the state elections.

The major political event in 1978 was the reemergence of Mrs. Gandhi, who in January created her own party—the "Indira" Congress—and carried away the larger part of the Congress organization. By winning two large southern states in the February elections, she demonstrated her continued appeal. Mrs. Gandhi herself returned to parliament in November by winning a by-election from a safe seat. The CPM viewed these developments with alarm and reacted by reaffirming its support of the ruling Janata Party.

The CPI had been discarded by Mrs. Gandhi during the last months of the Emergency and the party's eight-year "unity and struggle" relationship with Congress was in tatters. While the party now officially brands Mrs. Gandhi a "reactionary," there remains considerable support for the "unity and struggle" line. To reclaim some measure of influence, the CPI has called, so far unsuccessfully, for a "leftist" third political front in which "progressive" Congress elements, but not Janata, would be included.

Both the CPM and CPI held national congresses in April to work out their strategies in the changed political situation of post-Emergency India.

CPM: *Organization and Strategy.* The CPM's Tenth Congress left the leadership structure largely intact. E. M. S. Namboodiripad was retained as general secretary as were all sitting members of the Politburo, the party's highest policy-making body. The Politburo was expanded from 9 to 12 members. The Central Committee was also increased from 31 to 44 members, with 27 of the sitting members included in the enlarged body. The expansions reflect the party's desire to expand its influence outside its regional bases in West Bengal and Kerala.

The party establishment is aging. Only 33 of the 572 delegates at the party congress were 33 years or less, and only a fourth had joined the party after 1964. Most of the delegates were from urban middle-class backgrounds.

Party membership, estimated at some 100,000 in 1978, has remained stable for over a decade. It is concentrated in Kerala (40,000) and West Bengal (30,000) with smaller contingents in Tamil Nadu, Punjab, Andhra Pradesh, and Assam. There are very few in the strategically important Hindi-speaking states, although the party's expanded national bodies underscore its intention to enroll new members there. Attached to the party is the Centre of India Trade Unions (900,000 members), the Students' Federation of India (160,000 members), and a peasant front, the All-India Kisan Sabha (1,100,000 members).

While the Tenth Congress labeled the Janata Party a representative of the "bourgeois-landlord" class, it also reaffirmed its "support with opposition" line because of the ruling party's role in "restoring democracy" and in "resisting authoritarianism" (i.e., Mrs. Gandhi). The Politburo in July declared that under present conditions there is no alternative to Janata Party rule at the center (*Statesman,* 24 July).

Nevertheless, the party congress did propose building a left alternative that would eventually replace the "bourgeois" parties. The party executive met with its CPI counterpart at the conclusion of the national conclave to explore coordinating activities in the student, labor, and peasant fields, but political cooperation was not included in the talks. This was the first time since 1969 that the two parties had met jointly to discuss such cooperation. There are, moreover, prominent figures, like former General Secretary Sundaraya, who oppose the CPM's "support with opposition" line. Sundaraya submitted a dissenting note to the Central Committee, warning that the party's cooperation with the Janata could undermine the CPM's efforts to mobilize the Muslims and the untouchables (*New Age,* 9 July).

General Secretary Namboodiripad wrote in the CPM's official journal that the talks between the two communist parties were only a "modest beginning" and that a wide gulf still separates them

(*People's Democracy,* 13 April). The CPM's differences with the CPI revolve around the latter's continuing links with the Congress Party, its participation in a united front ministry in Kerala that includes the Congress Party, and its close identification with the international policies of the Soviet Union. Namboodiripad in mid-October harshly attacked the CPI for not opposing Mrs. Gandhi's bid to reenter parliament (*New Age,* 22 October).

Since taking control of two state governments, the CPM has put forward a "govern and mobilize" line to demonstrate that it can govern effectively, advance the living standards of the underprivileged, and thus mobilize support. The tactic requires close coordination between the party and the government. In West Bengal, for example, major policies are made by the party executive and subsequently transmitted to the government as "recommendations."

This tactic also requires some organizational structure to mobilize mass support. The government of West Bengal decided to hold elections to *panchayat* councils on a partisan basis. The CPM won about two-thirds of the seats. The government is now preparing to transfer substantial resources and developmental functions to these councils; however, any structural changes in the local economy are likely to be gradual since the CPM wants to avoid the revival of rural unrest that tarnished its image ten years ago and that eventually brought down upon it the wrath of the central government.

Attitudes on Internal and External Issues. The central leadership has concluded that socialism in one state is unrealistic as long as the center is controlled by a "bourgeois" government. Consequently, it must prove that the Communists can provide good government in its regional base. Within this framework, it has called for labor peace and a minimal use of the strike weapon in West Bengal and Tripura (although it has not hesitated to advocate strikes elsewhere). The West Bengal government promised the business community that the state would work for stability, administrative efficiency, and increased productivity. This approach was challenged in mid-1978 by a work slowdown that threatened a significant curtailment of power generation. The government moved vigorously to end the labor unrest. A major establishment newspaper in Calcutta observed that the communist government in West Bengal is "widely accepted as moderate, businesslike and well-intentioned" (*Statesman,* 21 June).

The party's ability to achieve the objectives of the "govern and mobilize" line depends to a certain extent on increased state autonomy. The West Bengal government has called for a substantial devolution of power and of development resources to the states. The West Bengal cabinet on 1 December 1977 presented Prime Minister Desai with a memorandum proposing that the power of the central government be limited to defense, transport and communications, finance, and foreign affairs (ibid., 2 December 1977), but Prime Minister Desai rejected the proposal. The CPM also supports removing from the Indian constitution those provisions that give New Delhi the power to declare a state of emergency, to engage in preventive detention, and to remove state governments.

International Views. The CPM officially welcomes rapprochement between India and China, although not at the expense of good relations with the USSR. The nationalist orientation of the CPM's foreign policy is reflected in its rather magnanimous stance toward Eurocommunism. Its independence is further underscored by the absence of foreign delegates at the Tenth Party Congress. Moreover, neither the PRC nor the USSR sent fraternal messages.

CPI: *Organization and Strategy.* The Indian press had speculated early in the year that the CPI was on the verge of a split over the question of its support for the 1975–77 Emergency. At the Eleventh Party Congress, discipline and unity ultimately prevailed. S. A. Dange, who had been associated with the pro-Emergency view, was reelected chairman, and C. Rajeswara Rao, who took a hard line against the Emergency, remained the general secretary. Only two new members were elected to the eleven-member Central Secretariat.

Like the CPM, the party leadership is urban, well-educated and aging. The CPI claims 546,000 members, of whom over one-half are in Bihar (100,000), Andhra Pradesh (85,000), Kerala (80,000), and Uttar Pradesh (35,000). The party's major front groups are the All-India Students' Federation (105,000 members), the All-India Trade Union Conference (2,600,000 members) and the All-India Kisan Samiti (175,000 members).

Two strategy issues dominated the Eleventh Congress: (a) placing distance between the party and its earlier support of the Emergency and of Mrs. Gandhi and (b) consolidating the Left.

The reappraisal of its reaction to the Emergency elicited a painful confession of sins. Party Chairman Dange was the architect of the party's close ties with the ruling Congress Party. He resigned his position in December 1977 "for health reasons," when the 114-member National Council publicly admitted that the party had erred in supporting the Emergency. (Dange's resignation was not accepted.) While the *Political Report* of the party congress upheld the National Council's December verdict (1,125 in favor and 111 abstentions), the delegates rejected by a vote of 774 to 232 an anti-Dange amendment that condemned the party's 1969—75 "unity and struggle" relationship with the Congress Party. However, the delegates also turned down, 712 to 403, an amendment that proposed that the party's initial support of the Emergency was acceptable in light of the challenge from "right reactionary" forces.

The delegates strongly supported the leadership's moves to bring the various leftist parties together as a third political alternative. The *Political Report* stated that "The country can no longer be saved either by continuation of the Janata rule or by restoration of Congress rule. It can be salvaged only . . . by a left and democratic national alternative . . . for which our party and its mass organisations have to play a significant initiating and leading role."

Despite the official move away from a unified front approach with "bourgeois" parties, many CPI leaders clearly did not think the "unity and struggle" line a bankrupt policy. Moreover, even the third alternative tactic left open the door for the participation of "progressive" Congress members.

So far, the CPM has refused to consider political cooperation with the CPI seriously and will not cooperate with the CPI as long as the CPI remains in the Kerala united front government, agrees to electoral adjustments with the Congress (even if selective), and refuses to cooperate with Janata in blocking the political comeback of Mrs. Gandhi.

General Strategy. Having performed its mea culpa on the Emergency, the party congress pledged its support to the "full democratic rights" of the people, to the efforts to delete the internal emergency provisions from the constitution, and to the devolution of power to the states. On the economic front, it continues to advocate the nationalization of "monopoly" houses and the state control of wholesale trading in food grains and essential commodities. It attacks the Janata government's shift away from heavy industry as a retrograde step.

The executive leadership met in May and outlined a program of mass struggle to protest "police repression," the "harassment" of the minority communities, unemployment, and the nonimplementation of reforms (*New Age,* 23 May). In July the executive called for a nonviolent resistance campaign to commence on 7 September (ibid., 16 July). The party claims that over 243,000 people participated in this campaign (ibid., 17 September). Despite this effort to capitalize on popular frustrations, the CPI has failed to generate mass support and remains politically isolated.

On foreign policy issues, the CPI maintains its unwavering support of Moscow. The Eleventh Congress declared that "Indo-Soviet friendship is an example to all who cherish peace and friendship." On China, the party executive declared that its rulers "have forged a common global front with imperialism and extreme reaction and aligned themselves fully with the NATO moves" (ibid., 16 July). Party Secretary Rao blasted the CPM's "equidistance" line as "shameful at a time when the Soviet Union is performing its internationalist duty by giving all help to those fighting against imperialism" (*WMR*, July). The Eleventh Congress denounced the Desai government's "genuine non-alignment" policy as an attempt to undermine India's traditionally close ties with the Soviet Union.

Communist Party—Marxist-Leninist. Both the CPI and the CPM demanded the release of "Naxalite" (extremist communist) detainees when the Emergency was lifted. Both advised the Maoist ideologues to participate in the parliamentary process. CPI General Secretary Rao included them in the fraternal groups that should coalesce together in the proposed left alternative (*New Age,* 30 April). While the CPM also welcomed their inclusion in a leftist front, the draft resolution on the subject at the Tenth Congress advised the Naxalites that their tactics were wrong and that they needed ideological guidance, presumably from the more mature communist parties (*Indian Express,* 24 January).

Some Naxalites have abandoned revolutionary tactics. Various groups ran candidates in the West Bengal and Tripura state elections, winning one seat in each legislative assembly. In July Naxalites reportedly established a trade union federation (*Ananda Bazar Patrika,* 17 July).

There are, however, indications that some factions are again resorting to their traditional tactics. India's official news agency reported that the police in Andhra Pradesh had discovered that the Naxalites were regrouping in that state and that they had in April attacked eighteen police stations (Agence France Presse, Hong Kong, 8 April). That same month, two bombs were thrown at the Soviet Trade Mission in Calcutta. It is widely believed that the Naxalites are responsible for this as well as for some scattered acts of violence in rural West Bengal. Whatever the validity of these rumors, the CPM government in West Bengal has warned the Naxalites that it would not tolerate a resumption of violence.

Arlington, Virginia   Walter K. Andersen

Indonesia

Founded on 23 May 1920, the Indonesian Communist Party (Partai Komunis Indonesia; PKI) in the aftermath of an abortive coup attempt in 1965 divided into small Moscow- and Peking-oriented factions, most of whose adherents live in exile. Since 1966 the movement has been formally proscribed and organizationally shattered after tens of thousands of members and sympathizers were killed or arrested and incarcerated without trial. The government officially considers the PKI a continuing "latent" threat to the country, however, and a handful of underground party activists are said either to have joined the North Kalimantan (Borneo) communist guerrillas (*see* Malaysia) or to be attempting to infiltrate or form new antigovernment front organizations.

PKI activities at the moment consist primarily of the issuance of statements by the two factions on conditions in Indonesia, congratulatory messages to friendly parties, and mutual denunciations. The pro-Peking faction is led by Jusuf Adjitorop, a PKI Politburo member before the 1965 coup, and its 200 or so adherents are resident either in Peking or Tirana, where they publish their principal organs, *Indonesian Tribune* and *API*. A few are active under deep cover in Indonesia itself. The Peking-oriented PKI group in the past has referred to itself as the "Delegation of the PKI" or the "Delegation of the Central Committee of the PKI," but during the past two years references to the word "delegation" have been dropped, and the Peking group now calls itself simply the "Communist Party of Indonesia." There is no customarily identified single leader of or spokesman for the Moscow-oriented PKI faction, a number of whose followers also appear to reside in Prague or other East European capitals. A dozen or so are also said to be in India and Sri Lanka. Spokesmen for this group are usually identified as members of "the leadership, Communist Party of Indonesia."

Reelection of Suharto to a third five-year term as president provided impetus for a number of critical PKI assessments. Satiajaya Sudiman of the pro-Moscow faction particularly cited alleged government economic failures, such as the inability to achieve self-sufficiency in food production as well as the "growing sway of imperialist monopolies" in the country, which he claimed were ruining national enterprises and leaving thousands unemployed. Amid mounting dissent, according to Sudiman, the PKI was calling on all patriots "regardless of their party affiliation or religious beliefs" to cooperate in a joint effort to "renew society," an effort which would not require anyone to "renounce his convictions." Instead the unity of all "patriotic forces" was being sought in order to give further impetus to "the great tide of protest" presently said to be occurring in Indonesia. Sudiman reiterated an earlier party call, made in January, demanding the release of all political prisoners and the full restitution of their civic rights. (*WMR*, April, pp. 86–89.)

The organ of the Moscow-oriented PKI faction, *Tekad Rakjat* (Will of the people), in May carried a letter of its Central Committee sharply attacking the leadership of China and accusing it of weakening world socialism and undermining the unity of revolutionary and anti-imperialist forces in the world. Indonesian Communists, according to the letter, have expressed their "profound disappointment" with the policies of the Chinese leadership. (*FBIS*, 5 June.)

The most important statement made by the Peking faction during the year was the message of Jusuf Adjitorop on 23 May commemorating the PKI's fifty-eighth anniversary, read over the Voice of the Malayan Revolution (*see* Malaysia) on 8 June. According to this anniversary message, having revealed itself as a "military dictatorship," the Suharto regime has aroused today a broadly based national opposition movement. "People of all classes and strata, political parties and groups, personages in religious circles, various nationalities, and students of universities and middle schools" are condemning and accusing the regime and its policies. According to Adjitorop's message, Suharto's basic threefold policy aims, i.e., domestic stability, a high rate of economic development, and the achievement of social justice, have turned out to be so much "demagogic propaganda." A new, just and prosperous society can only be realized in Indonesia "by taking the road of armed struggle" and by uniting "all patriotic forces" and receiving their help. (Ibid., 22 June.)

The Voice of the Malayan Revolution broadcast the text of an article on problems of the Suharto regime which had originally appeared in the PKI Peking faction's new journal, *Voice of the People of Indonesia*. Like other statements by both factions, this article also took note of public dissent in Indonesia, where college students allegedly are raising the slogan: "Democracy is dead." The antigovernment struggle has become particularly apparent since the beginning of 1978, according to the same article, and is bound to be successful because "this era does not belong to Suharto and his clique. Suharto's fascist totalitarian regime goes against historical development." (Ibid., 22 March.)

Subsequently, the same radio station broadcast the text of another commentary from the *Voice of the Indonesian People*, this one dealing with the new cabinet. Although Suharto had promised he would accelerate economic development, in fact he supposedly has not been able to hide the steady economic decline of the country. Meanwhile, "the university students' resistance movement" exposes the "ugly features" of the Suharto regime. (Ibid., 15 May.)

Apart from the expected criticism of Suharto's economic policies, perhaps the important feature of these and similar statements by the two PKI factions is their expectation of a continuing broad-based antigovernment movement in the country, a movement that can become a joint front of all "patriotic" forces. A similar communist tactic is evident in the Philippines.

The organs of the PKI Peking faction have particularly noted over the years the persisting regional resistance movements in Indonesia, notably in West Irian (New Guinea) and East Timor. *API*, the irregularly appearing publication of the group's "youth movement," made mention last year of the "freedom struggle" by the so-called Fretilin resistance movement in East Timor. This year it called attention to the guerrilla independence struggle of the Free Papua Organization in Irian Jaya or West New Guinea, where five "fascist" Indonesian officials had recently been captured by insurgents. (*API*, Tirana, June.)

Domestic Developments. As in previous years, Indonesian officials frequently referred to subversive threats. Official concern with domestic security and stability, including the potential of an underground communist exploitation of divisive public issues, appeared in connection with the planned election of General Suharto to a third five-year term as president. Toward the end of 1977, thousands of university and high school students demonstrated in Djakarta and other major cities on Java, attacking the failure of the government's anticorruption campaign, the increasing poverty, and the third-term presidency. Top military commanders, coming to the government's aid, repeatedly warned that they would take severe measures to insure public order. Admiral Sudomo, chief of staff for the security agency Kopkamtib, stated that the government "would accept any consequences or risks in dealing with demonstrations" (*FBIS*, 14 January).

Although Suharto was reelected on 22 March to another presidential term by the People's Consultative Congress, the country's highest policy-making body, shortly thereafter student unrest began to subside. Nevertheless, the government continued its strict security measures.

Meanwhile, Muslim insurgents in northern Sumatra, calling themselves the National Liberation Front for Acheh (NLFA), seem determined, under their principal leader, Hasan Tiro, to emulate the Moro National Liberation Front in the Philippines. The Indonesian army command at Acheh began distributing leaflets urging the public to report the whereabouts and capture the nine principal NLFA leaders "dead or alive" (*FBIS*, 6 July). An NLFA band attacked the Arun natural gas field, killing an American construction worker (*Far Eastern Economic Review*, 25 August).

North Sumatra is not, however, the only scene of antigovernment insurgent activity. In East Timor, formerly a Portuguese colony, resistance continues against Indonesia's annexation. Despite defections and the capture of some leaders, about 1,000 members of the Revolutionary Front for Independent East Timor or Fretilin (essentially a Marxist organization which has won the endorsement of China, Vietnam, and other communist-ruled states and groups) are keeping up a guerrilla struggle against some 20,000 Indonesian troups (*NYT*, 19 April). Fretilin representatives have indicated that they intend to keep the East Timor issue before the U.N. General Assembly "and not let Indonesia have a free hand" (*l'Humanité*, Paris, 18 September; *FBIS*, 28 September).

Indonesian spokesmen indicated that they have no intention of negotiating with the Fretilin, whose strength is estimated by Djakarta to be only 200 hard-core guerrillas, and asserted that "a completely civilian administration" will take over the administration of the territory by April 1979 (*FBIS*, 21 April, 19 May).

In Irian Jaya or West New Guinea, the Indonesian military during July increased action against the guerrilla forces of the Free Papua Organization (Organisasi Papua Merdeka; OPM). In so doing, they repeatedly crossed the boundary of adjacent Papua—New Guinea, where several hundred anti-

Indonesian dissidents have found sanctuary for some time (*De Volkskrant*, Amsterdam, 1 August). As a result of these military activities, an addition 640 Irian Jaya villagers crossed into Papua−New Guinea according to official estimates, and Indonesian authorities have admitted dropping "nonlethal" plastic bombs on suspected OPM positions close to the border (*Post Courier*, Port Moresby, 24 and 26 July).

OPM resistance is now more than a decade old, and despite factional disputes and leadership squabbles in the OPM (*Far Eastern Economic Review*, 10 March), the struggle appears to persist. OPM sources claim continuous uprisings and spontaneous guerrilla attacks (*News Bulletin*, Republic of West Papua−New Guinea, London Office, 13 August). Indonesia asserts there is no unrest, however, and Irian Jaya regional military commander Brigadier General Imam Munandar claimed that "security in Irian Jaya is excellent, everything is in order and development efforts are unhampered" (*FBIS*, 2 June). At least one OPM faction appears to have a Marxist orientation, but little is known about the ideological complexion of the Papuan resistance movement as a whole.

Slow progress was made during the year concerning Indonesia's political prisoners, most of them suspected Communists or sympathizers, who had been arrested following the abortive 1965 coup. Some 10,000 were freed at the close of December 1977, the government plans to release another 10,000 in 1978 and the remainder in 1979 (*Washington Post*, 21 December 1977). Thousands of prisoners were given psychological tests to determine the degree of their "communist inclination" so that the communities to which they returned could "control their attitude" (*NYT*, 26 April). Doubts have been expressed whether all will be released because of reports that new arrests are taking place for security reasons.

Vice-president Walter Mondale met with President Suharto concerning the recent and intended release of prisoners. He declared afterwards that recent Indonesian actions in the area of human rights had received a "very favorable reaction" in the United States (*NYT*, 7 May).

Government spokesmen have expressed the belief that after having been subjected to supervision, the detainees "will be aware of their past mistakes" and return to society "in good faith" (*FBIS*, 5 July).

International Aspects. Indonesia's strongly anticommunist domestic policy continues to affect relations with communist-ruled countries, even though the frequency of contact with these states has been increasing. Suharto announced that his government had agreed to restore normal diplomatic relations with Kampuchea (Cambodia), which had been disrupted by the fall of the Lon Nol government in 1975. According to the foreign minister, Indonesia welcomed a recent Cambodian initiative to restore relations, which were expected to materialize later in the year (ibid., 23 February).

A Cuban delegation led by a former chargé in Djakarta, Jacinto Vasquez de la Garza, paid a visit. It was subsequently revealed that Havana had expressed a desire to exchange ambassadors with Djakarta and that Indonesia was prepared to do so. (Ibid., 10 April.)

Frequency of contact with Vietnam accelerated also, but no basic change occurred in the government policy of cautious watchfulness. At the end of last year, Hanoi's vice-premier and concurrent foreign minister visited Djakarta. In a joint statement, the two countries pledged to increase mutual scientific and technical exchange, particularly in agriculture. The two countries also declared that the present situation in Southeast Asia was favorable for all nations in the region to develop new relations on the basis of "peace, neutrality and independence" (ibid., 3 January). In the fall, Vietnam's premier spent four days in Indonesia. His visit was part of a general goodwill tour to ASEAN countries. In a joint statement, agreement was voiced on "further studies" to improve the scientific and technological cooperation between the two countries. (Ibid., 25 September.)

During this visit, endorsement of a policy change toward greater "independence" (code word for removal of foreign bases and elimination of joint military maneuvers, e.g., between Australia and

Indonesia) could not be obtained. The joint statement, while expressing the desirability of Southeast Asia being an area of "independence" as well as peace, freedom, and neutrality, also reiterated Suharto's personal commitment to ASEAN's striving for ZOPFAN or Zone of Peace, Freedom, and Neutrality (ibid., 25 September). Among the nuances in the joint statement, there was sufficient indication that Vietnam had not allayed Indonesia's basic suspicions of its policies in Southeast Asia.

Neither have there been any indications that Moscow-Djakarta relations improved. Trade did increase and contacts remain the same as during the past five years, i.e., formally correct. The Soviet press takes note of domestic Indonesian developments and has condemned foreign oil monopolies, which allegedly prevent development of national resources and even the marketing of oil. (Ibid., 5 October.)

However, the USSR also saw positive aspects in Indonesia's external relations. Caution in restoring diplomatic relations with China was lauded, and Moscow Radio asserted that Peking had been sending "spies to Indonesia to engage in antigovernment activities." It also took note of official statements that Sino-Indonesian normalization must await a solution to the problem of the 3.5 million Overseas Chinese in Indonesia. (Ibid., 2 May; *Indonesia Times*, 9 June.) Behind the question of political-legal status for the Chinese are Indonesian suspicions about their loyalty. It is feared that a normalization of relations with Peking would cause thousands of now "stateless" Chinese residents in Indonesia to opt for Chinese citizenship. Given its determined domestic anticommunist posture, the Djakarta government would then be confronted with a formidable security problem.

The press in general has reacted negatively to Peking's proposal that it and the ASEAN nations form a joint front against big power encroachments in Asia (*FBIS*, 26 April), although the sympathetic Chinese attitude toward ASEAN has met with approval in the Indonesian media.

Publications. The Moscow faction of the PKI primarily relies on three media: the irregularly appearing Indonesian-language journal *Tekad Rakjat* (Will of the people), edited by exiles in Moscow; for official statements, *World Marxist Review* and *Information Bulletin.* Main organs of the Peking-oriented faction are the bimonthly *Indonesian Tribune* and the irregularly appearing quarterly *API* (Api Pemuda Indonesia; Flame of Indonesian youth), both published in English at Tirana. The Communist Party of Malaya's clandestine transmitter, Voice of the Malayan Revolution, believed to be located in southern China, also periodically relays statements and messages of the pro-Chinese group. Over the past five years, media in Peking have paid only occasional attention to the pronouncements and activities of the PKI.

University of Bridgeport   Justus M. van der Kroef

Japan

The past year was an uneventful one for the Japanese Communist Party (JCP), as well as for other communist and leftist parties in Japan. No national elections were held, and the JCP's leadership remained unchanged, except for the expulsion from the party of one of its six vice-chairmen—who then publicly criticized the party, probably damaging the JCP's image. After two major election defeats, in December 1976 and July 1977, the JCP had to find a strategy that would allow it to recoup its losses. In October 1977 the JCP held its Fourteenth Party Congress, but no such new strategy appeared. Its problems, instead, were attributed to poor election tactics and the collusion of other parties to combat the JCP's growing strength. While this was true, the JCP also suffered from changing voting patterns and the loss of a major issue—the Vietnam War—that had helped the party in the past.

Indications now are that the JCP has done little to solve these problems, and had an election been held in 1978 the party would have suffered another defeat, although perhaps not so marked a defeat as in the last two elections when its strength in the Diet fell by half. A nationwide public opinion poll in May showed that mass support for the party had declined from 3.9 percent in December 1977 to 3.4 percent (Kyodo, 8 May). The poll also showed that the most important voting issue was commodity prices, followed by economic recovery; better social welfare programs, for which the JCP has strongly campaigned, was a paramount issue to only 18.9 percent of those questioned (ibid.). In the area of foreign policy, those polled were concerned with the 200-mile fishing zone and oil and other natural resources, issues which the JCP had not discussed (ibid.). The JCP had taken a strong stand against the Sino-Japanese peace treaty (particularly the antihegemony clause), in contrast to all other parties, and opposed the U.S.-Japan Defense Pact and the Japan Self-Defense Forces, even though its own membership failed to hold similar views. The JCP remained independent of both the Soviet Union and the People's Republic of China, and its attitude toward both can be described as hostile, although its hostility toward China was more evident in 1978.

Leadership and Party Line. The Fourteenth Party Congress, held in October 1977, reaffirmed the leadership of Miyamoto Kenji, chairman of the Presidium and de facto leader of the party. Nosaka Sanzo, the elder statesman of the party and chairman of the Central Committee, and Fuwa Tetsuzo, chief of the Secretariat of the Central Committee and Miyamoto's heir-apparent, retained their positions. Most other central party leaders were reelected at the congress and remained in the same posts during 1978. More changes were visible at the local level where some prefectural and district chairmanships changed hands.

At the close of the party congress, the party's Secretariat announced that the Central Committee comprised 141 full and 54 alternate members—an increase of some 10 percent. It also announced that the average age had declined by five years, from 60 to 55. The circulation of the party's newspaper, *Akahata* (Red flag), was unofficially reported to be 3,259,354—the highest ever. The goal for future party membership was set at 500,000. The party's real size was probably just over 300,000, about equal to its membership in 1973. It is also questionable whether *Akahata*'s circulation had exceeded earlier records. More likely, it fell rather than grew during 1978. The JCP made no official announcements of party strength or its paper's circulation during the year.

The party line remained unchanged. The JCP is a "Eurocommunist" party and espouses a "parliamentary road" to acquire political power. Chairman Miyamoto frequently reiterated this strategy during the year. The party continues to try to influence public opinion through its publications and by winning elections rather than initiating mass movements. It is not clear if the party will move away from using elections to educate the voters—a strategy which fielded too many candidates without their being elected and resulted in the party's serious defeats in the last two elections. (See *YICA, 1978*, pp. 265–66 for further details.)

The party continued to underscore its goal of resisting the anticommunist press and the collusion of the centrist parties linked with the right-wing ruling Liberal Democratic Party (LDP). It appears that the LDP's concern with communism subsided after July 1977 when the JCP suffered its second electoral defeat in seven months and lost considerable strength in the Diet. The same is true of the press. The JCP needed a rallying point; so it kept up its efforts to struggle against "anticommunist" elements.

The major leadership problem has revolved around Hakamada Satomi, who was stripped of his vice-chairmanship at the Fourteenth Party Congress. Hakamada had been a veteran party stalwart. Both he and Miyamoto had been imprisoned before the war and interrogated about the death of a party infiltrator. Later Miyamoto had been charged with the informer's murder but was acquitted after WWII. In January 1978 Hakamada wrote an article for an "anticommunist" magazine criticizing Miyamoto and the party. For this, the party expelled him, the first time in ten years that a top party leader had been expelled.

Hakamada criticized Miyamoto for being a dictator and for not allowing freedom of speech within the party. He also charged that the party line was anti—working class and ignored Marxism-Leninism in favor of scientific socialism. He went on to say that the bureaucratic administration of the party had caused over 130,000 members to leave the party. Finally, he raised some questions about the Miyamoto murder charge of 45 years ago.

The Hakamada article appeared in *Shukan Shincho* (New current weekly). It undoubtedly caused the party considerable loss of face. Another Japanese magazine has speculated that it could "cause the collapse of the Miyamoto empire." The party's retaliation against Hakamada encouraged him to write two more articles in which he attacked Miyamoto for "bourgeois methods" and gave further details on the murder incident. He disclosed some information about party recruitment and noted that *Akahata*'s circulation was 3.2 million, somewhat less than the party had claimed (*Asian Wall Street Journal*, 24 February).

In February Miyamoto and Nosaka initiated a libel suit against Hakamada, the editor of *Shincho*, and the president of the newspaper *Sankei Shimbun*. For several months *Akahata* carried stories about Hakamada, criticizing him for blindly following the Soviet Union and violating party discipline. *Akahata* also reported interviews and statements by Miyamoto boasting that the Hakamada case had actually helped the party's image and attracted more votes. Whether this is true is uncertain. The case has obviously deepened the split between old and new members of the party; the former support mass movements and are more militant, whereas the latter are committed to reforms and gaining more seats in parliament.

Party Meetings and Activities. The JCP convened the fourth Central Committee plenary meeting on 8–10 May to discuss means of reviving the party's influence. It was resolved to fight against the Shokyo Rengo (International Anticommunist and Conspiracy Organization) and repel rumors created by the "renegade" Hakamada. On 14 September the fifth plenum of the Central

Committee met to discuss the emergency legislation bill that would give the Self-Defense Forces special powers in crises. Other issues on the agenda included party building and mass movements. At this meeting, Miyamoto declared that progressive forces must unite to oppose the LDP's efforts to turn the country back to the "prewar order" (*FBIS*, 18 September). He expressed the hope that the Japanese Socialist Party and the Sohyo (Japan's largest labor union) would join in a struggle against this new legislation. By year's end, the emergency legislation was still pending and the LDP did not appear enthusiastic about pushing it through the Diet.

Less important party meetings were held during the year, including a celebration on 15 July of the party's "Foundation Day." A national meeting of prefectural and district party committees was held in June, and a national conference of chairmen of prefectural chapters took place in July.

The party has spoken out critically on U.S. Secretary of Defense Brown's February comments about U.S. strategy in the event of a Korean crisis. The JCP opposed the use of Japanese territory for the support of U.S. military forces. A JCP Diet member also asked the Diet to investigate reports of U.S. nuclear weapons at Kadena Air Force Base in Okinawa. The party accused the LDP and the government of bribery and corruption in the sale of Japanese-produced subway cars in Korea. The money had allegedly been transferred to the U.S. for influence-buying by Korean officials.

International Contacts. Chairman Miyamoto traveled to Yugoslavia and Romania in June and met top leaders of both countries. This trip was supposedly to learn more about Eurocommunism and Titoism, but it was clear that the visits also emphasized the JCP's independence from Moscow and Peking and its "parliamentary road" to power in Japan. Miyamoto was invited by the French Communist Party, but he decided not to go because of their setback in the French elections. He was also invited to Spain, but instead of going he invited leaders of the Spanish Communist Party to Japan.

Other party leaders visited Cuba and Vietnam. On 23 May the JCP gave a reception in Tokyo for Hoang Tong, editor in chief of *Nhan Dan*, the official paper of the Vietnamese Communist Party. Throughout the year *Akahata* favorably reported Vietnam's side in its dispute with China and Cambodia. In midyear Bulgarian party leaders visited Japan, but no official contacts were reported with the JCP.

Sino-Soviet Dispute. The JCP continued to remain independent of both Moscow and Peking. The party seemed to denounce China more strongly than the Soviet Union, and after the peace treaty was signed with China *Akahata* reported that the Communist Party of the Soviet Union has sought improved relations with the JCP.

During his visit to Europe, Miyamoto stressed that the JCP is the only Eurocommunist party in Asia and described Tito as a "leader who has maintained his party's independent road . . . and a forerunner of the international workers' movement." The party also criticized the Kremlin for its policies regarding the Kurile islands, which Japan has claimed and Moscow has agreed to negotiate a settlement over. On the other hand, this criticism was not nearly as strident as in the past.

Relations with China throughout the year were obviously cool. Delegates from all Japanese political parties except the JCP received invitations to visit China. JCP leaders explained this in terms of Peking's still regarding the JCP as an "opportunist" party. The JCP's most vitriolic criticism of China came after the signing of the peace treaty in August. JCP spokesmen said that they agreed with the treaty in principle but went on to assail Peking on a number of points. The JCP made it known that it felt the treaty was being signed on China's terms, and it did not approve of this—the only Japanese political party to take this position. More importantly, the JCP attacked China for supporting the U.S.-Japan Defense Pact. In a nationally televised interview, Miyamoto stated that this was "wrong for a socialist country." (*FBIS*, 26 September.) JCP officials also blasted China's policy of supporting the North Atlantic Treaty Organization. In October when Chinese Vice-premier Teng Hsiao-ping visited Japan, Miyamoto spurned an invitation to a banquet to which all party heads had been invited.

More bitter criticism followed the next month when Miyamoto spoke out on the anti-hegemony clause in the treaty: "On the contrary, the treaty expresses a desire for hegemony" (ibid., 21 September). He went on to say—again in a nationally televised interview—that China's actions toward Japan constitute "interference in the people's movement and run counter to the five principles of peace" (ibid.). He further declared that China's "theory of three worlds" boils down to "rallying all the forces that oppose the Soviet Union" (ibid.). Then he accused China of trying to establish ties with the Japanese Self-Defense Forces and cited the fact that the deputy chief of staff of the Chinese People's Liberation Army was the first Chinese leader to visit Japan after the conclusion of the peace treaty (ibid.). The party newspaper said at the time that this "exposes a U.S.-Japan-China alliance plot" (*Akahata*, 10 September).

Publications. See *YICA, 1978.*

Splinter Groups and Factions. A number of communist and leftist parties in Japan made news during the year by their terrorist activities, especially their demonstrations and destruction at Narita Airport outside Tokyo. The JCP does not maintain contacts with these groups and, in fact, criticizes their activities. JCP officials specifically condemned the activities at Narita. No contacts or reconciliations occurred between the JCP and the Voice of Japan, the pro-Moscow splinter group of the JCP, in spite of what appeared to have been warming relations with Moscow as a result of the JCP's criticism of China.

The Japanese Red Army, the most famous of all left-wing terrorist groups in Japan, sent statements supporting the Narita demonstrations, and some of its members were reportedly seen at Narita (*Far Eastern Economic Review*, 23 June). This small, militant group of about 20 members abroad and 100 supporters in Japan did not, however, attract world attention during the year as it had on other occasions. The head of the Japanese Farmer-Labor Party wrote threatening letters to Israeli Prime Minister Begin stating that there might be more airport shootings like that at Lod Airport in Tel Aviv in 1972 or the hijacking of a military plane loaded with atomic weapons. Okamoto Kozo had been involved in the Lod massacre and is still imprisoned in Israel (*FBIS*, 5 September). This did not appear to have any direct link to Red Army plans, however.

The Japanese Revolutionary Communist League (the Japanese section of the Fourth International) claimed at midyear that it was coordinating activities at Narita, but the truth of this is open to interpretation. The Narita demonstrators were made up of many left-wing groups and local farmers with little coordination among them. The Middle Core Faction, also an anti-Narita group, set off timed explosive devices at police firing ranges in Tokyo and Chiba in September.

In May a joint congress of the Communist Party of Japan (Leftist) and the Japanese Communist Party (Marxist/Leninist) convened to discuss questions relating to the merging of the two parties. A resolution to form a central organ to effect this unification was unanimously passed. This is not of much significance because the two groups are quite small.

Southwestern at Memphis   John F. Copper

Korea: Democratic People's Republic of Korea

Leadership and Organization. The Democratic People's Republic of Korea (DPRK) has a typical communist administrative structure. The center of decision making is in the Korean Workers' Party (Choson Nodong-dang; KWP), and the government merely executes party policy. All important leaders hold concurrent positions in the party and government.

KWP membership was recently extimated at 1.8 million, and the population of the DPRK is now slightly over 18 million.

The cult of the North Korean dictator and his family members continued unabated in 1978. DPRK media constantly stressed that loyalty to Kim Il-song and his ideology of *chuch'e* (self-identity or national identity) should continue from generation to generation, and the program of perpetuating his ideology and policies was given further institutional muscle.

Kim Il-song told Japanese visitors that the country's senior vice-president (number two man), Kim Il (66), resigned due to ill health 19 April.

Han Ik-su (66), a veteran North Korean military officer and politician, died on 5 September. At the time of his death, he was an alternate member of the KWP Political Committee and a member of the DPRK Supreme People's Assembly.

In late 1977 three prominent aides of the North Korean chieftain had been dropped from the Pyongyang leadership. They were Kim Tong-kyu, vice president; Yang Hyong-sop, Russian-educated party secretary for ideology; and Yi Yong-mu, director of the armed forces political bureau. The dismissal of Yi Yong-mu had something to do with his failure to tighten army discipline and improve relations with civilians. (Yi's post has been filled by So Chol.) All were members of the KWP's elite Political Committee.

Yang Hyong-sop and Kim Tong-kyu were apparently purged (or sacrificed) by the DPRK regime to placate the new post-Mao leadership of China under Hua Kuo-feng and Teng Hsiao-ping. The Pyongyang regime openly had applauded the second downfall of Teng in 1976 and welcomed the rise of the Gang of Four led by Mao's wife, Chiang Ching. But later the DPRK was to be disappointed by the purge of Chiang Ching and her radical faction by Hua, who emerged as Mao's successor, and embarrassed by the return to power of Teng. (*Far Eastern Economic Review*, 6 January.)

According to another theory, Yang and Kim, along with several others, really represented the pro-Soviet line and were defeated by pro-Chinese colleagues who wanted to improve relations with the West through the good offices of Peking.

During the first half of 1978 there was the rumored incapacitation of Kim Chong-il, 38-year-old son of Kim Il-song and political heir apparent. The junior Kim was rumored to have been wounded critically last year in an assassination attempt by a group of young North Korean army officers. *Tong-il Ilbo* (Unification daily), a Japanese-language newspaper published by pro-Seoul Korean residents in Japan, and the *Japan Times* reported this in early February, quoting "informed sources." The sources said that Chong-il suffered a serious head injury in mid-September when he was run down by a car and became comatose. The assailants, reportedly arrested and executed, were said to have been close to the former head of the General Political Department of the armed forces, Yi Yong-mu, who is known to have lost his post in October 1977. According to the same sources, North Korean agents recently asked top Japanese neurologists in Tokyo to visit Pyongyang to look at "a son of a VIP who had been in a deep coma for more than two months as a result of a traffic accident." Credence was apparently added to this story by circumstantial evidence concerning the status of Kim Chong-il. In 1975 and 1976 the junior Kim's birthday on 16 February was widely celebrated in North Korea with athletic events, youth rallies, and other festivities, which in turn led up to his father's birthday celebration on 15 April. This year, however, no such events took place. Chong-il's birthday was observed simply as a holiday for North Korean soldiers.

The pro-Pyongyang Federation of Korean Residents in Japan reportedly ordered early this year the withdrawal of books concerning the junior Kim, according to the mass-circulation Japanese daily *Yomiuri Shimbun.* It also skipped the annual rally celebrating the birthday of Chong-il, one of its major events for the past few years.

There is no way of verifying these rumors. Nevertheless, there are several reasons why they should not be taken seriously. *Tong-il Ilbo* has a reputation for reflecting strong anticommunist views, especially in dealing with North Korean affairs. Most major Japanese newspapers tend to have a thinly veiled anti-Korean bias, and the credibility of their reports on North Korea is suspect. It is important to remember that Kim Il-song and his son are among the most heavily guarded political personalities in the world. The special security unit (officially called the Escort Bureau) is an extremely well-trained "praetorian guard" of 7,000-10,000 men and is accountable to the senior Kim personally. It would be virtually impossible for any dissidents to find an opportunity to try to assassinate the North Korean dictator or his son.

In recent weeks, photos of Kim Chong-il began to reappear along with those of his father, indicating that a massive campaign to resurrect the faded image of the junior Kim as heir apparent to the Pyongyang leader is under way.

Domestic Attitudes and Activities. The second session of the Sixth Supreme People's Assembly was convened in Pyongyang in late April. The session adopted a new labor law calling for improvement of the working people's technical skill, for the first time since 1946. This legislation was prompted by the needs (*a*) to adjust the provisions of the previous law enacted in June 1946 to the present requirements for what the DPRK calls "the stage of socialist revolution" and (*b*) to enable the North Korean people to be mobilized fully and effectively to overcome their economic hardships by stepping up control of laborers.

A budget report to this session said that last year's state revenues were 13,789 million won (U.S. $5,365.4 million), with expenditures of 13,349.2 million won ($5,194.2 million), leaving a 439.8 million won ($171.1 million) surplus. The report also said that for the current fiscal year the DPRK would spend 16 percent of its total 15,293.2 million won ($5,950.7 million) state budget on defense "to cope with the ever growing acute situation" in the Korean peninsula. This defense spending would be 2,446.9 million won ($952.1 million), up from the 2,119.4 million won ($824.7 million) reported last year. (The actual defense budget would be higher because the Pyongyang regime makes it a rule to hide defense expenditures in other sectors.) Total armed forces in 1978 were believed to number around 470,000 actives and 1,600,000 civilian militia.

During 1978 the DPRK experienced severe economic difficulties. Recent droughts damaged crops, and provincial publications reported official workers helping farmers to dig wells. However, since half of the country's generating capacity is hydroelectric, a water shortage meant additional costly fuel imports.

The promotion of Yi Chong-ok, a veteran industrial administrator, to be the DPRK's new premier in December 1977 was one important indication that the Pyongyang regime was attempting to put first priority on straightening out the country's economic crisis, following apparently widespread mismanagement of the 1971−76 six-year plan. Whether the recent cabinet reshuffle can bring about the economic improvement the regime seeks is now anybody's guess. But given the economic slowdown of the past several years, mounting foreign debts, and only lukewarm Soviet-Chinese assistance, the going will certainly not be easy.

North Korea's balance of payments with the outside world continued to deteriorate during 1978. Figures on external debts vary, but reliable sources said that the DPRK owed a total of U.S. $2 billion to the Communist bloc, Western Europe, and Japan at the end of 1977. Of this, U.S. $400-500 million was already overdue for repayment to noncommunist creditors alone, and negotiations were continuing on a debt rescheduling at higher interest rates. Pyongyang's heavy outstanding foreign debts and its continuing default on payments, according to a recent U.S. Central Intelligence Agency report, have given the country a poor credit rating and thus "cut its access to further imports of advanced Western machinery and equipment," thereby forcing the DPRK to slow down its ambitious economic growth plan. More specifically, according to the same study, North Korea is expected to be able to buy only about U.S. $1,000 million worth of imports by 1983, half its level of imports between 1970 and 1976.

The DPRK announced the principal targets of the new seven-year plan (1978−1984). The plan calls for a 220 percent increase in gross industrial output value, with an average annual growth rate of 12.1 percent. By 1984 electricity output will be 56−60 billion kwh; coal output, 70−80 million tons; steel, 7.4−8 million tons; machine tools, 50,000 units; chemical fertilizer, 5 million tons; and cement, 12−13 million tons. Agriculture, too, will be enormously developed, with grain production reaching 10 million tons by 1984.

Except for electricity, all of the announced targets are either equal to or considerably below the goals previously enunciated by North Korea in 1974. This fact clearly suggests that the DPRK has readjusted its projections of economic growth for the next seven years in the light of current severe economic difficulties. Even so, outside experts believe that Pyongyang will have a hard time achieving the lowered targets unless assistance from the outside world—especially the Soviet Union and China—is forthcoming.

South Korea. During 1978 relations with South Korea continued to deteriorate. Talks on rapprochement have been suspended for more than five years. Meanwhile, the DPRK resumed violent propaganda attacks on the Republic of Korea, and tension between the two Koreas was at its highest level since the end of the Korean War in 1953. DPRK propaganda campaigns claimed that the danger of war was steadily increasing because of the southern regime's "war preparations."

Since talks have collapsed, the Pyongyang regime has shown no change in its intransigent attitude in dealing with the issue of national unification, merely reiterating its opposition both to any "cross-recognition" of Seoul and Pyongyang by outside, especially great powers, and to simultaneous admission of the two Koreas to the United Nations.

In July the DPRK rejected outright South Korean President Park Chung-hee's proposal for the establishment of a consultative body between the divided peninsula to promote economic exchange. At the same time Pyongyang refused to discuss unification with South Korea as long as President Park remained in power.

The military situation in Korea in 1978 was potentially as explosive as ever. American and South Korean troops in late October discovered a new North Korean underground invasion tunnel in the southern sector of the Demilitarized Zone. More than a million men were under arms in the divided peninsula, each side possessing the most sophisticated modern weapons short of the nuclear variety. While none of the great powers encouraged either Pyongyang or Seoul to reunify the peninsula by force, Korea presented at least as great a threat to world peace as did the Middle East.

International Views and Positions. During 1978 Pyongyang tried to undermine the international position of its rival regime in South Korea and develop world support for its policies. Parliamentary, trade, and other goodwill missions were dispatched abroad and invited to North Korea, and friendly diplomatic gestures were made to every corner of the earth, especially the Third World countries, whose bloc has increasingly dominated actions at the United Nations. In particular, the DPRK sought to prevent recognition of "the two Koreas" concept by the world community, to isolate South Korea from both the Third World and the Communist bloc, and to drum up diplomatic support for the annual United Nations debate on the withdrawal of United Nations (actually U.S.) forces from South Korea.

The DPRK has recently replaced its ambassadors assigned to sixteen countries while increasing the number of officials on foreign service in Asia, the Middle East, Africa, and Europe. This move was aimed at strengthening Pyongyang's diplomatic and economic ties with nonaligned countries as well as at intensifying anti-Republic of Korea activities.

President Nicolae Ceauşescu of Romania and the two top-ranking Chinese Communist leaders—Hua Kuo-feng and Teng Hsiao-ping—visited the DPRK during 1978.

Relations with the Soviet Union and China. Moscow and Peking still sought to preserve the status quo on the Korean peninsula and gave verbal and material support to please North Korea and to draw Pyongyang close to each of their sides. Moscow and Peking also urged the prompt withdrawal of American troops from South Korea.

In mid-January Kim Il-song accepted the Order of Lenin, one of the Soviet Union's highest decorations, at a meeting with Dinmukhamed A. Kunaev, a member of the Political Bureau of the Soviet communist party. Kim also received a personal letter from the Soviet leader, Leonid D. Brezhnev. In mid-October North Korea reaffirmed its "friendly and cooperative relations" with the Soviet Union on the occasion of the thirtieth anniversary of their opening diplomatic ties. The official North Korean Central News Agency (KCNA) said that the reaffirmation was made in the form of an exchange of messages between DPRK Foreign Minister Ho Tam and Soviet Foreign Minister Gromyko. In mid-October both Moscow and Pyongyang also signed an agreement concerning the exchange of scientific research materials between fisheries research institutes of the two countries. During 1977—78 Pyongyang failed to secure new aid commitments from Russia. Most observers believe that this was caused by the DPRK's inability to make good on its outstanding Soviet debts and that all Pyongyang got from Moscow was a concession on overdue financial claims.

Chinese Communist Party Chairman Hua Kuo-feng made a six-day visit to the DPRK in mid-May. In public speeches in North Korea, Hua endorsed Pyongyang's insistence on being the "only legitimate" government representing all of Korea. Expressing China's support for the "peaceful reunification" of the two Koreas "without foreign interference," he also called for the withdrawal of American troops from South Korea and the dissolution of the United Nations Command. But no joint communiqué was issued at the end of Hua's visit, and unresolved differences on some issues between Peking and Pyongyang probably remained.

Following the visit of Hua Kuo-feng, Chinese Vice-premier Teng Hsiao-ping and his four-member Chinese delegation arrived in Pyongyang in early September to take part in the thirtieth anniversary celebration of the DPRK on 9 September. He pledged to solidify further friendly ties between China and North Korea and gave perfunctory support to Pyongyang's demand for U.S. withdrawal from South Korea.

While Moscow appeared to be plain stingy as far as further aid to North Korea was concerned, Peking seemed more generous. Pyongyang also owed China a considerable sum of money, but Peking reportedly extended its moratorium for the repayment of these debts. During his visit to the DPRK in May, Hua Kuo-feng promised the North Koreans to supply cheap Chinese oil (one million tons of crude oil per year at U.S. $4 to $5 per barrel—half the U.S. $11 per barrel for crude oil imported by North Korea from the Soviet Union)—and to build several factories and plants.

The DPRK has kept silent on the Sino-Japanese peace and friendship treaty signed in Peking on August 12 and on Chinese Vice-premier Teng Hsiao-ping's visit to Japan in October to ratify the treaty. North Korea's silence could signify displeasure at the closer ties between China and Japan. Teng and former Japanese Prime Minister Fukuda had agreed during their talks in Tokyo that there was no danger of war on the Korean peninsula, a theme so often reiterated by North Korea. Teng's denial of war danger on the Korean peninsula represented a rejection of Pyongyang's familiar charges that a new Korean War can flare up at any moment because of "war preparation" in the South.

During 1978 the DPRK seemed to move closer to China, while maintaining its traditional nonaligned position friendly both to China and the Soviet Union. Reports and observations of Pyongyang's slightly pro-Chinese tilt had been apparent since Chinese Communist Party Chairman Hua Kuo-feng's visit to the DPRK in May; this impression was reinforced by frequent exchanges between North Korean and Chinese military delegations.

Such an observation seemed to be clear when Chinese Vice-premier Teng Hsiao-ping was the star name on the list of guests from the communist and Third World countries who came to Pyongyang to celebrate the thirtieth founding anniversary of the DPRK on 9 September. At that time North Korea gave a hearty welcome to Teng and his party. On the contrary, however, Pyongyang was reportedly cool to the Soviet delegation led by Vice-president Nazar M. Marchanov, a member of the Central Committee of the Soviet communist party but not of its Political Bureau. Kim Il-song had talks with Teng but did not meet the Soviet delegate during the celebration.

Yet there was no firm indication that the DPRK wanted to move away from its neutral position in the rivalry between the two major communist powers. Kim Il-song fully recognizes that Moscow, which has provded the DPRK with vast economic and military aid since the birth of his communist regime, is still valuable as an ally.

To Pyongyang's obvious chagrin, the Soviet Union appeared to have softened its policy toward South Korea conspicuously, showing an unprecedentedly favorable attitude toward Seoul during 1978. In early September *Kazakhstanskaya Pravda* (the organ of the Central Committee of the communist party, Supreme Council, and cabinet of the Kazakhstan Socialist Republic), for the first time referred to South Korea by its formal name, the "Republic of Korea." For the first time in the history of the United Nations, Soviet Foreign Minister Andrei Gromyko made no reference to the Korean peninsula situation in his keynote speech at the United Nations General Assembly conference on 26 September.

In addition to the above gestures, Moscow expanded its nongovernmental contacts with South Korea. The Soviet Union in the summer permitted the entry of a South Korean cabinet minister and allowed South Korean reporters to attend a World Health Organization meeting there. In late September four South Korean scholars were permitted to visit the Soviet Union to participate in an international conference in Moscow on the preservation of nature.

China accused the Soviet Union of "flirting and colluding" with South Korea and said that this signified Soviet support for a "two-Korea" policy. The Soviet Union lost no time in responding to this charge, saying that the aim of Peking's accusation was to drive a wedge between Moscow and Pyongyang. The Soviets retorted that China was trying to distract attention from its collusion with Washington by defending the United States bases and troops stationed in Japan; they even charged Peking's leaders with having assured American diplomats that China considered the presence of American troops in South Korea a stabilizing force in that part of the world.

Relations with Japan. The Japanese tried to get the North Koreans to repay overdue trade debts of an estimated U.S. $370 million in principal and interest owed to banks and companies. Agreement had been reached in 1976 for the DPRK to pay interest on those import debts in 1977 and to repay the principal in 1978. But, say the Japanese, the last payment by Pyongyang was in February when it sent U.S. $3.6 million in interest that was due last September.

Japan and North Korea agreed to extend a private interim fisheries agreement by two years until 1979. The agreement, which was to have expired on June 30, allows Japanese fishermen to operate within the DPRK's newly declared 200-mile economic zone up to its 50-mile military sea boundary in the Sea of Japan. Japanese Foreign Ministry officials said that this extension would not constitute a step toward recognition of the Pyongyang regime.

Relations with the United States. North Korean verbal attacks on the Carter administration continued during 1978. The North Korean Communists ended their fourteen-month moratorium on personal criticism of President Carter on March 28 and launched a blistering verbal attack. Pyongyang urged the United States to withdraw "immediately and totally" all troops and lethal weapons from South Korea, charging that the Carter administration was following a "deceptive Korean policy" in delaying its withdrawal of forces from the Korean peninsula. The DPRK charged that the United States was strengthening South Korea's war potential by carrying out a "double-faced policy of war and peace." An editorial of the official *Nodong Shinmun* in late June charged that arms reinforcement and war preparations by the United States behind the curtain of troop pullouts had "reached a very dangerous stage in its plot to start an adventurous war of aggression." The United States rejected North Korean chieftain Kim Il-song's reiteration of his proposal for direct talks with the Carter administration and urged him instead to resume direct discussions with the South Korean government.

Press reports in April that a U.S. table tennis team had accepted the DPRK's invitation to participate in the Thirty-fifth World Table Tennis Championships in Pyongyang next year, heightened Seoul's suspicions and uneasiness at a time when Washington-Seoul relations were at their worst due to the Tong Sun Park influence-buying scandal in the U.S. capital. South Korea feared that the visit of an American table tennis team to North Korea could be a repeat of the 1971 ping-pong diplomacy which paved the way for the United States and Mainland China to normalize their ties.

United Nations. United Nations Secretary General Kurt Waldheim told visiting South Korean Foreign Minister Park Tong-jin on 22 September that the DPRK had informed him two weeks previously of its plan not to bring up the Korean question at the thirty-third regular session of the United Nations General Assembly in 1978.

Publications. The KWP publishes a daily organ, *Nodong Shinmun,* and a journal, *Kulloja.* The DPRK government publishes *Minju Choson,* the organ of the Supreme People's Assembly and the cabinet. The *Pyongyang Times, People's Korea,* and *Korea Today* are weekly English-language publications. The official news agency is the Korean Central News Agency (KCNA).

Washington College   Tai Sung An

Laos

The leaders of Laos demonstrated their support for Vietnam in the latter's disputes with Cambodia and China during 1978. Although such support was predictable on the basis of past experience, there were signs that the final breakup of the unity cemented at the 1970 Indochinese summit conference of revolutionaries came as a traumatic shock to the Lao. Meanwhile, its economy in shambles with people being told to live on cassava, taro, and yams, Laos embarked on the first year of a three-year plan.

The country's governing party, the Lao People's Revolutionary Party (Phak Pasason Pativat Lao; PPPL) had in 1975 an estimated membership of 15,000 (*NYT*, 5 October 1975). The estimated population of Laos is 3.5 million.

Leadership and Organization. The PPPL has a Political Bureau of seven members: Kaysone Phomvihan (general secretary), Nouhak Phoumsavan, Phoumi Vongvichit, Phoun Sipaseut, Khamtai Siphandon, Sisomphon Lovansai, and (former Prince) Souphanouvong. The Central Committee includes these seven and sixteen others, one of whom died during 1978: Chanmi Douangboutdi, Khamsouk Saignaseng, Ma Khaikhamphithoun, Maichantan Sengmani, Maisouk Saisompheng, Meun Somvichit, Nhiavu Lobaliayao, Sali Vongkhamsao, Sanan Soutthichak, Sisavat Keobounphan, Somseun Khamphithoun (deceased), and Souk Vongsak. Alternate members are Khambou Soumisai, Mrs. Khampheng Boupha, Saman Vilaket, and Sisana Sisan.

Little is known about these people and their roles in the PPPL leadership. Although the PPPL has moved into the open, its procedures and deliberations are still kept secret.

Auxiliary and Mass Organizations. Official organs still refer to the Lao Patriotic Front (Neo Lao Hak Xat; NLHX, sometimes NLHS) on the anniversary of its founding on 6 January 1956. This body, which served as the PPPL's principal mass-mobilizing instrument during the long war years, appears to play little active role today, and its founding anniversary serves as an occasion to call for greater national unity among Laos's different ethnic minorities, who are greatly underrepresented in the leadership structure.

Party Internal Affairs. Few details of the PPPL's internal affairs are known, although it does provide the leadership of the Lao People's Democratic Republic (LPDR) and controls all important government positions.

Domestic Attitudes and Activities. The current role of the PPPL is officially said to be to lead Laos through the period of "socialist transformation and socialist construction." In the words of the statement issued by the Central Committee on the founding anniversary:

> Our party has grown stronger and bigger in all respects, especially with regard to internal unity and unification from the party central level down to party grass-roots organizations. Party cadres and members

have also grown stronger and come to grasp more firmly proletarian attitudes and principles. We are very proud of our party, which is the organizer and leader of all the victories of the Lao revolution. (Radio Vientiane, 22 March.)

Official organs cited 1978 as the first year of a three-year plan to mark a major step in the party's governance of the LPDR. Economic conditions were far from encouraging. To cope with a serious shortfall in rice production resulting from imposition of the country's first agricultural tax in 1976 and a severe drought in 1977, the regime urged farmers to plant maize, cassava, taro, and yams and to dig ditches to allow rivers and marshes to irrigate paddy fields. The economy also suffered from a shortage of trained technicians, a handicap offset only in part by foreign experts, mainly from the Soviet Union.

The anniversary of the LPDR on 2 December 1977 was without banquets, illuminations, or public festivities. In place of the military parade of 1976, only 30,000 people gathered in front of the former National Defense Ministry. In a demonstration intended to show unity, former Prime Minister Prince Souvanna Phouma appeared on the tribune along with the other LPDR leaders.

Many of the technicians of the former royal regime are still among the "tens of thousands" of persons who Kaysone, in a rally speech, claimed are in reeducation camps or, upon their release, have been "transformed by the revolution" (ibid., 2 December 1977).

Other persons with skills have joined the continuing outflow from Laos of refugees, which has totaled more than 100,000 people since 1975. Most of these have been housed in temporary refugee camps in Thailand.

Domestic security remained critical during 1978 as resistance to the regime flared up only to be repressed, and then reignite. There were still many people with arms and ammunition in the countryside to oppose the LPDR government. However, in what appeared to be the fiercest repression of the armed Hmong (Meo) tribesmen to date in the Phou Bia mountain range northeast of Vientiane, thousands of resistance members fled when their villages were destroyed by North Vietnamese artillery and aircraft. The lucky ones escaped across the Mekong River into Thailand. There were persistent reports that napalm and gas were used by the North Vietnamese. Refugees spoke of a white powder that caused coughing and death and of shells releasing poisonous fumes that induced vomiting; foreign doctors reported treating victims of gas inhalation (*International Herald Tribune*, 23 October).

In the vicinity of the towns of Phong Saly and Vieng Sai, "bandits and thieves" were reported to be creating disturbances (Radio Vientiane, 15 May). And in southern Laos, resistance by small bands, often made up of disaffected units of the Lao People's Liberation Army, continued to spread.

Although details were sketchy, there apparently were two attempts to assassinate Kaysone: in 1976 at the national day ceremonies and in 1977 during a trip to the Vientiane airport. The KPL news agency reported on the trial of 26 persons before the People's High Court for the attempts. (*Far Eastern Economic Review*, 2 December 1977.) Security arrangements surrounding Kaysone's recent appearances in public have been strengthened.

International Views and Policies. An exchange of documents to ratify the 25-year treaty of friendship and cooperation and the border delimitation treaty was held in Hanoi between the Laos Deputy Prime Minister and Foreign Minister Phoun Sipaseut and the Vietnamese Deputy Prime Minister and Foreign Minister Nguyen Duy Trinh. This event consolidated the "special relationship" between the two countries.

Souphanouvong paid a visit to Democratic Cambodia from 17 to 22 December 1977, when tension between Cambodia and Vietnam worsened. Nothing was publicly reported about any discussions of the conflict that might have taken place. However, in separate meetings on 3 and 10 January,

Laos Foreign Minister Phoun Sipaseut received the Vietnamese and Cambodian ambassadors in Vientiane and expressed to both parties Laotian regret over the incidents that had occurred and the hope that a solution would soon be found to the border dispute (Radio Vientiane, 4 and 11 January). On 17 January the KPL news agency denied a report by Reuters that a Vietnamese division had moved down from Laos to the northern sector of the Cambodian border. The statement said:

> It is the policy of the Lao party and government not to allow any country to use Lao territory to invade another country. On the other hand, they have always been persistent in pursuing their policy of solidarity with Vietnam and Cambodia. Since the founding of the Lao People's Democratic Republic, there has never been any military operation carried out by Vietnam armed forces through Lao territory. (KPL, 17 January.)

This statement was worded to exclude any reference to the estimated 30,000 Vietnamese troops stationed in Laos since the end of the war, whose presence is now permitted by the recent treaty between Laos and Vietnam.

However, this evenhanded treatment of the Vietnam-Cambodia dispute dissolved into a partisan attitude by the LPDR government as 1978 wore on. On 16 January the Supreme People's Council and the Council of Ministers convened to discuss the world situation as well as the conflict's influence upon Laos. On 17 and 18 January Kaysone dispatched letters to Le Duan, Pham Van Dong, and Pol Pot, deploring the armed incidents but for the first time approving the Vietnamese proposals to Cambodia for negotiation of the conflict.

Nothing further was said publicly by Lao leaders on the conflict until 2 March when Kaysone reported on international and internal affairs to a joint session of the Supreme People's Council and the Council of Ministers. He noted the long history of border disputes in Indochina and said that the three-point proposal made by Vietnam on 5 February was a "rational" one. (Radio Vientiane, 6 March.) Further support of Vietnam's position came in July when Kaysone and Souphanouvong said the following to Vietnamese leaders:

> We support Vietnam's stand on the settlement of differences between countries by negotiations on the basis of sincerity and mutual respect.

Using the jargon "international reactionaries" to refer to China, the two leaders implied that Laos sided with Vietnam in the latter's growing dispute with Peking:

> We once again reaffirm that we always stand by the side of the Vietnamese people and wholeheartedly support the fraternal Vietnamese people's just struggle to defend their independence, sovereignty, and territorial integrity against threats, pressure, trouble-making, provocation, violation, slander, and sabotage conducted by the imperialists and the international reactionaries (KPL, 17 July).

An editorial in the party newspaper *Siang Pasason* on the same occasion seemed to blame China for Cambodia's refusal to negotiate the border question with Vietnam:

> All attitudes and acts of great-nation chauvinism and narrow nationalism by any country to force other states to depend on it and sacrifice the interests of other nations are outmoded, reactionary, and contrary to the trend of history. They cannot avoid humiliating defeats. (Radio Vientiane, 18 July.)

As for the conflict between Cambodia and Vietnam, the LPDR leaders probably see Vietnam's offer to negotiate as an opportunity to avoid publicly criticizing Cambodia. This might explain why they urge the Cambodians to negotiate the difficult border question. If Vietnam was moving its troops across Lao territory into the area of Cambodia west of Stung Treng (on the Mekong River), as was reported, this act must have made the LPDR leaders ponder just how far the Vietnamese expect to push their "special relationship" and what the reactions of the Chinese will be.

In mid-1978 China reportedly pulled out its three engineer regiments and support troops used in Laos for constructing roads in the northern part of the country (*Los Angeles Times*, 15 June). Whatever the move signified in the context of Sino-Lao relations and even in Sino-Soviet relations in the Indochina area, it was an important and unexpected event. A protocol for China's building aid to Laos had been signed in Vientiane on 20 January, and the Lao had been counting on continued Chinese aid. Whether Peking decided to cut off all aid to Laos, as it did in the case of Vietnam during 1978, remains to be seen.

A cooling with Peking left only the Soviet Union as the most important foreign aid donor to Laos, and new agreements were signed during late 1977 and 1978. One such agreement signed in Moscow on 23 December 1977 covered economic assistance in 1978, and another in February 1978 followed a visit to Laos by a Soviet economic delegation. The Soviet Union also furnished unspecified military aid to Laos, and there were reports that the Soviets had built a large radar installation at Savannakhet and were manning it (*Bangkok Post*, 28 May).

Aside from the agreements with Vietnam for trade, road and bridge construction, and other projects, Laos entered into economic agreements with North Korea.

International Activities and Contacts. Just as in 1977 when more than 40 foreign delegations visited Laos, the PPPL and LPDR government in 1978 engaged in many exchanges with socialist and other countries. There were visits by delegations from East Germany and Czechoslovakia, a Soviet military delegation, a Chinese road delegation, Vietnamese trades unions and Foreign Minister Nguyen Duy Trinh, and a state visit by Romanian President Nicolae Ceauşescu on his Asian tour.

Kaysone visited Moscow to attend the sixtieth anniversary celebrations of the October Revolution; Foreign Minister Phoun Sipaseut visited Thailand, Malaysia, and Czechoslovakia and attended the nonaligned nations meeting in Belgrade in July; and Phoumi Vongvichit visited East Germany and Czechoslovakia.

Publications. The central organ of the PPPL is the newspaper *Siang Pasason* (Voice of the people), published in Vientiane. There is also an army newspaper. Official news is released by the Pathet Lao News Agency (Khaosan Pathet Lao; KPL), which has daily Lao and French transmissions for internal consumption and a daily English transmission intended for foreign listeners, reportedly prepared in Hanoi by KPL representatives who use material received from Laos and transmitted over Vietnam News Agency facilities. Sisanan Sengnanouvong is both editor in chief of *Siang Pasason* and director general of KPL.

Radio Vientiane broadcasts 22 hours a day. Apart from broadcasting news in Lao and in the languages of Laos's ethnic minorities, Radio Vientiane broadcasts in Vietnamese, Cambodian, Thai, French, and English. Local transmitters are located in provincial capitals, and there are loudspeakers in district towns.

Bethesda, Maryland   Arthur J. Dommen

Malaysia

Communism in Malaysia involves four parties and two distinct regions, peninsular Malaya and the Borneo stae of Sarawak. In west Malaysia (i.e., the eleven states of the Malay peninsula), there exist three groups with various satellite organizations: the Communist Party of Malaya (CPM), founded in 1930, and two rival offshoots, the Communist Party of Malaya/Revolutionary Faction (CPM-RF), founded in 1970, and the Communist Party of Malaya/Marxist-Leninist (CPM-ML), founded in 1974. (For origins of the last two see *YICA*, 1976, pp. 334−336.) The North Kalimantan Communist Party (NKCP) gradually evolved in Sarawak during the 1950s from various communist-infiltrated interest groups of youth, farmers, women, and others. (Kalimantan is the local name for Borneo.)

CPM guerrilla forces are called the Malayan National Liberation Army (MNLA), whereas those of the CPM-RF and CPM-ML designate themselves the Malayan People's Liberation Army (MPLA). Additionally the CPM has employed a covert political network for infiltration and proselytizing, the Malayan National Liberation League (MNLL), at times also known as the Malayan National Liberation Front (MNLF). The CPM-RF has a similar organization called the Malayan People's Liberation Front (MPLF), as does the CPM-ML in its Malayan People's Liberation League (MPLL). The NKCP also maintains a guerrilla army, the North Kalimantan People's Guerrilla Force (NKPGF), but no separate political front organization.

The CPM has about 2,000 hard-core followers, the CPM-RF some 700, the CPM-ML about 300, and the NKCP around 150 members. Affiliation with parties and respective guerrilla forces tends to overlap, but the main CPM faction is thought to have an additional 1,000 or so sympathizers (some with the MNLL) among the inhabitants of the Thai-Malaysian jungle frontier and border towns and villages. All movements claim to have functioning central committees. But the names of only two leaders appear regularly in party literature: Chin Peng, the CPM secretary general for more than three decades, and Wen Ming-chuan, NKPGF chairman since 1974. All parties also claim to have special interest groups for women, youth and others. The Islamic Solidarity Party (Parti Persuadaraan Islam or "Paperi"), the Malayan Peasants' Front (Barisan Tani Melaya), and the Malayan Communist Youth League are CPM affiliates and attempt to influence the Malay Islamic community, rubber tappers and other farmers and teenage youth, respectively. But like the NKCP's Sarawak Farmers Association, these groups are little more than paper organizations to be used periodically as forums to enunciate specific CPM policies.

For many years the CPM main guerrilla forces have operated from bases in southern Thailand. E.g., the MNLA Twelfth Regiment maintains its headquarters in the border district of Betong, Yala province. The Tenth Regiment, consisting largely of Malay and Thai Muslims, is stationed in the southern border zone of Narathiwat province across from Malaysia's Kelantan state. The Eighth Regiment has usually been headquartered along the southwestern border of Songkhla province. Periodic raids on military patrols and convoys as well as development of a network of supporters among Chinese rubber estate workers, farmers and traders, students in private schools and other youths on both sides of the border, and Sino-Thai businessmen have been among the west Malaysian parties' main preoccupations.

All four Malaysian communist movements are Peking oriented in their international outlook. They acknowledge Mao Tse-tung's thoughts as a major doctrinal inspiration and stress the necessity for operational self-reliance, guerrilla-style people's war, and tactical encirclement of cities from the countryside. All four parties also favor the breakup of the Malaysian Federation, whose establishment (1963) they consider to have occurred by undemocratic means and as a part of "imperialist" machinations by Britain and the United States. They envisage a "democratic socialist Malaya" (consisting of the peninsular Malay states plus Singapore) but political self-determination and presumably independence for Sarawak and Sabah (the two states in Malaysian Borneo). Operationally the NKCP-NKPGF is wholly independent from the CPM and the other two west Malaysian parties, although the CPM and NKCP do consider each other in fraternal terms and periodically exchange greetings. The continuing differences between the CPM and its two minor rivals, the CPM-RF and CPM-ML, appear to involve primarily leadership quarrels and personality clashes with few programmatic or tactical differences. In the 1970s a fear of extensive purges led dissidents to leave CPM and eventually form the CPM-ML and CPM-RF. The parent CPM continues to have the more extensive program reaching out to landless peasants, hard-pressed rubber smallholders, unemployed but educated youths, and others with grievances against the economic system and government in power. There were no significant programmatic or organizational changes in any of the four parties. A statement over the Voice of the Malayan Revolution claimed that the MNLA had won "tremendous victories" in some "133 battles and other military operations" and that more than 560 enemies had been "wiped out" during the preceding year (*FBIS*, 3 February). Three weeks later the CPM's "fraternal" party, Paperi, broadcast a message which condemned the Hussein Onn government's "oppressive atrocities" against Malay Muslims (ibid., 1 March).

In a retrospective statement broadcast over Voice of the Malayan Revolution, the CPM declared that it had united itself closely with "the great Chinese Communist Party" in the struggle against modern revisionism and that the "protracted revolutionary armed struggle" had tempered the party, educated the people, and enhanced the "new nationalist revolution" in the country (ibid., 4 May).

A CPM Central Committe statement commemorated the thirtieth anniversary of the outbreak of the "national liberation war" against British control of Malaya. It reviewed and reaffirmed party policy positions. The "basic contradiction" in Malayan society is between "imperialism, the landlords and bureaucrat-bourgeoisie" and the "nationalities and people of all walks of life." To overcome this contradiction, the CPM seeks a "new democratic revolution," based on an alliance of workers and peasants and supported by a national united front composed of all classes. Tactically the CPM is enjoined to use various contradictions in society to its own advantage, to solve the land problem, and to end the nationality problem, i.e., the often tense relations between the principal racial and ethnic groups in Malayan society. The latter requires a "proletarian" viewpoint: "It is necessary to propagate the idea that workers and peasants of all nationalities belong to one family and that the working people of all nationalities are class brothers." (Ibid., 29 June.)

Considering the relative lack of contact between the two groups in the past, a letter from NKCP chairman Wen Ming-chuan to the CPM Central Committee on 25 June was noteworthy, particularly because the NKCP evidently continues to support the parent Malayan party against criticism by its two rival offshoots, the CPM-RF and CPM-ML. Wen stated in his letter that the CPM has always supported the revolutionary struggle in North Kalimantan and that CPM-NKCP relations are close because they face common enemies and because their "revolutionary conditions are similar in many respects." Wen's letter also mentioned the defections and acceptances of government amnesty by several hundred NKCP members in recent years (see *YICA, 1975*, pp. 384–385). But he also noted that the "renegades" were now out of the party, that "daring revolutionary fighters" of the party were persisting in their struggle, and that "no reactionary force" would be able to put out the "raging fires" of the struggle to liberate the people. (Voice of the Malayan Revolution, 22 July; *FBIS*, 26 July.)

Domestic Developments. On 8 July general elections were held with 154 seats at stake in parliament or Chamber of the People, which had been dissolved four weeks earlier. The coalition of parties in the National Front, led by Premier Hussein Onn, obtained 131 seats, four fewer than in the 1974 elections. (It also won control of all state legislative assemblies.) Sixteen seats were taken by the main opposition party, the Democratic Action Party (DAP), compared with nine in the old parliament. The opposition Pan-Malayan Islamic Party won five seats; the newly formed Sarawak People's Organization took one, as did a progovernment independent from Sabah. The conservative Malayan Chinese Association (MCA) won seventeen seats versus twenty previously. (*Far Eastern Economic Review*, 21 July; *FBIS*, 26 July.)

Although the results were free of fraud and accurately mirrored the state of opinion, restrictions had been placed on election campaigning, ostensibly in the interests of public security. On 19 June, for example, the government banned open-air public rallies, on the grounds, as the premier explained, that Communists might provoke incidents. The DAP leader in Perak state protested that "the Communists will always be there" and that "since the government knows it can never wipe out the remaining isolated pockets (of the Communists), they feel they can use this as a reason for banning rallies" (*Far Eastern Economic Review*, 28 July).

The election gains made by the DAP were a warning to the government that significant segments of the Chinese community (36 percent of Malaysia's twelve million population) remain estranged from economic development and educational policies. Security policies represent another source of grievance among Chinese and DAP supporters. There are only 70 political prisoners in Malaysia, held on charges of alleged subversion or security violations (*Amnesty International Report*, 1977, p. 199); virtually all of them are Chinese. Two DAP members, one of whom obtained the largest majority of votes by any of the successful candidates in the election, could not campaign because they were in jail for alleged subversive activity (*NYT*, 11 July).

Not surprisingly, the CPM sharply denounced the general elections and their results. Over its clandestine radio transmitter, the CPM charged the government with "relying on the gun" by using a so-called "maintenance of law and order" policy to intimidate the masses and to frighten the opposition parties. According to the CPM, the announcement of nomination and voting dates was closely followed by "large-scale searches and arrests" in such states as Perak, Negri Sembilan, Selangor, and Pinang, "thus overshadowing the whole country with terror." Moreover, some 64,000 troops also were placed in combat readiness by the government according to the CPM. From these and other developments, "it can be seen that the Hussein (Onn) clique could not have won the majority of seats if it had not resorted to force and the threat of force." Finally, the government was accused of resorting to bribery. Even though limits had been established on expenses of political candidates, monies spent by the ruling coalition allegedly exceeded stipulated amounts by as much as twenty times in some cases. (Voice of the Malayan Revolution, 15 July; *FBIS*, 20 July.)

During the year arrests of suspected Communists and sweeps by security forces of CPM strongholds continued. It was announced that police in Malacca had arrested 56 "communist underground" members and had killed two others. Substantial quantities of arms and ammunition, including homemade weapons, and printing materials belonging to the Communists reportedly were discovered in three tunnels, two in the Alor Gajah district and one in the Jassin district (*Straits Times*, 28 February). The attorney general reported the arrest of 60 "agents" at Triang, Pahang state, in connection with an alleged communist attempt to establish a covert "logistical base" in the area.

The following month, security forces engaged in three running gun battles with a group of 20 to 30 communist guerrillas in the Ulu Muda Forest Reserve near the Thai-Malaysian border. Several Communists were reported to have been killed. Ammunition and documents were also captured. (Ibid., 17 March.) Subsequently, the home affairs minister announced that a "communist underground movement" in the state of Negri Sembilan had been smashed by police actions. Ninety-six had been arrested last year and 35 in the present year, he said. (*FBIS*, 6 April.) During June, a sequence of five clashes, described as "major" in nature, took palce with bands of communist insurgents. The deputy inspector general of police noted that these had occurred on the thirtieth anniversary of the "liberation struggle," and he appeared to suggest that Communists had been turning to acts of violence in connection with the forthcoming general elections (ibid., 6 July).

Concern over the effects of communist psychological warfare and proselytizing was expressed in several official quarters during the year. The minister of home affairs stated that authorites had proof Communists were trying to infiltrate schools in Kampar, Batu Gajah, Ipoh, Kuala Lumpur, and other places. He urged parents and teachers to be vigilant, adding that both secret societies and communist terrorist activities had implications threatening to public order and national security (ibid., 16 May).

Meanwhile, the government security committee in Perak announced the publication of *A New Life*, aimed at communist insurgents and other "subversive elements" operating in the state. Written in Chinese, the magazine is distributed in "security sensitive areas" where Communists are "known to be present," according to an official spokesman. Articles and photographs have as their theme "the happy and prosperous lives Malaysians in general are leading" and the "futility of the communist struggle to overthrow the government" (*Straits Times*, 20 April). Included in the magazine are statements of former Communists in which conditions of their lives in the jungle are contrasted with their improved circumstances since they rejoined society.

As in previous years, close coordination continued between the Malaysian and Thai military for the purpose of joint operations against CPM insurgents and the two rival offshoot parties operating on both sides of the border. Malaysian communist insurgents (generally referred to as "Chinese communist guerrillas" in the Bangkok media) were reportedly fleeing from Thai security sweeps in the Than To and Betong districts of Yala province. The Thai defense minister, during a visit to Kuala Lumpur, declared that the combined operations were designed to "apply continuous pressure" on the guerrillas in order to prevent them from regrouping. He admitted that insurgents had managed to regroup "on a minor scale," but failed to regain influence among the local population. (*Sarawak Tribune*, 29 April).

Toward the end of last year, the Sarawak state government announced that 21 persons had been released from its Center of Protective Custody. They had been held over periods ranging between one and fifteen years for "communist and antinational activities." (*FBIS*, 14 December, 1977.) The chief executive officer of RASCOM, the principal counterinsurgency command in Sarawak, advised "all concerned" not to be complacent over the government's success against the guerrillas but to "continue to be vigilant," since the threat posed by the Communists still remained great (*Sarawak Tribune*, 31 March). Operationally, NKPGF appears not to have recovered from massive defections three years ago, and there were few clashes with Malaysian security forces during the year. Last year a RASCOM spokesman estimated the total strength of the NKPGF at 107 (ibid., 28 March 1977). However, the Malaysian army chief of staff announced that "about 150 Communists" were hiding on Sarawak (*FBIS*, 4 August).

Officials have expressed their satisfaction with the effectiveness of the joint anti-communist border operations with Thailand and Indonesia. Reviewing them, the Malaysian defense minister declared that both had been successful, the number of Communists in the jungle had been decreasing, and communist attempts to infiltrate from Thailand had been thwarted. He expressed general satisfaction with the state of security in the country. (*FBIS,* 11 August.)

International Aspects. During the year, both the CPM and the NKCP sent messages to the Chinese Communist Party, indicating their continued close identification with Peking in the international communist movement. The CPM on the occasion of the conclusion of the Fifth National People's Congress praised it for "upholding the great banner of Mao Tse-tung thought" and declared that the congress "marked the beginning of a world-shaking long march to be made by the Chinese people who account for one-fifth of the world's population." Under Hua Kuo-feng, "socialist China is a strong bulwark for world revolution," and its prosperity and vitality are perceived as "vigorously" aiding the struggles of the Third World's peoples against "imperialism, colonialism and hegemony." (Voice of the Malayan Revolution, 11 March.)

A letter sent by the NKCP chairman congratulated the Central Committee of the Chinese Communist Party on its third plenary session. It praised Hua Kuo-feng, "Chairman Mao's good student and successor," who is carrying forward "the behests of the great revolutionary teacher" and has decisively broken the machinations of the "Gang of Four." The letter added that "confirmation" of Hua Kuo-feng's position as chairman and his leadership of the People's Liberation Army were facts of "great and far-reaching significance" in consolidating both the party and the dictatorship of the proletariat in China. (New China News Agency, 6 August.)

During the year, Malaysia continued to make informal efforts within the Association of Southeast Asian Nations (ASEAN) to foster improved relations with the new communist regimes in Indochina. Vietnam's vice-foreign-minister visited Kuala Lumpur in July. He described the relationship between his country and ASEAN member states in various fields as "encouraging." In a meeting with the Malaysian premier, he indicated that it was his country's policy to establish "practical cooperation" with countries in Southeast Asia on the basis of mutual respect and peaceful coexistence. The premier, in turn, expressed the hope that Vietnam's border conflict with Cambodia and its difficulties with China would be solved peacefully in the interests of regional stability. (*FBIS,* 24 July.)

During his visit, Vietnam's vice-foreign minister reportedly declared that conditions were favorable for establishment of a zone of peace and neutrality in Southeast Asia. Malaysian commentators generally praised this suggestion and pointed out that the new approach contrasted with Hanoi's earlier position that the 1971 ASEAN peace and neutrality proposal had been nothing more than a "neocolonialist plot" (ibid., 26 July). It soon became apparent that Hanoi's friendlier posture toward ASEAN reflected increasingly tense relations with China. Vietnam's premier, Pham Van Dong, visited Kuala Lumpur as part of a general goodwill tour of the five ASEAN capitals. In a pointed display of neutrality, the Malaysian government planned to receive Peking's vice-premier, Teng Hsiao-ping, toward the middle of October (*Asiaweek,* 29 September).

An agreement was announced between the visiting foreign minister of Laos and Malaysia to work for "promotion of peace, stability, and economic progress in Southeast Asia." Kuala Lumpur reportedly offered training facilities in broadcasting and development administration. Both states would also "continue their dialog" on establishment of a "zone of peace, freedom, and neutrality" in Southeast Asia. (*FBIS,* 16 May.)

The political views of Malaysian students abroad, many of whom have increasingly vented antigovernment criticism, aroused concern during the year. The premier said that his government knew about a small group of students in Australia who were "procommunist, anti-Malaysia, and antigovernment." This was based on several of their publications, he said, and from their involvement in hostile demonstrations on 13 February in Sydney, when the premier attended a meeting of Commonwealth governments in the Pacific and Asia. Some 40 students were involved in the demonstration, whose aims reportedly were to advance the cause of the communist struggle in Malaysia and mar the government's image. (*Sarawak Tribune*, 28 March.)

Publications. Malaysian communism's principal medium of communication is the Voice of the Malayan Revolution, a clandestine transmitter believed to be located at Hengyang in southern China, about 200 miles south of Changsha. Under CPM control, it also has occasionally relayed statements of Indonesian and Philippine (Peking-oriented) communist parties. Broadcasts are mainly in Mandarin but occasionally in Malay and Indonesian. The CPM-ML is believed to have a transmitter calling itself the Voice of the People of Malaya, but its signal is weak. Since an initial broadcast on 4 May, 1976, little has been heard of it. In the past three years, the Voice of the Malayan Revolution has also transmitted main NKCP policy statements and messages. But the latter group, like the CPM-RF, relies primarily on poorly stenciled leaflets for propaganda and recruiting purposes. Malaysian security officials periodically claim to have found printed materials of the MNLL, MNLF, and other front groups, but the nature of these has not been revealed. Apart from use of its radio transmitter for dissemination of statements which it believes to be important also for those outside Malaya, the CPM, as well as its rival offshoots, seems to depend principally on word-of-mouth communication and close cadre contact. Supporters in Britain publish a monthly, the *Malayan Monitor and General News.* Its appearance is subject to delays, however; issues in 1978 carried world news as well as long excerpts from the writings of Mao Tse-tung. The media in Peking, both foreign language and domestic, devote little or no attention to the CPM, unlike two decades ago when its statements and activities were frequently reported in the Chinese press.

University of Bridgeport   Justus M. van der Kroef

Mongolia

A fusion of two revolutionary groups produced the Mongolian People's Party in 1921. The party held its First Congress in March of that year at Kyakhta, on Soviet territory. It became known as the Mongolian People's Revolutionary Party (MPRP) in 1924. Fiftieth anniversary celebrations in November 1974 commemorated this shift to "socialism" in 1924, but Russian dominance had already been established in 1921. The designation of the country as the Mongolian People's Republic (MPR) was adopted in 1924, as was the name of the capital, Ulan Bator (formerly Urga). At that time a noncapitalist and antibourgeois line was announced by the party's Third Congress and the first Great Khural (the structural equivalent of the USSR Supreme Soviet).

In 1976 the MPRP claimed 67,000 members (compared with 58,000 in 1971). The population of the MPR in 1977 was estimated at just over 1,500,000.

Organization and Leadership. Tsedenbal's annual August meeting with Brezhnev in the Crimea confirmed his number one position as leader of the MPR, while Batmunkh, the prime minister, continued as number two man. General Avkhia (b. 1923) succeeded General Dorj (b. 1914) as minister of defense. Major General Gunsen (b. 1923) became state prosecutor, while G. Ish (b. 1924) succeeded Gunsen as chairman of the Supreme Court. Avkhia had been first deputy minister of public security and state prosecutor; Dorj had earlier been minister of public security; Gunsen had formerly been deputy minister of public security; and Ish served for a time as first deputy state prosecutor. Thus, the close interrelationship of the Defense Ministry, the Public Security Ministry, the Supreme Court, and the Prosecutor's Office continues. In June Major General Tumendemberel, first deputy minister of defense and director of Mongolian civil defense since February 1975, toured installations and discussed civil defense in Lithuania in company with the USSR's deputy chief of civil defense.

The minister of education since 1965, Ishtseren, died in March and was succeeded by R. Sajaasuren. P. Jasray, who had been head of the Central Committee's Department for Economics and Planning, became first deputy chairman of Gosplan and received assimilated rank of government minister in May. Tsedenbal's Russian wife enjoyed renewed press attention after comparative obscurity in the preceding year. Direct connection of USSR ministries with MPR ministries bypassing the central government continues the trend to "convergence" specifically noted by Politburo member Molomjamts in February and by Tsedenbal in October. Announcement of MPR consular officials in Tashkent emphasizes closer ties with Soviet Central Asia.

Domestic Attitudes and Activities. Related developments were the continued decline in total livestock and the imposition of controls to limit and even reduce urban population. Tighter controls were also imposed on private ownership of animals, and requirements were added for compulsory delivery of livestock products. The flight from the rural areas, mainly to the capital city of Ulan Bator but also to the new development at the copper-molybdenum project city of Erdenet, has exceeded natural population increases and probably caused manpower shortage for care of the herds. Larger urban population, however, still does not compensate for the loss of the construction workers provided by immigrant Chinese in the 1950s, and some Vietnamese laborers were building various projects in the MPR in 1978.

The USSR subsidy to Mongolia—the excess of Soviet exports over their imports from the MPR—increased once again, partly due to continued outlays for new projects, such as Erdenet. The mines have not yet begun production but are supposed to do so in 1979. The total Erdenet output is scheduled to go to the Soviet Union.

Russian-language study was emphasized even more than before and combines with the ever closer military-defense and economic integration, so that the "nationalistic-independent" portion of MPR decision-making and administration becomes even less important, while the part directly subject to USSR direction grows more important.

International Views and Contacts. A major force driving the MPR closer to the Soviet Union is the continuing dispute with China. The themes dominant in MPR publications and statements in 1978 included accusations that China plans to annex Mongolia, that Chinese incursions on Mongolian territory continue, that Soviet troops must stay in Mongolia to defend against the immediate threat of aggressive China, and that China mistreats its own Mongols, Tibetans, and other ethnic minorities. The MPR also expresses its pro-USSR, anti-China policy by increasing favorable attention to Vietnam and Laos, including employment of propagandistic Buddhist connections.

On its side, China vigorously attacks the Mongolian claims and accusations and particularly expresses outrage about the Soviet troops stationed in the MPR. China once again refused to permit

Mongolian representatives into Manchuria and Inner Mongolia to hold memorial services at the monuments commemorating MPR participation in World War II and loss of lives there at that time. But "normal" relations also continue, with trade negotiations in March and announcement of a new Chinese ambassador in Ulan Bator—Meng Ying, who had been a consular official in the MPR in 1960.

Special economic arrangements with Japan, and proposed similar deals with Great Britain, are still small but have already begun to extend MPR economic activity beyond communist countries. The Japanese are actually building a small factory in Ulan Bator, and Britain may soon be supplying textile machinery. The Indian minister of foreign affairs received his Mongolian counterpart with some effusiveness, calling attention particularly to ancient religious-philosophical ties of the two countries and emphasizing the significance of Sanskrit sources in Mongolian libraries and archives to India's understanding of its past.

Publications. The MPRP issues *Unen* (Truth), *Namyn Amdral* (Party life), the Russian-language *Novosti Mongolii* (News of Mongolia), and a Chinese-language weekly *Meng-ku hsiao-hsi-pao* (News of Mongolia). *Ediyn Dzasag* (Economics) is issued by the MPRP Central Committee and *Shine Hodoo* (New countryside) by the Ministry of Agriculture. The MPR assigns a representative to the editorial board of *Problems of Peace and Socialism.* There are radio broadcasts in Mongolian, Russian, English, Chinese, and Kazakh. Television broadcasting was begun in 1970.

University of North Carolina   Robert A. Rupen
Chapel Hill

Nepal

The Communist Party of Nepal (CPN), like all parties in the kingdom, is proscribed. Reliable information on the total number of CPN members is not available, but for various reasons the membership estimate has been revised downward to 4,000. Nepal's population is estimated at 13,680,000.

Leadership and Organization. Keshar Jung Raimajhi remains general secretary of the moderate faction of the openly divided CPN. Through selective support of the monarchy, the Raimajhi CPN and its sympathizers have occasionally been given official, if not significant, positions. In August Raimajhi was among those the king nominated as members of the Council of State. In addition, D. P. Adhikari, a CPN cofounder, has been minister of state for water and power since September 1977.

Pushpa Lal Shrestha, a longtime leader of more extreme CPN elements, died in India last July. It is still unclear how much of an effect his death will have on the leadership and policies of the revolutionary CPN exiles. The extremist elements remain factionalized, and Man Mohan Adhikari continues to head the extremist faction within Nepal.

Both CPN organizations apparently still focus their efforts on students and intellectuals in the Katmandu valley and urban areas of the Tarai in southern Nepal. CPN influence, however, appears limited.

Domestic Attitudes and Activities. K. J. Raimajhi was one of four politicians who issued a joint statement in November 1977 calling for parliamentary democracy, although not specifically for a multiparty system. The group was a disparate one—at least two members are considered pro-Soviet and one is reputedly pro-Chinese. The statement criticized administrative corruption and incompetence, warned against foreign involvement in Nepal, and also contained criticism of Nepali Congress leader B. P. Koirala.

In a measured response soon afterward, Prime Minister K. N. Bista said that the government's new "liberal" attitude stemmed from self-confidence, not weakness, and warned that his government would not hesitate to deal with hostile elements (*Far Eastern Economic Review*, Hong Kong, 23 December 1977). During the latter part of 1977, however, statements from government organizations indicated that there could be no basic changes in the Panchayat system.

The pro-Soviet newspaper *Samiksha* was again banned in April. The government gave no reason for its action, but political observers considered the paper's strongly antigovernment stance the likely cause (*FBIS*, 3 May).

The death of revolutionary CPN General Secretary Pushpa Lal Shrestha evoked expressions of grief and tributes from a large number of noncommunist as well as communist politicians in both Nepal and India. CPN supporters held condolence meetings for several weeks afterward; in some cases participants were arrested, apparently because the government considered the meetings to be political demonstrations (*Arati*, Katmandu, 26 July, 2 August).

Activity by Naxalite terrorists was reported in western Nepal as well as in the eastern districts, their traditional area of operation (*Far Eastern Economic Review*, 9 June). There is no indication, however, of a major resurgence of terrorist activity such as that of several years ago.

Meanwhile, a key political issue continues to be the fate of B. P. Koirala, who has now been acquitted of the most serious charges against him, including subversion. The elderly opposition leader met with King Birendra in October and reportedly said later that he supported the monarchy and felt "hopeful" about his proposal for "national reconciliation" (*Nepal Post*, Katmandu, 5 November). Koirala, nevertheless, remains a controversial figure, and rivalry, rather than cooperation, seems to mark his relations with other opposition elements.

International Views and Policies. The moderate CPN, recognized and financially assisted by the USSR, continues to urge closer Nepali-Soviet relations. Chinese involvement with factions of the extremist CPN appears limited to some financial support.

Publications. The weekly *Samiksha* reflects views of the moderate CPN.

Alexandria, Va.   Barbara Reid

New Zealand

The Communist Party of New Zealand (CPNZ), founded in 1921, is unique among communist parties in that it has been aligned first with the Soviet Union, then with China, and now (since 1978) with Albania. Soviet supporters split off in 1966 to form a separate organization, the Socialist Unity Party (SUP), which has gained recognition as a member of the world communist movement. Chinese supporters defected in May 1978 and set up a Preparatory Committee for the Formation of the Communist Party of New Zealand (Marxist-Leninist). Among the possible components of this projected party are such earlier pro-Chinese groupings as the Wellington Marxist-Leninist Organisation (known locally as MILO) and the group of supporters around the journal *Struggle*, as well as the recently formed Northern Communist Organization in Auckland and Hamilton. The major Trotskyite group in New Zealand is the Socialist Action League (SAL), which was founded in 1969.

These organizations all function legally. Membership figures have not been published, but the combined strength of all Marxist groupings can be estimated at 500. The SUP is largest with perhaps 200 members, followed by the CPNZ with an estimated 150 and the SAL with up to 100. The population of New Zealand is 3,116,000.

Leadership and Organization. The CPNZ is required by its constitution to hold a national conference at intervals not exceeding three years. No such conference has been held since 1966, and elected offices which fell vacant could not be constitutionally filled. For many years now the party has had no national chairman, and about half the members of the National Committee elected in 1966 have since died, resigned, or been expelled. This year it was revealed that the party no longer had a general secretary; V. G. Wilcox, who has held this office since 1951, was removed from all posts of responsibility (though not expelled or replaced) in March 1977.

Wilcox's demotion was kept secret even from party members as the National Committee hoped to "solve the contradiction in a nonantagonistic manner." The decision was however communicated to the Central Committee of the Chinese Communist Party. Rumors filtered back to New Zealand through visitors to China, but the first hard news was an article "Unite all Marxist-Leninists in Oceania," which appeared on 2 March 1978 in *Vanguard*, the organ of the Communist Party of Australia (Marxist-Leninist) — CPA(M-L). It stressed that support for Mao's theory differentiating the three worlds was the touchstone of true Marxist-Leninists and denounced "all those who in the name of communism oppose the revolutionary essence of communism, either by silence, attempted suppression of comrades like comrade Wilcox, lies, slanders, intrigues and conspiracies."

Copies of this article were sent anonymously to CPNZ members and sympathizers throughout New Zealand. The CPNZ reacted strongly to this "crude attempt to split the CPNZ" and "outrageous interference in the internal affairs of one party by another." Wilcox, it said in reply, was not "suppressed" but "under criticism" over questions of principle dating back several years and totally unconnected with the three worlds theory. As regards the latter, the party would resolve its attitude "in its own time." (*People's Voice*, 3 April.)

On 7 April *Peking Review* reprinted excerpts from the *Vanguard* article, a clear sign that it had Chinese approval. The CPNZ cabled a protest to Peking, which was ignored, and another *Vanguard* article commenting on New Zealand affairs followed on 27 April. At about this time the Chinese party canceled its orders for the *People's Voice* and the *N. Z. Communist Review*. Since substantial quantities were involved, the CPNZ characterized this action as "a deliberate blow at the economics of the *People's Voice* and hence at our Party" (*CPNZ's Firm Stand Against the New Revisionism*, Auckland, 1978, p. 28).

The CPNZ National Committee next issued a statement setting out its differences with the CPA(M-L): "The basic contradiction in New Zealand, a developed capitalist country, is that between the working class and the capitalist class headed by the monopoly section. Consequently the working class faces a directly socialist revolution. Any attempt to try to insert an intermediate stage between capitalism and the dictatorship of the proletariat is opportunism and revisionism." (*People's Voice*, 22 May.)

The great majority of members and all but two out of about a dozen branches rallied around the party leadership. On 23 May Wilcox and three other members (one of them a member of the CPNZ National Committee, another the national president of the New Zealand—China Friendship Society) announced the setting up of a Preparatory Committee for the Formation of a CPNZ(M-L). They stressed their support for the three worlds theory and for cooperation with the CPA(M-L). On 24 June in Auckland they held an enlarged initial meeting of the committee but decided to postpone the setting up of a new party until they gained wider support.

The CPNZ also held an extended plenum of its National Committee on 2—3 September and published the full text of the resolution adopted there with the title *CPNZ's Firm Stand Against the New Revisionism*. The leadership announced that Wilcox's removal had made it possible to convene the long postponed national conference; the date is still uncertain but preconference discussion material which denounces the three worlds theory as incorrect and non-Marxist has been issued to party members. According to the Wilcox group, the leadership of the CPNZ is now in the hands of an "Albanian Gang of Three"—R. C. Wolf, H. Crook and R. Nunes—who form the National Secretariat located in Auckland.

The SUP, unlike the CPNZ, has been remarkably stable. G. E. Jackson, who celebrated his seventieth birthday during the year, has been general secretary of the party since its foundation. Two other founding members, G. H. Andersen and Ella Ayo, hold the offices of president and vice-president respectively. There are eleven SUP branches throughout the country, five of them in Auckland where the party has a regional committee as well as its head office with the National Executive. The last triennial conference of the SUP met in 1976.

The SAL held its fifth biennial conference in Otaki in the last week of 1977, with over 80 delegates and observers in attendance. The organizational report claimed that the league had grown considerably, that more members had jobs in industry, and that the league had established a presence in major working-class areas. A new National Committee was elected of ten full and five alternate members. In May this committee elected Russell Johnson the League's national secretary. Later in the year the league moved its headquarters and editorial staff from Wellington to Auckland. It has branches in Auckland, Wellington, and Christchurch.

Auxiliary Organizations. The Progressive Youth Movement, associated with the CPNZ, appears to be defunct, although no formal announcement has been made of its demise. The Democratic Youth Front (DYF) has expanded its activities during the year. It is aligned with the SUP but claims to be an independent organization of young people based on the theory and practice of Marxism-Leninism. Ten New Zealanders, including members of the DYF, attended the Eleventh World Festival of Youth and Students in Cuba in July-August. The DYF is now making plans to launch its own journal, the *Young Worker*.

Four representatives of the Romanian Union of Communist Youth led by Nicu Ceauşescu, son of the president, came to New Zealand in October. Their visit was part of an international visiting program organized by the New Zealand National Youth Council.

The youth organization associated with the SAL is called Young Socialists. They held their fourth national conference in Wellington in June. The Young Socialists' main strength is in the universities where they contest student elections with some success. Their journal, *Young Socialist*, has been published since 1975.

The SUP also has influence in the small Union of New Zealand Women, which dates its origin to 1950. Two delegates from this organization attended a women's conference in Moscow in May at the invitation of the Women's International Democratic Federation.

A branch of the World Peace Council was formed in Wellington early in the year. Another branch exists in Auckland, and they have been active in collecting signatures for the New Stockholm Peace Appeal. Two representatives of the World Peace Council visited New Zealand in July.

Friendship societies work in support of the Soviet Union, China, and the Democratic People's Republic of Korea. Chile solidarity committees exist in several cities. In July for the first time a three-man delegation from North Korea visited New Zealand. The New Zealand–China Friendship Society, which used to be closely aligned with the CPNZ, is now viewed as "no longer a body for promoting friendship between the people of China and New Zealand but an agency for pushing China's great-power chauvinist policy centering on the theory of the three worlds" (*CPNZ's Firm Stand Against the New Revisionism*, p. 8). The CPNZ sees "the petty-bourgeois elements who had collected in the China Society" as the main base of support of Wilcox and his Preparatory Committee.

Domestic Attitudes and Activities. CPNZ, SUP, and SAL have all been active in the trade unions, among the growing number of unemployed, in the woman's movement, and in support of Maori land struggles. The SUP has been able to extend its influence in the N. Z. Federation of Labour, the country's central trade union organization. One of its leaders, K. G. Douglas of the Wellington Drivers' Union, was reelected to the National Executive. Douglas is also secretary of the Wellington Trades Council. G. H. Andersen, the SUP president, is secretary of the Northern Drivers' Union and president of the Auckland Trades Council, the country's largest. SUP members hold other key positions in trade unions, but the party suffered a defeat when one of its leaders lost the secretaryship of the important Meat Workers' Union.

The extent of communist influence in industrial disputes remained a matter of controversy. While the prime minister, R. D. Muldoon, claimed that "a few reds stir a lot," his minister of labour denied significant communist involvement. "The Communists are certainly not a dominant concern," he told the press, "although I do get concerned about one or two instances. When you are sitting at this desk dealing with up to ten disputes a day, you don't see much Communist influence." (*Auckland Star*, 14 June.)

Nineteen seventy-eight was the year of the triennial national elections, and both the SUP and the SAL again put forward candidates for Parliament. The CPNZ, which has not contested elections since 1969, boycotted what it calls "the parliamentary circus." The SUP stood five candidates, compared with fifteen in the previous general elections in 1975. It urged its supporters to "vote SUP where our candidates are standing. Vote Labour in all other electorates to ensure the defeat of the National Government at the polls." (*New Zealand Tribune*, 9 October.)

The SAL announced that it would stand six candidates, compared with four in 1975, but it then withdrew two candidates a few weeks before the elections. The league also urged its supporters to vote for the opposition Labour Party in districts where no SAL candidates were standing: "We call on working people to kick out Muldoon and elect a Labour government. We must put the Labour Party in office and insist that it represents our needs." (*Socialist Action*, 29 September.)

The elections resulted in a return of the National government, though with a reduced majority. The SUP and SAL campaigns received very little publicity, and as in 1975 their candidates polled badly. The preliminary election-night results showed a total of 183 votes for the five SUP candidates, and 125 votes for the four SAL candidates. The final count will slightly increase these figures, but in no instance did the SUP or SAL vote exceed half a percent of the votes cast in the electorates contested.

International Activities and Contacts. No CPNZ overseas visits were reported during the year, but the Albanian Party of Labor welcomed the CPNZ's stand in an article in *Zëri i popullit* (18 June). So too did the Communist Party of Italy (M-L) in a statement in *Nuova Unità* (11 July). Messages of support also came from the communist parties of Spain (M-L) and Japan (Left) and from the Ceylon Communist Party.

G. H. Andersen, the SUP president, visited the Soviet Union for the first time in April at the invitation of the Communist Party of the Soviet Union. His month-long tour also took in the Ninth Congress of the World Federation of Trade Unions in Prague (where he was joined by four other New Zealand observers), the GDR, Denmark, and Italy. A four-man delegation of the Central Committee of the Hungarian Socialist Workers' Party, led by A. Bondar, came to New Zealand in October at the invitation of the SUP. A joint statement of the two parties was signed on 12 October (text in *New Zealand Tribune*, 23 October). G. E. Jackson and the Hungarians later attended the Third Congress of the Socialist Party of Australia.

Two Australian delegates attended the SAL national conference, one of them representing the United Secretariat of the Fourth International. G. Fyson represented the SAL at the fusion conference of the Australian Socialist Workers' Party with the Communist League in Sydney in January.

Publications. The CPNZ publishes a weekly journal, *People's Voice*, and a monthly theoretical journal, *N. Z. Communist Review*. Much of the latter used to consist of reprints of overseas material (mostly Chinese and Albanian), but in future local material is to predominate. The SUP publishes the fortnightly *New Zealand Tribune* and the theoretical journal *Socialist Politics*, which appears about three times a year. *Socialist Action*, the organ of the SAL, is also published fortnightly.

A pro-Chinese theoretical journal, *Struggle*, produced by a group of defectors from the CPNZ, has been published in Porirua near Wellington since 1975. Another pro-Chinese group, the Wellington Marxist-Leninist Organisation, began publication of a monthly bulletin, *Unity*, in March. Wilcox's Preparatory Committee publishes its own bulletin, and the first issue of *Class Struggle*, magazine of the Northern Communist Organization, made its appearance in November.

No circulation figures are available, but *Socialist Action* probably has the widest distribution within New Zealand, with about 2,500 copies, followed closely by the *New Zealand Tribune* and the *People's Voice*.

University of Auckland   H. Roth

Pakistan

In late 1978 the illegal Communist Party of Pakistan (CPP) continued to pose no discernible overt threat to the government of Pakistan. The CPP, an offshoot of the Communist Party of India, was formed shortly after Pakistan became independent with the partitioning of British India in August 1947. In 1954 the government banned the CPP as a subversive and illegal organization under the provisions of the Criminal Law (Amendment) Act of 1908. Moreover, the Political Parties Act of 1962 prohibits the formation or functioning of any party that the government defines as detrimental to "Islamic ideology" or the "integrity and security of Pakistan."

Foreign observers speculated that in the mid-1970s the CPP had perhaps 1,500 members, a tiny fraction of the country's estimated 77.7 million (mid-1978) population. Intelligence officials of the United States government profess not to know the exact number but suggest that although formal CPP membership was probably less than 1,500, several thousand students, workers, intellectuals, and ethnic and regional dissidents privately espoused variations of communist doctrines and were members or supporters of various clandestine, little-known communist organizations. Despite Pakistan's close official relations with the People's Republic of China, most adherents of communist ideology were believed to be pro-Soviet.

On 16 October Pakistan's martial law government promulgated an ordinance amending the Political Parties Act of 1962 to specify that no political party would be allowed to exist that received aid from or was associated in any way with a foreign country or its nationals. The amendments stipulated that officers of parties which had been dissolved by the government may not engage in any political activity for seven years from the date of dissolution. The amendments were made retroactive to 5 July 1977, the date of the military coup d'etat.

The government's ordinance presumably was prompted by the formation in Pakistan of one or more avowedly communist parties and by the violent coup d'etat in neighboring Afghanistan by the pro-Soviet People's Democratic Party in April 1978. The 20 October issue of the *Far Eastern Economic Review* carried a report that a new communist party had publicly enunciated its political goals. A spokesman for the Awami Jamhurriya Ittehad (United People's Democratic Party; UPDP) asserted that the UPDP would "follow the example of the coup in Kabul to capture power," adding that this would be accomplished in two years. The spokesman, Anis Hashmi, said that he was the president of the Sind province branch of the party. C. R. Aslam, a longtime and well-known activist in pro-Soviet organizations, was identified as the president of the national party.

Foreign observers opined that the pro-Soviet coup in Afghanistan had not only contributed to the creation of the UPDP, and possibly other similar groups, but had also heightened the military government's concern that the several dissident and separatist groups in Pakistan might seek and receive aid from the new regime in Kabul. In mid-1978 Mir Hazar, the leader of the self-described Marxist-Leninist organization, Baluch Awami Azadi Mahaiz (Baluch People's Liberation Front), was residing in the party's guerrilla base in southeastern Afghanistan. This political-cum-guerrilla group emerged during the 1973-1977 "war" that was waged in Pakistan's Baluchistan province between the

Pakistani armed forces and large segments of the Baluch people. In an article in the fall issue of *Foreign Policy*, Selig Harrison, a longtime and highly respected observer of South Asian affairs, estimated that "at least 3,300 Pakistan military men and 5,300 Baluch guerrillas, as well as hundreds of women and children caught in the crossfire, were killed in the four-year war." In mid-1978 Baluch public opinion, at least as voiced by the more prominent Baluch leaders, ranged from demands for considerable provincial autonomy within Pakistan to demands for a sovereign, independent Baluchistan. According to Harrison, one of the most influential Baluch spokesmen, Khair Baksh Marri, does not exclude the possibility of an independent Baluchistan under "a form of national communism" that would be aligned with neither the Soviet Union nor China.

The 1977 military coup resulted from the political chaos that followed the parliamentary election held in March 1977—the second direct, universal election in Pakistan's history. Prime Minister Zulfikar Ali Bhutto's Pakistan People's Party (PPP) had been expected to win a majority of the seats, but the PPP's margin of victory was so overwhelming that the opposition coalition—the Pakistan National Alliance (PNA)—charged that the election had been rigged. The PNA consisted of the National Democratic Party, formed in 1975 by former members of the proscribed National Awami Party, led by Sardar Sher Baz Mazari; the branch of the Pakistan Muslim League led by the Pir of Pagaro; Tehrik-i-Istiqlal led by Air Marshall (retired) Mohammad Asghar Khan; the Pakistan Democratic Party led by Nawabzada Nasrullah Khan; the Jamaat-i-Islami led by Tofail Mohammad; the Jamiat-ul-Ulema-i-Pakistan led by Maulana Shah Ahmad Noorani; and the Jamiat-ul-Ulema-i-Islam led by Maulana Mufti Mahmud. Ideologically, the groups ranged from socialists and liberals, who were generally dedicated to parliamentary democracy, to Islamic fundamentalists, who desired to institute the observance of the letter as well as the spirit of *sharia* (Islamic religious law). The groups and their members were united, however, in their fear and hatred of Bhutto and his party and what the PNA leaders came to refer to as "Bhuttoism."

During the campaign the PNA leaders—particularly Asghar Khan and Mufti Mahmud—had warned that Bhutto's supporters might attempt to steal the election and had asserted that the PNA would not accept the results of a rigged election. When the results of the election were made public, the leaders of the PNA announced that the PNA would boycott the elections to the provincial legislatures scheduled four days later, that the few PNA members who had been elected to the National Assembly would not take their seats, and that the PNA would formally protest the election results. Throughout the country, but particularly in Punjab and Sind provinces, massive rioting broke out. Within a few weeks hundreds had been killed and hundreds more wounded. Bhutto responded by increasing the activities of his special police, the Federal Security Force, and, in Lahore and a few other major cities, calling on the army to restore and maintain order. At the same time Bhutto began to charge that his opponents were being supported by foreign powers, and he later made clear that he meant the Central Intelligence Agency of the United States.

The senior military officers had all been selected by Bhutto and had in fact been promoted over officers senior to them, several of whom were exiled to diplomatic posts abroad. Although a number of middle-grade officers and at least three brigadiers were known to be distressed that the army was engaged in police work of a repressive nature, the chiefs of staff continued through the spring and early summer to express their support for Bhutto as the head of government. When what had appeared to be an agreement between Bhutto and the PNA collapsed and rioting seemed about to start again, the army on 5 July 1977 placed Bhutto under house arrest and imposed martial law. Army General Mohammad Zia ul Haq assumed the position of chief martial law administrator, chief of state, and head of government. In December 1978 he still held that post.

General Zia almost immediately announced that new elections would be held in October 1977. In September 1977, however, he postponed the elections until charges brought against Bhutto by the martial law authorities had been heard and tried by the High Court in Lahore. The charges ranged from allegations of official corruption to conspiracy to commit murder. On 18 March the High Court found Bhutto guilty on the charge of conspiracy to commit murder and condemned him to death by hanging. Bhutto appealed the decision to the Supreme Court but as of late November the Supreme Court had not handed down its opinion. General Zia has made clear his intention to accept the Supreme Court's ruling, which most observers, both Pakistani and foreign, expected would leave standing the High Court's death sentence.

Bhutto's many enemies publicly endorsed the High Court decision, even if some of them found the court's reasoning something less than judicially compelling. Bhutto's large body of supporters and admirers, however, were bitterly and at times violently critical of the ruling. Although most of the officials of Bhutto's PPP who remained loyal to him were in jail in November 1978—as were an estimated 10,000 adherents of Bhuttoism—observers expected that Bhutto's death would provoke a violent reaction, particularly in Punjab and Sind. In September and October, for example, in protest against the sentence and Bhutto's expected death, six individuals engaged in self-immolation; one person died, and the others were not expected to survive.

The severe public punishments for political and serious criminal acts imposed by the martial law authorities were applauded by some, who endorsed General Zia's wish to adhere to the letter of the centuries-old Islamic law, but were viewed with dismay and repugnance by the secularist majority of Pakistan's literate minority. In March 1978, for example, a former member of the prorogued National Assembly, an ardent supporter of Bhutto, emerged from hiding to lead a demonstration against the imprisonment and trial of Bhutto. The individual was seized and sentenced the same day to imprisonment for one year and five lashes by the cane. The flogging was carried out the following day; no appeal had been allowed. At about the same time three men were publicly hanged after conviction on charges of kidnapping, murder, and rape; these were the first public executions in Pakistan's history. In May Amnesty International reported that at least 160 people had been flogged after conviction for political crimes. Again, the sentences were imposed by martial law courts and were not reviewed by civil courts. And in June, 4 of the 150 journalists jailed for participating in a hunger strike against government restrictions of the press were publicly flogged.

Foreign observers concluded that in late 1978 the political system was more seriously and widely split than at any time in the nation's history. The example of the secession of East Pakistan and the creation of Bangladesh remained a topic of constant discussion. These observers and numerous Pakistanis feared that the groups most alienated by the death of Bhutto and the increasingly draconian measures of the martial law regime—i.e., the students, intellectuals, and ethnic, religious, and linguistic-regional separatists—might seek a solution to their perceived problems by embracing the dogma and ideology of either the Soviet or Chinese model and by seeking and accepting help from the new communist government in Kabul. A few more pessimistic observers feared that the dissolution of Pakistan was at hand.

The American University   Richard F. Nyrop

Philippines

There are two communist parties in the Philippines. The older is the Philippine Communist Party (Partido Kommunista ng Pilipinas; PKP) founded on 7 November 1930, essentially oriented toward Moscow. The other, with a Maoist-influenced program and leaning toward Peking in the Sino-Soviet dispute, is the Communist Party of the Philippines/Marxist-Leninist (CPP-ML) founded on 26 December, 1968. Both are officially proscribed. Republic Act 1700, the so-called "Antisubversion Law" of 17 June 1957, has never been repealed and formally declared the PKP to be an illegal organization. Its provisions have been formally applied to the CPP-ML as well. President Ferdinand Marcos cited the threat posed by the latter's guerrilla forces as justification for the martial law proclaimed on 22 September 1972 and still in force.

The PKP policy of favoring constitutional rather than violent change has made its leaders more acceptable to the present government, and PKP leaders have at times even attended occasions at Malacanang, the Philippine White House. PKP Secretary General Felicisimo Macapagal has emphasized that his group is an "independent" Filipino party, although he has admitted that the PKP generally has tended to support the position of the USSR because of the its "progressive and principled position" in contrast to the allegedly "chauvinistic and pro-imperialist position" of the Chinese (Letter to the Editor, *Asiaweek*, Hong Kong, 28 October 1977). More recently, Macapagal has praised Marcos as "one of the strongest and most determined Filipino presidents," whose policies have marked an "unprecedented public assertion of Philippine sovereignty" against U.S. and other "imperialist" interests (*WMR*, August). Marcos "represents essentially the reformist and industrialising sector of the national bourgeoisie," and while his "pragmatic centrist position" is historically "a step forward," the "imperialist forces" are attempting to "destabilize" his regime as economic conditions worsen. The PKP is estimated as having about 250 members. But the party has additional sympathizers in some trade union and intellectual circles, and it serves the government as an informal conduit in relations with the Soviet bloc. PKP Central Committee members, like former Secretary General José Lava, have continued to give modest praise as well as mild criticism for the economic development and foreign policies of Marcos (ibid., December 1977).

Since the capture on 10 November 1977 in the town of San Fernando, La Union province, of José Maria Sison, CPP-ML chairman, the latter organization has been in a leadership crisis. It is estimated to have about 2,000 members, most of them also affiliated with the party's guerrilla New People's Army (NPA). Like the PKP, the CPP-ML claims to have a functioning central committee. But partly because of the dispersed, insular nature of Philippine territory and partly because of the shifting tactical demands of guerrilla warfare, the CPP-ML organization is considerably decentralizd with provincial and local party committees and NPA units exercising a high degree of autonomy.

Founded on 29 March 1969 and described in the CPP-ML Constitution (Art. IX, Sect. 3) as the "main weapon of the Party in the people's democratic revolution and in the subsequent socialist stage," the NPA has ceaselessly engaged in ambushes of and running gun battles with the Philippine police and other security forces. From time to time, it also has established de facto control over several villages and small towns in the northern and central Philippines (see author's article in *Issues and Studies*, March 1978).

Next to waging "liberation war," the CPP-ML sees itself as committed to developing a broad-based mass movement, joining "with all forces that are opposed to the fascist dictatorship of the U.S.-Marcos clique" and involving peasants, trade unions, students, intelligentsia, petite and national bourgeoisie, and ethnic minorities, including those affiliated with the so-called Moro (Muslim) rebellion in the southern provinces (see below). According to its self-defined "tasks," the CPP-ML is required to "coordinate" the southern Muslim struggle with the revolutionary armed struggle in Luzon and the Visayas, so that the U.S.-Marcos dictatorship will become exhausted. There is little indication that such tactical coordination has occurred, however, and Muslim suspicions of the NPA and indeed of all Marxism allow for only occasional tactical alliances.

As martial law over the years has drawn an increasing amount of domestic and international criticism, CPP-ML's front-building efforts have met with a measure of success. This does not mean, of course, that the whole anti-Marcos opposition is CPP-ML inspired; however, the party has to some extent been able to capitalize on that opposition which ranges widely from church and missionary circles to intellectuals and partisan political opinion. On 5 January Marcos told a special U.S. congressional mission that "the active communist movement in the Philippines now centers around the National Democratic Front, a relatively new organization serving as an umbrella for all subversive groups." He also stated that "communist insurgents [presumably the NPA] are being assisted by the Communist Party of the People's Republic of China" (U.S. Congress, House Committee on International Relations, *Prospects for Regional Stability: Asia and the Pacific. Report Submitted by a Special Study Mission to Asia and the Pacific*, 2–22 January 1978, p. 11).

Actually, the National Democratic Front (NDF) is a CPP-ML sponsored group and had been in the process of formation since April 1973. CPP-ML oriented support groups abroad describe the NDF as continuing "to organize all progressive forces against the U.S. backed Marcos regime" (*Makibaka: Join Us in Struggle*, London, Blackrose Press, 1978, p. 29). NDF publications assert the existence of a "secret army of activists" who, though belonging to different organizations like the Federation of Filipino Workers or the Union of Nationalist Urban Poor, presumably also are in sympathy with the aims of the "umbrella" NDF (*Liberation*, 15 June; cited by *Philippine Liberation Courier*, Oakland, 18 August). Thus, the CPP-ML, the more dynamic part of Philippine communism, appears to be repeating some of the communist strategy of the middle and later 1960s, when a broadly based complex of leftist and radical nationalist organizations also had come into existence as a general antigovernment mass movement, led by Sison and subsequent heads of the CPP-ML.

Despite the CPP-ML's apparent emphasis on building a broad-based united front, NPA guerrilla activity also has continued. There have been NPA ambushes and running battles with small NPA units on Mindanao (*FBIS*, 4 March, 26 April). However, NPA guerrilla leader Roberto Guevara ("Commander Kamonte") was captured in a gun battle in the mountains of Bamban on Luzon (*Straits Times*, 10 March). Later fighting near Capas in Tarlac province reportedly wounded the second ranking NPA leader, Juanito Rivera ("Commander Juaning"), though he was able to escape (*FBIS*, 15 May). Clashes also took place with NPA units near Libog, Camarines Sur, Chuayan, and Isabela, resulting in capture of Luelhati Agril, CPP-ML secretary for eastern Mindanao (ibid., 3 August, 19 September).

Ernesto Dizon ("Commander Darmo"), Cagayan valley NPA commander, surrendered in May. The following month 22 persons, including 3 American servicemen stationed in the Philippines, were arrested in Manila on charges of having sold high-powered firearms to the NPA (*FBIS*, 25 May; *NYI*, 13 June). Most of them had been employed at the U.S. naval base on Subic Bay.

Preliminary trial proceedings began against CPP-ML Chairman José M. Sison, captured the previous November, before a military court at Fort Bonifacio. Sison is charged with violating Republic Act 1700 and is linked with the ambush killings of three American military personnel outside Manila in

1974 (*FBIS*, 23 June). NPA units staged attacks in such widely separated areas as Kalinga-Apayao province, 200 miles northeast of Manila and the town of Baganga in Davao Oriental province, 600 miles south of the capital (ibid., 27 September). CPP-ML media claim that coordination proceeds through liaison teams, which also maintain contacts with the masses.

Domestic Developments. Formally, overwhelming support continued to be expressed for the government. On 18 December 1977, about 89 percent of the 22 million electorate voted in a popular referendum for continuation of Marcos as both president and prime minister (*Keesing's Contemporary Archives*, 17 February, p. 28,831). On 7 April general elections took place for the 165 elected seats of the 199-member interim National Assembly. Some 629 candidates contested the seats, but there were only two major political parties: the progovernment Movement for a New Society and the main opposition People's Power Movement. Except for the Visayas (where thirteen candidates of another local anti-Marcos opposition group won) and a few seats in southeastern Mindanao and the central Bicol regions, the progovernment party won. But controversy erupted over the fairness of election procedures. Mass demonstrations occurred in Manila as a protest. (*Asia Research Bulletin*, 31 May, pp. 442–443.)

Already on 27 March, shortly before the elections, Marcos charged that a "communist plot" to "create a revolutionary situation" leading to the overthrow of his government had been uncovered. A week later, unidentified persons bombed two power stations and a government party headquarters in Manila (*FBIS*, 28 March; *Straits Times*, 4 April). Constabulary chief, General Fidel V. Ramos, stated that the Philippine Communist Party (presumably the CPP-ML) had decided to use arson as a major weapon in urban centers, and he blamed a "substantial number" of recent fires in the capital on the communists (*FBIS*, 31 March). Marcos, accusing "anarchists, radicals, and terrorists" and other "subversives" of planning a full-scale armed offensive, reimposed martial law restrictions on free assembly and public political debate (*Straits Times*, 11 April).

In the aftermath of the elections, officials frequently raised the specter of new subversive movements. The Defense Department announced that a new plot, linked to anti-Marcos opposition groups and designed to stir up violence and disorders in Manila and in nearby provinces had been uncovered (*FBIS*, 13 April). Marcos later warned against the persistent threat to national security, declaring that a new socialist group was forming a united front against the government. It had its own armed forces, though it remained "pragmatic" and disavowed some of the overt principles of communism while nevertheless being committed to the use of violence to gain political power. The new group, the United Democratic Socialist Party of the Philippines, is supposedly distinct from the CPP-ML (*Straits Times*, 21 June).

Marcos spoke soon after Defense Minister Juan Ponce Enrile had given an extensive report to the newly elected National Assembly on security and defense. An underground communist organization (presumably the CPP-ML) had succeeded in establishing a National Democratic Front and formed alliances with various disparate groups, including students, professionals, and intellectuals, trade unionists, and religious elements. Enrile noted particularly that some clergymen were security risks, declaring that "the potential of the clergy as a base for subversion cannot be overemphasized" (*Asiaweek*, 30 June).

Amid speculation on how Marcos would attempt to stabilize his government, he named his wife (a political power in her own right) deputy prime minister and successor to himself (*Economist*, 19 August). He continued to improve his image abroad by accelerating release of political prisoners arrested since martial law was proclaimed.

At the close of the previous year, Marcos had granted amnesty to 1,646 persons, said to be "radical student activists and suspected subversives," in accordance with the announced policy of "reconciliation, unity and compassion" (*FBIS*, 29 December 1977). Six months later, the government released another 1,483 martial law detainees in the Visayas in the central Philippines. Among them were those charged with common crimes "as well as those facing charges of subversion" (ibid., 30 June).

Not only NPA insurgents but also guerrilla forces of the secessionist Muslim movement called the Moro National Liberation Front (MNLF) fight against Philippine security forces. In early 1978, a serious rift had become public in the MNLF leadership, and Hashim Salamat replaced Nur Misuari as chairman. According to the Defense Department, the ouster of Misuari reflected dissatisfaction with his alleged tendency to direct the MNLF in a more "Marxist-Maoist direction" (ibid., 15 February).

Although official Philippine sources claim continuing mass surrenders of Muslim dissidents, fighting has persisted. Defense Minister Enrile declared that he was ready to resume peace talks with the MNLF. Enrile said this shortly after Marcos, in an obvious response to recent international expressions of concern over the Muslim problem, had emphasized that the MNLF question "is a Filipino affair and must be settled without any intervention from any foreign country" (ibid., 21 July). Meanwhile, fighting was particularly heavy on the island of Basilan in the south, where Philippine army troops were trying to capture MNLF strongholds in the mountainous regions.

International Aspects. In line with government policy of improving and diversifying foreign relations, including with communist powers, in order to offset Manila's continuing heavy economic and strategic reliance on Washington, contacts with Hanoi, Moscow, and Peking increased notably during the year. On 6 January, the foreign minister of Vietnam, Nguyen Duy Trinh, arrived on an official visit with his deputy. The latter called for a "new form" of regional cooperation in Southeast Asia, reflecting Hanoi's opposition to the Association of Southeast Asian Nations (ASEAN) and the American military presence in the area.

On 12 March Chinese vice-premier Li Hsien-nien arrived in Manila for a visit. Three days later, Marcos announced that the Philippines had come to an agreement with the People's Republic and with Vietnam on the "peaceful settlement" of the dispute over the Spratly islands. The exact nature of the agreement was not announced. Moscow predictably took a dim view of these developments in Sino-Filipino relations. It warned that the "hope that the Chinese leaders would stop supporting the so-called New People's Army has not been realized" and that activities of the Chinese embassy in Manila "had created dissension" among ethnic Chinese in the Philippines. According to the Soviets, further normalization of relations between China and the rest of Southeast Asia, as suggested by the Philippine example, would only "further complicate" the domestic difficulties of Southeast Asian countries. (Ibid., 13 March.)

Publications. Both the PKP and CPP-ML rely on irregularly appearing periodicals, which sometimes have English-language editions. The PKP's main journal is *Ang Kommunista* (The communist), which has usually appeared in stenciled form. The international organs of Moscow-oriented communist parties, *World Marxist Review* and *Information Bulletin*, occasionally publish statements by PKP leaders and reports on activities. The principal organ of the CPP-ML is *Ang Bayan* (The nation), which also has an English-language edition. During the last two years, media in the People's Republic of China have all but ignored the CPP-ML. However, the Peking-oriented clandestine radio transmitter of the Communist Party of Malaya, the Voice of the Malayan Revolution (believed to be located in southern China) continues to broadcast CPP-ML statements. The principal organ of the Maoist wing of the Indonesian Communist Party, *Indonesian Tribune* (still being published in Tirana), occasionally also carries reports on and messages of the CPP-ML.

University of Bridgeport   Justus M. van der Kroef

Singapore

Singapore has no distinctive communist party of its own. Members are formally considered to be affiliated with the Communist Party of Malaya (CPM) and with its satellite organizations like the Malayan National Liberation Army (MNLA) because the CPM, Singapore communists, and their sympathizers view the formation of the Malaysian Federation in 1963 to have occurred illegally and undemocratically. That year, Singapore joined the states of the Malayan peninsula, as well as the Borneo states of Sarawak and Sabah in the formation of Malaysia. But in 1965, after protracted political difficulties with the federal Malaysian government in Kuala Lumpur, Singapore seceded from Malaysia and became an independent republic.

While the CPM, its satellites, or any other formal distinctively communist organization would be illegal, the Singapore government has considered the opposition Barisan Sosialis Malaya (Malayan SocialistFront) to be a communist infiltrated or front organization. However, the latter party since its founding on 26 July 1961 has been legal in Singapore and regularly participates in general elections. While formally retaining their CPM orientation, communists are believed to be affiliated with or to have infiltrated the Barisan Sosialis Malaya. However, Chairman Dr. Lee Siew Choh has repeatedly denied government allegations that the party is a CPM or communist front. Barisan's aim is "merger," i.e., a fusion of Singapore and peninsular Malaya into a "democratic socialist Malaya," permitting the Borneo states of Malaysia (Sabah and Sarawak) to determine their own political destinies.

Domestic Developments. During 1978 the strict security surveillance exercised by the Singapore government over all partisan political activity continued. There were few public Barisan meetings, and the party's appeal to those in Singapore committed to greater political democratization and less security-conscious national policy diminished. Critics of the government have tended to be more attracted to such movements as the Workers' Party and the United Front Party. Neither the Barisan nor other smaller groups hold any seats in the Singapore parliament, the People's Action Party having made a clean sweep of all 63 contested seats in the general elections of 22 December 1976 (*YICA*, *1978*, p. 313).

The communist underground in Singapore during the year appeared not to have revived after elimination in June-July 1976 of an alleged CPM satellite organization, the Malayan New Democratic Youth League (MNDYL), when a dozen arrests were made. Documents captured at the time of these arrests described MNDYL aims, according to the Singapore government, as ranging from covert manufacture of grenades and mines to recruitment of factory workers and infiltration of government departments and parties (*Straits Times*, 7 September 1976). There has been no indication thus far that MNDYL aims were realized to any significant degree. During the year, no publicized arrests under the Internal Security Act or any release of those detained under the act for reasons of alleged subversion occurred. The number of those held is probably more than the figure of 61 given by Premier Lee Kuan Yew on 25 May 1977 (*Amnesty International Report*, 1977, p. 213), and the government remains committed not only to a policy of preventive arrest and detention without trial but also to encouragement of self-incriminatory confessions by political detainees as a condition for release.

In the prevailing political atmosphere, any threat to the present pattern of orderly, rapid economic growth is seen as essentially subversive. As in previous years, not just suspected communists or Barisan candidates but political spokesmen of other political parties as well, particularly at election time, continue to run the risk of arrest and imprisonment or heavy fines because of campaign statements. While there is no overt press censorship, newspapers and other media are unofficially expected, and during the year continued, to practice a certain self-censorship. Meanwhile, prevailing licensure statutes provide the government with effective controls over the appearance of any new publications or any public organizations of whatever kind, including political ones.

During the year, the sensitive question of Chinese-language education, historically exploited by communists, was raised again. In mid-February, the premier announced that the chief language of instruction for the 2,000 students at Nanyang University would be changed from Chinese to English. The use of Chinese for some time allegedly had been linked with communist exploitation of cultural and linguistic pride. As in peninsular Malaya, attempts to curtail or regulate the use of it as a medium of instruction in private schools always have prompted communist charges that the government was seeking to "destroy" Chinese language and culture.

In recent years the daily use of Mandarin among Chinese educated in Singapore has been declining, and between 1959 and 1977 students registering in Chinese-language schools fell from 45.9 to 10.8 percent (*Far Eastern Economic Review*, 7 April, p. 31). Stringent supervision over Barisan publications thus far has limited open Barisan protest against the premier's decision to change Nanyang's instructional language to English, but Barisan spokesmen have indicated that they intend to make the matter a political issue.

Of the 2.4 million population, some 76 percent are Chinese, 15 percent Malay, 7 percent Indian and Pakistani, and 2 percent other backgrounds. The uneven participation of these major groups in the benefits of Singapore's economic development continues to open tactical possibilities to communist and other critics of the government. The unemployment rate fell from 4.5 percent in 1976 to 3.9 percent in 1977 (*Straits Times*, 27 February), but conditions of employment for Malaysian contract workers—mostly ethnic Malays—apparently leave much to be desired. Ethnic Malays thus far have not represented a significant communist or MNLA recruiting ground, but the contract laborers' plight could change that.

International Aspects. Singapore continued to refuse to open diplomatic relations with the People's Republic of China (PRC), although other members of the Association of Southeast Asian Nations (ASEAN) have done so. Indonesia's relations with the Peking government, though not formally broken, have remained "frozen" since the abortive 1965 communist coup in Djakarta. The PRC, according to official Indonesian views, is alleged to have been involved. Singapore officials repeatedly have stated that they will open formal diplomatic relations with the PRC only after Djakarta has done so. Although the Singapore press has welcomed PRC expressions of support for ASEAN, it sharply rejected a Chinese suggestion that ASEAN and Peking establish a "joint front" to balance big power pressures in Asia (ibid, 25 April).

However, Singapore's contacts with the USSR are expanding. On 1 June, their foreign ministers exchanged greetings on the occasion of the tenth anniversary of the establishment of formal diplomatic ties. Somewhat earlier, at the close of May, Soviet Ambassador Yuri I. Razdukhov had commented that during the previous decade the average annual rate of growth in trade between the two countries had been about 7 percent but during 1977 had increased by nearly 25 percent with two-way trade reaching $260 million. He also revealed that the USSR had offered State Minister of Communications Ong Teng Cheong assistance in building a rapid transit system in Singapore (*FBIS*, 1 June).

Singapore has also been interested in improving relations with communist regimes in former Indochina. A trade delegation visited Cambodia, and agreement was reached to resume direct shipping between the two countries "as soon as goods are ready to be shipped." During the visit, a Phnom Penh spokesman said that "as long as we adhere to the principles of mutual respect for independence, sovereignty, and territorial integrity" efforts would be "crowned with success" (*FBIS*, 15, 18 May). During the year, implementation of this agreement occurred slowly, however, although Singapore spokesmen have continued to express themselves sympathetic to closer commercial ties. Recent overtures by Vietnam for improved relations with the ASEAN countries in general have been received with cautious optimism.

Singapore's neutrality has been called into question, however, with the report that U.S. aircraft (mainly P-3 Orions) engaged in long-range reconnaissance flights over the Indian Ocean are serviced and repaired at the Tengah military airbase. Singapore thus has become a peripheral support facility for American military operations centered on the Indian Ocean island of Diego Garcia (*Far Eastern Economic Review*, 19 May, p. 10).

Publications. The main Barisan publication, *Plebeian*, at one time a weekly, now appears only irregularly, allegedly because necessary government permits cannot be obtained. Partisan publications critical of the government are, in any case, few in number except at election time. Poorly stenciled handouts and leaflets represent the principal Barisan media prior to elections. The government has claimed in the past that MNLA materials, (i.e., posters, handbills and leaflets) also have been found. There is no regular opposition medium of the Left or otherwise in Singapore today, and papers and periodicals practice self-censorship. The CPM clandestine radio transmitter, Voice of the Malayan Revolution, in recent years has had occasional broadcasts attacking the government.

University of Bridgeport   Justus M. van der Kroef

Sri Lanka

The Sri Lanka Communist Party (SLCP) observed its thirty-fifth anniversary during the past year, a period in which Sri Lanka's leftist parties have been attempting to recover from overwhelming defeat in the 1977 elections. The Trotskyist Lanka Sama Samaja Party (LSSP) remains the country's other major Marxist party. Communist party membership is estimated at 6,000, with the pro-Soviet SLCP accounting for virtually all of it. The influence of the pro-Chinese factions appears negligible. Sri Lanka's estimated population is 14,283,000.

Leadership and Organization: *The LSSP.* Tensions between the party's traditional leadership and young militants have culminated in the expulsion of the rebels, whose leader, V. Nanayakkara, formed his own party early last year (*Far Eastern Economic Review*, Hong Kong, 20 January).

In its first post-election conference in March, the LSSP undertook a reappraisal of what it called a "critical phase" in the leftist movement. While admitting some tactical errors, the party decided that parliament should remain the primary focus of the United Left Front's (ULF) efforts despite the fact that the Left now holds no seats. In discussing the leadership-drafted "political resolution," the conference also expressed fears of right-wing repression under the United National Party (UNP) government and warned of the dangers of "ultra-adventurism" (*FEER*, 31 March).

The Pro-Soviet SLCP. The SLCP also reassessed its situation and policies prior to holding its Tenth Congress on 22—26 March. The SLCP's candid reappraisal was reflected in the Central Committee's "draft thesis" for the Congress and in General Secretary Pieter Keuneman's comments on the meeting's results. The party acknowledged mistakes in its previous cooperation with the social-democratic Sri Lanka Freedom Party, but asserted that strengthening of the ULF was still of "paramount importance." It admitted internal differences and stated the need to end "rightist trends" while avoiding "ultra-leftism" (*World Marxist Review*, Information Bulletins 17 of 1977 and 14 of 1978; *WMR*, August). The Congress also elected a new 35-member Central Committee including Keuneman and S. A. Wickremasinghe (*FBIS*, 27 March).

After outlining its future course, the Congress concluded that "mass extra-parliamentary struggle" is becoming the main form of activity. It called for a joint program for the ULF and set specific tasks such as greater recruiting and organizational efforts, particularly among the peasantry for the first time, but also among industrial workers and the youth. The party also demanded a new agrarian reform (*WMR*, August).

The Pro-Chinese Communist Parties. The Communist Party of Sri Lanka (Marxist-Leninist) has elected a secretariat whose most prominent member appears to be V. A. Kandasamy (*FBIS*, 2 December 1977). N. Sanmugathasan's faction continues to control the Ceylon Trade Union Federation.

The Revolutionary JVP. There has been little evidence that the strength of Janatha Vimukthi Peramuna (JVP) has grown since the release of Rohan Wijeweera in late 1977. During party rallies early last year Wijeweera noted that he was no longer general secretary and hinted at financial problems for the party.

Domestic Attitudes and Activities. The UNP political and economic programs—including constitutional changes permitting a presidential system of government and austerity measures involving cuts in traditional rice subsidies—have provoked widespread criticism from the leftist groups. One government step in particular apparently sparked a new solidarity among many of Sri Lanka's trade unions over which the LSSP and Communists exert a significant influence.

Following the release in January of the government's proposed labor regulations, virtually all major labor organizations except UNP affiliates formed a Joint Trade Union Action Committee to protest these proposals. The Committee launched a wall poster campaign and picketing activities. Thirteen unions later published a joint declaration rejecting the government "white paper" and resolved to oppose any government efforts to restrict labor's "fundamental rights." This alliance included the LSSP, SLCP and Sanmugathasan's group (*FEER*, 20 January; *Intercontinental Press*, New York, 1 and 22 May).

International Views and Policies. The SLCP Congress reaffirmed the party's "friendship" with the USSR while passing resolutions condemning Maoism and protesting U.S. neutron bomb production. The party also supported Vietnam's position in the latter's dispute with Cambodia (*WMR*, August; *FBIS*, 27 and 30 March, 5 April). The CPSU was one of several communist delegations attending the Congress.

For its part, the pro-Chinese Communist Party (Marxist-Leninist) praised Chairman Hua Kuo-feng's European trip and has demanded that Vietnam cease "its hostilities against China and invasion of Kampuchea" (*FBIS*, 8 September; *Peking Review*, 6 October).

Party Publications. The SLCP publishes *Aththa, Mawbima, Deshabimani,* and *Forward.* LSSP newspapers include *Samasamajaya* and *Janadina.*

Alexandria, Va.   Barbara Reid

Thailand

During 1978 the Communist Party of Thailand (CPT) remained an illegal clandestine organization waging a scattered and intermittent struggle against the government of Thailand from numerous rural border provinces. Estimated at a combined total of 8,000 to 9,000 insurgents in the southern, northern, and northeastern provinces, the CPT has been able to stage attacks against Thai army and police units which have drained sizable resources from the economic development of the kingdom. The ranks of the communist insurgents continue to have considerable numbers of socialists, students, and trade union activists who fled to the rural areas after the military coup in October 1976. Leadership of the insurgent movement is reported to be directed by Udom Sisuwan, the first secretary of the CPT; Bunyen Wothing and Chamni Sakdiset, former socialist members of the National Assembly; Thirayut Bunmi, a former leader of the National Students Center of Thailand; and Thoetphum Chaidi, a former trade union leader.

Student activists have also been involved in broadcasting propaganda messages throughout the kingdom from a clandestine radio station, thought to be located in Laos, called the "Voice of the People of Thailand." According to numerous reports, the CPT, in addition to its armed attacks and radio broadcasts, is seeking to infiltrate youth groups in Thailand, especially the village scout movement, in an attempt to foment antigovernment hostility (*Ban Muang*, 4 January). Yet in spite of some dramatic armed attacks against the government forces, the communist insurgency has been plagued by a growing number of defectors to the government side. These persons have cited a growing disillusionment with the communist movement and personal hardships as major reasons for abandoning the insurgent cause (*Bangkok Post*, 5 May). The Kriangsak government has repeatedly sought to persuade disgruntled students, union leaders, and peasants to leave the communist underground organization and return to their homes. This conciliatory policy is likely to meet with increasing success in the future due to the amnesty law passed by the National Assembly in September, granting freedom to the eighteen Thammasat University students being tried for acts against the government and the monarchy in the events which precipitated the October 1976 coup (*Far Eastern Economic Review*, 29 September). This action has supplemented an earlier executive decree which granted amnesty to all students who fled to the rural areas following the overthrow of the last constitutional government led by Seni Pramoj.

The Southern Insurgency. The communist insurgency in the southern provinces still takes place in an area with several dissident organizations. Chinese communist guerrillas in the Communist Party of Malaysia (CPM) are continuing to wage an armed struggle against the Malaysian government along the Thai-Malaysian border by using Thai territory for staging bases. Thai communist insurgents are active in several provinces further to the north, and the clandestine organization of Thai-Muslim separatists called the Pattani United Liberation Organization (PULO) is also active in the four border provinces. During 1978 all three insurgent groups were involved in armed attacks against Thai government installations and personnel, with the major attacks coming from the two communist guerrilla movements. The Malaysian Chinese Communists have adopted a new method of operating in smaller groups in an effort to obtain food, conduct propaganda campaigns, recruit new members, and gather intelligence on Thai and Malaysian security forces. These guerrillas have staged scattered attacks along the border, but they have become increasingly on the defensive since a major joint military operation called "Selamat-Sawadti" was launched by sizable Thai and Malaysian military forces. (*Bangkok Post*, 11 June.)

Communist rebels have also been active in the provinces to the north. On several occasions they have made surprise attacks against small police outposts and caused extensive destruction before being driven into the jungles by government reinforcements. In June they attacked a government camp at Phattalung and killed 14 border policemen and wounded 28 others. There have been reliable reports that the Thai Communists and the Chinese Communists from Malaysia are cooperating in joint actions against the Thai government. Chinese communist cadres have provided training in guerrilla warfare to their Thai counterparts in return for weapons and supplies. There have also been indications that some cooperation has been achieved between the communist insurgents in these provinces and the Thai-Muslim separatists. (*Nation Review,* 19 August.) To cope with a possible resurgence of communist terrorism, the Thai government has sponsored large-scale demonstrations, including marches by several thousand people to isolated villages, in an effort to bolster stability and morale in these vulnerable areas.

The Northern Insurgency. Like the dissident movements in the South, the communist insurgency in the northern provinces has continued to occur in a region where government security is weak and armed attacks have been made by different hostile groups. Some of these clandestine organizations are involved in the lucrative opium trade between the "Golden Triangle" in Burma, Laos, and Thailand and the channels of the international narcotics market (*Bangkok Post*, 25 August). Other dissident groups are armed minorities involved in antigovernment operations in Burma. Most communist insurgents in the northern Thai provinces are Meo tribesmen who have been trained and armed by foreign cadres. They continue to operate on a somewhat larger scale than the insurgents in the South, and one of their major goals has been to stop road construction in this large mountainous region. They are also better armed than most communist insurgents in other areas and often use rockets and grenade launchers in their attacks against Thai security forces.

In March a communist band of 300 terrorists blocked a road near the provincial city of Phitsanulok and held it for several days before being driven off by government troops. Road construction companies in this area have again been forced to abandon their work because of frequent harassment by the communist insurgents. Armed attacks have also been made by communist terrorists in the provinces of Chiang Mai and Chiang Rai adjoining the Thai-Burmese border. As in the South, the Thai government has launched sizable ground and air attacks against communist strongholds with both army and border police forces. (Ibid., 18 May.)

The Northeastern Insurgency. Except for the areas along the Thai-Cambodian border, the communist terrorists in the northeastern provinces have been somewhat less active during 1978 than in recent years. For several years this densely populated and impoverished region has been the target of gradual infiltration and subversion by the CPT rather than an area of extensive overt military action. Some communist insurgents have continued to launch attacks against Thai government outposts, but they have generally sought to avoid large-scale encounters with Thai army or police forces. (Ibid., 23 July.) This reduced phase of guerrilla warfare has encouraged the Thai government to increase its efforts to eliminate communist influence in this strategic region. As in the South, the Thai army early in the year launched a major suppression drive called the "Naresuan Operation" to reduce communist strength. Eleven communist camps were captured and destroyed, and increasing numbers of insurgents surrendered to the government.

The Role of International Politics. Since the emergence of communist regimes in Indochina in 1975, communist activities in some border provinces of Thailand have markedly changed. The smallest change has taken place in the areas along the Thai-Lao border. A few skirmishes between Pathet Lao military forces and Thai villagers have occurred along the Mekong River, but these disruptions have not spread to the internal provinces intermittently attacked by Thai communist guerrillas. Many of these border incidents have been caused by disgruntled Laotian people and Meo tribesmen seeking political asylum in Thailand. (*Bangkok World*, 8 March.)

A recent development in the influence of Laos on communist insurgency in northeastern Thailand has been the disclosure of the use of Laotian territory by Thai communist insurgents for training in guerrilla warfare. Reports by Thai defectors claim that several hundred Thai students and young people are training at a special base in Sayaboung province in Laos located about six kilometers from the Thai-Lao border. (*Bangkok Post*, 17 August.) Thus far, the attacks staged by these new members of the communist insurgency in northeastern Thailand have not been on a large scale. A major reason for the lack of sizable military attacks by Thai insurgents trained and based in Laos has been the policy of the Thai government to improve diplomatic and economic relations with the new communist regime in Vientiane. During 1978 the Kriangsak government held top-level talks with Laotian officials, and both governments agreed to improve political and economic relations. The Thai government provided small amounts of rice and salt to cope with a food shortage in Laos, and both countries signed trade and transit agreements to improve the transshipment of goods in Laos.

A similar effort by the Thai government to improve relations with Vietnam has also reduced the likelihood of large-scale external support to Thai communist insurgents in the northeastern provinces. High-level diplomatic visits were made during 1978 by officials of both governments, and in January they signed a trade and economic cooperation agreement. The following month diplomatic missions were opened by both governments, and new diplomatic talks were held. The Hanoi government dropped its opposition to the Association of Southeast Asian Nations (ASEAN), of which Thailand is a member, and it declared that it would also like to form a zone of peace, independence, and neutrality. In September Vietnamese Prime Minister Pham Van Dong made an official state visit to Bangkok and declared at a press conference that his government would not support communist insurgencies in Thailand or take actions which could harm "the independence and sovereignty" of Thailand. (Ibid., 11 September.)

The most significant change in the communist insurgency in the Northeast has occurred in the region along the Thai-Cambodian border. In an effort to deter military conflict in this vulnerable area, the Thai government has sought desperately to expand its diplomatic offensive in Indochina and establish normal diplomatic and trade relations with the new communist government in Phnom Penh. In January the Thai foreign minister, Dr. Uppadit Panchariyangkhum, visited Cambodia in an attempt to start diplomatic relations and economic and trade cooperation. An agreement was made during this visit to exchange ambassadors and to respect the independence of each country. Six months later the Cambodian foreign minister, Ieng Sary, visited Thailand to discuss the implementation of this agreement. (*Far Eastern Economic Review*, 28 July.)

But progress toward normal diplomatic relations between the two countries has been hampered by numerous attacks by Khmer Rouge military forces against Thai villagers near the Thai-Cambodian border. These forays into Thai territory have included savage attacks against unarmed Thai villagers and the abduction of Thai nationals to Cambodian territory. In April the Khmer Rouge launched a heavy attack with rockets and grenades against the large border city of Aranyaprathet. Some of these attacks have involved Thai communist insurgents operating with the Cambodian invaders and aiding in the abduction of Thai villagers. Reliable reports indicate that the CPT has formed a special insurgent group called the "Siem Organization," which maintains a series of special training bases inside Cambodian territory for Thai nationals seized by the Khmer Rouge and Thai communist forces. (*Bangkok Nation*, 24 April). At times the savage raids by Cambodian and Thai communist groups along the border have caused the Kriangsak government to counterattack with artillery and aircraft. Some decrease in the intensity of Cambodian military attacks against Thailand has resulted from the expansion of military conflict between Cambodia and Vietnam along their common national border.

De Pauw University   Frank Darling

Vietnam

Communist Vietnam, as the result of military victory in the spring of 1975, now comprises the whole of the Vietnamese portion of the Indochina peninsula. For a brief history of the Vietnamese communist party under its various names see earlier editions of *YICA*, particularly 1976 and 1977.

The Position in 1978. The year 1978 was marked by difficulties and setbacks which rivaled the darkest days of the war. Internally there were acute food shortages, a steadily sagging economy, rampant official mismanagement and corruption. Politically this was translated into harsher rule, sullen opposition in the South, and a doubling in the rate of refugee flight. The ailing economy was exacerbated by farmers planting less and withholding shipment to market, by bad weather, and by severe transportation snarls. This in turn left food shortages everywhere and doubled the price of food on the uncontrolled or free market. These economic ills, as much as political repression, were the reasons for the exodus from Vietnam during 1978 of some 240,000 persons, including about 160,000 ethnic Chinese.

Externally it was a year of turmoil in which Indochinese communist alliances were torn apart, warfare between Vietnam and Cambodia intensified, and the confrontation between Vietnam and China grew more dangerous. Vietnam's general security position thus deteriorated, which also had implications in foreign economic terms, since it meant further delays in attracting foreign investment, trade, and aid.

In sum the Vietnamese scene was characterized by the theme of force—by repression and forced socialization at home, by confrontation abroad. It was as if, after a lifetime of warfare, the leadership in Hanoi was unable to adjust to the ways of peace and returned almost inadvertently to war or to the policies of force which lead to war.

Little of what was to come—this ominous downturn in Vietnam's fortunes—was apparent when the year began. There were a few dark clouds on the horizon but the same could be said for every country facing the new year. True, much of the euphoria of total victory three years earlier had dissipated, but a buoyant spirit remained, at least officially. This official New Year ebullience was captured in Vietnamese Communist Party official Nguyen Huu Chinh's New Year's Day commentary on Radio Hanoi, titled "Reviewing the Past Year with Great Enthusiasm and Confidence." (Hanoi Domestic Service, 9 January.) He declared: "Today, looking at the new calendar, we are filled with enthusiasm and confidence. We are enthusiastic because 1977, which is now history, was a year of continued advances made by forces around the world who love peace, democracy, independence and socialism. We are enthusiastic because our country recorded many diplomatic successes in 1977. We are confident because the world situation over the past year eloquently and convincingly testified to the correctness of the international line pursued by our party and state, a line adopted by the Fourth Party Congress."

As Politburo officials' pessimistic speeches later in the year were to indicate, the party already was painfully aware that not only were past troubles, which the party had managed to escape for so long, were catching up with it, but a host of new or postwar difficulties was descending on the country.

Party Leadership and Organization. Within the party during the year the scene was marked by still another reorganization, by the expulsion of most ethnic Chinese members and by the demotion or retirement of certain officials and cadres regarded as pro-Chinese. These changes were a follow-on from Fourth Party Congress actions, late 1976, which retired Hoang Van Hoan and most other top-level officials with a past close association with China (including Ly Ban, Hanoi's top expert on Chinese foreign aid and three former Vietnamese ambassadors to Peking: Nguyen Trong Vinh, Ngo Minh Loan and Ngo Thuyen). Also transferred from line officer duty to less sensitive staff positions were three ethnic minority generals of the People's Army of Vietnam (PAVN): General Chu Van Tan and General Le Hien Mai, both Nungs, and General Le Quang Ba, a Tay. However, during the year there were no known truly significant party developments, such as massive purges, nor any leadership changes, such as generational transfer of power. The composition of the Politburo remained the same, aging a year of course (the average age is now 67; the average age of the Central Committee about 65).

Party plenums were held in February and July. The first session was devoted to restructuring the social order in the South (including the matter of ethnic Chinese there) and the July meeting dealt with general economic problems and the deteriorating situation with China.

Party cadres and lower level officials were once again made the regime's whipping boys in documents coming out of these meetings. Also, for the first time, the country's armed forces were singled out for criticism, specifically for slack discipline, failure to maintain military equipment (said to be the reason for such heavy casualties in the Cambodian border war) and generally for "incorrect motivation" which led to "hedonistic attitudes and indolence" on the part of officers and troops alike.

In May the Politburo established a new Party Department of Economic Management. It was given responsibility for supervising the overall administration of the national economic sector. Two specific tasks were assigned: to insure the ideological purity of various national economic programs and policies and to monitor personnel affairs of upper echelon economic cadres (i.e., their training, assignment and promotion). This change appears to be an effort by the party to increase its control of those who manage the economic sector.

Trouble with China revived the nearly defunct thesis that the Vietnamese top leadership could be divided into pro- and anti-Chinese elements. This developed largely as the result of charges and accounts of recent history appearing in the official Peking press. The anti-Chinese tilt, say the Peking accounts, began after the death of Ho Chi Minh. Ethnic Chinese were denied higher echelon cadre jobs, were expelled from the party because of minor or trumped up infractions and were made the scapegoats for local troubles. In general, Chinese in the Vietnamese Communist Party were treated like "bees up one's sleeve" as a Peking editorial writer put it.

The central fact of leadership in Vietnam during the year was demonstration of incredible incompetency in running a modern or semimodern society. Not only did the economic system fail to develop during the year, it lost much of the gain achieved in the previous first two years of peace.

The clearest example of bungling leadership was in the country's most important economic activity, the production of food. The South, in the year after the end of the war, made a remarkable comeback in farming and at the end of the second postwar harvest was self-sufficient in rice production. Then production dropped in 1977 and again in 1978. Thus the agricultural decline is a wholly postwar phenomenon. There were several reasons for the drop in production, including some beyond the control of anyone, such as bad weather. But the central reason was that the Politburo made some bad decisions and issued some wrong orders.

Technical reorganization of the government continued during the year, part of the long-range plan to eliminate the traditional village and relocate farmers into large "agro-industrial" units. The ultimate plan is to divide Vietnam into 400 districts within some 38 provinces and municipalities each of which is a combined governmental administrative headquarters and an agricultural production center. The district also will be a security center and headquarters for a militia division, which means eventually Vietnam will have a 400-division, million-man militia as part of its armed forces.

Changes in governmental institutions during the year also extended to the country's armed forces. Since the end of the war PAVN has been almost constantly reorganized. Previously there were three major elements: PAVN; Peoples Liberation Armed Force (PLAF) or Viet Cong army (divided into two elements, the full-military and the paramilitary or guerrilla force); and the People's Militia.

In 1978 a five-year development plan for PAVN was launched under the supervision of Major General Cao Van Khanh, Deputy Chief of PAVN for Recruiting and Training. It had a three-fold purpose.

The first was an intensified recruiting effort. A new draft law, termed a "military obligation decree," was issued 17 April 1978. It ordered the registration of all 18-year-olds, men and women alike, for five years of military service. The order amounted to full military mobilization for Vietnam. As of the end of the year Vietnam was conscripting from ages 16 to 55 although only those in the 18 to 35 age bracket were being sent into combat. Each village, North and South, was assigned a quarterly quota of draftees. Exempted were party officials, some professionals and persons in essential industries, fathers with three or more children, only remaining sons in "Hero families" (i.e., gold star) and college students (who get a form of ROTC). Draft resisters were dealt with harshly.

Apparently much of the initial trouble with the ethnic Chinese beginning in 1977 stemmed from the resistance of young Chinese to being drafted to fight in Cambodia.

The second purpose of the PAVN developmental program was to increase specialized understaffed elements such as fighter pilots, navy personnel, radar operators and coast defense personnel. This was in keeping with the general restructuring of PAVN and the enlargement of those services, particularly naval, now considered under strength.

The third purpose was to train or retrain PAVN troops so as to heighten discipline; to strengthen what was called "the military's observance of socialist laws and regulations," meaning strict enforcement of PAVN regulations; and in general to increase the individual soldier's sense of "socialist patriotism." Retraining was aimed at reducing slackness, self-indulgence, and corruption, which increased sharply after the end of the war (particularly among garrison troops on duty in the South), and to increase the spirit of dedication among those shipped off to the Cambodian front.

Domestic Attitudes and Activities. Agricultural production dropped during 1978 because of bad weather, because of governmental mismanagement particularly in the supply and transportation sectors, and because the country's antiquated agricultural plant grew a year older without significant modernization. A fifth of the rice eaten, which previously came from China, now had to be garnered from other sources or there had to be further belt tightening, which became the case. Rice rations during the year dropped to half a pound a day, from the previous 20—35 pounds per month (depending on job category). The "officially guaranteed" food intake for the country was 1,300 calories per day or 200 calories short of what nutritionists consider subsistence level.

Rice production, the key economic indicator, dropped during 1978 but exactly how much was not clear at year's end. Beginning with the fifth month crop in 1977 new emphasis was placed on agriculture and priority given to meeting its needs. Despite this the 1977 target of 13.3 million metric tons (MT) was off by 18 percent. Target for 1978 was unrealistically set at 15 million MT which could not have been reached under any circumstances. The 1978 fifth month harvest was fairly good (compared to recent years) but flooding of some half million hectares of rice land in Central Vietnam and the northern part of the Mekong Delta severely reduced the tenth month crop. Hanoi officials in October set this loss at 2.9 million MT (which would be a catastrophic 20 percent of the anticipated yield if the 15 million MT figure were accepted as a base). However this claim appears exaggerated, to encourage outside assistance; probably the loss more realistically was about 1.2 million MT, still a significant figure. In any event the grain situation worsened during 1978, with a shortfall of about two million MT and possibly as high as four million MT, and the halt in shipment of food from China. Some of the shortage was made up with USSR grain.

Collectivization of southern agriculture was pressed during the year, but slowly and carefully, because the regime did not want to risk a violent reaction from farmers as had occurred in the North in 1956 when collectivization was introduced there. The southern collective administrative cadre structure, which averaged about 500 per province in 1978 is expected to be about 25,000 per province by 1980. About one third of the farm households in the South were somewhere in the collectivization process by mid-1978. In addition there were 184 state farms. Collectivization in the Highlands appeared to be most advanced, with the Mekong Delta region least advanced.

The North has about 11,500 collectives and eventually the number in the South will be about equal to that. Separate from these are the state farms, most of which are larger than a collective, with as many as 25,000 farm laborers on a single state farm.

Briefly, there were these other developments in the economic sector during the year:

—The country's industrial plant, three and a half years after the end of the war, was running at about 55 percent capacity (as opposed to 65 percent at war's end) although industrial production in some sectors increased during the year. Major difficulties in the industrial sector included scarcity of energy, particularly electricity; shortage of construction materials; and lack of sufficient technicians and specialists.

—Oil exploration contracts for Vietnam's continental shelf were signed in September with four Canadian firms. Earlier, contracts were signed with French and Norwegian companies. Reportedly, if oil is found, the companies will be paid for their exploration work, get a percentage of the oil produced at below world cost and will have the option of buying more of the production at world price. Hong Kong reports during the year said that small-scale mining of uranium had begun recently in the Hoang Lien—Son Yunnan border area.

—Vietnam's decrepit transportation system lost capacity during the year. One third of the country's trucks were red-lined, out of service for one reason or another (as opposed to about 5 percent at the end of the war). Distribution suffered as a result. Fertilizer was stacked up at the ports but farmers could not plant for lack of fertilizer. District towns in the North were completely out of rice while Nha Trang farmers in the South fed rice to their ducks.

—There was a serious manpower shortage in various economic sectors. Part of this was due to drafting of key technicians into the armed forces. Vietnam has the world's fourth largest armed forces (after the People's Republic of China with 2.5 million, the USSR with 1.8 million, and the United States with 785,000). Its 700,000-man armed force is drawn out of a population of 50 million.

Labor unrest was reported widespread. There was a strike, something unheard of in communist Vietnam, at the Hong Kao coal mine. "Worker demoralization" was the official reason given. Worse was the fact that the Hong Kao miners were among the country's best paid and most coddled industrial workers.

—Exports increased about 35 percent during the fiscal year ending July 1978. Exports ran at about $300 million per year, as compared to imports of about $1.5 billion (giving Vietnam one of the worse trade deficits of any country). About one-fourth of the imports are for petroleum and one-fourth for food. (Vietnam needs to import an average minimum of 1.4 million MT of grain annually to keep above the starvation level.) In the past this trade deficit was made up by bloc assistance: 50 percent from the USSR; from East Europe and China about 22 percent each; the remainder from the noncommunist world. Now a greater burden has been shifted to the USSR because of the halt in Chinese aid.

—The New Economic Zone (NEZ) continued to be a drain on the nation's economy, rather than a contribution to it. An estimated one million persons from cities and towns were relocated to the NEZ during the year. As the war with Cambodia continued, a new dimension was added to the program, what was called the "rational reassignment of the labor force into strategic regions," meaning use of the "strategic hamlet" concept along the border.

By every indication corruption in the South was worse than it had been under any Saigon government. The press reported examples of high-level corruption. The chief of the Motion Picture Department of the Ministry of Culture was caught smuggling diamonds on a trip to Europe to attend a film festival. Wives of high-ranking cadres made killings in the real estate market in the South. New measures were implemented during the year in an attempt to tighten controls. However these often simply facilitated corruption by adding new opportunities to solicit bribes and in any event tended to snarl economic activity in further red tape.

The most dramatic moment of the year on the economic scene came in the early hours of 23 March in cities across South Vietnam but chiefly in Saigon's sister city of Cholon, home of a million business-oriented ethnic Chinese. The night, later to be called the night of the bourgeois coup d'etat, saw nearly a million cadres, soldiers, and party youths staging raids on the shops, factories, warehouses, and homes of the nation's domestic traders.

The blow was the start of Phase Two of the "socialist transformation of the South." Phase One, termed the "policy of moderation," had begun with the communist military occupation of the South in May 1975. It had sought to gain administrative control of the southern economy without frightening the entrepreneurial class. The Communists took over the reins of the economy while also keeping it functioning. This phase ceased by the end of 1975.

Then began a systematic program to socialize the economy. In early 1976 all sizable southern economic enterprises—about 1,600 of them accounting for 80 percent of the GNP in the South—were nationalized under a complex program involving five separate ownership/management arrangements which temporarily permitted previous owners varying degrees of residual control and profit-taking. Some businesses—import-export firms, banks, service companies—were simply put out of business although most had been inoperative since May 1975 in any case.

Then came Phase Two, "breaking the machine." In official language this meant shifting "the national merchant bourgeoisie in the southern provinces into the production sector," and the end of all private domestic trade. Its mastermind was Do Muoi, alternate Politburo member and longtime economic czar in Hanoi. His Politburo's Commission for Transformation of Private Industry and Trade implemented Phase Two with two decrees in early 1978.

The first decree, issued 31 March, ordered that all small one-man or one-family businesses— usually retail shops—be closed, their inventories seized, and their owners denied the right to their former occupation. It also required most of them to relocate to the New Economic Zone and become farmers. The order applied to an estimated 60,000 enterprises in South Vietnam, about half of them in Saigon-Cholon.

The second decree, dated 7 April, abolished the trade of all groups below the shop owner level, that is, the street vendors and market stall operators, most of them women, so common throughout Asia.

The party implemented these decrees by creating a strike force of young people, the "ubiquitous eyes of the party," who could be trusted more than older officials. The youths were mobilized into 75 and 100 person teams. During the curfew the night and morning of 22–23 March police and army roadblocks were established and the business areas of South Vietnam's cities cordoned off. At dawn the young inspection teams arrived—large numbers of persons so as to reduce the possibility of bribery—with orders to remain until all inventory work was completed. The teams made detailed lists of property, plant equipment, supplies, and goods, a huge operation involving at least 30,000 separate enterprises in Saigon-Cholon alone. These young Vietnamese completed their work with a zeal and vengeance, in the eyes of the ethnic Chinese.

By dawn state control of domestic trade in the South had risen from about 30 percent to about 90 percent. This compared well with state control in the North where even today an estimated 20 percent of the domestic food trade business is outside of state control.

Finally, the nation's money systems were unified. PM Decree 88-CP of 25 April 1978 merged the two currencies, North and South, that had been installed in the summer of 1975. (Previously the northern *dong* rate was ND2.40 = U.S. $1.00, while the southern *dong* rate was SD2.82 = U.S. $1.00. There was a special tourist rate for foreigners of ND3.65 = U.S. $1.00. Officially the exchange rate from North to South was ND1.00 = SD1.25 while the black market rate was SD1.00 = ND 2.50.) The official reason given for the switch was to prevent inflation from spreading to the North.

The socialist transformation of the South—at least in institutional terms—was complete. *Nhan Dan* hailed it as a "victory for ideology."

This transformation affected about 1.8 million South Vietnamese (including 365,000 from Saigon-Cholon) and represented a class war action, for the attack was never narrowly conceived in economic terms but regarded as a restructuring of the social system. Its purpose was not to destroy capitalism as represented by the market economy—that had been done the day the Communists won in the South—but to destory the social system represented by capitalism. Thus when property was seized and indemnification with government bonds offered, it was not on the basis of equity but on "estimated fixed social value," meaning an inverse graduated scale in which the richer you were the less you were indemnified and the more you lost. The very rich wound up with less payment in absolute terms than did the middle class.

Cadres were ordered to retain technical skills, such as typewriter repairing, where possible, because this would continue to serve the society economically. But the noneconomic or class conflict dimension of the transformation became apparent when professionals—doctors, lawyers, and teachers—were barred from their professions and told to become artisans or to take proletarian jobs. Blandly the world was informed that Vietnam had abolished private trade. What it had actually done was to depose its middle class, transfer its property to the national inventory, and ship the people involved off to a New Economic Zone to plant bananas. Thus ended Vietnam's great economic blitz of 1978. As the dust settled it became evident that it had not distributed the wealth, only impoverished all more equally. Domestic trade was not improved, it was ruined. State control had been established but over an economic desert.

Reeducation camps continued to operate throughout the country during the year although at diminished levels, having processed and released an estimated 1.1 million persons in the previous three years. Five levels remained in operation, ranging from the mild Level One camp which was little more than a lecture center (people attended during the day and returned home at night) to the infamous Level Five camp where the detainees (nicknamed *tchais*) are the more important former leaders in the South (government officials and professionals such as teachers and editors) being held under three-year or five-year "sentences." Initially, in mid-1975, these Level Five *tchais* were told to expect to remain for either three or five years (others were released when their jailers considered them "reeducated"). In the spring of 1978 when some of the three-year "sentences" were completed some of the *tchais* were released, most were not. They, and those under five-year "sentences," clearly were regarded as natural leaders within the society and too dangerous to release. (These include virtually all members of the National Assembly; leading editors; Vietnam's most prominent writer, Doan Quoc Sy; its leading poet, Tran Da Tu and his wife Nha Ca, also a poet; and intellectual Nguyen Man Con.) Numbers involved here varied according to source. *Le Monde* in April 1978 estimated the figure at 50,000–80,000. The regime has admitted privately 30,000. Vietnamese refugee organizations in Paris fix the number at 800,000. Probably the entire reeducation camp population during the year stood at about 300,000, of whom perhaps 50,000 were *tchais* in Level Four and Level Five camps and could be considered political prisoners under the Amnesty International definition. (That is, a person incarcerated for what he believes or thinks, not for what he has done.)

Officially these camps are not prisons. No judicial process is involved in sending a person to be reeducated. The Vietnam prison system is quite separate. Here are incarcerated those deemed truly dangerous to the regime, former police and security personnel, military officers, those judged "war criminals" as well as common criminals. New prisons were opened during the year and old ones expanded. The Chi Hoa prison outside of Ho Chi Minh City, which held 5,000 prisoners under the Thieu government, in 1978 housed 15,000. The prison population in the South was estimated at triple the number under the former government.

Resistance to the regime in the South continued to be widespread, but at a low level and poorly organized and led. Reports filtered out of occasional guerrilla raids and ambushes and some high-level assassinations—Dinh Ba Thi and supposedly Do Muoi—but armed opposition to the government apparently did not significantly increase, nor become a serious concern. Dinh Ba Thi, former SRV ambassador to the U.N., expelled after a spy scandal, officially died in an automobile accident near Cholon, but refugees in the United States said his car was ambushed. Do Muoi, the Hanoi economic czar, supposedly was ambushed and killed near Nha Trang in late 1978, again according to refugee sources. At year's end it was not possible to verify whether Do Muoi was still alive. Hostility to the regime chiefly took the form of passive psychological gestures. In January Radio Hanoi reported that some 10,000 Hoa Hao sect members in Cho Moi district of An Giang province were militantly opposing the provincial government, the largest single act of opposition admitted by the media. Efforts went forward to tighten control of Buddhist organizations in the South and, according to refugees, there was a general increase in religious persecution. The drive against Buddhism however appeared to be an attempt to destroy it organizationally rather than to attack its religious tenets.

The flow of refugees from Vietnam rose sharply during the year and threatened to become a flood by year's end. Their plight, once out, worsened. By the end of 1978 more than a half million Vietnamese had fled their country since communist victory in the South. An estimated 160,000 ethnic Chinese, most of them from the North, left Vietnam for China. Another 100,000, many of them ethnic Chinese from the South, fled the country in some 5,000 boats and ships during the year. There was reason to believe, late in the year, that the regime was allowing the refugees to "escape" after paying sufficient "bribes" to the State, in what amounted to an official policy of covertly pushing them out of the country.

International Views and Attitudes. Grim as Vietnam's internal condition was during the year, its external relations were, if anything, in a worse state. Warfare, actual and potential, obviously eclipsed all other foreign difficulties.

Vietnam, by late 1978, was on a full wartime footing, as she had been in the decade of 1965−75. There was a general mobilization, new wartime emulation campaigns to increase production in agriculture and industry, and a massive agitprop campaign built around patriotic themes.

The border war with Cambodia bled and bled and seemed to defy all efforts at resolution, either by military campaign or negotiation.

The specter of war with China, which most observers a year earlier would have dismissed as being so remote as to be absurd, suddenly became not absurd at all, but a possibility that daily grew more menacing.

The overriding characteristic of Vietnam's foreign relations to emerge during the year perhaps was the marked and extensive rise in the stakes in the current Indochina struggle for power. In part this was due to the rebirth and growth of narrow nationalism within Indochina. In part it was due to the fact that the Sino-Soviet dispute had become central to politics throughout Southeast Asia. The Cambodian war took on new meaning because of moves by Moscow and Peking. Some observers went so far as to assert that China and the USSR were deliberaely on a collision course, that each wanted a regional showdown (short of war of course), and that each saw Indochina as the place where it should come. Vietnam's face-off with China was thrust into the very center of the Sino-Soviet dispute when Hanoi and Moscow signed what amounted to a military alliance. Not only within Indochina or within the Sino-Soviet context but well beyond—in Japan, in the United States, in the entire Pacific basin—the power struggle took on added dimension, one whose significance at year's end was largely an imponderable.

There was no reason to believe that Hanoi's top military planners were excessively worried about Vietnam's strategic condition. It had, after all, a powerful army, fourth largest in the world, well trained and battle hardened. It had, after November, a mutual security arrangement with the USSR which if nothing else served as a deterrent against adventurist moves by China. And the war with Cambodia, while a serious irritant, was not one which could be lost in the sense that the Cambodians could achieve military victory, outnumbered as they were seven to one and with an even greater imbalance of military strength.

Many official statements about Vietnam's basic strategic position came out of Hanoi during the year, the most revealing perhaps being a study by the country's top line officer, General Van Tien Dung, writing in the August *Tap Chi Quan Doi Nhan Dan*, the party's theoretical journal for the armed forces, on "Defense in a New Era."

General Dung listed what he considered to be the six basic sources of Vietnamese strategic strength. The six were: 1.) The Vietnamese heritage of unity and national spirit. 2.) The country's socioeconomic system of collectivism. 3.) The nation's reorganized and technically developed armed forces. 4.) A leadership experienced in application of Marxist military science (people's war) doctrine to produce superior strategy. 5.) A just cause. 6.) International support as well as the support of history (i.e., movement in the direction history is taking the world).

Some of the six, General Dung indicated, are existing strengths: numbers one, four and five. Number two required nurturing. The remaining numbers, three and six, he indicated, were conditions not yet sufficiently achieved to be considered true strengths.

All in all, the Dung list represented an accurate and authoritative perception of Vietnam's geopolitical situation as seen from Hanoi.

The Vietnam-Cambodia war, which became known to the world in late 1977, when the Cambodians went public, has been the result of Vietnamese actions. As the Chinese Cambodians noted, Vietnam launched the war with American weapons, Chinese oil, and USSR advisers. The Vietnamese war strategy was to use high technology. There were major incursions in mid-1977, late 1977, and again in late 1978, involving as many as 120,000 Vietnamese troops who were opposed by the entire Cambodian army, estimated at about 70,000 men. These Vietnamese strikes appear to have been aimed at destroying much of the Cambodian military and at triggering a palace coup d'etat in Phnom Penh.

At the same time, the Vietnamese have resorted to a strategy of protracted conflict. They have created a Cambodian *troika* organization of the following:

—A Cambodian Liberation Army drawn from the 150,000 Cambodian refugees in Vietnam and defectors from the Cambodian army. Midyear official Vietnamese reports spoke vaguely of a "headquarters command" of seven Cambodian military officers. One name to appear in press references was former Cambodian Vice-president So Phim, a longtime Cambodian communist party figure from western Cambodia, the region that logically would become the "liberated area" of an anti-Pol Pot organization. Reportedly he defected to Vietnam after his troops mutinied and he dared not stay and face Pol Pot's wrath.

—A Cambodian United Front, a collection of Cambodian mass organizations specifically created for their utility inside Cambodia, built around a newly created Cambodian Communist Party.

—Eventually, a Cambodian Provisional Government, essentially a "cabinet" of a dozen or so persons (rather than a full-scale government in exile) which would operate out of a "liberated area"—probably the 15 mile by 60 mile strip along the Vietnamese border opposite Tay Ninh province but with sanctuary within Vietnam.

This strategy had been employed successfully in South Vietnam, and there is no reason for Hanoi officials to believe it would not work in Cambodia. Its chief weakness is that it takes a great deal of time to accomplish, and time may not always be on the Vietnamese side.

The major neighboring country influencing the Cambodia war is China. In mid-1978 Peking apparently sought to deter or inhibit Vietnamese military actions in Cambodia. During the year China made it clear that it intends to remain committed to an independent Cambodia (that is, a non-Vietnamese dominated Cambodia) even though it may not underwrite the career of Pol Pot or any other specific leader. China reportedly has about 6,000 advisers, military and otherwise, in Cambodia, slightly less than the number of USSR advisers in Vietnam. A steady flow of Chinese arms arrived in Cambodia during the year. There were also reports of Chinese pilots flying (and training Cambodians) in MIG-19 fighter planes (with similar reports of Soviet pilots in MIG-21's in Vietnam. Late in the year, as the dry season in Cambodia approached, the Vietnamese stepped up military actions. There were heavy artillery barrages along the long border and increased air strikes, as many as 40 per day.

Hanoi's economic troubleshooter, Nguyen Chanh, arrived in Peking 2 January for the annual Goods Exchange and Payment Agreement negotiations, which was duly signed 10 January and Chanh made his usual obligatory visit to the Chungshan Botanical Garden. It was the same agenda followed for twenty years.

Chinese Premier Hua Kuo-feng's annual report to the nation on foreign affairs, in March, assured all socialist nations of China's continuing dedication to proletarian internationalism, but while North Korea was singled out for specific mention there was no reference at all to Vietnam. Hanoi in March, ostensibly with the Philippines in mind, made some new comments about the contested offshore islands which Peking found provocative. Then the border incidents began; the first came in February but both sides remained silent. A more serious incident came in late March at Highway Four where it crosses from Vietnam to China. Subsequent reports, by Swedish Radio and others, said that 30 persons were killed in the clash which involved the use of tanks on both sides and lasted nearly two days.

April was the month of decision. Deputy Foreign Minister Phan Hien went to Hanoi in mid-April to deal with a problem in which he is a specialist—border disputes. Hien and the Vietnamese had probably gotten wind of Peking's decision to reduce or eliminate economic assistance to Vietnam, a decision apparently taken in early April. Aid was reduced by about half in late April or early May, then eliminated entirely in June. Actually there had been a steady drop in assistance for several years. Chou En-lai in early 1973 promised Vietnam five years of economic aid at the 1973 level. In 1975 China ended its nonreimbursable loan (i.e. gift aid) arrangement and began regarding assistance as a repayable debt. At the same time it ended military aid. Technically China had met its original aid obligation and was free to halt assistance in mid-1978, having given Vietnam, it said, $10 billion in twenty years. The cut off was announced 9 June and China ordered home some 1,000 technicians and construction supervisors from twenty major aid projects.

On 19 June China ordered closed the three Vietnamese consulates in China (Canton, Kunming and Nanning) which had been operating since 1956.

A significant exodus of ethnic Chinese had begun in late 1977, with the economic crackdown, and by the end of the year some 15,000 had left. In early 1978 the rate increased slowly, then after the 24 March "economic coup d'etat" it became a flood. The 22—23 March Cholon raids used PAVN troops who were not always gentle with the Chinese. Some 30,000 Chinese families lost their businesses that night. Within a week some 50,000 Chinese had been dispatched to the New Economic Zone. Regulations published at the same time forbade the Chinese from practicing certain professions (such as teaching) and from working as fishermen, foresters, radio repairmen, bus drivers, typists, photocopiers or printers.

Somewhat unexpected was the reaction of Chinese in the North. Foreign Ministry official Xuan Thuy in a 4 May interview with VNA introduced the subject. On 18 May he told Peking newsmen in answer to a question on ethnic Chinese being free to leave Vietnam: "If anyone wants to return to China he has only to make an open request." The following day there were long lines outside the Chinese embassy in Hanoi of ethnic Chinese seeking visas to leave for China. There were disorders, followed by clashes with police.

The exodus from the North also began to increase sharply. In May it was running at about 2,500 a week and by August at double this rate. The alarmed Chinese closed the border although they blamed the halt on the Vietnamese. Even so, by the end of the year an estimated 175,000 ethnic Chinese had left Vietnam, most of them going to China although some by boat to Southeast Asia. About 75 percent of those departing were from the North.

Border clashes continued and various military strategic moves were reported. A Soviet airlift of arms pumped weapons and other military supplies into Vietnam during the whole of the month of November. There were additional shipments of Soviet-built MIG-23 fighter planes, some of which

Vietnam positioned closer to the China border than ever before. The Chinese replied by installing additional missile batteries along the border.

Hanoi-Moscow relations warmed during the year. The two major official acts were SRV admission into Comecon in August and the signing of the USSR-SRV Treaty of Friendship and Cooperation in November.

The treaty was the first such signed by the two nations. In addition to the friendship and cooperation treaty, five other agreements were signed, dealing with defense, economic aid, science, technology and cultural exchange. The signing came 3 November 1978, by Party Secretary Le Duan and Premier Pham Van Dong for Vietnam and by President Leonid Brezhnev and Premier Alexei Kosygin for the USSR.

Exactly what the USSR committed itself to under the treaty was not at all clear. The operative clause, with respect to security guarantees was Article Six which read: "In case either party is attacked or threatened with attack the two parties signatory to the treaty shall immediately consult each other with a view to eliminating the threat, and shall take appropriate and effective measures to safeguard peace and the security of the two countries. . . ." (Treaty text was broadcast by Hanoi VNA in English, 3 November 1978.)

Moscow spokesmen stated that the treaty threatens no one and is similar to those signed with noncommunist nations such as Finland, Iraq, and Ethiopia, as well as those treaties with Warsaw Pact nations. The language of the treaty with India (and the unspoken reference to Pakistan) is the same as in the Vietnamese treaty.

Reaction to the signing in Asia was strong and hostile. The PRC of course saw it as a direct threat and asserted that it was an out and out military alliance aimed at serving the USSR's hegemonistic dreams in Southeast Asia and the Vietnamese goal of a Federation of Indochina. Peking said Vietnam had become the tool of big power hegemonists and had become the Cuba of the East. Two days after the signing, Peking dispatched a high-level delegation, including military figures, on a mission to Cambodia. The treaty also drew strong response in Tokyo where the Japanese saw it as a move by the USSR to increase its influence in Southeast Asia at Japan's expense. Some critics of the government in Japan suggested that the treaty was a USSR reaction to the signing earlier in the year of the PRC-Japan treaty.

At the year's end the new relationship had begun to pay off for the Vietnamese, in terms of military aid. A month-long airlift in arms built up the Vietnamese Air Force. More MIG-23 fighter planes were delivered. There were reports of new USSR missile installations at Hon Gai and elsewhere in the China border area. Also, once again, there were unsubstantiated reports that Cam Ranh Bay was about to become a USSR naval base.

Vietnam moved from cautious wooing of ASEAN members early in the year to outright solicitation by the year's end. The same was essentially true with Vietnamese-Japanese and Vietnamese-American relations; both conditions and prospects changed markedly during the year.

The central fact of regional relations to emerge was the growing USSR-PRC rivalry over Vietnam. Moscow saw China attempting to shut the USSR out of the region; Peking saw the USSR as attempting to encircle China. The USSR responded to Peking by pursuing unilateral arrangements. The PRC tried to forge an anti-Moscow united front throughout Asia.

In some ways the new conditions were beneficial to the smaller nations of the region. Premier Pham Van Dong went to Bangkok and in the 9 September 1978 final communiqué promised not to support Thai insurgents, something which could hardly have been envisioned even a year earlier. The final communiqué signed 9 September 1978 said that both sides promised not to engage in direct or indirect subversion and also to refrain from the use of force against the other. Reportedly Vietnam wanted a treaty of friendship with Thailand but could not persuade the Bangkok government. The Thais quite obviously, at year's end, sensed a definite advantage over the SRV and were exploiting it. They were, for instance, pressing Vietnam to repatriate the Vietnamese who have been living in Thailand for several decades and presumably wish to return to Vietnam. These number some 40,000 and have been in Thailand since the Viet Minh war.

Japanese-Vietnamese relations continued to be dominated by economic considerations. In August Japan approved a $450 million Bank of Tokyo loan to Vietnam. Japan also sought World Bank loans. Reports from Tokyo late in the year however indicated that Japan was cooling to the idea of extensive economic aid to Vietnam and that the current rate of assistance, about $50 million a year, might be the price Hanoi would pay if it actively opposed the Japanese policy of preserving Southeast Asia as a nonaligned region.

American-Vietnamese officials met during the year, in Paris and in New York, on the question of normalization of relations. Vietnam softened, but did not entirely abandon, its position that war reparations must precede an exchange of embassies.

Publications. See *YICA, 1978.*

Washington, D.C.   Douglas Pike

Argentina

The Communist Party of Argentina (Partido Comunista de Argentina; PCA), founded in 1918, is considered the oldest Marxist-Leninist party in Latin America. Other Marxist and Marxist-Leninist organizations in the country include the Revolutionary Communist Party (Partido Comunista Revolucionario; PCR); the Socialist Vanguard Party (Partido Socialista de la Vanguardia; PSV), sometimes known as the Argentine Marxist-Leninist Communist Party (Partido Comunista Marxista-Leninista de Argentina; PCMLA); the Socialist Workers' Party (Partido Socialista de los Trabajadores; PST); the Social Democratic Party (Partido Socialista Democrático; PSD); the Montonero Peronist Movement (Movimiento Peronista Montoneros; MPM), formerly known simply as the Montoneros; and the People's Revolutionary Army (Ejército Revolucionario del Pueblo; ERP). Little information is available on the membership figures of these organizations, although the U.S. Government (*Basic Factbook,* July) estimated PCA membership at 70,000. The population of Argentina in 1978 was approximately 26,487,000.

The Setting. Like other Argentines, the local Marxists were swept up by nationalist sentiment during 1978 as the military government got tough with Chile over a territorial dispute, and they shared vicariously in the honor of Argentina's winning the World Cup soccer matches. Even the once self-professed Marxist Montoneros guerrillas took a sort of holiday from their terrorism of the past three years. (*La Vanguardia,* Buenos Aires, 24 August; *Observer,* London, 25 June).) But the military government headed by General Jorge Videla continued its open war against Communists and subversives as before and even invented a special acronym to cover its Marxist enemies: BDSM, Delinquent Subversive Marxist Bands (Bandas de Delincuentes Subversivos Marxistas). And yet at times, and with respect to some groups, the government tolerated and even cooperated with Marxist political organizations domestically and continued friendy trade and diplomatic relations with Cuba and the USSR internationally.

The consensus seemed to be, however, that inflation and economic stagnation were Argentina's principal foes. The Videla regime claimed to have reduced inflation to around 100 percent annually during 1978, as contrasted with some 20,812 percent cumulatively since 1970 (*Intercontinental Press,* 20 February). Argentine financial experts consulted by this writer agreed generally with the above figures. But, as seen below, there was little general agreement in the reporting on Marxist parties and activities during the year. Contradictory information was forthcoming about Peronism and the entire political spectrum. A few desperate guerrilla actions took place, but it was difficult to identify them ideologically. Questions were raised about the alleged involvement of former Argentine terrorists with the Red Brigades of Italy and other such European associations. The Videla government continued to work in concert with various members of the Marxist spectrum, most conspicuously with Social Democratic (PSD) leader Américo Ghioldi, who continued to serve as Argentina's ambassador to Portugal.

The Argentine Communist Party (PCA). This pro-Moscow party celebrated its sixtieth birthday on 6 January. Secretary General Gerónimo Arnedo Alvarez issued an open letter which spoke of the party's struggle against the outmoded structures still prevailing in Argentina but carefully avoided direct attacks on the military government. He honored the party's founders, Victorio Codovilla and Rodolfo Ghioldi, and lauded the Soviet Union as the leading developed state of the socialist world. He attacked Peronism generally as reactionary and warned of the danger that Pinochet-style (the current Chilean dictator) fascism could grow in Argentina if the PCA and its members did not maintain a constant vigil. (*IB,* no. 6.) The PCA publicly opposed any boycott of the 1978 World Cup soccer matches. As reported by the Italian publication *Corriere della Sera* on 14 March, PCA Central Committee member Fernando Nadra explained that his party supported the Videla government's effort to unite Argentines around a common set of goals that would lead eventually to the restoration of political democracy and that support for the World Cup event was a symbolic start in the right direction. Arnedo Alvarez met with Italian Communist Party leader Enrico Berlinguer in Rome during July, and the latter gave assurances of the Italian party's solidarity with their Moscow-oriented comrades in Argentina (*L'Unità,* Milan, 11 July). Earlier in July Arnedo Alvarez had been received in Hungary by János Kádár, the first secretary of the Hungarian Socialist Workers' Party and there received similar pledges of international solidarity. It was disclosed in June that Executive Committee members Fernando Nadra and Athos Fava had traveled about the United States as formal guests of the Communist Party of the United States (*La Nación,* Buenos Aires, 18 June), the first such visit since the PCA was founded in 1918.

The PCA, through its official spokesman, Jesús Mirá, sent a letter to the military government denouncing the assassination attempt on Admiral Armando Lambruschini in August, an attack that claimed the life of the admiral's daughter. The letter said that those who placed the bomb were trying to prevent the continuation of talks that would lead to military-civilian rapprochement and fruitful ideological dialogue among all Argentines (*Noticias Argentinas,* telex, 3 August). Little information was available on party membership, publications, or domestic activities during 1978.

The Revolutionary Communist Party (PCR). This Maoist and pro-Chinese party issued a document in January criticizing both the United States and the Soviet Union for preparing for war when peace could be a realistic and humane possibility. The PCR's statement, reproduced in the *Peking Review* (no. 33, August), especially condemned the Soviets for having sabotaged Arab unity in the Middle East and for seeking to embroil Angola in a widespread African war. The statement accused the Soviet Union of planning the takeover of all of South America and condemned Soviet troop buildups on China's northern border. The PCR charged that by using "revisionist theories" (like claiming that war can be avoided), the Soviets are setting up a smoke screen for their own war preparations. The PCR document clearly makes the U.S. seem the lesser of the two evils in the scenario, with China the hero and the remainder of the Third World being the principal victims. The PCR holds up China to the world as "a bulwark of world proletarian revolution and anti-imperialist struggle for liberation."

A delegation from the PCR visited the Peoples' Republic of China (PRC) during 1978 and was received by Vice-chairman Li Hsien-nien. The *Peking Review* (28 July) identified the leader of the PCR delegation only as "Aguirre," a member of the Argentine party's Central Committee. Chinese Central Committee member Keng Piao greeted the Argentine delegation, saying that "since its founding in 1968 the Argentine Revolutionary Communist Party (PCR) has actively participated in the revolutionary mass movement at home . . . [and] has persevered in the struggle against imperialism and revisionism." Comrade "Aguirre" stated publicly that the two superpowers, of which the USSR was clearly the worse, were on a collision course that inevitably would lead to world war. There was little information from domestic sources about the PCR.

Socialist Vanguard Party (PSV). There was also a shortage of news within Argentina on the PSV, generally known in 1978 as the Argentine Marxist-Leninist Communist Party (PCMLA). But the Mexican review *Proceso* (4 September) reported that Elias Semán, titular head of the PSV, and Roberto Cristina, identified as PCMLA secretary general, disappeared in Argentina between May and August along with almost 500 other persons. Both men had begun their Marxist careers in 1957 when the PSV broke away from the old Socialist Party of Argentina (founded in 1896), and both were identified with the 1969 *cordobazo* of militant labor unions and student groups. The *Proceso* article continued that the PSV had been formed to combat both North American and Soviet imperialism and reported that Semán and Cristina had visited the PRC in April and been toasted warmly by Chairman Hua Kuo-feng. A PSV delegation— identified by the PCMLA name— under the leadership of Guillermo Juárez visited the PRC and Cambodia during April and was toasted by communist party officials in both countries. The PCMLA paper *No Transar* (29 November 1977) editorialized that Mao Tse-tung had been correct in claiming that both formerly and currently colonized nations of the Third World were the vanguard of the true world proletarian revolution against the United States and the Soviet Union, and Chairman Hua publicly hailed Juárez as a defender of Mao's doctrine during the April visit. The PCMLA accused the Soviet Union of having converted itself into a virtual capitalist state and denounced the Russians as "latecomers" in the imperialist effort to divide up the world.

The Socialist Workers' Party (PST). Reports sent to me from Buenos Aires on the PST said only that the party functioned during 1978 under the "utmost of strict discretion" and that its titular leader, Nahuel Moreno (pseudonym of Hugo Brezzano), traveled actively outside Argentina. Moreno and Juan Carlos Coral maintained contacts with the Socialist Workers Party in the United States. My informants continued to feel that the PST was weak organizationally but had the sympathy of many Argentine workers as a result of the political charisma developed over the years by Moreno and Coral. It is not possible to make estimates of the size of the PST, but my informed sources continued to feel that the PST could beat the PCA in an honest election for deputies throughout Buenos Aires province. Moreno's flirtation with international Trotskyism continued, and it was alleged that Moreno's stepbrother, also named Brezzano, was a close associate of Admiral Emilio Massera.

This is significant because Massera, after retiring in 1978, began organizing a new "centrist" political movement intended to regroup the most respectable proletarian remnants of the discredited Peronism and unite them with some middle class sectors into a progressive party of the future. Although it was not clear whether the PST might be coopted into a coalition of parties to be led by Admiral Massera, it is significant that this possibility was being discussed in Buenos Aires and that the door had been left open for participation of the PST Marxists. The PCA "Stalinists" appeared to have been excluded from this growing rapprochement.

What apparently was not reported in Buenos Aires was the fact that Nahuel Moreno and Rita Strasberg were arrested and jailed in August by the Brazilian federal police (Intercontinental Press, 25 September). The two were described as leading members of "the Argentine Trotskyite organization PST," and it was suggested that their arrests in Brazil might have been at the request of Argentine authorities. Keeping in mind the possible rapprochement between the PST Marxists and Admiral Massera, this may be evidence of a split within the Argentine military establishment over the issue of collaboration with Marxists. It is also noteworthy that the *Intercontinental Press* referred to the PST as a Trotskyite organization when it has been generally believed that the official Trotskyite party in Argentina was the defunct PRT (see below). Expressions of support for Nahuel Morena or Rita Strasberg came from Brazilian Labor Party officials, themselves in prison, who carried out a hunger strike from 1 to 13 September. Parties in France, Spain, Sweden, Italy, and Venezuela also demanded freedom for the two Argentines. The *Intercontinental Press* carried a protest from the PST in its 9 October issue concerning the incarceration of more PST leaders within Argentina and denouncing the continued imprisonment without charges of Juan Carlos Herrero, editor of the publication *Avanzada Socialista,* which had also been shut down by the military but reportedly still circulated clandestinely. It seemed, then, that the importance and potential of the PST was considerable both internationally and within the Argentine domestic political scene as 1978 came to a close.

The Social Democratic Party (PSD). The PSD remained the most promising member of the Marxist spectrum in Argentina. It is a nationalistic party paralleling many European socialist movements in its relative independence from the intrigues of international Marxist organizations. It has strong institutional and human figure symbols of identification within Argentina. This is the only Marxist-oriented party in Argentina which conserved a genuinely functioning party apparatus into the year 1978, albeit with careful discretion. The party's official publication, *La Vanguardia,* continued to circulate openly via subscription and at an occasional newsstand. During 1978 it was possible to establish in concrete detail, more so than had been the case during the previous two years, what were the actual organizational roots of the PSD.

According to my respondents in Buenos Aires, the PSD had twelve federated chapters in as many provinces during 1978. In addition it had over 100 local study centers and reading and meeting rooms, always under the guise of a social club or study center. The party had an estimated 25,000 solid, active members and potentially 70,000 nominal members. In addition *La Vanguardia* was published in the capital city, and a number of provincial weekly publications under various names were PSD-controlled. The PSD continued to operate its cooperative "El Hogar Obrero," which is believed to be the largest popularly operated distribution system and credit union existing under the aegis of any political party in Latin America. The party's Juan B. Justo library, with nearly 250,000 volumes and some 80 branch libraries, reaches out from the capital to various provinces. The PSD, likened by some to the British Fabian Socialist Society of the past century, advocates progressive socialism by peaceful means. During 1978 it had underway a ten-story building intended eventually to house its social welfare center and future party functions. This activity was carried out openly and with the approval of the military government.

A sampling of *La Vanguardia,* still under the editorship of Raúl T. Dellepiane, revealed continued polite support for the Videla government and PSD leader Américo Ghioldi still served as Argentina's ambassador to Portugal. In its 24 August edition, *La Vanguardia* supported the determination of the military government not to yield to Chilean territorial demands in the south and criticized influences which since the end of World War II have contributed to the socioeconomic distress of Argentina, including excessive state intervention in the economy, which did not have truly popular goals. The edition solicited donations for the rebuilding of the Casa del Pueblo (House of the People), which was burned and pillaged on 15 April 1953 during the first Perón era. Although avoiding direct mention of the PSD by name, the publication referred openly to "our leaders" and cited Juan Antonio Solari, Emilio J. Giannoni, and others as members of the House of the People reconstruction committee *La Vanguardia* reported the General Motors decision to close its plants in Argentina, with the consequent loss of some 9,000 jobs, but said that in the broad picture of things there were already too many auto manufacturers in Argentina and suggested that the displaced workers should be incorporated into a prefabricated housing industry, one of the dearest needs of the Argentine people according to the PSD analysis. The defect in the Argentine economy, said the PSD, was in the absence of state planning and blind adherence to "free marketplace economic theories." High tariff protectionism was criticized for allowing uneconomic production practices and inflated costs to be charged to the Argentine consumer, a direct challenge to the policies of Economics Minister José Martínez de Hoz. The PSD called for a return to free and democratic unionism, eschewing the yoke of Peronism or any other authoritarian leadership.

The 21 September edition of *La Vanguardia* carried a front-page editorial indicting nearly all sectors of Argentine political life for contributing to institutional instability and corruption. A signed open letter criticized the military government for allowing deposed President Isabel Perón to live under luxurious "house arrest" and expressed the fear that tolerance by the military government for such corrupt personages would lead eventually to the Peronists again taking over the government — stronger sounding criticism of the military regime than was reported in last year's *Yearbook*. My informed sources believed that continued military dependency on the PSD for external Third World and domestic popular support had resulted in concessions of greater press freedom to the party. The 19 October issue of *La Vanguardia* carried a nintieth birthday homage to Teodoro Bronzini, a PSD leader in Mar del Plata whose political machine has dominated that city's political life during recent decades. Bronzini received a letter of greeting from President Videla that was published as an open acknowledgment of the PSD's good standing with the military government. Moreover, the presence of limited commercial advertising in *La Vanguardia* (mostly for professional services) meant that the PSD's scope of activity was growing within the political scene and that its ability to function as a party had not been seriously impaired by the junta.

Marxism and the Guerrilla Sector (in Exile). Confusion prevails in this sector. There are still substantial reasons to doubt that the Montoneros, formerly professed Marxists (1973—76), were ever more than fellow travelers of convenience. But the Argentine government still insisted during 1978 that the Montoneros— who renamed themselves the Montonero Peronist Movement (MPM) in 1977 —were proscribed Marxist terrorists. The MPM functioned almost exclusively in exile during 1978, but its declarations were directed at the Argentine political arena, and the party professed to have "units" operating within the home nation.

The Montonero paradox— Marxism for profit—continued during 1978 with the group's exiled leader, Mario Firmenich, jumping about Europe, apparently well financed, and representing himself as a popular champion of the coming Argentine "liberation." Firmenich, the self-confessed assassin of former Argentine interim president General Pedro Aramburu (in 1970), appeared alongside Palestinian leader Yassir Arafat in a photo published by the *London Times* on 23 June. The accompanying story cited the tactical schooling received by the Montoneros, along with the Palestine Liberation Organization and the Irish Republican Army, at Cuban training centers and in the Middle East. This account cited terrorism as Argentina's most successful, albeit tragic, export during 1978. Yet the article contended that separation of the Marxist terrorists from the fascists and from some opportunistic commercial entrepreneurs would be a difficult task. The *Times* mentioned that forged documents, easily obtainable in Sweden, gave the guerrilla leaders remarkable mobility. It also said that the practice of carrying cyanide pills— to end one's life before information could be extracted under torture— had been employed to frustrate inquiries into the group's ties and ideological coloration.

MPM leaders claimed to have held a clandestine meeting with foreign newsmen in Buenos Aires during June. Montonero representatives Armando Croatto, Norberto Habegger, and Juan Gelman stressed their fight to gain control over the abandoned proletarian apparatus which had brought the Peronist movement back to power during the second Perón era (1973—76). The statements did not, however, mention socialist or Marxist principles and could well be interpreted as a fascist appeal to workers in the style of Perón or Mussolini, the bitter irony of the fascist-Marxist ideological clash being that both compete for the loyalty of the same social classes.

Other developments further entangled the MPM in ideological ambiguity. Despite the Argentine government's having branded them as Marxist subversives, Montonero leaders in Paris offered to meet with retired Admiral Emilio Massera, according to an Agence France Presse report on 20 April. This story accompanied speculation in Argentina that Massera would try to regroup the untarnished Peronist elements surviving the second Perón era to build a new centrist party with an eye to Argentina's future return to a democratic political life. Adriana Lesgart, a Montonero spokeswoman, told the Paris daily *Le Monde* that her organization wanted to end the political war in Argentina. Moreover, Montonero leader Juan Gelman, later exiled in Rome, told the press that the Montoneros had nothing to do with the murder of former Italian Prime Minister Aldo Moro and said that a communiqué disseminated in Buenos Aires, signed by Mario Firmenich and praising the Red Brigades of Italy, was a forgery. Firmenich himself was interviewed by the Swedish press and stated that while in Europe the Montoneros wanted nothing to do with terrorists (*La Prensa,* Buenos Aires, 22 March). This offer from Paris-based Montoneros to meet with Massera was in contrast to a comment by Oscar Bidegain, first secretary of the Montoneros in exile, who stated from Spain that there would be no negotiation with the Argentine military junta. Bidegain, once Peronist governor of Buenos Aires province, said the Montoneros' goal would be to rid Argentina of despotism, be it military or otherwise (*El País,* Madrid, 3 May). Clearly the exiled Montoneros were not in agreement on goals or strategy. Although the original Montonero organization had been created in Argentina in 1968, said Bidegain, the MPM was a new formation branching out of the old. He said it had been formally set up in exile in Rome on 20 April 1977. He stressed that the Montonero Army was a related entity but that it stood apart from the MPM. The movement's new broad goal was to be Peronist reunification and the democratization of Argentina. No mention of Marxism was made, but the appeal was clearly proletarian. The MPM, stated Bidegain, "is not a party, but it is a movement seeking to create a broad social liberation front in Argentina." He condemned the Videla government's hiring of a public relations firm in New York to mold a new image for the military regime. No matter what image was paid for outside Argentina, he said, the regime of terror is well known within the country, and one day the people would rise to support the MPM.

Montonero Army tactician Horacio Alberto Mendizábal gave a clandestine interview to a European reporter in which he claimed that a Montonero unit had hit the Casa Rosada (the government palace) with a bazooka on 10 June while the World Cup soccer matches were in progress. Mendizábal pledged to bring down the Videla government with bazooka fire. He spoke of the intensive logistics training then being carried out by the Montoneros inside Argentina, including weapons factories and the establishment of new underground networks and "people's jails," but he added that the Montoneros' principal weapon would be the Soviet made RPG-7 bazooka. (*L'Espresso,* Rome, 16 July). However, Mendizábal denied that the Montoneros had ties wih the Italian Red Brigades, saying that guerrilla action is necessary only in countries like Argentina where there is no freedom of speech, press, or political organization. He criticized the Red Brigades for playing into the hands of reactionary elements by carrying out unnecessary terrorism. He said that the Montoneros were welcome in Cuba and expressed admiration for Fidel Castro but denied that the Havana government had received Montonero exiles. He said the movement still lives from the more than U.S. $60-million-plus ransom that was collected for the kidnapped Born brothers in 1975 and that with Argentina's monetary devaluation continuing, the peso value of the Montoneros' dollar reserves was going up "admirably." Mendizábal associated the Montoneros with the Argentine workers' struggle but criticized the PCA for its collaborationist stance. He also stressed that the Montoneros still consider themselves a Catholic organization and have their own chaplain, Father Jorge Adur. He said that just as Catholicism has diverse elements, so does Peronism. But the truly popular Peronism, said Mendizábal, is that associated with former President Cámpora (still exiled in Mexico's embassy in Buenos Aires) and others who tried to save Perón in his final years from reactionary influences around him, in particular, Perón's third wife, Isabel, who succeeded him as president, and José López Rega, who served briefly as minister of welfare and turned that ministry into a base for right-wing terrorism. Although Mendizábal talked in socialist-sounding terms and lauded Fidel Castro and the class struggle, he did not say that the Montoneros were still professing Marxism or communism, nor did he deny it. It is believed that the Montoneros' source for Russian weapons was the Palestine Liberation Organization and the Basque (ETA) guerrillas of Spain.

Much of the credibility ascribed to the Montonero organization seems to stem from the attention it has received in the normally "respectable" press in Europe, as has been noted above. A Latin American counterpart to this phenomenon is the Mexican journal *Proceso,* whose editor is widely thought to be one of the more progressive journalists writing in the Spanish language. It is likely that such journalists have been deceived into thinking that the Montoneros are truly a patriotic organization, not just Marxists and/or fascists for entrepreneurial convenience. But such attention as that paid to the Montoneros by *Proceso* in several interviews published during 1978 lent credibility to the Montoneros' claim to the role of a patriotic movement in exile, just as permitting the Montoneros to set up a political exile center in Mexico also contributed to that image. A case in point is the interview published by *Proceso* (18 September) with Adriana Gauda, a woman Montonero who was listed as exiled in Beirut, Lebanon. The woman stated that the Montoneros' long-range strategy was to set up "shops" throughout the Third World as well as in Europe and to exert pressures which would "isolate" the military junta in Buenos Aires. The MPM would enlist the allegiance of national liberation movements in the Middle East and elsewhere to "oppose the fascist tyrants of South America." She cited as important the symbolic protests of Argentine workers but stressed an activity that has come to be known as the "crazy women of the Plaza de Mayo," a group of mothers and widows who paraded silently during 1978 before the government palace demanding to know the fate of their missing children and husbands. Adriana Gauda also lauded the action within Argentina of "Montonero militias" but did not offer specific details. Contrary to this published testimony, my sources in Buenos Aires ascribed the "crazy women" phenomenon to the Third World Priests movement and to elements within the proscribed Christian Democratic Party. Specifically, my sources contended that the "crazy women" had been organized by Alicia Moreau de Justo, a prominent female activist in Argentine socialist circles for many years, and denied that the women protesters had anything to do with the Montoneros. Yet these same sources did not mention to me the disappearance in Brazil of Norberto Habegger, a journalist who often serves as a spokesman for the Montoneros in various countries of Latin America (*Argentina Outreach,* Berkeley, October/November). So one should weigh carefully all claims about the guerrilla sector in Argentina as severe discrepancies and information "gaps" appear to exist as of this writing.

As far as the remainder of the former Argentine guerrilla sector was concerned, the last available comment from the People's Revolutionary Army (ERP) came from Spain where Luis Mattini, self-appointed commander of the ERP in exile, told the Madrid publication *Diario 16* in December 1977 that during 1978 his group would offer Argentines of the political "center" an opportunity to oppose the Videla junta. Mattini criticized the Montoneros for too much political "separatism" and denounced the pro-Moscow PCA for collaborating with the military government. Informed sources in Buenos Aires assured me, however, that the ERP (along with its political arm, the Revolutionary Workers' Party) had ceased to exist during 1978 and that for all intents and purposes the guerrilla sector of the Marxist spectrum could be considered liquidated. Agreeing with that, the Videla government could then also publish in an early October issue of *Time* magazine an impressive supplement called "Advertising from Argentina" in which American investors were assured that Argentina had once again been made safe from Marxist terrorists.

Publications. Aside from periodicals and newspapers mentioned in the text above, several other publications carry information on various groups across the Marxist and Marxist-Leninist spectrum. Among them are the Buenos Aires monthly *Redacción* and the Buenos Aires weekly *Ultima Clave*. Such formerly accessible guerrilla news and propaganda sheets as *Evita Montonera* and *Estrella Roja* were reportedly nonexistent during 1978.

University of Missouri   Kenneth F. Johnson
St. Louis

Bolivia

The far Left in Bolivia is exceedingly splintered. Virtually all of the parties and tendencies have their origin in one of five original groups: (*a*), the heirs of the pro-Stalinist Party of the Revolutionary Left (Partido de Izquierda Revolucionario; PIR), established in 1940, include the pro-Moscow Communist Party of Bolivia (Partido Comunista de Bolivia; PCB), and the pro-Chinese Marxist-Leninist Communist Party of Bolivia (Partido Comunista de Bolivia Marxista-Leninista; PCB-ML); (*b*), the Trotskyite Revolutionary Workers' Party (Partido Obrero Revolucionario; POR), also organized in 1940, has given rise to at least five parties, most of which still use the name POR; (*c*), the National Liberation Army (Ejército de Liberación Nacional; ELN), Ernesto "Che" Guevara's guerrilla group organized in 1966, established in 1975 the Revolutionary Party of Bolivian Workers (Partido Revolucionario de los Trabajadores de Bolivia; PRTB); (*d*), from the middle-of-the-road Christian Democratic Party (Partido Democrata Cristiano; PDC) there broke away in 1971 the Movement of the Revolutionary Left (Movimiento de Izquierda Revolucionario; MIR); (*e*), finally, from the center-left Nationalist Revolutionary Movement (Movimiento Nacionalista Revolucionario; MNR), a dissident left-wing group, formed the Socialist Party (Partido Socialista de Bolivia; PSB) in the early 1970s. The total membership of the communist factions was estimated at 500. The population of Bolivia was 5,081,000.

During 1978 almost all of the far Left groups took part in the aborted move to supplant the military dictatorship of President Hugo Banzer with a democratically elected regime. As a result of a hunger strike involving several hundred people in January, President Banzer declared a general amnesty to allow all exiles to return and to permit both parties and labor unions to reorganize freely. Most of the far-left parties were aligned with one or another of the coalitions which were organized to participate in the 8 July general election. Although the election results were upset, and the government's presidential candidate General Pereda Asbun seized power, all parties, including the far-leftist ones, continued to function relatively freely during the remainder of the year.

The PCB: Leadership and Organization. The first secretary of the PCB is Jorge Kolle Cueto. Others prominent in the party include Mario Monje Molina, a former first secretary, and Central

Committee members Simón Reyes, Arturo Lanza, Carlos Alba, and Luis Padilla, the latter a frequent international spokesman for the party. The PCB's youth organization, the Communist Youth of Bolivia (Juventud Comunista de Bolivia; JCB), was illegal until 1978. Among its leaders in recent years have been Jorge Escalera and Carlos Soria Galvarro. Simón Reyes, the head of the PCB's mining activities, assumed a leading position in the miners' federation (FSTMB) when it resumed legal activities early in 1978.

The PCB: Domestic and International Attitudes and Activities. In connection with the general election in July, the PCB issued a new political platform in May. It started by stating that "the PCB is the vanguard detachment of the Bolivian working class, the highest working class organization, and the leading force which will lead that class to achieve political power and later to the construction of socialism and to the building of a communist society. The PCB bases its action on Marxist-Leninist doctrine and on the political line approved by its congress, whose ideals are characterized by the anti-imperialist and popular character of the Bolivian revolution." It also stated that "within the party there exists only one political line and one organic unity that is guided by the existence and enforcement of only one statute, one leadership and one conscious discipline." The platform called for the "breaking of relations with the IMF, [a state foreign trade monopoly] management of public affairs, of state enterprises, and of municipal and local authorities through popular organizations; equal rights for women, raising of the people's living standards, and "full equality of rights of the various nationalities, guaranteeing the development of their cultures," apparently a reference to the various Indian linguistic groups in Bolivia. (*Presencia,* La Paz, 30 May.)

During the election campaign the PCB formed part of the Democratic and Popular Unity Front (Frente de Unidad Democrática y Popular; FUDP), the largest element of which was the Left Nationalist Revolutionary Movement (Movimiento Revolucionario de Izquierda; MNRI), headed by ex-president Hernán Siles Suazo, the Front's presidential nominee. Other members of the Front included the MIR and the PSB. The PCB platform proclaimed the Front to be the "political instrument" which would create "a democratic civilian-military government which would unite the working class, the peasants, the petite bourgeoisie, and some nonfascist levels of the Bolivian bourgeoisie."

On international issues, the platform proclaimed strict adherence to proletarian internationalism. In an interview in April, First Secretary Jorge Kolle Cueto said the PCB "maintains fraternal relations, based on the principle of proletarian internationalism, with all communist and workers parties of the world. It is obvious that this same relationship applies to the CPSU." (*FBIS*, 1 May.)

Publications. The PCB publishes irregularly a newspaper, *Unidad,* and occasional pamphlets and bulletins distributed among workers, peasants, and intellectuals.

The PCB-ML. The PCB-ML was founded as a result of a split in the PCB in 1965. It has long been torn by dissension. The faction headed by Oscar Zamora Medinacelli has given its blessing to Hua Kuo-feng and continued to be recognized by the People's Republic of China. It was the only pro-Chinese group which was registered for the 1978 election and is thought to have had some 150 members, although the number may have increased during the year.

In its election statement, issued in May, the PCB-ML proclaimed itself "the vanguard detachment of the Bolivian working class, its superior form of organization." It also said that it was "guided in its actions by Marxism—Leninism—Mao Tse-tung Thought" and that "the Leninist principles of democratic centralism, collective leadership, and criticism and self-criticism rule the party's life." (*Presencia,* 31 May.) The PCB-ML formed a part of the Revolutionary Front of the Left (Frente Revolucionario de Izquierda; FRI), the main constituent of which was Juan Lechín's Revolutionary Party of the

Nationalist Left (Partido Revolucionario de la Izquierda Nacionalista; PRIN) but which also included two factions of the Trotskyites and some elements formerly associated with the ELN.

The pro-Chinese Communists have some following among the miners. Also, one faction of the much splintered peasant movement, the National Independent Peasant Workers' Confederation (Confederación Nacional de Trabajadores Campesinos; CNTC), is headed by a member of the PCB-ML.

The Trotskyites. In 1978 the Trotskyites were reportedly divided into at least five different groups, four of which were registered for the 1978 election. The POR headed by Hugo Gonzalez is affiliated with the United Secretariat of the Fourth International and supported the Revolutionary Front of the Left in the election, as did the Communist Vanguard of the Revolutionary Workers' Party (Vanguardia Comunista del Partido Obrero Revolucionario; VCPOR), a split off from the Gonzalez party led by mine leader Filemon Escobar. On the other hand, the POR led by Guillermo Lora, which is affiliated with a Fourth International faction based in Paris, and the Posadista POR, the Bolivian affiliate of the Fourth International faction led by the Argentinian J. Posadas, did not support any presidential candidate in the 1978 election.

Although the original POR had substantial influence in the labor movement in the 1940s and 1950s, particularly among the miners, Trotskyite influence is presently much smaller. However, the Gonzalez POR, the Lora POR, and the Communist Vanguard POR still have some following among the miners.

Other Revolutionary Organizations and Activities. The Revolutionary Party of Bolivian Workers (PRTB), the political heir of the Ché Guevara guerrilla effort in 1966–67, first supported the political campaign of the Revolutionary Front of the Left in the 1978 election. However, at the end of May it switched its support to the Democratic and Popular Unity Front. (*Presencia*, 1 June.) The Socialist Party, which was formed by a splinter group of the MNR during the government of General Juan José Torres in 1970–71, was a member of the Democratic and Popular Unity Front, as was the MIR, formed by members of the Youth Development of the Christian Democratic Party (PDC), which launched an abortive guerrilla movement after General Banzer seized power in 1971. The MIR was particularly closely aligned with the Front's presidential candidate, Hernán Siles.

Rutgers University   Robert J. Alexander

Brazil

The original Communist Party of Brazil (Partido Comunista do Brasil; PCdoB), founded in March 1922, remains the most important Marxist-Leninist organization in the nation. Several small groups that broke away or were expelled from the party in the first decade formed a Trotskyite movement which subsequently split into several factions. Two of these factions still maintain a precarious existence. In 1960, in a bid for legal recognition, the original pro-Soviet party dropped all international slogans from its statutes and changed its name to Brazilian Communist Party (Partido Comunista Brasiliero; PCB). A pro-Chinese element broke away the following year and in February 1962 adopted the original party name, Communist Party of Brazil. Another source of far-leftist groups was Popular Action (Acão Popular; AP), which originated in the Catholic student movement in the late 1950s. In the following decade a segment of AP identified itself as the Marxist-Leninist Popular Action (Acão Popular Marxista Leninista; APML).

Dissidence within these parties after the military coup of 1964 led to the formation of numerous splinter groups, predominantly of Maoist and Castroite tendencies, which strongly advocated the use of armed violence to overthrow the regime. There may have been as many as sixteen such organizations at one point. Some of them, using urban guerrilla or terrorist tactics, gained considerable notoriety for a time, but between 1969 and 1972 the deaths of their most prominent leaders, the wholesale arrests of militants, and continued public apathy or hostility drastically reduced their number and effectiveness. An attempt to launch a rural guerrilla movement undertaken by the PCdoB and three other groups in the early 1970s was suppressed by the military.

The communist movement has been illegal in Brazil throughout most of its existence, though it has at times operated with varying degrees of freedom. The military regime which came to power in March 1964 drove the PCB and other far-left groups deeply underground and banned existing communist-influenced organizations. Since 1969 certain acts of subversion have been punishable by banishment or death. In practice, the death penalty has not been applied by the courts, but several dozen Brazilian terrorists have been exiled and others have died in prison or have been killed in clashes with the police and the military.

The PCB and PCdoB are thought to have had some 6,000 members combined, the majority found in the former. Little is known of the strength of other Marxist-Leninist groups. The population of Brazil is something over 115,415,000.

The PCB: Organization and Leadership. The PCB apparatus is supposed to include a 21-member Executive Commission, a Central Committee, state committees, municipal committees, and local cells in residential districts and places of employment. However, government persecution has made it impossible for the party to maintain a full panoply of organization.

Party General Secretary Luiz Carlos Prestes, who has lived in exile most of the time since 1964 and in Moscow since 1971, explained the situation in an article published in March. He noted that "despite . . . long experience and the efforts made by our Central Committee, by the whole party, to maintain vigilance and use new methods of illegal work, the truth is that these methods, adopted by various sections of the party, beginning from the CC, were not adequate to the new devices employed by the repressive agencies. . . ." He added that "in the face of repression and violence aimed at physically destroying the party's leaders, the PCB Central Committee passed a decision that the most prominent members of the party leadership should leave the country. This enabled the Central Committee to reorganize all its activity on a new basis." (*WMR*, March 1978.)

The last congress of the PCB (the sixth) took place in December 1967. Since then occasional plenary sessions of the Central Committee have been held. It held such a session in December 1977, which adopted a political resolution to guide the party's thinking and action.

The party draws its leadership and members from the ranks of students, intellectuals, and organized labor. Consistently, there has been a substantial turnover in membership, especially among white-collar elements, as individuals become inactive because of boredom, fear of arrest, or—in the past decade and a half—impatience with the nonviolent policies of the PCB.

Domestic Activities and Attitudes. The PCB is an orthodox pro-Soviet party, which seeks to mobilize and manipulate the masses to achieve power. It long ago recognized the impossibility of achieving power in Brazil by violence and thus advocates popular front tactics. Within its limited possibilities, the PCB seeks to identify with—and to claim responsibility for articulating—the legitimate grievances and aspirations of broad sectors of Brazilian society. The total failure of the "reckless adventures" of extremist left-wing guerrilla organizations has reinforced the belief of PCB leaders in the correctness of the party's domestic policies.

On various recent occasions the leaders of the PCB have published analyses of the current Brazilian situation and the party's reaction to it, most recently after the Central Committee meeting of December 1977. Its Political Resolution proclaimed that "we are struggling to set up an anti-fascist and patriotic front. This aim corresponds to the idea of 'forming and developing an anti-dictatorship front' which we expressed ten years ago at the Sixth PCB Congress. It is a question of the content, not the form, since it would be futile to try to determine the form such a front might assume." The Central Committee stated: "We realize the fundamental importance of using every legitimate opportunity to continue the struggle; we are prepared to cooperate with all trends moving in that direction, even if in some cases the prospects of their clashing with the regime are limited and partial. The attainment of democratic freedoms is at the center of our struggle. Great importance attaches to every successful step in that direction, however small. We understand, however, that only a democracy, having eliminated the constitutional and repressive mechanisms on which the fascist power rests, will open the way for the changes urgently needed by Brazil." The resolution also noted: "We should concentrate our attention on the working-class and trade union movement. Its present upsurge is distinguished by the fact that it links the struggle for specific demands, starting with the demand for higher wages, with general issues concerning the entire people." It added: "The question of mobilizing the peasant masses should remain an object of our attention. The stepped-up struggle of the agricultural workers against the policy of growing unemployment, the peasant actions against the policy of ruining their farms and strengthening the big capitalists and latifundists, the struggle of the small owners against eviction from their lands, create better conditions for enhancing and strengthening the organization of rural workers." The resolution concluded with a comment on the need to reorganize the party: "It is essential to surmount the disparity between the political influence of the PCB and the weakness of its organization. This is a political task that requires—proceeding from a correct approach to present and future demands of revolutionary work—at once a correct assessment of the balance of forces and concrete opportunities, skill, flexibility and a clear awareness of the limits within which steps can be taken with assurance." (*IB*, no. 9.)

During 1978 there was some public controversy among Brazilian politicians and military men over whether the PCB should be legalized. Army Minister Fernando Belfort Bethlem said in February that the army was "united and dedicated in its permanent struggle against antifatherland and pseudodemocratic communists who, in Brazil and abroad, plot against Brazil" (*Latin*, 21 February). In June, the government's presidential candidate, General João Baptista de Figueiredo, announced that the Communist Party would never be legalized during his tenure as president (Agence France Presse, 27 June). In August, Antonio Delfin Neto, former minister of finance of the military regime, and aspirant to the governorship of São Paulo, came out in support of legalizing the party.

During the year, people accused of trying to reorganize the PCB were tried and convicted by courts of the military regime. However, in September, Luiz Carlos Prestes, the PCB secretary general, was reportedly cleared in absentia by a military court of charges of trying to reorganize the party.

International Views and Contacts. The PCB continued to be a loyal member of the pro-Moscow group of communist parties. Luiz Carlos Prestes indicated his party's loyalty to the Soviet Union in a midyear interview. Asked about the significance of "Eurocommunism," he commented that " 'Eurocommunism' is a term dreamed up by certain journalists. At the back of it is the bourgeoisie's intention to divide the communist movement, to separate certain West European communist parties from the communist movement in the East, from the socialist community. . . . We do not oppose the West European communist parties in France, Italy, and Spain having certain differing opinions on political tactics and strategy. But we are against the way the bourgeoisie is abusing this to introduce conflicts among the communist parties, against the way it is trying to strengthen anticommunism and anti-Sovietism." (*Rudé Právo*, Prague 24 May.) Prestes continued to reinforce his party's relations with East European countries by visiting them and conferring with their leaders. In January he visited Bulgaria, where he was received by Todor Zhivkov and other party leaders, and in April he spent several days in Czechoslovakia, where he conferred with Gustav Husák and other Czech communist figures.

Publications. The PCB paper *Voz Operaria* circulated illegally throughout 1978. An article on the paper in *World Marxist Review* noted that "now, as before, the paper popularizes the party's slogans." It also noted that "the paper publishes resolutions and other documents issued by the party's Central Committee, and materials signed by the PCB General Secretary." The article claimed that "the communist newspaper is winning growing prestige and significance under conditions of the social and political crisis and the mounting struggles of the masses." (*WMR*, January.)

The PCdoB. The organizational structure of the PCdoB, which was founded by men who had long held leadership positions in the PCB, is believed to be patterned after that of the parent party. Little is known about the number or distribution of currently functioning units.

Although the PCdoB originated as a party loyal to the Chinese communist regime, during 1978 there was evidence that it had broken with the heirs of Mao Tse-tung. In August it sent a message to the Albanian Communist Party expressing its support for that party in its break with the Chinese. The message noted: "We have long observed with revolutionary concern the contemptuous attitude of the Chinese leaders toward the forces that genuinely defend socialism and their arrogant and imposing revisionism, imperialism and world reaction. . . . They have now gone to the extreme [of] vileness and by economically attacking a socialist country like Albania, which is admired and respected for its adherence to principles, its military spirit and its revolutionary honesty, intend to weaken its economy and national defense." It concluded that "They call themselves Marxists and internationalists, whereas in practice they act, in everything, like a big power, seeking unconditional submissions to their nationalist line and policy from those who receive their aid." (*FBIS*, 12 August.)

Other Organizations. Of the numerous extremist and terrorist organizations that operated in Brazil in the late 1960s and early 1970s, only a few appear to have survived into 1978. A pro-Moscow group, the Revolutionary Communist Party (Partido Revolucionario Comunista; PRC) is apparently still active. In April, four people who had been convicted of activity in it the year before were captured by the police. (*O Estado de São Paulo*, 9 April.) In late September, an Italian deacon, Domenico Corcione, was arrested on the same charge (*FBIS*, 3 October).

The Trotskyites also remained active. In September, 22 people, including Nahuel Moreno and Rita Strasberg, leaders of the Argentine Trotskyite party, Socialist Party of the Workers (PST), were arrested in São Paulo. They were accused of belonging to the Liga Operaria, the Brazilian group associated with the United Secretariat of the Fourth International and of participating in organizing Socialist Convergence, (Convergencia Socialista; CS), a new party which was seeking legal recognition. In October, Moreno and Strasberg were freed.

Rutgers University   Robert J. Alexander

Canada

The Communist Party of Canada was founded in 1921. This legal party claims a membership of under 5,000; some sources estimate it to be about 2,000. The population of Canada is 23,632,000 (estimated 1978). There are a number of other small Marxist-Leninist groups. The Communist Party of Canada/Marxist-Leninist (CPC/M-L), which has recently come to refer to itself as the Marxist-Leninist Communist Party of Canada, is Maoist and takes its present orientation from Albania. It is especially active in the province of Quebec, with headquarters at Montreal. The Maoist group that now enjoys the Peking franchise is the Canadian Communist League (M-L) and it appears to be the more dynamic organization.

In addition there are various Trotskyist organizations. The Revolutionary Workers' League (RWL) was formed in 1977 through a merger of the League for Socialist Action/Ligue socialiste ouvrière (LSA/LSO), the Group marxiste révolutionnaire (GMR), and the Revolutionary Marxist Group (RMG), which was originally formed in 1973 by LSA/LSO breakaways. The second oldest is the Groupe socialiste des travailleurs du Quebec, formed in 1973 and associated with the Fourth International. In addition there are such groups as The Socialist League, founded in 1973 by Ross Dowson, who split from the LSA over the issue of Canadian nationalism and supported Quebec's independence as a step towards the socialist revolution in North America. The International Socialists (IS) came into being as a faction of the so-called Waffle group who were expelled by the more moderately socialist New Democratic Party, the third party which forms the government in Saskatchewan province. The Trotskyist League (TL) is the result of a merger of the Spartacus League and the Leninist-Bolshevik Tendency (LBT); it sees its role as a left opposition to the Revolutionary

Workers' League. These groups tend to be highly critical of one another amidst charges of different forms of revisionism.

It used to be said that most CPC members were elderly persons of East European origin, but that is no longer true. There has been energetic recruitment of younger members and these are active in the party. In anticipation of a federal election in 1978, the CPC nominated representatives to run in various ridings and these tended to be middle aged and younger. No general election was held, but CPC candidates did contest some of the October by-elections. None was elected. Thus the CPC has neither federal nor provincial representation. There are, however, CPC members or sympathizers who serve on municipal councils and local school boards.

The United Fishermen and the Allied Workers' Union, on the west coast, and the United Electrical, Radio, and Allied Workers' Union are unions in which Communists hold some leadership positions. A number of CPC members are officers in union locals and regional labor councils as well as being influential in district and town labor councils, especially in British Columbia. Some ethnic organizations of East European origin reflect CPC influence. However, the strong support the CPC has given the establishment of a Palestinian state has been a source of friction with the leaders of some Jewish groups which had been in friendly association with the CPC. The CPC (M-L) has worked among Canadians of East Indian origin who have been the victims of racial prejudice in the Toronto area. Recruiters have been active in factories and recently the CPC (M-L) has been successful among Montreal hospital workers, obtaining offices in local union executive committees.

CPC: Leadership and Organization. William Kashtan continues as CPC general secretary and party leader; Alfred Dewhurst, editor of *Communist Viewpoint*, is a member of the Central Executive Committee and director of its ideological work through a weekly column on Marxist-Leninist theory as it relates to contemporary problems, in the *Canadian Tribune*. Bruce Magnuson serves as labor secretary on the Central Executive Committee and as president, publisher, and labor columnist of the *Canadian Tribune*. Mel Doig, Rod Dran and Elizabeth Hill continue as Central Executive Committee members. William Stewart is leader of the party in Ontario, and John Bizzell chairman of the metropolitan Toronto organization. Gerry Van Houten serves as research director of the CPC. Mike Gidora continues as general secretary of the Young Communist League.

Sam Walsh is president of the Parti Communiste du Québec (PCQ), the fraternal organization which enjoys a certain autonomy within the CPC; he is also a member of the Central Executive Committee. Maurice Rush replaced Nigel Morgan (who died in June) as leader of the party in British Columbia. Tom Hill also died this past year; he had been a party member since the early 1920s and had served in Kingston penitentiary with Tim Buck from 1931 to 1934 when the party was illegal.

Domestic Attitudes and Activities. The crisis in Canadian unity which came after the election victory of René Lévesque's Parti Québécois, with its objective of sovereignty for the province of Quebec, continued to be a leading problem. Prime Minister Trudeau had originally won in 1968 on a one country—one nation platform. However, his failure to solve the economic problems of inflation and high unemployment damaged his popularity in recent months. It had been thought he would call for an election before the autumn, but when his standing in the polls sank to 35 percent in contrast to the 45 percent given conservative leader Joe Clark, Trudeau postponed the election until 1979.

The CPC defended a united Canada but called for a reformed constitution which would recognize the right of the French people to enjoy a measure of self-determination. In contrast, Maoist parties supported Quebec's independence, believing such a disruption would hasten the socialist revolution. The CPC regarded the Parti Québécois as a bourgeois middle-class group whose success would only further the takeover of Canada by the imperialistic United States. As the Canadian dollar declined to 85 cents against the U.S. dollar, the CPC tried to emphasize the contradictions in

Canadian capitalism. A great deal of attention was paid to layoffs in the auto industry and to such events as strikes at Inco in Sudbury. Officially, the New Democratic Party is linked to the labor unions. This moderate socialist party is highly critical of the Soviet Union. Thus, the CPC press berates the NDP yet supports it in some elections as a better alternative than the traditional liberal or conservative parties. When the Royal Canadian Mounted Police counterespionage force was forced to reveal that it had committed illegal acts in the name of national security, this admission, and some bungled attempts to recruit agents from among USSR foreign trade personnel, provided grist for the CPC mills of protest.

International Views and Policies. The CPC generally supports positions taken by the Communist Party of the Soviet Union (CPSU) on international issues. Thus early in 1978 a great campaign was waged in editorials, news stories and cartoons against development of the neutron bomb by the United States. After President Carter decided to postpone its production, this campaign slacked off. In contrast, relatively little attention was paid to the theme of détente or to news of the SALT talks. There was the usual negative attitude toward Canada's participation in NATO and NORAD, but in general less was said on these matters.

There was criticism of the United States for alleged denial of human rights to the Wilmington Ten, and Andrew Young's statements about American "political prisoners" were pounced on with great glee. The movement of Eurocommunism was repudiated and the communist parties of Britain, France, and Italy were rebuked for supporting such Soviet dissenters as Shcharansky, Filatov, and Ginzberg. The shortcomings of Iran, Nicaragua, Rhodesia, and, of course, South Africa, in the realm of human rights, were repeatedly underlined. Countries like Chile and Zaire, favored by Peking, were exposed often in negative reports.

The German Democratic Republic received most favorable treatment, with laudatory articles on its devotion to culture, sport, and women's equality. Nor was Cuba neglected in the handing out of praise. The space achievements of the USSR provided a series of articles on the success of socialism in scientific endeavors. Friends of the Soviet Union, such as Ethiopia and Vietnam, were treated well, as was Afghanistan later in the year.

Terrorism of the Red Brigades which resulted in the murder of former premier Aldo Moro in Italy was roundly condemned, and Dewhurst analyzed in his column what he regarded as the differences between working for the revolution and the adventurism of the ultraleft terrorist groups.

Israel came in for criticism regularly, while the PLO was supported. The overtures Sadat made toward peace early in the year were treated negatively, and the Camp David accords were ignored along with whatever else President Carter tried to do to promote peace in the Middle East.

International Activities and Contacts. William Kashtan visited Romania and Bulgaria in July on his way to a six-day visit to Vietnam from 5 to 10 August. He then returned to Canada via the Soviet Union, where he reported on the progress being made in Vietnam. A delegation from the Young Communist League, led by Mike Gidora and including Anna Larsen and Mike Constable, attended the Eleventh World Youth Festival at Havana, Cuba during late July and early August.

Publications. The CPC publishes a theoretical journal, *Communist Viewpoint*, six times a year, and two weeklies, *Canadian Tribune* (Toronto) and *Pacific Tribune* (Vancouver). The PCQ issues the weekly *Combat* (Montreal). The organ of the YCL, *Young Worker* (Toronto), changed its name to *New Horizons* and will appear ten times a year. Party members edit and publish various ethnic papers in languages other than English and French; the Italian *Lotta Unitaria*, which began in April 1977, continued into 1978.

The North American edition of the Prague-based *World Marxist Review* and its companion publication, the fortnightly *Information Bulletin*, are published in Toronto.

The CPC (M-L) organ, the *People's Canada Daily News*, appears regularly out of Montreal and follows a Maoist line—as set forth by Radio Tirana in Albania—primarily by its spokesman, Hardial Bains. The Canadian Communist League (M-L) produces a weekly, *The Forge*, in French and English editions; it extols the Maoist leadership of Third World forces. A theoretical journal, *October*, appears bimonthly, and a weekly, *Alive Magazine*, edited at Guelph in Ontario, features Hsinhua news releases.

The fortnightly *Socialist Voice* serves as organ of the Revolutionary Workers' League, with *Lutte ouvrière* (Montreal) focusing on labor and nationalist movements in Quebec.

University of San Francisco   Desmond J. FitzGerald

Chile

The Communist Party of Chile (Partido Comunista de Chile; PCCh) was first established as the Socialist Workers' Party in 1912. The name PCCh was adopted in January 1922 following the party's decision in 1921 to join the Communist International. The party was illegal between 1948 and 1958. A pro-Chinese party, the Revolutionary Communist Party of Chile (Partido Comunista Revolucionario de Chile; PCRCh), was established in May 1966, primarily by a group of Communists expelled from the PCCh in 1963. The Movement of the Revolutionary Left (Movimiento de Izquierda Revolucionaria; MIR) brought together several leftist groups in 1965 and soon developed an affinity for the form of armed revolutionary struggle advocated during the middle and late 1960s by Che Guevara and Fidel Castro. All of these groups have been illegal since the military coup of September 1973.

The PCCh claimed 200,000 members in early 1973. Many party leaders have been killed, imprisoned, or forced into exile since September 1973, but most of the present 100,000 or so members in Chile are free though banned from political activities. At its height before the coup, the PCRCh probably had several hundred active members but, after internal dissension, there are fewer today. The MIR, which probably had from 5,000 to 10,000 active members in mid-1973, has been hard hit by Chilean security forces; its membership has been greatly reduced and its top pre-coup leaders are dead, in jail, or abroad.

Popular Unity Movement. Between 1956 and 1969 the PCCh allied itself for electoral purposes with the Socialist Party of Chile (Partido Socialista de Chile; PSCh) in the Popular Action Front (FRAP). Realizing that a still broader front had to be established to secure victory at the polls, the PCCh led in forming the Popular Unity (Unidad Popular; UP) in 1969, an alliance of leftist parties which enabled Salvador Allende to win a narrow plurality in the September 1970 elections. During 1978 the most important UP members—all of which were outlawed—were: the PCCh, the PSCh, the Radical Party (PR), and several leftist Christian splinter groups, essentially the composition of the original 1969 alliance.

Under the leadership of Socialist Salvador Allende, the UP alliance controlled the executive branch of government during the 1970-1973 period despite rising dissension within its ranks with respect to the proper strategy and tactics of revolution. During the Allende period the unity of the UP alliance was further weakened by disputes with non-UP revolutionary groups that adopted a more militant revolutionary line, particularly the MIR. Since the coup the PCCh has led the drive to build a broader and more secure leftist front, ranging from the Christian Democrats (PDC) in the center of the political spectrum to the MIR and other groups on what it has long considered the "ultra-left."

During 1978 the UP members sought to strengthen the alliance—in particular through cooperation with the Christian Democrats—held meetings abroad, organized and attended international Chile "solidarity" conferences, and issued statements on developments in the country. On 10 January the UP parties issued a statement saying that the plebiscite held by Chilean President Augusto Pinochet on 4 January—in which 75 percent of the voting population condemned "international aggression" against Chile and affirmed the "legitimacy of the government"—was a "great farce." It called for an "alliance of all democratic forces," including the PDC and the so-called democratic sectors of the military, "without which it would be almost impossible to overthrow Pinochet." The Popular Unity groups were particularly elated because Christian Democracy "has placed itself in frank and active opposition to the regime." (Agence France Press, Paris, 10 January.) The same parties attended the International Conference of Solidarity with the Chilean People, held in the Libyan city of Benghazi in April, the first meeting of the many national committees of solidarity with Chile. The conference, which aimed its discussions at "practical measures in the struggle against the fascist junta," was attended by delegates from most of the socialist countries, sixteen West European states, and many other countries as well. (*New Zealand Tribune*, 5 June.) Popular Unity exiles stated on 5 May in Caracas that the recent "liberalization" campaign announced by the Chilean government was "nothing but a political maneuver to deceive international public opinion and to ease pressures, both national and international, on the regime" (*El Nacional*, Caracas, 8 May). In mid-year the Prague-based *World Marxist Review* organized a seminar which included PCCh theoretician Volodia Teitelboim, Julio Silva, editor-in-chief of the Italy-based *Chile-America* magazine, and Radomiro Tomic, the PDC's 1970 presidential candidate. In the discussions Tomic reiterated his party's 30 March statement "resolutely denying all rumors about negotiations with the Popular Unity parties and categorically rejecting all proposals for a broad front, though this does not mean rejection of certain joint actions aimed at reestablishing democracy in Chile." Teitelboim reiterated the UP interest in a "more or less broad alliance" that will operate as "a joint effort to implement practical ideas on which the views of both sides coincide." The PCCh leader continued: "In the present Chilean situation, with fascism continuing to oppress the people and the country, Popular Unity strategy is based on the belief that socialism must be preceded by a stage consisting of a number of transition periods. The most practical changes have been in tactics, and by carrying out this change the Popular Unity has demonstrated its ability realistically to assess the situation." He called upon Chilean "democrats" to have "enmity toward the fascists within the army but not toward all servicemen." (*WMR*, October.) PCCh secretary general Luis Corvalán and other UP leaders attended the World Conference of Solidarity with the People of Chile held in Madrid in mid-November, a meeting reportedly attended by delegates from 50 countries. Besides condemning the "gross violations of human rights and basic democratic liberties" in Chile, the delegates from Cuba, Vietnam, and other countries condemned U.S. and Chinese communist "imperialisms." (Tass, Moscow, 11 November; Havana Radio, 10 November.)

PCCh: Leadership and Organization. PCCh general secretary Luis Corvalán has been in exile since December 1976 when he was released from a Chilean prison in exchange for the freedom of a Soviet political prisoner. Political Commission members and alternate members who are active in exile include Orlando Millas, Rodrigo Rojas, Volodia Teitelboim, José Cademártori, Jorge Insunza, Manuel Cantero, and Gladys Marín, the latter also general secretary of the Communist Youth (Juventud Comunista de Chile; JCCh). The once-powerful communist-dominated Single Center of Chilean Workers (CUT or CUTCh) has been outlawed, and the Communist Youth, for years a powerful force in university politics, has been driven underground. Both the CUT and the JCCh remain active abroad, the labor central in particular getting strong support from such international labor organizations as the World Federation of Trade Unions and issuing statements periodically from Havana or some other city. In September the "Ranquil" Peasant and Indian Federation, long dominated by the Communist Party and its youth organization, reappeared for the first time in five years in Chile to voice its support, via its president, Sergio Villalobos, for the leftist National Union Coordinating Board (CNS) and its proposed labor reforms.

PCCh: Domestic Attitudes and Activities. Although isolated communist statements were circulated within Chile during the year, most published analyses were made by party leaders in exile. Commentaries focused on such topics as the "lessons" of the Allende years (1970-73), the need for broad "antifascist" unity, what the party saw as the deterioration of the Pinochet government, and the kind of government and political system to be established in Chile once the military government is vanquished.

The PCCh issued statements immediately before and after the 4 January plebiscite, which the party branded a "crude farce" and a "political swindle," and called for a "genuine popular plebiscite" in its place (*IB*, No. 5). A more extensive party statement in March set forth the fundamental positions of the PCCh during the year. According to the Communists, the Pinochet government's economic policy is directed from outside the country, by the so-called "Chicago boys," and his foreign policy has isolated Chile from the international community and resulted in the country's worst relations with its neighbors in the present century. Under internal and external pressures, Pinochet is having to introduce changes which will pacify critics but maintain his control. Popular opposition to the government is increasing but as yet inadequate. What should be done? The majority of Chileans who oppose fascism should: (1) expand the mass struggle and united actions, (2) expand the areas of mutual understanding between all antifascist and nonfascist groups, civilian and military alike, and (3) achieve mutual understanding on the state system that is to replace fascism, and come up with a minimum socioeconomic program. The party expressed particular regret over the misunderstandings still existing between Popular Unity parties and the Christian Democrats, and proposed additional effort to resolve fundamental and surface differences between those concerned. The party stated that two ways are open to "democratic" forces in Chile: (1) "overthrow the tyranny, and then separate, so that each party can advance its own political plan," and (2) "together to overthrow the tyranny, maintain unity, and on the basis of a single political plan advance the objective of creating jointly a broad-based democratic representative government." The PCCh repeated its September 1976 proposals that call for "unity to overthrow the fascist dictatorship, an agreement enabling the creation of a new democracy, and formation of a government in which all the antifascist forces would be represented." Immediately after the overthrow of the "fascist tyranny," a "provisional government" should be set up to "lead the country from a fascist dictatorship to a lawful state, to implement a deep-going process of eradicating fascism and of general democratization, beginning with the convening of a Constituent Assembly, which will draft a new political constitution, and culminating in democratic elections, at which the people will elect their lawful bodies of power." The provisional government "must proceed from the minimum program envisaging economic and social measures that will ensure the country's return to the road of progress." (Statement abridged in *IB*, No. 11.) Teitelboim told the Italian communist newspaper *L'Unitá* (10 April) that the main reason for the crisis of the Pinochet government is the inquiry into the September 1976 assassination in Washington, D.C. of PSCh leader Orlando Letelier, former foreign minister of the Allende government. According to Teitelboim, "it is now clear, and it has been proved, that the orders came from Pinochet himself." The Communists hailed the decision of the Inter-American Regional Organization of Workers in late November to institute a trade boycott against the Pinochet government, noting this action as a major step forward in the international campaign against Chilean "fascism."

On a number of occasions during the year the Chilean security forces announced the breaking up of alleged communist cells and the discovery of printing presses, or charged the PCCh with participating in or organizing disruptive activities around the country. For example, in September the government accused the PCCh of working with the Christian Democrats in a united campaign to create difficulties for the government and "to disturb the tranquillity of the people," charging communist involvement in the extended strike at the Chiquicamata copper mine.

PCCh: International Attitudes and Activities. Prior to the 1973 coup, the PCCh was extraordinarily interested in international affairs, but since the coup its concerns have shifted. Although pro forma denunciations of the Chinese Communists continued, in 1978, as in recent years generally, proletarian internationalism meant chiefly international support for efforts to overthrow the Chilean military government. Exiled PCCh leaders travelled ceaselessly, particularly in Eastern and Western Europe and the Soviet Union, but also to friendly countries as far afield as Vietnam, promoting international opposition to the Chilean government and support for its "antifascist" front. Support groups operate in and out of many countries, the most important in the Western Hemisphere being Cuba, the United States, Canada, Venezuela, and Mexico. The PCCh received strong support from assorted pro-Soviet international front organizations, such as the World Federation of Trade Unions, and played an important role in a variety of international meetings, such as the World Conference of Solidarity with the People of Chile held in Madrid in mid-November.

The Movement of the Revolutionary Left. The MIR has been particularly hard-hit by government security forces since September 1973, one exiled leader estimating that some 5,000 miristas have been killed (*Caretas*, Lima, 18 September). Prominent MIR spokesmen in exile included Victor Toro and Andrés Pascal Allende. MIR statements during the year uniformly noted the strength of the Pinochet government, but added that since 1977 internal contradictions have increased and the mass movement has been reactivated. According to one party leader, "the military regime has entered a phase of immobility and decline. . . . The speeding-up of the recovery process of the mass movement has emerged as the most distinctive trait of the present Chilean political situation. . . . Today it is possible to forge a great popular resistance movement, capable of toppling the dictatorship and installing a revolutionary, popular, democratic government." The mirista warned, however, that this eventuality would not be easy to achieve. "We still need to advance a great deal more in the organization of the popular resistance movement. It is necessary to reach greater levels of coordination among the diverse struggles in order to confront conflicts with the dictatorship with nationwide force. We have to be capable of combining all forms of struggle and of reaching every part of Chile." (*Chile Newsletter*, Berkeley, Winter.) A MIR Political Commission declaration dated April 1978 called for a broadening of unity on the left, between the MIR and the UP, on the one hand, and all of these leftists and the anti-dictatorial sectors of the Christian Democrats, on the other (*Chile Newsletter*, Fall). Pascal Allende, in an interview given in Havana in September, reiterated the MIR call for "a front that will unite all leftist and democratic forces to fight the dictatorship," but sounded a scarcely-concealed decade-long animosity toward the PCCh; despite his call for "all forms of struggle," he emphasized the importance of armed struggle far beyond the level advocated by the PCCh or the UP generally. (*Caretas*, 18 September.) An unidentified leader quoted in *Chile Newsletter* (Fall), said that in view of the new conditions emerging in Chile, the popular resistance movement must seek to build a rearguard on more dynamic and flexible bases of support, one that is able to respond with greater capacity, quantitatively and qualitatively, to the growing needs of the MIR in Chile. This must be a rearguard prepared tactically and strategically to provide material, political, ideological, propagandistic, and human resources help for the struggle in Chile. The MIR confronted government security forces with increasing frquency during the year, staged propaganda operations, and had members captured or sent into exile.

Publications. The illegal Marxist and Marxist-Leninist parties and organizations of Chile circulate irregular clandestine papers and leaflets domestically and publish limited-circulation but legal newspapers abroad. These include *Unidad Antifascista* and *Principios* (PCCh), *Liberación* (JCCh), *El Rebelde* (MIR), *La Chispa* (PSCh), *Frente Antifascista* (UP), and three publications of the ultraleftist factions of the PDC, *Resistencia Democrática, Venceremos,* and *Pueblo Cristiano.* Communist Party statements circulate most widely in the regular journals of individual pro-Soviet communist parties around the world, as well as in the Prague-based *World Marxist Review* and its *Information Bulletin.* MIR (as well as PCCh) statements appear periodically in Cuban and sympathetic U.S. and European papers and journals.

Hoover Institution   William E. Ratliff
Stanford University

Colombia

The Communist movement in Colombia has undergone various transformations in both name and organization since the party's initial formation in December 1926. The Communist Party of Colombia (Partido Comunista de Colombia; PCC) was publicly proclaimed on 17 July 1930. In July 1965 a schism within the PCC between pro-Soviet and pro-Chinese factions resulted in the latter becoming the Communist Party of Colombia, Marxist-Leninist (PCC-ML). Only the PCC has legal status. It has been allowed to participate in elections under its own banners since 1972.

The PCC took part in the 26 February 1978 general elections as a member of the leftist coalition UNO-ANAPO-MIL (National Opposition Union—National Popular Alliance—Independent Liberal Movement). The coalition won one seat in the 112-member Senate and two seats in the 199-member Lower Chamber, compared with two Senate seats and five Lower Chamber seats in 1976 when the PCC/UNO's major coalition partner was the pro-Chinese Independent Revolutionary Workers' Movement (MOIR). At the state assembly level, the UNO maintained the same number of deputies, twelve, as in the 1976 election. Of 173 municipal councilmen elected in 1976, the PCC recognized the loss of at least 23 seats in 1978.

The PCC and the left-wing opposition in general failed to profit from popular discontent over high prices and low wages in the 1978 presidential elections held on 4 June. The abstention rate approached 70 percent, with all three candidates of the Left doing considerably worse than in the February elections. As can be seen from the results listed below, the candidate endorsed by the PCC, ex-ANAPO congressman Julio César Pernía, received less than 2 percent of the total popular vote, while the total vote for leftist candidates was less than 4 percent:

1978 Presidential Election

Candidate and Party	Votes	Percent
Julio César Turbay Ayala (Liberal)	2,506,228	49.9
Belisario Betancur (Conservative)	2,358,644	46.4
Julio César Pernía (PCC/UNO-ANAPO-MIL)	97,234	1.9
Alvaro Valencia Tovar (National Renewal Movement)	65,961	1.3
Jaime Piedrahita Cardona (MOIR/FUP— Front for the Unity of the People)	27,059	0.5
Socorro Ramirez (Socialist)	1,643	0.03
Regina Betancur de Liska (Independent)	126	
Blank Votes	9,923	
Null Votes	6,641	
Total	5,073,459	

A more detailed analysis of the elections is discussed below (see "Domestic Attitudes and Activities").

According to U.S. intelligence estimates, the PCC has 10,000−12,000 members. Although the party is confident that its ranks have increased in recent years, the 1978 elections provide compelling evidence that the party's growth has been less than hoped for in general and especially disappointing in the large cities. The PCC continues to exercise only marginal influence in national affairs. The population of Colombia is 25,559,000 (estimated 1978).

Guerrilla Warfare. Although not a serious threat to the government, guerrilla warfare has been a feature of Colombian life since the late 1940s, the current wave beginning in 1964. The three main guerrilla organizations are the Revolutionary Armed Forces of Colombia (FARC), long controlled by the PCC; the pro-Chinese People's Liberation Army (EPL), which is the guerrilla arm of the PCC-ML; and the Castroite National Liberation Army (ELN). Colombian military sources avoided giving estimates of the guerrillas' strength in 1978, although the FARC and the ELN probably have between 250 and 300 guerrillas each, along with an undetermined number of urban supporters. The EPL is believed to have fewer than 100 members.

Serious ideological and tactical differences continued to divide Colombia's guerrilla movements in 1978 despite periodic appeals for "unified action." In its final clandestine bulletin of 1977, the FARC announced that "there is no insurmountable reason to prevent unified guerrilla action in 1978" (*Alternativa,* 13 February). For its part, the EPL declared that it was not interested in "unity for unity's sake" and proposed total abstention from the 1978 elections (ibid., 23 January). In July, official spokesmen reported a "virtual war" between members of the two guerrilla organizations, citing a series of attacks that occurred between them on the borders of Antioquia and Córdoba. The conflicts apparently reflected "serious disagreement" over the construction of the Urrá Dam, which is being built by Soviet engineers. According to sources in Medellín, FARC guerrillas have been deployed in the region to prevent the EPL from carrying out threatened acts of sabotage (*El Tiempo,* 18 July).

The most concerted appeal for guerrilla unity came from the M-19, a predominantly urban guerrilla organization which claims to be the armed hand of ANAPO. In July the M-19 proposed a joint meeting with the FARC and the ELN to discuss a coordinated plan of action (*Alternativa,* 17 July). In its first reaction to the proposal, the FARC replied that the policy of unified guerrilla action is interpreted differently by some groups. However, it added that "all our armed movements agree on the urgent need for such a unity." While the FARC agrees with the ELN on the basic issue of unity of action, no mention of the EPL was made in the exchange of messages. In August the FARC announced the movement's merger with the ELN and the creation of new fronts in a movement to be called "FARC Plus People Equals Victory" (*Resistencia,* no. 70, August). Nevertheless, the continuation of independent operations by both groups, together with FARC's virulent attacks against the EPL and the PCC-ML, strongly suggests that Colombia's guerrilla movement will remain highly factionalized.

For its part, the M-19 has demonstrated a growing capacity to carry out acts of violence in different regions of the country. In March the M-19 claimed that it had taken part in a series of terrorist attacks in various Colombian cities since the first of the year in conjunction with the FARC and the ELN (RCN, 20 March). On 12 September the M-19 claimed credit for the assassination of former Government Minister Rafael Pardo Buelvas, although it should be noted that credit for Pardo's assassination was also claimed by the Marxist-Leninist Workers' Self-Defense Committee (Autodefensa Obrera; ADO).

Guerrilla offensives, particularly by the FARC, during late 1977 and early 1978 prompted a statement by the Defense Ministry in March outlining plans for a large-scale campaign against guerrilla groups (*El Tiempo,* 21 March). On 28 July the army announced that it had launched a "mammoth offensive" against guerrilla groups that had been assaulting townships and hamlets in remote highland regions of Córdoba (*El Espectador,* 29 July). In a speech before a Senate commission on 30 August, Defense Minister General Luis Carlos Camacho Leyva discussed preparations for "an unrestrained offensive" against guerrilla activities. The minister stated that "guerrilla leaders have been acting as true bandits in their attacks against peasants in areas of Santander and central Magdalena." He complained about the people's indifference toward political problems such as the one in Cimitarra where "the Communist Party is promoting violence and is forcing the people to sell their property at low prices." Camacho attributed peasant killings in the area to the adverse results experienced by the Communists in the elections: "The FARC credits itself with eliminating alleged criminals, but its members are actually murdering people and acting as bandits and common criminals" (*El Siglo,* 31 August). Antiguerrilla warfare intensified in early September when three specialized battalions were deployed in areas affected by an escalation in guerrilla activity; El Pato and Guayabero in the southwestern part of the country and Cimitarra in the northeast. Military spokesmen said the troops had received specific orders to "entirely exterminate the subversive pockets" (Agence France Presse, 3 September). As of late November, there was no evidence to indicate that the military had succeeded in its mission.

The PCC: Leadership and Organization. The PCC is headed by its 12-member Executive Committee and 54-member Central Committee. The highest party authority is the Congress, convened by the Central Committee at four-year intervals. The PCC held its Twelfth Congress on 5−9 December 1975. Gilberto Vieira is general secretary of the PCC. (For more detail, see *YICA, 1978,* p. 353.)

A major source of PCC's influence lies in its control of the Trade Union Confederation of Workers of Colombia (CSTC), which claims a membership of 300,000. The CSTC was granted legal status by the Colombian government in August 1974 and is a member of the World Federation of Trade Unions (WFTU). The president of the CSTC is Pástor Pérez. The CSTC was instrumental in achieving an unprecedented degree of cooperation among Colombia's four major labor centrals in 1977, culminating in the 14 September national strike and the formation of a National Labor Council (CNS; see *YICA*, 1978, pp. 353−54), which Pástor Pérez called "a major advance in collaborative action within the labor movement" (*Voz Proletaria*, 24 November 1977). The CSTC met in plenary session on 5−6 December 1977 in Bogotá to plan activities for 1978 and to further its goal of organizational and tactical solidarity with the other labor syndicates. The final resolution adopted called upon workers, peasants, students, and intellectuals to support and vote for candidates of the UNO. On a more pragmatic political level, the document noted that the UNO's slate of candidates for assembly and municipal offices included a number of labor and peasant leaders from the CSTC's directorship and the central's affiliates (ibid., 15 December 1977). On 20 December the CSTC announced that there would be no boycott of the February electoral debate, although Pérez declared that "after the elections there will be a greater mobilization, with more strikes and agitation than in 1977" (*El Espectador*, 21 December 1977). For his part, Gilberto Vieira called the creation of the National Labor Council and the cooperative action on the part of Colombia's four major labor unions "the most significant event of 1977" (*Voz Proletaria*, 22 December 1977).

On 15 February the CNS issued a plan of action for 1978 (ibid., 23 February). On 13 March the four labor centrals comprising the CNS announced they would stage "an unprecedented protest demonstration" on 1 May to demand that the López government provide concrete solutions to the economic and social problems being experienced by the Colombian working class (*El Espectador*, 14 March). On 28 March President López met with the leaders of the major labor centrals in the first meeting in the country's history between the chief of state and confederations representing all political persuasions.

But it took the new president less than one month to sow the seeds of discord among the labor centrals comprising the CNS. On 6 September President Turbay met with leaders of the more moderate Union of Workers of Colombia (UTC) and the Confederation of Workers of Colombia (CTC) to discuss the country's socioeconomic problems. CSTC Vice-president Miguel Antonio Caro argued weakly that "the fact that two of the centrals met separately with the president does not mean that there is a split in labor unity" (*Voz Proletaria*, 12 September). Any pretense of further unity of action was abruptly broken on 25 October when the UTC and the CTC stayed away from meetings called by the CNS. The break came about after the government systematically excluded the CSTC and the General Confederation of Workers (CGT) from meetings called to reform the labor code and from the convening of the government's national wage and trade union councils. The practical, if not official, dissolution of the CNS was a major setback for the PCC, and the party finds itself once again in the position of having to pursue its objective of working-class unity primarily through the CSTC. The PCC tries to influence peasants through the National Federation of Agrarian Syndicates (FENSA), which functions as a part of the CSTC. (See *YICA, 1978*, p. 354.) A number of FENSA officials appeared on UNO-ANAPO-MIL's electoral lists in 1978, especially at the municipal level.

The PCC's youth organization, the Communist Youth of Colombia (JUCO) has an estimated membership of 2,000. JUCO has its own National Directorate, Executive Committee, and Central Committee. The general secretary is Jaime Caycedo. As a militant adjunct of the PCC, the JUCO plays an active role in promoting party policy among university and secondary school students. On 1 December 1977 the JUCO organized a March of Youth in Bogotá to support the candidacy of Julio César Pernía. According to PCC estimates, some 5,000 youth participated in an UNO-ANAPO-MIL demonstration sanctioned by the authorites on 9 February. During the week preceding the 26 February elections, the JUCO was responsible for ensuring the enthusiastic support of youth for the parent coalition. The JUCO exercised a controlling vote within the national committee responsible for Colombia's participation in the World Festival of Youth held in Havana in July. Through its control of the national committee, the JUCO was able to determine both the organization and the number of delegates that each youth organization would be allowed to elect to the festival (*Alternativa,* 1 May). The JUCO is occasionally called upon to serve as the enforcing arm of the PCC. In the hours preceding the International Workers' Day demonstration on 1 May, JUCO's strong-arm tactics and the PCC's obvious partisan electioneering prompted some of the party's leftist critics to question its "sincerity" in proclaiming support for "unified action" (ibid., 8 May).

The PCC has controlled the peasant guerrilla FARC since 1966. Party leaders have maintained an ambivalent attitude in recent years toward the use of armed struggle in furthering the revolutionary process. Although the political resolution adopted at the Twelfth Congress affirmed that "the guerrilla movement in the rural areas has always been a notable factor in the general popular struggle and is a component of the tactics of correctly combining all forms of action," the general position of the party is that armed struggle cannot yet be the chief means of resistance (*IB,* 31 January 1976). The PCC demonstrated once again in 1978 that it does not wish to jeopardize its quest to gain power through an electoral coalition of opposition groups. The party's lack of total commitment to armed struggle remains a continuous source of irritation to FARC leaders, especially to its supreme commander, Mario Marulanda Vélez, who once served as a member of the PCC's Central Committee.

The FARC maintained at least five active guerrilla fronts in 1978: the first and second in Caquetá; the third in the central Cordillera; the fourth in middle Magdalena; and the fifth in Antioquia. Its general headquarters are located somewhere in the border zone between Caquetá and Huila. Each unit is in essence a communist cell. The minimal guerrilla unit consists of twelve men. The leadership mechanisms and general policy of the FARC are determined by the PCC's bylaws and political resolutions emitted at various congresses and plenums and presumably transmitted to the various fronts through Marulanda's directives.

The FARC was the most active of Colombia's rural guerrilla movements in 1978. Marulanda anticipated the intensification of guerrilla warfare in a clandestine bulletin released in late December (RCN, 30 December 1977). In February the Army's Fifth Brigade announced a major operation against the FARC in Magdalena, which tends to confirm the belief that the FARC has largely displaced the ELN as the major guerrilla group operating in that region (*Alternativa,* 13 February). FARC units were especially active in the plains region of El Meta during the first part of the year. In a communiqué released on 8 June, FARC guerrillas operating in Colombia's eastern region announced an all-out struggle against "latifundists and the government for their violence against the masses" (Agence France Presse, 8 June). Following the June elections, during which the FARC reaffirmed its economic and military support for the UNO coalition, guerrilla operations were concentrated in the central portion of the country. Military authorities confirmed in August that the American biologist Richard Starr, who was kidnapped by a FARC unit on 14 January 1977, was still being held somewhere in the border region between Caquetá and Huila (*El Siglo,* 15 August). More than 40 peasants had been murdered in the Campo Capote area by September 1978 (RCN, 5 September). Army sources also claimed that during the first week of September FARC guerrillas killed fifteen peasants in the Urabá region (*Latin American Political Report,* London, 15 September). In response to these actions and many other crimes of violence not directly attributable to guerrillas, the Turbay administration published a security statute on 6 September which includes stiff penalties for crimes of violence and terrorism and for "disturbing public order." The PCC, which has become a favorite target of attacks by Defense Minister Camacho, explained that the decree stemmed from the fact that "reactionaries" have established "preeminence" in the Turbay government (*Voz Proletaria,* 2 October).

Domestic Attitudes and Activities. By the end of 1977 the PCC had achieved to a large degree its objective of expanding the ranks of UNO (see *YICA, 1978,* p. 357). The ANAPO faction headed by UNO's presidential candidate, Julio César Pernía, brought to the coalition former ANAPO leaders from various departments. PCC leaders believed that the Independent Liberal Movement's presence in the alliance would open the way for other dissident liberal sectors to join forces with those seeking more radical changes in the economic and social structure (*Voz Proletaria,* 22 December 1977). By early 1978 the PCC's principal objectives were twofold: (*a*), to consolidate its position as the leading opposition movement, and (*b*), to unleash a vigorous ideological campaign against the MOIR and the smaller parties comprising the Front for the Unity of the People (FUP). Even during the preelection debates it became clear that the PCC did not really want to join any broad electoral alliance with the MOIR, without whose participation it would be impossible to talk about "unity" among leftist forces, since for the first time in decades the PCC had the opportunity to project itself as the major choice for popular opposition to the government. PCC spokesmen adopted the position that the acrimonious division could prove to be beneficial insofar as it served to clarify positions about the "real enemy" of the Colombian people. The pro-Peking groups, headed by MOIR, argued that the Soviet Union, together with "the other imperialism," is the enemy of the Colombian people, which makes any alliance with the PCC illusory, if not impossible, until such time that it "abandons its role as an agent of social-imperialist expansion in Latin America" (*Alternitiva,* 30 January). The international alignments emerged most clearly in the 1978 elections with respect to each group's position toward Cuba. While the PCC called for unconditional support for the Cuban revolution against "imperialist aggression," the MOIR viewed Cuba as "an outpost of the Soviet Union's socialist imperialism" (ibid., 13 February).

The PCC approached the February elections with unbridled optimism. Gilberto Vieira's assessment of the PCC's preelectoral activity emphasized the party's success in advancing the formation of "a united anti-imperialist and antioligarchical front." However, in a moment of candor, Vieira admitted the validity of one reporter's observation that the Communists can fill public plazas for their demonstrations, but they consistently fail to produce a similar turnout at the ballot box. The 1978 elections were no exception. The fact that the various leftist coalitions were unable to convert the charges of immorality, corruption, and inefficiency of the López administration into concrete electoral support attests to their general state of ideological confusion and fundamental lack of mass appeal. Vieira blamed the government and the Maoists for the PCC's poor showing (*Voz Proletaria,* 2 March, 14 April).

The PCC expressed concern early in 1978 with what it considered "the serious threat" of a coup d'etat that had "suddenly arisen" as the result of a public statement by military authorities. The statement, issued on 19 December 1977 by 33 top-ranking officers, demanded that the López administration take greater control of the press and adopt more drastic measures against what they described as "subversive activity" by the Left (*El Tiempo,* 31 December 1977). The Central Committee warned of "the grave danger threatening the public—the putschist elements in the armed forces, headed by General Camacho, who have launched on a road that can only signify stepped-up repressions, impunity for the oligarchy's illegal deals, and unhampered plunder of Colombia on the part of U.S. imperialism" (*Voz Proletaria,* 5 January). The military reiterated its concern in a statement published prior to the June elections. It prompted a response from the Central Committee in the form of an appeal to "all patriotically minded officers, noncommissioned officers, and soldiers who are watching with horror how the forces of imperialism and the oligarchy are misusing them for suppressive measures" (ibid., 23 March). In commenting on armed resistance against "repressive operations" by the military, Gilberto Vieira stated during an interview in Poland that the FARC is continually becoming stronger. He was questioned about the Colombian Communists "special situation" in which they operate legally, have representation in congress, and engage in publishing activites but at the same time they actively take part in guerrilla warfare against the government. Vieira responded that the PCC's "special method" employed a combination of various forms of legal and illegal warfare—a policy reaffirmed by the party at its Twelfth Congress.

The Central Committee met in Bogotá on 17—18 August to formulate the party's position regarding the Turbay administration and to outline new tasks for the various party affiliates. It adopted a resolution calling for participation in the 1 September convention of the UNO-ANAPO-MIL coalition and the Socialist Workers' Party (PST). The committee also agreed on a policy to deal with the emergence of the "Firmes" movement, which grew out of a preelection campaign organized by the weekly *Alternativa* to channel popular discontent into a unified left-wing party. The movement attracted a number of left-wing ANAPO members following the dismal electoral performance of the FUP coalition, along with several prominent former members of the MOIR who resigned in protest over the party's sectarian policies. Several small groups such as the Socialist Revolutionary Union, the ANAPO Socialist, and a faction of the PST have aligned themselves with Firmes, along with other independent sectors. During September the PCC praised the policy Firmes developed at its national convention, while Firmes, for its part, supported the PCC's position regarding the security statute. Although Firmes is unlikely to avoid internal dissension for long, some Colombian observers expect it to develop into a more radical version of the MRL.

In the aftermath of the 1978 elections, three leftist sectors are now clearly definable: the PCC and what remains of the UNO-ANAPO-MIL coalition, Firmes, and the MOIR. With its Maoist front, the MOIR is in open conflict with the PCC. On the other hand, there is some indication of a possible "union of convenience" between Firmes and the PCC on certain issues of mutual interest. This can be observed in the editorial flirtation which has taken place between them through their respective news organs, *Alternativa* and *Voz Proletaria* (*El Espectador,* 23 September).

International Views and Positions. The PCC faithfully follows the Soviet line in its international positions. The PCC stated the major tenets of its international policy early in the year when it called for a clear stand in relation to real socialism, of which Cuba is an embodiment on the American continent and pointed to the need for irreconcilable ideological struggle against imperialism and the various leftist deviations, such as Maoism and Trotskyism, whose defeat will bring nearer the final victory of socialism throughout the world" (*Voz Proletaria*, 6 April).

Along with its unwavering support of Cuba, the party is critical of anti-Sovietism of every type, whether from the Right, the Maoists, or the Trotskyites. The party spent a good portion of its resources in 1978 in ideological and tactical jousting with the pro-Chinese MOIR, and as a result, the PCC's domestic position suffered, both at the polls and within the trade union movement.

Party Contacts. A delegation of UNO-ANAPO-MIL headed by Julio César Pernía and Central Committee member Juan Arteta visited Cuba in December 1977 and met with Fidel Castro. A delegation from the Central Committee of the Communist Party of the Soviet Union visited Colombia in May at the invitation of the PCC. In turn, Gilberto Vieira headed a PCC delegation that visited Eastern European countries and the Soviet Union in May-June. Jaime Caycedo headed JUCO's representatives to the World Youth Festival held in Havana in July.

Publications. The PCC publishes a weekly newspaper, *Voz Proletaria* (reported circulation 40,000), a theoretical journal, *Documentos Políticos* (5,000), and a Colombian edition of *World Marxist Review* (7,500). The FARC publishes a clandestine bulletin, *Resistencia.*

The Maoists. The Communist Party of Colombia, Marxist-Leninist (PCC-ML), is firmly pro-Chinese. Its present leadership hierarchy is not clearly known, although Arturo Acero was cited by the Chinese press in September 1977 as the political secretary of a group referred to as the Marxist-Leninist League of Colombia. The PCC-ML has never recovered from the setback it received in July 1975 when its general secretary, Pedro León Arboleda, was killed by police in Cali. The PCC-ML has an estimated membership of 1,000. Unlike the PCC, it has not attempted to obtain legal status. Its impact in terms of national political life is insignificant. Its official organ is *Revolución*. The Marxist-Leninist League of Colombia has a monthly publication, *Nueva Democracia*. PCC-ML statements are sometimes found in Chinese publications and those of pro-Chinese parties in Europe and Latin America.

The basic form of struggle adopted and approved by the PCC-ML is rural guerrilla warfare, peasant indoctrination, and the creation of a popular liberation army that will eventually achieve revolutionary victory. The PCC-ML's guerrilla arm, the EPL, was the first attempt to stage a revolutionary "people's war" in Latin America. The EPL has limited its operations largely to urban areas since 1975, although several rural attacks and kidnappings were attributed to the group in 1978. On 16 December 1977 a special unit of the EPL claimed credit for the assassination of Jairo Ochoa Franco, an employee of the Colombian Textile Company charged with "persecuting workers" (RCN, 16 December). In a December communiqué the EPL proposed that total abstention from the 1978 elections should become "the rallying cry for organizing the masses" (*Alternativa*, 23 January). Government authorities charged the EPL with a variety of minor incidents intended to disrupt the February elections. The "Pedro León Arboleda" command was the most active guerrilla group operating in Bogotá between February and June (*El Tiempo*, 21 June). During a two week period in July, EPL guerrillas reportedly attacked and briefly occupied the towns of Puerto Libertador and Callejos in Córdoba (*El Espectador*, 13 July). Despite its relative weakness, the EPL continues on ideological grounds to reject any attempt at unified guerrilla action.

The Independent Revolutionary Workers' Movement (MOIR), established in 1971, aspires to become the first mass-based Maoist party in Latin America, with leadership and organization independent from those of the PCC-ML. The general secretary is Francisco Mosquera. Politically, the MOIR committed its electoral support in 1978 to the Front for the Unity of the People (FUP) and its presidential candidate, Jaime Piedrahita Cardona, ex-ANAPO senator from Antioquia. Piedrahita received less than 1 percent of the popular vote, while the MOIR also did poorly with its separate lists of candidates in the February elections. The MOIR retained the one assembly seat it had won in Cundinamarca in 1976, but the party was able to elect only 15 municipal councilmen throughout the country, compared with 29 in 1976. The party's national leadership hierarchy was severely weakened at midyear when two of its most prominent members, Carlos Bula Camacho and César Pardo Villalba, resigned in a dispute over the MOIR's sectarianism. The MOIR's official news organ is *Tribuna Roja*.

The ELN. The National Liberation Army was formed in Santander in 1964 under the inspiration of the Cuban revolution. It undertook its first military action in January 1965.

Once recognized as the largest and most militant of the guerrilla forces operating in the country, the ELN has never recovered from the toll exacted on its leadership and urban network in recent years by government forces, including the defection in 1976 of its principal founder and maximum leader, Fabio Vásquez Castaño. The movement was further weakened in 1977 by serious internal divisions (see *YICA*, 1978, p. 360). In November 1977 the ELN issued a bulletin claiming credit for the kidnapping and killing of several industrialists. The release also denied any conflict with the M-19 and stated that the two groups shared similar political interests and objectives. While admitting to internal crisis within its ranks, the bulletin proclaimed that through self-analysis, the ELN would emerge with greater strength "because we are trying to correct our mistakes and follow the course of the people's war more closely in order to take over power" (*El Tiempo*, 23 November).

In February security forces announced the capture of Segundo Galeano Lopéz, reportedly responsible for organizing and operating the ELN's urban support apparatus in Bucaramanga (*El Espectador,* 27 February). On May Day, the ELN "Jaime Andrade Sosa" guerrilla command reaffirmed its support for the working class in a communiqué distributed to news media. Symptomatic of the internal problems within the movement, the message contained a basic reformulation of the ELN's revolutionary strategy: "In homage to the working class we wish to reaffirm its indisputable condition as vanguard of the Colombian revolutionary process. We have reached this conclusion after having first unsuccessfully attempted to advance our revolutionary cause outside the class struggle. We now recognize the error of that policy." (*Alternativa,* 11 May.)

On 6 October the body of José Manuel Martínez Quiroz was found by peasants near the town of Fusagasugá, located south of Bogotá. During the 1960's, Martínez Quiroz was, along with Fabio Vásquez Castaño and Ricardo Lara Parada, one of the founders of the ELN (*El Tiempo,* 7 October). Although military spokesmen are confident that the ELN is no longer a serious menace, the movement's capacity for survival suggests that it would be imprudent to predict a permanent end to its existence at this time.

Washington College   Daniel L. Premo

Costa Rica

The Costa Rican Marxist movement is composed of several different political groups. The Popular Vanguard Party (Partido Vanguardia Popular; PVP) is pro-Soviet; the Socialist Party (Partido Socialista; PS) leans toward Cuba; and the Revolutionary Movement of the People (Movimiento Revolucionario del Pueblo; MRP), the most radical of the three, is the only one theoretically committed to violent revolution. Two other groups are the anti-Soviet Costa Rican People's Front (Frente Popular Costarricense; FPC) and the Socialist Organization of Workers (Organización Socialista de los Trabajadores; OST), tending toward Trotskyism, which is headed by Alejandra Calderón, the younger sister of the Costa Rican minister of foreign relations. The PVP is estimated to have some 3,200 members (*Basic Factbook*, July). The population of Costa Rica is estimated at 2,119,000.

Within the Costa Rican electoral system, the PVP, PS, and MRP formed a coalition known as the United People's Party (Partido Pueblo Unido; PPU), while at the same time maintaining their individual internal structures and medium- and long-term objectives. The PPU ran its own presidential candidate, Dr. Rodrigo Gutiérrez, the independent dean of the University of Costa Rica Medical School, as well as its own congressional candidates, in the February national elections. PPU congressional candidates received some 62,564 votes (7 percent of the total cast) and ended up with 3 of the 57 congressmen—Humberto Vargas Carbonel, Mario Devandas, and Rodrigo Ureña Quiros—a one-seat gain over their 1974—78 coalition representation. But Gutiérrez took only 22,744 votes (2.74 percent), suggesting that some PPU supporters voted either for the candidate of the incumbent National Liberation Party (PLN) or, in an effort to radicalize the political process, for the more conservative (and victorious) candidate of the Opposition Unity (UO) coalition. The Frente Popular, which was rumored to be receiving financial support from the UO, elected its leader, Rodolfo Cerdas, to congress (with 1.5 percent of the vote), and Cerdas subsequently tended to collaborate with the government. When the PPU sector began flinging all sorts of epithets at Cerdas, including the accusation that he was a collaborator with the U.S. Central Intelligence Agency, the Frente Popular leader fired back that the PPU members were revisionists and collaborators with the PLN, but the latter charge was not supported by subsequent voting patterns.

Leadership and Organization. Effective control of the PVP is retained by the traditional leadership, particularly Manuel Mora Valverde, Arnoldo Ferreto, and Eduardo Mora, although some other individuals are now formally recognized as party leaders and several members are national congressmen. The PPU coalition has established a strong presence in national politics and may provide the structural scaffolding for a new, permanent, leftist organization. It should be noted, however, that the Socialist Party has suffered an apparently irreconcilable split that has led to a separation of the PS leadership from the Executive Committee of the PPU coalition.

Labor Activities. The communist General Confederation of Workers (Confederación General de Trabajadores; CGT) is superior to the noncommunist Confederation of Democratic Workers (CTD) in economic and numerical strength and is a cause of apprehension in government and business circles. It is said to have an annual income of more than $90,000, a sum that permits it to have a permanent staff of 32 well-trained activists and a group of thirteen lawyers, with a particularly active role played by the Socialist Party. CGT Secretary General Rodrigo Paniagua reports that the confederation, organized on a national level—rather than by plant as is the CTD—represents 45 unions with some 48,500 active members. The public workers' unions are also under the control of communist-oriented leaders, with the National Federation of Public Workers (FENETRAP) drawing unions away from the CTD.

University and Students Movements. Although the Pueblo Unido groups are relatively strong in both of Costa Rica's universities, there is a clear erosion of influence in academic circles due to internal divisions on Marxist dogma and uncertainties regarding political strategy on the Left. Perhaps the major strength of the communist intellectuals is in the National University, in Heredia, where erosion is only beginning to take place. The University of Costa Rica in San José is more traditionally oriented. One important tendency in the Communists' university strategy is to give support in elections to progressive noncommunist individuals and then gradually surround them so as to acquire strong influence in critical situations.

Attitudes toward Nicaraguan Sandinistas. The anti-Somoza movement in Nicaragua has drawn considerable sympathy from the Costa Rican people, including some prominent leaders of the National Liberation Party. This has resulted in assorted anti-Somoza demonstrations and the use of Costa Rican territory as a haven for Sandinist guerrillas, thus creating a serious conflict with the Nicaraguan government. The Costa Rican Revolutionary Movement of the People, a member of the PPU coalition, has been described by some (*Latin America Political Report*, 14 October 1977) as a "support group for the Sandinists."

Other International Positions. The PVP played a leading role in promoting the improved relations between the Costa Rican government and the pro-Soviet communist world that came about during the National Liberation Party administration that ended in early 1978. The new Costa Rican government, under strong pressure from conservative groups and over the objections of the Left, has taken a harder stand toward communist countries by reducing the level of Costa Rican diplomatic representation and limiting contacts to the commercial and consular spheres. Leftist pressure and the fear of losing communist markets will probably prevent a more serious break in relations with the communist world. The government is also concerned that a more severe policy could drive the PVP and other leftist forces into the arms of the National Liberation Party and thus cause another swing in political predominance at the next election.

Universidad Nacional
Heredia, Costa Rica

Rodrigo Carreras Jimenez

Cuba

The Communist Party of Cuba (Partido Comunista de Cuba; PCC) is the country's ruling party and the only one permitted under the 1976 national constitution. The population of Cuba at the end of 1978 was approximately 9,797,000. PCC membership was estimated at 200,000.

PCC Leadership and Organization of State Authority. The leadership and organization of the PCC remained unchanged in 1978. In June Havana announced that the sixth plenary meeting of the party's Central Committee took place but indicated neither the agenda, the length of the gathering, nor its results. Late in 1977 Raúl Valdés Vivó, a member of the Central Committee, was elected to the party Secretariat to work in the field of foreign relations under Carlos Rafael Rodríguez, who retains this responsibility at the state and party levels.

The administrative organs of state authority continued to be strengthened, and their functions were clarified, according to Havana's weekly *Bohemia* (30 June). The National People's Government Assembly—Cuba's parliament—was composed of 481 deputies elected in the 169 municipal people's government assemblies in the country's fourteen provinces. Of the total, 55.5 percent were rank-and-file delegates—representatives elected directly by the people—while the remainder were appointed by the local assemblies and the party. The National Assembly is the highest state organ and the only one with legislative power. The Council of State is the organ that represents the National Assembly between its sessions and is the supreme representative of the Cuban state nationally and internationally. It includes a chairman and 30 other members elected by the National Assembly from among its members. The chairman of the Council of State, Fidel Castro, is the chief of state, head of the Council of Ministers, head of the government, and the supreme chief of the armed forces. Thus, the Cuban constitution places the leadership of the state, government and the armed forces in one person.

There are three types of central state administrative agencies: state committees, ministries, and institutes. The state committees carry out at the national level duties analogous to those performed by the functional administrative offices in the local people's government organs. Under the new decentralized economic management system, the role of these committees is to supply the main economic guidelines to the different ministries and institutes and, in general, to all state agencies and institutions. The 23 ministries are equivalent to the sectorial administrative offices of the local people's government organs. They are in charge of the management and administration of one or more branches of the economy, culture, education, international relations, security, defense, etc. The nine institutes are in charge of sectorial activities of smaller scope.

Because of the administrative decentralization produced by establishing the people's government throughout the country, functions of the great majority of central state administrative agencies are no longer predominantly executive. Rather, they establish normative and methodological guidelines for and give advice to the local administrative offices of the people's government and the production and service units under them.

The Council of Ministers, the country's highest executive and administrative organ, is appointed by the National People's Government Assembly. Its chairman and deputy chairmen constitute its executive committee.

The People's Supreme Tribunal is the highest judicial authority, and its decisions are final. Through its government council, it has legislative initiative and ordinance power. It makes decisions and dictates norms that must be followed by all people's tribunals. The People's Supreme Tribunal is elected by the National People's Government Assembly and must report to it. The National Assembly has the power to recall judges.

The primary objective of the Office of the Prosecutor General of the Republic is to control socialist legality by maintaining strict compliance with the law and other legal provisions by state agencies, economic and social organizations, and citizens.

As Blas Roca, head of the National Assembly, said: "The people's government is a new experiment. Local organs of the people's government do not always have the resources necessary to carry out their tasks . . . there are functions that remain a bit up in the air."

The Cuban governmental structure was faced in 1978 with seemingly unending economic problems, as well as its own inadequacy. The Cuban economy—increasingly tied to the Soviet bloc—was performing relatively better than in recent years. The sugar harvest, the country's economic mainstay, totaled 7,300,000 tons, the second largest in the nation's history. But at the same time, Soviet aid to Cuba was much greater than before. U.S. analysts estimated that Moscow was sending to Cuba about $6 million worth of goods a day, including 200,000 barrels of oil, almost 100 percent of the country's consumption. The Soviets were charging Cuba half the world oil price and paying four times the world price for the four million tons of sugar imported from Cuba. In addition, Soviet military aid continued to flow to Cuba—and to Cuban troops abroad—at no cost to the Havana government. But the Soviet aid was not open-ended. In a revealing speech on 24 December 1977, Castro said that some Cuban investment projects had to be "sacrificed" and that the country was going through a "period of austerity . . . and [economic] adjustment. . . . Until 1985 we cannot talk about [improving] standards of living, only about consolidation of what we have. . . . For the next seven or eight years, our spendings and investments will be guided by economic, not social criteria . . . we have to fight against indolence, bourgeois spirit, delinquency. . . . This generation has to make sacrifices." Castro also disclosed that Cuba's 1978 budget was about U.S. $11.5 billion. (*Granma*, 2 January.)

Mass Organizations. Cuba's mass organizations were maintained essentially at the same level in 1978 as in the previous year. The Committees for the Defense of the Revolution (Comités de Defensa de la Revolución; CDR) organized a new grouping, apparently within their ranks, called the Exemplary

Parents Movement, which in October had 1.2 million members, according to the Havana press. The Federation of Cuban Women (Federación de Mujeres Cubanas; FMC) had 2,264,454 members, or 81.5 percent of all Cuban women aged 14 to 65, according to *Granma*. Women continued to toil hard at home and at work; an official survey has found that the average housewife devotes an average of nine hours and fourteen minutes a day to housework. (Ibid., 7 June.)

The Revolutionary Armed Forces and Africa. Cuba's combined military forces, known as the Revolutionary Armed Forces (Fuerzas Armadas Revolucionarias; FAR), received special domestic and international attention during 1978 because of Cuba's involvement in Ethiopia and Africa generally. According to London's Institute for Strategic Studies (1977), the FAR had 189,000 members, some 160,000 of whom were in the army. (The army also had 90,000 reservists.) Army forces comprised fifteen infantry divisions, three armored regiments, and several independent regiments, with more than 600 tanks. The Cuban navy's personnel was 9,000 strong, with 1 escort patrol vessel, 18 submarine chasers, 25 speed patrol boats with guided missiles, 24 motor-torpedo boats, 29 patrol boats under 100 tons, and 50 surface-to-surface missiles. The air force, with 20,000 members, had about 210 combat aircraft, including 15 MIG-15s, 75 MIG-17s, 4 MIG-19s, 80 MIG-21s, more than 50 transport planes, and about 60 helicopters. In the second half of 1978, according to U.S. intelligence sources, the Soviet Union supplied Cuba with about 20 advanced MIG-23 jets. Cuba's paramilitary forces included 10,000 state security troops, 3,000 border guards and 100,000 people's militia and regular uniformed policemen.

At the beginning of 1978, Cuban military involvement abroad practically doubled compared with the country's military presence overseas in the previous year. According to U.S. State Department figures, there are about 45,000 Cubans in thirteen African countries, including 20,000 soldiers in Angola and more than 16,000 troops in Ethiopia. Several thousand Cubans are civilians—doctors, nurses, engineers, technicians, and bureaucrats. Western intelligence sources estimate that the number of Cubans killed in the last three years is about 1,500, including over 1,000 in Angola. Over 4,500 Cubans have been wounded, these sources say. (*NYT*, 12 November.) There are few reports about the performance of Cuban soldiers in Angola and Ethiopia. They are obviously far superior to local forces, and they were victorious against equally inferior troops. But Cubans are said to have been badly mauled by South African regulars in a brief confrontation in Angola three years ago, their only encounter so far with well-trained adversaries.

Beginning in December 1977, thousands of Cuban regular army and air force personnel were sent to Ethiopia, where the Mengistu government was losing its struggle with Somali guerrillas and army troops in the Ogaden desert. Cuban soldiers took over the training of Ethiopian tank, artillery, and aviation units. When they were unable to train enough Ethiopians in the use of a large quantity of Soviet arms in so short a time, Cuban soldiers and airmen took over much of the fighting against the Somalis. In February and March "medium-sized" Cuban regular units were thrown into battle, according to Castro, soundly defeating the Somalis (*Granma*, 26 March). The Cubans remained in Ethiopia after the victory in the Ogaden, and for a while it looked as though they might be engaged in Ethiopia's "second front," its fight against Marxist guerrillas in Eritrea. But Cuba apparently thought better of enlarging its military involvement. At the end of 1978, even though its Ethiopian contingents did not actually diminish, there were no reports of any direct participation of FAR personnel in the Eritrean fighting.

During a September trip to Ethiopia, Castro met with Rhodesian black nationalist leaders Robert Mugabe and Joshua Nkomo, who head the Patriotic Front guerrilla alliance. Cuban specialists are reportedly training the front's guerrillas, although the extent of that involvement has not been documented.

Developments in 1978 did not provide a clear-cut answer to a question that analysts of Cuban affairs have been posing: Is Havana's presence in Africa the result of its subservience to the Soviet Union, or did Cuba volunteer and then get Moscow's approval to help its allies in Africa militarily? One thing is clear: without massive Soviet military and economic support, Cuba could not maintain 45,000 people abroad.

International Positions. Having cast a long shadow over parts of Africa, Cuba gained some friends in that continent but also a number of influential enemies, whose number is likely to grow as the Cuban presence continued with no end in sight. (While the military victories have undoubtedly revitalized revolutionary zeal at home, this is unlikely to last forever. There is no glamour in repairing roads in Angola or guarding American-owned oil installations in Cabinda.) Certainly Cuba's African venture did not enhance its stature among Third World and Latin American countries, and it practically stopped rapprochement talks with the United States.

In August the U.S. State Department declared that no significant improvement of relations with Cuba was possible without a "drastic" withdrawal of Cuban troops from Africa. The statement indicated that other outstanding issues between the two countries were the freeing of political prisoners in Cuban jails, repatriation of Americans in Cuba, and reunification of families. Two weeks later Castro invited Cuban exiles to Havana to discuss prisoner release and family reunification, and Washington applauded that initiative. Throughout the year Cuba maintained a relatively conciliatory posture toward the Carter administration, especially toward the president. "In my opinion," Castro told American journalists in Havana, "Carter is a decent person, personally an honest man" (ibid., 18 June). Whether the arrival in Cuba of the MIG-23s, which could have the capability to deliver nuclear weapons, will damage the prospects for improvement of relations was not immediately known. Concerned over the presence of these advanced aircraft in Cuba, President Carter ordered resumption of reconnaissance flights over the island in late October for the first time since January 1977. The principal source of pressure for the resumption of relations with Cuba continued to be the American business community. A number of U.S. industrialists visited Cuba to establish contacts with Cuban trade officials. According to Lawrence Theriot, a U.S. Commerce Department expert who visited Cuba in February 1978, the island represented an "interesting and profitable market." If trade with Cuba is resumed, he estimated that the volume of American sales will reach $400 million by 1981. In addition to the continuing operations of special interest sections of the two governments in their respective capitals, late in May Secretary of State Cyrus Vance met in New York his Cuban counterpart, Carlos Rafael Rodríguez, the highest level official contact between the United States and Cuban officials since 1960.

The Cuban-Chinese controversy continued unabated in 1978. In June *Granma* reported a Peking charge that Cubans were "plundering Angola, including equipment in factories left abandoned by the Portuguese." On 11 June *Granma* published a special anti-Chinese supplement with anti-Peking charges of its own; large-type headlines read: "The Chinese Leaders' Great Betrayal of the Revolutionary and National Liberation Movements of Asia, Africa, and Latin America" and "Repugnant Crimes of the Chinese Leadership." Elsewhere, the Peking leaders were called "the scum" by *Granma*. In July Castro added his own voice to the campaign. "Vietnam, Angola, and Cuba are now victims of brutal attacks, hostility, and slander from the traitorous Chinese leadership. . . . There is no longer any difference between the imperialist wire services and that of China."

On the other hand, Castro showed a hands-off attitude toward Eurocommunism. Asked about Santiago Carrillo, the Spanish communist leader and Eurocommunism's spokesman, Castro said in September: "It is not for us to tell the Spanish [party] leaders how they should apply the principle of Marxism or what they should do. That's strictly their affair." (Ibid., 6 September.)

While the Cuban government was preparing for the September 1979 meeting of nonaligned nations in Havana, its African involvement was causing it some problems in that international grouping, which Castro aspires to lead, possibly in the post-Tito period. At the July meeting in Belgrade of 85 nonaligned countries, there was surprisingly strong criticism of Cuba and its efforts to link the Third World nations more closely to the Soviet Union. Cuba was called a Soviet surrogate, if not a stooge, and some 30 countries indicated they might boycott the Havana gathering next year. (*NYT*, 28 June.) Countries like India, Indonesia, Yugoslavia, and Egypt opposed Cuba's moves for adoption of pro-Soviet resolutions. Somalia even asked that Cuba be expelled from the group. In Germany, commenting on the Belgrade discussion, Chancellor Helmut Schmidt said that in view of Havana's military involvement in Africa, "to call Cuba nonaligned is a bad joke." The Cuban position has been that troops in Africa were requested by legitimate governments of host countries and are operating there legally.

Domestic Affairs. There was a notable toning down of revolutionary fervor in Cuba during 1978, as though the Castro regime, twenty years old this year, has exhausted its at times strident rhetoric. According to foreign journalists visiting the island country, there was a general feeling of boredom, monotony, and conformity. This ennui has pervaded even the young, Western journalists reported. People talk less about the virtues of the Revolution and more about their daily chores. They complain about long working hours, endless lines for rationed goods, bureaucratic red tape, and perennial scarcities. Salaries continue to be modest, ranging from the $120 or so a farm worker receives monthly to $1,200, the highest salary, paid to a top scientist. Fidel Castro reportedly gets about $725 a month. But a "new class" continues to grow—government and party "apparatchiki" who have access to special stores, get new cars, and can travel abroad. Discrimination on the basis of skin or sex has not disappeared. There are probably fewer blacks among the leaders of the country than in the days of Batista, twenty years ago. (Ibid., 28 June.) Cuba's ten million population is 37 percent white, 11 percent black, 1 percent Asian and 51 percent racially mixed. There are said to be about 3,000 Russians in Cuba, living in completely segregated areas, and intermarriage—even intermingling—with Cubans is reportedly forbidden to them.

International Contacts. In January the Romanian minister of national defense visited Havana, as did a U.S. Coast Guard delegation that met with Cuban border patrol troops of the Interior Ministry to discuss improved communications, search and rescue operations, and activities aimed at curbing drug traffic and terrorism. Fidel Castro met with the secretary of state of the Dominican Republic and a Dominican governmental delegation. In February Cuban Defense Minister Raúl Castro, who visited Angola in December 1977, traveled to Moscow and was received by Leonid Brezhnev. Visiting Havana were the bishop of Cuernavaca, Mexico, the deputy secretary general of the Polisario Front, and the deputy chief of the Soviet air force. In March the first deputy defense minister of Bulgaria visited Havana, as did the deputy chairman of the East German Council of Ministers and a delegation from the Dominican Communist Party. In April visitors to Cuba included Ethiopian leader Lieutenant Colonel Mengistu and a delegation of the Chilean Communist Party led by Volodia Teitelboim. In May the vice-president of Iraq and the president of the People's Republic of the Congo visited Havana. In June the prime minister of Angola met with Castro in Havana. In July Michael Manley, prime minister of Jamaica, reviewed "all range of subjects" in a conversation with Castro in Havana. In September the prime minister of Spain, during a two-day visit to Cuba, started negotiations for the signing of a new trade agreement between the two countries. Spain was to extend a line of credit to Cuba, and both countries agreed to solve the issues of reparation claims by Spanish citizens affected by Cuban nationalization laws as well as the repatriation of Spanish nationals and their families living in Cuba. Later that month after a brief stopover in Moscow, Castro flew to Ethiopia, Libya, and Algeria. Gus Hall, secretary general of the Communist Party of the U.S., stayed in Cuba for two weeks.

Publications. *Granma*, the official organ of the PCC Central Committee, is published six times a week in Havana, with an average daily circulation of 600,000. Its editor is Jorge Enrique Mendoza, a Central Committee member. *Granma* also appears in weekly editions in Spanish, English, and French, which circulate widely abroad. The Central Committee's Secretariat publishes a journal, *Militante Comunista*, which gives news about the PCC and its contacts with other fraternal parties. Its circulation is 150,000. The Union of Young Communists publishes the daily *Juventud Rebelde*, the country's second national newspaper, with a circulation of 200,000. National weeklies are *Verde Olivo*, the organ of the FAR, and *Bohemia*, a general news magazine, whose circulation is 300,000. Among the provincial party dailies are *Guerrillero*, Pinar del Río (circulation 15,000); *Girón*, Matanzas (15,000); *Vanguardia*, Santa Clara (25,000); *Adelante*, Camagüey (25,000); *Sierra Maestra*, Santiago de Cuba (45,000); *Ahora*, Holguín (10,000); and *Venceremos*, Guantánamo (4,500).

University of Miami

George Volsky

Dominican Republic

Leftist forces in the Dominican Republic in 1978 continued to present a picture of extreme fragmentation, which was possibly without parallel in the political history of Spanish America. This long-standing balkanization showed no signs of diminishing during the year despite the relative weakness of the Marxist groups.

By the end of 1978 there were fourteen different Marxist groups in the Dominican Republic, some of which were subdivided into antagonistic factions. Since divisions and subdivisions of the groupings have occurred almost every month, any list is perforce incomplete. The groups are the Dominican Communist Party (Partido Comunista Dominicano; PCD), a pro-Soviet group led by Narciso Isa Conde; the Dominican People's Movement (Movimiento Popular Dominicano; MPD), a pro-Chinese group, which was divided into two sectors, one led by Onelio Espaillat and Jorge Puello Soriano, and the other by Rafael Chaljub Mejia; the Nucleus of Communist Workers (Núcleo de los Trabajadores Comunistas; NTC), led by Rafael (Fafa) Taveras; the Dominican Liberation Party (Partido de Liberación Dominicana; PLD), presided over by former President Juan Bosch; the Red Line of the 14th of June Movement (Movimiento Línea Roja del 14 de Junio), headed by Esteban Días Jáques; the Proletarian Banner (Bandera Proletaria), whose leader was Juan B. Mejia; the Patriotic Anti-imperialist Union (Unión Patriótica Antiimperialista; UPA), led by Franklin Franco; the Camilo Torres Revolutionary Committee (Comité Revolucionario Camilo Torres; CORECATO); the Marxist-Leninist Path (Via Marxista-Leninista), headed by Fidelio Despradel; the Dominican Liberation Movement (Movimiento de Liberación Dominicana; MLD), presided over by Agustín Alvarez; the Trinitarian National Liberation Movement (Movimiento de Liberación Nacional de los

Trinitarios), led by Juan Bautista Castillo Pujols; the Communist Party of the Dominican Republic (Partido Comunista de la República Dominicana; PACOREDO), whose leader was Luis Montás (Pin); the New Republic Revolutionary Movement (Movimiento Revolucionario Nueva República; MORENURE), headed by Rafael Gamundy Cordero; and the Popular Socialist Party (Partido Socialista Popular; PSR), led by Félix Servio Ducoudray.

It is impossible to know how many people were in each of these parties and other smaller Marxist groups, but it is estimated that the total membership was approximately 5,000.

The fourteen-year-long government ban on political activities of the extreme left was abandoned in November 1977 when President Joaquín Balaguer authorized the PDC to resume legal operations, a concession apparently made in exchange for that party's agreement to participate in the May 1978 presidential election. While the PDC had originally intended to enter the campaign in alliance with progressive non-Marxist parties, it finally had to conduct its own campaign, running its secretary general, Narciso Isa Conde, and Pericles Franco Ornes as its presidential and vice-presidential candidates, respectively. In the election, out of the approximately 1,700,000 votes cast, less than 3 percent went to candidates on the Left. Antonio Guzmán Fernández of the Dominican Revolutionary Party (PRD) was elected with almost 860,000 votes, while President Balaguer of the Reformist Party (PR) obtained some 700,000. The Dominican Army, seeing that the vote was going against Balaguer, interrupted the counting one day after the 16 May election, but a decisive intervention by President Carter avoided a constitutional crisis, and in August Guzmán, a left-of-center businessman, was sworn in as president. It was the first peaceful transfer of the presidency to an opposition candidate in the history of the republic.

The new condition of legality has not changed the relationships among different Marxist groupings, which continued to outdo themselves in mutual attacks, accusations, and personal invectives. The PCD, trying to adjust to the new situation, moved toward the policy line of Eurocommunism. The MPD, which was active on the very politicized campus of the Autonomous University of Santo Domingo (UASD), and other Marxist groups followed developments in China and adjusted their policies to the winds of change blowing from Peking.

PCD leaders, as usual, traveled to Cuba to exchange views with leaders of the Communist Party of Cuba. But Havana has shown restraint in appearing too concerned about Dominican affairs, as it hoped the Dominican government would soon establish relations with Cuba. Guzmán, however, said that his government would continue the same policies toward Cuba as the Balaguer regime; that is, it will establish relations with Cuba only after the United States has done so.

While adopting a tolerant attitude toward the Marxist Left, Guzmán stated that he would not permit Communists to hold public posts of responsibility in his government. But knowledgeable observers assert that PCD members have long since infiltrated the middle-level ranks of the Dominican bureaucracy and have exerted influence from early in the Balaguer era to the present. Also, the MPD is said to have a number of its followers in fairly high governmental jobs, and even the armed forces are not thought to have remained immune to Marxist penetration.

Dominican students continue to be very active politically, albeit disunited organizationally, with several anarchist factions present on the UASD campus. The organized labor movement is also in a state of flux, with communist influence on the decline. Since the principal adversary of most labor bodies was President Balaguer, union leaders were looking to President Guzmàn to satisfy their economic demands and have been inclined to collaborate with the government for the time being.

The Guzmán victory has debilitated the influence of Marxist groups in the Dominican Republic. It has also diminished violence. Guerrilla activities are a thing of the past, as all groups, the extreme left included, have adopted the posture of participating in the country's political life. Thus, in August the Red Line of the 14th of June Movement and the Proletarian Banner—two pro-Peking groups—announced at a joint national conference that they had decided to "operate publicly in view of the PRD's promise to establish a regime of political freedom (EFE Agency, Madrid, 18 August).

Pro-Chinese Dominican groups continued to attack the Soviet Union and Cuba in their official pronouncements. The Dominican Maoists and the Communist Party (Marxist-Leninist) of the United States issued a statement saying that their common enemies were "U.S. imperialism, Soviet social-imperialism, modern revisionism and all reaction . . . They also denounced the danger that social-imperialism poses for the Dominican people and for the Dominican Revolution, since Cuba has been converted into a base of support and a shock force for expansionism and aggression of Soviet social-imperialism in Africa and Latin America and a direct threat to the Dominican Revolution." (*Peking Review*, 8 September.)

As in the past, communist groups tried in 1978 to unify their forces. Esteban Díaz Jáquez, head of the 14th of June Red Line, said it was necessary to create "a vanguard party of the working class, the Party of Dominican Workers (Partido de los Trabajadores Dominicanos; PTD)." He said that he has been working toward the creation of the PTD for a number of years and that it will be formed "sooner or later." According to Díaz Jáquez, the repeal of anticommunist legislation forces his organization to "better utilize, within new conditions, legal forms of struggle and work, and to maintain vigilance against all deviations, either toward the right or the left . . . We have always postulated and practiced a policy of unity of those who believe in the ideas of Marx, Engels, Lenin, Stalin, and Mao Tse-tung, as well as of popular masses." (*Ahora*, Santo Domingo, 2 October.)

Pro-Moscow communist party leader Isa Conde, paying lip service to unity of the Left, believed that his group has found the "only way" to mobilize public opinion in the country and that the PCD "has the capacity to organize and mobilize important sectors of the masses." He dismissed other leftists as "small sectarian groups . . . moved exclusively by personal passions of their leaders" and said it would be a "waste of time" to even think about unity with such groupings. Isa Conde attacked pro-Chinese Dominicans and stated they have become "incoherent" when faced with the new political situation in that country. In contrast, "the PCD long ago traced a political path within the Dominican process which applies Marxism creatively to the new reality and investigates and studies problems to arrive at a course of political action and programs aimed at transforming our country's system jointly with all socialist and anti-imperialist forces in the world." (Ibid.) Statements by NTC leader Rafael Taveras and by Rafael Chaljub Mejia, head of a faction of the MPD, have also indicated that the Dominican Left is a very long way from uniting and even from comprehending the reasons for its prolonged disunity. Dominican Communists, said Taveras, have a "low theoretical level" and because of "this theoretical incapacity, we never understood Dominican society, especially of the proletariat in whose name we act." (Ibid.)

Publications. Until 1976 the PCD published a clandestine weekly, *El Popular*. Now it is issuing a legal magazine, *Impacto Socialista*.

University of Miami   George Volsky

Ecuador

In 1926, representatives of Marxist discussion groups founded the Ecuadorian Socialist Party, from which the "Friends of Lenin" group split two years later adopting the name Communist Party of Ecuador (Partido Comunista del Ecuador; PCE) in October 1931. A Maoist splinter group, the Marxist-Leninist Communist Party of Ecuador (Partido Comunista Marxista-Leninista del Ecuador; PCMLE) dates from 1963. Factional disputes have repeatedly fragmented the Socialist Party; the most important offshoot is a frankly Fidelista group, the Ecuadorian Revolutionary Socialist Party (Partido Socialista Revolucionario Ecuatoriano; PSRE). The membership of the PCE was approximately 1,000, and that of the PCMLE around 250; PSRE membership was estimated at between 250 and 500.

The PCE and Electoral Politics. For the first time in eight years, elections were held in Ecuador in 1978. Moreover, not since 1968 had the PCE or any other Marxist organization competed in the quest for votes. The military triumvirate, attempting to negotiate its return to the barracks and concomitantly assure itself the selection of a sympathetic civilian government, first oversaw a constitutional referendum on 15 January. By a margin of 43 to 32 percent, the electorate chose a new draft constitution rather than a revision of the 1945 document. Relatively progressive in its provisions, the new document was supported by the majority of political parties, incuding the PCE. The PCE had earlier endorsed the plebiscitary initiation of the process to reestablish constitutional government. In its view, the vote for a new charter would open "new perspectives on the road to liberation, justice, and democracy," and at the same time broaden the scope of democracy and derogate "antilabor decrees while guaranteeing the representation of the workers" (*El Comercio*, 21 November 1977). Following the vote, the PCE hailed the results as endorsing "broader political rights for the citizens, including voting rights for the illiterates, [and] strengthening the state sector of the national economy and an independent foreign policy" (*FBIS*, 25 January).

This paved the way for national elections on 16 July, in which the PCE participated as senior partner of the Marxist coalition Broad Front of the Left (Frente Amplio de la Izquierda; FADI). Its task was defined as an effort to "broaden trade union rights, speed up the development of industry, especially the entire state sector, ensure a policy of peace and friendship with all peoples in the foreign policy field, condemn colonialism, neocolonialism and racism, and support the liberation struggle of the people" (*FBIS*, 25 January). In constructing a leftist alliance, the PCE joined together with the PSRE and such minuscule groups as the Committee of the People (Comité del Pueblo; CP), Revolutionary Movement of the Christian Left (Movimiento Revolucionario de Izquierda Cristiana; MRIC), Second Independence Movement (Movimiento Segunda Independencia; MSI), and Movement for Unity of the Left (Movimiento por la Unidad de la Izquierda; MUI). Following extended debate, the FADI chose PCE Central Committee member René Maugé Mosquera as its presidential nominee, accompanied by Aníbal Muñoz Quirola of the PSRE for vice-president.

The FADI announced its objective to be a "socialist, democratic Ecuador that is free from any dependency," and outlined a platform calling for true democracy, a classless society, and control over the economy through expansion of state-run enterprises and the nationalization of transnational businesses and foreign banks (*FBIS*, 26 April). Opposition from pro-Chinese critics took the form of the new Popular Democratic Movement (Movimiento Popular Democrático; MPD), which nominated Camilo Mena Mena for president. It failed to gain legal recognition from the Supreme Electoral Tribunal (Tribunal Supremo Electoral), however, leaving the FADI as the only Marxist organization in the race. Sharing the skepticism of other parties over the sincerity of the military in withdrawing from the exercise of power, the FADI moved away from the tacit approval which it had extended the government in earlier years. A postreferendum declaration, contending that civil and labor rights were being constantly violated, concluded that "we Ecuadorians have endured severe setbacks in all facets of our national life" (*JPRS*, 12 April). Particularly harsh criticism was repeatedly directed at the officialist candidacy of former Quito mayor Sixto Durán Ballén—widely regarded as the front-runner—on the grounds that his campaign was enjoying the support of North American, Israeli, and South Korean economic interests (*FBIS*, 13 July).

Despite repeated government intervention to ban or harrass unsympathetic candidates and their supporters, elections were held as scheduled on 16 July. The government's Electoral Information Service announced that 1,612,994 votes were cast, representing 77 percent of those registered. Dr. Jaime Roldós Aguilera, candidate of the populist-reformist Concentration of Popular Forces (Concentración de Fuerzas Populares; CFP), unexpectedly took a plurality with 31 percent of the vote but faced a runoff. The FADI ticket of Maugé and Muñoz finished last in a field of six, receiving 75,277 votes for a total of some 5 percent (*Boletín*, 559, Embajada del Ecuador, August). It was sixth in fourteen of the twenty provinces and fifth in the remainder. Two-thirds of its total came from the two most populous provinces, Guyas and Pichincha. Dismayed by the victory of a candidate to whom it was strongly opposed, the military regime sought means to prevent or delay Roldó's accession to the presidency. Although abstaining from any formal agreements, the FADI made clear its commitment to the convening of the second round and its preference for Roldós as the least unacceptable alternative. By November, the convening of the runoff remained uncertain, as did the posture of the government should Roldós win the majority, as seemed likely. A revised schedule promised the runoff for April 1979, to be accompanied as well by congressional races.

Organization and Leadership. While Secretary General Pedro Antonio Saad retained his domination of the party, the advent of national elections and the presidential candidacy of René Maugé encouraged greater participation by a new generation of activists. This was also evident in the communist-dominated Confederation of Ecuadorian Workers (Confederación de Trabajadores Ecuatorianos; CTE) founded by Saad in 1944. The CTE, a member of the communist-front World Federation of Trade Unions (WFTU), remained the largest of Ecuador's three national labor federations with an estimated 18 percent of the country's organized workers. It was closely followed by the Ecuadorian Center of Classist Organizations (Central Ecuatoriana de Organizaciones Clasistas; CEDOC) with 17 percent and the Ecuadorian Confederation of Free Workers' Organizations (Confederación Ecuatoriana de Organizaciones Sindicales Libres; CEOSL) with 15 percent. The remaining 50 percent of organized workers belonged to independent associations.

Labor unrest had mounted in 1977 with a series of strikes and had met increased governmental repression. In 1978 the rivalry of the three national federations, along with internal divisions of both CEDOC and CEOSL, produced greater disunity within the national labor movement. The customary May Day parades in Quito and Guayaquil were less successful than those of the two preceding years. From 20,000 to 30,000 workers participated in Quito, while in Guayaquil there were rival marches by the three organizations. Posters and slogans focused on economic issues, demanding an increase in the minimum wage, denouncing the high cost of living, and charging the government with antiworker repression. Speeches were delivered by the candidates of the FADI electoral coalition (*FBIS*, 2 May). The CTE, drawing 70 percent of its membership from urban labor, was plagued by Maoist dissension. Its Quito affiliate, the Pichincha Workers' Federation (Federación de Trabajadores de Pichincha; FTP) was briefly taken over by pro-Peking elements. While PCE labor leaders soon regained control, the FTP was left in a weakened condition. Similarly, the party's youth wing, the Communist Youth of Ecuador (Juventud Comunista Ecuatoriana; JCE), was unable to win control of the Federation of Ecuadorian University Students (Federación de Estudiantes Universitarios del Ecuador; FEUE) from Maoists. This was further illustrated by the generalized support of leftist students for the temporary presidential candidacy of Camilo Mena Mena, the rector of the Central University.

The posture of the government was manifested by the extensive use of the police to disperse April demonstrations in Quito protesting an increase in bus and cab fares. The CTE charged that "the constant baiting of students and workers is explained by the clear intention of preventing the return to constitutional government and the installation of a reactionary, violently repressive dictatorship" (*El Comercio*, 19 April). Although its commitment to the electoral process was communicated through the CTE, the contribution of labor to the FADI campaign proved ineffective.

Domestic Views. The electoral process provided a major forum for the expression of PCE policies, with René Maugé its major spokesman. Particular attention was directed toward agrarian reform, property rights, natural resources, and the role of the working class. A call for the liquidation of the *latifundio* was coupled with proposals for cooperatives, state enterprises, the provision for credit, and creation of a viable internal market. Expansion of state activity in the economy was advocated, with stronger controls placed upon the private sector. Control of natural resources was framed within the context of petroleum, and the presence of foreign-based multinational corporations was to be terminated. Worker participation in a FADI government was viewed as the linchpin of a new government. Maugé accepted the nine-point proposal of the three labor federations as requisite for the establishment of true socialism in Ecuador (*Nueva*, June).

For the Marxist coalition, Maugé spoke at length in justification of PCE support for various measures adopted in earlier years by the military regime. Contending that the government had taken a marked turn toward capitalist dependency and had set aside its earlier nationalism, he further maintained that the post-1972 period had seen an intensification of the class struggle. The growth of revolutionary consciousness had been promoted by the continuing high cost of living, depressed working conditions, and the deepening economic crisis of world capitalism. For the campaign and thereafter, the PCE would "step up the struggle for national interests . . . and advance along the path of revolutionary change." In short, the immediate task was "to explain to the masses the program of the national-liberation revolution as a stage preceding the transition to socialism, and rally all patriotic, anti-imperialist and democratic forces in a united front." (*WMR*, February).

International Views. The FADI platform called for "an independent and sovereign international policy" free of the dictates of the United States and characterized by the reestablishment of relations with Cuba and North Korea (*Nueva*, June). Basic domestic problems were blamed in large part upon international capitalism and North American economic imperialism, especially as manifested in the exploitation of Ecuadorian oil. It was necessary for the nation to replace dependency on capitalism with the independence of socialism. In the words of the PCE "minimum program" adopted at its Ninth Congress in 1973, it was necessary to "remove the economic and political roots of imperialist domination; nationalize the entire oil industry . . . and pursue a sovereign, independent and peaceful foreign policy" (*WMR*, February).

The PCE also projected its positions through nonelectoral means. Expressions of solidarity with other socialist regimes were frequent, as in the 29 July message to Kim Il-song supporting "the Korean people's struggle for the independent and peaceful reunification of their fatherland" (*FBIS*, 8 August). Similar occasions were employed for reiteration of opposition to Maoism. During an April visit to the Soviet Union, Pedro Saad told a Tass correspondent that the Chinese were weakening the camp of socialism, threatening world peace, and aiding the warmongering North American imperialists. "The Maoists and their accomplices are enemies of the struggling peoples in all continents . . . trying to undermine the unity of the Communist parties all over the world . . . a full and total denial of proletarian internationalism" (ibid., 11 April).

The PCMLE. The Marxist-Leninist Communist Party of Ecuador (PCMLE) is a Maoist splinter group dating from 1963. It enjoys its greatest support among university students and in 1978 centered its activities on the formation of a party to contest with FADI for leftist votes. In March the first convention of the Popular Democratic Movement (MPD) gathered 5,000 delegates to nominate Camilo Mena Mena as its standard bearer (ibid., 20 March). Denying explicit Maoist overtones, Mena characterized his candidacy as representing the lower classes and promised a goverment of national dignity in which "decisions will result from the experience of the lower classes" (*El Comercio*, 7 April). While denying that his candidacy was intended to compete with that of FADI, Dr. Mena viewed his movement as the only true representative of marginal groups demanding a transformation of politics and society. He pledged basic structural change based on the will of the populace. Agrarian reform would have high priority, private enterprise would be controlled to permit effective defense of national sovereignty, foreign oil companies would be expelled, and diplomatic relations would be established with socialist regimes. Soviet-Chinese discrepancies were "ideological problems deserving of study" (*Cambio*, April). When the MPD was denied legal recognition by the Supreme Electoral Tribunal, it announced the initiation of a campaign in favor of electoral abstention, but the effort had minimal impact on the vote.

Other Marxist Organizations. Although their numerical membership is very small, several other Marxist groups emerged in the months preceding the vote and joined the PCE in the FADI electoral alliance. Most important of these was the Ecuadorian Revolutionary Socialist Party, a Fidelista offshoot of the original Socialist Party, which embraced elements more radical than those found in the PCE. The Revolutionary Movement of the Christian Left had split away from the centrist Christian Democrats, the Movement for Unity of the Left was a group of intellectuals gathered about longtime socialist Benjamín Carrión, and the Second Independence Movement similarly followed the noted leftist popularizer, author Jaime Galarza Zavala.

By the close of 1978, the Ecuadorian left was enjoying its greatest political activity and visibility of the decade but still was fundamentally weak and fragmented, with the Communists retaining relatively greater viability than any of the smaller mini-parties. Its political participation in the immediate future awaited resolution of the knotted electoral situation.

The Pennsylvania State University   John D. Martz

El Salvador

The Communist Party of El Salvador (Partido Comunista de El Salvador; PCES) was officially founded in 1930 but has been illegal since the communist-led uprising of 1932. The country's ruling group is the Party of National Conciliation (PCN), which holds regular but fraudulent elections and now maintains General Carlos Humberto Romero in power. The pro-Soviet PCES, with an estimated membership of 225, has no elected representatives in the government. The population of El Salvador is approximately 4,515,000.

Leadership and Organization. The PCES has as its secretary general Schafik Jorge Handal; other prominent party members include Jaime Barrios and Victor Montes. Although in the past Handal lived openly in San Salvador, he found it necessary to go underground during 1978 and spent much of his time abroad. There is a legal front organization, known as the Nationalist Democratic Union (UDN), which has joined with the Christian Democratic Party (PDC) and the National Revolutionary Movement (MNR), a socialist, noncommunist group, to form the opposition bloc called the National Opposition Union (UNO) for the purpose of contesting elections. As this purpose appears increasingly futile, there are signs that the UNO may break up.

The PCES maintains a moderate, nonviolent position, cooperating with the UNO and with such trade union organizations as the Federation of Salvadoran Unions (FUSS). However, there are a number of more extreme Marxist organizations which have challenged the claim of the PCES to speak for Salvadoran communism. These include the People's Revolutionary Army (ERP), a Maoist student group, and the Trotskyite Popular Liberation Forces (FPL), headed by former PCES Secretary General Salvador Cayetano Carpio. Both of these groups are committed to violence and have a nihilistic program which Handal declares "sets one's teeth on edge" (*Latinskaya Amerika*, Moscow, January-February). There is also the Marxist Unified Popular Action Front (FAPU), made up of a number of student, worker, and peasant groups. The government of El Salvador claims this is linked to the terrorist Armed Forces of National Resistance (FARN), whose head is said to be the lawyer Doroteo Gómez Ariaz, during 1978 a refugee in the Venezuelan embassy. A small group called the Workers' Revolutionary Organization (ORT) continues to enjoy a shadowy existence.

None of these groups are to be confused with the Popular Revolutionary Bloc (BPR), made up chiefly of two peasant organizations with a mixture of Marxist and Christian-social teachings, which is not linked to the PCES, despite government claims that it is. The BPR has denounced the PCES as "revisionist" and accused it of "betraying the Salvadoran people" (*El Salvador Reports*, August).

Publications. Because of government pressure, no group maintains regularly scheduled publications, though the PCES and FAPU have newspapers, *Voz Popular* and *Pueblo*, respectively.

Guerrilla Movements. The government of El Salvador continues a policy of extreme repressive violence against its opponents and especially against peasant organizations. Such events as the invasion of San Pedro Perulapan in March and the mass killings there have become the customary government response to FAPU and the BPR. To protest these policies, the BPR peacefully occupied various embassies in the capital while the FAPU organization twice seized the Red Cross headquarters. The BPR and the FPL also called for a boycott of the municipal and assembly elections held in March (*NYT*, 3 March).

In addition to these relatively peaceful actions, there were a number of instances of terrorism. The FPL celebrated the eighth anniversary of its founding by seizing a radio station and detonating a series of bombs throughout the country on April 3. Its "Farabundo Martí Brigade" kidnapped two prominent businessmen on May 14, and three days later two members of the FPL were shot by security forces during a demonstration. On 16 September FPL members machine-gunned the United States embassy, to little effect, and killed an ex-speaker of the Salvadoran Legislature. Two days later they killed two guards at the National University, and on 3 October they burned the offices of the Nicaraguan national airline, LANICA.

Meanwhile, the ERP, once believed nearly defunct, bombed the Argentine embassy on 19 June and the Guatemalan embassy on 24 July. On 10 August it kidnapped ex-mayor Tomás Antonio Monedero on the streets of Santa Anna, killing his chauffeur, an incident incorrectly blamed on the FARN. The ERP also bombed PCN headquarters in central San Salvador on 8 September.

Although three members of the FARN were seized by the government near Izalco in February, the organization remained active, its most spectacular deed being the kidnapping of a Japanese businessman on 18 May. Although a substantial ransom was demanded, he was in fact killed the same day; his body was discovered some months later, and Antonio Carranza Parada was picked up for this action on 10 August.

Eastern Connecticut State College   Thomas P. Anderson

Guadeloupe

Guadeloupe's Communist Party (Parti communiste guadeloupéen; PCG) experienced a bittersweet year in 1978. Although it happily celebrated its twentieth anniversary as an independent party, its single deputy to the French National Assembly, Hégésippe Ibéné, lost his seat in the March general elections. As a result the island group, a French overseas department, is now represented in the lower house of parliament by three members of the neo-Gaullist Rally for the Republic (RPR). Marcel Gargar and Georges Dagonier, allied with the party, continue to represent Guadeloupe in the Senate, however.

The Communists also comforted themselves with the fact they continued their control of elected offices in the major cities of Pointe-à-Pitre and Basse-Terre. In a by-election to the General Council, Hermann Songeons ran for the PCG and won the seat on 18 June.

Leadership and Organization. The defeat of Ibéné unleased bitter reappraisals of the party's organization and alliance with other left-wing parties, particularly since the March elections left all four "old colonies" (Guadeloupe, Martinique, French Guiana, and Réunion) without any communist representation in the National Assembly. Party leaders such as Guy Daninthe, secretary general, called for the annulment of the elections. He claimed that the abstention rate of almost 50 percent was due to threats emanating from the local newspaper *France-Antilles*, owned by Robert Hersant, who also controls *Figaro* in Paris. Leaders also blamed the Socialists for allegedly not living up to the leftist alliance, which had been forged in Guadeloupe as in France. Early in January the permanent Committee of the Guadeloupan Left had met, but the Socialists had refused to present a common electoral platform. Later in the month the PCG Central Committee decided it would not cooperate with Socialist candidates although they attempted to do so informally during the runoff elections on 19 March.

Party members forgot their anger for the time being on 7 April when 1,500 persons, or about half the party's members, joined together in Pointe-à-Pitre to celebrate the twentieth anniversary of the transformation of the former Guadeloupe Federation of the French Communist Party into an independent party. Allied organizations such as the Union of Guadeloupan Communist Youth, the General Confederation of Labor of Guadeloupe (CGTG), and the Union of Guadeloupan Women joined to celebrate the anniversary. The youth organization also announced the opening of its own office in Pointe-à-Pitre. And the Center for Marxist study announced that its collection of 3,000 books was at the disposal of party members.

Domestic Attitudes and Activities. Traditional local themes dominated party speeches, meetings, programs, and publications. The leadership again denounced what it called the colonial practices of Paris and supported the numerous strikes called by the CGTG and the Federation of National Education of Guadeloupe (FEN). It called for a revival of the sugar industry, a reduction in unemployment, a dynamic economic development program, and, most importantly, self-determination. The latter still meant the creation of an elected local assembly with more powers than the present General Council, a responsible executive, and an organ ensuring close cooperation with France. Because the PCG refused to call for a complete break with France, it was attacked by the Socialist Revolution Group (GRS) on the extreme left. The latter also accused the party of trying to control the trade unions.

At the same time that the party was calling for more autonomy and development, it found itself criticizing France's austerity program, which reduced aid to Guadeloupe. For example, the party said it feared the normal school might close because of a restricted budget, and it denounced the newly created Fruit Company of Marseille because it claimed that this company would put small banana producers out of business. The party condemned the Office of Migration from Overseas Departments (BUMIDOM) for assisting the departure of 3,000 young people to France because, in the PCG's view, they are condemned to menial jobs and racism.

On 1 May the party celebrated with the traditional parade in Pointe-à-Pitre. On 28 May the party also marked the heroic deaths of Ignace and Delgrès, who died fighting the French in 1802. In the last few years all nationalist movements and left-wing parties have adopted these two men as symbols of their programs and struggles. Along the same lines, the party praised the production and screening of a Guadeloupan film, "Coco La Fleur," which deals with customs and politics in the islands. Produced by Christian Lara, the film is in the Creole language, which the party has been tentatively praising as a symbol of Guadeloupan identity.

French military exercises brought loud criticism from the PCG. It seized the occasion to denounce French intervention in Zaire, Chad, and Mauritania.

International Views and Policies. The PCG's closest ties were naturally with the French Communist Party (PCF). Etienne Fajon, a member of the Political Bureau of the PCF, headed a delegation to Guadeloupe at the beginning of the year. Later in the year Georges Marchais, secretary general of the French party, sent a message to Guadeloupe urging support for the PCG.

Messages of congratulation and support were received at the twentieth anniversary celebration from the communist parties of the USSR and Romania. A cultural group from Trinidad visited, and a leader of the communist party of nearby Dominica—which became independent from Great Britain in November—spoke to the party members, and the PCG pledged to cooperate with it in the future.

Delegations left Guadeloupe to visit East Germany, Martinique, and France. The most important visits were to Cuba, however. A group participated in the Eleventh World Festival of Youth and Students in Cuba; Dr. Henri Bangou, mayor of Pointe-à-Pitre, studied development there; and another group examined sugar production in Cuba in the hope of finding a solution for Guadeloupe's faltering industry.

As an ally of the Soviet party, the PCG reported and praised Russian and Cuban initiatives in Ethiopia and Angola.

Publications. *L'Etincelle* (Spark), the party's main organ of expression, celebrated its thirty-fourth birthday and attracted thousands to its annual fête in June. It embarked on a particularly strong attack against the Jehovah's Witnesses, who, it asserted, had departed from their traditional apolitical position to urge followers to vote for the Rally for the Republic party in the March elections. A non-communist reader sued the paper for libel and won 1,500 francs.

Howard University   Brian Weinstein

Guatemala

The communist party in Guatemala, which since 1952 has been called the Guatemalan Party of Labor (Partido Guatemalteco del Trabajo; PGT), originated in the predominantly communist-controlled "Socialist Labor Unification," founded in 1921. The PGT operated legally between 1951 and 1954, playing an active role in the administration of Guatemalan President Jacobo Arbenz. Outlawed in 1954 following the overthrow of Arbenz, it has operated underground since then. Although the party has some influence among students, intellectuals, and workers, its does not play any significant role in national affairs.

According to U.S. intelligence sources, the PGT is estimated to have 750 members. The population of Guatemala is 6,621,000 (estimated 1978).

As an illegal party, the PGT did not participate in the 5 March presidential and congressional elections. Although the party's official position called for popular abstention, there is reason to believe that the Left, including the Communists, favored a victory by General Romeo Lucas García, a conservative backed by the Institutional Democratic Party (PID), the Revolutionary Party (PR), and the right-wing Central Aranista Organizada (CAO). Approximately 40 percent of the 1.8 million registered voters cast ballots. Amid widespread charges of fraud in the vote counting, reminiscent of the 1974 elections, Lucas emerged as the apparent victor among the three military candidates, although with less than the majority required. On 13 March the Guatemalan Congress selected Lucas as president-elect by a narrow majority. The election of Lucas, a 53-year-old former defense minister, provides the greatest assurances of a continuation of the state of affairs under his predecessor, General Kjell Laugerud Gardía, whose government proved to be weak, divided, and incapable of finding solutions to Guatemala's political and social crises. Some observers believe that as a result of Lucas's election, the Communists are likely to develop their strength in the labor movement, and along with guerrilla organizations, benefit from another example of electoral fraud and another government expected to be equally ineffective (*Latin American Political Report,* London, 17 March).

Guerrilla and General Violence. Various guerrilla groups have operated in Guatemala in recent years, including the Revolutionary Armed Forces, which is the military arm of the PGT, and the Rebel Armed Forces, (Fuerzas Armadas Rebeldes; FAR), at least some of whose members have claimed affiliation with the PGT. The Revolutionary Armed Forces and the FAR probably have fewer than 100 members each, plus several hundred sympathizers.

The most active of the guerrilla organizations in 1978, and now the largest, was the self-styled Guerrilla Army of the Poor (Ejército Guerrillero de los Pobres; EGP). The EGP began operations in November 1975 when it assumed responsibility for the murder of an anticommunist leader and proclaimed in bulletins to news media "a war to the death on U.S. imperialism and its local representatives." Its membership is believed to contain remnants of leftist guerrilla groups that succumbed to the effective counterinsurgency tactics of the Guatemalan military during the late 1960s and the "law and order" administration of General Carlos Arana Osorio (1970–74). Although the EGP has not claimed any direct affiliation with the PGT, there is strong evidence on which to base such an inference (for this reason, the EGP's operations are discussed below in connection with the PGT's domestic activities). The guerrilla situation is complicated by the continued existence of nonideological groups of common criminals who engage in kidnapping, extortion, robbery, and other acts of violence. Although the Laugerud presidency was relatively free of the extremist violence that convulsed Guatemala from 1966 to 1974, politically motivated killings involving leftist groups and right-wing paramilitary organizations remained a disturbingly common feature of Guatemalan daily life in 1978. Amnesty International issued a list of 113 people either killed or presumed to be kidnapped by paramilitary groups during the last three months of 1977 (ibid., 24 February). There is no indication that this alarming rate of political violence has diminished in 1978 or that security forces responsible for maintaining public order have been any more effective in controlling it.

In the postelection confusion prior to the Congress's selection of General Lucas, news media in Guatemala City received a bulletin announcing the emergence of yet another extremist organization characterized by its radical anti-Marxism, the self-styled Guatemalan Labor Militias (Milicias Obreras Guatemaltecas; MOG). During the months that followed, the MOG and the National Liberation Movement, whose candidate ran second in the presidential election, were accused of assorted bombing and terrorist acts around the country. Following Lucas' inauguration on 1 July, Guatemala's new police chief announced "a harsh campaign against guerrilla groups operating in the country." He added that street demonstrations would not be allowed without permission from the Government Ministry. (*Diario El Gráfico,* 7 July.) But by the end of the president's first month in office, the government admitted that "a new wave of violence" was sweeping the country, although the government characterized it as "more criminal than political." The assassination of a labor leader in Huehuetenango gave rise to speculation that the anticommunist Labor Militias had begun the elimination of trade union and labor leaders. Rumors circulated that the MOG might be a new edition of the "White Hand" or the "Eye-for-an-Eye" group which previously existed in Guatemala. The frequent discoveries of tortured or bullet-riddled bodies also generated reports of the reappearance of a "death squad." Government Minister Donaldo Alvarez Ruíz stated that police had no knowledge of the existence of such an organization and added that the bodies found recently in isolated spots were "probably the result of gangwars among criminals" (*El Imparcial,* 26 July). On 2 August the Government Minister declared that the so-called "death squad" appeared to have resumed operations, but he denied that it had any connection with the government. He announced that instructions had been issued for a "thorough investigation" of the organizations responsible for the continued killings (*Diario El Gráfico,* 2 August). On 4 August several thousand workers and students were attacked by antiriot police while staging a demonstration in Guatemala City to demand an end to violence and repression against labor organizations. A spokesman for the president said that the demonstrators had not requested permission from the government to hold the rally.

On 10 August urban transportation workers went on strike for the second time in less than a month to demand higher salaries. During the disputes over salaries and an increase in urban bus fares from five to ten cents in order to satisfy salary demands, demonstrations were organized. In the ten-day period of 2−12 October, at least 30 persons were killed, 350 injured, and 600 arrested in clashes between police and workers and students who opposed the bus fare increase. Students were joined by government employees throughout the country, including teachers, telephone workers, and municipal emloyees. By 10 October the general labor strike called by labor and popular organizations led by the National Committee for Labor Unity (CNUS) had spread to all of Guatemala, including Quezaltenango, the nation's second largest city, where disturbances on 5 October left a toll of six persons dead. Shortly after the initial demonstrations, government authorities reported that "well-organized agitators have taken advantage of disorders in the capital in an attempt to overthrow the government." According to the information secretary of the presidency, agitators were "following instructions from political groups identified with the extreme Left" (*Diario El Gráfico,* 5 October). The government subsequently charged that Nicaraguan Sandinistas and "international terrorists" were at work in the street disturbances. Guerrilla groups representing both the Left and the Right gave some credence to government charges when they announced their support for "the popular struggle" against the increase in urban bus fares. The self-styled Secret Anticommunist Army (ESA) announced on 5 October that it had ordered its combat units to intensify acts of sabotage and rebellion throughout the country. For its part, the Guerrilla Army of the Poor urged the people to struggle to keep bus fares at five cents. In a communiqué sent to news media, the guerrillas said that "the poor can only effect change by armed struggle" (*El Imparcial,* 6 October). Strikes continued into mid-October despite the fact that the Guatemala City municipality cancelled the fare increase on 7 October. The unions affiliated with CNUS announced that a demonstration would be held on 20 October "to protest against generalized and institutionalized repression." On 19 October the clandestine ESA announced that it had "tried and sentenced to death" two cabinet ministers, the chief of police, and 37 Guatemalan labor, university, political, and leftist leaders. In a press bulletin sent to newspapers, the ESA reiterated its determination "to fight international communism to the death." On October 20, the first person among the 40 Guatemalans whose names had appeared on the death list made public by the ESA was shot to death. Tension in Guatemala City was heightened on 26 October when the ESA announced that it planned to execute six more Guatemalan Communists "in the next few hours" (ibid., 27 October). At the end of October police reported that 20 persons had been killed in the previous 72 hours by clandestine groups engaged in executing persons considered ideological enemies (Agencia Centro Americano Noticias, 30 October). It remains to be seen whether such deep-rooted political differences can be resolved through negotiations between the Right and moderate leftist sectors.

The PGT: Leadership and Organization. Little information is available on the present leadership of the PGT or the party's structure. Since 1972, two general secretaries and nineteen ranking members of the Central Committee have "disappeared," apparently the victims of assassination. Following the murder of Humberto Alvarado Arrellano in December 1975, Isías de León became general secretary. Other prominent members of the Central Committee are Otto Sánchez, Jorge Muñoz, A. Bauer Pais, Antonio Fuentes, and Pedro González Torres.

The PGT has a youth auxiliary, the Patriotic Youth of Labor (Juventud Patriótica del Trabajo). Student agitators are active at the secondary and university levels, although direct affiliation with the PGT is disclaimed. Student leaders supported by the PGT have been unsuccessful in recent years in their efforts to gain control of the influential Association of University Students (AEU), although the association's statements on domestic issues tend to be strongly critical of the government and its inability to control right-wing paramilitary violence.

The PGT also controls the clandestine Guatemalan Autonomous Federation of Trade Unions, a small and relatively unimportant labor organization. The federation became an affiliated member of the communist-front World Federation of Trade Unions (WFTU) in October 1974. The National Committee for Labor Unity (CNUS), which includes some 70 unions, has become the most important voice for organized labor in Guatemala. Some observers believe that its militant activities in recent years have been the result of increasing PGT influence within its ranks.

Domestic Attitudes and Activities. It is difficult to determine whether the PGT's Central Committee met on a regular basis during 1978, or where. Similarly, there is little data to reveal the content of any political resolutions that may have been adopted. In order to characterize the PGT's attitudes on domestic and foreign issues, it is necessary to rely upon statements by party leaders who either publish abroad or grant interviews on an irregular basis. Clandestine bulletins attributed to the PGT appear occasionally in Guatemala, but their authenticity is open to question.

The Political Commission of the PGT published one of its most detailed statements of party policy in recent years in late 1977. It defined the most characteristic trait of the situation in Guatemala today as "the growth of the mass struggle in general and of the workers' and trade union movement in particular." The party views this struggle as "a prolonged process whose objective causes are to be found in the population's miserable living and working conditions, their merciless exploitation, and the violation of elementary democratic rights and freedoms." From the party's point of view, the upsurge in the mass struggle in recent years is the result of the growing level of consciousness and mass organization among students, workers, and peasants against a government weakened by acute internal contradictions and dominated by a system of capitalist exploitation. (*IB*, 15 September 1977.)

The PGT believes that the "reactionary bourgeois" Association of Trade, Industrial, and Financial Chambers (CACIF), together with the National Liberation Movement, is responsible for the most recent wave of terror and reprisals by rightist paramilitary organizations to maintain a repressive and authoritarian fascist-type military regime. It views the formation of the Secret Anticommunist Army (ESA) as "part of a plan by the reactionary ruling circles . . . to decapitate and crush the popular, revolutionary and anti-imperialist forces and split the workers', trade union, peasant, and student movements" (ibid.). (It should be noted that the "reactionary" role attributed to CACIF is a view widely shared by Guatemalan intellectuals who do not consider themselves "communists.")

For the PGT, recent elections have served only to permit the usurping of power by reactionary groups of the ruling class who, replacing each other in the government, protect the interests of the "bourgeois-landed oligarchy and U.S. imperialism." In anticipation of the 1978 elections, the PGT announced that it was not dogmatically opposed to elections in general, but that it rejected the content and aims of the March elections: "By their character, elections in our conditions are an oppressive, relatively violent constitutional form of perpetuating the domination of the exploiters" (ibid., 14 February). Therefore, the party contends that the only way for the people to establish their power is through a prolonged revolutionary war. Participation in elections at the present time signifies acceptance and legalization of fraud: "We revolutionaries hold that these elections are an anti-popular, anti-democratic farce in which only the parties representing the various bourgeois strata and imperialism are taking part" (ibid., 15 September 1977). During the week preceding the elections, the PGT was charged with exploding bombs in different parts of the capital and distributing "subversive propaganda" urging people to abstain from voting (*El Imparcial,* 2 March).

The party has expressed its support for setting up a broad alliance of forces to create the conditions for revolution and the election of a people's government responsible for implementing structural changes. The working class and its closest ally, the peasantry, are expected to form the backbone of this alliance. To achieve its goals, the party is prepared to use both legal and extralegal means of struggle. Precisely to what extent the PGT was responsible for the instigation of violent acts in 1978 is difficult to ascertain. On 16 February the FAR, which had been quiescent for several years, announced the resumption of guerrilla activity with the intention of establishing a socialist regime in Guatemala. In a press communiqué, the FAR stated that one of its units had clashed with police in the capital on 7 February, during which two of their members died. At the time they were identified as common criminals (ibid., 17 February). There were no subsequent guerrilla actions claimed by either the FAR or the Revolutionary Armed Forces in 1978, which casts some doubt on the validity of the former's February bulletin. On 15 June a mine explosion destroyed a vehicle, killing seventeen military patrolmen in Guatemala City. It was reported that the PGT issued a statement saying that the attack was "a reply with revolutionary violence to the repressive government forces which carried out the peasant massacre in Panzós" (Agence France Presse, 16 June). The PGT subsequently released a bulletin denying responsibility for the action. Party spokesmen condemned the usurpation of the party's name and stressed that "popular justice does not undertake indiscriminate retaliatory actions" (*Diario El Gráfico*, 20 June).

The most enigmatic aspect of the PGT's activities in 1978 was the degree of its involvement with the self-styled Guerrilla Army of the Poor. Given the ideological orientation of the EGP and the targets of its rural and urban attacks, some degree of PGT influence, if not control, appears highly likely. According to U.S. and Guatemalan sources, the EGP, which has become a force to be reckoned with since its initial appearance in 1975, descends directly from the Revolutionary Armed Forces. The guerrillas are believed to number about 300, divided into four independent commands, three in the countryside and one in Guatemala City. They have been most active in propaganda and organizing in El Quiché, a mountainous region in northern Guatemala; near Escuintla, along the tropical Pacific Coast; and to a lesser extent in the department of Zacapa, where the guerrillas had their strongest support ten years ago. Guatemalan intelligence reported in late 1976 that the EGP's principal leader is César Montes, who was a member of the Revolutionary Armed Forces until it was crushed with U.S. support in the late 1960s.

The influence of the PGT is believed to be greatest within the guerrilla unit operating in Guatemala City. U.S. and Guatemalan officials agree that the guerrillas are not under the direct command of the PGT, although a large percentage of urban guerrillas are believed to be party members. César Montes was at one time a member of the PGT's Central Committee, but he reportedly resigned in 1968 in protest over the party's failure to provide its full support to the guerrilla movement. On 4 January the EGP claimed responsibility for the kidnapping of former Government and Foreign Minister Roberto Herrera Ibarquen on 31 December 1977. As conditions for Herrera's release, the EGP demanded (*a*), the publication of Herrera's activities as government minister during the Arana administration in which the EGP claimed he had been responsible for the deaths of several revolutionary leaders and the formation of terrorist groups; and (*b*), the payment of a ransom (*El Imparcial,* 5 January). The EGP's demands were met, and Herrera was released on 30 January. The EGP also took credit for the December kidnapping and murder of industrialist Luis Canella Gutiérrez and the abduction of Luis Arimany. President Laugerud declared on 21 January that the kidnappings were "an attempt on the part of the left wing to obstruct the electoral process through terrorism." He stated that the EGP is a "strictly Castroite" movement, noting that the communiqué published as a condition to free Herrera carried a picture of Ché Guevara. From this he concluded that "there is no doubt where the EGP obtains all its support and even the instructions as to what it should do and how and why" (*Prensa Libre,* 21 January).

In perhaps the year's most controversial and tragic incident of violence, the Defense Ministry announced on 29 May that 43 "guerrillas" had been killed in Panzós, Alta Verapaz, during an armed clash with army units. According to the official report, seventeen other guerrillas and seven soldiers were wounded during a sudden attack on the Panzós garrison (Agencia Centro Americano Noticias, 30 May). On 30 May the public relations secretariat of the presidency issued a communiqué in which it confirmed that the military garrison in Panzós was in effect "attacked by a crowd of peasants who had been mobilized by subversive elements who have been encouraging the illegal occupation of land in the region" (*El Imparcial,* 31 May). On 1 June President Laugerud accused "Fidel Castro and his cohorts of the EGP" of being responsible for the killings in Panzós. Laugerud charged that the nomadic peasants of the northern part of the country had been instigated by EGP guerrillas to invade private ranches in Alta Verapaz and to attack the army garrison. He added that the Indian peasants of the region have also been incited by Catholic priests and Protestant ministers to undertake land invasions (*Prensa Libre,* 2 June). The president's "official" explanation was echoed by the defense minister, who in subsequent press releases claimed that the peasants had been spurred on by extreme leftist elements of the EGP. As contradictory versions of the incident began to reach the capital from eyewitnesses, and from peasant, church, labor, and student organizations, public opinion reacted to the official story with outrage. According to a report issued by the London-based Latin America Bureau, a church-based organization, several hundred unarmed Indian peasants were fired upon by an army detachment while protesting against efforts by large landowners to force them from lands to which they had traditional rights but no legal title. Catholic church workers in the area prepared a provisional list of 114 dead, including women and children.

On 15 June seventeen soldiers were killed in Guatemala City when a mine destroyed a military truck. Reports indicated that the attack may have been a form of revenge by elements of the EGP for the peasant deaths in Panzós on 29 May (AFP, 16 June). Among its actions following the inauguration of General Lucas, the EGP claimed credit in September for the shooting of Nicaragua's ambassador to Guatemala, whom they charged with coordinating police repression against guerrillas operating in Central America. The action was intended to demonstrate the EGP's solidarity with Nicaragua's Sandinista National Liberation Front (*El Imparcial,* 17 September).

International Positions and Contacts. The PGT's positions on international issues follow closely those of the USSR. The party sees the world situation constantly changing for the better for the forces fighting for "independence, democracy, and freedom." The socialist community headed by the Soviet Union represents "the main force ensuring that the successes achieved by democratic and progressive humanity are consolidated and further developed" (*IB,* 15 September 1977). In the past, party spokesmen have accused supporters of Trotskyism in Guatemala of attempting to split the revolutionary movement by belittling the prestige of the PGT, slandering the Soviet Union, and serving the interests of American imperialism (*Latinskaya Amerika,* July/August 1977).

The government's recurring discovery of "an international plan of terror" is viewed by the PGT as "an attempt to intimidate the masses and dampen popular discontent by inventing non-existing international conspiracies which nobody believes in and everybody ignores." The party also opposes the "chauvinistic slogans" adopted by the military "on the pretext of recovering Belize." The PGT has accused the Guatemalan government of stirring up conflict with Great Britain over Belize in order to divert the people's attention from Guatemala's acute social and economic problems. According to the party, a state of war would simplify the government's, the oligarchy's, and the paramilitary organizations' use of terror and reprisals "to behead the revolutionary, popular, trade union and peasant movements, and, if possible, brutally crush organized mass opposition." (*IB,* 15 September 1977.)

Publications. The party publishes a clandestine newspaper, *Verdad,* on an irregular basis.

Washington College   Daniel L. Premo

Guyana

The People's Progressive Party (PPP) of Guyana was founded in 1950. At its First Congress, in 1951, it declared itself a nationalist party, committed to socialism, national independence, and Caribbean unity. During most of the following two decades, the leadership of the PPP was predominantly Marxist-Leninist, but party followers in general were not knowledgeably so. In 1969 party leader Cheddi Jagan moved for the first time to align the PPP unequivocally with the Soviet Union, and in turn, the PPP was recognized by Soviet leaders as a bona fide communist party. Party leaders say that the process of transforming the PPP into a Leninist party began in 1969.

The PPP is a legal organization and represents the major opposition to the ruling People's National Congress (PNC), a party led by onetime PPP member, and present Guyanese prime minister, Forbes Burnham. Particularly since Burnham's break with the PPP in the mid-1950s, Guyanese politics have been heavily influenced, at times determined, by ethnic differences in the population—roughly 50 percent of the population is of East Indian descent (traditionally supporting the PPP), some 40 percent of African descent (generally supporting the PNC), and the remainder assorted Amerindians, Portuguese, Chinese, and racial mixtures. In 1973 Burnham was reelected for his third term while the PPP, still claiming to be the majority party in the country, received only 26 percent of the vote (and 14 out of 53 seats in parliament). Jagan with good reason protested that fraud and illegal maneuvers had prevailed. The PPP boycotted parliament in protest until May 1976.

Membership of the PPP is unknown, though the number of active and influential Marxist-Leninists is probably no more than several hundred. In the past few years, a number of blacks have joined the PPP while many East Indians have drifted into the PNC. The population of Guyana in 1978 was estimated at 850,000.

Leadership and Organization. At its Nineteenth Congress in 1976, the PPP returned Cheddi Jagan to his long-held position as secretary general and elected a 32-member Central Committee. Among the prominent party leaders, all of whom are among the fourteen PPP members of parliament, are Janet Jagan (PPP secretary for international affairs), Ram Karran (secretary for labor), Clinton Collymore (columnist for *Mirror*), Reepu Daman Persaud (chairman of the Auditing and Control Commission), Harry Persaud (organizing secretary), and Feroze Mohamed (secretary for youth affairs).

The Progressive Youth Organization (PYO), traditionally a source of strong personal support for Cheddi Jagan, held its three-day Tenth Congress during the first week of July in the eastern region of Berbice. The meeting of 700 delegates and observers took place under a banner proclaiming "Towards a Secure Future with a National Patriotic Front." The opening session, chaired by PYO First Secretary Navin Chandarpal, was addressed as always by Cheddi Jagan, who gave a critical analysis of the situation in Guyana and praised the revolutionary role taken by the PYO. Numerous documents and resolutions were approved, including one expressing support for the Eleventh World Festival of Youth and Students. The PYO also called for a truly national people's militia, condemned government violations of human rights, lamented the declining quality of social services and education, and urged a resolution of economic and political problems in the country by political means via a national patriotic front. (*Mirror*, 5, 9, 12 July.)

The PPP-controlled Guyana Agricultural and General Workers' Union (GAWU), based in the sugar industry, claims to be the largest trade union in the country with some 20,000 members. Ram Karran is president and Pariag Sukhai is secretary general. The GAWU is a member of the Guyana Trade Union Congress (TUC), though it is frequently critical of TUC administration and policies. The GAWU held its Eighth Congress in mid-June, attended by some 700 delegates and overseas observers, and examined both domestic and international issues, including the impact of the GAWU-sponsored sugar strike (August 1977 to January 1978), the government's use of "volunteer" workers to harvest the cane, and the need for a united front of opposition forces to act against the PNC.

The PPP also sponsors the Women's Progressive Organization (WPO) headed by Arai Tantoni.

Party Internal Affairs. The core leadership of the PPP has been shaken on several occasions since Jagan's 1969 decision to become affiliated with the pro-Soviet communist bloc. The most recent expulsion occurred in mid-1978 and involved Lalbachan Lalbahadur, a senior Central Committee member and an officer of the GAWU. Prime Minister Burnham has encouraged this dissension, in part by appointing several prominent PPP defectors—notably Ranji Chandisingh and Vincent Teekah—to important positions in the government and the PNC. In October Teekah was promoted to the position of senior minister in Burnham's government. Cheddi Jagan received the Order of Friendship from the Presidium of the Supreme Soviet of the USSR on his sixtieth birthday in March in recognition of his efforts on behalf of the Guyanese people, world peace, and "friendly relations between the peoples of Guyana and the Soviet Union" (*Mirror*, 24 March).

Domestic Attitudes and Activities. The PPP frequently outlines its overall position with respect to domestic policy: "The PPP reiterates its commitment to Marxism-Leninism (scientific socialism) and proletarian internationalism and to the creation of a National Patriotic Front Government of all left and democratic forces with an anti-imperialist socialist-oriented program as the only vehicle for uniting the people, transforming the economy, resolving the crisis, safeguarding our national independence and sovereignty, and achieving social progress" (*Mirror*, 28 May). Cheddi Jagan expressed the party's limited policy of "critical support" for the Burnham government in an interview with a Hungarian reporter (*Népszabadság*, Budapest, 8 September): "Although our views differ on numerous issues from those of the ruling PNC, we completely support the government in the struggle against the international monopolies, and we stand by it with regard to all of its steps consistent with the people's interests." But, Jagan warns, these steps on the people's behalf are too few, and domestic and international pressures on the PNC are increasing: "The international monopolies and the imperialist circles behind them are applying the 'Peruvian model.' Through economic pressure, they are trying to divert our country and people from the anti-imperialist and progressive trend they have chosen." While Jagan says the PPP responds to this pressure by calling for anti-imperialist unity, the PNC has been caving in and turning to the right. The government's talk of "socialist thrust" and its "road to socialism" is considered mere rhetoric (*Morning Star*, London, 10 July). As *Mirror* commented editorially on 13 April: "To claim that we are moving in the path of socialism is bunkum, a confidence trick by the PNC which is pretending to be what it is not! Guyanese must not be fooled by the humbug of the PNC."

The single issue that most troubled the PPP and many other Guyanese in 1978 was the government's successful effort to amend Article 73 of the country's constitution. The amendment was designed to (*a*) remove a provision in the constitution by which certain key clauses could only be changed if approved by a referendum, (*b*) put the PNC-dominated parliament in charge of writing a new constitution, and (*c*) postpone elections scheduled for 1978 so as to put current parliamentarians in charge of the rewriting. The fourteen PPP delegates walked out of parliament in April when the bill was approved by that body. Taking advantage of broad opposition to the PNC action, the PPP rallied other parties and groups, church leaders, professional associations, and unions of the Left and the Right into the Committee for the Defense of Democracy, which called for a boycott of the referendum held on 10 July. But the bill, described by Collymore as "perfidious, iniquitous, and the very final nail in the coffin of democracy in Guyana," was approved by what the government reported was a 97 percent to 3 percent margin of the 70 percent of registered voters participating. The PPP, other opposition groups, and independent foreign observers declared that the turnout was much smaller—the PPP claimed it was less than 10 percent, leading Jagan to comment the next month that "Guyana is being ruled by a 10 percent government propped up by police and military bayonets" (*Advocate-News*, Bridgetown, 11 August).

International Views and Contacts. In 1978 the PPP continued its warnings that the United States, upset by the leftward direction of events in Guyana, was trying to arrest and reverse trends in the country, in large part by economic means, such as the substantial IMF credits secured in July. Praise for the accomplishments of the Soviet Union and Soviet-bloc countries is complemented by criticism of the People's Republic of China. Cheddi Jagan traveled in most Soviet-bloc countries during the year, as did a number of other PPP leaders.

Publications. The PPP's newspaper, *Mirror*, is published in Georgetown and edited by Janet Jagan. The party's quarterly theoretical journal is *Thunder*.

Hoover Institution   William E. Ratliff
Stanford University

Haiti

The United Party of Haitian Communists (Parti unifié des communistes Haitiens; PUCH) was formed in November 1968 by merging several smaller leftist parties. The membership of the PUCH is unknown but presumed to be less than several hundred persons, most of whom are underground, in jail, or in exile. The population of Haiti in 1978 was approximately 5,534,000.

All political parties have been outlawed in Haiti since 1949. In April 1969 a law was passed declaring all forms of communist activity crimes against the state, the penalty for which would be both confiscation of property and death. Most PUCH activities have been carried on outside Haiti among exiles in Europe, the Soviet Union, and Cuba. Some PUCH members were among the political prisoners released and sent into exile in the past two years. The main party spokesman during the year was Jacques Dorcilien, a member of the Secretariat of the Central Committee. The party says it is disseminating revolutionary ideas, starting new cells in industry and agriculture, and forging links between the party and the workers, peasants, and other sectors of society.

Party Affairs. The PUCH held its first congress somewhere in Haiti during the final months of 1978. The congress elected members of its Central Committee, reelected Jacques Dorsilien as general secretary, adopted a party platform and rules, and expounded upon the domestic and international situation. Party members produced a document entitled "Struggle for Labor, Bread, and Liberty," confirmed their loyalty to the principles of Marxism-Leninism and proletarian internationalism, strongly condemned anti-Sovietism and the splitting activities of the Peking leaders. (Tass, 14 November; *Granma*, English ed., 26 November.)

Domestic and International Views. The Political Bureau of the PUCH charged that the "Haitian communists and people are facing the fascist dictatorship of the U.S.-imperialist-supported Duvalier clique" (message to Cambodian Communist Party, Phnom Penh domestic radio, 11 May). In reaction to the extreme poverty of the people and the political repression of the government, Dorcilien said that the Haitian people are going abroad illegally in increasing numbers and settling in the United States, the Dominican Republic, and other Caribbean islands. Despite talk of "liberalization," the Duvalier regime has become increasingly repressive since the strike movement of 1977, and the long arm of the police has reached into communities of Haitians living in the Dominican Republic. Thus, declarations of "liberalization" by the government are directed at improving the country's relations with foreign businesses and governments. The impact of U.S. business investments, the Central Intelligence Agency, and international banks and agencies is increasingly felt at all levels of society. The state budget is "balanced" by loans, credits, and other financial aid from U.S. banks and international institutions in which the United States has a decisive vote. The "ideological laboratories" of the CIA are said to be "preparing religious 'systems' especially adapted to the Haitian people" in order to convince them they must "become reconciled with the existing conditions of life in poverty, that everything in this world is 'predestined by God,' and that nothing can be changed." Under these conditions the PUCH sees its main tasks as the "struggle for democracy and freedom for the Haitian people." In order to achieve these objectives, "it is necessary to unite the efforts of all Haitian patriots and to win the abolition of anticommunist laws, to assert political freedom, and to liquidate the existing power structure, particularly the regime of Duvalier's lifetime presidency. The party demands free elections and the return of all political exiles." (Interview with Dorcilien published in *Rudé Právo*, Prague, 21 April.) The concluding declaration of the PUCH congress put forward demands that an end should be put to the imperialist pillage of the national wealth, that the anticommunist law of 1969 should be abrogated, that the system of lifelong and hereditary presidency should be liquidated, that all political prisoners should be released and a general amnesty proclaimed permitting all political emigres to return to the country unconditionally. (Tass, 14 November.)

Publications. The PUCH publishes the irregular, clandestine *Boukan* for limited circulation in Haiti. Several irregular PUCH press organs are published in Canada, Mexico, and France, and the party passes on its views through communist media throughout the world.

Hoover Institution   Lynn Ratliff
Stanford University

Honduras

The Communist Party of Honduras (Partido Comunista de Honduras; PCH) was organized in 1927, destroyed in 1932, and reorganized in 1954. A dispute over strategy and tactics in 1967 led to the expulsion of one group and the division of the PCH into rival factions. Since 1971 a self-proclaimed pro-Chinese Communist Party of Honduras/Marxist-Leninist (PCH-ML) has functioned, but little is known about its leadership and membership. The PCH has been illegal since 1957 but has operated openly in varying degrees under recent governments. The government of General Melgar Castro was ousted in August 1978, and the prospects for the PCH are not yet clear under the apparently more conservative regime of Army General Policarpo Paz Garcia.

Membership in the PCH is estimated at 650. Most statements by the PCH-ML emanate from Peking, raising the possibility that it is little more than a paper organization. The population of Honduras is 3,517,000 (1978 estimate).

Leadership and Organization. The secretary general of the PCH is Dionisio Ramos Bejarano. Other important leaders are Rigoberto Padilla Rush, deputy secretary general and secretary of the Central Committee; Milton René Paredes, a Central Committee member; Mario Sosa Navarro, a member of the Political Commission; and Rigoberto Luna, active in the party's work with labor unions. Longino Becerra, a propaganda spokesman in the 1960s, resurfaced in April 1977 after five years of unexplained absence, but his responsibilities at the present time are not known.

Data on the party's Third Congress emerged in an extensive interview with Padilla Rush published in Moscow's *Latinskaya Amerika* (March—April). While the party staged a "diversionary congress" in one city, "in order to divert the secret agents there," the real forum was held in the capital city of Tegucigalpa in late May and early June 1977. Padilla Rush said that 42 percent of the 150 delegates to the congress "represented the working class and the rest—the peasants, intellectuals, small-scale property owners, and housewives."

The party has been active in recruitment and organizational work among university and secondary students and claimed some years ago that students made up 20 percent of its membership. However, neither Padilla Rush nor other party officials during the year mentioned student participation in or attendance at the May-June congress. The PCH sponsors the Socialist Student Front (Frente Estudiantil Socialista; FES) and the Federation of Secondary Students (FESE). The FES is probably the second most important university student organization after the right-wing United Democratic University Front (FUUD), which dominates political activities on the campuses of the National Autonomous University of Honduras (UNAH) in Tegucigalpa and San Pedro Sula, the most important city on the north coast. The FESE was probably the principal organizer of a strike in the capital city on 12—13 July by over 15,000 secondary students who demanded lower tuition and enrollment fees and other reforms in education and administration. Secondary students also occupied the Vicente Caceres Central Institute, the nation's largest secondary school, for a short time during the strike, and one week later, several FESE leaders were among those arrested in demonstrations before the presidential palace in Tegucigalpa.

PCH influence in the trade union movement during 1978 was still recovering from losses suffered between March and June 1977 when a reformist Democratic Front group ousted Napoleon Acevedo Granados from the presidency of the Standard Fruit Company Workers' Union (SETUFSCO). Padilla Rush noted in his *Latinskaya Amerika* interview that "both in rural areas and in the city the workers are forced to wage an unequal and persistent struggle for their social and democratic rights through the Confederation of Honduran Workers [CTH] . . . the North Coast Federation of Workers' Unions [FESITRANH] and the Federation of Workers of the Capital District [FECESITLH] . . . into the leadership of which have penetrated agents of the entrepreneurs who enjoy the unlimited support of the minister of labor." Padilla Rush continued: "An adverse effect is also exerted on the workers' struggle by the attempts of the Maoist elements" in the trade union organizations of the north coast and in the Standard Fruit Company Workers' Union "to establish so-called 'parallel' trade unions" and a new federation. It is not known whether Padilla Rush was alluding to efforts of the PCH/ML or of some other group.

On two occasions in early 1978, Padilla Rush claimed that the PCH was taking part in negotiations with more moderate parties "towards finding a new political alternative for the country" (*Latinskaya Amerika*; *WMR*, May). In the *Latinskaya Amerika* interview, he also noted that the PCH was negotiating with the Democratic Left Front, the Liberal People's Alliance, and "a few leftist groups, which call themselves 'parties of the Marxist structure.' "

The PCH also claims some support within a "reformist" faction of the Honduran armed forces, which (in 1976) it said was "more or less agreeable to structural changes intended to end poverty, backwardness, and dependence." In 1978, Padilla Rush associated these "reformists" with the administration of former President López Arellano which was interested in agrarian reform and capitalist development (*Latinskaya Amerika*, March—April). However, elements which were identified in 1976 as conservative by the PCH are now divided by Padilla Rush into two groups, one led by Melgar Castro, which was identified with the large multinational firms and the business and industrial sectors of the country, and another led by Paz Garcia, which was linked to the National Party and large landowners who wanted little or no change, some of whom were involved in various "get-rich-quick" schemes involved the smuggling of drugs and emeralds.

Domestic Events and Views. The new election law, which went into effect on 1 January 1978, prohibits political parties which proclaim or practice doctrines "contrary to the democratic spirit of the Honduran people" or which act "according to or in subordination to any international organization" (*La Gaceta*, Tegucigalpa, 31 December 1977). This will probably prohibit the PCH from formally seeking and obtaining legal recognition to nominate candidates for the Constituent Assembly elections of 20 April 1980, although Padilla Rush and others have said that the 10,000 notarized signatures required by a party to be registered could easily be met.

In reviewing the events of the 1970s, Padilla Rush looked favorably upon some aspects of the "bourgeois-reformist" rule of General López Arellano, especially those portions of the National Development Plan dealing with agrarian reform and national development. The PCH, he claimed, pointed out "the need to . . . achieve the most rapid implementation of agrarian reform, dismissal of the foreign companies from the levers of the national economic system, establishing control over the export of capital, elimination of the system of economic privileges that enriched the small groups of entrepreneurial middlemen, legalization of the work of all the political forces supporting these measures [an oblique reference to the PCH's own illegal status], and carrying out an independent foreign policy." In his *Latinskaya Amerika* interview, Padilla Rush noted:

> Many reforms, especially the agrarian one, were carried out by sectarian methods, as a result of which the main blow was often inflicted not on the large-scale but on the small-scale property owners. This was furthered by the errors in the work of the National Agrarian Institute and also by the position of the ultraleftist groups, which did not distinguish between the small-scale landowners and the latifundists. . . . As a result, the rightist forces were able to turn public opinion not only against us but also against bourgeois reform. That is why the small-scale landowners, for example, of the Olancho Department . . . were so willing to take up weapons. The owners of a plot of land and of whole large areas took up positions in the same ranks. These improvised bands reached the point where they killed priests and monks, not to mention our comrades, who had explained the problems of agrarian reform.

The references to Olancho are apparently a rewriting of history by the PCH so that it can claim credit in the martyrdom of twelve Hondurans who, along with a Colombian priest and a North American priest, were killed on 25 June 1975 in Juticalpa, Olancho. In the view of the PCH—and many others—the program of the National Agrarian Institute has shifted away from agrarian reform to colonization of territories.

International Activities and Contacts. The PCH publicly said very little about international events in 1978. Central Committee member Milton Paredes participated in a "Roundtable on Imperialist Destabilization in the Developing Countries" in an unknown location during the year along with representatives from ten other communist and workers' parties. The meeting was sponsored by the Commission on National-Liberation Movements in Asian and African Countries. In an account of the meeting published in the *World Marxist Review* (September), Paredes commented on alleged U.S. efforts to "destabilize" a number of governments but did not discuss the Honduran situation at all. In his *Latinskaya Amerika* interview, Padilla Rush noted that Shafik Handal, general secretary of the Central Committee of the Communist Party of El Salvador, sent a warm message of greetings to the Third Party Congress of the PCH—which met in May-June 1977—calling on both peoples to "join forces in the struggle against senseless, fratricidal wars and noted that the fascism-imposing rulers of the countries surrounding Honduras had entered into a deal with the purpose of exerting pressure on Melgar Castro's government, so that the latter would persecute the Communists more cruelly and do away with the remnants of political tolerance in the country."

The PCH-ML. News of the Maoist PCH-ML came largely from abroad, as in years past. The party reportedly sent greetings to the government of Cambodia in June and, according to the New China News Agency, held a "friendly meeting" with the Marxist-Leninist Communist Party of Argentina in July. A joint declaration with the Argentine party branded the Soviet Union the "principal warmonger" in the world today and called for unity among Marxist-Leninist parties (*FBIS*, China, 24 July). Two months later, the New China News Agency said that a "friendly meeting" between delegations of the PCH-ML and the Marxist-Leninist Communist Party of Argentina took place at the end of May in Honduras" (*FBIS*, China, 24 July). (The Argentine group may be the Socialist Vanguard Party of Argentina.) The joint declaration reportedly said that "the intensified struggle between the two super-powers — the United States and the Soviet Union — for world hegemony carries the threat of leading to the outbreak of a third world war. The Soviet Union is the principal warmonger because it is an imperialism on the rise and pursuing an expansionist cause." The two parties were agreed on "the need to strengthen the relations between the Marxist-Leninist parties of all the continents on the basis of Marxism-Leninism and proletarian internationalism, equality, independence, and mutual respect" while also expressing their "determination to struggle against imperialism, social-imperialism, reaction and modern revisionism."

Publications. The PCH's principal publication is *Patria*, a weekly, which has appeared sporadically since June 1976 when it replaced *Vanguardia Revolucionaria*, which was forced out of existence by the Honduran government's Department of National Investigation (DIN). *El Trabajo*, a theoretical and informational journal, has not been circulated publicly in the past five years and has not been mentioned in international communist publications. Party statements are often found in the *World Marxist Review*, that journal's *Information Bulletin*, and in occasional press conferences or newspaper advertisements in Honduran newspapers.

Texas Tech University   Neale J. Pearson

Jamaica

A communist party was founded in Jamaica in December 1978 when the Workers' Liberation League (WLL), at its First Congress, transformed itself into the Jamaican Workers' Party (JWP). According to Trevor Munroe, WLL founder and JWP general secretary, the new party will be a "full member of the international community of communist and workers' parties" (*Canadian Tribune*, 4 December). A representative of the Communist Party of the Soviet Union attended the founding ceremony and the JWP has adopted a pro-Soviet stance.

The JWP expects to continue and expand the activities begun by the League in the labor and student movements, where Munroe claims WLL influence has been considerable. In recent years WLL members have been elected to positions of leadership at the University of the West Indies (UWI), where Munroe is a Senior Lecturer, and in the more than 800 Jamaican youth clubs.

Party Internal Affairs. The WLL was established in 1974, according to Munroe, when there was "a need for some form of communist activity in Jamaica, particularly in the area of broad anti-imperialist and democratic struggle." But by late 1978, he told a Canadian Communist Party leader just before the formal founding of the JWP, "the situation has matured to the point where it is possible to have a full communist party." He noted that domestic and international factors brought about this change, but asserted in particular: "There is a new receptiveness to socialist thought and ideas in Jamaica. Today there exists in all strata of the people of Jamaica a certain pro-socialist, pro-communist sentiment." (*Canadian Tribune*, 4 December.) On 17 December, in his first address as JWP secretary general, Munroe told an enthusiastic crowd of some 3,000 at the Regal Cinema that in order to qualify for membership in the JWP a person must be "serious about joining the communist party and about becoming a part of the communist movement in the world." He said that membership will require study, discipline, and willingness to sacrifice. "We want to be sure that when the imperialists attack us our comrades will stand up firmer than before as communists who never run, as communists who never bow before the imperialists." He declared that the JWP will work to "build the communist party of Jamaica, step by step," recognizing that the goals the party has set will not be easily achieved. (*Daily Gleaner*, Kingston, 18 December.) The congress that resulted in the formation of the JWP lasted for three days in Kingston and was attended by representatives of parties and organizations from the Soviet Union, Cuba, Guyana, the United States, Canada, Great Britain, St. Vincent, St. Lucia, Barbados, and Uruguay. The Regal Theater was decorated with pictures of Marx, Engels, and Lenin, as well as Jamaican national heroes Paul Bogle and Marcus Garvey. (*Granma*, Eng. ed., Havana, 31 December.)

Domestic and International Positions. In his 17 December address, Munroe charged that "imperialist forces" were responsible for increasing the suffering of the Jamaican people. American imperialism and the conditions imposed by the International Monetary Fund had caused mass layoffs of skilled workers in the country, land hunger among farmers in the rural areas, and other problems throughout society. He pledged "critical support" for the government of Prime Minister Michael Manley of the People's National Party, and Manley hailed the formation of the JWP and praised positions adopted by the organization. But though the JWP pledged its support for a number of government positions, the "critical" aspect of its stand was also emphasized. Munroe asserted on 17 December that the Manley government was "too soft" on "capitalists who are closing down businesses and laying off workers," on "colonialist elements inside the police force and inside the army," on "propagandists" in the Kingston press, on "bureaucratic civil servants," on Reynolds Bauxite Mines, on ministers who are "friending up with the capitalists and who forget that it is the people and not the capitalists who put them into power." As for the opposition Jamaica Labour Party, he proclaimed it an "agent of imperialism." (*Daily Gleaner*, 18 December; Havana Domestic Service, 14 December.)

On international issues, Munroe condemned "American imperialism" for backing "the racist regime of South Africa" and for trying to "strangle the baby of Angola." "American imperialism," he concluded, "will one day be buried deep beneath the oceans of the world." On the other hand, he praised the October Revolution in the Soviet Union and the Castro Revolution in Cuba, for "without them our party could never have come into being." Munroe pledged to combat all forms of Trotskyism and anti-Sovietism. (*Daily Gleaner*, 18 December; *Granma*, Eng. ed., 31 December.)

Publications. The JWP will publish *Struggle*, a newspaper that began as a WLL broadsheet and grew to be an eight-page tabloid. Like the WLL before it, the JWP has a weekly radio broadcast to spread socialist ideas in Jamaica.

Hoover Institution   William E. Ratliff
Stanford University

Martinique

Martinique's Communist Party (Parti communiste martiniquais; PCM) continued to play second violin on the Left to Aimé Césaire and his Martinique Progressive Party. The March elections to the French National Assembly sent the three incumbents back to the Palais Bourbon in Paris, and no Communist was among them. Césaire remained the only one of the three to represent the Left; he was joined by a member of the neo-Gaullist Rally for the Republic (RPR) and a third deputy allied with the RPR.

Deputy Césaire, who is also mayor of Fort-de-France, the major city, kept the spotlight on himself rather than on the PCM by articulating better than they the demands for self-determination. He defined this in terms of "Five Freedoms": customs, commerce, economy, culture, and politics. The PCM supported him.

Tensions grew during the political contests because of a strike by 6,000 construction workers, who at one point blocked the major streets of Fort-de-France. A bodyguard of an RPR candidate was murdered. Racial animosities grew, and PCM members accused the *Békés*, or locally born whites, of undermining Martinique's economy. Armand Nicolas, secretary general of the PCM, was the most vocal denouncer of the whites and sponsored a national conference of the PCM on 16−17 December 1977 to plan for action against the economic difficulties facing the island.

Fueling the fire were data released by the National Institute of Economic Statistics showing an island unemployment rate approaching 40 percent. It also announced that the average Martiniquan worker was earning about 40 percent of what his white metropolitan counterpart earned. Polls of 500 teenagers in Martinique found a deep malaise among them and a desire for political change short of independence.

The party denounced two French initiatives to resolve the economic problems. The minister for overseas departments sponsored a Conference for the Development of the Antilles in Martinique and Guadeloupe during December 1977, but the party said this was an affair of bureaucrats, local puppets, and business people only. At the same time a banana company, the Fruit Company of Marseille, planned to open a plant in Martinique. The PCM denounced both actions as futile and a threat to local initiative.

Violence increased as the year wore on. A French soldier shot and killed an eighteen-year-old Martiniquan. Strikes of students, teachers, and workers backed by the PCM spread.

The French Communist Party (PCF) supported the PCM fully in all its actions. A delegation, headed by Etienne Fajon, a secretary of the Central Committee of the PCF, visited in January and November. Robert Balanger, president of the communist group in the French National Assembly complained to the minister for overseas departments that RPR mayors in Martinique would not permit Communists and others to use municipal facilities.

Four East Germans were refused visas to travel to Martinique, but General Secretary Nicolas traveled to Eastern Europe, particularly to Romania. Philibert Duféal, a secretary of the Central Committee, traveled to Addis Ababa, Ethiopia, to attend the Afro-Arab Solidarity Conference. The party praised the Ethiopian revolution.

Justice, the party newspaper, celebrated its fifty-ninth anniversary. In addition to this important publication, the PCM also printed a booklet, *The Communists Explain: Democratic and Popular Autonomy*, to explain its current position on self-determination.

Howard University   Brian Weinstein

Mexico

The Mexican Communist Party (Partido Comunista Mexicano; PCM) was founded in 1919 as the Communist Party of the Mexican Proletariat, but has held its present name since 1920. The PCM has been legal in recent years but because it consistently failed to demonstrate the minimum membership necessary for official registration, it was not entitled to have candidates' names printed on election ballots, the Federal Electoral Commission's (FEC) notice that a candidacy has been recognized. However, in accordance with an electoral reform introduced by Mexican President José López Portillo in late 1977, the FEC granted the PCM conditional registration in May 1978, thus enabling the party to participate in the 1979 federal elections. If the PCM candidates receive as much as 1.5 percent of the popular vote in the 1979 election, the party will not need to demonstrate a membership of 65,000 in order to obtain definitive registration for future elections. The party claimed on March 12 that its much publicized membership campaign had exceeded its goal of 100,000 members, making the PCM unquestionably the largest of the numerous parties to the left of the Popular Socialist Party (PPS). The population of Mexico is 65,833,000 (estimated 1978).

The PCM plans to contest the 1979 elections as part of a leftist front, although its efforts in this direction had achieved only modest success by this writing in early November. In December 1977 the PCM, the Mexican People's Party (PPM), and the Revolutionary Socialist Party (PSR) signed a "Declaration of Unity" pledging to work for "the broadest possible alliances with all the parties favoring democratic development, with the population groups interested in independence, social progress, and freedom." The "Declaration" also called for the formation of a mass working-class party capable of uniting broad sectors of the population: "The party needed by the working class must be guided by Marxist-Leninist theory as applied to national reality. It must combat everything that hampers its growth, as well as such harmful trends as sectarianism, opportunism, revisionism, and dogmatism. . . . It must have a democratic, anti-imperialist and socialist program envisaging democratic development for the good of the people, providing for the people's participation in the management of every sphere of economic, political and social activity, and showing the people the way to socialism." The three parties agreed to set up unity committees at all organizational levels, promote collective research as the basis for cadre training, cooperate at all propaganda levels as a first step toward the publication of a common newspaper, set up committees to study problems and circulate alliance positions, and demand the electoral participation of all political parties. (*WMR*, August.) Electoral plans of the PCM, PPM, and PSR moved ahead during the year (*Oposición*, 29 June—5 July), but other parties of the center and left declined to become involved in the alliance.

Party Internal Affairs. Since the PCM's Eighteenth Congress in mid-1977, its Central Committee has consisted of 65 persons and the Executive Committee of 11 persons. Composition of delegates at the Congress was said to represent the composition of the party as a whole—workers (35 percent), peasants (25 percent), and white-collar workers, students, intelligentsia (40 percent). Prominent party members during 1978 included Arnoldo Martínez Verdugo, secretary general, and Alejo Mendez Garcia, J. Encarnación Pérez, Gilberto Rincón Gallardo, Arturo Martínez Nateras, and Jesús Sosa Castro. The Fourth Plenum of the Central Committee convened on 7-8 February to examine the national situation on the eve of the PCM's electoral registration and to plan the party's policies for the period ahead. The PCM weekly, *Oposición* (18 February), immediately published a "Resolution" for party members and a "Manifesto" directed to all Mexicans who want a "democratic political and social system." The primary tasks of party members during the early months of the year were to increase party membership, so that the PCM would be a true "mass party," and to raise some ten million pesos for party activities. Later in the year the party directed its attentions primarily toward the political and organizational strengthening of the party and toward building leftist unity in the country in anticipation of the 1979 elections (*Oposición*, 11—17 May).

Domestic Attitudes and Activities. According to the PCM, the government of President López Portillo carries out policies in the interests of the big bourgeoisie rather than the masses of Mexican people. The present period is characterized by the increasing differentiation and regrouping of political and social forces in the state and society. This is manifested in the reactivation of political struggle across the country, the confrontation of differing analyses and suggested policies to resolve the grave economic, social, and political problems of the nation, the growth of dissension and conflict within the government bloc, and the resurgence of labor activities and prospects. The aggravation of the national economic crisis has led to limited political reform, intended by the government to consolidate its position in troubled times by providing an escape valve for dissident groups. According to the PCM, all groups seeking democracy and socialism should welcome these reforms and use them to extend their own influence throughout the country. (*Oposición*, 18 February.) Secretary General Martínez Verdugo looks upon the elections as one form of struggle among many, one in which it should be possible to mobilize the masses in defense of their economic and political rights, strengthen their organization independently of the bourgeoisie and the state, and extend their education in the principles of socialism. At the same time he has warned that a failure to unite the left behind a common program could be detrimental to the cause of socialism since it would fracture the only potential strong opposition to the government party, the Institutional Revolutionary Party (PRI), pointing in particular to the negative attitudes of the Socialist Workers' Party (PST). (See *El Dia*, Mexico City, 11 May; *Oposición*, 11—17 May.) The PCM has been critical of "ultraleftists" generally, going so far as to suggest that the Communists must infiltrate such groups as part of their effort to eliminate divisive groups on the left (*Oposición*, 21 January), though it has also denounced government repression of suspected and former guerrillas and the assassinations carried out by the "White Brigade" antiguerrilla group. Acting upon its calls for broad unity of the left, PCM members have held discussions with receptive Christians, participated in demonstrations (at times side-by-side with the PST), and held its second "Festival," in mid-May, a large meeting attended by sympathetic Mexicans as well as newsmen and delegations from fifteen foreign countries, including Cuba, the Soviet Union, Vietnam, and the United States.

International Views and Positions. Martínez Verdugo has described the international independence of the PCM as similar to that of the Eurocommunists (*NYT*, 27 December 1977; *El Dia*, 11 May 1978), a position highlighted by the highly publicized visit of French Communist Party leader Georges Marchais to Mexico City in May. While maintaining ties with the Communist Party of the Soviet Union, the PCM was critical of the severity of Soviet sentences against dissidents during the year. The party has been strongly critical of the People's Republic of China on a number of issues and has supported Vietnam in that country's conflict with Cambodia. In October the PCM called for the expulsion from Mexico of a U.S. diplomat alleged to be the highest ranking CIA official in Latin America.

Publications. The primary PCM organ is *Oposición*, a weekly newspaper which received a new format and circulation push at mid-year.

Guerrillas and Terrorists. Again in 1978, most guerrilla and terrorist activity in Mexico was associated with the 23rd September Communist League (Liga Comunista 23 de Septiembre). Though it has been blamed for many bombings, kidnappings, and assassinations in recent years, the League—which took its name from the date of an attack on an army garrison in Chihuahua in 1965—remains a shadowy entity. Spreading from its original base in Madera, Chihuahua, it now operates off-and-on in a half-dozen states despite periodic police reports that it has been destroyed. It is often seen as a loosely bound collection of militant revolutionaries; it is sometimes taken to be little more than the name used by isolated bandits and terrorists who want publicity and a cloak of revolutionary legitimacy; it has occasionally been branded a Mexican police or U.S. CIA front, used as a provocateur to discredit the Mexican Left. Whatever its true identity, its name was linked with a number of actions in 1978, among them: the shoot-out and capture of League leader Mario Cartagena López (alias "El Guaymas") in April; a shoot-out with police in Monterrey in May; the firebombing of two large stores in Mexico City in May; the bungled kidnapping and death of the son of the Mexican ambassador to the United States in August; and the kidnapping of a wealthy heiress in October-November. According to some reports, the League merged early in the year with the Union of the People (Unión del Pueblo; UP) in Guadalajara. The UP attacked banks and operated on university campuses. Guerrillas, former guerrillas, terrorists, and others, were hard-hit by Mexican police forces and by the right-wing "White Brigades" counterterrorists.

Hoover Institution   William E. Ratliff
Stanford University

Nicaragua

The Marxist and radical leftist parties in Nicaragua gained strength in 1978 due to escalating opposition to the 41-year-old Somoza family dynasty. That opposition formed a Broad Opposition Front (Frente Amplio Opositor; FAO) in July, and at various times during the year the FAO either included leftist elements within its ranks or carried on extensive liaison with them.

The biggest gainer was the Sandinist Liberation Front (Frente Sandinista de Liberación Nacional; FSLN), a guerrilla organization whose leadership is decidedly Castroite, but whose rank-and-file membership includes individuals from all spectrums of political life in Nicaragua and is largely youth oriented. Founded in 1961, its membership stood at little more than 500 armed members at the start of 1978, but by the end of the year this total had swelled to perhaps 5,000. The Sandinist leadership carried on an extensive recruitment campaign in 1978.

The other two Marxist political parties that gained most in numerical strength and political clout through association with opposition groups were the socialist and communist parties.

The Socialist Party of Nicaragua (Partido Socialista Nicaraguense; PSN), is a pro-Soviet group founded in 1937. It was declared illegal a year later and has been a clandestine organization ever since. Its membership is estimated at 250, some of whom are linked with the Sandinist guerrillas. The Communist Party of Nicaragua (Partido Comunista Nicaraguense; PCN), is an anti-Soviet group formed in 1967 when an internal struggle in the PSN resulted in the expulsion of six party leaders. These six established the PCN, but have had limited success in attracting PSN members to their cause. The PCN's present strength is estimated at less than 50. The population of Nicaragua is 2,395,000.

The FSLN. Founded in 1961 by Carlos Fonseca Amador, the Sandinist National Liberation Front has consistently maintained the necessity of direct action against the Somoza government. During the 1970s, until early 1978, there was a split within Sandinist ranks between those favoring a more protracted struggle and those favoring random and immediate violence to achieve the downfall of General Anastasio Somoza Debayle. This latter group generally was the dominant wing of the FSLN, and its preeminent role was assured during 1978 when the Sandinists were hailed by many other Somoza opponents for their direct action against the general, particularly during September's bloody civil strife which engulfed much of the country and particularly the main cities.

The FSLN has long benefited from training and assistance from Cuba, and some of the group's leaders have spent time in Cuba. In addition, FSLN members have frequently used sanctuaries in Costa Rica and Honduras. During 1978, numerous border skirmishes, particularly along the San Juan River in southern Nicaragua near the Costa Rican border, resulted in the flight of FSLN members into Costa Rica. A number of the guerrillas were reported to be Costa Ricans and not Nicaraguans. This relationship nettled the Somoza government and it repeatedly accused Costa Rica of providing a haven for the guerrillas; Costa Rica in turn charged Nicaragua with violations of its border when Nicaraguan National Guardsmen allegedly crossed over into Costa Rican territory. On 21 November the Costa Rican government of Rodrigo Carazo Odio broke relations with Nicaragua because of a border incursion in which a Costa Rican was killed.

Sandinist guerrilla and terrorist activities continued throughout the year; in the wake of the 10 January assassination of opposition newspaper editor and publisher Pedro Joaquín Chamorro Cardenal, the Sandinists raided police stations, shot at government officials, and kidnapped businessmen in a show of force. But soon afterwards, when more conservative businessmen staged a month-long strike against the Somoza government, the Sandinists stopped action against such people and began coordinating, on a loose basis, their activities with other anti-Somoza forces. During February and March, Sandinist guerrillas fought battles with National Guardsmen in the cities of Masaya and Granada. The battles resulted in the deaths of at least 31 guerrillas and 24 Guardsmen. Both towns were badly battered in the fighting.

In the effort to coordinate activities against the Somoza government, the Sandinist guerrillas joined the so-called Group of Twelve (Grupo de Doce) that sought during the first half of 1978 to rally all Somoza opponents under one banner. While supporting the group, the Sandinist forces denied the group's authority to lead all the opposition. This struggle between the Sandinist guerrillas, on the one hand, and other opponents was a key factor in the collapse of the Group of Twelve at midyear and its replacement by the FAO, which proved a more effective umbrella over the whole opposition. It treated the various groups within it as equals and encouraged each opposition element to carry out its own program, requesting merely that efforts be made to coordinate these programs to give them greater meaning.

The Sandinist guerrillas carried out a daring seizure of the Nicaraguan National Palace in August, holding nearly 500 people hostage, including 20 parliamentarians, the Minister of Gobernación, and a first cousin of General Somoza who is a key figure in the pro-Somoza Liberal Party. A "war communique" issued by the guerrillas demanded $10 million, the release of nearly 100 political prisoners, and airplanes to fly guerrillas and prisoners out of the country. Some 25 guerrillas took part in the palace seizure. The leader was Eden Pastora who took the name "Commander Zero," a title that other Sandinist guerrillas had used in the past; his second in command was Dora María Téllez Arguello, a woman in her early twenties, who impressed the hostages with her articulateness and her ability to handle her fellow guerrillas. The palace was held for 45 hours and the Somoza government eventually released 56 prisoners, but did not deliver the full $10 million. The guerrillas and prisoners went off to Panama.

The palace raid preceded by weeks a massive Sandinist attack on half a dozen key cities — including Leon, Nicaragua's second largest, Chinandega, Estelí, and Matagalpa. The Sandinists attracted to their ranks hundreds of young men and women, many in their teens, and fighting continued in several cities for three weeks. The National Guard eventually defeated the guerrillas, but not before hundreds had been killed and the center parts of the towns largely destroyed. An estimated 5,000 persons were killed in the fighting, with perhaps as many as 1,000 actual guerrillas included in this number.

As the year ended, efforts by the United States, the Dominican Republic, and Guatemala to mediate the dispute between General Somoza and his opponents continued, but the Sandinist guerrillas threatened to resume fighting and a number of minor skirmishes took place along the Costa Rican frontier and in the countryside in general. Elements from the FSLN appeared to be grouped near the frontier and they were reportedly training for future fighting. The FSLN also received assistance, according to reports, from Costa Rica, Venezuela, Panama, and other sources, as well as Cuba. Arms used by the Sandinists apparently came from half a dozen countries, including the United States, but their method of arrival was unclear.

The PSN. The PSN had limited impact on the political situation in Nicaragua. Its small membership, together with the more attractive nature of Sandinist activities, led the PSN to merely support the FSLN activities with propaganda leaflets, clandestine radio broadcasts, and occasional financial assistance. Captured documents indicated that this financial aid was limited to small sums.

At the end of 1977, the PSN issued a statement supporting formation of a government of national unity "in which all political forces would participate, including the Sandinist National Liberation Front." This approach was followed in 1978 with at least two separate calls for formation of such a government to replace that of General Somoza. Luis Sanchez, the secretary general of the party, said in January: "we must stress the need for such a national unity government to replace the fascistic legions that now occupy the government of our homeland."

Publications. FSLN and PSN publications were limited mainly to circulars, handbills, and the like.

The Christian Science Monitor   James Nelson Goodsell
Boston, Massachusetts

Panama

The Communist Party of Panama (Partido Comunista de Panamá) was founded in 1930, but dissolved in 1943 in favor of the People's Party of Panama (Partido del Pueblo de Panamá; PPP). Since political activity in Panama has largely concentrated on the Panama Canal issue and the PPP generally supports the government of General Omar Torrijos Herrera, the communist apparatus enjoyed some freedom of action in 1978 despite the fact that it has been illegal since 1953. Since 1975, leftist political opposition to General Torrijos has been evident on a limited scale and the PPP has on occasion taken a slightly different tack than that of General Torrijos.

The PPP's membership is difficult to ascertain, but is generally put at between 450 and 600. The population of Panama is 1,850,000.

Other leftist groups in Panama include the Revolutionary Unity Movement (Movimiento de Unidad Revolucionario; MUR), the National Action Vanguard (Vanguardia de Acción Nacional; VAN), the Panamanian Revolutionary Union (Unión Revolucionaria Panameña; URP), and the National Liberation Movement of 29 November (Movimiento de Liberación Nacional de 29 de Noviembre; MLN-29-11). These groups have been largely inactive in recent years and showed little evidence of any change in 1978. Many of their members are either in prison or in exile. In 1976, the Revolutionary Socialist League (Liga Socialista Revolucionaria; LSR) emerged, replacing the Revolutionary Socialist Faction (Facción Socialista Revolucionaria; FSR). It issued a manifesto in late 1978 denouncing "foreign intermediaries" in Panama, but did not elucidate on the subject. Its membership is believed to be about 25.

The PPP. Rubén Darío Sousa is secretary of the PPP, a post he has held since 1951. In addition to its own activities, which include publication of the monthly newspaper *Unidad*, the PPP works through trade union and student groups. Its labor affiliate, the Trade Union Federation of Workers of the Republic of Panama (Federación Sindical de Trabajadores de la República de Panamá; FST), was disbanded by the Torrijos government in 1968 along with other labor organizations. But it has managed to keep some of its cadres together and occasional rumblings of discontent with the hiatus in labor activities were heard from the PPP in 1978. One document, issued apparently by a fringe element within the disbanded FST, called on General Torrijos to "restore trade union democracy." In the education sphere, the PPP worked through the Federation of Students of Panama (Federación de Estudiantes de Panamá; FEP), which is active on the campus of the University of Panama. Numerous FEP leaders are either members of the PPP or close to PPP leadership.

Much of PPP activity for 1978 was concentrated on the Panama Canal issue. It supported conclusion of the new treaty in 1977 and approved the Panamanian public's ratification of the document in late 1977. But in February 1978 the party's secretary general, Darío Souza, claimed that signing and ratifying the document is only the first step in gaining control of the waterway. "The struggle for complete liberation will continue even after the Canal Zone is abolished," he wrote in the *World Marxist Review*. In Moscow, Miguel Porcell Pana, a member of the PPP's politburo, echoed this theme in a speech saying that "we have only begun to cross the bridge to independence and freedom from Yankee domination."

This line was the main thrust of PPP propaganda during the year. In working with the FEP, the PPP leadership encouraged students to demand greater speed in getting control of the canal and in wall posters appearing all over Panama City in April, the PPP called on Panamanians "to resist continued Yankee aggression." It appeared that the party was determined to keep the heat on the issue, even while the U.S. Senate was in the midst of ratifying the two treaties.

The PPP's monthly newspaper *Unidad* devoted considerable attention to this issue, but also focused on the Sandinist guerrilla activities in Nicaragua and spoke glowingly of the Sandinist effort to topple the 41-year-old Somoza family dynasty in that country. The newspaper was particularly laudatory of the Sandinist guerrillas who held the National Palace in Managua, the Nicaraguan capital, for 45 hours in August and then went into exile in Panama along with 56 political prisoners who were released as part of the ransom for those held hostage by the guerrillas in the palace. "They proved their mettle," the paper said, "and spotlighted the nefarious ways of the Somoza government and its corrupt allies in the United States who have worked with the Somoza clique to keep it in power against the legitimate wishes of the Nicaraguan people." This fraternal solidarity was a continuing keynote of PPP propaganda during the year.

The Christian Science Monitor   James Nelson Goodsell
Boston, Massachusetts

Paraguay

The Paraguayan Communist Party (Partido Comunista Paraguayo; PCP) was founded in 1928 but did not hold its First Congress and adopt a party platform until 1941. The party has been illegal throughout its existence except for a period between August 1946 and January 1947. Onetime Secretary General Oscar Creydt formed a rival PCP in 1965, after being ousted from the main body of the party, and has maintained an essentially pro-Chinese stance since that time.

The membership of the Paraguayan communist movement, including factions and sympathizers, has been estimated at approximately 3,500. Many are exiles in various Latin American and European countries. The population of Paraguay was estimated in 1978 at 3,095,000.

Organization and Domestic Positions. The PCP held a plenary meeting of its Central Committee in June at an undisclosed location. The session elected Antonio Maidana as first secretary and Obdulio Barthe as president. Party leaders emphasized that they considered the session a demonstration of the increasing strength of the PCP in the face of continued oppression by the Paraguayan government. The PCP sees its tasks as developing the ideological and political enlightenment of the Paraguayan people. In order to accomplish this, the party is working to strengthen its ties with the working class, especially at large-scale enterprises, and claims to be both setting up action committees for higher wages and the satisfaction of other demands and striving to make the trade unions more class-oriented organizations by exposing government and police agents among trade unionists and explaining why the working-class movement must be united. (*Granma*, Havana, English ed., 16 July; *WMR*, June.)

According to the documents of the June plenum, the Stroessner regime is an obedient tool in the hands of multinational companies, foreign monopolies, and the local oligarchy (*Pravda*, 26 June). The Stroessner government must be defeated and replaced by a provisional government capable of leading the country along the path of freedom, democracy, and social progress (Havana International Service, 18 July). This is to be accomplished through the formation of a broad national front, which Maidana and Central Committee member Alfredo Alcorta write is presently the vital task of the Paraguayan Communists. They claim that the isolation of the Stroessner government has been growing and that "the most diverse forces have come out unanimously against the dictatorship." Stroessner's government enjoys extensive support only from the financial, political, and military sectors of U.S. imperialism and Brazilian ruling circles, backed up by the powerful *latifundistas* and bourgeois oligarchy at home. These reactionaries aside, "there is, on the whole, complete identity of the economic and democratic demands put forward by the communists, the Radical Liberals, the Febreristas, the Christian Democrats, MOPOCO, the Catholic Church, the students, a sizable section of the liberal professions, industrialists, merchants, and landowners and, of course, the working class and the toiling peasantry, whose alliance is designed to lay the foundation for a broad national anti-dictatorial coalition." The party calls for the formulation of a political and economic platform that will even take into account the interests of sizable sections of the national bourgeoisie and even some groups of landowners who are discontented with the dictatorship. Immediate demands include democratic liberties for all people's parties and organizations, without restrictions or exceptions; release of all political prisoners; an end to reprisals against and tortures and assassination of patriots; lifting of the state of siege; annulment of antidemocratic laws; raising of wages; an end to the layoffs of workers and urgent measures against the high cost of living and the shortage of goods; full reestablishment of the free activity of the trade unions; land and low-cost credits for the poor and middle peasants, fair prices and secure marketing for their produce; abolition and reduction of the burdensome taxes on industrialists, merchants, petty producers and the liberal professions; and renegotiation of the Itaipu Treaty. (*WMR*, June.)

International Positions and Activities. The June plenum emphasized that the chief force of our age is the community of socialist states, whose vanguard is the Soviet Union, the loyal and consistent friend of peoples struggling against imperialism and fascism, and it resolutely condemned the anti-Soviet and anticommunist policies of the present Chinese leadership in Peking (*Pravda*, 26 June). An article by Maidana, Alcorta, and Central Committee member Julio Rojas (*Pravda*, 7 April) specifically condemned the PRC for its policies toward Chile, Angola, Ethiopia, and the neutron bomb. Maidana, Alcorta, and Rojas spent most of 1978 residing or traveling in the Soviet Union, the German Democratic Republic, Czechoslovakia, Cuba, and other pro-Soviet communist countries. The GDR openly acknowledges its aid to the publication program of the PCP (Allgemeiner Deutscher Nachrichtendienst, East Berlin, 16 June).

PCP-Maoists. The pro-Chinese faction of the PCP, headed by Oscar Creydt, maintained its alignment with Peking. In a letter to Chinese leader Hua Kuo-feng, Creydt said the PCP Political Commission was "fundamentally in agreement with the ideas you have formulated in the principal report approved at the Eleventh Congress." The letter said the PCP is most satisfied with the fact that Chairman Hua has energetically reaffirmed the proletarian revolutionary line of Mao Tse-tung and demonstrated that "Russian revisionist imperialism is the greatest danger in the present world." (New China News Agency, 23 March.)

Hoover Institution   Lynn Ratliff
Stanford, University

Peru

The Peruvian Communist Party (Partido Comunista Peruano; PCP) took its present name in 1930 as a result of orders from the Communist International. Since 1964 the movement has been divided into a pro-Soviet party and several pro-Chinese splinter groups, some of which use the PCP name.

There also exist in Peru various Marxist-Leninist and Trotskyite parties and coalitions to the left of the PCP. These include the Castro-oriented Movement of the Revolutionary Left (MIR); the Revolutionary Vanguard (VR); the Popular Democratic Union (UDP), an eighteen-group coalition that includes the majority of the miners' federation leadership, some Trotskyites, and Maoists; and the Workers, Peasants, Students, and Popular Front (FOCEP), a thirteen-group coalition that comprises various Trotskyite organizations, including the Socialist Workers' Party (PST), the Front of the Revolutionary Left (FIR), and the Revolutionary Marxist Workers' Party (POMR).

U.S. intelligence estimates place the current hard-core membership of the pro-Soviet PCP at 2,000 and that of the pro-Chinese PCP groups at 1,200. Other Marxist-Leninist and Trotskyist groups are smaller, with the POMR, VR, and FIR believed to have the largest memberships. The population of Peru is about 16,818,000.

Elections were held in Peru on 18 June for the first time since the military assumed power in October 1968. At stake were 100 seats for the Constituent Assembly that will draft a new constitution in preparation for general elections and the transfer of power to civilians in 1980. An electoral law published on 16 November 1977 lowered the voting age from 21 to 18, but illiterates—estimated to total some 30 percent of the population—continue to be barred from voting. For the first time in its history, the PCP was permitted to participate openly in an election. Although eleven other parties (or party coalitions) put up slates of candidates, the election came down to a contest among the center-right Popular Christian Party of Luis Bedoya Reyes (PPC), the center-left APRA party of Víctor Raúl Haya de la Torre, and the six leftist and ultraleftist groups that qualified by submitting lists of at least 40,000 supporters and demonstrating the existence of a minimum of twelve departmental committees. The Popular Action Party headed by former president Fernando Belaúnde Terry decided against participating for tactical reasons, calling instead for general elections (*Washington Post*, 19 June). The National Electoral Tribunal published the official election results and the distribution of assembly seats on 15 July.

Constituent Assembly Elections

Party or Coalition	Votes	Percentage	Seats
APRA	1,241,174	35.3	37
PPC	835,294	23.8	25
FOCEP	433,413	12.3	12
PSR (Socialist Revolutionary Party)	232,520	6.6	6
PCP	207,612	5.9	6
UDP	160,741	4.6	4
FNTC (Peasants & Workers National Front)	135,552	3.9	4
PDC (Christian Democratic Party)	83,075	2.4	2
UNO (Odrista National Union)	74,137	2.1	2
MDP (Peruvian Democratic Movement)	68,619	1.9	2
ARS (Socialist Revolutionary Action)	20,164	0.6	—
MDRP (Peruvian Reformist Democratic Movement)	19,594	0.6	—
	3,511,895	100.0	100

The six leftist groups showed surprising strength in Lima and in Peru's mining and coastal cities and amassed almost 30 percent of the popular vote. According to a statement issued by the PCP's National Plenum on 26 July, the elections "demonstrated that the Peruvian Communist Party has grown considerably." Party spokesmen expressed the opinion that despite their various limitations and their lack of experience in electoral campaigns, the Communists worked well in the period preceding the election (Agence France Presse, Paris, 26 July). Viewed objectively, however, the elections represented a serious defeat for the PCP and the other parties, such as the PSR and the PDC, which supported the policies of former President Juan Velasco Alvarado.

The Pro-Soviet PCP: Leadership and Organization. The highest organ of the pro-Soviet PCP is officially the National Congress, which is supposed to meet every three years. Its Sixth Congress, the most recent, met in November 1973. The PCP is organized from cells upward through local and regional committees to its Central Committee. Regional committees exist in at least 22 cities. Lima has the largest number of local committees, concentrated in low-income neighborhoods and slum areas, which the government now refers to as "new towns." The PCP employs around 60 paid officials, including leadership and rank-and-file cadres. The party's expenditures include subsidies for the General Confederation of Workers of Peru (Confederación de Trabajadores del Perú; CGTP), the Peruvian Communist Youth (Juventud Comunista Peruana; JCP), and specific regional committees of the party. Jorge del Prado has served as general secretary of the party for eighteen years. Raúl Acosta Salas is under secretary. Jaime Figueroa is head of the party's National Propaganda Committee, and Mario Ugarte Hurtado serves as head of the Finance Committee. Other prominent members of the Central Committee are Isidro Gamarra, Guillermo Herrera, Eduardo Castillo Sánchez, Alejandro Olivera Vila, Luis Alberto Delgado, Juliano Sierra Corrales, Eteldrita Humala Aybar, Gustavo Espinoza, José Martínez, Vicente Ramírez, and José Reccio. According to del Prado, the oldest members in terms of active membership in the party besides himself are Raúl Acosta and Isidro Gamarra. The other members of the Political Committee and the Central Committee have been active for "only twenty years or less." Until the 1978 elections, the PCP's leaders had maintained that traditional elections were only "bourgeois practices." To understand better the bureaucratic nature of the PCP's leadership hierarchy, it is sufficient to note that the names on the party's list of candidates were ranked almost exclusively on the basis of seniority, a point clearly visible in the order of the six who were elected to the Constituent Assembly; del Prado, Gamarra, Acosta, Castillo, Olivera, and Delgado (*Expreso*, 26 March).

The PCP's youth group is relatively small and operates mainly at the university level. Jorge Tapia is the group's general secretary. In recent years the JCP has actively competed with Maoist and Trotskyite groups for control of the university student movement. According to del Prado, "the students have always been allies of the workers' movement, but in Latin America, Yankee imperialism has set in motion a strategy aimed at dividing the Left, and it has succeeded in separating the student movement from the anti-imperialist struggle" (*Oiga*, 10 June 1977). In January a faction of the JCP's national Executive Committee openly criticized the PCP's Central Committee for having supported the Velasco regime, even though this policy had been approved by the movement's highest leadership. Del Prado stated that a political center, which had been seized in mid-December by "infiltrated bourgeois elements," had just been recovered, while the JCP said the center had been taken from it by "revisionist elements." The JCP's Executive Committee further claimed that for some time "an internal struggle has been going on against reformist tendencies" within the party. It asserted that a group of reformists entrenched in the Political Committee, headed by Mario Ugarte and Gustavo Espinoza (the former general secretary of the CGTP), were directly responsible for initiating a "liquidation offensive" against progressive sectors within the JCP and the PCP itself (Agence France Presse, 4 January). On 7 January the PCP accused the "bourgeois press organs" of resorting to open slander in order to prevent the party from creating a united front. The party's statement dismissed as "absurd" the assertion that a split had occurred in the PCP's leadership or the CGTP (*Pravda*, 7 January). (Additional indications of a breach in party unity are discussed below.)

In October the JCP actively supported demonstrations against the government's 50 percent increase in transportation fares. Schools were closed in Lima on 24 October to prevent further clashes between police and students. The government charged that "interested groups" were attempting to involve the students in violent acts "with the object of using them for unspeakable political purposes" (Agence France Presse, 24 October).

A major source of the PCP's influence lies in its control over the CGTP. The CGTP, headed by PCP members Isidro Gamarra, president, and Eduardo Castillo Sánchez, secretary general, claims a membership of 700,000 workers.

On 11 February approximately 400 CGTP delegates voted to hold a nationwide strike on 27–28 February to demand reinstatement of some 3,000 trade union members, wage increases, and a price freeze on staples. The meeting also reaffirmed confidence in Gamarra and Castillo, whose order to call off a strike on 23 January was sharply criticized by ultraleftist sectors (ibid., 11 February). Three other labor centrals rejected the strike, stating that the CGTP measure was of "a political nature to undermine the stability of the regime" (*El Comercio*, 27 February). Government sources stated that only 10 percent of workers participated in the work stoppage, while a CGTP communiqué claimed that "a campaign of misinformation and lies unleashed by the media did not detract from the effectiveness of the strike" (*Unidad*, 2 March). The interior minister disclosed that 185 persons, including 25 labor leaders, were arrested in Lima alone on the first day of the strike, while prostrike spokesmen claimed that workers in Cuzco, Trujillo, Arrequipa, and Chimbote had also joined the protest. On 13 April police prevented a "unity march" called by the CGTP to demand full labor amnesty, job stability, and salary increases. The "march" was reduced to proclamations over loudspeakers from inside the CGTP's headquarters in Lima (Agence France Presse, 14 April).

On 15 May the government adopted drastic anti-inflationary measures in an effort to meet conditions stipulated by the International Monetary Fund to enable Peru to renegotiate its foreign debt. The CGTP was among Peru's most important labor unions to call for a nationwide strike for 22–23 May to protest increases of 50 to 100 percent in the prices of bread, cooking oil, bus fares, gasoline, and other essential goods and services which had been subsidized to protect low-income consumers. Faced with increasing levels of rioting, President Morales yielded to military pressure and declared a state of emergency on 20 May. He announced that Peru faced "an organized subversive movement" and postponed for two weeks the Constituent Assembly elections scheduled for 4 June (*El Comercio*, 21 May). According to official figures, 21 persons died as a result of street violence throughout the country. Political circles in Lima termed the strike a complete success. The capital, a city of five million inhabitants, was virtually paralyzed, along with most of the major cities in the interior. Taking advantage of the strike's apparent success, left-wing parties demanded the repeal of the emergency measures and urged that the government's economic and social policies be substantially modified. As activities returned to normal, the government announced on 25 May that it had deported thirteen people to Argentina, including nine candidates for the Constituent Assembly, among them retired General Leonidas Rodríguez, president of the Socialist Revolutionary Party (PSR), and Hugo Blanco, ex-guerrilla, member of the Fourth International, and an outspoken leader of FOCEP. They were subsequently permitted to return to Peru in July following their elections to the Assembly.

Factionalism based on ideological differences clearly exists within Peru's trade union movement. For example, the leadership of the CGTP failed to come out clearly in support of a strike by the United Federation of Educational Workers of Peru (SUTEP) in its fight for recognition by the government. The SUTEP is under Maoist leadership and does not belong to the CGTP. At a rally on 19 July the president of SUTEP's Lima unit called on the CGTP to set the date for a national general strike in support of the teachers' demands. CGTP spokesmen were careful to say nothing concrete as to when such a work stoppage might be called (*Intercontinental Press*: IP, 31 July). The SUTEP's 80-day strike ended on 27 July when the government granted most of the teachers' demands for union recognition, a wage increase, and better working conditions (*El Comercio*, 28 July). In August the CGTP leadership voted not to support the nationwide strike by the National Federation of Miners and Metalworkers of Peru (FNTMNP) that closed down virtually all of the nation's mines between 4 August and 8 September. According to FNTMNP President Víctor Cuadros, the CGTP's leaders claimed that calling a general strike to back up the miners' demands "could have caused the overthrow of the government and its replacement by a Chile-type fascist regime." The CGTP even refused to allow Cuadros to speak at its rally in Lima on 2 September (*Marka*, 14 September).

During the first part of 1978 the PCP attempted to exert some influence in the peasant sector through its participation in the National Agrarian Confederation (CNA). At the beginning of the year the CNA claimed to represent 3.5 million peasants, with twenty departmental agrarian federations, 170 agrarian leagues, and more than 3,800 rank-and-file organizations. At the end of its Sixth General Assembly held in December 1977, the CNA announced its decision to participate in the June elections. The National Electoral Tribunal subsequently refused to permit the CNA's registration on the grounds that it was a union and not, strictly speaking, a political organization similar to a party (*El Comercio*, 26 January). On 30 May the government decided to disband the CNA for "neglecting the legitimate interests of the Peruvian peasants and engaging in purely political activities." The dissolution of the CNA was the focal point of a concerted military and propaganda campaign against "subversion" following the general strike of 23–24 May. The CNA, established in 1974, was an uncomfortable remnant of the Velasco era, which the government had been anxious to deal with for months. Like SINAMOS before it, it has now been abolished. The government's decision received the support of various agrarian cooperatives and organizations, which claimed that the CNA had contributed to disunity among peasants by lapsing into political factionalism (*El Correo*, 3 June).

The PCP's principal opposition in the peasant sector comes from several Chinese-oriented parties belonging to the Confederation of Peruvian Peasants (CCP). According to Raúl Acosta Salas, one faction of the CCP is under the direction of the "Bandera Roja" and the other follows the dictates of the Revolutionary Vanguard. The latter managed to achieve majority strength within the CCP several years ago but has since been weakened by internal divisions.

Party Internal Affairs. The PCP has been forced to redefine its domestic position by the gradual erosion of the image of revolutionary development in Peru and the impending return to civilian government in 1980. The PCP gave virtually uncritical support to the government and the armed forces during the years of Velasco's rule (1968–1975). When General Morales Bermúdez replaced Velasco in August 1975, the PCP hailed the move as a "deepening of the revolution." As the Morales government became more openly conservative, the PCP followed a vacillating policy, on some occasions giving support to workers' and peasants' struggles—as in the July 1977 national strike—and at other times seeking a "dialogue" with the military to create and establish a more orthodox political role for the party in anticipation of the June elections (see *YICA, 1978*, pp. 407–8). The result has been rather widespread disillusionment with both the party's leadership and its policies. This is reflected not only in the growing influence of currents to the left of the PCP, as indicated by the relatively strong showing of the FOCEP, the PSR, and the UDP in the Assembly elections, but also in the evidence of existing differences within the party itself.

At the beginning of the year a Coordinating Committee of the Regions and the Youth (CCRJ) publicly challenged the PCP's Political Committee for control of the party. It claimed to represent 90 percent of the party's regional organizations and 95 percent of the youth, with particularly strong support in the CGTP. The CCRJ charged the party's leadership with adopting a "reformist, bourgeois-liquidationist policy," placing "excessive confidence in the military left," and bureaucratically violating the party's statutes. Jorge del Prado and his faction of the Political Committee responded by calling the oppositionists "Trotskyite" and accusing them of links with the police. In turn, CCRJ leaders affirmed their loyalty to "the world communist movement and its vanguard, the Communist Party of the Soviet Union," and criticized the Political Committee for espousing "typically Eurocommunist positions" (IP, 13 March).

One of the reasons for the split in the PCP and the CGTP can be attributed to the latter's reluctance to struggle more vigorously for the reinstatement of the workers fired after the general strike in July 1977. Many of those dismissed belong to the new generation of militant working-class leaders, including some members of the Communist party. When the PCP and the CGTP took no real initiative, and even backed out of actions that had already been decided on (e.g., the 23–24 January strike), opposition developed inside the party and the CGTP. Gradually the oppositionists broke from the PCP and have been expelled from both the party and the CGTP. It is difficult to ascertain precisely how much damage the PCP incurred as a result of the split. However, internal disunity probably contributed to the breakdown of negotiations between the PCP and the UDP on the formation of a broad-based popular front, damaged the PCP's prestige in general, and enhanced the appeal of other left-wing groups, such as the PSR and especially FOCEP. The *Mayoría* faction of the PCP ran in the June elections in a bloc with the UDP. It continues to attack the "old-line Stalinist leadership" of the party through its newspaper, *Mayoría*, from which it takes its name. Although the size of the *Mayoría* faction's membership is unknown at this time, it purports to hold the allegiance of most of the major trade union leaders within the CGTP (ibid., 24 July), although more objective sources believe that the PCP continues to exercise decisive influence in the trade union movement.

Domestic Attitudes and Activities. In Jorge del Prado's assessment of the situation in Peru at the end of 1977, he cited the main danger as "the present government's attempt to solve economic problems by encouraging private national and foreign investment, with the financial help of organizations controlled by U.S. imperialism" (*WMR*, December 1977). In January the Central Committee's Political Commission called for the creation of a broad anti-imperialist, antioligarchic front to participate in the Constituent Assembly and defend the main achievements of the revolution against the "regressive policy" of reactionary circles (*Unidad*, 5 January). During a television interview on 1 February, del Prado commented on the future of the church and the armed forces, stressing that "we have to respect the people's religious feelings and to support the armed forces so long as they defend the interests of the nation and the people." He later spoke in favor of state enterprises, calling them the most efficient means of national advancement. He also remarked that workers' participation in the leadership of the enterprises is indispensable and that "imperialist and private firms should be replaced with state firms that conform to the national interest" (*El Comercio*, 2 February).

On 15 February the PCP released a communiqué calling for the unity of popular forces in order to prevent the danger that the Constituent Assembly would be "artificially dominated by reactionary and proimperialist parties." The party demanded "political and labor amnesty, the opening of the information media to popular parties, the right of illiterates to vote, and the direct representation of peasant and labor organizations in the assembly" (*Unidad*, 16 February).

The PCP justified its participation in the elections as consistent with its policy of "critical support," adding that it was necessary "to prevent the rightist sectors from introducing antidemocratic and antipopular measures in the new constitution." Party spokesmen also stated that direct participation in the assembly would be accompanied by the PCP's continued involvement in "the general struggle of the masses, public demonstrations, and the ideological struggle" (ibid., 30 March). On 23 June del Prado described as a "shameless intervention" a declaration made by the U.S. Department of State in connection with the elections and the country's political future. Del Prado charged that under the auspices of the State Department, negotiations that would allow the continuation in Peru of the

IMF's economic policy were already underway between APRA and the PPC. He asserted that "a profascist threat looms over Peru" because of APRA's "proimperialist past" and the PPC's identification with Chile's economic policy (Agence France Presse, 23 June).

In an editorial commentary on the election results, del Prado stated that despite the "scandalous restrictions and intimidating measures implemented against the Left before, during, and after the elections," the PCP had emerged as "an indisputable force and the backbone of the Left." He added that the extreme Left—"simply rebellious groups"—enjoyed a degree of electoral support "to which it is not entitled" (*Unidad*, 29 June). In a statement issued by the National Plenum on 26 July, the party pledged to direct its political struggle "against the oligarchy, the imperialists, and their allies" both within and outside the Constituent Assembly (ibid.). In August various left-wing deputies in the Assembly, including del Prado, Antonio Meza Cuadra (PSR), and Genaro Ledesma (FOCEP), agreed on the need for unity in order to give the new constitution a popular character. Del Prado stated that the PCP favors an alliance of all parties and fronts that represent the masses, both for work within the Assembly and action outside of it. He proposed the formation of a popular, anti-imperialist and anti-oligarchic coalition consisting of the Communist, Socialist Revolutionary, and Christian Democratic parties, together with the FOCEP and UDP. He added that the new constitution should incorporate structural changes carried out during the Velasco regime, including the agrarian and private enterprise reforms and the expansion of state-controlled enterprises (*Granma*, Havana, English edition, 20 August). At a meeting of the Political Commission on 28 August, the party expressed the goal of coordinating the efforts of its members and those of other leftist groups in promoting action in the Constituent Assembly (*El Comercio*, 29 August). The likelihood of the PCP's achieving such a goal appears remote. The role of the various left-wing groups in the Assembly is highly unpredictable—especially that of the FOCEP, which is more a collection of small and belligerent Trotskyite factions than a cohesive political organization. The charismatic personalities of such leaders as Hugo Blanco, Genaro Ledesma, and Ricardo Napuri were FOCEP's greatest asset in the June elections, but the bases of their support are all different and have already led to friction (see below). Party officials also discussed the PCP's participation in future elections and suggested that the PCP intends to present its own candidates in the forthcoming municipal elections (ibid.).

International Views and Positions. The PCP continues to follow the Soviet line closely in its international positions. In response to conservative criticism that the PCP is simply a tool of international communism, del Prado has stated that "the PCP is in fact playing the role of the vanguard of the Peruvian working class and is a recognized detachment in the struggle against imperialism and the oligarchy and for socialism on Peruvian soil." In this respect, the party attaches great importance to the expansion of trade, as well as scientific and technological cooperation between Peru and the socialist countries (*WMR*, December 1977).

The PCP is opposed to seeking credits from international monetary organizations, increasing private investment, and assisting capitalist enterprises at what it considers to be the detriment of the state and at the cost of greater exploitation of the working people. In discussing Peru's foreign debt, del Prado stated on 13 January: "We should not exclusively seek financing from imperialism's financial institutions, nor should we subject ourselves to the conditions imposed by the International Monetary Fund" (*El Comercio*, 14 January).

In March the PCP circulated a statement in Lima analyzing the foreign policy of the People's Republic of China. The document contends that the present Peking leadership has "fully renounced the international Communist and working class movement, aligns ever more closely with the most reactionary imperialist forces, and continues to follow this shameful road of betrayal." The statement condemns "the subversive activities of the Maoists in Asian, African and Latin American countries."

The PCP further claims that the Maoists' operations in the foreign policy field are at variance with Peking's "demagogic" assertion that it "supports the peoples fighting for their national and social liberation." (*IB*, no. 10.)

The PCP maintained a variety of international contacts in 1978. In April a delegation of the CGTP attended the Ninth Congress of the World Federation of Trade Unions in Prague. In July the JCP sent a delegation to the World Festival of Youth and Students in Cuba. On 3 October a delegation from the Cuban Communist Party arrived in Lima to participate in activities commemorating the fiftieth anniversary of the PCP.

Publications. The PCP weekly organ is *Unidad*, which claims a circulation of more than 10,000.

Other Parties. From their inception in the 1960s, the pro-Chinese groups have experienced continuous internal dissension and splits. As many as twenty Marxist political organizations have been identified in the past, many of which, strictly speaking, no longer exist.

In recent years there have been at least three major factions of the pro-Chinese PCP. The one which enjoys more or less official recognition from the Chinese Communist Party is known as the Peruvian Communist Party, Marxist-Leninist (PCC-ML), headed by Antonio Fernández Arce. Its members are affiliated with the Peru-China Cultural Institute. A second pro-Chinese faction is headed by Saturnino Paredes Macedo and, from its somewhat sporadic periodical, *Bandera Roja*, is generally known as the PCP-Bandera Roja. The Red Fatherland faction, so-called because of its periodical, *Patria Roja*, is believed to have the largest following of all pro-Chinese groups among students and labor. It reportedly exercises control over national labor organizations with memberships in excess of 100,000. The Bandera Roja faction, on the other hand, heads only local organizations with fewer than 100,000 affiliates. The Patria Roja also controls one of the labor "unification organizations" that has engaged in fierce competition with a similar unifying organization controlled by the CGTP. The pro-Chinese groups have had relatively little success in acquiring influence within the peasant movement, although the Confederation of Peruvian Peasants (CCP) has a pro-Chinese orientation.

In addition to the pro-Chinese groups, there are numerous Marxist-Leninist parties and movements of Castroite and Trotskyite orientation. Although these groups are individually small compared with their size in the early 1960s, most of them joined either the FOCEP or the UDP coalition for electoral purposes. The UDP is a political front that claims to follow democratic centralism. Maoists exercise a majority influence through the Revolutionary Vanguard (VR), sections of the Revolutionary Communist Party (PCR), and the Movement of the Revolutionary Left (MIR). There are also two Trotskyite groups in the UDP—the FIR-Fourth International and the FIR-Combate. The UDP's governmental slogan is a "revolutionary people's government," a version of the Maoist slogan of a "bloc of four classes," i.e., workers, peasants, the middle class, and the national bourgeoisie (*IP*, 24 July). While most of these groups have been accustomed to operating underground in the past, the majority participated openly in one of the aforementioned electoral fronts. Their major points of agreement lie in their opposition to the military government and the pro-Soviet PCP.

The Socialist Revolutionary Party (PSR) was founded in November 1976 by leftist officers forced to retire following Velasco's removal. It considers itself to be fundamentally an autonomous, national movement not dependent "on foreign political organizations" (*Caretas*, 20 April). The PSR suffered a serious split in July with the expulsion of a group of prominent party militants led by Antonio Aragón, a former activist in one of the shantytowns outside Lima. The split came as no surprise to local observers, who had marveled that the PSR's ill-assorted coalition had held together as long as it did (*Latin America Political Report*, 14 July). On 17 July the FOCEP and UDP confirmed that they had severed political ties with the PSR and would henceforth recognize only the dissident faction led by Aragón.

The PSR held its First Congress in September, at which time the delegates elected General Leonidas Rodríguez as party chairman and Antonio Meza Cuadra as general secretary. The congress unanimously passed a motion expressing full solidarity with Cuba and identifying U.S. imperialism as the main enemy of the people. The resolution called on all peoples of the continent "to unite in the struggle to break imperialist domination" (*Granma*, 8 October). In October the PSR officially split into two factions. The dissident group, headed by Jorge Castro, rejected the "reformist" line of General Rodríguez and proclaimed itself to be Marxist-Leninist. As national coordinator of the "Popular PSR," Castro claimed the support of 21 of the 23 departmental committees and said that the three "Popular PRS" members in the Constituent Assembly would align themselves with the Trotskyite front and the Maoist UDP, with which they profess to have more political affinity. Castro's declarations came at the conclusion of his faction's First National Congress on 1 October (EFE, Madrid, 3 October).

Perhaps the greatest surprise in the outcome of the June elections was the strong showing of the FOCEP coalition, whose main leaders are Hugo Blanco and Genaro Ledesma. Although loosely organized in comparison with the PCP, the FOCEP successfully mobilized thousands of activists. Apart from Blanco's charismatic leadership, it was the FOCEP more than the PCP that best reflected the combativeness of the workers expressed in the 22−23 May general strike. The FOCEP also had the clearest policy of independence from the military government. As the coalition claimed in the PST's newspaper on 26 June: "It was the FOCEP that most clearly put forward a socialist solution to the crisis which the country is going through" (*Palabra Socialista*, 26 June). In an evaluation of the election results, Blanco concluded that the basis had been laid for creating a large working-class and socialist party as an alternative political expression for the more than one million voters who voted for leftist parties in June. On 8 October the Commission for Trotskyite Unification, which includes the majority of the Trotskyite groups in Peru, founded a united section of the Fourth International. On 11 October Blanco announced the merger of three Trotskyite groups to form the Workers' Revolutionary Party (PRT), a new front comprised of the FIR, the Revolutionary Left Front−Fourth International, and the Socialist Workers' Party (PST). Blanco explained that he had created the new movement "to fight against capitalism and imperialism and to implement socialism in Peru" (Agence France Press, 12 October).

Washington College   Daniel L. Premo

Puerto Rico

The Puerto Rican Communist Party (Partido Comunista Puertorriqueño; PCP) has long been closely associated with the Communist Party of the United States (CPUSA), and has shared its pro-Soviet views. The Armed Forces of Puerto Rican National Liberation (Fuerzas Armadas de Liberación Nacional Puertorriqueña; FALN) appears to have its origins in predecessor terrorist groups. The Puerto Rican Socialist Party (Partido Socialista Puertorriqueño; PSP), formerly the Pro-Independence Movement (Movimiento Pro-Independencia; MPI), maintains close ties with Cuba and appears to maintain an independent stance in the Sino-Soviet dispute. The International Workers League (Liga Internacionalista de los Trabajadores; LIT) is reported to be associated with the Fourth (Trotskyist) International. The Puerto Rican Socialist League (Liga Socialista Puertorriqueña; LSA) is reported to have ties with the Progressive Labor Party (PLP) of the United States, and, like the PLP, to have dropped its pro-Chinese platform in 1971. The Armed Commandos of Liberation (Comandos Armados de Liberación; CAL) were active during the late 1960s and early 1970s, and were allegedly involved in at least one incident during 1978.

Membership estimates include: PCP, 125; FALN, 12; PSP, several thousand. The PSP polled approximately eleven thousand votes in the island's 1976 gubernatorial elections. With the exception of the PSP, none of these groups has ever participated in a gubernatorial election, and, at least since 1948, none but the PSP has been represented in either house of the insular legislature.

The population of Puerto Rico has been estimated (1977) at 3,200,000.

The PCP: Organization. The Puerto Rican Communist Party was founded in 1934, dissolved in 1944, and refounded in 1946. Party institutions include the National Party Congress (the second Congress was held in December 1975), the Central Committee, the Politburo, and the General Secretariat. As was noted in last year's *Yearbook*, a Czech study has claimed that three-fourths of the party members are salaried peasants and workers and 40 percent are 30 years of age or older.

Domestic and International Views. The party asserts that "United States imperialism" has economically oppressed the Puerto Rican people and denied them their right to self-determination. It claims that Puerto Rico has been utilized by the United States as a base for hemispheric military aggression. The PCP seeks economic and political independence for Puerto Rico, and joined other independence and socialist groups in celebrating Lares Day, commemorating the 1868 independence rebellion.

The PCP has attacked "colonialism" and supported anti-imperialist movements around the world. In the past it has tended to support Moscow's foreign policy, and the various policies of Cuba.

Publications. The PCP publishes the newspapers *El Pueblo* and *El Proletario*.

The FALN. The Armed Forces of National Liberation is an underground revolutionary group advocating national independence for Puerto Rico. Little is known of its membership, organization, or ideology. As is detailed below, the FALN may have emerged from several earlier revolutionary groups. Its goals include independence for Puerto Rico and freedom for Puerto Rican nationalists imprisoned in the United States. It is alleged to have been implicated in 65 bombings by October 1977 (*Time*, 24 October 1977). Multinational corporations are its primary targets (*NYT*, 4 August 1977). FALN reportedly took credit for two bombings in New York City on 31 January. One device exploded outside a utility company office, and the other under a police automobile. (*NYT*, 31 January.) On 22 May, bombs exploded outside the Justice Department in Washington, D.C., in the New York metropolitan area, and at the Newark, LaGuardia, and Kennedy airports. A bomb threat was received in Chicago. In each instance the FALN reportedly claimed credit by phone (*NYT*, 23 May). On 12 July, an explosion occurred in a New York City apartment in which the police said the FALN was manufacturing bombs, an incident that may have been related to the detonation of devices in two New York City department stores on that same day (*NYT*, 13, 14, and 15 July). Investigations have taken place, and a Federal grand jury has held some persons for months for alleged lack of cooperation with its activities (see, for example, *NYT*, 25 January and 9 May).

The PSP. The Puerto Rican Socialist Party was founded in November 1971 at the Eighth Annual Assembly of the Pro-Independence Movement. It participated in the 1976 insular elections, and its gubernatorial candidate, Lic. Juan Marí Bras, received approximately eleven thousand votes.

Organization and Leadership. The PSP is guided by the Party Congress, the first of which was convened in 1971, and the second in 1975. Additional major organs include the Central Committee and Political Commission. The Cuban paper *Granma* reported on 27 February 1977 that PSP leaders included: Julio Vivres Vásquez (chairman), Marí Bras (general secretary), Carlos Gallisá (first deputy general secretary), Pedro Biagés (second deputy general secretary), and Lucia Romero (organizing secretary).

Domestic Attitudes and Activities. The PSP has traditionally maintained that the island is an oppressed colony of the United States, and has advocated economic and political independence, following the socialist path.

On 20 February the PSP organized a march and demonstration in the Puerto Rican capitol in support of striking electrical workers (*Granma*, English ed., 5 March).

Since 1972 the United Nation's Special Committee on Colonialism has maintained the status of Puerto Rico as an agenda item, without final resolution, and the PSP has been one of the groups in the forefront of the fight to convince the U.N. and its various organs that the island remains a colony of the United States and should be granted its independence. On 31 August, PSP General Secretary Marí Bras addressed the General Assembly's Special Committee and stressed that "his party rejected any kind of political association with the United States." According to a U.N. press release, the PSP considered statehood a form of "annexation," not a "form of decolonization," and one that "would impinge on the inalienable right of the Puerto Rican people to self-determination and independence." Marí Bras complained of personal harrassment by the U.S. Federal Bureau of Investigation (FBI), charged that "FBI crimes committed against the Puerto Rican independence movement" have been covered over, and added that "such persecution . . . had created a collective fear among the people which made it impossible for them to exercise their right to self-determination." The PSP leader concluded that "his party wanted a peaceful transition, but would not hesitate to confront the violence of the enemy with the violence of the Puerto Rican revolutionary spirit." (U.N. Press Release, 1128th Meeting of the Committee, GA/COL/1970, 31 August.)

On 12 September, the Special Committee issued a nine-point resolution, which included the reaffirmation of "the inalienable right of the people of Puerto Rico to self-determination and independence in accordance with General Assembly resolution 1514 (XV)," and added that "by virtue of that right the people of Puerto Rico should freely determine their political status and pursue their further economic, social and cultural development. . . ." It concluded by declaring its intention "to keep under review the question of Puerto Rico. . . ." (U.N. General Assembly doc. A/AC.109/574, 13 September.) With respect to that resolution Marí Bras sent a letter on 8 November to the chairman of the General Assembly's Fourth Committee, which was scheduled to consider the resolution of the Special Committee, and the Cuban Permanent Representative requested that the letter be deemed an official document of the Fourth Committee. In that communication Marí Bras sought permission to give the Fourth Committee "at least a summary of the statement we made to the Special Committee," and added that "it is our understanding that, as a result of the adoption of the Special Committee's resolution . . . and the extraordinary impact it has had on the political life of the Puerto Rican people, situations have arisen which should be made known to the General Assembly before it approves the report of the Special Committee." He said the PSP believed that "representatives of the other three political parties in Puerto Rico, namely, the Puerto Rican Independence Party, the Popular Democratic Party and the New Progressive Party" should also be heard. (U.N. General Assembly doc. A/C.4/33/14, 21 November.)

International Attitudes and Activities. At the Lares Day festival, while cautioning against badly organized armed struggle for independence, the PSP general secretary pledged both moral and tangible assistance to the Sandinista rebels of Nicaragua, and was reported to have said after the ceremonies that this included dispatching Puerto Ricans to Nicaragua if needed (*The San Juan Star*, 24 September). The PSP has traditionally refused to take sides in the Sino-Soviet dispute. It has maintained a close relationship with the Cuban government and has vocally supported several governments which have emerged victorious from national liberation struggles, such as those in Angola and Vietnam. Carlos Rivera Lugo, the head of the PSP office in Cuba, had high praise for the Cuban revolution and its support of independence for Puerto Rico, and emphasized the fraternity between the two lands (*JPRS*, 14 February). However, the PSP reportedly criticized the People's Republic of China's relations with the current regime in Chile. While PSP looks favorably upon Eurocommunism, it does not see it as applicable to the island of Puerto Rico. (*The San Juan Star*, 17 September.)

Publication. The PSP publishes the daily newspaper *Claridad.*

The LSP. The Puerto Rican Socialist League is led by Secretary General Juan Antonio Corretjei, a former assistant to the late Pedro Albizú Campos, leader of the Partido Nacionalista (PN). The party was founded in 1964.

On 31 August, the secretary general appeared before the U.N. General Assembly's Special Committee of Twenty-four on Decolonization. He claimed that the people of Puerto Rico seek independence, and that while he wished that the United States could appreciate this quest on the part of the people of the island for self-determination, it was "like expecting the eloquence of Demosthenes from a police dog." The press release of his statements added that "Yankee imperialism had banned all patriotic organizations, and thus a kind of guerrilla warfare was being waged. The enemy, in the meantime, was able to launch attacks wherever it pleased." He noted that "clandestine organizations" were at work on the mainland and on the island, and that they were "operating with heroism and prudence. Puerto Rican forces would move forward until there was victory in the United Nations." (U.N. Press Release, 1128th Meeting of the Committee, GA/COL/1970, 31 August). The secretary general also participated in the Lares Day celebrations and affirmed support of the Sandinistas in Nicaragua.

CAL. This militant organization was active during the late 1960s and early 1970s. A message left near a small fire in a New York City department store on 23 January claimed CAL responsibility and threatened similar activities (*NYT*, 13 January).

St. John's University   Frank Paul Le Veness
New York

United States of America

The Communist Party, U.S.A. (CPUSA) remains the largest and most influential Marxist-Leninist organization in the United States. It is descended from the Communist Labor Party and the Communist Party, both formed in 1919. At various times CPUSA has also been called the Workers Party and, for a brief period of time during World War II, the Communist Political Association. CPUSA is a legal party. Restrictive laws which hindered access to the ballot in some areas have been removed. In 1976 the party's presidential ticket of Gus Hall and Jarvis Tyner was on the ballot in nineteen states and the District of Columbia and received about 16,000 votes. The party's gubernatorial candidate in NY in the 1978 election received 11,279 votes. At present the party has no representation either in Congress or any state legislature.

The party does not release membership figures but claimed to have 18,000 members a few years ago; another, outside estimate was 5,000 (*Nation*, 25 September 1976). The membership is concentrated in a few industrial states and believed to be largely middle-aged or older. Recruitment efforts are aimed at minority groups (Blacks, Puerto Ricans, Chicanos) and young industrial workers. The population of the U.S.A is around 220 million.

The Socialist Workers Party (SWP) is the leading Trotskyite party. Organized formally in 1938, it traces its origin to 1928 when James Cannon and several other CPUSA leaders were expelled for backing Leon Trotsky. SWP has spawned numerous other small parties, including the Workers' World Party, the Spartacist League, and the Revolutionary Marxist Organizing Committee. Membership in SWP is probably somewhere between 1,500 and 2,500. Like CPUSA, SWP runs candidates for office, usually in more localities, and usually receives more votes. Although concentrated in the industrial states, SWP has established branches in areas of the South and Southwest where CPUSA has no presence. The Workers' World Party, a Trotskyite group, has a few hundred members.

The two most important Maoist groups are the Communist Party (Marxist-Leninist) [CP(M-L)] and the Revolutionary Communist Party (RCP). The latter splintered in two this past year. The Communist Labor Party has moved in the direction of Stalinism. There are dozens of other Maoist organizations including the Proletarian Unity League, Bay Area Communist Union, Marxist-Leninist Organizing Committee (which supports Albania), Central Organization of US Marxist-Leninists, Revolutionary Wing, Philadelphia Workers Organizing Committee, Workers Party for Proletarian

Socialism, El Comité-M.I.N.P., August 29th Movement, and I Wor Kuen. The CP(M-L) and the RCP have no more than a few thousand members; the others are much more limited, and, occasionally, all but invisible. The Progressive Labor Party (PLP), also small, is Stalinist.

CPUSA and SWP are active in a wide variety of organizations and causes, particularly those relating to civil rights, peace, and labor issues. The smaller Maoist sects, many of which sprang out of the campus upheavals during the 1960s, no longer seem capable of attracting more than a handful of students and, while receiving occasional publicity, have little influence. Many of them were particularly active in the anti-Bakke struggle.

CPUSA: Leadership and Organization. There were few changes in party leadership during 1978. Gus Hall and Henry Winston remain general secretary and national chairman. Arnold Bechetti is organizational secretary, Sid Taylor treasurer, and Betty Smith national administrative secretary. There appears to have been a revamping and renaming of units during the year. Their directors include Alva Buxenbaum (chairwoman, National Women's Rights Section), George Meyers (chairman, National Labor and Farm Department), Roscoe Proctor (secretary, National Labor and Farm Department), James Jackson (education director), Helen Winter (chairwoman, International Affairs Department), Si Gerson (chairman, Political Action and Democratic Rights Department), Tom Dennis (chairman, Nationalities Department), Daniel Rubin (chairman, Economic and Social Rights Department), Victor Perlo (chairman, Economics Section), Lorenzo Torres (chairman, Chicano Section), Alex Kolkin (chairman, Jewish Section), Carl Winter (editor, *Daily World*), Carl Bloice (editor, *People's World*).

Leaders in key states are Jarvis Tyner (New York), Jack Kling and Ishmael Flory (Illinois), Jim West (Ohio), Mike Boyer (Indiana), Matt Berkelhammer and Kendra Alexander (California), Helvi Savola (Minnesota), Ed Texieira (Massachusetts), B. J. Mangaoang (Washington).

CPUSA does not formally have any affiliated organizations, but the Young Workers Liberation League (YWLL) serves, in fact, as the party's youth arm. YWLL has an estimated 3,000 members, apparently having not grown much since 1976. James Steele is chairman, Jay Schaffner organizational secretary, and Judith LeBlanc national educational director. Lack of funds caused suspension of the March issue of the *Young Worker*. The major focus of YWLL activity is youth unemployment. The organization was active in promoting a "Youth March for Jobs" on Washington, which drew a claimed 12,000 demonstrators (*Daily World,* 11 April). It included demands for passage of the Harrington Youth Jobs Bill. James Steele attacked President Carter for not providing jobs to unemployed youths. YWLL also strongly opposed Alan Bakke and urged support for both affirmative action and quotas (ibid., 18 January).

Several other organizations, although not tied as directly to CPUSA, are dominated by the party and controlled and led by its functionaries. The most prominent and successful of these united front groups continues to be the National Alliance against Racist and Political Repression (NARPR). Charlene Mitchell, one time CPUSA candidate for the U.S. presidency, is executive director. Other key figures include Angela Davis and Judge Margaret Burnham of Massachusetts. NARPR has focused its efforts over several years on North Carolina, seeking freedom for the Wilmington 10 and charging that the state is the most repressive in America. The group claimed 10,000 people had marched on Washington to demand freedom for the Wilmington 10.

The Trade Unionists for Action and Democracy (TUAD), founded in 1970, is the party's major vehicle for increasing its influence in that field. Rayfield Mooty and Fred Gaboury are TUAD leaders. Other party-dominated organizations include Committee for a Just Peace in the Middle East, National Council of American-Soviet Friendship, Chile Solidarity Committee, Metropolitan Council on Housing, and National Anti-Imperialist Movement in Solidarity with African Liberation.

The party's most important front for women is Women for Racial and Economic Equality (WREE). Among WREE leaders are Georgia Henning, Sondra Patrinos and Vinnie Burrows. Carmen Teixidor is editor of *WREE View.*

Party Internal Affairs. In a report to the National Council and the Central Committee, Gus Hall criticized certain unnamed party members for sectarianism. He charged that some communists resisted united front activites not controlled by CPUSA in the peace field. Specifically, they were accused of opposition to taking part in a 27 May demonstration at the United Nations for fear it would be anti-U.N. and anti-Soviet (ibid., 22 June).

Domestic Attitudes and Activities. CPUSA has intensified its calls for independent political action. The two-party system is seen as bankrupt. Denunciations of the Carter administration by Douglas Fraser of the United Auto Workers and William Winpisinger of the Machinists' Union as well as the retirement of Albert Fitzgerald of the United Electrical Workers to help organize a new labor party were cited as encouraging evidence of independent, progressive politics (ibid., 26 September). Hall insisted that CPUSA must run its own candidates. However, it could not be indifferent to the Democratic and Republican parties, particularly in cases of crucial differences between candidates. Hall noted that mostly this meant "a matter of differentiation, a shading in our criticism" (ibid., 22 June).

In the trade union field and working-class movements, CPUSA has called for left-center unity. The party sees numerous opportunities for such cooperation as the developing crisis of capitalism further weakens rightist forces. Hall argued that the Left is the initiating force, that it is willing to work with both the center rank-and-file and leadership, but that it must understand the reluctance of centrist forces to take leftist positions. He also warned that ultraleftists and "crazies" are antiunion, anticommunist elements used by corporations and the FBI (*Political Affairs,* January). The party gave strong support to the coal strike and the farmers' strike. In addition to calling for nationalization of the energy industry, the party also demanded that the federal government take over steel plants closing down in Youngstown, Ohio. The AFL-CIO was criticized for disregarding the rank-and-file upsurge in the steel and coal unions and also for its anti-Soviet positions on détente and human rights. Hall also criticized CPUSA for not making economic issues and struggles the center of party activity and for not being "involved or concerned with the economic problems or economic struggles of workers" (*Daily World,* 22 June).

In domestic economic affairs, the party strongly supported an effort in Congress to transfer $12 billion from defense to domestic programs for jobs and called for a 30-hour week, the closing of tax loopholes, and the hiring of the unemployed at union wages. In a speech, however, Hall called for a $100 billion cut in the military budget. California's Proposition 13 was attacked for benefiting big business and for being racist and part of the offensive against public employee unions, and the claim was made that a progressive tax system and the transfer bill would help reduce taxes. In a somewhat contradictory way, the party saw the vote on Proposition 13 as a protest against inflation and not as a turn to the right (ibid., 23 May, 15 June).

On civil liberties issues, CPUSA remained hostile to a proposed revision of the federal criminal code and gave strong support to the Wilmington 10, claiming that this case demonstrated American hypocrisy about human rights. The party strongly opposed the right of American Nazis to march in Skokie, Illinois, arguing that racist groups had no civil rights. Hall claimed, however, that charges that socialism was hostile to democracy were slanderous: "We are for the Bill of Rights and for all of the amendments to the Constitution." In an important and major policy shift, both CPUSA and WREE came out in support of the Equal Rights Amendment to the Constitution. Hall admitted that in the past CPUSA had placed too much emphasis on the legal aspects of ERA and insisted "we were never against the general, the overall objectives of ERA" (ibid., 22 June). The party argued that resolutions of intent should specify that ERA would not hurt affirmative action programs or women's benefits. CPUSA also supported the ERA time extension. In line with its views on affirmative action, CPUSA urged that the Bakke decision be reversed.

On other issues, CPUSA continued its strong support of détente and bitterly criticized presidential advisor Zbigniew Brzezinski, "the Rockefeller-cloned gusano" (ibid., 22 June). Pressure was urged on President Carter to stop production of the neutron bomb and to throw his weight on the side of prodétente forces within his administration. The party also supported efforts to block nuclear power plant construction because of capitalism's alleged inability to put safety first but argued that when the nuclear energy industry is nationalized, construction should go ahead.

International Views and Policies. CPUSA does not deviate from Soviet positions. Gus Hall admitted that one of the major party problems is its image of association with the USSR but warned that "we must not give in to the opportunistic pressures of denying the charges by joining in with the anti-Sovieteers" (ibid., 22 June).

Support for the USSR includes condemnation of other communist parties for challenging Soviet views. China has been bitterly criticized for its activities, including the conflict with Vietnam and links with the United States. Eurocommunism has come in for attack. Hall noted that CPUSA disagreed with "the viewpoint of some communist leaders in some of the communist parties" (ibid.). CPUSA concentrated its main fire on the Spanish party and its leader Santiago Carrillo, charging him with abandoning Marxism-Leninism. President Carter was accused of violating the Helsinki agreement for his attack on the French and Italian parties, and CPUSA expressed its solidarity with both of them—but not its agreement.

The Middle East also received considerable attention. Throughout the year, CPUSA condemned Carter, Sadat, and Begin for trying to avoid a Geneva conference negotiation with the PLO, and total Israeli withdrawal. Israel's invasion of Lebanon was regarded as a result of this collusion. A party statement, signed by Hall and Winston, did not mention Israel's right to exist, but a later editorial did note that right (ibid., 20 January, 6 May). The Camp David agreement was attacked for ignoring the PLO and Syria and for not constituting a step towards peace.

On African affairs, CPUSA fully supported revolutionary regimes and liberation movements. There was frequent support for Libya, Ethiopia, and Cuban troops. The United States, on the other hand, was accused of covertly trying to intervene in the Horn of Africa, and the party charged that NATO paratroopers invaded Zaire with American help. The conflict in Zaire was said to be a civil war to oppose a dictator, not an invasion from Angola. The internal settlement in Rhodesia was called a sham and support expressed for guerrilla leaders Joshua Nkomo and Robert Mugabe.

CPUSA supported the Panama Canal treaty, seeing it as a defeat for American reactionaries, but demanded that the right of military intervention be abolished. The murder of Aldo Moro was regarded as part of a reactionary effort to destabilize Italy by the CIA and to keep communists out of government. Red Brigade policies were claimed to "serve neo-fascism" (ibid., 11 May).

International Activities and Contacts. Henry Winston represented CPUSA at several meetings during the year. In April, he and Arnold Bechetti met with French party leaders. That same month, Winston and his wife were delegates to the Communist Party of India congress. In September, he and George Meyers met with Hungarian party leaders. He also was in the Soviet Union. Jim West was at the Greek party congress in May, and James Steele of YWLL went to Moscow for the Eighteenth Komsomol Congress. Two delegates from the Argentine party visited the United States for discussions and issued a joint communiqué in June. Gus Hall and Henry Winston met with Boris Ponomarev during the latter's trip to New York in February, and Hall visited Cuba in September.

Publications. The *Daily World,* appearing five times a week in New York, is CPUSA's major publication with a claimed circulation of 30,000 copies. *Political Affairs* is a monthly theoretical journal. Other party-linked papers are *People's World,* a San Francisco weekly; *Freedomways,* a black quarterly; *New World Review,* a bimonthly newsletter; *Cultural Reporter; African Agenda; Labor Today; Korea Forum;* and *Black Liberation Journal.* International Publishers has long been identified as the CPUSA publishing outlet.

SWP: Leadership and Organization. There was little change in the leadership of SWP during the past year. Jack Barnes is national secretary and Barry Shepard organizational secretary. Other party leaders include Mary-Alice Waters (editor, *Militant*), Peter Camejo (national field organizer), Linda Jenness, Bruce Levine, Lew Jones, Ed Heisler, Malik Miah, Cindy Jaquith, Larry Siegle, Susan Lamont, Maceo Dixon and Betsy Stone.

The party's most important auxiliary is the Young Socialist Alliance (YSA). Cathy Sedwick is national chairperson, Betsy Farley organizational secretary, and Chuck Petrin national secretary. YSA still has not recovered from the 1977 decision to send over 600 members into SWP. The loss of so many experienced cadres crippled YSA activities, depleted finances, and forced organizational cutbacks. YSA membership is around 700; about 10 percent high school students and 78 percent college students. Only about 100 members are from minority groups, while nearly half of the 57-member national committee is composed of minorities. Major YSA activities have included demonstrations against the Bakke decision, a campaign to prevent deportation of YSA member Hector Marroquin to Mexico, and defense of the revolution in Africa.

Other party organizations include Political Rights Defense Fund, National Student Coalition against Racism, U.S. Committee for Justice to Latin American Politcal Prisoners, and Committee for Artistic and Intellectual Freedom in Iran.

Party Internal Affairs. A National Committee meeting approved plans in February to move party workers into industry. SWP has concluded that there is growing radicalization of workers and that the proper response is to concentrate its efforts on industry. Many SWP members have been students. These cadres sent into factories are to lead a drive for union democracy, solidarity, and independent political action. They are to build party factions in key unions and try to recruit workers for SWP (*Militant,* 1 September). Some 1,500 party members and supporters attended an Active Workers' and Socialist Educational Conference in Ohio, during which the new party line was emphasized.

Domestic Attitudes and Activities. SWP was active in anti-Bakke activities and supported affirmative action programs. The party also has been a strong supporter of the Equal Rights Amendment but has faced efforts by some in the National Organization of Women to oust SWP members on the grounds that they have a hidden agenda.

SWP continues to press its lawsuit against the FBI for political harassment. A federal judge has ordered the FBI to release the names of more than 50 informers within SWP, and Attorney-General Bell has risked contempt of court by refusing to do so. Party candidates in local elections fared poorly in 1977, rarely winning more than 1 percent of the vote. In the 1978 New York mayoral election, the SWP candidate received 3,300 votes or 0.86 percent.

International Views and Policies. SWP considers the Soviet Union to be less dangerous than the United States. It continues to criticize the USSR for its treatment of dissidents, particularly Anatoly Shcharansky, and for collaboration with capitalism. The party supports Cuban involvement in Angola but disagrees that the latter has a socialist government. SWP also supports Eritrean forces and expressed satisfaction that Cuban troops in Ethiopia had not been used against the rebels (ibid., 7 July). SWP supports the PLO call for dissolution of Israel; consequently it found nothing to applaud in the Camp David agreements, alleging them to be a victory for American imperialism.

Publications. SWP publishes the weekly *Militant,* the monthly *Young Socialist,* and the Spanish-language biweekly *Perspectiva Mundial.*

Maoist Groups. The numerous Maoist sects have been quarreling more than usual as a result of the political situation in China. Although past differences were often based on theoretical hairsplitting, fundamental political issues now divide Maoists. The two largest groups are the Communist Party (Marxist-Leninist) and the Revolutionary Communist Party, which underwent a split. The *Guardian,* published in New York City, represents still another Maoist line.

The CP(M-L) led by Chairman Michael Klonsky, is recognized by the Chinese government as the official Maoist party. It met in Chicago during June to celebrate its first anniversary with 1,200 people attending. The CP(M-L) has been trying to unite with various other Maoist groups, notably the I Wor Kuen (made up of West Coast Asians) and the Chicano August 29th Movement. All three accept the validity of China's three-world theory. That theory urges unity between the third world and advanced capitalist nations against the superpowers, with the main enemy being the USSR (*Guardian,* 14 June). In line with this theory, CP(M-L) has attacked Soviet activities in Africa and opposed détente.

One of the party's leaders, Harry Haywood, met with Chinese leaders in June. The moving force behind CPUSA's adoption of self-determination for the southern "Black Belt" in the U.S.A. during 1928, Haywood never abandoned his position, and CP(M-L) currently espouses it. Daniel Burstein, editor of the party journal, *The Call,* visited Cambodia in April and charged that reports of widespread killings were CIA fabrications (*NYT,* 12 May).

The Revolutionary Communist Party, the largest Maoist group last year, was split apart in 1978 by disagreement on China. The majority, under party leader Robert Avakian, charged that revisionists have seized power in China and are leading the country down the capitalist path. The conflict had been building ever since the arrest of the "Gang of Four." Avakian, who leans toward the Albanian position, charged that China has abandoned the class struggle and opted for expertise over politics, elitism in education, and leniency in art and culture. He attacked the reintroduction of Shakespeare, Beethoven, Chopin, Bach, and Rembrandt in China (*Guardian,* 22 March). Some 1,200 people, most of them party members, attended a New York meeting where Avakian called the Chinese government "a fascist bourgeois dictatorship over the masses seeking to undertake the restoration of capitalism" (ibid., 20 September). RCP members resigned from the U.S.-China People's Friendship Association and sponsored Mao memorial meetings.

The minority faction, led by Mickey Jarvis and Nick Unger, claimed that 40 percent of the party followed it into a new organization called the Revolutionary Workers Headquarters. The dissidence was centered in the New York area and on the West Coast. The Jarvis group claims that the "Gang of Four" represented a cancer and denies that China has become revisionist. It backs Hua Kuo-feng but does not mention Teng Hsiao-ping. Despite its support for the Chinese government, it has rejected any thought of coalition with CP(M-L). The Jarvis group has accused RCP "goons" of beating up its supporters and published a cartoon of Avakian with the caption "This short person's got no reason to live" (ibid., 22 March, 20 September). RCP publishes *Revolution.*

Other Groups. The Progressive Labor Party (PLP) is resolutely Stalinist. It does not provide information about organization or leaders, although Mitt Rosen is known to be chairman. PLP rhetoric remains blunt and crude. Giving support to striking miners, it noted that "only through such working-class violence, combined with communist ideas, will we be able to smash the bosses' state apparatus" (*Challenge,* 5 January). The group devoted particular attention to preventing Nazis and

Ku Klux Klansmen from marching and participating in "Kill Nazi" rallies. PLP also launched campaigns to prevent sociobiology from being taught on college campuses. Its most prominent front is the Committee against Racism (CAR).

Emory University   Harvey Klehr

Uruguay

The Communist Party of Uruguay (Partido Comunista del Uruguay; PCU) dates from September 1920. It is firmly pro-Soviet and has been illegal since 1973. Several other leftist organizations operate underground or in exile and display Soviet, Chinese, Cuban, or nationalistic leanings or combinations thereof. Among these are the National Liberation Movement (Movimiento de Liberación Nacional; MLN), better known as the Tupamaros, and the Uruguayan Revolutionary Communist Party (Partido Comunista Revolucionario del Uruguay; PCRU), which broke away from the PCU and in 1978 proclaimed ties to the Khmer Communist Party in Cambodia. The Broad Front (Frente Amplio; FA) was formed by the PCU and a number of other leftist groups and individuals in time for the 1971 national elections, in which it won 18 percent of the vote. All these groups were outlawed in 1978.

PCU membership, long estimated at 30,000, may have fallen to a third of that today. All other Marxist parties are smaller. The population of Uruguay is approximately 2,893,000.

A decree of 15 August 1977, signed by the Uruguayan president and his cabinet ministers, proclaimed that elections scheduled for 1981 will be held with "traditional parties" participating. This has been interpreted to mean that the Colorado and Blanco parties will be on the ballot but not the PCU and other leftist parties or the Broad Front coalition. All the same, a prominent military spokesman said in mid-1978 that as civilian leadership returned to Uruguay after 1981, he foresaw that some leftists, perhaps even ex-PCU members, might be ready to participate individually in the national life.

The PCU: Organization and Leadership. PCU First Secretary Rodney Arismendi continued to reside in Moscow during 1978 and issued communications from there as official head of the PCU in exile; clandestine announcements from the PCU in Uruguay referred to Arismendi as first secretary in absentia. The party Central Committee has 48 members and 27 alternates when every position is filled. The five-member Secretariat consists of Arismendi, Enrique Pastorino, Jaime Pérez, Enrique Rodríguez, and Alberto Suárez. Despite the fact that Arismendi, Pastorino, and Suárez lived abroad during 1978 and Pérez remained imprisoned, the PCU announced no official substitute Secretariat, remaining silent about the underground group presumed to be functioning inside Uruguay. Pastorino remains president of the pro-Soviet World Federation of Trade Unions (WFTU) and, through the International Labor Office in Geneva, enjoys United Nations diplomatic immunity, while Julia

Arévalo, in jail since 1976, is a vice-president of the Women's International Democratic Federation. Pérez, imprisoned in Montevideo in October 1974 on charges of attempting to overthrow the government, has been the object of a "Freedom for Pérez" campaign directed by Arismendi in news releases from Moscow and Havana, a campaign echoed by Western left-wing publications and groups (Tass, 20 January).

The PCU's youth organization, the Union of Communist Youth (Unión de la Juventud Comunista; UJC), founded in 1955, claimed a membership of 22,000 when outlawed in 1973 but is probably not more than several thousand strong today. In comments on the Eleventh World Festival of Youth and Students held in Havana at midyear, Arismendi stressed his party's commitment to the youth activists who replenish the ranks of those fighting against imperialism.

During the year Arismendi challenged outspoken European social democrats to recognize the peculiar contributions of Lenin to the twentieth-century revolutionary scene. Leninism, he wrote in a long article in *World Marxist Review* (October), is the "Marxism of our epoch," and Lenin's theory and practice provide an overview of the foreseeable future and the political organization by which to promote socialism today. He acknowledged that for all their thematic range, Lenin's works "do not furnish ready-made solutions to all the problems posed by the revolutionary practice of our time," but that that is no reason to "belittle the epochal importance of Leninism," as some "socialist" writers are doing today.

Domestic Attitudes and Activities. The PCU gave a comprehensive analysis of the situation in Uruguay as of the beginning of the year in a Central Committee manifesto dated 30 December 1977 and originally issued clandestinely in Montevideo. (An abridged version is in *IB* 1978, no. 14.) According to the PCU, the Uruguayan government is "essentially a terrorist dictatorship of finance capital and certain big latifundists in the service of U.S. imperialism, supported solely by the most retrogressive sectors of the armed forces." The manifesto quoted with approval from a recent Broad Front document which stated: "The preservation of the dictatorship is due primarily to lack of concerted actions by the opposition forces which, though they comprise the overwhelming majority, have failed to unite their forces in a single stream on the basis of common views reflecting the sentiments and aspirations of the Uruguayan people." The nature of "fascism" and the need for unity among opposition forces remained principal themes for the PCU throughout the year. Sergio Sierra, a member of the PCU Central Committee, contributed a long analysis of "fascism in Latin America" to *World Marxist Review* (August) in which he concluded that the failure to understand the specific features of the phenomenon, and thus the inability of Latin Americans to work out the strategy and tactics necessary to defeat it, stems largely from "petty-bourgeois revolutionism." He reported that the PCU's policy in this sector of the ideological struggle is determined by (*a*) "the need to characterize 'leftism' in class terms and to determine its place in the revolutionary process; (*b*) the elaboration of a tactical line relying on the immediate experience of the mass struggle; and (*c*) ideological struggle as an important means for attaining political goals, primarily invigorating the struggle and achieving anti-fascist unity." He noted that "our primary task today is to rout fascism. The immediate alternative is not capitalism vs socialism, but fascism vs democracy." Although the Uruguayan military controlled the country and administered the fascism, he said that the PCU attitude toward the armed forces is "neither vulgar anti-militarism nor military paternalism."

What the party needed now was vigorous tactics, not contemplation of events and moralizing. He quoted Arismendi: "The important thing to remember is that what the imperialists want is one thing, and what can happen if the people unite, if all the anti-fascist forces pool their efforts, is quite another, and this, incidentally, is the only possible way for the earliest overthrow of the present dictatorship." (Ibid.) Late in the year Arismendi presented what he considered a generally optimistic view of the present and immediate future in Uruguay. He told a correspondent from the East German *Neues Deutschland* (26 September) that "despite the machinations of U.S. imperialism and the reactionary forces in Uruguay," the dictatorship is in increasing decline and falling to a position of internal as well as international isolation. The government has failed to resolve economic problems, and Uruguay now has one of the lowest economic growth rates in Latin America. Resistance to the regime involves the working class but stretches as well into the bourgeoisie and all political parties. With opposition building among cattle ranchers, churchmen, and even within the ranks of the armed forces, the "political-military crisis is growing more aggravated." Arismendi asserts that the PCU is playing a leading role in this movement, in particular by "holding aloft the banner of the Broad Front."

On a number of occasions during 1978 the Uruguayan government charged the PCU and its youth arm with working actively to overthrow the existing leadership. A PCU militant was convicted of espionage in January on the grounds that in his position as a government employee he had obtained data about military and police installations. According to the Montevideo daily *El País* (10 January), he passed this information to the PCU Central Committee, which hoped to sell it to guerrilla groups for funds to finance the party's clandestine activities. The same paper (11 May) reported that captured documents of the Group for Unified Action (GAU), formed in 1972 with assistance from Cuba, indicate regular contacts between this organization and the PCU.

International Attitudes and Activities. The PCU, with many of its top leaders living and traveling in the Soviet Union and Eastern Europe, maintained its customary reputation as one of the most dependable of pro-Soviet parties in Latin America. Arismendi and other leaders, although not primarily concerned with international affairs, condemned the People's Republic of China (*IB*, no. 12) and spoke out predictably on other issues of concern to the USSR. PCU members have protested that Uruguay's diplomatic representation to the Arab countries, once in Lebanon, was moved to Iran rather than Algeria (Radio Havana, 17 May). Arismendi received congratulations from all over the pro-Soviet communist world on his sixty-fifth birthday in March and was given the Karl Marx Order, the highest decoration authorized by the East German government.

Publications. PCU statements are found largely in the *World Marxist Review* and its *Information Bulletin* as well as in the media releases of pro-Soviet governments around the world.

The Tupamaros. In Uruguay, the Tupamaros are currently in a state of almost complete disrepair, although incidents occasionally occur. In February the Argentine police in Buenos Aires arrested Andrés Cultelli Chiribao, a deputy of imprisoned MLN leader Raúl Sendic until 1972 when he moved to Chile to help revolutionaries during the presidency of Salvador Allende. After living in Sweden, from which he traveled through Europe collecting funds to help the MLN, he returned to Argentina where he was captured. (*El País*, 25 February.) News correspondent Claire Sterling noted numerous cases of cooperation among the Tupamaros and other now internationally minded guerrilla terrorists—including the Argentine Montoneros, the Italian Red Brigade, the Popular Front for the Liberation of Palestine, the Baader-Meinhof gang, and the Revolutionary Coordinating Committee (JCR)—in an article in the U.S. monthly *Atlantic* (November).

Arizona State University   Marvin Alisky

Venezuela

Founded in 1931, the Communist Party of Venezuela (Partido Comunista de Venezuela; PCV) is the oldest, but no longer the most important, Marxist force in the country. Participation in the guerrilla warfare of the 1960s undermined the PCV's once strong popular base. At the same time, its rigid adherence to the Moscow line alienated many of the party's most promising leaders. Disenchanted with old-guard intolerance, a large group broke away in 1970 and founded the Movement toward Socialism (Movimiento al Socialismo; MAS). The MAS rapidly took first place among leftist parties. Still weak from this massive desertion, the PCV suffered another split in 1974, with part of the old guard itself leaving to form the Communist Vanguard (Vanguardia Comunista; VC), later renamed the United Communist Vanguard (Vanguardia Unitaria Comunista; VUC). Another Marxist-Leninist group, the Movement of the Revolutionary Left (Movimiento de Izquierda Revolucionaria; MIR), has shown marked progress in the past year, displacing the MAS in the student movement. The MIR originated from a split in the Democratic Action Party (Acción Democrática; AD) which controlled the government from 1959 to 1969 and returned to power early in 1974. Most Maoist and Trotskyite groups have announced their support for one or another of the Marxist candidates in the 3 December presidential elections. Increased guerrilla activity was characteristic of the election year. All communist factions combined are estimated to have some 10,000 members. The population of Venezuela is estimated at 14,058,000.

Opportunities for a unified Left to increase parliamentary and state assembly representation in the 1978 election were the best in two decades. But the parties failed to agree upon a unity candidate and conversations to this end were abandoned in February 1978, with all energies and efforts thereafter dedicated to the campaigns of four separate leftist presidential candidates—the PCV, MAS, MIR, and the People's Electoral Movement (Movimiento Electoral del Pueblo; MEP). Although avowedly non-Marxist, the MEP, born from an AD split in 1968, is always included in this list. Its program now differs very little from those of the so-called "patriotic socialists"—the MAS and MIR—and the MEP would have formed part of any popular front agreed upon by the Marxist parties. The MIR proposed a postelectoral program for a leftist parliamentary bloc and unified slates in expectation of the June 1979 municipal elections. (*El Nacional,* Caracas, 24 August.) The MAS won 6 percent of the congressional vote and has 2 (of 47) senate seats and 11 (of 195) deputy seats. The MIR and the MEP have 4 deputies each; the PCV, VC, and Socialist League have 1 each. There are 6.13 million registered voters, and the voting is obligatory.

The PVC: *Organization and Leadership.* The top leadership of the PCV is its eighteen-member Politburo. This body includes President Gustavo Machado, Secretary General Jesús Faría, and Radamés Larrazábal, who directed the party's presidential campaign.

Until the December 1970 split, the PCV's Venezuelan Communist Youth (Juventud Comunista Venezolana; JCV) was the largest political group in the student movement. The split deprived it of most of its leaders and members, but current JCV Secretary General Noel Sirit maintains that the communist youth movement is slowly recovering from these losses: "We are now the first leftist force in the secondary schools, as evidenced by nationwide elections of the past two years. [We have also made] strong advances among the young people of the working class and popular neighborhoods." (Ibid., 1 October.)

The principal center of PCV influence in the labor movement is the United Workers' Confederation of Venezuela (Confederación Unitaria de Trabajadores de Venezuela; CUTV), established in the early 1960s when the PCV lost virtually all influence in the majority Confederation of Workers of Venezuela (Confederación de Trabajadores de Venezuela; CTV). PCV Labor Secretary Pedro Ortega Díaz recently defended the continued existence of the CUTV as a necessary base for working toward a unified labor movement free of all political party domination: "This obviously will not be possible until the system is changed. Meanwhile, the PCV has members and leaders in CTV federations and unions, and these fight as Cetevistas [representatives of the CTV]" (ibid., 20 October). The attorney general has asked the Supreme Court to declare unconstitutional eight articles of the labor law regulations which limit the right to strike as a result of a proposal submitted to him last April by the PCV Labor Committee (*Tribuna Popular*, 17–23 November; *El Nacional*, 17 November). The PCV presidential candidate (see below) consistently advocated the formulation of a new labor code to unify and correct present legislation. The code would guarantee the right to strike, job stability, efficient social security, industrial security and hygiene, and genuine full employment, which can only be achieved in a planned economy.

Domestic Attitudes and Activities. The PCV has not fielded a presidential candidate of its own since 1947 when Gustavo Machado polled 3.29 percent of the vote. During the Pérez Jiménez dictatorship the only effective resistance came from the AD and the PCV. The Communists reached the peak of their influence with the overthrow of Pérez Jiménez in 1958, but their coalition candidate, Wolfgang Larrazábal, lost to AD founder Rómulo Betancourt. Guerrilla warfare and internal dissension have contributed to the steady decline of the party since then. Aware of its weakness, popular and financial, the PCV held out until the last for a popular unity candidate. Under the circumstances, the decision forced upon it could not have been happier. PCV candidate Héctor Mujica received a minuscule vote, but he did more in a few months for the image of the party than would have been accomplished in years of dedicated committee work. Mujica is a talented writer, sociologist, director of the faculty of social communication of the Central University (Universidad Central de Venezuela; UCV), and president of the National Journalists Association (Colegio Nacional de Periodistas; CNP). An extremely sympathetic intellectual, he centered his attack on the economic monopolies, their political power, and the resulting evils of inflation, inequitable distribution of income, inadequate public services, and administrative corruption and waste.

International Views and Positions. Never overstepping the lines of orthodox pro-Moscow orientation, Mujica answered the usual criticisms with statements to the effect that the "PCV is not an international, but an internationalist party" and "the 'great fatherland' [gran patria] is Venezuela, not the Soviet Union" (Channel 8 television, debate, 26 November). Jesús Faría was less ambiguous. He quoted Lenin to the effect that revolutions should be tailored to national reality but followed up with a 1930s-style panegyric on Soviet society (*Tribuna Popular*, 17–23 November). Radamés Larrazábal capped this with the statement that "those of the MAS today are neither Marxist nor communist, and the same goes for the little group of Eduardo Machado and Guillermo Ponce (VUC) which is pro-COPEI. . . . the PCV, an international workers' party, does not have to hang on the skirts of any bourgeois party in the country" (*El Nacional*, 26 September).

Along with the rest of the Left, the PCV was totally preempted by President Carlos Andrés Pérez on the most immediate international issue, Nicaragua. Belated statements of support for government action were unavoidable. Jesús Faría later attacked Betancourt's criticism of Cuban interven-tion in Africa as illogical if the AD government is "willing to send military aid to Costa Rica when re-quested" (ibid., 8 November). Author Miguel Otero Silva, whose wife heads the Nicaraguan Solida-rity Committee, suggested the creation of a voluntary Venezuelan brigade to fight against Somoza and recalled the "valiant action of Gustavo Machado (and other Venezuelans) at the side of Augusto César Sandino" (ibid., 25 September). Gustavo Machado was awarded the "Jorge Dimitrov" order on his eightieth birthday by the People's Republic of Bulgaria, becoming the first North or South American to receive this distinction (ibid., 4 November). In Cuba for the 26 July anniversary, Politburo member Eduardo Gallegos visited the Vietnamese embassy to express PCV solidarity with the Vietnam Communist Party and the Socialist Republic of Vietnam, who now face the malignant action of the Chinese leadership and its followers, the Kampuchean authorities (*FBIS,* 6 August).

Publications. The PCV publishes the weekly *Tribuna Popular,* which, like all Venezuelan leftist periodicals, tends to be somewhat irregular.

MAS. The Movement toward Socialism was formed late in 1970 following the first major PCV split. Teodoro Petkoff led the rebellion against old-guard dogmatism and gained the support of Politburo member Pompeyo Márquez. Together they took with them a large part of the leadership cadres of the PCV, a majority of the former PCV rank and file, and virtually all of the JCV. Márquez and Petkoff are now secretary general and assistant secretary general, respectively, of the MAS.

The MAS youth organization, originally called Communist Youth—MAS (Juventud Comunista—MAS; JC-MAS), but now called Youth-MAS (Juventud-MAS; J-MAS), initially dominated most of the stu-dent bodies of Venezuelan universities but has now been displaced by the MIR (see below). J-MAS Secretary General Hugo Negretti admits that mistakes such as a tendency to exclusivity, have been made, but attributes the university defeats to a lack of prepared student leaders: "a problem common to all parties. Uninformed students ingenuously voted for alternatives which were the same as, or worse than, our own." (*El Nacional,* 22 August.)

At its inception the MAS had some influence in the CUTV trade union movement. Those who went with the MAS first formed the "CUT Clasista" as a rival organization. In 1974, the MAS Central Committee decided to have its supporters enter the CTV, and the MAS now has one seat on the CTV Executive Committee. Apart from a series of labor reforms, the MAS program gives priority to increased worker participation in management at all levels. Labor secretariats of the parties and movements supporting the candidacy of José Vicente Rangel (see below) formed the Unitary Soci-alist Labor Movement (Movimiento Unitario Sindical Socialista; MUSS). (Ibid., 22 August.)

Internal Dissension. Differences which were visible in 1976—77, particularly after Petkoff failed to receive the presidential nomination, were patched over for campaign purposes but apparently not eliminated. The need to present an outwardly united image has, however, greatly reduced the availability of reliable information. Petkoff's group reportedly failed in an attempt to prevent the si-multaneous nomination of José Vincente Rangel to both the presidency and the Chamber of Depu-ties. According to a Venezuelan newsweekly, Petkoff told a group of university professors in August that the MAS ticket as a whole must poll a larger percentage than the presidential candidate in order to assure the triumph of the "Teodorista" (Petkoff) faction. The same source stated that Pompeyo Márquez will abandon his usual position of relative obscurity to make sure that Rangel receives the larger vote, while Rangel, an independent, has promised to join the party and will bring his intellectual supporters to assist Márquez in the struggle for control of the MAS. Petkoff allegedly assured his listeners that the party would follow him, "even without the party name, if necessary." (*Zeta,* Caracas, 26 November.) The magazine is pro-MIR and may overstate the case, but the "Teo-dorista" revolt is commonly, if not officially, acknowledged. Petkoff is not only miffed by the rejection of his presidential aspirations but is disturbed by increasing signs of antidemocratic tendencies in internal party affairs. He is reportedly backed by the MAS youth and intellectuals.

Domestic Attitudes and Activities. MAS slates were presented in every district of the country, but the two-party AD-COPEI "polarization," which MAS hoped to break, was stronger than ever at the end of the 1978 campaign, and Rangel's predicted share of the vote declined steadily from June. Analysts attribute this primarily to the bewildering array of leftist candidates, all saying more or less the same thing. The MAS refusal to accept any unification proposal which entailed sacrifice of its own candidate is largely responsible for the situation. Rangel, who won 4.26 percent of the vote on a MAS-MIR ticket in 1973, is the best candidate, and ideological reasons could be adduced for reluctance to join forces with PCV or MEP. Rejection of proffered MIR cooperation is less easily explained, except by overconfidence. The MAS did accept the unbinding support of some recognized national parties—the VUC, the Revolutionary Action Group (Grupo de Acción Revolucionaria; GAR), and the Socialist League (Liga Socialista; LS), as well as that of smaller groups, including the Partido Socialista de los Trabajadores (PST), El Pueblo Avanza (EPA), Patria Joven, and the intellectual Independent Socialists' Movement led by D. F. Maza Zavala.

The MAS program, in brief, proposed: the conversion of an electoral democracy into a participatory democracy; a pluralistic society, rather than one dominated by a few powerful groups; personal well-being for all through statistical economic growth; human rights as a reality instead of an abstraction; and socialization of the economy, ridding it of the oligarchy in the private sector and excessive bureaucracy in the public sector (presentation in the Teatro Metropolitano, Caracas, 19 September). The socialist society will be pluralistic and democratic with direct elections for all public offices, and the election of a nonsocialist government will be respected. Means of production will be socialized, with a fade-out of initially necessary state action, but expropriations will be cautious and gradual, with only banks nationalized in the first phase. Monopolistic economic groups will be eliminated through some constitutional reforms and the removal of their corrupt political power bases. According to Rangel, a genuine enforcement of the 1961 constitution would be perfectly adequate for establishment of the first phase of socialism. (Alfredo Peña, *Conversaciones con José Vicente Rangel,* Caracas, 1978.)

International Views. The MAS was upstaged by Carlos Andrés Pérez on Nicaragua but covered with subsequent calls for solidarity and condemnation of U.S. support for Somoza. Rangel said that "a word from Carter, the State Department, or the Pentagon" would be sufficient to topple Somoza (*El Nacional,* 27 September). A MAS government would maintain relations with all countries, although the petroleum industry dictates priority for the U.S., with Western Europe and Japan coming next, in order to diversify the market. The MAS approved of African liberation movements but "does not understand the continuing presence of Cuban troops in the continent" (*Conversaciones con José Vicente Rangel*). The CTV sent Jesús Urbieta, Executive Committee member and national labor leader of MAS, as its delegate to the Congress of Solidarity with the Chilean People in October in Madrid.

Publication. The principle MAS organ is the newspaper *Punto.*

VUC. Following a split in the PCV old guard in 1974, two of the party's traditional leaders, Eduardo Machado (brother of Gustavo) and Guillermo García Ponce, left to form the Communist Vanguard, later renamed the United Communist Vanguard. The VC's First Congress, held in 1974, elected Machado president and García Ponce secretary general. It also proclaimed the new group to be a Marxist-Leninist party, faithful to the traditions of international solidarity. A Central Committee plenum in 1977 decided not to run a presidential candidate in the 1978 elections. The VUC supported Rangel and presented its own electoral slates in ten regions; in others it fielded tickets jointly with the LS, GAR, and EPA. Machado and García Ponce headed VUC lists for senators and deputies, respectively, in the Federal District. (*El Nacional,* 4 and 9 September.)

MIR. The MIR was established in 1960 by AD dissidents unhappy with Betancourt's policy of economic austerity. These included some members of the Executive Committee, led by Domingo Alberto Rangel, and virtually all of the youth movement. A number of splits preceded both the MIR's formal decision to enter the armed struggle in 1964 and its official withdrawal in 1969. D. A. Rangel, opposing continued guerrilla participation, left the party in the middle sixties and now leads a small group of independent leftists boycotting elections. After the MAS rejected MIR's offer of support and later unity proposals fell through, MIR nominated Américo Martín as its presidential candidate. The former guerrilla leader, amnestied under former President Caldera's pacification program, is MIR's only representative in the Chamber of Deputies.

In the November 1977 Central University elections, the MIR doubled its previous vote, displacing the MAS in the presidency of the Federation of University Student Centers (FCU). University authorities complained in 1978 of "agitation and violence" from the new student leaders. The occupation of administrative offices and aggressive language were primarily related to the university's decision to increase token payments for intensive summer courses. (*El Universal,* Caracas, 22 November.) FCU President Eduardo Semtei was a candidate for deputy from Caracas. Martín, at 40, is the youngest presidential candidate, and MIR congressional tickets have the largest percentage of young persons. The MIR won in the elections of the Pedagogical Institute of Caracas on 5 October.

The MIR has made some inroads in the labor movement, particularly with its victory in the steelworkers' union in 1977, but its predominant message continues to be an appeal for leftist labor unity. Martín underscored the urgency of this appeal by listing important events coming up in 1979: (*a*) 2,000 collective bargaining contracts; (*b*) 1,800 union elections; (*c*) congresses of the CTV and its most important affiliates; (*d*) discussions of reforms in the labor law, establishing new labor union organization; and (*e*) a MIR initiative for inflation-indexed wage scales.

There is essentially no difference in the MIR and MAS programs of democratic socialism. The MIR, however, has taken the lead in promoting leftist unity. A proposal released in August called for (*a*) creation of a left-wing parliamentary bloc; (*b*) unified slates for the June 1979 municipal elections; (*c*) unified ballots for the 1979 labor union and CTV elections; (*d*) unified slates for elections in agrarian leagues, unions, and the Venezuelan Federation of Peasants and Farm Workers (Federación Campesina de Venezuela; FCV); (*e*) unified action in teacher and student movements; and (*f*) unified action in professional and technical associations.

MEP. Inclusion of this party may be disputed, as noted above. Luis Beltrán Prieto Figueroa, founder of the People's Electoral Movement (MEP), is a Venezuelan institution, universally respected. One of the founders of the AD, he left the party in 1968 when convention maneuvers deprived him of the presidential nomination. As an MEP candidate the same year, he won almost 20 percent of the vote, which contributed decisively to the AD defeat. With its strongest base in the labor unions, the party moved toward the left, and many supporters returned to the AD. According to the party's labor secretary, the MEP is still the second strongest party in the labor movement, after the AD (*El Nacional,* 18 October).

Prieto says MEP objectives are national liberation and democratic socialism, with state ownership of basic industry. The party supports the original theses of the AD—a pluralistic democracy (which is) anti-imperialistic, antifeudalistic, and anti-oligarchist—and objects to the AD's betrayal of those principles. (Alfredo Peña, *Conversaciones con Luis Beltrán Prieto,* Caracas, 1978, pp. 171–2.)

Andrés Caleca, national youth secretary of the MEP, was a delegate to the World Youth Festival in Havana and is a representative of the MEP on the Executive Committee of the World Federation of Youth (*El Nacional*, 2 October). Salom Mesa headed the MEP list for the Chamber of Deputies in Caracas, although he has not been able to campaign. He was arrested two years ago in connection with the Niehous kidnapping but has been neither charged nor released.

Maoists. The most important Maoist groups are the Party of the Venezuelan Revolution (Partido de la Revolución Venezolana; PRV) and the Ruptura movement. The latter functions legally and participates, with some small successes, in university elections. Argelia Melet, wife of Douglas Bravo, is secretary general of Ruptura. The PRV is still clandestine, but leader Douglas Bravo has indicated that it might agree to form part of a united front in the 1979 municipal elections. This will be decided in a national conference to be convened for this purpose, according to Alfredo Peña's best-selling *Conversaciones con Douglas Bravo* (Caracas, 1978, p. 185). Peña interviewed Bravo in his secret headquarters "somewhere in Colombia." Bravo said the PRV ceased military operations in March 1974 when Carlos Andrés Pérez took office because of conditions created by increased petroleum wealth and the political bloc, including some leftist parties, which formed around the government, plus international socialist praise of Pérez as an anti-imperialist president. This "conciliation" weakened the revolutionary movement, making armed struggle inadvisable. Priority has since been given to promoting political, social, and economic objectives of the masses. Conditions are still not adequate for legalization of the group (i.e., the lack of democratic freedom), and Pérez has made no pacification offers, according to Bravo, but this does not necessarily mean that the PRV is retrenching for a return to guerrilla warfare, which "cannot be decreed capriciously." (Ibid. pp. 173−8.) Delegations from both the PRV and Ruptura visited China during 1978 (*FBIS*, 10 July; *Peking Review*, 7 July). Ruptura publishes a newspaper of the same name. The Revolutionary Communist Movement (Movimiento Comunista Revolucionario; MCR) has placed paid notices in national newspapers, signed by MCR President Douglas Crespo, calling for defense of the "purity of Marxism-Leninism−Mao Tse-tung thought" (*El Nacional*, 14 November).

Trotskyites. The Venezuelan Trotskyist Group made its appearance in 1972 and in 1973 took the name of Socialist Workers' Party (Partido Socialista de los Trabajadores; PST). The PST supported J. V. Rangel's candidacy in the 1973 elections. It was presumed to have merged with the groups which in 1974 formed the Socialist League (Liga Socialista; LS), but a PST, which claims to publish *Voz Socialista,* supported Rangel again this year (mimeographed sheet distributed at the presentation of the MAS program, Teatro Metropolitano, 19 September). The LS, also supporting Rangel, is the Venezuelan section of the United Secretariat of the Fourth International. The International Secretariat is represented by the Revolutionary Workers' Party, Trotskyist-Posadist (Partido Obrero Revolucionario Trotskista-Posadista; PORT-Posadista), which supported the PCV candidate.

The LS is the only national-regional party among the three, a recognition gained in 1978 after long legal battles and much government opposition. The LS has had a stormy history, which will probably be clarified only when and if the Niehous kidnapping case is solved. In July 1976 LS founder and Secretary General Jorge Rodríguez was arrested as a presumed courier for the kidnappers and tortured to death by the intelligence police (DISIP). Niehous was kidnapped by an unknown "Revolutionary Command, Argimiro Gabaldón." A court martial summary at the time said: "It has been established that members of this command come from the Organization of Revolutionaries (OR), from the LS, which is a front organization for the OR, and a dissident military detachment from the PRV" (*Latin American Report*, San Francisco, August 1976). (See below.) Carmelo Laborit, a former MIR member, and Juan Medina Figueredo are president and secretary general, respectively, of the LS. The party has presented congressional candidates in all states, including Laborit and David Nieves (also arrested in 1976) for the Federal District.

Guerrillas. Rural guerrilla activity this year was concentrated principally in the states of Guárico, Anzoátegui, and Monagas. Attacks against army patrols and military and police posts, some harassment of villages, and extortion of landowners were usually attributed to the Red Flag (Bandera Roja) group or to "pseudoguerrillas" (bandits). In the cities, a series of spectacular bank robberies has been linked to former guerrillas, but police have been parsimonious with statements.

Both Bandera Roja and the OR were formed in 1969 when the MIR split over the question of abandoning armed resistance. Little has been heard of the OR recently, and Bandera Roja has suffered a number of divisions. According to documents captured by police, one of the most important was the 1975 division which produced Bandera Roja and Bandera Roja Marxista-Leninista, the latter apparently led by the Carlos Betancourt faction. At that time Betancourt and other leaders allegedly ordered the execution of Miguel Salas, "Comandante César." Arrested guerrillas led police to his grave this year (*El Universal,* 17 October). What is left of the groups—and perhaps new ones—has nonetheless been active enough to keep fairly strong contingents of military and police patrols occupied almost permanently during the year, particularly in the eastern states. The only tangible results seem to be a further decimation of guerrilla forces through deaths and arrests.

In October police presented their prize arrest to the press: Rubén Ricardi, "Comandante Indio," fourth man in the Américo Silva front of Bandera Roja, led by Gabriel Puerta Aponte. The interview was garbled and often contradictory. Although admitting participation in several spectacular kidnappings, Ricardi denied any connection with the Niehous case. He first seemed to give the OR credit for this and then switched the responsibility to a dissident "PRV group led by Rodríguez Lanz." (*El Nacional,* 29 October.) In an interview with Alfredo Peña, Douglas Bravo condemned the kidnapping and refused to comment upon it, saying he had absolutely no clues as to the identity of those involved (*Conversaciones con Douglas Bravo,* pp. 189–92).

The EPA denied reports that three persons arrested for the attempted kidnapping of a bank manager in Ciudad Bolivar are militants of the party. EPA has applied for its first regional recognition in the state of Bolivar. (*El Universal,* 28 November.) The GAR defended the action of its regional secretary in Mérida, detained in connection with land invasions which the party insists were socially justified (*El Nacional,* 26 November).

Caracas, Venezuela.   Carole Merten

AFRICA AND THE MIDDLE EAST

Egypt

The Communist Party of Egypt (al-Hizb al-Shuy'i al-Misri; CPE) was founded in 1921. It was proscribed at its inception, and in 1965 it dissolved itself and merged with the Arab Socialist Union (ASU), the country's sole legal party organization. Under the new Egyptian policy of liberalization and democratic pluralism which began in 1976, Egyptian leftists formed a faction within the ASU which subsequently developed into a legitimate party, the National Progressive Unionist Party (NPUP), embracing Marxists, Nasserites, trade unionists, and intellectuals under the leadership of Khalid Muhyi al-Din. During February the NPUP held its first constituent conference to select its leadership. During the same month it began to publish a weekly newspaper, *al-Ahali* (The people), which by May had a circulation of 135,000. Three of the 375 seats in the People's Assembly are held by NPUP members Khalid Muhyi al-Din, Qabbari 'Abdallah, and Abu al-'Izz al-Hariri. The NPUP maintains close, unofficial ties with the five proscribed Egyptian communist parties: the Beirut-based Egyptian Communist Party, responsible for publishing the underground journal *Victory*, the Egyptian Communist Workers' Party, the Revolutionary Current (Maoist), the Revolutionary Egyptian Communist Party, and the 8th of January Organization.

Political Positions of the NPUP. As to domestic issues, in May Khalid Muhyi al-Din declared that "economic difficulties require a radical change of economic policy, and the government has no political boldness for that." He pointed out that the NPUP has consistently called for measures to resolve the problems of the working sections of the population and to reduce the gap between the poor and the rich. He emphasized that "our economic cooperation with other countries be of producing and not consuming character." (*al-Usbu' al-'Arabi*, Beirut, 27 May.) In regard to Egyptian foreign policy, the NPUP, alone among Egyptian parties, has voiced open opposition to President Sadat's negotiations with Israel. It supports the convening of the Geneva peace conference. In July Khalid Muhyi al-Din declared that "our main purpose must be putting an end to Israeli occupation of Arab lands including Jerusalem . . . setting up an independent Palestinian state, and recognition of the PLO as the only legitimate representative of the Palestinian people" (*FBIS*, 26 July). On 27 September the NPUP denounced the Camp David agreements, declaring that the agreements would mean drastic changes in the political map of the region and the cancellation of all commitments undertaken by Egypt under the accords signed within the framework of the Arab League (*FBIS*, 29 September). The NPUP strongly advocates Arab solidarity and urges a resumption of relations with the Arab states of Syria, Libya, Iraq, and South Yemen. The NPUP also calls for a return to a policy of nonalignment through a loosening of ties with the U.S. and a reestablishment of contacts with the Soviet Union. The NPUP criticized Egypt's supplying military aid to Somalia while Egypt does not have enough arms for itself. And, as a strong supporter of the Lebanese national movement, the NPUP accused Egypt of standing idle during the Israeli aggression against southern Lebanon. The NPUP holds the government responsible for the incident in which fifteen Egyptian soldiers were killed by the Cyprus National Guard while attempting to free hostages.

Government Repression of the NPUP. Anwar Sadat's government has tried both to restrain the leadership and restrict the influence of the NPUP without proscribing it. The government has arrested many NPUP members, accusing them of cooperating with clandestine communist parties and attempting to organize antigovernment demonstrations. Various issues of the newspaper *al-Ahali* have been confiscated.

The most direct effort to restrain the NPUP came with the holding of a referendum on May 21. The referendum aimed at pressuring the two opposition parties (the NPUP and the rightist New Wafd) to purge their ranks of the principal leaders who have been challenging government policies. Egypt's eleven million eligible voters were asked to endorse six principles. According to these principles anyone espousing an ideology contrary to religious teaching (i.e., the Communists) and anyone who corrupted the nation's political life before or after the 1952 revolution (aimed at the Wafdists) is banned from holding senior posts in the government or state industry, from joining trade unions, from holding posts in the media, and from writing in the press. The referendum also binds journalists and political parties to three principles: national unity, social peace, and the inevitability of the socialist solution. The day before the voting, the Egyptian Bar Association denounced the referendum as "unconstitutional, illegal, and a setback to democracy" (*Intercontinental Press*, 5 June). While some sources charged that government figures were highly inflated, the official result of the referendum claimed that 85 percent of the electorate voted and 98.29 percent of these supported the referendum. Two days after the vote was taken, President Sadat told editors and journalists that he had erred in allowing "rotten elements" created and supported by the Soviet Union to enter Egyptian politics. He declared that the referendum was "above all, support for sound democracy" (*Middle East News Agency*, 23 May). On 1 June the People's Assembly, with only nine opposing votes, approved a draft law to implement the results of the referendum. While the other opposition party, the New Wafd, dissolved itself, the members of the NPUP voted on 11 June to freeze public activity, including the publication of *al-Ahali* and the enrollment of new members, in protest to the law but decided not to dissolve. *Al-Ahali*, however, resumed publication on 13 July after a stoppage of about six weeks. Action to implement the law began immediately with an escalation of arrests of NPUP members. Parliamentary immunity was withdrawn from Khalid Muhyi al-Din, as it had been earlier from Abu al-'Izz al-Hariri. When *al-Ahali* resumed publication, it was subject to almost regular confiscation.

While the NPUP declares that the Marxists are only one group within the party, constant accusations in the Egyptian press declare that "Marxists" or "Communists" control the party. The strongest charge against the party came on 6 June from President Sadat who declared that "the Marxist groups . . . have regrettably grown up under the sponsorship of the Soviet Union . . . Through their newspaper and their method they are inciting one class against another . . . We will not accept . . . having the communists continue to control the leftist organization. Nor will we accept having any communist hold a key state post in information or other fields" (*FBIS*, 7 June). In a speech on 14 August, President Sadat said that the New Wafd party had dissolved itself and that the NPUP must follow suit for "there is no place for it among us." Both parties, he charged, corrupted political life before and after the revolution, sold their consciences, and bought foreign ideologies. (*Arab Report and Record*, London, 1–15 August.)

The NPUP clearly has a greater impact on the Egyptian political scene than its small membership would indicate. This can be attributed to its amalgamation of the leftist opposition into one active, cohesive bloc; its existence as the only real opposition to the policies of President Sadat; and finally, its interaction with the various communist parties who give it strength through their clandestine operations.

The Egyptian Communist Parties. The five communist parties mentioned earlier, the Egyptian Communist Party, the Egyptian Communist Workers' Party, the Revolutionary Current, the Revolutionary Egyptian Communist Party, and the 8th of January Organization, have very small but active memberships. They work almost exclusively at clandestine organizing on campuses and in factories. They rarely surface to issue public statements or participate in conferences. Two notable exceptions involve the Egyptian Communist Party (ECP). During mid-April the ECP participated in the meeting of eight Arab communist and workers' parties held in Cyprus. The parties condemned the Israeli invasion of southern Lebanon and asserted their support for both the Palestinian resistance and the Lebanese national movement. A Beirut newspaper reported that the meeting also discussed measures to topple the governments of a number of Arab countries, particularly South Yemen and Iraq, so that communist forces could eventually dominate them (*al-Hawadeth*, Beirut, 28 July). The party also issued a statement, published in Beirut, which called for the overthrow of President Sadat's government. The statement attacked what it called "the political authority's prejudice in favor of local capitalism and reaction and in favor of imperialism and its allies abroad." The statement also denounced "parasite capitalism" in the Egyptian economy, which it claimed was "led by a few politicians, their relatives and followers." (*al-Safir*, Beirut, 10 June.)

Beyond a few such exceptions, the communist parties generally have become visible only when members are arrested by Egyptian authorities. The government of President Sadat was active during the year in trying to uncover communist activities. On 28 January three Communists were arrested in Alexandria. On 18 February, 34 people were indicted on charges of forming a secret communist organization to overthrow the government. On 7 March seventeen Palestinian students in Asyut University who had allegedly formed a secret communist organization were detained for investigation. A trial of 176 alleged Communists, charged with trying to overthrow the regime by force, committing terrorism, and participating in the January 1977 riots began in April. A prosecution witness in this case said that the "Communists" had received "material support" from the USSR and a radical Palestinian group and testified that these members of the "Communist Workers' Party" aimed to "seize power in Egypt by any means" (*Middle East Reporter*, Beirut, 27 April). On 28 May the public prosecutor at the Tanta Court of Appeals announced the sentencing of 24 defendants in cases involving communist activities. Such efforts by the government were exerted with even greater intensity after the May referendum. On 13 June the Socialist Public Prosecutor submitted four lists of 131 names of politicians and former government officials to be restrained under the new law. One of these lists, categorized as those "advocating doctrines contrary to religion," consisted of 22 alleged Communists. Further lists of this sort are to be issued later. Also in June the labor movement was purged of leaders because of "declared affiliation with communism." In mid-July six Egyptians were sentenced to jail terms and fines on the charge of organizing and operating the proscribed Egyptian Communist Party and Egyptian Communist Workers' Party. On 7 October the state security intelligence forces arrested 85 members of the 8th of January Organization (that is the date when it is alleged that most of the communist parties unified). The five communist parties are clearly not a significant threat to the Egyptian government.

Death of ECP Cofounder. On 4 May Henri Curiel, cofounder of the ECP, was assassinated in Paris by unknown assailants. He had been a principal organizer of meetings between Israeli leftists and the Palestine Liberation Organization. He had been accused by some sources of having close links with international terrorism and of being a KGB agent.

Stanford University   Patricia Mihaly

Iran

Since 1941 communism in Iran has been represented by the Tudeh Party (Party of the Masses). In 1953 the Communists were suppressed, but a number of leaders managed to escape and reorganized the Tudeh Party in East Germany.

Iranian communist activity is confined primarily to groups operating outside the country. Within Iran, Tudeh Party membership probably does not exceed a few thousand. (Other estimates put it at about 1,000. *NYT,* 8 December.) Iradj Eskandari has been first secretary of the party since 1971. Eskandari and his colleagues have consistently attacked the government and the shah while emphasizing the regime's alleged corruption, injustice, and oppression. In 1978 the Tudeh Party's criticisms were repeated by Iranians throughout the country who rose in mass protest against the shah's government. The Tudeh partisans were, however, only a tiny fraction of the opposition forces.

Other Marxist-Leninist groups include the Revolutionary Tudeh Party organized in 1965, the Organization of Marxist-Leninists formed in 1967 by two Maoist former Tudeh members, the Guerrilla Organization of the Devotees for the People established in Iran in 1971, and a tiny section of the National Front which embraced Marxist doctrines beginning in 1972. Because of the widespread upheaval in 1978 and the government's reaction by force, there is evidence that membership in these groups increased somewhat during the year. By the end of the year, approximately 30,000 Iranians were associated with them in one way or another. This represents, however, only a very small part of the overall mosaic of opposition to the shah and his policies.

A Year of Domestic Opposition and Upheaval. In 1978 Iran was the scene of domestic upheaval on a scale unprecedented since the days of the Constitutional Movement of 1906-1911. Since 9 January when military forces fired on 2,000 unarmed demonstrators in Qom, the country has witnessed violent confrontation between masses of anti-shah demonstrators and the army in hundreds of Iranian cities and towns. During the first eleven months of the year, over 3,000 persons were killed in the riots. During the last months of the year, the shah instituted military rule throughout the country and hung on precariously to his throne.

The political opposition that erupted in 1978 cut across all class lines and took on the proportions of a mass movement. During the first week of September, for example, over three million people joined antigovernment demonstrations. Although the Shi'ite religious leadership helped guide and direct the opposition, the movement consisted of workers, merchants, writers, students, bureaucrats, teachers, lawyers, clerks, and craftsmen. Thousands of women joined the demonstrators. The demands of these groups included political participation, an end to corruption, an equitable system of justice, quality health and education systems, and freedom of speech, press, and assembly. The opposition was united in its call for a return to rule according to the constitution of 1906. The religious leaders also demanded an end to the government's ten-year-old policy of attempting to destroy the organization and influence of the Shi'ite establishment. These demands were exacerbated by a series of economic problems that converged in the early part of the year. These included runaway inflation, a stagnant agricultural growth rate, and a widening urban-rural income distribution gap.

Throughout the year, the shah was unable to bring the opposition forces under control. Numerous minor political and economic concessions only served to further alienate the crowds, who came to demand nothing less than the abdication of the shah himself. By the end of November the shah ruled behind bayonets, as large numbers of Iranian citizens engaged in strikes, sabotage, and passive opposition of many kinds.

Tudeh Party Policy. The leadership of the Tudeh Party viewed the turbulent events of 1978 as the inevitable culmination of years of alleged repression and corruption practiced by members of the Iranian political elite. On 11 September, Iradj Eskandari described the upheaval against the shah as "popular, democratic, and revolutionary." According to Eskandari, "this situation is not unexpected for our party." In noting that the Shi'ite religious leaders were directing the movement, he rushed to stress the Tudeh Party's respect for Shi'i Islam. "We have never attacked religion. We find in the precepts of Islam many principles which we share, such as that of the equality of all men." The Tudeh Party consistently called for a united front against the shah's rule. Eskandari assured his compatriots that "our party . . . has always respected the religious beliefs that are solidly rooted in the vast majority of the Iranian population . . . We are in favor of a union with all democratic forces, including religious ones" (*Pravda,* 13 September).

Tudeh efforts at collegiality and a coalition of opposition forces were not reciprocated by the other leaders of the anti-shah movement, Karim Sanjabi, head of the National Front, a large movement of opposition middle-class nationalists, stated in August that a reconciliation of national forces could not extend to the Tudeh Party since it was not a genuinely independent party. The religious leaders also constantly and consistently repeated their abhorrence of any communist alternative to the shah. Thus, although Tudeh Party sympathizers constituted a small but dedicated part of the mass of opposition forces, they were a group not trusted by the overwhelming majority of the Iranians who joined hands to challenge the shah and his 37-year regime.

International Activities. The party has taken a consistently pro-Soviet line. According to Eskandari, the shah's principal support derives from American imperialism. But, Eskandari believes, the PRC backs the shah as well; Peking is in "shameless and unprincipled collusion" with Washington (*Problemy mira i sotialisma,* November, 1978, pp.45−46).

University of Texas, Austin   James A. Bill

Iraq

The Iraqi Communisty Party (ICP) was founded in 1934. Its membership remains essentially confined to minority groups—ethnic and religious—and to intellectuals. It now operates in alliance with the ruling Ba'th Party as part of the Ba'th-dominated Progressive National Front (PNF). The ICP has some representatives within the cabinet, but its effective influence is limited. There are no reliable figures concerning party membership, estimated in the past at about 2,000. (Iraq's population is about 12 million.)

Domestic Attitudes and Activities. The ICP leaders who represent the party in the cabinet—Mukarram al-Talabani and 'Amir 'Abd-Allah—as well as 'Aziz Muhammad (secretary of the Central Committee) and Karim Ahmad have incurred censure from dissidents for alleged subservience to the Ba'th. The malcontents have organized a dissident communist group which in 1978 distributed circulars denouncing the ICP leaders for toeing the Ba'th line.

International Views and Policies. Iraqi-Soviet relations were strained by Soviet support given to Ethiopia against the nationalist rebels in Somalia and Eritrea with whom the Ba'th Party sympathizes. These differences were reflected in the cooling of Ba'th-ICP relations, even though many Iraqi Communists sympathize with Ethiopia's adversaries. Iraqi-Soviet relations were further affected when the nationalist regime of President Daoud of Afghanistan was overthrown by a communist coup in April. The prompt Soviet recognition of Afghanistan's new regime was regarded as an indirect encouragement of communist activities in the Arab world. In Iraq, the dissident communist group, encouraged by the events in Afghanistan, seems to have contemplated a similar coup in Iraq. All suspects were rounded up, and 21 culprits, already under arrest, were executed. Ba'thi action was regarded in some Arab nationalist circles as retaliation for Soviet support of Communists rather than Arab nationalist elements in the Horn of Africa. The Soviet leaders, however, have kept quiet about the matter, and the Soviet press has made statements in support of the Ba'th regime. In a statement on 5 June, Na'im Haddad, secretary of the PNF and a Ba'th spokesman, declared that his country still regarded the Soviet Union as a strategic ally.

Arab Policy. According to the Central Committee of the ICP (10 March), the Arab national liberation movement faced serious difficulties during 1977—78 because of the bitter imperialist-Zionist-reactionary offensive against it. This offensive was described as part of the global strategy of imperialism in confrontation with the world revolutionary movement, wherein the forces of reaction—landlords, bourgeoisie, and the bureaucracy—have made an alignment with imperialism and Zionism. Sadat's visit to Jerusalem in November 1977 was seen as the expression of the alignment between Egypt's reactionary forces and the United States and Israel. In a meeting on 3 December 1977, the Central Committee stated that Sadat's visit to Jerusalem was a step hostile to the Arab national liberation movement. According to the ICP, the trip marked the perpetutation of the consequences of the

1967 aggression, the liquidation of the Palestine question and the Palestine Liberation Organization, and the disruption of the progressive Arab ranks. Sadat's visit was viewed as having the effect of encouraging Zionist aggressive circles to display greater insolence, intransigence, and insistence on territorial expansion. As a result, Israel was encouraged to threaten Syria, attack southern Lebanon, and strike at Palestinian settlements. In brief, Sadat has undermined Soviet-Arab friendship and supported Zionist and imperialist ringleaders.

The termination of the civil war in Lebanon is regarded as a victory for the Lebanese national movement and for the Arab national liberation movement as a whole. But, in communist eyes, the imperialist and Zionist forces have tried to exercise their influence to prolong the tension and oppose all efforts to restore a normal situation in the country. For this reason, the aftermath of the civil war resulted in a triangular contest among the Lebanese, Palestinian, and Syrian forces, ultimately benefiting the Zionists and imperialists.

In the ICP view, only a front composed of Syria, Iraq, and the PLO and supported by the national liberation movement can stand in the way of the disruptive forces of Zionism and imperialism. Syria's reconciliation with Iraq is viewed as the first step in the right direction, which, the ICP hopes, will lead to a mobilization of the progressive forces at summit meetings in Baghdad.

Relations with other Communist Parties. In 1977 a delegation of the Central Committee, headed by 'Umar 'Ali al-Shayk, visited the Hungarian People's Republic (21—29 October). In a joint statement, the two parties condemned the Israelis and declared their solidarity with the peoples struggling for the elimination of colonial systems.

On 13 October 1977 the ICP celebrated the sixtieth anniversary of the Great October Revolution, which it hailed as a highlight for all peoples. In an article published in the journal *al-Thaqafa al-Jadida*, 'Aziz Muhammad noted the great impact of the October Revolution on the development of the Arab national liberation movement.

On 29—30 December 1977 a delegation of the ICP, headed by 'Aziz Muhammad, visited Moscow. A meeting with Mikhail Suslov, secretary of the Political Bureau of the Soviet party's Central Committee, Boris Ponomarev, Mikhail Zimianin, and Karen Brutent was held at the Central Committee. The ICP delegation stated that Iraqi Communists have always appreciated the USSR's efforts in support of the just cause of the Arabs. They also expressed their solidarity with the democratic anti-imperialist forces of the Middle East, which oppose neocolonialist plans and condemn the anti-Soviet and anticommunist actions of reactionary circles.

On 9 January a delegation of the Lebanese nationalist movement met with Saddam Husayn, vice-president of the Revolutionary Command Council. Included in the Lebanese delegation were George Hani, assistant secretary general of the Lebanese Communist Party and vice-president of the Central Political Council, and Muhsin Ibrahim, secretary general of the Communist Action Organization and executive secretary of the Central Political Council. They exchanged views on the current situation in the Arab world and the developments in Lebanon.

On 24 January Ahmad Hasan al-Bakr, president of Iraq, received a delegation of the Italian Communist Party (PCI), headed by Giancarlo Pajetta, member of the Secretariat of the PCI and official in charge of the party's foreign relations. They reviewed the situation in the Arab world and discussed current international issues. In addition, they discussed the existing cooperation between the Ba'th Party and the PCI and the means of further developing relations between the two parties.

In February the Vietnamese ambassador in Baghdad, Hoang Duc Phuong, talked with the head of the Foreign Relations Committee of the ICP Central Committee. Also in February a delegation of the Bulgarian Communist Party, led by Ivan Prumov, secretary of the Central Committee, visited Baghdad. Included in the delegation was Elena Lagadinov, chairwoman of the Committee of Bulgarian Women and a member of the Central Committee. The delegation talked with a number of high government officials during its one-week visit and expressed its admiration for the progress achieved by Iraq, especially in the agricultural field. In February and March delegations of Soviet Communist and Ba'th Party cadres exchanged visits to each other's countries.

On 25 March Nadim 'Abd al-Samad, secretary general of the Lebanese Communist Party, visited Baghdad. He stated that he intended to exchange views with leaders of the Ba'th Party National Command on the situation in Lebanon in the wake of the Israeli aggression in southern Lebanon.

In April an agricultural delegation, led by Amir Mahdi al-Khishali, deputy minister of agriculture and agrarian reform, visited Peking, and while there he said: "Having seen for ourselves the developments in China's agriculture, our delegation is convinced that led by Chairman Hua and the Central Committee of the Communist Party of China, the Chinese people will surely achieve still greater successes in the days to come." However, during a visit to Moscow, Zaki Khayri, a member of the ICP Central Committee, declared on 30 April that the Maoist policy had rendered a direct service to the sworn enemies of the Arabs—imperialism and Zionism—and that Maoist policy had converged with the policy of the most die-hard imperialist reaction.

In June a delegation of the ICP, led by 'Aziz Muhammad, visited Prague. The delegation met with Josef Kempry, Presidium member and secretary of the Czechoslovak Communist Party Central Committee, exchanged views on the situation in the Middle East, and informed each other concerning the activities of their respective parties.

In mid-July a delegation of the ICP, led by Karim Ahmad, a member of the Central Committee, visited the Soviet Union, including the Republic of Uzbekistan. The delegation visited industrial and agricultural projects and acquainted itself with activities of the Communist Party of the Soviet Union.

Publications. The ICP publishes *Tariq al-Sha'b* (People's road), a daily newspaper. Other ICP publications are *al-Fikr al-Jadid* (New thought), a weekly, and *al-Thaqafa al-Jadida* (New culture), a monthly magazine.

The Johns Hopkins University   Majid Khadduri

Israel

The communist movement in Palestine dates back to 1920. Two years later, a Palestine Communist Party (Palestinische Kommunistische Partei; PKP) was established, and it joined the Comintern in 1924. Following periodic appearance of factional divisions, the PKP split along ethnic lines in 1943. While the Jewish group retained the original name, the Arab faction called itself the League for National Liberation ('Usbah al-Tahrir al-Watani). In October 1948, with the new state of Israel in control of most of Palestine, both groups reunited to form the Israeli Communist Party (Miflaga Kommunistit Isra'elit; MAKI).

The movement split again in 1965, partly along ethnic lines. The "New Communist List" (Reshima Kommunistit Hadasha; RAKAH)—pro-Moscow, strongly anti-Zionist, and drawing a majority of its members from the Arab population—emerged as the main party and increasingly gained international recognition as the Communist Party of Israel (CPI). MAKI, which became an almost completely Jewish organization and moderate in its opposition to government policies, was eclipsed. In 1975, MAKI disappeared as a separate organization after merger with MOKED (Focus), a Zionist socialist organization moderate in attitude toward the Arabs. In 1977, MOKED united with other noncommunist groups in the "peace camp" to form Peace for Israel (Shalom le-Israel; SHELLI). By this time, some former (post-1965) MAKI members had joined or at least supported RAKAH as the country's only communist party.

In keeping with Israel's competitive political party system, Communists have been free to organize and participate in public life. The prevailing system of proportional representation has facilitated election of candidates from small parties, including the Communists, to the Knesset (parliament).

From the beginning of the state, MAKI (and later RAKAH) found its main support among the Arab minority. This resulted from the absence of an Arab nationalist party in Israel, which left the Communists the only alternative to Zionist parties. Communists also gained Arab support because of their stand against official policies toward the Arab minority and toward the Arab world but not because of any espousal of Marxism-Leninism by a large number of Arab voters. Increasingly they have gained support of young, educated Arabs. Although RAKAH's membership is about 80 percent Arab, many of its leaders (including a majority on top party organs) are Jews. The party presents itself as a model for Arab-Jewish cooperation.

RAKAH membership is estimated at about 1,500 for an Israeli population of 3,708,300 in September 1978 (not including occupied territories).

However, RAKAH is isolated from the mainstream of Israeli politics. No communist party has ever participated in the cabinet. Since the December 1977 election, the RAKAH-led coalition, Democratic Front for Peace and Equality (DFPE) has had five seats in the Knesset, one of which belongs to each of the two noncommunist coalition partners: the Black Panthers (an Afro-Asian Jewish group protesting against alleged discrimination by Jews of European origin) and the Arab Local Council Heads. The less radical SHELLI, with two seats, sometimes votes with DFPE.

Leadership and Organization. RAKAH congresses meet at four-year intervals. The Eighteenth Congress (actually the fourth congress of RAKAH, which sees itself as the direct successor to the 1920 organization, the PKP, and to the pre-1965 MAKI as the Communist Party of Israel) met in December 1976 at Haifa. It elected a Central Committee of 31 members and five candidates, as well as a Central Control Commission. (*Information Bulletin,* no. 9—10, 1976). Meeting in plenary session on 25 December 1976, the Central Committee elected a Political Bureau of nine and a Secretariat of seven members. (See *YICA,* 1978, pp. 434—435 for names of members.)

Auxiliary and Mass Organizations. RAKAH provides the dominant core of the Nazareth Democratic Front and other antiestablishment electoral lists in smaller Arab towns as well as of the DFPE (see above). It sponsors an active children's Young Pioneer movement and a youth organization, the Young Communist League. RAKAH also participates in the Democratic Women's Movement, the Israeli Association of Anti-Fascist Fighters and Victims of Nazism, and the Israeli-USSR Friendship Movement.

Domestic Attitudes and Activities. During 1978, RAKAH leaders continued to stress the economic consequences of Israel's foreign policy. An article, entitled "Israel: The Cost of Militarism" (*WMR*, January), blamed the "militarists" for "a serious disruption of the system of foreign payments and recurrent breakdowns of the monetary and financial machinery." It pointed to the 1976 balance of payments deficit that reached $4 billion and a foreign debt of $9 billion, a reduction in productive capability, high taxes, and inflation that allegedly reduced "real wages by 13.8 percent" during 1977. In an interview (ibid., May), a spokesman mentioned "hysterical attacks on CPI policy" and "concentrated efforts to isolate our party." The Political Bureau called for resignation of the government, and RAKAH deputies later supported an unsuccessful no-confidence motion.

In January, a Greek communist journalist from Cyprus and Hans Lebrecht (RAKAH Central Committee member and correspondent for several European communist publications) were arrested on charges of collecting information for the Palestine Liberation Organization. Lebrecht was later acquitted, but the Cypriot received a five-year sentence. The Central Committee called the charges "absurd" and "an onslaught on democracy and human rights." (*FBIS*, 25 March.)

International Activity and Contacts. In February, Politburo member David Burnstein led a delegation on a visit to Bucharest, while his colleague Emile Habibi visited Budapest during the same month. Secretary General Meir Vilner headed a delegation that visited the Soviet Union, Poland, and Bulgaria during April. He also traveled to Hungary and Mongolia in July. Wolf Erlich, president of the Central Control Commission, was a guest of the Hugarian Communist Party during May. A delegation of about 50, headed by the secretary of the youth movement Yehuda Goshansky, attended the Eleventh World Festival of Youth and Students at Havana in July.

International Views and Policies. A report of the Central Committee in January praised the Soviet Union and its "principled and consistent peace policies" (*IB*, 15 March). Emile Tuma, a Central Committee member, declared "solidarity with the CPSU an expression of proletarian internationalism" (*WMR*, May). A joint statement issued by Vilner and Mongolian communist leaders "resolutely condemned the antisocialist, anti-Soviet, great power chauvinist, and militarist policies and activities of China's Maoist leadership" and supported Vietnam against "the Peking leadership's slanderous campaign" (Summary of World Broadcasts, 22 July).

The bulk of RAKAH's attention during the year was directed toward the Arab-Israeli conflict. Statements repeatedly emphasized the necessity of a settlement that would involve Israeli withdrawal from all territories occupied in 1967, the right of Palestinians to establish an independent state, guarantees for security of all states in the region, and the right to use international waterways. Such a peace treaty can be achieved through resumption of the Geneva conference, with PLO participation. While rejecting Zionism, the party supports the continued existence of Israel but attacks its "aggressive" policies.

Egyptian President Anwar Sadat's visit to Israel in November 1977 was described as a "capitulation" that "shocked Arab public opinion and true peace fighters the world over" (*WMR*, August). Politburo member Ruth Lubitz called the initiative an attempt to wreck the Geneva conference, split the Arab world, undermine progressive regimes, and establish a " 'pax Americana' in the Near East" (*FBIS*, 17 March). In a Knesset speech, Vilner described Begin's proposal for Palestinian autonomy as "nothing but an attempt to create an Israeli colony" (ibid., 30 December 1977). The Central Committee described the "creating of new settlements" as proof "that the sole purpose" of all of Begin's talk is to camouflage the policy of annexation and war (ibid., 12 January).

In an article (*WMR*, August), Habibi stated that "The imperialist-Zionist-Arab reaction triangle had come out into the open because of its deepening crisis and because of the growing liberation movement." He described U.S. attempts "to bring about a temporary normalization between the reactionary rulers of Israel and Egypt" as an effort to use them against revolutionary forces in Africa. The sale of American arms to Saudi Arabia, Egypt, and Israel was cited as "plots of the U.S.-Egypt-Israel triangle."

In a press conference, Vilner described the Camp David conference as an attempt to create, "under the U.S. and NATO aegis of a military bloc . . . directed against the independent progressive states of the region" (*FBIS,* 9 September). DFPE deputies in the Knesset voted against the subsequent Camp David agreements.

Various RAKAH statements condemned the Israeli invasion of Lebanon. Habibi (*WMR,* August) spoke of "Israeli aggression" and "barbaric crimes against the Lebanese and Palestinian peoples."

Publications. RAKAH's newspaper, *al-Ittihad* (Union), is an Arabic biweekly published in Haifa, edited by Tawfiq Tubi and Habibi. A Hebrew weekly, *Zo Ha-Derekh* (This is the way), is edited by Vilner in Tel Aviv. Other party publications are *al-Jadid* (The new), a monthly literary and cultural magazine published in Haifa; *al-Ghad* (Tomorrow), a youth magazine; the Yiddish *Der Weg* (The way), published weekly by Vilner in Tel Aviv; the Bulgarian *Tovaye Putnam* (This is the way), published every two weeks in Jaffa; the theoretical *Arakim: Be'ayot ha-Shalom ve-ha-Soatziyalizm* (Values: Problems of peace and socialism), published six times a year in Tel Aviv; and a sporadic English *Information Bulletin, Communist Party of Israel,* published in Tel Aviv by the Foreign Relations Department of the Central Committee.

Other Marxist Organizations. Several other groups exist in Israel, but none of them is comparable to RAKAH as a political force. Each consists of a handful of members, mostly young Jews, but none offers its own list of electoral candidates.

The most radical trend is represented by the Israeli Socialist Organization (Irgun Sotziyalisti Isra'eli; ISO), formed by a group expelled in 1962 from MAKI. Widely known by the name of its monthly Hebrew publication, *Matzpen* (Compass), issued from Tel Aviv, ISO condemns establishment of Israel at the expense of Palestinian Arabs and its "open alliance with . . . imperialism, and collusion with the most reactionary forces in the Arab world." The ISO recognizes the continued existence of a Hebrew nation in Palestine but calls for "de-Zionification" and "a socialist revolution," as well as "integration into a unified, socialist Middle East." It criticizes USSR policy of "peaceful coexistence," Soviet "bureaucracy," and RAKAH's acceptance of the Soviet line. It also has censured Peking's policies. The *Matzpen* viewpoint has received most attention outside Israel. Several splits in the organization occurred during the early 1970s. Breakaway splinter groups include the Revolutionary Communist League (Brit Kommunistit Mahapkhanit), which is associated with the Fourth (Trotskyite) International; the Workers' League (Brit ha-Po'alim), also Trotskyite; and the Maoist-oriented Revolutionary Communist Alliance-Struggle (Brit Kommunistit Mahapkhanit-Ma'avak).

The Israeli New Left (Smol Yisrael Chadash; SIAH) was launched in 1968. It consists of a few youths, mainly students, previously associated with MAKI and MAPAM (the United Workers' Party, formerly a far-left party but now a part of the Labor Alignment). SIAH, which identifies with the radical student movement in Europe, professes devotion to a combination of Zionism and Marxism and calls for the creation of an independent Palestinian state to exist alongside Israel. Its publications include *Siah* (published irregularly in Hebrew) and *Israleft,* a biweekly English newsletter that disseminates statements by various leftist and peace groups.

Indiana State University   Glenn E. Perry
Terre Haute

Jordan

The Communist Party of Jordan (al-Hizb al-Shuyu'i al-Urdunni; CPJ) was officially established in June 1951 and has operated under the guise of various popular front organizations since that time. Its center of activity has been the West Bank, where it has drawn support from students, teachers, professional workers, and the "lower middle class."

The CPJ has been illegal since 1957, although the government's normally repressive measures on occasion have been relaxed. At present, party membership is punishable by jail sentences of three to fifteen years. Few other radical organizations are active in Jordan; however, various Palestinian groups, such as the Marxist-oriented Popular Front for the Liberation of Palestine (embittered by "repression" of the Palestinians during 1970–71), urge the overthrow of King Hussein. They appear to have little overt influence in Jordan. Beginning in 1972, Israel clamped down on the party in the West Bank because it had engaged in terrorist activities. More recently, the West Bank Communists have returned to more conventional political action, perhaps in preparation for Israel's implementation of an autonomy plan for the West Bank.

The CPJ has perhaps no more than 500 members, mostly Palestinians. Jordan's population of about 2,990,000 includes more than 700,000 in Israeli-occupied East Jerusalem and the West Bank.

Leadership and Organization. The CPJ is said to be a tightly organized, well-disciplined network of small cells. Due to secrecy, little information is available on the party leadership. Fu'ad Nassar, who died in late 1976, was the party's first secretary general. Fayiq Muhammad Warrad then succeeded to that post. There are two West Bank communist factions. The Palestine Communist Organization, an establishment-oriented group headed by Bashir Barghuti, a well-known Marxist from Ramallah, is reportedly the larger of the two. The Palestinian Communist Party is a small, militant organization affiliated with the Leninist Lodge, which seceded from the CPJ in the early 1970s because of ideological and personal differences. Both factions engage in organizational and propaganda activity and recruit from the five small West Bank colleges. They have made their influence felt by penetrating municipalities, professional associations, trade unions, and welfare organizations. Recently they have become more open about their Marxist orientation. The Communists are among the few groups with a political organization operating throughout the West Bank.

Prominent party members reportedly include 'Abd al-Muhsin Abu Maizar, also of the Palestine National Front (PNF) and Ishaq al-Khatib. 'Arabi 'Awad, CPJ Central Committee member and PNF leader has spent more than ten years in Jordanian or Israeli jails. Jiryas Qawwas is an associate of 'Awad and also a prominent West Bank communist PNF official; a former teacher, he claims to have spent more than thirteen years in Jordanian and Israeli jails. Other members of the Central Committee include 'Isa Madanat, Na'im Ashhab, and Ya'qub Diya' al-Din.

Auxiliary and Mass Organizations. The PNF is composed of professional and labor union representatives and "patriotic personalities." It was established in August 1973 on the West Bank, evidently on CPJ initiative. The PNF generally follows the Palestine Liberation Organization (PLO) line, advocating an independent Palestinian state on the West Bank together with the Gaza Strip. Its program includes mass political struggle and armed resistance in the occupied territories.

The PNF's precise relationship to the CPJ is unknown. According to Israeli officials, the CPJ forms the core of the PNF. The PNF is a member of the PLO, and its Central Committee includes representatives of most Palestinian factions and commando organizations. At least some of its leadership comes from the CPJ. West Bank Communists have thus become closely associated with Palestinian nationalist forces.

Party Internal Affairs. The CPJ has been described officially as the working-class party of two fraternal peoples—Jordanian and Palestinian. Despite its support of Palestinian statehood, the CPJ remains somewhat suspicious of the PLO, an attitude that is reciprocated. In 1975, West Bank Communists began signing official statements "Communist Party of the West Bank," as did affiliated student, labor, and women's associations. The CPJ's West Bank newspaper *al-Watan* appeared under the auspices of the "Palestine Communist Party," a name apparently adopted by West Bank cells without prior approval by the CPJ Central Committee.

Domestic Attitudes and Activities. The CPJ seemingly has devoted little attention to purely domestic issues. Like other Palestinians of whatever ideological persuasion who are anti-Hussein, party leaders denounce the "reactionary regime" in Amman and its links to "imperialism." They advocate establishment in Jordan of a "democratic independent state" whose goal is social development. The CPJ considers its efforts to establish a national front in Jordan a precondition for establishment of a national liberation regime. These activities are designed, among other things, to eliminate "imperialism" on the East Bank.

The Palestine issue has vexed the party since its inception. As a generally pro-Soviet organization, the CPJ evidently has not been entirely free to take an independent stand. Consequently, it has lost support to more committed and radical Palestinian liberation movements. In fact, the CPJ's basic position on Palestine is similar to that of the main Palestinian groups. The party recognizes the PLO as the sole representative of the Palestinian people.

International Activities and Attitudes. Representatives of the CPJ and the Syrian Communist Party met in Damascus and denounced President Sadat's visit to Jerusalem as a "crime," a "conspiracy," a betrayal of the Arab national liberation movement, and a blow to the Palestinian cause. They also "hailed the steadfastness of the popular masses in the West Bank and Gaza," praising their boycott of Sadat's visit and their support of the PLO. The two parties also noted the importance of cooperating with the USSR in the march toward socialism and Arab national liberation. They reaffirmed the need to strengthen the bonds between the Syrian and Jordanian parties, noting that the genuine basis for Arab solidarity is the struggle against imperialism and Zionism (summary of World Broadcasts, 6 December 1977).

In March, Secretary General Warrad visited Hungary and met with János Kádár; the two leaders condemned Israel's invasion of Lebanon. CPJ officials met at an undisclosed location in April with representatives of communist and workers' parties from Algeria, Sudan, Syria, Iraq, Lebanon, Egypt, and Morocco. In a joint statement, they declared their solidarity with the Palestinian resistance and the Lebanese National Movement, a grouping of leftwing parties. The statement refers to the "imperialist U.S. onslaught" in the Middle East and emphasizes the importance of protecting national sovereignty, strengthening ties with the socialist bloc, and consolidating the "nationalist and progressive fronts" that have been established in several Arab countries (*FBIS*, 27 April). In May, the CPJ denounced the execution of 21 Communists in Iraq.

The CPJ favors a comprehensive peace settlement in the Middle East, total Israeli withdrawal from all occupied territories, and the right of the Palestinians to establish their own state. In a statement issued in *al-Nida'* (ibid., 3 October), the CPJ denounced the Camp David accords between Israel and Egypt as evidence of a growing imperialist-Zionist offensive against the Arabs. The statement accused Sadat of capitulating under U.S. pressure to Israeli demands and ignoring the Palestinian problem. It also expressed the fear that other "reactionary" Arab regimes might join the Israeli-Egyptian alliance. It urged all patriotic and progressive forces to rally to thwart the Cairo—Tel Aviv—Washington "plot." Secretary General Warrad has also referred to Sadat's "capitulatory policy" and noted that Arab "reaction" is merging with Zionism. He declared that the true friends of the Arabs are the USSR and other Socialist countries (ibid., 2 August).

Publications. The CPJ publishes *al-Jamahir* (Masses) and an underground newspaper, *al-Watan* (Homeland); both appear once or twice a month, the former in Jordan and the latter on the West Bank. The party also issues a political and theoretical magazine *al-Haqiqah* (Truth), distributed in Jordan and the West Bank. These publications are distributed clandestinely on both sides of the Jordan River, except for *al-Watan,* which is restricted mainly to the West Bank. In early 1978, *al-Taliyah* (Vanguard), an Arabic weekly published in East Jerusalem with the knowledge of the Israeli authorities, appeared on the West Bank. Its editor-in-chief and founder is Elias Nasralla, a member of the Israeli Communist Party RAKAH; senior editor is Bashir Barghuti. Shortly after its appearance, Israeli military authorites ordered *al-Taliyah* to stop publication because it did not have a permit. Another CPJ organ, *al-Shaab* (The people), also appeared in 1978. The PNF publishes its own newspaper, *Filastin* (Palestine). News of CPJ activities also appears in the organs of the Lebanese Communist Party, *al-Akhbar* and *al-Nida'.* Many communists and communist-inspired pamphlets have appeared recently on the West Bank.

U.S. Department of State   Norman F. Howard
Washington, D.C.

(Note: Views expressed in this article are the author's own and do not represent those of the State Department.)

Lebanon

The Lebanese Communist Party (al-Hizb al-Shuyu'i al-Lubnani; LCP) was established in 1924. In 1965 it became a member of the Front of Progressive Parties and National Forces (FPPNF), under the leadership of the Progressive Socialists, now led by Walid Jumblat. The LCP more recently has become a member of the Lebanese National Movement (LNM) and functions legally. It is estimated to have about 2,500 members and sympathizers. The population of Lebanon is about 2.5 million. Authority is vested in the 24-member Central Committee, which in turn elects the 11-man Political

Bureau, five secretaries, a Central Control Commission, and Financial Commission (see *YICA 1978*, p. 440 for names).

Domestic Views and Activities. The LCP primarily operates through the LNM. According to Ghassan al-Rifa'i, a member of the Political Bureau (*WMR,* May), Lebanon faces a "foreign-inspired conflict," rather than a "civil war in its well-known classical sense." It is the victim of a vast imperialist conspiracy that aims at destroying the Palestine resistance movement, itself an important factor in the Arab national liberation movement. The LCP condemned the Israeli occupation of southern Lebanon and subsequent replacement of Israeli troops by right-wing Lebanese forces of Major Sa'd Haddad. LCP Secretary General Niqula al-Shawi called on Lebanese authorities to give inter-Arab peace-keeping forces the task of ensuring security in place of factional militias. The LCP rejected the U.S. proposal for an international conference on Lebanon, lest Israeli intervention be legalized and Egypt be drawn into the settlement of the crisis. (*al-Nida'*, 11 September.)

International Views and Activities. The LCP consistently has expressed solidarity with the USSR. It considers "anti-Sovietism" a "rallying point" for imperialism, Zionism, Arab reaction, and PRC leadership. The LCP has urged China to give up anti-Sovietism and has denounced the Sino-American rapprochement as a threat to the world communist and working-class movement, and to national liberation forces all over the world (*FBIS,* 12 September, citing *Tass*). In the LCP's view, support given by China to President Sadat prompted Israeli aggression against Lebanon and the Palestinian resistance movement (ibid., 23 September). George Hawi, head of the LCP Secretariat, condemned "the oppressive measures taken by the Sadat government against democratic liberties and parties." He claimed that "the Sadat regime is passing through an advanced crisis following Sadat's renunciation of the 23 July revolution and his treasonable visit to occupied Jerusalem (ibid., 9 June, citing Iraq News Agency). According to Niqula al-Shawi, the talks at Camp David aimed at forcing Sadat to accept Israeli conditions for a separate peace and later drawing Jordan into the settlement.

LCP Participation in the LNM. Hawi served as vice-president of the LNM Central Political Council. On 31 May, this body formed an Executive committee of 11 members, holding two-year terms, responsible to the 23-member Central Political Council. The first Executive Council is composed of Dr. 'Abd al-Majid al-Rafi'i, secretary of the regional command, pro-Iraqi Ba'th Party; Hawi; Muhsin Ibrahim, Organization of Communist Action in Lebanon (OCAL); In'am Ra'd, National Syrian Socialist Party; Walid Jumblat, Progressive Socialist Party; Ibrahim Qulaylat, Independent Nasserite Movement (al-Murabitun); three independents: 'Isam Nu'man, Muhammad Qabbani and Albert Mansur; and two members that were yet to be elected by the Council. It decided to leave the post of the chairman vacant and consider the first five members of the Executive Committee as vice-chairmen, exercising collective leadership (*Arab Report and Record.* 1–15 June).

The LCP has played an integral role in LMN whose actions enjoy full and active LCP assistance The LNM supported a comprehensive security plan for Lebanon. It opposed exclusion of certain areas from national security arrangements, lest such an arrangement eventually lead to partition of Lebanon. The LCP called for establishment of a balanced Lebanese national army to achieve comprehensive national security.

In mid-March, the LNM strongly denounced the Israeli incursion into southern Lebanon and credited itself, supported by the Palestinian resistance, with halting expansion of the Israeli occupation. The LNM called for implementation of the Security Council resolution stipulating total Israeli withdrawal from Lebanon and the deployment of U.N. forces along the border.

In April, the LNM rejected a proposal by Interior Minister Salah Salman to consider withdrawal of Syrian and Arab forces from Lebanon. The LNM pointed out that despite its own dispute with Syria, the latter's presence was necessary in view of the Israeli occupation. The LNM asked the Lebanese government for swift implementation of the U.N. Security Council resolution. It likewise demanded that the government expel Major Sa'd Haddad, Sami Shidyaq, and their forces from the army and try them for the high treason of collaborating with Israel. The LMN denounced the replacement of Israeli forces by the factional sectarian army of Major Haddad, rather than by U.N. forces, inter-Arab peace-keeping forces, or a reorganized Lebanese army.

On international issues, the LNM denounced the "oppression" of democratic liberties in Egypt and expressed solidarity with the Egyptian people on the first anniversary of the uprising against the Sadat regime during 18–19 January. Later in the year, the LNM condemned the Camp David accords. On 21 September, the LNM sent a telegram to the Steadfastness Summit Meeting in Damascus "calling for decisive military measures to end the battle with the isolationists" (*Arab Report and Record,* 16–30 September). LMN delegations, inlcuding Hawi and Muhsin Ibrahim, visited Libya, Iraq, and Syria. Hawi and Muhsin Ibrahim also conferred with Lebanese Prime Minister Salim Hoss on 18 September to stress the need for renewing the mandate of the inter-Arab peace-keeping force.

Meeting of Arab Communist Parties. The LCP joined with seven other Arab communist and workers' parties from Jordan, Algeria, Sudan, Syria, Iraq, Egypt, and Morocco in secret meetings on Cyprus during mid-April. They issued a joint statement condemning the Israeli invasion of southern Lebanon and Zionist ambitions. The parties expressed full support of Palestinian national rights and the LNM. Another statement called for establishment of an effective nationalist progressive front throughout the Arab homeland against imperialism and Zionism (*FBIS,* 19 April). Participants supposedly also discussed the formation of internal revolutionary fronts to overthrow existing Arab regimes, particularly in Iraq and South Yemen (PDRY) to prepare the ground for domination by communist forces (*al-Hawadith,* Beirut, 28 July).

Publications. The LCP publishes a daily newspaper, *al-Nida'* (The call); a weekly magazine, *al-Akhbur* (News); and a literary and ideological monthly, *al-Tariq* (The road). These organs also serve as general information media for illegal communist parties in the Middle East. Since the outbreak of the Lebanese civil war in 1975, publication and distribution of periodicals have been disrupted to varying degrees.

Other Communist Organizations. The Organization of Communist Action in Lebanon (OCAL) is led by Secretary General Muhsin Ibrahim. Fawwaz Tarabulsi is a member of its Politburo. OCAL strongly denounced decisions taken by the Arab League Council against South Yemen in the following words: "It is indicative that those who put their signatures to these decisions did not react at all to the capitulationist visit of Egyptian President Sadat to occupied Jerusalem, to the Israeli aggression against Lebanon, and to actions of British and Iranian troops in Oman." (*FBIS,* 17 July, citing Tass.) OCAL forms part of the FPPNF and of the LNM.

Three other Lebanese communist organizations have been mentioned in the news media: the Revolutionary Communist Group (Trotskyite), the Communist Labor Organization, and the Lebanese Communist Union.

Stanford University   Michel Nabti

Lesotho

Lesotho, a small agrarian state completely surrounded by the territory of the Republic of South Africa, is largely dependent upon South Africa. The Communist Party of Lesotho (CPL) has its origins in the South African Communist Party and much of the CPL's policy and many of its goals are oriented toward South Africa. The CPL was founded in 1962 (*WMR*, July), but its membership is quite small. The party was banned in 1970 and has operated clandestinely since that time. A recent publication does, however, give a current mailing address as P.O. Box 330, Maseru, Lesotho (*Africa Yearbook and Who's Who*, 1977).

Leadership and Organization. The secretary of the CPL is John Motloheloa (ibid.). J. M. Kena and R. Matji have been mentioned as secretary general and chairman respectively. Jeremiah Mosotho is an infrequent contributor and representative of the CPL to the *World Marxist Review*. The supreme organ of the CPL is its Congress, which elects the Central Committee; at the lower echelons there are district and village committees. The CPL is active in trade unions and other mass organizations (*WMR*, July).

Domestic Attitudes and Activities. "The Party's main social base" is among workers, but most of Lesotho's workers are in South Africa. However, the CPL is seeking recruits among peasants and "peasant-workers," i.e., those employed as laborers by "rich" farmers. Thus, the CPL stresses the development of rural cooperatives and organizing unions to fight for peasant rights. The model of noncapitalist development presented by Angola and Mozambique is important and shows that Lesotho can "bypass the capitalist stage of development." The CPL does not presently cooperate with other political parties in Lesotho. (Ibid.)

International Views and Positions. The CPL is a pro-Soviet organization. The Soviet victory in World War II was a great "upsurge [for] the national-liberation movement," and African countries owe their independence to the "process begun by the Great October Socialist Revolution" (ibid.). The foreign policy of the Lesotho government receives the CPL's support, especially in its nonaligned and anti—South African stances. However, nonalignment does not mean equidistance from the two world camps, one of which exploits the poor states while the other helps the poor states. (Ibid.) South Africa oppresses its own people and is also "attempting to force Lesotho into a neo-colonialist game" (ibid., May). Lesotho and South African progressives must collaborate in the overthrow of South Africa's racist system.

The CPL believes that "solidarity with the national-liberation movement is an inalienable part of proletarian internationalism" It therefore works in concert with "the progressive forces of the world, the socialist countries and especially the Soviet Union." (Ibid., July.)

Publications. The CPL currently has no publications although a recent book review in the *African Communist* (no. 73, 1978) heralds a "Marxist reader for Lesotho"—a new economics text for university use—published in Lesotho. (Michael Sefali, *An Introduction to Political Economy.* Lesotho: Morija Printing Works, 1977.)

University of South Carolina   Mark W. DeLancey

The Maghreb

ALGERIA

The Algerian Communist Party (Parti communiste algérien; PCA) was founded in 1920 as an extension of the French Communist Party. It existed independently after October 1936. The PCA participated in the nationalist struggle against France but was proscribed in December 1962, only five months after Algerian independence. Dissident left-wing elements of the legal National Liberation Front (NLF) joined with Communists to form the Popular Resistance Organization, which in January 1966 was renamed the Socialist Vanguard Party (Parti de l'avant-garde-socialiste; PAGS), which is recognized in the communist world as the official Algerian communist party. Membership in the barely tolerated PAGS is now estimated to be about 500. The population of Algeria is just under 18 million.

Leadership and Party Affairs. Little is known about the present PAGS leadership or organization. Sadiq Hadjeres is believed to be its secretary general. Other prominent members of the party in recent years are believed to include Larbi Bukhali, former PCA secretary general, Bashir Hadj 'Ali, Ahmad Karim, and 'Ali Malki. 'Ali Malki has contributed to the *World Marxist Review* and represented the PAGS in at least one *WMR* conference.

Domestic Views. In an article in the April issue of *WMR,* 'Ali Malki reaffirmed PAGS support for the National Charter approved in a referendum in June 1976. The Charter asserts Algeria's "choice of a noncapitalist road of development with a socialist perspective." Malki explained that the Charter strives for national unity, guarantees all social freedoms, and calls for closer solidarity among the anti-imperialist forces of the world, especially between the nonaligned states and the socialist countries. He noted that the Charter has weak points and inconsistencies, which he attributes to the pressure of rightists and inadequate ideological maturity of many Algerian progressives.
The PAGS has consistently called for the development of two forms of political organization: (*a*), a broad front of patriotic and anti-imperialist forces aiming at liberation, construction, development, democracy, and social progress and (*b*), a strong vanguard party guided by the theory of "scientific socialism." The latter is often discussed within the context of renewing and strengthening the only

legal Algerian party, the NLF, so that it might perform the function of a "revolutionary democratic party." The PAGS speaks of the NLF as a "bureaucratic apparatus" that hinders change and which, while socialist in orientation, lacks the ideological maturity to embrace the concept of scientific socialism. It is thus unclear whether the PAGS sees itself or a renewed NLF as the desired vanguard party.

The PAGS stresses the need to mobilize the masses and progressive forces now rather than waiting until social problems reach disastrous dimensions. The PAGS objects to the idea that only the president of the republic should initiate action. The party also asserts that making greater demands regarding the content and nature of NLF policy does not imply opposition to the NLF or the Charter but rather facilitates the NLF's "democratic and revolutionary renovation" (*IB,* no. 2).

International Views. The PAGS has strongly supported the Algerian government over "the right of the people of Western Sahara to self-determination." 'Ali Malki, on the other hand, attacked President Sadat's visit to Israel on the grounds that the trip was designed by imperialists to sabotage the Geneva peace conference; achieve a separate peace between Egypt and Israel at the expense of the Palestinians; split the common Arab, anti-imperialist, anti-Zionist front; isolate Egypt from the socialist countries; and strike at "Algeria and its progressive regime that supports the cause of freedom and social progress in the region and the world." According to 'Ali Malki, the swift approval given to Sadat's initiative by Morocco's King Hassan lent further support to this interpretation. (*WMR,* April).

.According to the PAGS, the imperialist countries increasingly divide their work while relying on closer cooperation. French neocolonialism is more closely aligned with the U.S. than before and is becoming more aggressive in Africa. The imperialist countries are making additional use of reactionary regimes in Asia and Africa. U.N. and Organization of Arab Unity investigations have allegedly revealed the involvement of Gabon and Morocco in the invasion of Benin. Reactionary governments in Asia and Africa have been used to broadcast anticommunist and anti-Soviet propaganda. (Ibid., May.)

The PAGS participated with seven other Arab communist and workers' parties in secret meetings held in Cyprus during mid-April.

Publications. The PAGS continues to issue at infrequent intervals its clandestine journal *Sawt al-Sha'b* (Voice of the people).

MOROCCO

The Moroccan Communist Party (Parti communiste marocain; PCM) was founded in 1943 as a branch of the French Communist Party, restricted in membership to European emigrés. Banned by the French protectorate in 1952, it experienced three years of open operations in independent Morocco before being banned again in 1959. Renamed the Party of Progress and Socialism (Parti du progrès et du socialisme; PPS), it was granted legal status in August 1974. The PPS participated in the Moroccan national elections of November 1976 but won no offices. Membership in the PPS is estimated at about 700. Morocco's population is approximately 19 million.

Leadership and Organization. A PPS party congress held in 1975 confirmed 'Ali Yata as secretary general and elected a secretariat (see *YICA,* 1977, p. 532).

Domestic Issues. Simon Levy, a member of the Political Bureau, represented the PPS at a conference of sixteen communist and workers' parties reported in the May issue of *WMR*. At the conference, Levy declared that in Morocco the oligarchy—consisting of local capitalists, bourgeois feudalists, and the elite of the bureaucracy—are seeking greater cooperation with imperialism. He noted that this is further enhanced by the opportunity for the oligarchy to acquire shares in foreign companies. He explained that in opposition to this situation, the masses are demanding democracy, freedom, and nationalization; they assert that the national wealth must be considered the property of the people as a whole. Levy called for the mobilization of the masses against reaction and imperialism, observing, however, that an organic link exists between unhampered anti-imperialist action and the struggle for democracy.

International Issues. The PPS broke away from a consistently pro-Soviet posture over the issue of the Spanish Sahara, choosing to support the government's 1976 partition and annexation of the phosphate-rich territory between Morocco and Mauritania. The PPS, however, did not support the Moroccan government in regard to its intervention in Zaïre (*Arab Report and Record,* London, 1–15 June). In early March a PPS delegation led by Ali Yata visited Cuba at the invitation of the Cuban Communist Party. The delegation met with Fidel Castro and other Cuban leaders. After returning to Morocco, 'Ali Yata told reporters that there were no Cubans fighting in Western Sahara or with the Polisario Front. He expressed his understanding that Cuba did not want to become involved in the issue, favoring a peaceful solution based on self-determination for the people of Western Sahara. In the interview, 'Ali Yata denied rumors that he had played any role in alleged mediation efforts between Morocco and Algeria. He further asserted that he had gone to Cuba in his role as leader of the PPS and not as an envoy of the Moroccan government seeking Cuban mediation in the conflict over Western Sahara (ibid., 1–15 April). The PPS participated with seven other Arab communist and workers' parties in secret meetings held in Cyprus during mid-April (see Lebanon).

Publications. Since November 1972 the PPS has legally distributed in Rabat a weekly publication, *al-Bayan* (The bulletin). It also publishes *al-Mukafih* (The fighter), which appears in Casablanca daily in Arabic and monthly in French.

TUNISIA

The Tunisian Communist Party (Parti communiste tunisien; PCT) was founded in 1920 and banned in 1963. Supposedly, the PCT has no more than a few hundred members. The population of Tunisia is about 6 million.

Leadership. Muhammad al-Nafa' is secretary general of the PCT, and Muhammad Harmel is its secretary. Tahar 'Ali and K. Tahar represented the PCT at two conferences organized by the *WMR*'s Commission on Problems of the National-Liberation Movement in African and Asian Countries. A. Ben Mustafa has also been cited as a member of the PCT leadership.

Domestic Issues. PCT leaders al-Nafa', Harmel, and Ben Mustafa issued a statement in Tunis in regard to the general strike and the subsequent government action at the end of January which resulted in an estimated 130 killed and 450 wounded. The PCT statement asserted that the general strike called by the Tunisian Federation of Labor (Union Générale tunisienne du travail; UGTT) was not intended as an insurrection but was a protest aimed at the increasing threat to union autonomy. The PCT charged that the repression struck a blow at the most precious gains of the working people and those who seek progress and democracy—the powerful trade union organization, which had gained considerable influence in the country's development within the framework of a genuine national alliance. The statement urged that the country's fundamental problems be resolved through "rejection of all forms of repression, repeal of the state of emergency, release of Habib Ashour [UGTT secretary general] and other detained trade union leaders and activists, recognition of the UGTT's right to autonomy, a general amnesty, establishment of democratic freedoms and the launching of a national dialog with the aim of a free and responsible discussion of the solutions needed by the country" (*L'Unità,* 10 February, in *IB,* no 7).

At a conference reported in the January issue of *WMR,* PCT member Tahar 'Ali explained that the assumption of power by the nationalist petite bourgeoisie over the national liberation movement of Tunisia led to a quickened pace of social differentiation. This, he said, expressed itself in the form of a new capitalist class and in the policy of the Destourian Socialist Party changing from the fairly major structural reforms of Ahmad Ben Salah, ousted in 1969, to the capitalist orientation of his successor, Hadi Nouira. He noted that the Salah reforms were accompanied by repression of the Left and curtailment of democratic freedoms. 'Ali pointed out that Tunisia's Communists stress "the need for a broad national democratic alliance" while at the same time insisting that "the existence of an independent party of the working class is a vital necessity at the moment." (*WMR,* January.)

At a second *WMR* conference, whose proceedings were published in May, K. Tahar warned that Tunisian legislation encouraging the "interpenetration of local and foreign capital" undermines independence and ultimately threatens the country with becoming an appendage "of state-monopoly capitalism" (*WMR,* May).

The PCT apparently did not participate in the secret meetings of eight Arab communist and workers' parties which were held in mid-April in Cyprus.

Publications. The PCT has had no official organ since its banning and the proscription of its publications, *al-Tali'ah* (The vanguard) and *Tribune du Progrès,* in 1963. In 1971 the party's request to publish a periodical entitled *Dialog* was denied by the Ministry of Interior. At the end of 1977, Muhammad Harmel applied for permission to publish a daily newspaper in two languages, Arabic and French, under the title *al-Jadid* (The new). This request was apparently also denied.

Stanford University   Michel Nabti

Réunion

The Réunion Communist Party (Parti communiste réunionnais; PCR) became an independent political organization when the Réunion federation of the French Communist Party became autonomous in 1959. Réunion is a French overseas department, and the PCR is a legal party. The population of Réunion is approximately 500,000. Membership in the PCR has been estimated at 2,000 (*Témoignages*, 29–30 January, 2 February 1977). Over 1,200 delegates participated in a special party conference held on 29 January (ibid., 30 January).

The island of Réunion combines unstable politics with economic contraction, unemployment estimated at between 30,000 and 60,000 persons, and emigration of nearly 6,000 persons a year. Although the PCR and its trade union counterpart, the Réunion General Confederation of Labor (Confédération générale du travail réunionnais; CGTR), have increased their strength and the scope of their activities in recent years, the electoral showing of the party has not been impressive. In the Réunion elections in March, government-supported candidates won all three seats in the French National Assembly. Paul Vergès, Elie Hoarau, and Bruny Payet were the defeated PCR candidates. There was outright hostility between Socialists and the PCR prior to the first round of the elections, carrying over from recent contests in which Socialist candidates had failed to stand aside for leading PCR candidates in second-round elections (ibid., 1 March). Results of the 12 March balloting showed an increase in votes won by government-supported candidates over the 1973 legislative elections, but the PCR's total of 32.8 percent was up from the 28 and 29 percent the party had garnered in departmental and municipal elections in 1976 and 1977 (*Le Monde*, 14 March).

Party Organization and Internal Affairs. Paul Vergès remains the party's secretary general (See *YICA, 1977*, p. 537). Party ranks were broken this year with the defection of former Political Bureau and Secretariat member Jean-Baptiste Ponoma, who ran against Vergès in the March legislative elections. Other members of the Central Committee include Laurence Vergès, Hippolite Piot, Roger Hoarau, Gervais Barret, and Ary Payet (*IB*, no. 10, 1977; *Témoignages*, 28 February 1977, 9 March).

Other associations affiliated with the PCR include the CGTR, the party's Women's League, and the Réunion Youth Front for Autonomy (Front de la jeunesse autonomiste de la Réunion; FJAR). The PCR is the keystone in a new organization created in August to assemble a united force of all "progressive" groups fighting for the island's autonomy. The Anticolonialist Front for the Self-Determination of Réunion (Front anticolonialiste pour l'autodétermination de la Réunion; FRAPAR) includes labor unions, the youth organization, and planters' associations (ibid., 28 August).

Domestic Policies and Activities. Key to the overall political goals of the PCR is the question of autonomy and self-determination for Réunion. Virtually all policy statements and speeches of party leaders, such as Paul Vergès and Elie Hoarau, stress that only the eventual freedom of Réunion from the evils of arbitrary commodity price-fixing and political manipulation from the mainland can permit the island's working-class population to achieve social and economic emancipation.

Vergès's report to the party's special conference in January serves as a summary of the PCR's immediate economic and social objectives. The secretary general called for an expansion of welfare relief measures; an increase in the minimum wage to the level applied in mainland France and the extension of minimum-wage protection to thousands of day laborers and employees; establishment of work projects for the unemployed; thorough revision of financing for sugarcane planters; extension of social benefits to small-business owners; technical education programs; and anti-inflationary measures tied to an immediate decrease in the price of rice, which had risen nearly 40 percent in 1977 (*Témoignages*, 1 February).

After the legislative elections, Vergés and the PCR gave the autonomy issue top priority in both domestic and international forums. With Elie Hoarau, Vergès undertook a series of islandwide conferences on the subject of "democratic and popular autonomy," defined as the "economic, social, cultural, and political solution to the problems of the populace at large" (ibid., 20 July). The formation of the FRAPAR organization is the domestic elaboration of this policy goal.

The PCR continues to collaborate with its labor union partner, the CGTR, in support of work stoppages. According to party spokesmen, the PCR's organizational network was in large part responsible for the complete shutdown of Réunion's cargo operations for nearly two weeks (ibid., 20 April). In November the PCR organized a general strike to mark the visit of French Premier Raymond Barre (ibid., 4–5 November).

International Activities. The PCR maintains close relations with left-wing organizations and parties both in its immediate region and in the Third World generally. The autonomy issue afforded the party a particularly wide audience in 1978. Libya announced the formation of a Réunion liberation committee in February (*Revue française des études politiques africaines*, March), and the Organization of African Unity enhanced the prestige of the autonomy movement by demanding independence for Réunion at its Khartoum congress in June (*L'Humanité*, 26 June). Vergès has developed particularly close relations with the French Communist Party, which sent representatives to help with the elections. The party sends delegates to meetings of the World Federation of Trade Unions and to regional leftist international conferences, such as those held in 1978 in the Seychelles (April), Madagascar (May), and Ethiopia (September). The PCR's Youth organization sent a delegation to the international youth congress in Cuba (*Témoignages*, 28 July).

At a July conference, Vergès summed up the PCR's foreign policy objectives: Africanization of the autonomy problem, dismantling of Indian Ocean military bases and evacuation of Western troops, and direct exploitation of raw materials by Third World countries (ibid., 20 July).

Publications. The PCR publishes a daily newspaper, *Témoignages*, which has an estimated circulation of 5,000. The CGTR publishes the *Travailleur réunionnais* twice a month.

Stanford University   Peter S. Stern

Senegal

There are three communist-inspired political parties in Senegal. The only legally recognized one is the African Independence Party (Parti africain de l'indépendance; PAI), founded in 1957. It became clandestine in 1960 when banned by the newly independent government of Léopold Senghor. A faction of the party emerged into legality in 1976 when Majmout Diop, its exiled leader, received a pardon and returned to Senegal. In August 1976 the PAI was designated as the country's legal "Marxist-Leninist" party. Its current membership is estimated at 1,000 (*Africa,* London, February). The population of Senegal is about 5,380,000.

Diop's PAI, however, represents only a small portion of organized communist opinion in Senegal. There is also an unofficial faction of the PAI, nominally clandestine but free to operate publicly. The most influential force on the Senegalese Left is the National Democratic Rally (Rassemblement national democratique; RND), directed by Cheikh Anto Diop. The RND rejected a 1976 offer from Senghor to be the official Marxist-Leninist party but has since made efforts to gain legal recognition without having an official label. The unofficial PAI faction has unsuccessfully sought legal recognition. At its seventh Central Committee plenum in October 1977, it deputized Politburo member Amath Dansoko to write Senghor requesting legaliztion (*African Communist,* 2nd quarter), but the minister of the interior rejected this request.

During the presidential elections in Feburary the official PAI decided not to put up candidates. (*Le Monde,* 24 February). The PAI did, however, field candidates for the Assembly elections. Majmout Diop campaigned on a conventional Marxist-Leninist platform of economic progress through access to power of the proletariat. The PAI, however, could not shake loose from charges of outright collaboration with Senghor (*Africa,* London, February). As *Andè Sopi* pointed out, there was direct coordination between the government's attacks on members of the illegal opposition and campaign speeches by PAI spokesmen against these same figures (*Andè Sopi,* February). The PAI ran a slate of 57 workers, twelve farmers, and three civil servants for the 72 seats it contested (out of 100 in the Assembly) but the peasant and working-class voters responded to the appeal for abstention put forward by former Premier Mamadou Dia of the RND. Hence, the official PAI candidates received only 3,111 votes— 0.32 percent of the total—and won no seats in the Assembly (*Voix d'Afrique,* 6—19 March). According to some observers, Diop and the legal PAI have been completely discredited by the elections (*Africa,* London, April) and any future activity on the part of an organized communist force would have to come from either a legalized RND or the integration of the presently clandestine wing of the PAI with the legal party (ibid., February; *L'Année politique africaine,* 1977).

Party Organization and Internal Affairs. The legal PAI is headed by a central committee and a politburo, served by a five-member secretariat (see *YICA, 1978,* p. 444). In spite of a recruitment campaign in mid-1977 among workers and farmers (*Africa,* Dakar, August—September 1977), the official PAI has only about 1,000 members (*Africa,* London, February).

The unofficial PAI held the seventh and eight plenums of its Central Committee in October and December 1977 (*Andè Sopi.* February). Its secretary general is Seydou Cissoko (*WMR,* May), and its principal spokesman both domestically and internationally is Amath Dansoko, who sits on the Central Committee. Magatte Thiam, its assistant secretary general, is leader of the United and Democratic Union of Senegalese Teachers (Syndicat unique et dèmocratique d'enseignants sénégalais; SUDES) and coeditor of the monthly *Andè Sopi.* The party also has the support of former Premier Mamadou Dia. Unofficial estimates attribute to the faction somewhat over 1,000 members (*Africa.* London, February).

Domestic Policies and Activities. The PAI's program stands for "the application of the principles of scientific socialism in order to consolidate the independence of Senegal and to construct a Senegalese socialist society based upon the respect for the principles of national sovereignty and democracy" (*Le Soleil.* 1 September 1976). The PAI holds that the future of Africa and the world rests on the struggle of the proletariat for emancipation from bourgeois and capitalist domination, represented in Senegal by the exploitation of the people under Senghor's elitist bureaucracy (*Voix d'Afrique.* 20 February−5 March). Majmout Diop justifies his reputed cooperation with Senghor by claiming that the cause of the proletariat "has nothing to lose by coming into the open. We can benefit from the electoral campaign to rebuild the party and make our programs known." His program has been characterized as Marxism-Leninism minus atheism; Diop ended his speeches during the recent campaign with a few verses from the Koran (*Le Monde,* 24 February).

The unofficial PAI faction calls for its own legalization; it also demands complete freedom for political organizations in the country. *Andè Sopi's* platform statement prior to the February elections, while not officially representing the unofficial PAI, puts forward most of its goals: identification with the struggle of the Senegalese proletariat, development of popular resistance to the vested powers through the creation of a truly socialist vision of the world, a reestablishment of popular culture, political freedom, cessation of all cooperation with international imperialism, nationalization and economic planning, and international cooperation to defeat imperialist strategy (*Andè Sopi,* February).

International Activities. The legal PAI is not recognized by international communist organizations. The unofficial faction, on the other hand, sends representatives to international communist gatherings. Amath Dansoko is on the editorial board of the *World Marxist Review* and contributes occasionally to that publication. He represented the PAI at the first meeting of Communist Parties of Tropical and Southern Africa held in 1978.

Publications. The legal PAI publishes a monthly, *La Lutte* (Struggle), and a weekly, *Monsarev* (Independence). The clandestine PAI publishes its own version of *Monsarev* and airs its opinions in the monthly *Andè Sopi* (Unite for change).

Stanford University   Peter S. Stern

South Africa

The South African Communist Party (SACP), formed in 1953 as an underground organization, continues to operate clandestinely in South Africa and from exile in Africa and Europe. As the direct successor of the continent's first communist party, the Communist Party of South Africa (founded in legality in 1921, but dissolved in 1950 immediately prior to its banning by the Nationalist government), the SACP maintains cadres and conducts propaganda in major South African cities despite unrelenting government hostility. Almost certainly the bulk of its own leadership, including the majority of the members of the Central Committee, live and work outside the country. Africans are "the overwhelming majority of the leadership and membership" of the SACP (*African Communist*, no. 65, p. 28), but the party's membership is nonracial. It is not possible to determine the total membership of the widely dispersed party; very probably it is numerically small but heavily concentrated in organizations allied to the SACP.

Leadership and Organization. The SACP describes itself "as an integral part of the national liberation movement" (ibid., no. 68, p. 46), of which the African National Congress (ANC) is recognized as the paramount body. The ANC, founded in 1912 as the first countrywide African nationalist organization but banned in 1960, operates, like the SACP, clandestinely within South Africa and from exile. The activities of the ANC (including those of its military wing, Umkhonto we Sizwe, charged with preparing and conducting armed struggle within South Africa) are directed from offices in friendly black African states by Oliver Tambo (acting president), Alfred Nzo (secretary general), and other ANC leaders, both in exile and underground. The ANC estimates that it "is making steady and unimpeded progress towards the consolidation of its revolutionary base at the mass level. The strength of white democrats—who together with the South African Indian Congress, the South African Congress of Trade Union and the Coloured Peoples Congress accept the leadership of the ANC . . .—is growing at a rate alarming to the enemy." (*Sechaba*, 3rd quarter, 1977, p. 6.) The latter organizations, unlike the ANC and the SACP, operate on the fringe of legality inside the country, regularly subject to police surveillance and harassment.

Although the lines between the SACP and its allies, particularly the ANC, are blurred, in part as a consequence of the underground and exile nature of their activities, the SACP determinedly maintains the "absolute right of our Party to exist as an independent organization and to continue to exercise its public role as the advance vanguard of the working class" (*African Communist*, no. 70, p. 44). Simultaneously it vigorously denies charges that it seeks to control the other organizations in the national liberation movement.

The publicly acknowledged leaders of the SACP have been older members of the party, active both in the period of legality prior to 1950 and subsequently. (See *YICA, 1978*, p. 446).

Domestic Activities and Attitudes. The SACP remains committed to a party program adopted at a clandestine meeting in South Africa in 1962, with subsequent elaborations and modifications made at irregular meetings of party bodies; the most recently publicly announced gathering was a plenary meeting of the Central Committee held at an unnamed location in April 1977. The SACP and the ANC are equally committed to the overthrow of the racist regime and the installing of a revolutionary government which would take effective measures against monopoly capital and revolutionize the economic, political, social, and military structures and institutions (*WMR*, July, p. 32).

The SACP remains optimistic about the long-term prospects for revolutionary change in South Africa. In its estimation both heightened black militancy, symbolized by the Soweto events of mid-1976, and subsequent government repressive actions have enhanced the attractiveness and validity of the program of action advocated by the SACP and ANC. Further inspiration continues to be derived from the experiences of the MPLA regime in Angola and the FRELIMO regime in Mozambique, both of which are explicitly committed to the achievement of socialism under the leadership of their respective Marxist-Leninist vanguard parties.

The SACP still regards the South African government as a formidable foe, particularly since the Western powers continue to support South Africa. But, according to the SACP, the government's attempts to crush the Soweto militants and to ban eighteen opposition groups willing to work within the narrow confines of legality have clarified the alternatives available to the opponents of apartheid. In the words of Dr. Yusef M. Dadoo, the party's chairman: "Armed struggle has become the most significant factor in the revolutionary struggle"; it is incumbent on the ANC and the SACP to "strengthen our underground structures" in order "to ensure that armed activities have a firm basis in every part of the country and to give direction and leadership to the mass discontent and militant actions of the people" (ibid., pp. 29–30). The armed struggle will, however, be protracted and suffer many setbacks at the hands of the enemy. Statements by South African government officials about the apprehension of armed members of Umkhonto we Sizwe and the discovery of arms caches testify both to the extension of activity within South Africa and to the continuing difficulties of establishing a strong guerrilla presence inside the country.

The SACP is also committed to the utilization of complementary nonmilitary actions to advance its cause: "We have to become even more professional in acquiring the necessary skills to combine different forms of struggle, armed and unarmed, legal and illegal, and mass militant actions." Hence, "a crucial aspect of our work is to forge greater unity between the oppressed Blacks—Africans, Coloured and Indians. The mass organizations through which so many of the youth and students articulated their grievances and aspirations need to be injected with a clearer revolutionary and political content. The SACP "is now working with redoubled energy within the various classes and sections of the population, including democratic and progressive elements among the white population. The SACP has undertaken with renewed vigor the necessary steps to organize the working class, especially at the factory level, and to disseminate even more widely the science of Marxism-Leninism. We fully support the South African Congress of Trade Unions—which is an integral part of the national-liberation movement—in its fight to improve the working conditions and wages of the Black workers, to extend the meager rights of the African trade unions, to organize the Black workers into militant trade unions, to mobilize them for nationwide unity of purpose and action and to develop viable illegal structures in the production area." Great significance is also attached to the need for "galvanizing . . . the rural masses into even more effective political actions"; the mobilization and organization of "the rural working people" is additionally regarded as important for the expansion of guerrilla warfare. The black middle strata, with its record of support for youth and workers during the Soweto confrontations, is also regarded as a group which can support the national liberation struggle. (Ibid., pp. 29–31.) But the SACP opposes those who attempt to seek to change the system while accepting positions within the government-supported institutions of separate development. The SACP thus condemns Inkatha, the organization led by Chief Gatsha Buthelezi of Kwazulu, and its alliance with the Coloured Labour Party, led until recently by Sonny Leon, and the Indian Reform Party, led by Y. S. Chinsamy, which calls for a national convention to draw up a new nonracial constitution for South Africa. According to a party spokesman, the alliance, "by spreading the illusion about a peaceful solution to the South African problem and declaring its opposition to armed struggle is attempting to render the revolutionary forces ineffective . . . those who propose compromise when the strength and resolve of the people are growing must be swept aside" (*African Communist*, no. 74, pp. 98—99).

Dr. Dadoo considers that the successful armed struggles in Angola and Mozambique and the subsequent policies of both regimes have not only "altered the geopolitical situation in Southern Africa and given an incalculable boost to the fighting morale and militant spirit of the oppressed toiling masses in Namibia, Zimbabwe and South Africa." These developments have also "brought into sharp focus the difference between people's power and that exercised by a privileged minority, the pawns of imperialism and neo-colonialism" (*WMR*, July, p. 25). In lengthy articles in the *African Communist* (nos. 73, 74, 75), Joe Slovo, a publicly prominent party theoretician, has analyzed in detail the policies of both regimes before and after their accession to power. In his opinion "many lessons of more general relevance can be learnt from a study of the Mozambican revolutionary experience" (*African Communist*, no. 73, p. 20), and "the kaleidoscope of MPLA experiences reflects the widest variety of problems which are common to the revolutionary process in much of our continent. The answers you [MPLA] have found and are continuing to find to these problems are instructive for revolutionaries everywhere." (Ibid., no. 74, p. 20.)

International Views and Activities. The SACP participated with an unidentified "number of communist and workers' parties of Africa" in a conference at an unnamed location. The conference elaborated "A Communist Call to Africa" as "the synthesis of their collective thought on the situation in Tropical and Southern Africa" and as "a basis for discussion among all parties, militants, patriots, progressives, revolutionaries and Marxists in Africa" (ibid., no. 75, p. 5). The four-part document analyzed economic, political, and social trends throughout the continent; it found that prospects for socialist-oriented regimes are increasing, along with the numbers of Africans looking beyond revolutionary democracy to Marxism-Leninism. The document concluded that "this first meeting of the Communist parties of Tropical and Southern Africa is of great historical significance both for the World Communist movement and for the struggle for national and social liberation of our continent. We feel that the Communists and revolutionary democrats should hold joint forums, on a bilateral and multilateral basis, which would facilitate the further consolidation of the unity of the anti-imperialist front of the Communist and revolutionary democrats, as the vanguard of all socialist, revolutionary and democratic forces." (Ibid., pp. 32—33.) In "A Communist Call to Africa" and elsewhere, the SACP rejected Maoism in all forms; in this fashion the SACP maintained its long-standing opposition to the policies of the Communist Party of China and its close identification with the Communist Party of the Soviet Union as the leader of the socialist countries.

John Nkosi represented the SACP at the first meeting of the Communist parties of Tropical and Southern Africa held in 1978.

Publications. Within South Africa since 1971, the SACP has circulated *Inkululeko-Freedom*, a theoretical journal originating in the country, as well as a clandestine edition of *African Communist*, its overseas quarterly founded in 1959 and presently printed in the German Democratic Republic but distributed from London. It has also irregularly issued party proclamations and pocket-sized Marxist-Leninist classics. Its ally, the South African Congress of Trade Unions, publishes a newssheet, *Workers' Unity*, in London, while the ANC publishes a quarterly, *Sechaba*, distributed from London but printed in the German Democratic Republic. Both organizations certainly issue irregular underground publications within South Africa; the ANC supplements its printed media with daily broadcasts from African radio stations in Dar es Salaam, Luanda, and Lusaka.

Duke University   Sheridan Johns

[Document: Africa]
FOR FREEDOM AND SOCIAL PROGRESS

The conference of communist and workers' parties of tropical and southern African countries, held recently, drew up a document entitled "For the Freedom, Independence, National Rebirth, and Social Progress of the Peoples of Tropical and Southern Africa."

Today, more than ever, the document stresses, international imperialism and its principal instrument—multinational corporations—are the main enemy of the African peoples. Africa's economic, social, and technical backwardness is the consequence of the overthrown colonial rule and the present imperialist policy of plundering and exploiting the African peoples. As recent events have shown genuinely patriotic and anti-imperialist forces in the African countries oppose reactionary, feudal, and tribalist elements, the bureaucratic bourgeoisie, neocolonialist politickers, and the agents of international imperialism.

A struggle between the forces of progress and reaction—which reflects the two opposing trends of social development, toward capitalism or toward socialism—is taking place in Africa. The continent's special conditions have made their mark on both of these trends.

Capitalism is incapable of satisfying our people's ardent desire for a better, fuller life free from the fetters of exploitation, poverty, hunger, disease, and ignorance. The particular feature of capitalist development in Africa is that imperialist monopolies remain the dominant force whereas national capitalism develops in backward and dependent forms, retaining many links with the older modes of production. National capitalism is developing chiefly in the area of services and trade. As a result, even the positive processes which could objectively develop on the basis of capitalism are extremely limited.

Our people's hopes and aspirations cannot be realized without resolute progress toward socialism. Recently, increasingly large detachments of the broad national liberation movements have come out in support of not only anti-imperialist but anticapitalist positions. These progressive aspirations, which are of historic importance, have been displayed in Angola, Mozambique, Ethiopia, Benin, and Madagascar, which have aligned themselves with the other African countries traveling the socialist-oriented path.

The experience of a number of countries shows that a socialist orientation in domestic and foreign policy means the strengthening of political independence on the basis of an uncompromising struggle against imperialist exploitation; the establishment of people's state power; development of the economy; improvement of the working population's social, material, and cultural standards; the elimination of feudal exploitation; the restriction of rapacious tendencies on the part of the local capitalists; a growth in employment; strengthening the public sector in industry and the cooperative movement in agriculture; the application of scientific principles in the sphere of economic planning; an alliance with the socialist community; and the gradual creation of the political, material, social, and cultural preconditions for the transition to building socialism.

Today, when mass, including armed, action against the reactionary, inhuman apartheid system in southern Africa has reached an unprecedented degree and when the armed struggle of the people of Zimbabwe and Namibia has risen to a new level, the conditions have emerged for eliminating the odious Vorster and Smith regimes. The repression and murders perpetrated by the fascists and racists will never be able to break the will of the heroic and courageous fighters for freedom and independence. In this situation, the United States and the imperialist Western European powers are making desperate attempts to ensure the conditions whereby they may dominate our life and our economy. They are doing everything to make it possible to continue plundering and intensively exploiting the labor of our peoples and our wealth, our natural resources and raw materials. As recent events have demonstrated, the NATO powers, headed by U.S. imperialism, have intensified their multifaceted reactionary activity on our continent under the spurious pretext of saving it from the "Soviet-Cuban Threat."

Coordinating their actions, the NATO powers are resorting more and more often to direct military aggression and open intervention in Africa. Events in Zaire, Chad, and the Western Sahara are evidence of this.

An exceptionally dangerous aspect of this activity is the attempt to concoct, with the connivance of the most reactionary African states, so-called "inter-African forces" and military blocs on the continent. The main aims of these reactionary military blocs are certainly to legitimize any imperialist aggressions and interference by the United States and the former European colonialists in African affairs, to undermine African unity by setting African against African, kindle interstate conflicts, and paralyze progressive, revolutionary processes on our continent.

While demagogically toying with the slogan "Africa for the Africans," the imperialists in reality continue to treat our continent as their own preserve and regard Africa's peoples in a racist way as incapable of handling their own affairs and choosing their own paths of development. Both national and international reactionary forces utilize anticommunism, chauvinsim, tribalism, and religious fanaticism in order to sow disorder in the ranks of the people's masses and to reverse the revolutionary process.

More and more, the Chinese leadership is acting in concert with imperialism and pursues a policy aimed at undermining and weakening the struggle for national independence, peace, democracy, social progress, and socialism throughout the world and in our continent.

We, the document goes on to say, appeal to all African parties, organizations, activists, patriots, progressive figures, revolutionaries, and Marxist-Leninists.

The major achievement of the African peoples is the elimination of colonialism and the gaining of political independence. We cannot and will not allow neocolonialism and its new collective form to enslave our peoples once again. Therefore, it is very important to utilize every available means to prevent the neocolonialists from returning to Africa with their weapons in hand.

A high degree of mobilization among the masses, strengthening the unity of progressive, democratic forces and coordinating their joint action within the framework of individual countries, the entire continent, and the former mother countries are necessary to stop and defeat imperialist intrigues and aggressive action.

In view of the fact that the imperialist powers and their allies in Africa are doing everything possible to destabilize countries with socialist and anti-imperialist orientations, it is the sacred international and patriotic duty of all progressive African forces to support and defend these states totally.

We call on all fighters against imperialism and racism, democrats, patriots, and revolutionaries of our long-suffering continent, to strengthen their unity in the name of ending once and for all the racist and colonial dominance of southern Africa. We urge them to give material, moral, and political aid to the genuine revolutionary forces headed by the African National Congress, the South African Communist Party, the South West African People's Organization (Namibia), and the Zimbabwe Patriotic Front.

The unity of Communists and revolutionary democrats is acquiring a paramount importance for the success of the struggle against imperialism and neocolonialism.

The Communists and revolutionary democrats, the document stresses, are consistent patriots. They have no interest other than the interest of their peoples. They struggle resolutely against imperialism, neocolonialism, and racism; boldly uphold the sovereignty and independence of African states; advocate peace, friendship, and comprehensive co-operation among them; respect and support the noble principles of the OAU; and strive to strengthen that organization's unity and cohesion.

The Communists and revolutionary democrats know that Africa's peoples are not alone in their struggle. The socialist community's international influence is a factor of tremendous importance for the African states. The active revolutionary struggle by progressive forces in support of the freedom and independence of African peoples is growing throughout the world.

It is necessary to wage a principled struggle against all forms of chauvinism, anticommunism, anti-Sovietism and Maoism, to deepen the alliance with the socialist community, particularly with the Soviet Union, and to strengthen the international solidarity of the working class and democratic and peace-loving forces throughout the world.

Loyal to the principles of proletarian internationalism, Africa's Communists express their fraternal militant solidarity with the communist parties and all inti-imperialist forces in Asia, Latin

America, and Europe which are struggling for national independence, against monopoly capital, and for democracy, peace, and socialism.

Together with all democratic, progressive forces, the African Communists actively support the policy of peaceful coexistence and détente in the relations between states with different social systems and the growing struggle of all the people for disarmament and the prohibition of nuclear weapons. They also advocate that Africa be genuinely transformed into a nuclear-free zone, the Indian Ocean be proclaimed a zone of peace, and all military bases be liquidated. They actively support the Final Act of the European Conference on Security and Cooperation signed in Helsinki, and they are striving for the widest possible dissemination of its spirit and principles in the African Continent.

The African Communists, the document says in conclusion, solemnly declare that they are an integral part of the international workers', communist, and national liberation movements. They are sincere friends of the Soviet Union and the other socialist-community countries, of all socialist-oriented states, and of the peoples waging the anti-imperialist struggle and defending the cause of freedom and independence. They have been and will always be active fighters for a firm, inviolable alliance between the African liberation movement, the socialist world, and the international workers and communist and national liberation movements on all continents.

Source: *Pravda*, 26 August.

Sudan

The Sudanese Communist Party (al-Hizb al-Shuyu'i al-Sudani; SCP) traces its origins to 1946 when a group of revolutionary intellectuals and members of the working class founded the Sudanese Movement for National Liberation under the leadership of 'Abd al-Khaliq Mahjub. At its Third Congress in 1956, the movement was renamed the SCP. At times the party operated in relative freedom and had elected representatives in the national legislature. Even Ja'far Numayri, president of the Sudan since May 1969, at one time had two Communist members in his cabinet. The SCP gradually became a focal point of opposition. Having been implicated in an attempted coup, the party was banned in 1971 (see *YICA, 1972,* pp. 290–292). Numerous SCP leaders, including Mahjub, were executed, and thousands of party members were arrested and held without trial. The SCP has also been accused of participating in more recent plots against the government. No reliable figures exist on present SCP membership. Before the 1971 coup attempt, the party was estimated to have from 5,000 to 10,000 active members; more recent estimates put the figure at 3,500. An unknown number are continuing party activities in exile or clandestinely within Sudan.

Leadership and Organization. The secretary general of the SCP is Muhammad Ibrahim Nuqud. Ibrahim Zakariya, Sulaiman Hamid, Su'udi Daraj, and 'Abd al-Majid Shakak are known members of the Central Committee, and Ahmad Salim is a member of the SCP Economic Commission. Both

Zakariya and Salim are occasional contributors to the *World Marxist Review*. Other important SCP leaders now in exile include Dr. 'Izz al-Din 'Ali 'Amir, Dr. Mustafa Khujali, and Dr. Khalid Hasan al-Tum.

The SCP has always been active in establishing and participating in mass organizations—trade unions and youth, women's, and other associations. The party operates through local party branches established at places of residence and work and integrated within regional organizations. The party has held four congresses: 1950, 1951, 1956, and 1967.

A breakaway faction of the SCP, led by Mu'awiya Ibrahim, is currently cooperating with the government of Ja'far Numayri. Other prominent members of this faction include Ahmad Sulaiman, Faruq Abu 'isa, and 'Abdin Isma'il. The latter is a member of the Central Committee of the Sudanese Socialist Union. A pro-Chinese splinter group led by Muhammad Ahmad Khair is also active in Sudan.

Relations with the Sudanese Government. In mid-1977 President Numayri initiated a program of national reconciliation to reintegrate into the political system members of the Sudanese opposition who were in exile, in jail, or were operating clandestinely within Sudan. By the end of March 1978, all former opposition political parties had reportedly reconciled themselves with the Numayri regime except the SCP (*Arab Report andRecord*, London, 16—31 March). A group of SCP dissidents entered the Sudanese Socialist Union, but the official SCP continued to be resolutely opposed to the Numayri government and thus had not benefited from the national reconciliation program or the amnesty related to it. On 4 May President Numayri released from detention 29 members of the SCP, including 10 members of the party's Central Committee. Despite estimates made prior to the release that at least 100 SCP members were still in jail, the national news agency declared that these were the last political prisoners remaining in Sudanese detention. It is not clear whether this gesture was related to Soviet-Sudanese efforts in early May to restore bilateral relations or whether it was the result of a purely domestic government decision to draw the SCP into national reconciliation. In response to the amnesty for the SCP members, the Soviet news agency Tass reported on 14 May that the World Federation of Trade Unions, based in Prague, had issued a message "to the Sudanese people and the progressive forces of Sudan" congratulating them on the success of their struggle (ibid., 1—15 May).

About the same time, reports from Khartoum indicated that government contacts were currently underway with former SCP leaders in Europe, including Dr. Mustafa Khujali, who was premier in the short-lived communist government of 1970, Dr. 'Izz al-Din 'Ali 'Amir, Dr. Khalid Hasan al-Tum, and Secretary General Muhammad Ibrahim Nuqud (*Sudanow*, Khartoum, May). Reports of these contacts indicate that the SCP representatives praised the repeal of repressive laws in Sudan. But negotiations probably reached a stalemate when President Numayri was unwilling to compromise with the SCP on the creation of a national front formula for the national constitution of Sudan (*Arabia and the Gulf*, London, 15 May). President Numayri, in a televised address on 1 August, insisted that "the Sudanese people have rejected communism on several occasions and will reject it forever." According to President Numayri, the Communists were trying to make up for the failure of their 1971 coup attempt by imposing ideological influence "supported by bases bordering Sudan and by elements within the country." Furthermore, he accused them of being behind recent strikes in Sudan organized by the unions. (*Arab Report and Record*, 1—15 August.)

International Views and Activities. The SCP has consistently taken a pro-Soviet stance on political and ideological issues. In a report on a 1977 plenary session published early in 1978, the SCP declared that "the socialist community and its vanguard the Soviet Union . . . together constitute the bulwark of all progressive forces throughout the world in their struggle for socialism, progress, democracy and peace." The plenum denounced the "excessively reactionary role of the huge reserves of petrodollars in the hands of Saudi Arabia and other Persian Gulf states," charging that they "constitute a new form of neocolonialist penetration, and a direct instrument of its expansion in the Arab region."

Moreover, it reaffirmed its commitment to the document adopted at the 1975 conference of Arab communist and workers' parties, which asserted the vital necessity of increasing the role of the communist parties in the Arab national liberation movement, owing to the intensifying struggle between national and progressive forces on one side and the forces of neocolonialism, Zionism, and local reaction on the other. (*IB*, no. 3.)

The SCP participated with seven other Arab communist and workers' parties from Jordan, Syria, Algeria, Lebanon, Iraq, Egypt, and Morocco in secret meetings held in Cyprus during mid-April. The parties condemned the Israeli invasion of southern Lebanon and asserted their support for both the Palestinian resistance and the Lebanese national movement. A Beirut newspaper reported that the participants also discussed measures to overthrow the governments of a number of Arab countries, particularly South Yemen and Iraq, in preparation for their eventual domination by communist forces (*al-Hawadeth*, Beirut, 28 July). Ahmed Salim represented the SCP at the first meeting of the Communist Parties of Tropical and Southern Africa held in 1978.

Stanford University   Patricia Mihaly

Syria

The Syrian Communist Party (al-Hizb al-Shuyu'i al-Suri; SCP) is an offshoot of the Lebanese Communist Party (LCP) established in 1924. Membership in the SCP is believed to be about 4,000 with another 10,000 sympathizers, although once source has estimated 30,000 card-carrying members. The population of Syria is about 8.7 million (1976 government census).

Leadership and Organization. The SCP continues to be led by Khalid Bakdash, a Syrian Kurd (For the leadership, see *YICA, 1978,* p. 450). In August 1977, six SCP members were elected to the Syrian legislature. The dissident SCP faction, led by Riyad al-Turk, has no representation either in the Syrian cabinet or the National Progressive Front (NPF).

SCP Relations with the Syrian Government. The SCP is represented within the leading NPF. According to President Hafiz Asad, this body "represents a political, social and economic safety valve . . . that . . . unifies the efforts of all political forces for . . . achieving all . . . proposed national objectives" (*al-Ba'th,* Damascus, 29 March). The SCP retained its two portfolios in the new cabinet formed on 30 March. The delegation that accompanied President Asad on his visit to the Soviet Union in October included Daniel Ni'mah, a Political Bureau member, in his capacity as SCP representative within NPF. According to a Central Committee plenum, the NPF needs to be strengthened in order to expand democratic liberties, raise living standards of the masses, and strengthen the country's defenses.

International Views and Activities. The SCP condemned Egyptian President Sadat for his alleged cooperation with Zionism and American imperialism. It also denounced the "American-

Israeli-Egyptian alliance" to frustrate serious efforts toward peace, eliminate the Palestinian resistance movement, impose capitulation upon the Arabs, and police Arab and African national liberation movements. The SCP consistently advocated a resumption of the Geneva peace conference, calling this the only international forum competent to settle peacefully the Middle East problem with participation of all sides, including the PLO, the sole legitimate representative of the Palestinian people. According to Bakdash, "this solution can only be based on Israel's withdrawal from all Arab territories occupied in 1967, and ensurance of the rights of the Palestinian Arabs, including the right to set up their own independent state" (*Information Bulletin,* no. 8).

A plenary meeting of the SCP Central Committee, reported on 3 January, called for strengthening cooperation among Syria, Algeria, Libya, South Yemen, and the PLO and expressed the hope that Iraq would also join this front of progressive Arab states.

The SCP denounced the Israeli occupation of southern Lebanon in mid-March and demanded immediate and unconditional withdrawal. It declared its support for the PLO, "which is defending its existence and the sovereignty of Lebanon, as well as for all democratic progressive forces on the side of the Palestinian fighters." The SCP asserted that we "must defeat the attempts of imperialism, Zionism and reaction to use Lebanese events to prevent Sadat's isolation in the Arab World under the guise of 'uniting the Arabs'" (ibid., no. 10).

After the Arab League council passed a resolution freezing diplomatic and political relations between member states and South Yemen (PDRY), the SCP denounced it and demanded a cancellation, claiming that it contradicted the League's charter and constituted gross interference in PDRY domestic affairs. The SCP charged Saudi Arabia, North Yemen (YAR), and Oman, prompted by U.S. imperialism, with putting blatant pressure on PDRY and preparing an armed attack against its people (*FBIS,* 17 July).

The SCP, which is consistently pro-Soviet, addressed a message in May to the Communist Party of China appealing that its leadership reconsider the USSR's initiative to normalize relations. Subsequently, the SCP revealed the extent of its antagonism toward China in a message to the Communist Party of Vietnam on its National Day, declaring that "we condemn the provocations made against Vietnam by the Peking authorities, the new ally of imperialism and reaction" (ibid., 12 September).

During 1978 the SCP kept contact with various countries aligned with the Soviet Union. Khalid Hammami, a member of the Political Bureau, led a delegation to Hungary in February; Bakdash visited the USSR in April; and a delegation led by Political Bureau member Ramu Shaikhu traveled to East Germany and Bulgaria during August-September. These SCP delegations joined with the leadership of each country in expressing mutual support and solidarity on such issues as international communism, national liberation movements, and the Middle East.

The SCP and Other Arab Communist Parties. Together with seven other Arab communist and workers' parties from Jordan, Algeria, Sudan, Iraq, Egypt, Lebanon, and Morocco, the SCP conducted secret meetings in Cyprus during mid-April. Participants condemned the Israeli invasion of southern Lebanon and asserted their support for both Palestinian resistance and the Lebanese National Movement. A Beirut newspaper reported that the meeting also discussed measures to topple the governments of a number of Arab countries, particularly South Yemen and Iraq, so that communist forces could eventually dominate them (*al-Hawadeth,* 28 July).

Publications. The official SCP organ is the fortnightly newspaper *Nidal al-Sha'b* (People's struggle), which is banned but has been circulating freely since the party joined the National Progressive Front. The SCP also disseminates its news through the two legal publications of the Lebanese communist party in Beirut, *al-Nida'* and *al-Akhbar,* as the situation permits.

Stanford University   Patricia Mihaly

INTERNATIONAL COMMUNIST FRONT ORGANIZATIONS

A network of international organizations, while allegedly democratic and nongovernmental, are in fact fronts for USSR policies. It dates back to 1921 when Lenin conceived the idea of propagating communism through trade unions, youth movements, cooperatives and other bodies. The strongest evidence of Soviet control, despite a pretense of independence and nonalignment, has been the faithful adherence by front organizations to the Moscow party line. Fronts coordinate and interact with one another, usually stressing the same propaganda themes at any given time. The most widely reiterated has been hostility to U.S. weapons development, most recently the neutron bomb. When the Sino-Soviet feud erupted, the fronts sided with Moscow, and officials suspected of pro-Peking sympathies were ousted.

Most present-day front organizations were begun during the late 1940s when the USSR launched them or secured control over existing ones. According to a CIA study, the fronts are funded by the Soviet Union (*U.S. News and World Report,* 7 August).

The following eleven have been selected for this annual review of international communist front organization activities: Afro-Asian People's Solidarity Organization (AAPSO), Christian Peace Conference (CPC), International Association of Democratic Lawyers (IADL), International Federation of Resistance Fighters (FIR), International Organization of Journalists (IOJ), International Union of Students (IUS), Women's International Democratic Federation (WIDF), World Federation of Democratic Youth (WFDY), World Federation of Scientific Workers (WFSW), World Federation of Trade Unions (WFTU), and World Peace Council (WPC). WFTU is the largest and has been the most active, but internal dissension has developed recently. WPC is perhaps the most important front from the Soviet point of view, with WFDY closely following.

Afro-Asian Peoples' Solidarity Organization. Set up at Cairo in 1958 as an anticolonialist offshoot from the World Peace Council (WPC), AAPSO during its first years was jointly controlled by the USSR, China, and the United Arab Republic. The Sino-Soviet dispute led to disruption of AAPSO conferences in 1963 and 1965 and finally to a split following the 1967 WPC meeting at Nicosia. The Chinese boycotted that meeting, which decided to hold the next AAPSO conference in Algiers rather than in Peking as planned. Since then, Soviet domination of AAPSO has continued.

Structure and Leadership. AAPSO's organizational framework has been and is relatively loose. Although meetings of its Congress and Council are held, in a practical sense the Secretariat has been the key organizational unit. The eleventh Council meeting in 1974 established the Presidium, which apparently will bear primary responsibility, along with the Secretariat, for development and execution of policy.

Yusuf al-Sebai, AAPSO secretary general since its foundation, was shot in February. He was replaced by the noted Egyptian writer and publicist Abdul Rahman al-Sharqawi. Nuri Abdul Razzaq Hussein and Edward al-Kharrat continue as deputy and assistant general secretaries, respectively.

Views and Activities. On the surface, the most important AAPSO activity seemed to be the meeting of its Presidium during 17−18 February at Nicosia, where its secretary general was killed "by terrorists." According to Soviet sources, they were enemies of the Palestine Liberation Organization (PLO) and inspired by proimperialist forces (*Pravda,* 19 February). Perhaps more important for the long run was the subsequent selection of a successor by President Sadat, exercising a right of the headquarters country (Middle East News Agency, 6 March). Possibly related to this leadership change is the continued postponement of the AAPSO Sixth Congress, originally scheduled for December 1977, rescheduled for March, and then postponed until the end of the year.

At the Nicosia meeting, resolutions were passed that reflected established propaganda lines—anticolonialism and anti-imperialism, support for the PLO and liberation struggles in Africa and Asia, peaceful settlement of the conflict between Vietnam and Cambodia (with a clear indication that the former is right). A special resolution on disarmament condemned U.S. plans to produce the neutron bomb. (*Cyprus Mail,* 18 February.)

At a conference on AAPSO tasks, held in Colombo during June, some 40 delegates from Asia, Africa, Latin America, Europe, and "socialist countries" approved a declaration stressing the necessity of stepping up the struggle against imperialism, colonialism, apartheid, and Zionism. Conferences also adopted a special resolution calling upon the People's Republic of China to accept the constructive proposals of Vietnam, which would put an end to their differences (Tass, 29 June).

Other resolutions called for a negotiated settlement in the Horn of Africa (*Izvestiia,* 26 February), condemned opposition to the "progressive" regime of South Yemen (Tass, 9, 24 July), and criticized the Camp David agreements (*FBIS,* 6 October). An AAPSO delegation visited Vietnam and received the Order of Friendship. It expressed alarm over the situation on the borders and, as a sign of solidarity, announced that the Presidium meeting would be held in Hanoi during January 1979 (*FBIS,* 13, 24 October).

Publications. A new quarterly, *Development and Socio-Economic Progress,* will be published in English, French, and Arabic.

Christian Peace Conference. With headquarters in Prague, the CPC has been under Soviet domination since 1968 but describes itself as a forum for Christians everywhere to "search for God's will concerning current political, social and economic problems." It claims to have members in about 50 countries. During the past two years, great effort has been devoted to establishment of new regional groups, especially in Africa and Latin America.

Structure and Leadership. The CPC's highest organ is the All-Christian Peace Assembly. The president for the past decade, USSR Metropolitan Nikodim, in 1978 was made honorary president and died not long afterward. He was replaced by Bishop Karoly Toth, for many years CPC secretary general. The new secretary general is Lubomir Mirejovsky, a minister in the Church of Czech Brethren. In addition to the Secretariat, there are several study commissions.

Views and Activities. The most important event was the All-Christian Peace Assembly at Prague. More than 680 delegates, guests, and observers from nearly 100 countries participated in workshops on disarmament, racism, economic problems, theological questions, cooperation with the U.N., and the contribution of Christians to world peace (*Neues Deutschland,* 21−29 June). Greetings came from many state leaders, including Kosygin, who asked the gathering to support the struggle against the armaments race.

Approved were a message to churches and to Christians; an appeal to governments concerning dangers to peace in Africa, Latin America, and the Middle East, and the proposed production of the neutron bomb; and resoltuions on disarmament and détente, colonialism and neocolonialism,

China's militaristic moves, and the need to solve the Vietnam-Cambodian dispute peacefully. The assembly also endorsed the Soviet call for a world disarmament conference.

Problems of church life in communist-ruled states were not on the agenda. Neither the massacre of missionaries and their families in Rhodesia nor the imprisonment of priests in such countries as Czechoslovakia, Ethiopia, and the USSR was mentioned. The protest by churches in East Germany against expansion of premilitary education in the schools never came up.

The CPC Commission on Disarmament met at Sofia and called for mobilization of Christians in the struggle for peace and against imperialism, racism, militarism (Bulgarska telegrafna agentsiya, 5 March). At an Asian continuation committee meeting in New Delhi later that month, documents were adopted on disarmament, demilitarization of the Indian Ocean, poverty in Asia, and the Vietnam-Cambodia border dispute (*CPC Information,* 23 March).

Publications. The principal media outlet is *CPC Information.* Because of its close ties with the World Peace Council, most CPC activities are reported in WPC publications.

International Association of Democratic Lawyers. An "International Congress of Jurists," meeting at Paris in October 1946 under the auspices of a para-communist organization (Mouvement national judiciaire) and attended by lawyers from 25 countries, founded the International Association of Democratic Lawyers. The leading role in the IADL was played by leftist French lawyers, and by 1949 most noncommunists had resigned. In 1950 the French government expelled the IADL from its base in Paris. It then moved to Brussels, where it remains, although some organization work has been carried out from Warsaw.

Membership is open to lawyers' organizations or groups, and to individual lawyers, and may be on a "corresponding," "donation," or "permanent" basis. Lawyers holding membership through organizations or individually are estimated to number about 25,000. While publishing no details of its finances the IADL claims to be supported by membership fees and donations. It holds consultative status, Category C, with the U.N. Economic and Social Council.

Structure and Leadership. The highest organ of the IADL is the Congress, in which each member organization is represented. The latest one met at Algiers in April 1975. The Congress elects the Council, which is supposed to meet yearly and consists of the Bureau, the Secretariat, and a representative of each member organization. Following the deaths in 1976 and 1977 of its two principal officers (see *YICA, 1978,* p. 455), Joe Nordmann (France) was elected president and Dr. Gerhard Stuby (Federal Republic of Germany) secretary general (*Neues Deutschland,* 23–24 June).

Views and Activities. At the Bureau meeting in Algiers during January, IADL programs for 1978 and 1979 were discussed and twelve resolutions passed on Africa, the Middle East, Chile, Vietnam and Cambodia, as well as the arms race and the neutron bomb.

The president and secretary general visited Vietnam, at which time they issued statements criticizing past and present U.S. actions, Peking's interference in Hanoi's internal affairs, and Cambodian aggression. They also proclaimed that legal and human rights were fully protected in Vietnam. (*FBIS,* 30 June.)

IADL continued to issue periodic statements about legal and human-rights abuses in noncommunist states (e.g., Chile and the Federal Republic of Germany) and announced that its president would assist the defense in a trial in West Germany (*Neues Deutschland,* 23 November 1977; *L'Humanité,* 3 March). The IADL has not, however, scored any violations of human rights in communist-ruled countries, nor has it sent observers to these countries, as it did to Greece, Chile, Egypt, and other nonbloc states.

Publications. Principal IADL media, *Review of Contemporary Laws* and *Information Bulletin,* appear irregularly in both English and French.

International Federation of Resistance Fighters. The FIR (Fédération internationale des résistants) was founded in 1951 at Vienna as successor to the International Federation of Former Political Prisoners (Fédération internationale des anciens prisonniers politiques). After the name change, membership eligibility was widened to include former partisans and resistance fighters as well as victims of nazism and fascism and their descendants.

FIR claims three million full members. In 1971 it boasted affiliated groups and representation in every country of Europe (*Résistance unie,* no. 14). Headquarters are in Vienna, and a small secretariat is maintained in Paris. FIR was granted Status B with the U.N. Economic and Social Council in 1972 and with UNESCO in 1978.

Structure and Leadership. Organs of FIR include a Congress, General Council, Bureau, and Secretariat. The Congress, which is to meet every four years, elects the president, vice-president, and Bureau members and approves members of the General Council after they have been nominated by national associations. The General Council supposedly meets at least once a year. The Bureau supervises implementation of decisions reached by the Congress and the General Council, and is responsible for the budget; from among its members, it elects the Secretariat. Arialdo Banfi (Italy) is president and Alex Lhote (France) secretary general.

Views and Activities. The principal event of the year was the Eighth Congress at Minsk during 24–26 May. Some 350 delegates, representing over 60 organizations, took part. A message from Brezhnev was read. In a declaration, FIR reiterated its dedication to the struggle against fascism and war, proclaiming its determination to work for security and cooperation in Europe, as well as détente and disarmament. It also passed a resolution in favor of banning the neutron bomb.

It was also decided at the congress to hold an international antifascist symposium on problems such as terrorism. The president also made known in an interview that a world conference of war veterans and former resistance fighters would be held at Rome in 1979 to discuss disarmament.

Publications. FIR publishes *Résistance unie/Service d'information.*

International Organization of Journalists. IOJ was founded in June 1946 at Copenhagen. Merging with it at the time were the International Federation of Journalists (IFJ) and the International Federation of Journalists of Allied and Free Countries. IOJ headquarters, originally in London, moved to Prague in 1947. By 1952 participating noncommunist unions had withdrawn in order to refound IFJ. Since 1955 IOJ has made unsuccessful overtures to IFJ for a new world organization of journalists. It was for this purpose that IOJ founded the International Committee for Cooperation of Journalists (ICCJ). No IFJ member is known to have become affiliated with ICCJ, perhaps because most ICCJ officers are also leading members of the parent IOJ.

A rival organization, the Afro-Asian Journalists' Association, became established in 1963 by pro-Chinese journalists and appears to have drawn little other support.

IOJ claims 150,000 members in 110 countries. It holds consultative status, Category II, with the U.N. Economic and Social Council.

Structure and Leadership. The highest IOJ body, the Congress, meets approximately every four years. It elects the Executive Committee, made up of the Presidium (president, vice-presidents, secretary general), other officers (secretaries and treasurer), and ordinary members. At the Eighth Congress in Helsinki during 21–23 September 1976, professor of journalism Kaarle Nordenstreng (Finland), was elected president. Jiří Kubka (Czechoslovakia) remained as secretary general. Jean-

Maurice Herman (France), the outgoing president, was named honorary president. Also elected to the Presidium, all as vice-presidents, were the chairman of the USSR Union of Journalists, the secretary general of the Somali Journalists' Association, a representative of the IOJ Puerto Rican Committee, the secretary general of the National Syndicate of Press Workers in Venezuela, the chairman of the National Union of Journalists in Mali, the assistant director of *Horoya* (Guinea), the secretary general of the National Syndicate of Journalists (France), the chairman of the Iraqi Journalists' Union, a representative of the Chilean IOJ Committee, and a representative of the Union of Democratic Journalists (Mexico), according to *Democratic Journalist,* no. 12, 1976.

Views and Activities. The Presidium met for the first time in Paris, where the president delivered a report on the responsibility of journalists for the comprehensive fulfillment of the Helskini agreements. (*FBIS,* 22 November 1977.) Other questions discussed were "imbalances" in information, especially with respect to developing countries, and the "concentration" of the press in West European capitalist countries. Representatives from Asia, Africa, and Latin America spoke in favor of "decolonization" of information.

At various times during the year, IOJ issued statements (*a*) against apartheid in South Africa, (*b*) welcoming the U.N. Special Session on Disarmament, (*c*) denouncing new weapons of mass destruction, especially the neutron bomb, and (*d*) supporting Vietnam in its border conflict with Cambodia. IOJ prizes went to Gabriel Garcia Marquez (Colombia), Helao Vinnia Ndadi (Namibia), and the National Federation of Italian Press (*Journalists' Affairs,* no. 23/24, 1977).

Publications. The IOJ fortnightly *Journalists' Affairs* and monthly *Democratic Journalist* appear in English, French, Spanish, and Russian editions. A special publication entitled *The IOJ in the Struggle Against Apartheid* came out during 1978.

International Union of Students. A congress at Prague in August 1946, attended by students of varying political persuasions, established the International Union of Students. In 1951 most of the noncommunist student unions withdrew because of IUS domination by pro-Soviet groups. The 1960s were marked by bitter debates between pro-Moscow and pro-Peking students. In the middle 1960s the Chinese withdrew from active participation.

IUS claims to have 99 organizations with members totaling ten million, mostly in communist-ruled countries. It has consultative Category C status with UNESCO. Applications for Category B status have been deferred repeatedly.

Structure and Leadership. IUS has headquarters in Prague. Its highest governing body, the Congress, is supposed to meet every three years. Each affiliated and associated organization is permitted to send delegates. The Congress elects the national unions to be represented on the Executive Commitee; the national unions then determine which individual(s) will represent them. The Executive Committee meets once a year.

The Twelfth Congress, held at Sofia on 1 November 1977, elected Miroslav Stepan from the Czech Student Center, as president. Fathi al-Fadl of the Sudanese Students' Federation was reelected secretary general. Vice-presidents are representatives from the following: Organization of Dakar University Students; Council of Presidents, Federation of Chilean Universities; University Students' Federation, Cuba; All-Indian Federation of Students; (North) Korean Committee of Students; National Union of Students, Mozambique; General Union of Palestinian Students; Federation of Students, Panama; Socialist Union of Polish Students; Soviet Council of Students; National Union of Vietnamese Students; and National Student Council, Bulgaria. The new secretaries represent organizations in Cyprus, Ghana, Hungary, Ireland, Namibia, Puerto Rico, Romania, Somalia, Uruguay, and the People's Republic of Yemen.

Views and Activities. Much of early 1978 was spent by IUS activists in helping WFDY plan the Eleventh World Youth Festival at Havana. IUS engaged in some actions of its own. An extraordinary meeting of the Secretariat held at Prague condemned U.S. plans to produce the neutron bomb and appealed for a student protest campaign (CETEKA, 13 December 1977). In early February, the IUS was represented at a meeting in Tripoli to express solidarity with the people and students of Palestine (*World Student News,* no. 3). Two months later, representatives of IUS and student organizations from Britain, Ireland, France, and Poland took part in a "student journalists' solidarity trip" to Lebanon, where they met with PLO leaders (CETEKA, 18 April).

IUS President Miroslav Stepan attended the Eighteenth Komsomol Congress in Moscow and praised Soviet peace activities. At the same time he announced that the IUS's highest award, the November 17 Medal, would be presented to the Komsomol organization (Tass, 25 April).

Several appeals to students were announced during the year: to redouble their efforts against U.S. plans to produce the neutron bomb; fight against racism and for civil rights in the U.S.; and for solidarity with the peoples of Cyprus and Nicaragua. IUS also praised the patient and correct stand of Vietnam in its difficulties with Cambodia. IUS offices announced that a youth conference on solidarity with the peoples of southern Africa would be held during early 1979, probably in Europe (CETEKA, 17 May).

Publications. IUS issues a monthly magazine, *World Student News,* in English, French, German, and Spanish, as well as a fortnightly bulletin, *IUS News Service,* in English, French, and Spanish.

Women's International Democratic Federation. WIDF was founded at Paris in December 1945 at a "Congress of Women" organized by the communist-dominated Union des femmes françaises. Headquarters were in Paris until 1951, when expelled by the French government. They moved to East Berlin.

WIDF holds Category A status with the U.N. Economic and Social Council and Category B with UNESCO. It is also on the Special List of the International Labor Organization (ILO) and chairs the Non-Governmental Organization (NGO) subcommittee on the Status of Women in the framework of the NGO Human Rights Commission. WIDF has 123 national affiliated organizations in 109 countries but has not published figures since 1966, when it claimed "over 200 million members."

Structure and Leadership. WIDF's highest governing body is the Congress which meets every four years. Next in authority is the Council, which meets annually and is in control between congresses; it elects the Bureau and the Secretariat. The Bureau meets at least twice a year and implements decisions taken by the Congress and the Council. It is assisted by the Secretariat. In 1978, Mirjam Vire-Tuominen (Finland) was elected secretary general, replacing Fanny Edelman (Argentina). Freda Brown (Australia) remains president.

WIDF membership is open to all women's organizations and groups and, in exceptional cases, to individuals. It seeks to maintain contact with nonaffiliated women's groups through an International Liaison Bureau which has general headquarters at Copenhagen and a secretariat at Brussels. New affiliates accepted in 1978 came from Afghanistan, Jamaica, Libya, Turkey, Northern Ireland, and the Western Sahara.

Views and Activities. At a Bureau meeting in East Berlin, delegates from 27 countries discussed new activities in the struggle for disarmament and adopted statements condemning the neutron bomb, apartheid, fascism, and racial discrimination (ADN, 20 February).

The Council convened at Moscow, with 292 delegates from 118 countries. Greetings from Brezhnev were read. The principal speech by President Freda Brown stressed the need for disarmament. She branded allegations that the Soviet Union threatens world peace as lies and called upon member organizations to explain the "consistent and patient policy" of the USSR (*FBIS,* 17 May). The Council, apart from a general solidarity declaration, adopted resolutions condemning apartheid and neutron bomb production, and formulated a message to the U.N. Special Session on Disarmament (Tass, 15, 19 May).

At different times during the year, WIDF issued statements protesting the violation of human rights in Bolivia, Chile, and Guatemala. It also called for abolition of "imperialist" military bases in the Indian Ocean; condemned Israel's "criminal aggression" against Lebanon; expressed support for Vietnam in its border dispute with Cambodia; and condemned aggression against Angola.

WIDF announced that a conference would be held in Algiers during May or June 1979 in connection with International Children's Year, on the theme "A Peaceful and Secure Future for All Children." A preparatory meeting on this topic was held at New Delhi during 30 January–2 February.

Publications. WIDF publishes a quarterly, *Women of the Whole World,* in English, French, Spanish, German, and Russian and also issues various pamphlets and bulletins.

World Federation of Democratic Youth. Founded in November 1945 at a "World Youth Conference" convened in London by the World Youth Council, WFDY appeared to represent varying shades of political opinion, but key offices were taken by Communists. By 1950 most noncommunists had withdrawn and established their own organization, the World Assembly of Youth. Originally based in Paris, WFDY was expelled by the French government in 1951. Headquarters have since been in Budapest.

All youth organizations that contribute to safeguarding activities of young persons are eligible for membership in WFDY, which claims to enroll 150 million persons from 210 organizations in 104 countries. Most members live in communist-ruled countries.

Structure and Leadership. The highest governing body of WFDY is the Assembly, which convenes every three years and to which all affiliated organizations send representatives. The Assembly elects the Executive Committee, which meets at least twice a year. Day-to-day work is conducted by the Bureau and the Secretariat. Ernesto Ottone (Chile) is president, and Miklos Barabas (Hungary) secretary general.

Views and Activities. Overshadowing everything else was the Eleventh World Youth Festival, sponsored jointly by WFDY and the much smaller International Union of Students and held at Havana between 25 July and 5 August. From time to time, WFDY issued statements expressing solidarity with the people of Africa; unity with the Arab people; hostility toward colonialism, imperialism, racism, and the neutron bomb; and support for détente and disarmament. These positions were reiterated especially at the Tenth Assembly, held in East Berlin during 22–28 February, and indicate the subjects taken up by the Assembly. Delegates from 130 countries received cabled greetings from Brezhnev and were addressed by the communist party secretary general of the host country, Erich Honecker.

Eleventh World Youth Festival. A large part of the previous year had been spent in preparation for this event (see *YICA, 1978,* p. 462). It attracted some 25,000 participants, including about 18,500 delegates representing nearly 2,000 organizations from 145 countries, plus guests, journalists and tourists. China, Cambodia, and North Korea did not send delegations (*L'Humanité,* 31 July). Separate days were set aside for discussion of solidarity with the peoples of Africa, Latin America, and the Arab countries; concern of youth and students with peace and détente; the struggle against imperialism and colonialism; the situation of youth in capitalist countries; and the striving by youth to build socialism in Cuba (*Juventud Rebelde,* 28 July–4 August). Raul Castro opened the festival, and Fidel Castro gave the closing speech.

Two manifestations tended to overshadow other aspects of the festival: (*a*) its carnival atmosphere and (*b*) the discord that developed among many delegates. Sparing no cost, the Cubans formally opened the proceedings in the largest sports stadium, filled with 60,000 persons and bright fireworks. During subsequent days, thousands of Cubans were mobilized to provide colorful parades, athletic contests, and cultural events. Previously held festivals at Moscow, Sofia, and East Berlin had been conformist exercises in comparison.

While hailed as a great success by the USSR and the Soviet-allied press (e.g. *Rudé Právo,* 7 August), the festival produced considerable discord. Several national delegations protested the nature of the program. For example, the Italians wanted to discuss the conflict in the Horn of Africa. The British and the Italians sought to condemn violation of human rights in communist as well as noncommunist countries (*Morning Star,* 2 August; *L'Unità,* 5 August). Some 400 U.S. delegates, most of them Puerto Ricans, Blacks, Indians, and Chicanos, spent a good deal of time squabbling with their Communist Party USA organizers (*NYT,* 6 August; *Wall Street Journal,* 15 September). Yugoslavs refused to sign the festival's final document because it smacked of the Cold War period when such festivals "constituted a special kind of forum to express the positions and the ideas of the East European countries" (*Mladost,* as reported by Tanjug, 14 August).

At the end, participants adopted two documents. One expressed gratitude to the people and youth of Cuba for their hospitality and contributions to the festival. The other called on young people in all countries to step up their actions for peace, détente and international cooperation, ending the arms race and imperialist wars, general and complete disarmament, raising a protest against manufacture of new destructive weapons such as the neutron bomb, and a continuing struggle against colonialism, racism, and fascism (Tass, 7 August). The latter document was adopted with important reservations on the part of a large number of delegations, mainly from Western European countries. Vietnamese and Soviet delegations attempted to have China condemned but without success (*Le Monde,* 8 August; *L'Humanité,* 7 August).

Publications. WDFY publishes a bimonthly, *World Youth,* in English, French, German, and Arabic. A monthly, *WDFY News,* appears in English, French, and Spanish.

World Federation of Scientific Workers. WFSW was founded at London in 1946 on initiative of the British Association of Scientific Workers, with organizations of scientists from fourteen countries taking part. Although it purported to be a scientific rather than a political organization, Communists obtained most official posts at the start and have kept control since. Headquarters are in London, but the secretary general's office is at Paris.

WFSW membership is open to organizations of scientific workers everywhere and to individual scientists in countries where no affiliated groups are active. It claims to represent 300,000 scientists in 28 countries, most of the membership deriving from fourteen groups in communist-ruled countries. The only large noncommunist affiliate, the British Association of Scientific Workers, has 21,000 members. Scientists of distinction who do not belong to an affiliated organization may be nominated for "corresponding membership." WFSW has a constitution and a "Charter for Scientific Workers" to which affiliates must subscribe.

Structure and Leadership. The governing body of WFSW is the General Assembly, in which all affiliated organizations are represented. Eleven Assembly meetings have been held, the most recent being in September 1976 in London. Between assemblies, the Executive Council and its Bureau are responsible for operations. There are three standing committees: Science Policy, Socio-Economic, and Peace and Disarmament. Eric Burhop (U.K.) is president and chairman of the Executive Council; J. M. Legay (France) is secretary general, having been elected to this position at the Eleventh Assembly (*Scientific World,* no. 4, 1976).

Views and Activities. At the Bureau meeting in Warsaw, a resolution demanding a ban on the neutron bomb and cruise missile and documents on educational policy, the brain drain, and multi-national companies were prepared (Polska Agencia Prasowa, 15 and 16 September 1977). The Executive Committee met for three days at Varna, Bulgaria, to discuss the responsibility of scientists in the struggle for peace and disarmament and against the neutron bomb (Tass, 21 May).

In an editorial, *Scientific World* (April/June) called upon its members, as well as those in organizations such as WPC, to contribute to a U.N. conference on "science, technology, and development" in Vienna during the summer of 1979.

New WFSW affiliates include the Union of Algerian Engineers; the Democratic Association of Greek Scientists in Great Britain; the Bangladesh Association of Scientists and Scientific Professions; and the Official College of Doctors and Graduates in Philosophy, Literature, and Science of Madrid District University (ibid.).

Publications. Aside from *Scientific World,* issued in French, English, German, Russian, Czech, and Spanish, the organization issues the *WFSW Bulletin* irregularly and only to members. Toward the end of 1977, the WFSW published a book-sized brochure in German and English, entitled *Ending the Arms Race: The Task of the Scientist.*

World Federation of Trade Unions. WFTU, set up at the initiative of the British Trades Union Congress, held its founding congress in October 1945 at Paris, where its first headquarters was established. Expelled from Paris and then Vienna for subversive activities, the headquarters has been at Prague since 1956. Some noncommunist affiliates gave up membership in 1949 to found an alternative organization, the International Confederation of Free Trade Unions (ICFTU). WFTU claims to have about 150 million members in 68 countries, but some 90 percent are from communist-ruled countries, including over 107 million in the Soviet Union.

Structure and Leadership. The highest WFTU authority, the Congress, meets every four years and is composed of delegates from affiliates in proportion to the number of their members. The Congress, which has no policy-making function and is too large to transact much specific business, elects the General Council, Executive Bureau, and Secretariat. The General Council has 85 regular and 87 candidate members representing national affiliates and eleven Trade Union Internationals (TUIs). The 28-member Executive Bureau is the most powerful organ and since 1969 has assumed much of the authority earlier enjoyed by the Secretariat, which is now reduced to a secretary general and seven members. At the latest congress (1978) the post of secretary general was given for the first time to a non-Frenchman, Enrique Pastorino (Uruguay), the outgoing president. The new president is Sándor Gáspár (Hungary).

TUIs represent workers of particular trades and crafts. One of their main purposes is to recruit local unions which do not, through their national centers, belong to WFTU. Though TUIs are in theory independent, their policies and finances are controlled by the WFTU department having supervision over their particular areas. The WFTU General Council in December 1966 decided that each TUI should have its own constitution; this move, taken to bolster the appearance of independence, had the purpose of allowing TUIs to join international bodies as individual organizations.

In recent years WFTU has moved vigorously to establish working relationships with noncommunist trade unions and intergovernmental organizations. In this area of operation one of the most important structural linkages is the WFTU "Special Commission on U.N. Agencies," created in 1967 to facilitate WFTU activities in the U.N. WFTU enjoys Category A status with a number of U.N. agencies. It has permanent representatives at the U.N in New York and at the International Labor Organization (ILO), the Food and Agriculture Organization (FAO), and UNESCO.

Views and Activities. The highlight of activities was the Ninth Congress held at Prague during 16–22 April. Nearly 1,000 delegates, observers, and guests arrived from 126 countries. representing over 300 national, international, and regional organizations, most of them from Soviet-bloc countries. Seventeen new members were accepted at the congress, including the Zimbabwe African Trade Union Congress as well as organizations from Angola and Ethiopia (Moscow radio, 17 April).

The congress was preceded by a growing split between representatives from the Soviet bloc and the West, made evident at Executive Bureau meetings. The rift, which has been some years in the making, involves opposing views on (*a*) the place of trade unions in society, including the nature of workers' rights, and (*b*) the structure and operation of WFTU.

This split was dramatized by actions of the communist-controlled Italian General Confederation of Labor (CGIL), which announced before the congress that it was leaving WFTU, an action presaged by CGIL downgrading its membership to "associate" five years earlier (*Times,* London, 15 March).

The other incident involved Georges Séguy, secretary general of the communist-controlled French General Labor Confederation (CGT), who told the congress that CGT had lost faith in WFTU's ability to reform itself; hence, no Frenchman would be available as a candidate for the position of secretary general, a post traditionally held by a citizen of France (*FBIS,* 19 April). Moreover, he hinted that in a year the CGT might follow CGIL, which had sent only observers to Prague, in complete disaffiliation.

For Italians, the choice of Prague as congress site represented a "provocation" (*Corriere della Sera,* 29 September 1977). They did not approve WFTU portrayal of conditions in the West as bad and in the Soviet bloc as good. And they found advance documents of the congress incompatible with unity and openness. WFTU is "an outdated and useless instrument," according to *L'Unità,* 15 March.

The French insisted that WFTU be subject to structural and statutory changes so that the rights of trade unions in East and West be recognized "to take all steps toward the organization and support of union actions, including strikes, and must not be subjected to penalties, fines, sanctions, or repressive measures before, during, or after these actions" (*L'Humanité,* 13 April). French spokesman Séguy asserted that CGT's views were shared by trade unionists in Spain and Portugal and by a number from Africa (ibid., 18 April), a position confirmed by speakers from several of these countries (*L'Unità,* 18 and 22 April).

In a press interview, a USSR trade union secretary regretted the French stand but claimed that WFTU was receptive to differing views. The WFTU would "continue to exist as it has always existed" whatever the Italian and French views (Tass, 18 April).

These negative actions by the two strongest Western trade unions in the WFTU did not prevent the congress from adopting well-known propaganda lines. Among several documents adopted, two tend to stand out: a long-term program for the international trade union movement, and a declaration of trade union rights which are threatened by "multinational monopolies in capitalist countries" (ibid., 23 April). Nothing was said about the right to strike. These documents stressed the struggles for peace, détente, and cooperation among all states, against the arms race, and especially against the neutron bomb (*FBIS,* 25 April). Targets for future propaganda include Chile, Iran, Brazil, Argentina, Israel, South Africa, Nicaragua, Indonesia, and other countries.

Throughout the year, WFTU issued statements in a variety of contexts: against the Pinochet dictatorship in Chile, against apartheid, for solidarity with Vietnam, and against the Camp David agreements.

A conference on solidarity with the struggle of African and Arab peoples against imperialism and reaction was scheduled to be held at Addis Ababa in September. It decided in April to convene in 1979 the Fourth World Trade Union Conference on "problems of employed women."

Publications. The most important WFTU medium is an illustrated magazine, *World Trade Union Movement,* circulated in some 70 countries in English, French, Spanish, German, Russian, and other languages. *Flashes,* appearing several times a month in four languages, is a four- to five-page information bulletin.

World Peace Council. The "world peace movement" headed by WPC dates from August 1948, when a "World Congress of Intellectuals for Peace" at Wroclaw, Poland, set up an organization called the International Liaison Committee of Intellectuals. In April 1949, it convened a "First World Peace Congress" in Paris. The congress launched a "World Committee of Partisans of Peace" which in November 1950 was renamed the World Peace Council. Originally based in Paris, WPC was expelled in 1951 by the French government. It moved first to Prague and then in 1954 to Vienna, where it adopted the name "World Council of Peace." Although outlawed by Austria in 1957, it continued its operations in Vienna under the cover of a new organization, the International Institute of Peace (IIP), subsequently referred to by WPC members as the "Scientific-Theoretical Workshop of the WPC." In September 1968, the World Council of Peace transferred its headquarters to Helsinki, while IIP remained in Vienna and reverted to its earlier name: World Peace Council.

Structure and Leadership. The WPC is organized on a national basis with peace committees and other affiliated groups claimed in 120 countries. No precise figure is available on total individual membership. The highest authority is the 600-member Council, which elects the 101-member Presidential Committee, which in turn elects the 24-member Bureau and 18-member Secretariat. Membership in these groups is divided among representatives from various countries. Communist-front organizations such as IUS, WFDY, WFSW, WFTU, and WIDF are represented on the Presidential Committee.

Amendments adopted at the February 1974 meeting of the Council require it to meet once every three years, instead of every two, and urge the national peace committees to convene annually. The Presidential Committee meets annually while the Bureau meets three or four times a year to review international events and the Council's work and to implement decisions of the Presidential Committee. It appears, however, that the Bureau has authority to act independently on a wide range of matters. Executive bodies of IIP—ostensibly independent of WPC, but in fact elected by the Council—are the seven-member Presidium and thirty-person Executive Committee. At the May 1977 Council session in Warsaw, a new Council was elected, with former Secretary General Romesh Chandra elected president. Twenty vice-presidents, a Bureau, and a Presidential Committee also were chosen. (*New Perspectives,* no. 6, 1976, and no. 1, 1977.) See Biographies, p. 449.

WPC has "Consultation and Association, Category A status" with UNESCO.

Views and Activities. WPC sponsored several conferences, held a Presidium meeting, and issued a number of statements in support of its general line. While a major concern seemed to be the threat to peace represented by Western powers and "reactionary" regimes in the less developed states of the world, a good deal of WPC attention focused on troubles in the communist camp (China and the Vietnam-Cambodia conflict).

The end of 1977 witnessed the awarding of the Frederic Joliot Curie Gold Medal, WPC's highest award, to Romanian leader Nicolae Ceauşescu (*FBIS,* 21 November 1977) and the announcement of a program for 1978 (ibid., 9 December 1977). President Chandra asserted that the WPC would deal with the struggle to end the arms race, the pursuit of a just settlement in the Middle East, the campaign against U.S. plans to produce the neutron bomb, and the struggle against apartheid, racism, and racial discrimination (Tass, 8 December 1977). Subsequently he pointed to such "negative" signs as China's rejection of Soviet initiatives toward normalization of relations and Chinese/Cambodian aggression against Vietnam (ibid., 22 March, 2 August).

The WPC Bureau met in Washington, D.C., its first meeting in the U.S.A., and called on all world peace forces to step up the struggle for relaxation of tension; against the arms race, especially manufacture of the neutron bomb; and for détente and disarmament (*FBIS*, 31 January).

WPC organized two "peace conferences," one at Mexico City and the other at Athens. At the first, designated as the "Latin American and Caribbean Continental Conference for Peace, Sovereignty, and Economic Independence," resolutions or declarations were adopted condemning imperialism, especially the U.S.A. and the neutron bomb; calling for a world disarmament conference; and dealing with Chile, Guatemala, Panama, Puerto Rico, El Salvador, and Korea. At the other one, called the "International Conference for Peace, Security, and Cooperation in the Mediterranean," there were resolutions on Cyprus, the Middle East, Korea, the Vietnam-Cambodia dispute, the "liberation struggle" in South Africa, and disarmament and the neutron bomb. (*Neues Deutschland*, 3–14 February.)

WPC later sponsored the Second World Conference on "Ways of Development and International Cooperation" at Tripoli with resolutions calling for struggle against imperialism, colonialism, racial discrimination, and production of the neutron bomb. Delegates also expressed themselves for détente and disarmament, adopting documents on problems of economic development in the "liberated" countries (*FBIS*, 17 April).

The WPC Presidium met in Moscow to discuss the arms race, which obstructs the processes of détente; the Cyprus tragedy; "loss of freedom" in Chile; and failure of Korean reunification (Tass, 10–14 July). The WPC president condemned Peking for splitting "the peace-loving and patriotic forces" and announced that the next regular Council session will be held at Varna, Bulgaria, in September 1980 (ibid., 14 July).

The WPC Human Rights Commission met at San Jose, Costa Rica, with the purpose of investigating "crimes of the dictatorial regimes" in Haiti, Nicaragua, and El Salvador. It called on nonaligned countries and the U.N. Human Rights Commission to act. It also asked the U.S. to halt political, economic, and military aid to these three countries. Moreover, it demanded that the U.S., Israeli, and West German governments end their assistance to "Latin American regimes which violated human rights" (*FBIS*, 15 August).

The WPC Bureau held a meeting in Wroclaw, Poland, at the time of the World Congress of Intellectuals in Defense of Peace. It adopted several resolutions expressing deep concern at "unilateral" action of the U.S., Israel, and Egypt at Camp David; solidarity with the people of Nicaragua suffering under the Somoza dictatorship; recognition of the threat to peace by the decision of NATO countries to increase their spending on armaments; an urgent need to convene a world disarmament conference; and condemnation of China and Cambodia for aggravating relations with Vietnam (ibid., 11 October).

At other times, acting through its president or Bureau or Presidium, WPC reiterated views discussed above. No event of any consequence from President Sadat's ban on the Egyptian Peace Council to the U.S. shipment of arms to Israel passed without a statement.

As indicated, WPC frequently expressed concern over deteriorating relations between Vietnam and Cambodia. President Chandra led a delegation to Vietnam which blamed Cambodia, being abetted by Peking (ibid., 6–12 January). WPC also awarded the Frederic Joliot Curie Medal to Nguyen Huu Tho, vice-president of Vietnam in return for the earlier Friendship Order from that country. At various times, WPC praised Vietnam for its peace initiatives. The existence of military conflict between communist-ruled states, all supposedly dedicated to peace, continued to represent a problem for WPC.

Publications. WPC issues a semimonthly bulletin, *Peace Courier,* in English, French, Spanish, and German; a quarterly journal, *New Perspectives,* in English and French; an occasional *Letter to National Committees;* and a *Letter* to members. Booklets published in 1978 included the following: *The World Peace Council at the Special Session of the U.N. General Assembly Devoted to Disarmament and Peace; Peace, Sovereignty, and Economic Independence; Ban the Neutron Bomb; The Way to Peace and Justice in the Middle East; World Peace Council Solidarity With Vietnam; Problems of Socio-Economic Transformation in the Developing Countries;* and *World Conference on the Path to Development and International Cooperation.*

Hoover Institution   Alex N. Dragnich
Stanford University

BIOGRAPHIES OF PROMINENT INTERNATIONAL COMMUNIST FIGURES

ROMESH CHANDRA

The World Peace Council (WPC), the major Soviet-controlled international front organization, honored Romesh Chandra, an Indian Communist, by elevating him from secretary general to president at its 1977 meeting in Warsaw.

The honor was well deserved from the Soviet point of view because Chandra, possibly the best known among all front officials, has faithfully followed the Moscow line throughout his quarter century in the front movement. Year after year, Chandra has praised Soviet peace initiatives and condemned Western "imperialists." The WPC, Chandra said at Moscow in 1975, "positively reacts to all Soviet initiatives in international affairs." Two years earlier at a 1973 Moscow peace conference, Chandra asserted that those peace organizations which took an anti-Soviet stance "ceased to be genuine peace organizations." He has never strayed, not even during such periods of stress as the Warsaw Pact invasion of Czechoslovakia in 1968. He supported Moscow then, although there were widespread protests from some other front group leaders, who subsequently were ousted from office.

Chandra, now 59, travels to scores of countries annually as part of his WPC assignment. He speaks at WPC seminars, regional and planning conferences, and before United Nations committees. He is cited in countless WPC news releases as an authority on peace.

He has been with the WPC practically from its beginning and has been active in international front gatherings since at least 1950. He became a member of the WPC Executive Committee and one of its secretaries in 1953. The following year he helped launch another major Soviet front, the Afro-Asian People's Solidarity Organization (AAPSO), Moscow's response to being banned from the 1955 Afro-Asian Conference in Bandung. Chandra has helped to guide AAPSO ever since, including its participation in many WPC propaganda campaigns. He is founder and former director of the International Institute for Peace, a separate front group which remains under WPC control, and also heads some front subsidiary groups.

Clever, ambitious, and vain, Chandra has been known in India for years as the Indian with Russian contacts. In 1953 Moscow used him as a go-between with the Indian Communist Party, advising the party to refrain from criticizing Jawaharlal Nehru so as to keep him neutral. In 1963 Chandra made a secret trip to Moscow to uphold India's case in the Sino-Indian dispute. He makes frequent stopovers in Moscow during his travels as WPC spokesman. Those familiar with the workings of the WPC say that the Kremlin uses these visits to keep Chandra posted on the party line.

The Russians, while thus keeping a short rein on Chandra, also exercise other means of control. They keep a representative of the Soviet communist party at his side in WPC headquarters, with authority to overrule him whenever deemed necessary. Igor Belyayev, although listed only as a secretary, is the Soviet representative who currenty wields this power in WPC affairs.

Source: U.S. Congress, House, Permanent Select Committee on Intelligence, Subcommittee on Oversight, *Hearings*. Washington, D.C., 20 April 1978, pp. 570—71.

KONSTANTIN USTINOVICH CHERNENKO

Born into a peasant family on 24 September 1911 in the village of Bolshaya Tes in south-central Siberia, Chernenko is an ethnic Russian, who joined the CPSU at age twenty. During the early 1940s, he served as secretary for his native Krasnoyarsk *krai* party organization. After graduating from the higher school for CPSU organizers at Moscow in 1945, he became secretary of Penza *oblast'* committee. From 1948 to 1952 he was head of agitprop for the Moldavian Republic and completed the pedagogical institute at Kishinev in 1953. It was here that his association began with Brezhnev, who was Moldavia's first CPSU secretary during 1950—1952. Four years later, Chernenko became chief of the mass agitation section in the Central Committee's agitprop department at Moscow. In 1960 he was transferred to head the Secretariat of the Supreme Soviet Presidium which Brezhnev chaired.

In 1965 Chernenko was made head of the CPSU Central Committee's General Department, involving among other things coordination of Politburo work. Selected a candidate member in the Central Committee a year later, he also became a deputy of the Supreme Soviet. Since his promotion to Central Committee full member in 1971, he was named a national secretary in 1976, candidate Politburo member in October 1977, and full member on 26 November 1978.

Chernenko accompanied Brezhnev on several trips abroad, including Ghana in 1961 and Helsinki during July-August 1975 for the Final Act of the Conference on Security and Cooperation in Europe. He has been awarded the Red Banner of Labor and two Orders of Lenin.

Sources: *Bolshaya sovetskaya entsiklopediya*, 3rd. ed. Moscow, 1978, vol. 29, p. 84; *Christian Science Monitor*, 30 November 1978.

STANE DOLANC

Born at Hrastnik in Slovenia on 16 November 1925, Stane Dolanc joined Tito's partisans and the Communist Party of Yugoslavia in 1944. Before then he had lived in the part of Slovenia annexed by the Third Reich and reportedly belonged to the *Hitler Jugend* as a high school student. Dolanc served in military counterintelligence until 1960 and has engaged in full-time party work since then. As director of the Higher School for Political Science and concurrently the party secretary of the university conference in Ljubljana, his career developed rapidly. The Fifth and Sixth Congresses of the party in Slovenia (1964 and 1968) elected him member of the central committee and of its executive committee, respectively.

The Ninth National Congress in March 1969 promoted Dolanc to the newly formed 52-member LCY presidium and the 15-member executive bureau headed by Tito. At the Second LCY conference in January 1972, a new 8-member executive bureau was elected, with Dolanc as secretary. Since then, he has been confirmed as the party's executive secretary, both at the Tenth LCY Congress in May 1974 and the Eleventh Congress in June 1978, with his title being changed from secretary of the executive committee to secretary-general of the central committee's presidium.

Dolanc, a graduate in law from Ljubljana University, has been regarded as Tito's protege, but his real strength lies in the organizational sphere. He played a key role during the 1971 purges from the LCY of "nationalists" in Croatia and of "anarcho-liberals" during 1972 in Serbia. Dolanc is married, has two children, and speaks good German as well as some Italian.

Sources: Borys Lewytzkyj and Juliusz Stroynowski, *Who's Who in the Socialist Countries* (New York: K. G. Saur, 1978), p. 130; *New York Times Magazine* (3 December 1978); Dusko Doder, *The Yugoslavs* (New York: Random House, 1978), p. 74.

JOACHIM HERRMANN

Born on 29 October 1928 at Berlin the son of a worker, Herrmann began his career as a journalist immediately after World War II and joined the SED in 1946 when it was founded. Employed on the communist youth newspaper *Junge Welt*, he served as deputy and then editor in chief from 1949 to 1960. Part of this time, Herrmann studied for a diploma in journalism and also during 1958−59 was a secretary of the communist youth organization FDJ.

Subsequently, he worked for the SED Central Committee apparatus until his appointment two years later as editor in chief of *Berliner Zeitung*. In 1965 he became state secretary for All-German Affairs (or West German Affairs, the new name given that government agency in 1969) and was transferred to editor in chief in July 1971 of the principal SED newspaper, *Neues Deutschland*. During this period, he also rose in party rank; he was made a candidate Central Committee member at the June 1971 congress, promoted to candidate Politburo member in October 1973, and made a national secretary at the May 1976 congress.

Relieved of his post as *Neues Deutschland* chief editor in March 1978, Herrmann became SED secretary responsible for agitation and propaganda in place of Werner Lamberz, who had been killed in Libya after a helicopter crash. He has been decorated with the Order of Merit (bronze, silver, and gold) and the Banner of Labor and on his fiftieth birthday received the Order of Karl Marx.

Sources: Günther Buch (comp.), *Namen und Daten*. Berlin, Dietz, 1973, p. 111; Bundesanstalt für gesamtdeutsche Aufgaben, *Staats- und Parteiapparat der DDR*. Bonn, 20 August 1978, pp. 28−30.

POL POT

Born 19 May 1928 into a peasant family in the village of Prey Svau north of Phnom Penh in Kompong Thom province, Pol Pot received his elementary education at a Buddhist temple. After working in the rice paddies with his parents, he attended a trade school in the capital. He next spent three years at the Ecole de radio electricité in Paris on a government scholarship but returned home in January 1953 without graduating.

Pot joined an underground "people's group" and from 1954 to 1963 taught geography and history at a private school in Phnom Penh. It was during this period that he reportedly assumed the name Saloth Sar and was arrested in 1955 for opposing the U.S.-Cambodian military agreement in his magazine *Solidarity*. One of the founders of the communist party (KCP), he became a Central Committee member at its First Congress in September 1960. The following year he already was KCP deputy secretary, and the Second Congress in 1963 made him secretary.

About this time Prince Sihanouk invited 34 known leftists, including Sar-Pot, to join the government. Believing this to be a prelude to repression, Pol Pot fled and spent four years in clandestine work. Between 1968 and March 1970 he reportedly directed guerrilla activities in the Northeast and then served as KCP Military Committee chairman during the next five years.

Meanwhile, the third and fourth party congresses (September 1971 and January 1976) reelected Pot to the post of KCP secretary. In addition, he became prime minister in April 1976.

Sources: Pyongyang radio, 3 October 1977; *Far Eastern Economic Review*, 21 October 1977; *Sekai Shuho*, 14 February 1978; Belgrade radio, 18 March 1978.

NUR MUHAMMED TARAKI

Born in 1917 into a family of Pushtu shepherds, Taraki received his primary education in the city of Nukur. While employed by the British chamber of commerce in Bombay, he completed courses for translators from English into Pushtu and Dari.

During the mid-1940s Taraki became one of the founders of the social-literary movement "Vish Zalmiian" (Awakened Youth) and took part in publication of the newspaper *Angar* (Burning coals). Through the latter, Awakened Youth declared its support for transformation of political and economic life in Afghanistan. During 1957 Taraki visited both the USSR and Eastern Europe.

After 1952 as a journalist, storyteller, and pamphleteer, he worked in the government's press department. Taraki next received an assignment as press attaché to the Afghanistan embassy in Washington, D.C. After his departure, the newspaper was closed down, but the organization continued to exist. Taraki published a manifesto against the king in one of the Washington newspapers. As a result, he was deprived of his Afghan citizenship.

In 1953 the government at Kabul was succeeded by one which proclaimed a new course. Taraki returned to Afghanistan and opened a private translating office. He also began to write on social themes.

His ideas supposedly inspired the organizers of the People's Democratic Party of Afghanistan (PDPA), which held its First Congress in January 1965. Taraki was elected PDPA general secretary and has remained party leader ever since. Shortly before the coup of 27 April 1978, Taraki had been placed under arrest but emerged as head of the Revolutionary Council on 2 May. Toward the end of the year, he paid an official visit to Moscow, where he signed a twenty-year treaty of friendship and cooperation on 5 December.

Sources: *Literaturnaia gazeta*, 17 May 1978, p. 9; *NYT*, 6 December 1978.

SELECT BIBLIOGRAPHY 1977-78

GENERAL ON COMMUNISM

Afanas'ev, V. G. *Fundamentals of Scientific Communism.* Moscow: Progress, 1977. 278 pp.

Ali, Tariq. *1968 and After: Inside the Revolution.* London: Blond & Briggs, 1978. 218 pp.

Balibar, Etienne. *On the Dictatorship of the Proletariat.* Atlantic Highlands, N.J.: Humanities Press, 1977. 237 pp.

Beam, Jacob D. *Multiple Exposure: An American Ambassador's Unique Perspective on East-West Relations.* New York: Norton, 1978. 317 pp.

Becker, James F. *Marxian Political Economy.* New York: Cambridge University Press, 1977. 326 pp.

Belknap, Michael. *Cold War Political Justice.* Westport, Conn.: Greenwood Press, 1977. 322 pp.

Berger, Martin. *Engels, Armies, and Revolution.* Hamden, Conn.: Archon, 1977. 239 pp.

Bergson, Abram. *Productivity and the Social System: The USSR and the West.* Cambridge, Mass.: Harvard University Press, 1978. 256 pp.

Bertsch, Gary K. *Power and Policy in Communist Systems.* New York: Wiley, 1978. 186 pp.

Besançon Alain. *Les origines intellectuals du léninisme.* Paris: Calmann-Levy, 1977. 327 pp.

_____. *The Soviet Syndrome.* New York: Harcourt, Brace & Jovanovich, 1978. 128 pp.

Breitman, Georg, ed. *Leon Trotsky on Black Nationalism and Self-Determination.* New York: Pathfinder Press, 1978. 96 pp.

Brutens, K. N. *National Liberation Revolutions Today.* Moscow: Progress, 1977. 2 vols.

Butler, William E., ed. *Source Book on Socialist International Organizations.* Leiden: Sijthoff, 1978. 1,000 pp.

Carlebach, Julius. *Karl Marx and the Radical Critique of Judaism.* London: Routledge & Kegan Paul, 1978. 466 pp.

Chao, Paul. *Women under Communism: Family in Russia and China.* New York: General Hall Publishers, 1977. 231 pp.

Connor, Walter D. et al. *Public Opinion in European Socialist Systems.* New York: Praeger, 1977. 240 pp.

Fleron, Frederick J., ed. *Technology and Communist Culture.* New York: Praeger, 1977. 518 pp.

Fraentzki, Ekkehard. *Der missverstandene Marx.* Pfuellingen: Guenther Neske, 1978. 293 pp.

Gastil, Raymond D., ed. *Freedom in the World: Political Rights and Civil Liberties.* Boston: G. K. Hall, 1978. 325 pp.

Geller, Evelyn, ed. *Communism: End of the Monolith?* New York: H. W.Wilson, 1978. 243 pp.

Gould, Carol C. *Marx's Social Ontology.* Cambridge, Mass.: MIT Press, 1978. 208 pp.

Gyorgy, Andrew, and James A. Kuhlman, eds. *Innovations in Communist Systems.* Boulder, Colo.: Westview, 1978. 224 pp.

Hacker, Frederick J. *Crusaders, Criminals and Crazies: Terror and Terrorism in Our Time.* New York: Norton, 1978. 355 pp.

Herspring, Dale R., and Ivan Voelgyes, eds. *Civil-Military Relations in Communist Systems.* Boulder, Colo.: Westview, 1978. 315 pp.

Howard, Dick. *The Marxian Legacy.* London: Macmillan, 1977. 340 pp.

Hunt, Alan, ed. *Class and Class Structure.* London: Lawrence & Wishart, 1977. 190 pp.

Jancar, Barbara Wolfe. *Women under Communism.* Baltimore, Md.: Johns Hopkins University Press, 1978. 291 pp.

Knei-Paz, Baruch. *The Social and Political Thought of Leon Trotsky.* Oxford: Clarendon Press, 1978. 629 pp.

Kolakowski. Leszek. *Main Currents of Marxism: Its Rise, Growth and Dissolution.* New York: Oxford University Press, 1978. 3 vols.

Laclau, Ernesto. *Politics and Ideology in Marxist Theory.* Atlantic Highlands, N.J.: Humanities Press, 1977. 203 pp.

Lebedev, N. I. *A New State in International Relations.* New York: Pergamon Press, 1978. 288 pp.

Leonhard, Wolfgang. *The Three Faces of Marxism: The Political Concepts of Soviet Ideology, Maoism, and Humanist Marxism.* New York: Putnam's, 1978. 497 pp.

Lewytzkyj, Boris, and Juliusz Stroynowski, eds. *Who's Who in the Socialist Countries.* New York: K. G. Saur, 1978. 736 pp.

Marie, Jean-Jacques. *Le Trotskysme.* Paris: Flammarion, 1977. 192 pp.

Miliband, Ralph. *Marxism and Politics.* New York: Oxford University Press, 1977. 199 pp.

Miliband, Ralph, and John Saville, eds. *The Socialist Register, 1977.* London: Feklin Press, 1977. 276 pp.

Parsons, Howard L., ed. *Marx and Engels on Sociology.* Westport, Conn.: Greenwood Press, 1977. 262 pp.

Peery, Sue, ed. *Outline for the Study of Marxism-Leninism.* Chicago: Workers Press, 1977. 190 pp.

Possony, Stephan T., and L. Francis Bouchey. *International Terrorism: The Communist Connection.* Washington, D.C.: American Council on World Freedom, 1978. 172 pp.

Possony, Stephan T., and Kurt Glaser. *Victims of Politics.* New York: Columbia University Press, 1978. 582 pp.

Ruben, David. *Marxism and Materialism.* Atlantic Highlands, N.J.: Humanities Press, 1977. 199 pp.

Rudenko, G. F. et al. *The Revolutionary Movement of Our Time and Nationalism.* Chicago: Imported Publications, 1978. 285 pp.

Schwarz, Hans-Peter. *Zwischenbilanz der KSZE.* Stuttgart: Seewald, 1977. 136 pp.

Seliger, Martin. *The Marxist Conception of Ideology.* New York: Cambridge University Press, 1977. 229 pp.

Seve, Lucien. *Man in Marxist Theory: and the Psychology of Personality.* Atlantic Highlands, N.J.: Humanities Press, 1978. 508 pp.

Sheldon, W. Della, ed. *Dimensions of Détente.* New York: Praeger, 1978. 240 pp.

Simon, Jeffrey. *Comparative Communist Foreign Policy.* Santa Monica, Ca.: Rand Corp., 1977. 158 pp.

Simons, William B. *The Constitutions of the Communist World.* The Hague: Sijthoff, 1978. 246 pp.

Svanidze, K. N., ed. *Konferentsiya kommunisticheskikh i rabochikh partii Evropy.* Moscow: Politizdat, 1977. 296 pp.

Trotsky, Leon. *Writings of Leon Trotsky, 1936—1937.* New York: Pathfinder Press, 1978. 576 pp.

Wesson, Robert G. *Communism and Communist Systems.* Englewood Cliffs, N.J.: Prentice Hall, 1978. 227 pp.

Woerdemann, Franz. *Terrorismus: Motive, Taeter, Strategien.* Munich: Piper, 1977. 392 pp.

Zarodov, K. I. *Sotsializm, mir, revolyutsiya.* Moscow: Politizdat, 1977. 304 pp.

SOVIET UNION

Academy of Sciences of the USSR. *Leonid I. Brezhnev: Pages from His Life.* New York: Simon & Schuster, 1978. 320 pp.

Adams, Jan S. *Citizen Inspectors in the Soviet Union: The People's Control Committee.* New York: Praeger, 1977. 232 pp.

Ammann, R. et al., eds. *The Technological Level of Soviet Industry.* New Haven: Yale University Press, 1977. 575 pp.

Apel, Hans. *Umfrage UdSSR und offener Brief an Andrei Sacharow.* Cologne: Pahl-Rugenstein, 1977. 176 pp.

Aranyossy, Georges, ed. *La presse antisémite en U.R.S.S.* Paris: Editions Albatros, 1978. 217 pp.

Atkinson, Dorothy, Alexander Dallin, and Gail Lapidus, eds. *Women in Russia.* Stanford, Ca.: Stanford University Press, 1977. 410 pp.

Azrael, Jeremy R., ed. *Soviet Nationality Policies and Practices.* New York: Praeger, 1978. 395 pp.

Baglay, M. V., ed. *Kommunisty i profsoyuzy.* Moscow: Profizdat, 1977. 335 pp.

Bailes, Kendall E. *Technology and Society under Lenin and Stalin.* Princeton, N.J.: Princeton University Press, 1978. 472 pp.

Barry, Donald, and Carol Barner-Barry. *Contemporary Soviet Politics.* Englewood Cliffs, N.J.: Prentice Hall, 1978. 406 pp.

Barry, Donald D. et al., eds. *Soviet Law under Stalin.* Leiden: Sijthoff, 1977. 303 pp.

Berlin, Isaiah. *Russian Thinkers.* London: Hogarth Press, 1977. 336 pp.

Berner, Wolfgang, ed. *Sowjetunion, 1976/77.* Munich: Carl Hanser, 1977. 299 pp.

Bethell, Nicholas. *Russia Besieged.* Alexandria, Va.: Time-Life Books, 1977. 208 pp.

Bettelheim, Charles. *Class Struggles in the USSR: Second Period, 1923–1930.* New York: Monthly Press, 1978. 640 pp.

Bogolyubov, K. M. et al., eds. *Spravochnik partiinogo rabotnika, 1977.* Moscow: Politizdat, 1977. 512 pp.

Borisov, O. B., and T. B. Koloskov. *Sino-Soviet Relations, 1945–1973.* Chicago: Imported Publications, 1978. 366 pp.

Borst, Gert et al. *Militaerwesen in der Sowjetunion.* Munich: Bernard & Graefe, 1977. 114 pp.

Breyer, Siegfried. *Guide to the Soviet Navy.* Annapolis, Md.: U.S. Naval Institute, 1977. 610 pp.

Brezhnev, L. I. *Leninskim kursom: Rechi i stati.* Moscow: Politizdat, 1978. 680 pp.

―――― . *O vneshnei politike KPSS i sovetskogo gosudarstva.* Moscow: Politizdat, 1978. 758 pp.

―――― . *Voprosy razvitiya politicheskoi sistemy sovetskogo obshchestva.* Moscow: Politizdat, 1977. 488 pp.

Brook-Shephard, Gordon. *The Storm Petrels: The Flight of the Soviet Defectors.* New York: Harcourt, Brace & Jovanovich, 1977. 241 pp.

Brule, Jean-Pierre. *Demain . . . l'armée soviétique.* Paris: Editions Copernic, 1978. 304 pp.

Brunner, Georg. *Politische Soziologie der UdSSR.* Wiesbaden: Akademische Verlagsgesellschaft, 1977. 2 vols.

Butler, William E., ed. *Russian Law: Historical and Political Perspectives.* Leiden: Sijthoff, 1977. 276 pp.

Carmichael, Joel. *Trotsky: An Appreciation of His Life.* New York: St. Martin's Press, 1978. 512 pp.

Carrière, Pierre. *L'Economie de l'U.R.S.S.* Paris: Masson, 1977. 250 pp.

Carter, Stephen. *The Politics of Solzhenitsyn.* London: Macmillan, 1977. 162 pp.

Chernenko, Konstantin Ustinovich. *Soviet Democracy: Principles and Practice.* New York: Vantage Press, 1977. 77 pp.

Chinn, Jeff. *Manipulating Soviet Population Resources.* New York: Holmes & Meier, 1977. 163 pp.

Collins, John M. *American and Soviet Military Trends since the Cuban Missile Crisis.* Washington, D.C.: Center for Strategic and International Studies, 1978. 500 pp.

Conquest, Robert. *Kolyma: The Arctic Death Camps.* New York: Viking, 1978. 254 pp.

Demou, Dimitros. *Le Sourire de Staline.* Paris: Jean-Pierre Delarge, 1977. 252 pp.

Dolgopolov, E. I. *Natsional'no-osvobodite'nye voiny na sovremennom etape.* Moscow: Voenizdat, 1977. 157 pp.

Dudko, Dmitrii. *Our Hope.* Crestwood, N.Y.: St. Vladimir's Seminary, 1977. 299 pp.

Dunn, Dennis J. *The Catholic Church and the Soviet Government, 1939—1949.* New York: Columbia University Press, 1977. 267 pp.

Dunn, Stephen P., and Ethel Dunn. *Kulturwandel im sowjetischen Dorf.* Berlin: Duncker & Humblot, 1977. 200 pp.

Dunnigan, F., ed. *The Russian Front: Germany's War in the East, 1941—1945.* London: Arms & Armour Press, 1978. 184 pp.

Eeman, Harold. *Inside Stalin's Russia: Memoirs of a Diplomat, 1936—1941.* London: Tritan, 1977. 202 pp.

Elwood, Ralph Carter. *Roman Malinovsky: A Life without a Cause.* Newtonville, Mass.: Oriental Research Partners, 1977. 107 pp.

Esakov, V. D. et al. *Kul'tura razvitogo sotsializma: Nekotorye voprosy teorii i istorii.* Moscow: Nauka, 1978. 457 pp.

Etkind, Efim. *Notes on a Non-Conspirator.* New York: Oxford University Press, 1978. 265 pp.

Feldbrugge, F. J. M., ed. *The Constitution of the USSR.* Leiden: Sijthoff, 1978. 150 pp.

Fic, Victor. *Revolutionary War for Independence and the Russian Question: Czechoslovak Army in Russia, 1914—1918.* New Delhi: Abhinav Publications, 1977. 270 pp.

Fisher, Alan. *The Crimean Tartars.* Stanford, Ca.: Hoover Institution Press, 1978. 264 pp.

Ginsburgs, George, and Alvin Z. Rubinstein, eds. *Soviet Foreign Policy Toward Western Europe.* New York: Praeger, 1978. 280 pp.

Gnedin, Evgenii. *Katastrofa i vtoroe rozhdenie: Memuarnye zapiski.* Amsterdam: Biblioteka Samizdata, 1978. 328 pp.

Godson, Roy. *The Kremlin and Labor: A Study in National Security Policy.* New York: Crane & Russak, 1977. 78 pp.

Golikova, M. I., ed. *Velikaia Okiabr'skaia sotsialisticheskaia revoliutsiia: Entsiklopediia.* Moscow: Sovetskaya entsiklopediia, 1977. 712 pp.

Gorodetsky, Gabriel. *The Precarious Truce: Anglo-Soviet Relations, 1924—1927.* New York: Cambridge University Press, 1977. 289 pp.

Gross-Solomon, Susan. *The Soviet Agrarian Debate: A Controversy in Social Science, 1923—1929.* Boulder, Colo.: Westview, 1978. 325 pp.

Hackenberg, Maria. *Die Entwicklung der Disziplinar und Strafmassnahmen im sowjetischen Arbeitsrecht im Zusammenhang mit der forcierten Industrialisierung, 1925—1935.* Berlin: Weinert-Druck, 1978. 210 pp.

Harasowska, Marta, and Orest Olhovych. *The International Sakharov Hearing.* Baltimore, Md.: Smoloskyp Publ., 1977. 336 pp.

Heiter, Heinrich. *Vom friedlichen Weg zum Sozialismus zur Diktatur Proletariats: Wandlung der sowjetischen Konzeption der Volksdemokratie, 1945—1949.* Frankfurt/M.: Haag & Herchen, 1977. 316 pp.

Hewer, Ulrich. *Zentrale Plannung und technischer Progress: Probleme seiner Organisation und Durchsetzung am Beispiel der sowjetischen Industrie.* Berlin: Duncker & Humblot, 1977. 225 pp.

Hollander, Paul. *Soviet and American Society: A Comparison.* Chicago: University of Chicago Press, 1978. 476 pp.

Hough, Jerry F. *The Soviet Union and Social Science Theory*. Cambridge, Mass.: Harvard University Press, 1978. 275 pp.

Howe, Irving. *Leon Trotsky*. New York: Viking Press, 1978. 214 pp.

Hunczak, Taras, ed. *The Ukraine, 1917—1921: A Study in Revolution*. Cambridge, Mass.: Harvard University Press, 1977. 424 pp.

Hunter, Holland, ed. *The Future of the Soviet Economy, 1978—1985*. Boulder, Colo.: Westview, 1978. 177 pp.

Huyn, Hans Graf. *Der Angriff: Der Vorstoss Moskaus zur Weltherrschaft*. Vienna: Fritz Molden, 1978. 276 pp.

Inozemtsev, N. N. et al., eds. *Leninskaia teoriia imperializma i sovremennost*. Moscow: Mysl, 1977. 454 pp.

Iovchik, M. T., ed. *Proletarskii sotsialisticheskii internatsionalizm*. Moscow: Mysl, 1978. 336 pp.

Ivinskaia, Olga. *A Captive of Time*. Garden City, N.Y.: Doubleday, 1978. 462 pp.

Jones, Lesya, and Bohdan Jasen, eds. *Dissent in Ukraine*. Baltimore, Md.: Smoloskyp, 1977. 215 pp.

Jurrjens, Rudolf Thodoor. *The Free Flow: People, Ideas and Information in Soviet Ideology and Politics*. Amsterdam: Vrije Universiteit te Amsterdam, 1978. 447 pp.

Kamenetsky, Ihor, ed. *Nationalism and Human Rights: Process of Modernization in the USSR*. Littleton, Colo.: Libraries Unlimited, 1977. 246 pp.

Kass, Ilana. *Soviet Involvement in the Middle East: Policy Formulation, 1966—1973*. Boulder, Colo.: Westview, 1978. 275 pp.

Katsenelinboigen, Aron. *Studies in Soviet Economic Planning*. White Plains, N.Y.: Sharpe, 1978. 224 pp.

Kenez, Peter. *The Defeat of the Whites: Civil War in South Russia, 1919—1920*. Berkeley: University of California Press, 1977. 378 pp.

Kerr, Walter B. *The Secret of Stalingrad*. Garden City, N.Y.: Doubleday, 1978. 274 pp.

Kiselev, Aleksandr. *Oblik Generala A. A. Vlasova: Zapiski voennogo sviashchennika*. New York: St. Seraphim Foundation, n.d. 204 pp.

Koeder, Kurt W. *Das Bildungswesen der UdSSR: Von der Oktoberrevolution zum 25. Parteitag der KPdSU*. Munich: Ehrenwirth, 1977. 127 pp.

Koropeckyj, I. S., ed. *The Ukraine within the USSR*. New York: Praeger, 1977. 352 pp.

Kozhevnikov, M. N. *Komandovanie i shtab VVS sovetskoi armii v Velikoi Otechestvennoi voine, 1941—1945*. Moscow: Nauka, 1977. 287 pp.

Kozlov, S. N., ed. *The Officer's Handbook: A Soviet View*. Washington, D.C.: United States Air Force, 1977. 358 pp.

Krasin, Y. A. *Teoria sotsialisticheskoi revolutsii: Leninskoye naslediye i sovremennost*. Moscow: Mysl, 1977. 192 pp.

Kudirka, Simas, and Larry Eichel. *For Those Still at Sea: The Defection of a Lithuanian Sailor*. New York: Dial Press, 1978. 226 pp.

Lane, Christel. *Christian Religion in the Soviet Union: A Sociological Study*. Albany, N.Y.: Allen Unwin, 1978. 256 pp.

Lapidus, Gail Warshofsky. *Women in Soviet Society: Equality, Development and Social Change*. Berkeley: University of California Press, 1978. 391 pp.

Larson, Thomas B. *Soviet-American Rivalry*. New York: Norton, 1978. 308 pp.

Lee, William T. *The Estimation of Soviet Defense Expenditures, 1955—1975: An Unconventional Approach*. New York: Praeger, 1977. 358 pp.

Lévesque, Jacques. *The Soviet Union and the Cuban Revolution, 1959—1977*. New York: Praeger, 1978. 220 pp.

Libbey, James K. *Alexander Gumberg & Soviet-American Relations, 1917—1933*. Lexington: University of Kentucky Press, 1977. 229 pp.

McCagg, William O. *Stalin Embattled, 1943—1948.* Detroit: Wayne State University Press, 1978. 423 pp.

McLellan, David, ed. *Karl Marx: Selected Writings.* New York: Oxford University Press, 1978. 640 pp.

Matthews, Mervyn. *Privilege in the Soviet Union: A Study of Elite Life-Styles under Communism.* London: Allen & Unwin, 1978. 197 pp.

Mawdsley, Evan. *The Russian Revolution and the Baltic Fleet.* New York: Harper & Row, 1978. 363 pp.

Medvedev, Roy A. *Political Essays.* Nottingham, England: Spokesman Books, 1977. 151 pp.

————. *Problems in the Literary Biography of Mikhail Sholokhov.* Cambridge: Cambridge University Press, 1978. 277 pp.

Medvedev, Zhores A. *Soviet Science.* New York: Norton, 1978. 249 pp.

Meerson-Aksenov, Michael, and Boris Shragin, eds. *The Political, Social and Religious Thought of Russian "Samizdat": An Anthology.* Belmont, Mass.: Nordland, 1977. 624 pp.

Meyer, Gerd. *Buerokratischer Sozialismus: Eine Analyse des sowjetischen Herrschaftssystems.* Stuttgart: Frommann-Holzbog, 1977. 331 pp.

Nekrich, Aleksandr M. *The Punished Peoples: The Deportation and Fate of Soviet Minorities at the End of the Second World War.* New York: Norton, 1978. 238 pp.

North Atlantic Treaty Organization. *The USSR in the 1980s: The Soviet Economy in the 1980s and the Role of Foreign Trade.* Brussels: NATO, Directorate of Economic Affairs, 1978. 241 pp.

Nove, Alec. *The Soviet Economic System.* London: Allen & Unwin, 1977. 399 pp.

Pilster, Hans-Christian. *Friede und Gewalt: Der militaerische Aspekt der sowjetischen Koexistenzpolitik.* Stuttgart: Seewald, 1977. 286 pp.

Portier, Jacqueline. *Convergence des systèmes et coexistence pacifique: La Position soviétique.* Paris: Presses des sciences politiques, 1977. 196 pp.

Reichel, Hans-Christian. *Das Praesidium des Obersten Sowjets der UdSSR.* Baden-Baden: Nomos, 1978. 159 pp.

Revész, László. *Menschenrechte in der UdSSR.* Bern: Verlag SOI, 1977. 320 pp.

Riordan, James. *Sport and Soviet Society.* New York: Cambridge University Press, 1977. 435 pp.

Salisbury, Harrison E. *Black Night, White Snow: Russia's Revolutions, 1905—1917.* Garden City, N.Y.: Doubleday, 1978. 746 pp.

Sawicki, Stanislaw J. *Soviet Land and Housing Law: A Historical Comparative Study.* New York: Praeger, 1977. 199 pp.

Schapiro, Leonard. *The Origins of the Communist Autocracy. Political Opposition in the Soviet State: First Phase, 1917—1922.* Cambridge, Mass.: Harvard University Press, 1977. 397 pp.

Scherer, John L., ed. *USSR Facts & Figures Annual, 1978.* Gulf Breeze, Fl.: Academic International Press, 1978. 559 pp.

Schlesinger, Rudolf. *History of the Communist Party of USSR: Past and Present.* Columbia, Mo.: South Asia Books, 1977. 485 pp.

Schneider, Eberhard. *"Einheit" und "Gegensatz" in der Sowjetphilosophie.* Cologne: Wissenschaft & Politik, 1978. 150 pp.

Schulze, Peter W. *Herrschaft und Klassen in der Sowjetgesellschaft.* Frankfurt/M.: Campus Verlag, 1977. 268 pp.

Scott, Harriet F., and William F. Scott. *The Armed Forces of the USSR.* Boulder, Colo.: Westview, 1978. 400 pp.

Sel'chuk, V. V. *Istoriia kommunisticheskoi partii Sovetskogo Soiuza: Rekomendatel'nyi ukazatel' literatury.* Moscow: Kniga, 1977. 271 pp.

Serge, Victor, and Lev Trotskii. *La lutte contre stalinisme.* Paris: F. Maspero, 1977. 270 pp.

Seton-Watson, Hugh. *The Imperialist Revolutionaries.* Stanford, Ca.: Hoover Institution Press, 1978. 157 pp.

Shafarevich, I. R. *Sotsialism kak iavlenie mirovoi istorii.* Paris: YMCA Press, 1977. 390 pp.

Sharlet, Robert. *The New Soviet Constitution of 1977: Analysis and Text.* Brunswick, Ohio: King's Court Communications, 1978. 132 pp.

Simons, William B. *The Soviet Codes of Law.* Leiden: Sijthoff, 1978. 400 pp.

Smith, R. E. E., ed. *The Russian Peasant, 1920 and 1984.* Totowa, N.J.: Frank Cass, 1977. 120 pp.

Solomon, Peter H. *Soviet Criminologists and Criminal Policy.* New York: Columbia University Press, 1977. 253 pp.

Solomon, Susan Gross. *The Soviet Agrarian Debate: A Controversy in Social Science, 1923–1929.* Boulder, Colo.: Westview, 1977. 309 pp.

Solzhenitsyn, Alexander I. *The Gulag Archipelago, Vol. 3, 1918–1956.* New York: Harper & Row, 1978. 752 pp.

Souvarine, Boris. *Staline: Aperçu historique du bolschevisme.* Paris: Champ Libre, 1977. 639 pp.

Spielman, Karl F. *Analyzing Soviet Strategic Arms Decisions.* Boulder, Colo.: Westview, 1978. 190 pp.

Starikov, Sergei, and Roy Medvedev. *Philip Mironov and the Russian Civil War.* New York: Knopf, 1978. 267 pp.

Stern, August, ed. *The USSR vs. Dr. Mikhail Stern.* New York: Urizen Books, 1977. 267 pp.

Swearingen, Rodger. *The Soviet Union and Postwar Japan.* Stanford, Ca.: Hoover Institution Press, 1978. 340 pp.

Teckenberg, Wolfgang. *Die soziale Struktur der sowjetischen Arbeiterklasse im internationalen Vergleich.* Munich: Oldenbourg, 1977. 228 pp.

Thomas, John R., and Ursula M. Kraus-Vaucienne. *Soviet Science and Technology: Domestic and Foreign Perspective.* Washington, D.C.: National Science Foundation, 1977. 455 pp.

Tolstoy, Nikolai. *Victims of Yalta.* London: Hodder & Stoughton, 1978. 496 pp.

Turchin, Valentin. *Inertsia strakha.* New York: Khronika Press, 1977. 296 pp.

Turpin, William Nelson. *Soviet Foreign Trade: Purpose and Performance.* Lexington, Mass.: Lexington Books, 1977. 172 pp.

Twentieth Century Fund. *The Raised Curtain: Report on the Twentieth Century Fund Task Force on Soviet-American Scholarly and Cultural Exchanges.* New York: The Fund, 1977. 101 pp.

Tyazhel'nikov, E. M. *Soyuz molodykh lenintsev.* Moscow: Politizdat, 1977. 350 pp.

U.S.S.R. Ministerstvo Inostrannykh Del SSSR. *Sovetsko-vengerskie otnosheniya, 1917–1976.* Moscow: Politizdat, 1977. 574 pp.

Van Heijenoort, Jean. *With Trotsky in Exile.* Cambridge, Mass.: Harvard University Press, 1978. 164 pp.

Wagenlehner, Guenther. *Staat oder Kommunismus: Lenins Entscheidung gegen die kommunistische Gesellschaft.* Stuttgart: Seewald, 1978. 260 pp.

Walker, Gregory. *Soviet Book Publishing Policy.* Cambridge: Cambridge University Press, 1978. 165 pp.

Warner, Edward L., III. *The Military in Contemporary Soviet Politics: An Institutional Analysis.* New York: Praeger, 1978. 328 pp.

Warth, Robert D. *Leon Trotsky.* Boston: Twayne, 1977. 215 pp.

Wesson, Robert G. *Lenin's Legacy: The Story of the CPSU.* Stanford, Ca.: Hoover Institution Press, 1978. 318 pp.

Yanov, Alexander. *The Russian New Right: Right-Wing Ideologies in the Contemporary USSR.* Berkeley: University of California Press, 1978. 185 pp.

Zorin, V. A. *Osnovy diplomatischeskoi sluzhby.* Moscow: Mezhdunarodnye otnosheniia, 1977. 367 pp.

EASTERN EUROPE

Adriányi, Gábriel et al., eds. *Ungarn-Jahrbuch.* Munich: Trofenik, 1977. 304 pp.

Allworth, Edward, ed. *Nationality Group Survival in Multi-Ethnic States: Shifting Patterns in the Soviet Baltic Region.* New York: Praeger, 1977. 299 pp.

Ancsel, Eva. *The Dilemmas of Freedom.* Budapest: Akadémiai Kaidó, 1978. 103 pp.

Ardissone, Grazia. *Classes sociales et lutte politique en Pologne.* Lyon: Fédérop, 1978. 256 pp.

Association of the Polish Congress. *Dissent in Poland, 1976—1977: Reports and Documents in Translation.* Toronto, Canada: APC, 1977. 200 pp.

Barberini, Giovanni, Martin Stoehr, and Erich Weingaertner, eds. *Kirchen in Sozialismus: Kirche und Staat in den Osteuropaeischen sozialistischen Republiken.* Frankfurt/M.: Otto Lembeck, 1977. 287 pp.

Berend, Iván T., and Gyoergy Ránki. *East Central Europe in the 19th and 20th Centuries.* Budapest: Akadémiai Kaidó, 1977. 164 pp.

Bock, K., and B. Bock. *Die Roten Handelsflotten: Die Handelschiffe der COMECON-Laender.* Herford: Koehlers Verlagsgesellschaft, 1977. 248 pp.

Borowiec, Andrew. *Yugoslavia after Tito.* New York: Praeger, 1977. 122 pp.

Brasch, Thomas. *Vor den Vaetern sterben die Soehne.* Berlin: Rotbuch Verlag, 1977. 109 pp.

Braun, Aurel. *Romanian Foreign Policy since 1965: The Political and Military Limits of Autonomy.* New York: Praeger, 1978. 218 pp.

Bukh, M. E. *Problemy effektivnosti sel'skogo khozyaistva v evropeiskikh stranakh SEV.* Moscow: Nauka, 1978. 168 pp.

Canapa, Marie-Paule. *Les rapports entre les communautés religieuses et l'état en Yougoslavie.* Paris: Presses des sciences politiques, 1977. 204 pp.

Collegium Carolinum. *Tschechoslowakei.* Munich: Carl Hanser, 1977. 340 pp.

Csizmadia, Ernö. *Socialist Agriculture in Hungary.* Budapest: Akadémiai Kaidó, 1977. 179 pp.

Doder, Duško. *The Yugoslavs.* New York: Random House, 1978. 256 pp.

Dunn, William N., and Josip Obradović. *Workers' Self-management and Organizational Power in Yugoslavia.* Pittsburgh: University of Pittsburgh Press, 1978. 448 pp.

Dyakin, B. G., and P. G. Pankov. *SEV: Problemy integratsii.* Moscow: Molodaya gvardiya, 1978. 176 pp.

Eckhardt, Karl-Heinz. *Die DDR im Systemvergleich.* Reinbek/Hamburg: Rowohlt, 1978. 332 pp.

Erard, Z., and M. Zygier, eds. *La Pologne: Une société en dissidence.* Paris: Maspero, 1978. 195 pp.

Fic, Victor M. *The Bolsheviks and the Czechoslovak Legion: The Origins of their Armed Conflict, March—May 1918.* New Delhi: Abhinav Publications, 1978. 495 pp.

Franck, Nicolette. *La Roumanie dans l'engrenage.* Paris: Elsevier Sequoia, 1977. 269 pp.

Fuchs, Juergen. *Gedaechtnisprotokolle.* Reinbek/Hamburg: Rowohlt, 1977. 117 pp.

Gosztony, Peter, ed. *Paramilitaerische Organisationen im Sowjetblock.* Bonn: Hohwacht, 1977. 332 pp.

Grothusen, Klaus-Detlev, ed. *Rumaenien.* Goettingen: Vandenhoeck & Ruprecht, 1977. 711 pp.

Haberl, Othmar Nikola. *Die Abwanderung von Arbeitskraeften aus Jugoslawien.* Munich: Oldenbourg, 1978. 337 pp.

Hájek. Jiří. *Dix ans après Prague 1968—1978.* Paris: Editions du seuil, 1978. 203 pp.

Haraszti, Miklos. *A Worker in a Workers' State.* Harmondsworth: Penguin, 1977. 175 pp.

Hartl, Hans. *Der "einige" und "unabhaengige" Balkan.* Munich: Oldenbourg, 1977. 234 pp.

Henrich, Wolfgang, ed. *Wehrkunde in der DDR.* Bonn: Hohwacht, 1978. 168 pp.

Hoehmann, Hans Hermann, ed. *Arbeitsmarkt und Wirtschaftsplanung: Beitraege zur Beschaeftigungsstruktur und Arbeitskraeftepolitik in Osteuropa.* Cologne: Europaeischer Verlagsanstalt, 1977. 250 pp.

Hunáček, Zdeněk. *Rechtliche Aspekte der Kooperation in der Landwirtschaft der CSSR and der DDR.* Berlin: Duncker & Humblot, 1977. 135 pp.

International Committee for the Support of Charter 77. *White Paper on Czechoslovakia.* Paris: ICSC-77, 1977. 269 pp.

Kabos, Ernö, and A. Zsilak, eds. *Studies on the History of the Hungarian Trade-Union Movement.* Budapest: Akadémiai Kiadó, 1977. 308 pp.

Kalvoda, Joseph. *Czechoslovakia's Role in Soviet Strategy.* Washington, D.C.: University Press of America, 1978. 391 pp.

Kaplan, Frank L. *Winter into Spring: The Czechoslovak Press and the Reform Movement, 1963–1968.* Boulder, Colo.: East European Quarterly, 1977. 208 pp.

Kende, Pierre, and Krzysztof Pomian. *1956 Varsovie-Budapest: La Deuxième révolution d'octobre.* Paris: Editions du seuil, 1978. 262 pp.

King, Robert R., and James F. Brown, eds. *Eastern Europe's Uncertain Future.* New York: Praeger, 1977. 359 pp.

Király, Béla, and Paul Jonas, eds. *The Hungarian Revolution of 1956 in Retrospect.* New York: Columbia University Press, 1978. 157 pp.

Korboński, Stefan. *The Polish Underground State: A Guide to the Underground, 1939–1945.* New York: Columbia University Press, 1978. 272 pp.

Korotkova, E. K. et al. *Sotsialisticheskaya Respublika Rumyniya.* Moscow: Iuridizdat, 1977. 304 pp.

Kostanick, Huey Louis. *Population and Migration Trends in Eastern Europe.* Boulder, Colo.: Westview, 1978. 247 pp.

Kuhlman, James A., ed. *The Foreign Policies of Eastern Europe.* Leiden: Sijthoff, 1978. 302 pp.

Kusin, Vladimir. *From Dubček to Charter 77.* New York: St. Martin's Press, 1978. 216 pp.

Lemberg, Hans, and Peter Nitsche et al., eds. *Osteuropa in Geschichte und Gegenwart.* Cologne: Boehlau, 1977. 461 pp.

Lohmann, Ulrich. *Verfassung und Programm in der DDR.* Berlin: de Gruyter, 1977. 200 pp.

Lopatka, Adam et al. *Probleme der Gesetzlichkeit im Staatsapparat der Volksrepublik Polen.* Berlin: Duncker & Humblot, 1977. 168 pp.

Lukacs, John. *1945: Year Zero.* Garden City, N.Y.: Doubleday, 1978. 322 pp.

Lukács, József, ed. *Ensemble pour une bonne cause: L'Etat socialiste et l'église en Hongroi.* Budapest: Corvina, 1978. 299 pp.

Lukas, Richard C. *The Strange Allies: United States and Poland, 1941–1945.* Knoxville: University of Tennessee Press, 1978. 230 pp.

Maoduš, Stevo, ed. *Tito's Military Accomplishment.* Belgrade: Narodna Armija, 1977. 318 pp.

Martin, André. *La Pologne défend son âme.* Paris: Editions Saint-Paul, 1977. 311 pp.

Molnar, Miklos. *A Short History of the Hungarian Communist Party.* Boulder, Colo.: Westview, 1978. 136 pp.

Morawski, Dominik. *Polonia—pane e libertà: Raccolta di scritti e documenti, 1976–1977.* Rome: Nuove Edizione Operaie, 1977. 190 pp.

Moreton, N. Edwina. *East Germany and the Warsaw Alliance.* Boulder, Colo.: Westview, 1978. 275 pp.

Neugebauer, Gero. *Partei und Staatsapparat in der DDR.* Opladen: Westdeutscher Verlag, 1978. 180 pp.

North Atlantic Treaty Organization. *COMECON: Progress and Prospects.* Brussels: NATO, Directorate of Economic Affairs, 1977. 282 pp.

Pelikán, Jiří, and Manfred Wilke. *Menschenrechte: Ein Jahrbuch zu Osteuropa.* Hamburg: Rowohlt, 1977. 477 pp.

Petrović-Šane, Dušan. *Self-Management In Yugoslavia.* London: Summerfield Press, 1977. 163 pp.

Prifti, Peter R. *Socialist Albania since 1944: Domestic and Foreign Developments.* Cambridge, Mass.: MIT Press, 1978. 311 pp.

Raina, Peter. *Political Opposition in Poland, 1954–1977.* London: Arlington Books, 1978. 584 pp.

Rakowski, Marc. *Toward an East European Marxism.* New York: St. Martin's Press, 1978. 1,144 pp.

Robinson, Gertrude J. *Tito's Maverick Media.* Urbana: University of Illinois Press, 1977. 263 pp.

Rodionov, N. N. et al., eds. *Sovetsko-chekhoslovatskie otnosheniya, 1972–1976: Dokumenty i materialy.* Moscow: Politizdat, 1977. 465 pp.

Scheidegger, Ursula. *Industrialisierung und sozialer Wandel in Polen.* Bern: P. Haupt, 1977. 148 pp.

Scheidegger, Ursula. *Industrialisierung und sozialer Wandel in Plen.* Bern: P. Haupt, 1977. 148 pp.

Schreiber, Thomas. *La Yougoslavie de Tito.* Paris: Presses de la cité, 1977. 111 pp.

Semerdzhiev, Atanas. *Geschichte der bulgarischen Volksarmee.* East Berlin: Militaerverlag der DDR, 1977. 331 pp.

Shchetinin, V. P., ed. *Ekonomicheskaya integratsiya stran chlenov SEV.* Moscow: Prosveshchenie, 1977. 168 pp.

Shiryaev, Yu. S. *Mezhdunarodnoe sotsialisticheskoe razdelenie truda.* Moscow: Nauka, 1977. 176 pp.

Sikora, Franz. *Sozialistische Solidaritaet und nationale Interessen Polen, Tschechoslowakei, DDR.* Cologne: Wissenschaft & Politik, 1977. 249 pp.

Simmonds, George W., ed. *Nationalism in the USSR & Eastern Europe in the Era of Brezhnev and Kosygin.* Detroit: University of Detroit Press, 1977. 534 pp.

Singer, Ladislaus. *Der ungarische Weg.* Stuttgart: Seewald, 1978. 192 pp.

Sinor, Denis, ed. *Modern Hungary: Readings from "The New Hungarian Quarterly."* Bloomington: Indiana University Press, 1978. 424 pp.

Slama, Jiri. *Die sozio-oekonomische Umgestaltung der Nachkriegs-Tschechoslowakei.* Wiesbaden: Harrassowitz, 1977. 143 pp.

Sólyom-Fekete, William. *Legal Restrictions on Foreign Travel and Emigration in the Hungarian People's Republic.* Washington, D.C.: Library of Congress, 1977. 120 pp.

Staar, Richard F., ed. *Yearbook on International Communist Affairs, 1978.* Stanford, Ca.: Hoover Institution Press, 1978. 276 pp.

Steele, Jonathan. *Red Prussia: Socialism with a German Face.* London: Cape, 1977. 256 pp.

Stepanek-Stemmer, Michael. *Der wahre Dubček: Woran der Prager Fruehling scheiterte.* Cologne: Ellenberg, 1978. 182 pp.

Stetskevich, S. M. *Sotsialisticheskie strany Evropy.* Moscow: Prosveshchenie, 1977. 224 pp.

Turnock, David. *Eastern Europe.* Boulder, Colo.: Westview, 1978. 288 pp.

Vanek, Jan. *The Economics of Worker's Management: A Yugoslav Case Study.* Winchester, Mass.: Allen & Unwin, 1978. 320 pp.

Völgyes, Ivan. *Social Deviance in Eastern Europe.* Boulder, Colo.: Westview, 1978. 210 pp.

Volovski, Aleksandr. *La vie quotidienne à Varsovie sous l'occupation nazie, 1939–1945.* Paris: Hachette, 1977. 381 pp.

Waedekin, Karl-Eugen. *Sozialistische Agrarpolitik in Osteuropa: Entwicklung und Probleme, 1960–1976.* Berlin: Duncker & Humblot, 1978. 335 pp.

Wallace, William V. *Czechoslovakia.* Boulder, Colo.: Westview, 1977. 374 pp.

Werner, Steffen. *Kybernetik statt Marx?* Stuttgart: Bonn Aktuell, 1977. 250 pp.

Wettig, Gerhard. *Broadcasting and Détente: Eastern Policies and Their Implication for East-West Relations.* New York: St. Martin's Press, 1977. 110 pp.

Weydenthal, Jan B. de. *The Communists of Poland.* Stanford, Ca.: Hoover Institution Press, 1978. 217 pp.

Zawodny, J. K. *Nothing but Honour: The Story of the Warsaw Uprising, 1944.* Stanford, Ca.: Hoover Institution Press, 1978. 328 pp.

WESTERN EUROPE

Albiac Lopiz, Gabriel. *Debate sobre Eurocomunismo.* Madrid: Taller do Sociologia, 1978. 200 pp.

Albonetti, Achille. *Gli stati uniti, l'Italia e l'Eurocomunismo.* Rome: Stato e Libertà, 1977. 272 pp.

Althusser, Louis, *Ce qui ne peut plus durer dans le parti communiste.* Paris: Maspero, 1978. 128 pp.

Alvarez, Santiago. *El Partido comunista y el campo.* Madrid: Ediciones de la Torre, 1977. 258 pp.

Anilov, V. F., comp. *VIII s'ezd Portugal'skoi kommunisticheskoi partii (11–14. XI. 1976).* Moscow: Politizdat, 1977. 239 pp.

Arrabal, Fernando. *Carta a los militantes comunistas españoles*. Barcelona: Ediciones Actuales, 1978. 125 pp.

Averoff-Tossizza, Evangelos. *By Fire and Axe: The Communist Party and the Civil War in Greece*. New Rochelle, N.Y.: Caratzas Bros., 1978. 438 pp.

Barnes, Samuel H. *Representation in Italy, Institutionalized Tradition and Electoral Choice*. Chicago: University of Chicago Press, 1977. 187 pp.

Bauss, Gerhard. *Die Studentenbewegung der sechziger Jahre in der Bundesrepublik und Westberlin: Handbuch*. Cologne: Pahl-Rugenstein, 1977. 353 pp.

Benedikter, Hans. *Eurokommunismus: Der grosse Bluff*. Bozen: Athesia, 1978. 363 pp.

Biard, Roland. *Dictionnaire de l'extrême-gauche de 1945 à nos jours*. Paris: Belfond, 1978. 411 pp.

Bloomfield, Jon, ed. *Papers on Class, Hegemony and Party*. London: Lawrence & Wishart, 1977. 125 pp.

Boeck, Walter. *Deutschland: Zwei Staaten, Zwei Systeme*. Freiburg: Ploetz, 1977. 112 pp.

Bourgois, Christian, ed. *El Partido comunista español, italiano y frances cara al poder*. Madrid: Editorial Cambio 16, 1977. 258 pp.

Brueckner, Peter. *Ulrike Marie Meinhoff und die deutschen Verhaeltnisse*. Berlin: Klaus Wagenbach, 1977. 192 pp.

Carrillo, Santiago. *Escritos sobre Eurocomunismo*. Madrid: Forma, 1977. 2 vols.

———. *Eurocommunism and the State*. New York: Lawrence Hill, 1978. 172 pp.

Castellacci, Claudio. *Manipulite: I comunisti e le amministrazioni degli enti locali*. Milan: Sugar Co., 1977. 175 pp.

Cecchi, Alberto. *Storia del P.C.I attraverso i congressi: Dal dopoguerra a oggi*. Rome: Newton Compton, 1977. 573 pp.

Cerny, Karl H., ed. *Germany at the Polls: Bundestag Election of 1976*. Washington, D.C.: American Enterprise Institute, 1978. 251 pp.

Cesarini Sforza, Marco, and Enrico Nassi. *L'Eurocomunismo*. Milan: Rizzoli, 1977. 190 pp.

Chevenement, Jean-Pierre. *Les Socialistes, les communistes et les autres*. Paris: Aubier, 1977. 354 pp.

Chiaromonte, Gerardo. *L'Accordo programmatico e l'azione dei comunisti*. Rome: Riuniti, 1977. 116 pp.

Claudin, Fernando. *Documentos de una divergencia comunista*. Barcelona: Iniciativas Editoriales, 1978. 315 pp.

———. *Eurocommunism and Socialism*. New York: Schocken, 1978. 168 pp.

Clutterbuck, Richard. *Britain in Agony: The Growth of Political Violence*. London: Faber & Faber, 1978. 335 pp.

Cunhal, Alvaro. *Entre duas eleições*. Lisbon: Avante, 1978. 216 pp.

———. *Uma politica ao serviço do povo*. Lisbon: Avante, 1977. 369 pp.

Debray, Régis. *Lettres aux communistes français et à quelques autres*. Paris: Seuil, 1978. 182 pp.

Denmark, Communist Party of. *XXV s'ezd Kommunicheskoi partii Danii: Kopenhagen, 23—26 sentyabrya 1976 goda*. Moscow: Politizdat, 1978. 155 pp.

Diaz, José Antonio. *Luchas internas en Comisiones Obreras*. Barcelona: Bruguera, 1977. 346 pp.

Elleinstein, Jean. *Lettre ouverte aux Français sur la République du Programme Commun*. Paris: Albin Michel, 1977. 215 pp.

Fauvet, Jacques. *Histoire du Parti communiste français: De 1920 à 1976*. Paris: Fayard, 1977. 621 pp.

Galkin, A. A., ed. *Kommunisty zapadnoi Yevropy v borbe za edinyi front proletariata, 1920—1923*. Moscow: Nauka, 1977. 344 pp.

Graziani, Pier Antonio. *Il PCI ieri e oggi*. Rome: Edizioni Cinque Lune, 1977. 535 pp.

Griffith, William E. *The Ostpolitik of the Federal Republic of Germany*. Cambridge, Mass.: MIT Press, 1978. 291 pp.

Haller, Michael. *Die eurokommunistische Offensive*. Neuwied: Luchterhand, 1978. 310 pp.

Hamel, Hannelore, ed. *BDR-DDR: Die Wirtschaftssysteme*. Munich: C. H. Beck, 1977. 365 pp.

Harvey, Robert. *Portugal: Birth of a Democracy.* New York: St. Martiň's Press, 1978. 200 pp.

Havemann, Robert. *Ein deutscher Kommunist.* Reinbek/Hamburg: Rowohlt, 1978. 159 pp.

Honecker, Erich et al. *Geschichte der Sozialistischen Einheitspartei Deutschlands.* East Berlin: Dietz, 1978. 676 pp.

Jones, Bill. *The Russia Complex: The British Labour Party and the Soviet Union.* Manchester: Manchester University Press, 1978. 299 pp.

Jones, Gareth S. et al. *Western Marxism: A Critical Reader.* Atlantic Highlands, N.J.: Humanities Press, 1977. 354 pp.

Josuttis, Manfred et al. *Pfarrer in der DKP: Theologische und kirchentliche Gutachten.* Munich: Kaiser, 1977. 178 pp.

Kolb, Eberhard. *Die Arbeiteraete in der deutschen Innenpolitik, 1918—1919.* Frankfurt/M.: Ullstein, 1978. 443 pp.

Kriegel, Annie. *Eurocommunism: A New Kind of Communism?* Stanford, Ca.: Hoover Institution Press, 1978. 131 pp.

Labbé, Dominique. *Le Discours communiste.* Paris: Presses de la Fondation nationale des sciences politiques, 1977. 204 pp.

Lammich, Siegfried. *Grundzuege des sozialistischen Parlamentarismus.* Baden-Baden: Nomos, 1977. 239 pp.

Leonhard, Wolfgang. *Euro-kommunismus: Herausforderung fuer Ost und West.* Munich: Bertelsmann, 1978. 413 pp.

Leubbe, Peter. *Kommunismus und Sozialdemokratie.* East Berlin, Dietz, 1978. 299 pp.

Levine-Meyer, Rosa. *Inside German Communism.* London: Pluto, 1977. 222 pp.

Luciani, Giacomo. *Il PCI e il capitalismo occidentale.* Milan: Longanesi, 1977. 184 pp.

Luelmo, Julio, and Henry Winston. *Eurocomunismo y estado.* Madrid: Akal Editor, 1978. 100 pp.

Mandel, Ernest. *Critique de l'eurocommunisme.* Paris: Maspero, 1978. 319 pp.

Marcou, Lilly. *Le Kominform: Le Communism de guerre froide.* Paris: Presses de la Fondation nationale des sciences politiques, 1977. 343 pp.

Mehnert, Klaus. *Twilight of the Young: The Radical Movements of the 1960's and Their Legacy.* New York: Holt, 1977. 428 pp.

Molina, Gérard, and Yves Vargas. *Dialogue à l'intérieur du Parti communiste français.* Paris: Maspero, 1978. 153 pp.

Monicelli, Mino. *L'Ultrasinistra in Italia, 1968—1978.* Bari: Laterza, 1978. 242 pp.

Olson, Gary L. *The Other Europe: Radical Critiques of Britain, France, West Germany and the Soviet Union.* Brunswick, Ohio: King's Court Communication, 1977. 339 pp.

Pajetta, Giancarlo. *La lunga marcia dell'internazionalismo.* Rome: Riuniti, 1978. 182 pp.

Penniman, Howard R., ed. *Ireland at the Polls: The Dail Elections of 1977.* Washington, D.C.: American Enterprise Institute, 1978. 199 pp.

——— . *Italy at the Polls.* Washington, D.C.: American Enterprise Institute, 1977. 386 pp.

Ramm, Hartmut. *The Marxism of Regis Debray: Between Lenin and Guevara.* Lawrence: Regents Press of Kansas, 1978. 240 pp.

Ranney, Austin, and Giovanni Sartori, eds. *Eurocommunism: The Italian Case.* Washington, D.C.: American Enterprise Institute, 1978. 196 pp.

Ravines, Eudocio. *Derrota mundial del comunismo.* Mexico City: G. de Anda, 1977. 337 pp.

Rizzo, Franco. *Il PCI tra societa e istituzioni.* Rome: Bulzoni, 1978. 192 pp.

Roskin, Michael. *Other Governments in Europe: Sweden, Spain, Italy, Yugoslavia and East Germany.* Englewood Cliffs, N.J.: Prentice Hall, 1977. 182 pp.

Ruiz, Fernando, and Joaquin Romero, eds. *Los Partidos marxistas.* Barcelona: Editorial Anagrama, 1977. 336 pp.

Salvadori, Massimo L. *Eurocomunismo e socialismo sovietico.* Turin: Einaudi, 1978. 161 pp.

Secchia, Pietro. *Chi sono i comunisti.* Milan: Mazzotta, 1977. 335 pp.

Semprun, Jorge. *Autobiografia de Federico Sanchez.* Barcelona: Planeta, 1977. 342 pp.

Steinkuehler, Manfred, ed. *Eurokommunismus im Widerspruch: Analyse und Dokumentation.* Cologne: Wissenschaft & Politik, 1977. 394 pp.

Tannahill, R. Neil. *The Communist Parties of Western Europe: A Comparative Study.* Westport, Conn.: Greenwood Press, 1978. 256 pp.

Thomas, Hugh. *The Spanish Civil War.* New York: Harper & Row, 1977. 1,115 pp.

Timmermann, Heinz, ed. *Eurokommunismus.* Frankfurt/M.: Fischer, 1978. 204 pp.

Toekes, Rudolf L., ed. *Eurocommunism and Détente.* New York: New York University Press, 1978. 544 pp.

Urban, G. R., ed., *Euro-Communism: Its Roots and Its Future in Italy and Elsewhere.* London: Maurice Temple Smith, 1978. 287 pp.

Vogt, Hermann. *Eurokommunismus: Ein Reader.* Berlin: Berlin Verlag, 1978. 224 pp.

Warwick, Paul. *The French Popular Front.* Chicago: University of Chicago Press, 1977. 212 pp.

Winkler, Karlheinz. *Auf der Suche nach der revolutionaeren Klasse: Das Dilemma der Marxisten in der Bundesrepublik.* Cologne: Edition Agrippa, 1977. 107 pp.

Wohlgemuth, Heinz. *Die Entstehung der Kommunistischen Partei Deutschlands.* East Berlin: Dietz, 1978. 308 pp.

Yglesias, José. *The Franco Years.* Indianapolis: Bobbs Merrill, 1977. 274 pp.

Zagladin, Vadim, ed. *Europe and the Communists.* Moscow: Progress, 1977. 286 pp.

Zak, L. M. *Oni predstavlyli narod Frantsii.* Moscow: Mysl, 1977. 280 pp.

ASIA AND THE PACIFIC

Andors, Stephen, ed. *Workers and Workplaces in Revolutionary China.* White Plains, N.Y.: Sharpe, 1977. 403 pp.

Armstrong, J. D. *Revolutionary Diplomacy: Chinese Foreign Policy and the United Front Doctrine.* Berkeley: University of California Press, 1977. 251 pp.

Banarjee, Jyotirmoy. *India in Soviet Global Strategy: A Conceptual Study.* Columbia, Mo.: South Asia Books, 1977. 201 pp.

Barnett, Doak. *China and the Major Powers in East Asia.* Washington, D.C.: Brookings Institution, 1977. 416 pp.

Bown, Colin. *China, 1949–1976.* London: Heinemann, 1977. 192 pp.

Broyelle, Claudie. *Women's Liberation in China.* New York: Humanities Press, 1977. 174 pp.

Brugger, Bill, ed. *China: The Impact of the Cultural Revolution.* New York: Barnes & Noble, 1978. 300 pp.

Burchett, Wilfred G. *Grasshoppers and Elephants: Why Vietnam Fell.* New York: Urizen Books, 1977. 265 pp.

Buss, Claude A. *The United States and the Philippines.* Washington, D.C.: American Enterprise Institute, 1977. 152 pp.

Chen, Jack. *The Sinkiang Story.* New York: Macmillan, 1977. 386 pp.

Chen, Jo-hsi. *The Execution of Mayor Yin and Other Stories from the Great Proletarian Cultural Revolution.* Bloomington: Indiana University Press, 1978. 220 pp.

Chung, Chin O. *P'yongyang Between Peking and Moscow.* University: University of Alabama Press, Press, 1977. 230 pp.

Colbert, Evelyn. *Southeast Asia in International Politics.* Ithaca, N.Y.: Cornell University Press, 1977, 372 pp.

Crouch, Harold. *The Army and Politics in Indonesia*. Ithaca, N.Y.: Cornell University Press, 1978. 377 pp.

Dawson, Alan. *55 Days: The Fall of South Vietnam*. Englewood Cliffs, N.J.: Prentice Hall, 1977. 366 pp.

Eckstein, Alexander. *China's Economic Revolution*. New York: Cambridge University Press, 1977. 340 pp.

Gamberg, Ruth. *Red and Expert: Education in the People's Republic of China*. New York: Schocken, 1977. 299 pp.

Gerbova, A. A., and A. V. Shurubovich, *Razvitie promyshlennosti MNR na sovremennom etape*. Moscow: Nauka, 1978. 115 pp.

Giap, Vo Nguyen. *Vooruzhen'e revolyutsionnykh mass i stroitel'stvo narodnoi armii*. Moscow: Voenizdat, 1977. 176 pp.

Hiro, Dilip. *Inside India Today*. New York: Monthly Review, 1977. 338 pp.

Howe, Christopher. *China's Economy: A Basic Guide*. New York: Basic Books, 1978. 248 pp.

Hsia, Chih-yen. *The Coldest Winter in Peking*. New York: Doubleday, 1978. 386 pp.

Hsin, Chi. *The Case of the Gang of Four*. Hong Kong: Cosmos Books, 1977. 295 pp.

Il'inskiy, M. M. *V'etnam*. Moscow: Nauka, 1978. 369 pp.

Jui, Li. *The Early Revolutionary Activities of Comrade Mao Tse-Tung*. White Plains, N.Y.: Sharpe, 1977. 355 pp.

Kerry, Tom. *The Mao Myth and the Legacy of Stalinism in China*. New York: Pathfinder, 1977. 190 pp.

Kim, G. F., and F. I., Shabshina. *Soyuz rabochego klassa s krest'yanstvom i opyt sotsialisticheskikh stran Azii*. Moscow: Nauka, 1977. 308 pp.

Kindermann, Gottfried-Karl. *Pekings chinesische Gegenspieler*. Düsseldorf: Droste, 1977. 290 pp.

Kooloskov, B. *Vneshniaia politika Kitaia, 1969–1976*. Moscow: Politizdat, 1977. 327 pp.

Le Duan. *Selected Writings*. Hanoi: Foreign Language Press, 1977. 540 pp.

Lee, Chong-Sik. *Korean Workers' Party*. Stanford, Ca.: Hoover Institution Press, 1978. 167 pp.

Lee, Hong Yung. *The Politics of the Chinese Cultural Revolution*. Berkeley: University of California Press, 1978. 369 pp.

Leys, Simon. *The Chairman's New Clothes: Mao and the Cultural Revolution*. New York: St. Martin's Press, 1978. 261 pp.

Low, Alfred D. *The Sino-Soviet Dispute*. Madison, N.J.: Fairleigh Dickinson University Press, 1978. 364 pp.

Mao Tse-Tung. *A Critique of Soviet Economics*. New York: Monthly Review, 1977. 157 pp.

Michael, Franz. *Mao and the Perpetual Revolution*. Woodbury, N.Y.: Barron's, 1977. 326 pp.

Militaergeschichtliches Forschungsamt. *Miliz, Wehrverfassung und Volkskriegsgedanken in der Volksrepublik China*. Boppard/Rh.: Harald Boldt, 1977. 195 pp.

Milne, R. S., and Diane K. Mauzy. *Politics and Government in Malaysia*. Vancouver: University of British Columbia Press, 1978. 406 pp.

Moody, Peter R. *Opposition and Dissent in Contemporary China*. Stanford, Ca.: Hoover Institution Press, 1977. 342 pp.

Munro, Donald J. *The Concept of Man in Contemporary China*. Ann Arbor: University of Michigan Press, 1978. 248 pp.

Opitz, Peter J. *Chinas Aussenpolitik*. Zurich: Interform AG, 1977. 107 pp.

Pauker, Guy J. et al. *Diversity and Development in Southeast Asia: The Coming Decade*. New York: McGraw-Hill, 1977. 191 pp.

Pepper, Suzanne. *Civil War in China*. Berkeley: University of California Press, 1978. 493 pp.

Perkins, Dwight. *Rural Small-scale Industry in the People's Republic of China*. Berkeley: University of California Press, 1977. 296 pp.

Pike, Douglas. *History of Vietnamese Communism, 1925–1976.* Stanford, Ca.: Hoover Institution Press, 1978. 181 pp.

Ponchaud, Francois. *Cambodia: Year Zero.* New York: Holt, Rinehart & Winston, 1978. 212 pp.

Porkert, Manfred. *China, Konstanten im Wandel.* Stuttgart: Hirzel, 1978. 197 pp.

Prybyla, Jan S. *The Chinese Economy: Problems and Policies.* Columbia: University of South Carolina Press, 1978. 258 pp.

Raddock, David M. *Political Behavior of Adolescents in China: The Cultural Revolution in Kwang-chow.* Tucson: University of Arizona Press, 1977. 242 pp.

Radványi, János. *Delusion and Reality: Gambits, Hoaxes, and Diplomatic One-upmanship in Vietnam.* South Bend, Ind.: Gateway, 1978. 295 pp.

Roger, Howard. *Mao Tse-Tung and the Chinese People.* New York: Monthly Review, 1977. 394 pp.

Romualdez, Daniel, and Philip Romualdez. *China: A Personal Encounter with the People's Republic.* Englewood Cliffs, N.J.: Prentice Hall, 1977. 164 pp.

Roots, John M. *Chou.* Garden City, N.Y.: Doubleday, 1978. 220 pp.

Sembdner, Friedrich. *Das kommunistische Regierungssystem in Vietnam.* Cologne: Wissenschaft & Politik, 1978. 292 pp.

Sergeeva, E. A. *Vneshnyaya politika i vneshnepolitischeskaya propaganda rukovodstva KPK.* Moscow: Nauka, 1978. 191 pp.

Sladkovskiy, M. I., ed. *Ideino-politicheskaya sushchnost' Maoizma.* Moscow: Nauka, 1977. 444 pp.

Sobolev, A. I. et al., eds. *Rol' i znachenie pomoshchi mezhdunarodnogo kommunisticheskogo dvizheniya v stanovlenii i razvitii MNRP.* Moscow: Politizdat, 1978. 264 pp.

Solomon, Richard H. *A Revolution is Not a Dinner Party: A Feast of Images of the Maoist Transformation of China.* New York: Anchor, 1978. 199 pp.

Strupp, Michael. *Chinas Grenzen mit Birma und mit der Sowjetunion.* Hamburg: Institut fuer Asienkunde, 1978. 472 pp.

Sutter, Robert G. *Chinese Foreign Policy after the Cultural Revolution, 1966–1977.* Boulder, Colo.: Westview, 1978. 176 pp.

Terrill, Ross. *The Future of China after Mao.* New York: Delacorte, 1978. 331 pp.

Trigubenko, M. E., ed. *Promyshlennost' Koreiskoi Narodno-demokraticheskoi Respubliki.* Moscow: Nauka, 1977. 181 pp.

Van Tien Dung. *Our Great Spring Victory: An Account of the Liberation of South Vietnam.* New York: Monthly Review, 1977. 275 pp.

Vasil'ev, V. F. *Rabochii klass Birmy.* Moscow: Nauka, 1978. 312 pp.

Ward, Robert E. *Japan's Political System,* 2nd ed. Englewood Cliffs, N.J.: Prentice Hall, 1978. 253 pp.

Weiner, Myron. *India at the Polls: The Parliamentary Elections of 1977.* Washington, D.C.: American Enterprise Institute, 1978. 150 pp.

White, Lynn T., III. *Careers in Shanghai.* Berkeley: University of California Press, 1978. 272 pp.

Whiting, Allen S., and Robert F. Dernberger. *China's Future: Foreign Policy and Economic Development in the Post-Mao Era.* New York: McGraw-Hill, 1977. 186 pp.

Yahuda, Michael B. *China's Role in World Affairs.* New York: St. Martin's Press, 1978. 336 pp.

Zasloff, Joseph J., and MacAlister Brown. *Communist Indochina and U.S. Foreign Policy.* Boulder, Colo.: Westview, 1978. 180 pp.

Ziring, Lawrence, Ralph Braibanti, and W. Howard Wriggins. *Pakistan: the Long View.* Durham: Duke University Press, 1977. 485 pp.

THE AMERICAS

Cantor, Milton. *The Divided Left: American Radicalism, 1900—1975*. New York: Hill & Wang, 1978. 248 pp.

Caute, David. *The Great Fear: The Anti-communist Purge under Truman and Eisenhower*. New York: Simon & Schuster, 1978. 671 pp.

Colombia, Communist Party of. *XII s'ezd Kommunisticheskoi partii Kolumbii (Bogota, 5—9 dekabrya 1975 g.)* Moscow: Politizdat, 1977. 128 pp.

Comin, Alfonso C. *Cristianos en el partido comunista en la iglesia*. Barcelona: Editorial Laia, 1977. 211 pp.

Dolgoff, Sam. *The Cuban Revolution*. Montreal: Black Rose Books, 1977. 199 pp.

Dominguez, Jorge I. *Cuba: Order and Revolution*. Cambridge, Mass.: Harvard University Press, 1978. 672 pp.

Drake, Paul W. *Socialism and Populism in Chile, 1932—1952*. Urbana: University of Illinois Press, 1978. 418 pp.

Edwards, Jorge. *Persona Non Grata: An Envoy in Castro's Cuba*. New York: Pomerica, 1977. 274 pp.

Fish, Hamilton. *An American Manifesto of Freedom in Answer to the Manifesto on Communism (1848)*. New York: Vantage Press, 1977. 209 pp.

Gornick, Vivian. *The Romance of American Communism*. New York: Basic Books, 1978. 265 pp.

Hansen, Joseph. *Dynamics of the Cuban Revolution: The Trotskyist View*. New York: Pathfinder Press, 1978. 393 pp.

Haywood, Harry. *Black Bolshevik*. Chicago: Liberator Press, 1978. 700 pp.

Hodges, Donald C., ed. *The Legacy of Che Guevara: A Documentary Study*. New York: Thames & Hudson, 1977. 216 pp.

Kaufman, Edy. *Uruguay in Transition: From Civilian to Military Rule*. New Brunswick, N.J.: Trans-Action Press, 1978. 200 pp.

Kostiainen, Auvo. *The Forging of Finnish-American Communism, 1917—1924*. Turku: Turun Ylio-pisto, 1978. 225 pp.

Kroes, Emmi. *Rabochee dvizhenie Venesuely*. Moscow: Progress, 1977. 184 pp.

Lewis, Oscar et al. *Neighbors: Living the Revolution, An Oral History of Contemporary Cuba*. Urbana: University of Illinois Press, 1978. 581 pp.

Llerena, Mario. *The Unsuspected Revolution: The Birth and Rise of Castroism*. Ithaca, N.Y.: Cornell University Press, 1978. 324 pp.

Martin, Lionel. *The Early Fidel: Roots of Castro's Communism*. Secaucus, N.J.: Lyle Stuart, 1978. 272 pp.

Mesa-Lago, Carmelo. *Cuba in the 1970's: Pragmatism and Institutionalization*. Albuquerque: University of New Mexico Press, 1978. 187 pp.

Roxborough, Ian et al. *Chile: the State and Revolution*. New York: Holmes & Meier, 1977. 304 pp.

Sigmund, Paul E. *The Overthrow of Allende and the Politics of Chile, 1964—1976*. Pittsburgh: University of Pittsburgh Press, 1977. 326 pp.

Sobel, Lester A., ed. *Castro's Cuba in the 1970s*. New York: Facts on File, 1978. 244 pp.

Sokolov, A. A. *Rabochee dvizhenie Meksiki, 1917—1929*. Moscow: Izdatelstvo Moskovskogo Universiteta, 1978. 264 pp.

Vieira, Gilberto et al. *Politica y revolucion en Colombia*. Bogota: Biblioteca Marxista Colombiana, 1977. 127 pp.

Ward, Fred. *Inside Cuba Today*. New York: Crown, 1978. 308 pp.

Weinstein, Alan. *Perjury: The Hiss-Chambers Case*. New York: Knopf, 1978. 674 pp.

Weinstein, Martin, ed. *Revolutionary Cuba in the World Arena*. Philadelphia: Institute for the Study of Human Issues, 1978. 192 pp.

AFRICA AND THE MIDDLE EAST

Ake, Claude. *Revolutionary Pressures in Africa.* London: Zed Press, 1978. 109 pp.

Association of Eritrean Students in North America. *In Defense of the Eritrean Revolution.* New York: n.p., 1978. 239 pp.

Austin, Dennis. *Politics in Africa.* Hanover: University Press for New England, 1978. 208 pp.

Gabbay, Rony. *Communism and Agrarian Reform in Iraq.* London: Croom Helm, 1978. 240 pp.

Gjerstad, Ole, and Chantal Sarrazin, eds. *Sowing the First Harvest: National Reconstruction in Guinea-Bissau.* Oakland, Ca.: LSM Information Center, 1978. 103 pp.

Golan, Galia. *Yom Kippur and After: The Soviet Union and the Middle East Crisis.* Cambridge: Cambridge University Press, 1977. 350 pp.

Greig, Ian. *The Communist Challenge to Africa: An Analysis of Contemporary Soviet, Chinese and Cuban Policies.* Richmond, Surrey: Foreign Affairs Publ., 1977. 306 pp.

Henriksen, Thomas H. *Mozambique.* London: Rex Collings, 1978. 276 pp.

Ivanov, M. S. *Iran v 60—70-kh godakh XX veka.* Moscow: Nauka, 1977. 272 pp.

Khadduri, Majid. *Socialist Iraq.* Washington, D.C.: Middle East Institute, 1978. 265 pp.

Marcum, John A. *The Angolan Revolution: Exile Politics and Guerrilla Warfare, 1962—1976.* Cambridge, Mass.: MIT Press, 1978. 2 vols.

Melotti, Umberto. *Marx and the Third World.* Atlantic Highlands, N.J.: Humanities Press, 1977. 222 pp.

Miske, Ahmed-Baba. *Front polisario: L'Ame d'un peuple.* Paris: Editions Rupture, 1978. 384 pp.

Moore, Robin. *Rhodesia.* New York: Condor, 1977. 313 pp.

Nohlen, Dieter, and Franz Nuscheler, eds. *Handbuch der dritten Welt.* Stuttgart: Hoffman & Campe, 1978. 4 vols.

O'Neill, Bard E. *Armed Struggle in Palestine: An Analysis of the Palestinian Guerrilla Movement.* Boulder, Colo.: Westview, 1978. 320 pp.

Ottaway, Marina, and David Ottaway, eds. *Ethiopia: Empire in Revolution.* New York: Africana Publ., 1978. 250 pp.

Penkin, F. P. *Irakskaya Respublika i ee vooruzhennye sily.* Moscow: Voenizdat, 1977. 111 pp.

Penrose, Edith, and E. F. Penrose. *Iraq: International Relations and National Development.* Boulder, Colo.: Westview, 1978. 569 pp.

Pir-Budagova, E. P. *Siriya.* Moscow: Nauka, 1978. 237 pp.

Rodinson, Maxime. *Marxism and the Muslim World.* Leiden: E. J. Brill, 1978. 368 pp.

Vinicios, Marco, and Maria João Saldanha. *Jonas Savimbi: Um desafio a ditadura comunista em Angola.* Lisbon: Ediçoes Armasilde, 1977. 206 pp.

Vivo, Raul Valdes. *Ethiopia, the Unknown Revolution.* Havana: Editorial de Ciencias Sociales, 1977. 147 pp.

Vorob'ev, V. P. *Policheskaya i gosudarstvennaya sistema Narodnoi Demokraticheskoi Respubliki Iemen.* Moscow: Nauka, 1978. 125 pp.

INDEX OF NAMES